Tanzania
Zanzibar & Pemba

Mary Fitzpatrick

LONELY PLANET PUBLICATIONS
Melbourne • Oakland • London • Paris

TANZANIA, ZANZIBAR & PEMBA

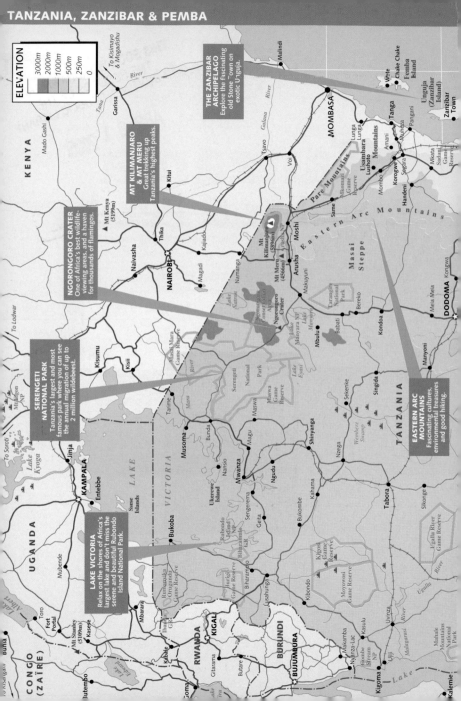

ELEVATION
3000m
2000m
1000m
500m
250m
0

THE ZANZIBAR ARCHIPELAGO
Explore the fascinating old Stone Town on exotic U'nguja.

MT KILIMANJARO & MT MERU
Great trekking up Tanzania's highest peaks.

NGORONGORO CRATER
One of Africa's best wildlife-viewing areas, and a haven for thousands of flamingos.

SERENGETI NATIONAL PARK
Tanzania's largest and most famous park where you can see the annual migration of up to 2 million wildebeest.

EASTERN ARC MOUNTAINS
Fascinating cultures, environmental treasures and good hiking.

LAKE VICTORIA
Relax on the shores of Africa's largest lake and don't miss the serene and beautiful Rubondo Island National Park.

KENYA

TANZANIA

UGANDA

RWANDA

BURUNDI

CONGO (ZAÏRE)

TANZANIA, ZANZIBAR & PEMBA

SOUTH-EASTERN TANZANIA
Remote and spectacular with beautiful beaches and the rugged Selous Game Reserve.

THE SOUTHERN HIGHLANDS
Pleasant climate, striking scenery and lots of colourful markets.

WESTERN TANZANIA
Historical towns, relaxing Lake Tanganyika and three seldom-visited national parks.

0   100   200 km

INDIAN OCEAN

MOZAMBIQUE

MALAWI

ZAMBIA

CONGO (ZAÏRE)

DAR ES SALAAM
LILONGWE

Lake Nyasa
Lake Tanganyika
Lake Rukwa

Livingstone Mountains

Selous Game Reserve

Mikumi National Park
Udzungwa Mountains National Park
Ruaha National Park
Rungwa Game Reserve
Kisigo Game Reserve
Uwanda Game Reserve
Katavi National Park

Uluguru Mtns
Ukaguru Mtns

To Nampula
To Blantyre
To Lusaka
To Kapiri Mposhi

Mafia Island
Pemba

Mtwara
Lindi
Mikindani
Palma
Mocimboa da Praia
Metoro
Montepuez
Masuguru
Newala
Masasi
Nachingwea
Mingoyo
Nangurukuru
Kilwa Masoko
Kilwa Kivinje
Kibiti
Bagamoyo
Ngerengere
Msata
Mwonero
Mpwapwa
Kilosa
Morogoro
Mikumi
Mangula
Ifakara
Iringa
Msembe
Makumbako
Mtema Njombe
Ibunga
Tukuyu
Mbeya
Tunduma
Chunya
Kipembawe
Rungwa
Kitunda
Namanyere
Mpanda
Sumbawanga
Mbala
Kasama
Shiwa Ngandu
Mpika
Mfuwe
Kapona
Chipata
Mzuzu
Karonga
Livingstonia
Nkhata Bay
Mbamba Bay
Liuli
Lituhi
Songea
Tunduru
Metangula
Lichinga
Liwale
Makumbako
Chiengi
Kapona
Moba

Rufiji River
Ruvuma River
Rungwa River
Kilombero River
Great Ruaha River
Kisigo River
Zambezi River
Luangwa River

Tanzania, Zanzibar & Pemba
1st edition – August 1999

Published by
Lonely Planet Publications Pty Ltd A.C.N. 005 607 983
192 Burwood Rd, Hawthorn, Victoria 3122, Australia

Lonely Planet Offices
Australia PO Box 617, Hawthorn, Victoria 3122
USA 150 Linden St, Oakland, CA 94607
UK 10a Spring Place, London NW5 3BH
France 1 rue du Dahomey, 75011 Paris

Photographs
Many of the images in this guide are available for licensing from
Lonely Planet Images.
email: lpi@lonelyplanet.com.au

Front cover photograph
Kilimanjaro (David Else)

ISBN 0 86442 726 3

text & maps © Lonely Planet 1999
photos © photographers as indicated 1999

Printed by Colorcraft Ltd, Hong Kong
Printed in China

**Although the authors
and Lonely Planet try
to make the informa-
tion as accurate as
possible, we accept
no responsibility for
any loss, injury or
inconvenience sus-
tained by anyone
using this book.**

Contents – Text

THE AUTHORS   **6**

THIS BOOK   **8**

FOREWORD   **9**

INTRODUCTION   **13**

FACTS ABOUT TANZANIA   **15**

History 15	National Parks &	Arts 32
Geography............................22	Game Reserves 26	Society & Conduct................36
Climate 23	Government & Politics 28	Religion 37
Ecology & Environment 24	Economy 30	Language...............................39
Flora 25	Population & People 31	
Fauna 25	Education...............................31	

SAFARI GUIDE   **41**

Primates................................42	Cats 50	Wild Pigs 57
Scaly Anteaters 45	Foxes & Dogs 53	Hippopotamus 58
Aardvark 45	Otters 54	Giraffe 59
Rodents 46	Badgers 55	Antelope 59
Dassies..................................46	Elephants 55	Birds 67
Small Predatory Mammals 47	Rhinoceros 56	
Hyaena 48	Zebra 57	

FACTS FOR THE VISITOR   **73**

Highlights 73	Radio & TV 85	Dangers & Annoyances 99
Suggested Itineraries 73	Photography & Video 85	Business Hours......................99
Planning 74	Time 86	Public Holidays &
Responsible Tourism..............76	Electricity 86	Special Events 99
Tourist Offices 76	Weights & Measures 86	Activities 100
Visas & Documents 77	Laundry 86	Courses 100
Embassies & Consulates 79	Toilets 86	Accommodation..................100
Customs................................80	Health 86	Food 101
Money..................................80	Women Travellers 98	Drinks 102
Post & Communications.......83	Gay & Lesbian Travellers 98	Entertainment 102
Internet Resources 84	Disabled Travellers 98	Spectator Sports.................102
Books....................................84	Senior Travellers....................98	Shopping 102
Newspapers & Magazines 85	Travel with Children 99	

GETTING THERE & AWAY   **104**

Air 104	Land 108	Sea & Lake..........................112

GETTING AROUND   **114**

Air 114	Car & Motorcycle................116	Boat.....................................118
Bus 114	Bicycle 117	Local Transport 119
Train 115	Hitching...............................117	Safaris 119

2 Contents – Text

DAR ES SALAAM 122

History 122
Orientation 122
Information.........................124
National Museum 127
Village Museum 127
Markets 127
Msasani 127
Bird Walks...........................127
Beaches...............................127
Diving 128
Places to Stay......................129
Places to Eat 132
Entertainment 134
Shopping 135
Getting There & Away 135
Getting Around...................137
Around Dar Es Salaam 137
Pugu Hills 137
Offshore Islands..................137
The Northern Beaches 139
The Southern Beaches 140

THE ZANZIBAR ARCHIPELAGO 142

History 142
Geography & Geology 145
Climate 145
Ecology & Environment 145
Government & Politics 145
Population & People 146
Society & Conduct..............146
Religion 146
Visas & Documents 146
Public Holidays
& Special Events..................146
Activities 146
Language Courses 148
Unguja (Zanzibar Island) 148
Orientation 148
Information 148
Stone Town 151
Places to Stay......................156
Places to Eat 159
Entertainment 160
Spectator Sports..................160
Shopping 160
Getting There & Away 160
Taarab Music 162
Getting Around 164
Around Zanzibar Town 166
Ruins 166
Spice Tours..........................166
Beaches 167
Offshore Islands..................172
Other Attractions................174
Pemba 175
History 176
Orientation 177
Information 177
Getting There & Away 178
Getting Around 178
Chake Chake 179
Mkoani 181
Wete 182
Other Destinations..............183

NORTH-EASTERN TANZANIA 186

Bagamoyo 186
Sadani Game Reserve..........189
Pangani 190
Tanga..................................192
Around Tanga 194
Muheza 196
Korogwe 196
Mkomazi Game Reserve 196
Usambara Mountains 197
Lushoto 198
Around Lushoto 200
Pare Mountains 201
Same 203
Mbaga.................................203
Mwanga 204
Usangi 204

NORTHERN TANZANIA 205

Moshi 205
Marangu 211
Arusha 212
Around Arusha....................221
Arusha National Park 221
Mt Kilimanjaro
National Park 223
Lake Manyara
National Park 224
Tarangire National Park 225
Serengeti National Park 227
Ngorongoro
Conservation Area..............230
The Crater Highlands..........231
Ngorongoro Crater 232
Olduvai Gorge 234
Engaruka 235
Lake Natron........................235
Lake Eyasi 236

TREKKING 237

When to Go.........................237
Kilimanjaro 237
Geography..........................237
Trekking Information 237
Places to Stay......................241
The Marangu Route............242
Mt Meru 245
Geography..........................245
Trekking Information 245
Places to Stay......................246
The Momela Route 246
The Crater Highlands..........249
Geography..........................249
Trekking Information 249

LAKE VICTORIA
251

Mwanza..............................251
Bukoba 258
Musoma 261
Rubondo Island
National Park 261
Shinyanga 262

WESTERN TANZANIA
263

Kigoma 263
Around Kigoma 267
Gombe Stream
National Park 268
Mahale Mountains
National Park 269
Uvinza 270
Tabora 271
Mpanda............................272
Katavi National Park 273
Sumbawanga.....................274

THE SOUTHERN HIGHLANDS
275

Dodoma............................275
Morogoro 280
Mikumi National Park 283
Udzungwa Mountains
National Park 284
Iringa 285
Around Iringa....................288
Ruaha National Park 288
Mbeya 290
Around Mbeya...................293
Tukuyu...............................294
Lake Nyasa 295
Songea...............................296
Njombe 297
Tunduru.............................297

SOUTH-EASTERN TANZANIA
299

Mtwara 299
Around Mtwara 306
The Makonde Plateau 308
Lindi 310
Kilwa Masoko 311
Around Kilwa Masoko 313
Mafia Island.......................315
Selous Game Reserve.........317

LANGUAGE
321

INDEX
338

Text 338
Boxed Text.........................343

MAP LEGEND
344

METRIC CONVERSION
inside back cover

Contents – Maps

FACTS ABOUT TANZANIA

National Parks & Game
Reserves.................................26

DAR ES SALAAM

Greater Dar es Salaam 123   Central Dar es Salaam 130   Around Dar es Salaam 139

THE ZANZIBAR ARCHIPELAGO

Unguja (Zanzibar Island) 143   Pemba 176
Zanzibar Town   Chake Chake 180
(Stone Town)........................154   Wete 182

NORTH-EASTERN TANZANIA

North-Eastern Tanzania 187   Tanga..................................193   Lushoto 198

NORTHERN TANZANIA

Northern Tanzania 206   Arusha National Park 222   Ngorongoro Conservation
Moshi 208   Tarangire National Park 226   Area.....................................231
Arusha 214   Serengeti National Park 227

TREKKING

Kilimanjaro Area..................238   Marangu Route 243   Momela Route 247

LAKE VICTORIA

Lake Victoria 252   Mwanza..............................254   Bukoba 260

WESTERN TANZANIA

Western Tanzania................264   Kigoma 266   Tabora 272

SOUTHERN HIGHLANDS

Southern Highlands 276   Morogoro 280   Mbeya 291
Dodoma..............................279   Iringa 287

SOUTH-EASTERN TANZANIA

South-Eastern Tanzania 300   Lindi 311   Selous Game Reserve..........318
Mtwara 302   Kilwa Masoko 312
Around Mtwara 306   Mafia Island.......................317

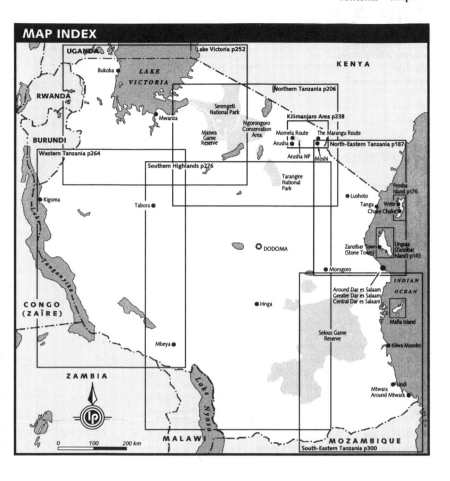

MAP INDEX

UGANDA

Bukoba

LAKE VICTORIA

Lake Victoria p252

KENYA

RWANDA

Mwanza

Serengeti National Park

Maswa Game Reserve

Ngorongoro Conservation Area

Northern Tanzania p206

Kilimanjaro Area p238

Momela Route

The Marangu Route

BURUNDI

Arusha

Arusha NP

Moshi

North-Eastern Tanzania p187

Western Tanzania p264

Southern Highlands p226

Tarangire National Park

Kigoma

Tabora

Lushoto

Tanga

Wete

Chake Chake

Pemba Island p176

Lake Tanganyika

⊙ DODOMA

Zanzibar Town (Stone Town)

Unguja (Zanzibar Island) p143

Morogoro

INDIAN OCEAN

CONGO (ZAÏRE)

Iringa

Around Dar es Salaam
Greater Dar es Salaam
Central Dar es Salaam

Mafia Island

Selous Game Reserve

Mbeya

Kilwa Masoko

ZAMBIA

Lake Nyasa

Mtwara
Around Mtwara

Lindi

0   100   200 km

MALAWI

MOZAMBIQUE

South-Eastern Tanzania p300

The Authors

Mary Fitzpatrick

Mary grew up in Washington, DC, and has travelled extensively in Africa, Asia and Europe. For the past five years she has worked in Africa, first on development projects in Mozambique, more recently as a freelance writer in Liberia and Sierra Leone. Her first visit to Tanzania was in 1993. Since then, she has travelled throughout the country while researching for this book. Mary also contributed to Lonely Planet's *West Africa* and *Africa on a shoestring*, and is presently working on a guide to Mozambique.

David Else

After hitchhiking through Europe for a couple of years, David Else kept heading south and first reached Africa in 1983. Since then, he has trekked all over the continent and written several Lonely Planet guidebooks to Africa including *Trekking in East Africa*. David contributed the trekking chapter in this book.

FROM MARY

I would like to extend special thanks to the following people: to my husband, Rick, for his unflagging encouragement and support, and for all the assistance with gathering research materials during what was supposed to be his vacation; to my sister, Margaret Michels Ohaion, and my father, Don Michels, for the countless hours which they spent perusing encyclopaedias and books, helping me to track down missing bits and pieces of information; to P. Leonhard Kessler, OSB for the very generous use of his printer, for sharing with me some of his computer expertise, and for coming to my rescue when my hard drive went down; to P. Thomas Blättler, OSB for spending so much time assisting me with research on language issues, and for placing his excellent library at my disposal; to Mary van Keuren for her hospitality and kindness in Lushoto; to Rusty and Irene Eads for their invaluable assistance in Dodoma; and, to Rogers Vincent Cidosa in Dar es Salaam for helping out a stranger.

I am also grateful to all of those who helped me at various points during my travels, including: Pia Kim, Chris Gilsenan and Huong Payson in Mwanza; Jessie Jentz, Ulrik Pedersen, Ditte Dahl, Richard Phillips, Jacky Barradale and Rhian Jenkins in Iringa; Brian Gunelson on Pemba; Christopher and Laurel McMullen, Graham Mercer, Ted Eull, Phil Muller and Josie Schaeffer in Dar es Salaam; Bill, Sandy and Christine Harrington, and Ben Harding and friends in Kigoma; Mr. Edeus T Massawe of the Mahale Mountains Wildlife Research Centre; Mr Nasir Hamiduddin, Marianne Blenkinsop and Troy van-de-l'Isle in Mtwara; Richard Cameron and James Dineen in Mikindani; Mr Danny Masasi, Mr Oscar Stevens and Mr Mohammed Chidoli in Kilwa Masoko; David Pinkerton and Damian Davies in Pangani; Mr John da Silva, Mr Seif Salim Saleh, Javed Jafferjies, Emerson Skeens, Nigel and Pilau Brown, and Mr Rashid Juma Hamad (Zanzibar Protected Areas Project) on Zanzibar; all the Peace Corps and VSO volunteers who assisted me with information; and, Sancha Simpson-Davis for taking the time to write such a detailed letter on Morogoro.

Finally, many thanks to David Else, contributor of the Trekking chapter and an East Africa expert, for his good-humoured and efficient collaboration, and for all the helpful insights and suggestions.

There is a Swahili saying which, roughly translated, reads, 'If you are going to give someone a bowl of porridge, then give them a full bowl, not just half'. Time and again, Tanzanians I met while researching put this adage into practice, going out of their way to help me when they did not have to, and when it may have inconvenienced them. For this, my sincere gratitude.

This Book

This guide grew out of the Tanzania chapter in Lonely Planet's *East Africa*. Geoff Crowther researched and wrote the original Tanzania chapter. Mary Fitzpatrick researched and wrote this book.

From the Publisher

Alan Murphy coordinated the editing of this first edition with help from Thalia Kalkipsakis, Monique Choy, Susan Holtham, Sam Carew and Justin Flynn. Anna Judd coordinated the mapping and design with cartographic assistance from Shahara Ahmed, Rodney Zandbergs, Katie Butterworth, Sonya Brooke and Sarah Sloane. Sarah Jolly provided the illustrations and Maria Vallianos designed the cover. Thanks to Quentin Frayne for organising the language chapter and to Paul Piaia for the climate charts. A special thanks to Luke Hunter for writing the safari guide and to William Steele for contributing the bird section.

Foreword

ABOUT LONELY PLANET GUIDEBOOKS

The story begins with a classic travel adventure: Tony and Maureen Wheeler's 1972 journey across Europe and Asia to Australia. Useful information about the overland trail did not exist at that time, so Tony and Maureen published the first Lonely Planet guidebook to meet a growing need.

From a kitchen table, then from a tiny office in Melbourne (Australia), Lonely Planet has become the largest independent travel publisher in the world, an international company with offices in Melbourne, Oakland (USA), London (UK) and Paris (France).

Today Lonely Planet guidebooks cover the globe. There is an ever-growing list of books and there's information in a variety of forms and media. Some things haven't changed. The main aim is still to help make it possible for adventurous travellers to get out there – to explore and better understand the world.

At Lonely Planet we believe travellers can make a positive contribution to the countries they visit – if they respect their host communities and spend their money wisely. Since 1986 a percentage of the income from each book has been donated to aid projects and human rights campaigns.

Updates Lonely Planet thoroughly updates each guidebook as often as possible. This usually means there are around two years between editions, although for more unusual or more stable destinations the gap can be longer. Check the imprint page (following the colour map at the beginning of the book) for publication dates.

Between editions up-to-date information is available in two free newsletters – the paper *Planet Talk* and email *Comet* (to subscribe, contact any Lonely Planet office) – and on our Web site at www.lonelyplanet.com. The *Upgrades* section of the Web site covers a number of important and volatile destinations and is regularly updated by Lonely Planet authors. *Scoop* covers news and current affairs relevant to travellers. And, lastly, the *Thorn Tree* bulletin board and *Postcards* section of the site carry unverified, but fascinating, reports from travellers.

Correspondence The process of creating new editions begins with the letters, postcards and emails received from travellers. This correspondence often includes suggestions, criticisms and comments about the current editions. Interesting excerpts are immediately passed on via newsletters and the Web site, and everything goes to our authors to be verified when they're researching on the road. We're keen to get more feedback from organisations or individuals who represent communities visited by travellers.

> Lonely Planet gathers information for everyone who's curious about the planet – and especially for those who explore it first-hand. Through guidebooks, phrasebooks, activity guides, maps, literature, newsletters, image library, TV series and Web site we act as an information exchange for a worldwide community of travellers.

Research Authors aim to gather sufficient practical information to enable travellers to make informed choices and to make the mechanics of a journey run smoothly. They also research historical and cultural background to help enrich the travel experience and allow travellers to understand and respond appropriately to cultural and environmental issues.

Authors don't stay in every hotel because that would mean spending a couple of months in each medium-sized city and, no, they don't eat at every restaurant because that would mean stretching belts beyond capacity. They do visit hotels and restaurants to check standards and prices, but feedback based on readers' direct experiences can be very helpful.

Many of our authors work undercover, others aren't so secretive. None of them accept freebies in exchange for positive write-ups. And none of our guidebooks contain any advertising.

Production Authors submit their raw manuscripts and maps to offices in Australia, USA, UK or France. Editors and cartographers – all experienced travellers themselves – then begin the process of assembling the pieces. When the book finally hits the shops, some things are already out of date, we start getting feedback from readers and the process begins again ...

WARNING & REQUEST

Things change – prices go up, schedules change, good places go bad and bad places go bankrupt – nothing stays the same. So, if you find things better or worse, recently opened or long since closed, please tell us and help make the next edition even more accurate and useful. We genuinely value all the feedback we receive. Julie Young coordinates a well travelled team that reads and acknowledges every letter, postcard and email and ensures that every morsel of information finds its way to the appropriate authors, editors and cartographers for verification.

Everyone who writes to us will find their name in the next edition of the appropriate guidebook. They will also receive the latest issue of *Planet Talk*, our quarterly printed newsletter, or *Comet*, our monthly email newsletter. Subscriptions to both newsletters are free. The very best contributions will be rewarded with a free guidebook.

Excerpts from your correspondence may appear in new editions of Lonely Planet guidebooks, the Lonely Planet Web site, *Planet Talk* or *Comet*, so please let us know if you *don't* want your letter published or your name acknowledged.

Send all correspondence to the Lonely Planet office closest to you:

Australia: PO Box 617, Hawthorn, Victoria 3122
USA: 150 Linden St, Oakland, CA 94607
UK: 10A Spring Place, London NW5 3BH
France: 1 rue du Dahomey, 75011 Paris

Or email us at: talk2us@lonelyplanet.com.au

For news, views and updates see our Web site: www.lonelyplanet.com

HOW TO USE A LONELY PLANET GUIDEBOOK

The best way to use a Lonely Planet guidebook is any way you choose. At Lonely Planet we believe the most memorable travel experiences are often those that are unexpected, and the finest discoveries are those you make yourself. Guidebooks are not intended to be used as if they provide a detailed set of infallible instructions!

Contents All Lonely Planet guidebooks follow roughly the same format. The Facts about the Destination chapters or sections give background information ranging from history to weather. Facts for the Visitor gives practical information on issues like visas and health. Getting There & Away gives a brief starting point for researching travel to and from the destination. Getting Around gives an overview of the transport options when you arrive.

The peculiar demands of each destination determine how subsequent chapters are broken up, but some things remain constant. We always start with background, then proceed to sights, places to stay, places to eat, entertainment, getting there and away, and getting around information – in that order.

Heading Hierarchy Lonely Planet headings are used in a strict hierarchical structure that can be visualised as a set of Russian dolls. Each heading (and its following text) is encompassed by any preceding heading that is higher on the hierarchical ladder.

Entry Points We do not assume guidebooks will be read from beginning to end, but that people will dip into them. The traditional entry points are the list of contents and the index. In addition, however, some books have a complete list of maps and an index map illustrating map coverage.

There may also be a colour map that shows highlights. These highlights are dealt with in greater detail in the Facts for the Visitor chapter, along with planning questions and suggested itineraries. Each chapter covering a geographical region usually begins with a locator map and another list of highlights. Once you find something of interest in a list of highlights, turn to the index.

Maps Maps play a crucial role in Lonely Planet guidebooks and include a huge amount of information. A legend is printed on the back page. We seek to have complete consistency between maps and text, and to have every important place in the text captured on a map. Map key numbers usually start in the top left corner.

Although inclusion in a guidebook usually implies a recommendation we cannot list every good place. Exclusion does not necessarily imply criticism. In fact there are a number of reasons why we might exclude a place – sometimes it is simply inappropriate to encourage an influx of travellers.

Introduction

Tanzania is a colourful fusion of peoples and cultures, a land where ancient coastal kingdoms meet with tribal peoples of the interior, a land where eastern mystique mixes with Africa's vibrancy and rhythms. It's a place of incredible contrasts, where endless stretches of palm-fringed beach rise to lushly forested mountains, where exotic, offshore islands offer relaxing respite from the rigors of climbing Africa's highest peak, where over 30 million people live in varying degrees of harmony with some of the largest herds of wildlife on the continent.

Tanzania has a geological past spanning more than 300 million years. It holds archaeological treasures that include hominid fossils more than three million years old, and has a historical legacy which reaches from

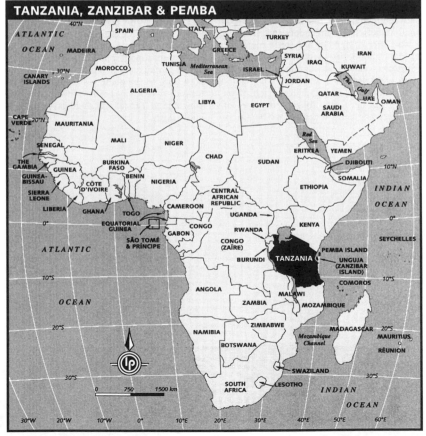

TANZANIA, ZANZIBAR & PEMBA

early tribal states through Julius Nyerere's idealistic attempts at nation-building, to recent steps towards multiparty democracy. It is a country of great natural wealth, where turquoise seas wash pristine coral reefs, and vast plains are home to millions of hoofed animals. It's a country of spectacular beauty, whose cool highland plateau is punctuated by the deep crevices of the Great Rift Valley, and whose inland lakes glimmer with the reflected shadows of countless water birds.

Tanzania's exceptional diversity encompasses more than 100 different tribal groups, each with its own language and customs. Thus far, frictions arising from this diversity – between Muslims and Christians, between members of one tribe and those of another, between mainlanders and islanders – have been bridged by a shared experience of nationhood, by a common language (Swahili), and by an ingrained sense and spirit of moderation.

Tanzania is a land that for much of its history has been seen through the eyes of outsiders and only recently has begun to define itself. It is a young nation forged together around the ideals of community and family, now struggling to come to terms with its limitations. It is a country of tremendous potential – a potential which will only begin to be harnessed if its more than 16 million children and youth are given access to a full education.

For travellers, one of Tanzania's most notable characteristics is its warmth and openness. It is a land whose culture and people are easily accessible for those who take the time to seek them, and where – in the markets, on the street, in homes and in remote villages – you will be greeted constantly with *karibu*, the Swahili word of welcome.

The aim of this book – in addition to providing all the necessary tips and information you will need to savour Tanzania's natural beauty, its topographical diversity, and its world-famous tourist sights – is to open the door a bit to the country's cultural and historical riches, to help visitors to know Tanzania as Tanzanians themselves see and know it.

Facts about Tanzania

HISTORY
Early History

Tanzania's human history spans a period of nearly 10,000 years, dating back to early hunter-gatherer communities that lived in the area south of the Olduvai Gorge. These peoples are believed to have been Khoisan speakers, distantly related to modern Tanzania's Sandawe group. Somewhere between 3000 and 5000 years ago, they were joined by Cushitic-speaking peoples from present-day Ethiopia who had begun to make their way south-west into the same territory. Moving sometimes in larger groups, but more often as individual clans or families, these newcomers brought with them basic techniques of agriculture, food production and, later, cattle tending. Gradually they absorbed the hunter-gatherer communities that had inhabited the area for so long.

From about 1000 BC, a series of migrations began which had a decisive impact on the settlement of the region. Bantu-speaking peoples from the distant Niger delta in West Africa started to move slowly east through Cameroon and Congo (Zaïre), arriving in East Africa around the 1st century BC, and spreading throughout much of present-day Tanzania. These new residents not only possessed more advanced agricultural skills, but also brought with them knowledge of iron-working and steel-production techniques. They absorbed many of the Cushitic peoples who had preceded them, as well as most of the remaining Khoisan-speaking inhabitants.

Somewhat later, smaller groups of Nilotic peoples began to arrive in Tanzania from what is now southern Sudan, both mixing and clashing with the Bantu speakers in the area. This influx continued through to the 18th century, with the most significant migrations taking place in the 15th and 16th centuries. Most of these Nilotic peoples were pastoralists, and many settled in the less fertile areas of north-central Tanzania where their large herds would have sufficient grazing space.

The Coast Meanwhile, coastal areas were being shaped by far different influences. Azania, as the East African coast was known to the early Greeks, was an important trading post as early as 400 BC, and had likely been inhabited by Bantu peoples well before then. In the early part of the first millennium AD, permanent settlements were established as traders, first from the Mediterranean and later from Arabia and Persia, came ashore and began to intermix with the indigenous Bantu speakers, gradually giving rise to Swahili language and culture. With the traders from Arabia came Islam, which by the 11th century had become entrenched.

Over the next few centuries, trading outposts were established all along the coast, including on the Zanzibar archipelago and Kilwa Kisiwani. Between the 13th and 15th centuries these settlements flourished, with trade in ivory, gold and other goods extending as far away as India and China. Things began to change in the early 16th century. In 1498, the Portuguese explorer Vasco da Gama became the first European to reach

Swahili

The word 'swahili' (literally, 'of the coast') is derived from the Arabic word *sahil*. It refers not only to the Swahili language (KiSwahili), but also to the Islamic culture of the peoples inhabiting the East African coast from Mogadishu in the north down to Mozambique in the south. Both language and culture are characterised by a mixture of Bantu, Arabic, Persian and Asian influences.

Although Swahili culture began to develop in the early part of the first millennium AD, it was not until the 18th century, with the ascendancy of the Omani Arabs on Zanzibar, that it came into its own. Swahili was initially used primarily as a language of commerce. During the 18th and 19th centuries, it spread from coastal areas throughout East and Central Africa along the great trade caravan routes. European missionaries and explorers soon adopted the language as the main means of communicating with locals. In the second half of the 19th century, missionaries – notably Johan Ludwig Krapf – also began applying the roman alphabet. Prior to this, Swahili had been written exclusively in Arabic script.

While there are an increasing number of Tanzanians for whom Swahili is their only mother tongue, most speak it as a second language, or as a second mother tongue together with their tribal language.

East Africa, and by 1525 the Portuguese had subdued the entire coast. Portuguese control lasted until the early 18th century, when Arabs from Oman established a foothold in the region. Under the Omani Arabs, the focus expanded westwards and powerful trade routes developed which stretched inland as far as Lake Tanganyika and Central Africa. Commerce grew at such a pace that in the 1840s the Sultan of Oman moved his capital to Unguja (Zanzibar island).

The slave trade also grew rapidly during this period, driven in part by demand from European plantation holders on the Indian Ocean islands of Réunion and Mauritius. Soon slave traders, including the notorious Tippu Tib, had established stations in Tabora, Ujiji and numerous other towns in the interior.

Beginning about the mid-19th century, European missionaries, explorers and, later, imperialists began to penetrate the Tanzanian mainland. The first missionaries to reach the interior of Tanzania were the Germans Johann Ludwig Krapf and Johannes Rebmann, who arrived at Mt Kilimanjaro in the 1840s. In the 1860s, Anglican and Catholic missionaries began to arrive on Unguja, and then in 1868 Catholic priests established the first mainland mission at Bagamoyo as a station for ransomed slaves. Over the next several decades, missionaries from a variety of denominations moved further inland, setting up mission stations as far west as Lake Tanganyika. Around the same time, European explorers began to 'discover' and map large areas of the interior, principally by following established caravan routes. Among the earliest of these explorers were Richard Francis Burton and John Hanning Speke, who traversed the country in 1857 in search of the source of the Nile. Shortly thereafter came the missionary-explorer David Livingstone and the journalist Henry Morton Stanley.

The Colonial Era

Reports from the missionaries and explorers made East Africa a known territory in the west and stimulated European interests, which until this point had been only lukewarm at best. By the late 1880s, Britain had established a sphere of influence on the Zanzibar archipelago and along the coast. In 1884, Carl Peters, a German acting independently of the German government, concluded various 'treaties' with unsuspecting local chiefs in order to secure a charter for his German East Africa Company (Deutsch-Ostafrikanische Gesellschaft or DOAG). The treaties were soon endorsed by the German government, which delegated the DOAG to administer the mainland. The challenge which this posed to Britain's coastal dominance was at least temporarily resolved in 1890, when Germany and Great Britain signed an agreement defining their spheres of influence and formally establishing a British protectorate over the Zanzibar archipelago. In 1891, most of what is now mainland Tanzania came under direct German control as German East Africa.

Colonialism brought western education and health care to German East Africa, as well as road and rail networks in the northern and central parts of the territory. However, these developments benefited relatively few Africans, and the German military administration was widely unpopular. Harsh labour policies, the imposition of a hut tax and numerous other measures contributed to the discontent and led to many uprisings. Local opposition culminated in the Maji Maji rebellion of 1905 to 1907, which decimated much of southern Tanzania and is considered to contain the first seeds of Tanzanian nationalism (see the boxed text 'The Maji Maji Rebellion' in The Southern Highlands chapter).

The German era lasted until the end of WWI, when German East Africa came under British administration as a League of Nations mandate and was renamed Tanganyika. This arrangement lasted until WWII, after which the country became a United Nations trust territory, again under British administration.

During the inter-war years, British administrators introduced a system of indirect rule which aimed at promoting the establishment of indigenous political institutions and leaders. While this gave Africans a say in political affairs, at least at the lower levels, it also resulted in many local chiefs being replaced with those who were considered to be more amenable to colonial interests. Corruption was an additional problem, and the system proved to be a dismal failure, intensifying discontent and widening the already existing rift between locals and the government.

The British were more successful with their policy of encouraging the cultivation of export crops. Effective marketing cooperatives were formed in several areas, notably among the Chagga around Kilimanjaro and the Haya around Bukoba. Many of these farmers' cooperatives soon took on an additional role as channels through which nationalist aspirations and protests against the colonial system could be expressed.

In 1929, a group similar to these cooperatives, but organised from the outset along political rather than economic lines, was founded in Dar es Salaam. This group, known initially as the African Association, assumed increasing importance as grass-roots resentment against colonial policies grew. In 1948 it was renamed the Tanganyika Africa Association (TAA) to reflect its broadening base of support.

A rallying point for the nationalist cause came in the early 1950s when several thousand Meru people were forcibly expelled from their lands in the western Kilimanjaro area in order to make room for a dozen European settlers to establish farms. When the Meru's protests were rebuffed via the normal channels – including in the United Nations General Assembly – they turned to local political groups to redress their grievances. These groups in turn looked to the TAA for leadership, and began to exert considerable pressure for more radical action.

Independence

In 1953 the TAA elected Julius Nyerere as its president. Nyerere was a teacher recently returned from studies in Europe, and one of only two Tanganyikans educated abroad at university level. Under his leadership, the TAA was quickly transformed into an effective political organisation. A new internal constitution was introduced on 7 July 1954 (an anniversary now celebrated as Saba Saba Day), and the TAA became the Tanganyika African National Union (TANU), which had as its slogan *uhuru na umoja*, or 'freedom and unity'. Within a year, Nyerere had given up his teaching profession to devote himself full-time to leadership of TANU.

One of the first items on TANU's agenda was independence. In 1958 and 1959, TANU-supported candidates decisively won general legislative elections, and in 1959 Britain agreed to the establishment of internal self-government, requesting Nyerere to be chief minister. On 9 December 1961 Tanganyika became independent and on 9 December 1962 it was established as a republic, with Nyerere as president.

In the meantime on the Zanzibar archipelago, which had been a British protectorate since 1890, the main push for independence came from the radical Afro-Shirazi Party (ASP). Opposing the ASP were two minority parties, the Zanzibar & Pemba People's Party (ZPPP) and the sultanate-oriented Zanzibar Nationalist Party (ZNP), both of which were strongly favoured by the British. As a result, at Zanzibari independence in December 1963, it was the two minority parties which formed the first government.

This government did not last long. Within a month, a Ugandan immigrant named John Okello initiated a violent revolution against the ruling ZPPP-ZNP coalition which led to the toppling of the government and the sultan, and the massacre or expulsion of most of the islands' Arab population. The sultan was replaced by an entity known as the Zanzibar Revolutionary Council, which was comprised of ASP members and headed by Abeid Karume.

On 26 April 1964 Nyerere signed an act of union with Karume, creating the United Republic of Tanganyika (renamed the United Republic of Tanzania the following October). Formation of the union, which was resented by many Zanzibaris from the outset, was motivated in part by the then-prevailing spirit of pan-Africanism, and in part as a cold war response to the ASP's socialist programme.

Karume's government lasted until 1972, when he was assassinated and succeeded as head of the Zanzibar Revolutionary Council by Aboud Jumbe. A few years later, in an effort to subdue the ongoing unrest resulting from the merger of the islands with the mainland, Nyerere authorised formation of a one-party state and combined TANU and the ASP into a new party known as Chama Cha Mapinduzi (CCM, or Party of the Revolution). This merger, which was ratified in a new union constitution on 27 April 1977, marked the beginning of the CCM's dominance of Tanzanian politics which endures to this day. Nyerere envisioned the CCM as an instrument for mobilising the population in all significant economic and political activities, and as a 'two-way street' for the flow of ideas and policy directives between the village level and the government.

Socialist Tanzania

Nyerere took the helm of a country which was economically foundering and politically fragile, its stability plagued in particular by the mainland's lack of control over the Zanzibar archipelago. Education had also been neglected, so that at independence there were said to be only 120 university graduates in the entire country.

This inauspicious beginning, and the problems it created, eventually led to the Arusha Declaration of 1967 which committed Tanzania to a policy of socialism and self-reliance (*ujamaa na kujitegemea*). The cornerstone of this policy was the *ujamaa* (familyhood) village – an agricultural collective run along traditional African lines, with an emphasis on self-reliance. Basic goods and tools were to be held in common and shared among members, while each individual was obligated to work on the land. Nyerere's proposals for education were seen as an essential part of this scheme. They were designed to encourage cooperative endeavour, to promote social equality and responsibility, and to discourage any tendency towards intellectual arrogance among the educated. Additional aspects of the Arusha Declaration included nationalisation of the economy, and tax increases aimed at redistributing individual wealth.

In the early days of the ujamaa system, progressive farmers were encouraged to expand in the hope that other peasants would follow their example. This enriched those who were the recipients of state funds but resulted in little improvement in rural poverty. The approach was therefore abandoned in favour of direct state control. Between 1973 and 1978, 85% of Tanzania's rural population was resettled, often forcibly, into over 7000 planned villages. These resettlements were aimed at modernisation of the agricultural sector and at making social services more accessible to rural dwellers. Yet, this new approach was also unsuccessful. The necessary finances exceeded the country's resources, and there was widespread resentment among large segments of the rural population towards compulsory resettlement. The government's authoritarian response to dissent further contributed to the discontent.

Tanzania's experiment in socialism and self-reliance was widely acclaimed in the days following independence. Despite the unpopularity of the ujamaa system, it marked a successful period of nation-building, and is credited with unifying the country, bridging ethnic and religious divisions, and expanding education and health care. Economically, however, the consensus is that it failed. Between 1978 and 1984, Tanzania's per capita income decreased by over 30%, agricultural production became stagnant, the industrial sector ran at less than 50% of capacity, and virtually all economic incentives were eliminated. This decline was precipitated by a combination of factors, including the steep rise in oil prices during the 1970s, sharp drops in the value of major exports such as coffee and sisal, the 1977 break-up of the East African Community (an economic and customs union between Tanzania, Kenya and Uganda) and prolonged drought during the early 1980s. Tanzania's regional activism, particularly its involvement in deposing Idi Amin Dada in Uganda in 1979, was also a significant drain on government resources.

Multiparty Politics

Nyerere was re-elected to a fifth term as president in 1980. During the next few years, economic decline worsened and dissatisfaction with socialist policies grew. In 1985, Nyerere resigned, handing over power to Ali Hassan Mwinyi. He retained his position as CCM chairman until 1990, when this post also went to Mwinyi. Mwinyi tried to distance himself from Nyerere and his policies, and instituted an economic recovery programme involving decreased government spending, price liberalization and encouragement of foreign investment. Yet the pace of change remained slow, and Mwinyi's presidency was unpopular; during its second half he was even condemned for incompetence by Nyerere, then still chairman of the CCM.

The fall of Communism in Europe at the beginning of the 1990s and increasing pressure from western donor nations accelerated the move towards multiparty politics. In 1991, a presidential commission published recommendations on the establishment of a multiparty system. In 1992, following a unanimous vote at an extraordinary sitting of the CCM, the constitution was amended to legalise opposition parties and a date was set for elections.

The first elections were held in October 1995 in an atmosphere of chaos. On the mainland, the CCM, under the leadership of Benjamin Mkapa, won 62% of the vote. Although the results were contested by the opposition, they were ultimately deemed to reflect the will of the people and were upheld.

The situation on the Zanzibar archipelago was different, with the voting for the Zanzibari presidency universally denounced for its dishonesty. The opposition Civic United Front (CUF) candidate, Seif Shariff Hamad, is widely believed to have narrowly won the presidential seat. Yet the official results came out as 50.2% of the vote in favour of the CCM incumbent Salmin Amour, against 49.8% for Hamad. In the ensuing uproar, foreign development assistance was suspended and most expatriates working on the islands decided to leave. The stalemate has still not been resolved, and more than a dozen CUF members are being held in indefinite custody on spurious treason charges, and harassment of the opposition continues.

Julius Nyerere

Julius Kambarage Nyerere, one of Africa's most renowned statesmen, was born in 1922 In the village of Butiama, just west of Lake Victoria. His father was chief of the small Zanaki tribe, which is based in the area. After attending mission schools in Tabora and Pugu, Nyerere studied at Makerere College in Uganda, and then taught for several years. Between 1949 and 1952, he pursued graduate studies in history and economics at Edinburgh University in Scotland, following which he returned to Tanganyika to begin a teaching profession.

It wasn't long, however, before Nyerere was drawn into politics. As president of the Tanganyika African National Union (TANU), Nyerere travelled within and outside of Tanzania advocating peaceful change, social equality and racial harmony. Soon his oratorical skills and political savvy earned him distinction as Tanganyika's pre-eminent nationalist spokesman. By 1962, he was president of the independent United Republic of Tanganyika, a position which he held until his resignation in 1985.

Nyerere is well known internationally for his philosophy of socialism and self-reliance, which was embodied in the Arusha Declaration of 1967. Many of the ideas contained in this programme had been inspired by his studies of Karl Marx, by his reading of the Bible, and by his observations of the Chinese Communist system. Nyerere brought these various elements together in the African context, reasoning that there could be no justification for social or other inequities in Tanzania given the value placed by traditional African culture on community and family. The African extended family cultivated its fields in common and shared its resources in times of need. Could not this communalism be extended to the entire nation, thereby avoiding large gaps between rich and poor? Nyerere chose the term *ujamaa* (familyhood) to describe his programme, and to emphasise the blend of economic cooperation, racial and tribal harmony, and moralistic self-sacrifice that he sought to achieve.

Nyerere gained widespread respect for his idealism, for his success in shaping a society which was politically stable and notably free of tribal rivalries, and for his contributions towards raising Tanzania's literacy rate, which during his tenure became one of the highest in Africa. He also earned international acclaim for his commitment to pan-Africanism and for his regional engagement – an area where he is still active.

Yet, the national unity which Nyerere was able to achieve came at a high price and, for all of his accomplishments, his legacy among his own countrymen is decidedly mixed. Nyerere is particularly resented for his authoritarian style, and for the forced resettlements of the

Negotiations moderated by the Commonwealth Secretary General are underway to try to resolve the impasse and lay the groundwork for credible, nonviolent elections in 2000. Meanwhile, Salmin Amour has indicated that he may try to run again, despite the constitutional two-term limitation. Optimistic observers do not feel that the union itself is in danger at this point. Yet, relations between the islands and the mainland are at their nadir, and the possibility of deterioration in the fragile status quo casts lurking shadows.

The Future

One of the effects which the introduction of multiparty politics has had on Tanzanian life has been the unmasking of underlying political, economic and religious frictions, both on the mainland and between the mainland and the Zanzibar archipelago. The tensions involving the archipelago are perhaps the most visible example. Yet – the Zanzibar situation notwithstanding – Tanzania as a whole remains reasonably well integrated, and has comparatively high levels of religious and ethnic tolerance, particularly on

Julius Nyerere

ujamaa period. During his rule, Tanzania became an increasingly rigid and ineffective single-party state, with his application of socialist ideology all but destroying the country's economy. Even Nyerere himself has acknowledged that from an economic perspective, his socialist experiment was a failure.

While it is too early to tell whether the passage of time will soften assessment of this era, Nyerere remains indisputably one of Africa's most influential leaders, and the person almost single-handedly responsible for putting Tanzania on the world stage as one of the continent's major players. He is widely acclaimed for his long-standing opposition to South Africa's apartheid system, and for his 1979 invasion of Uganda, which resulted in the deposition of the dictator Idi Amin Dada. In recent years, Nyerere has continued to be active as an elder statesman, taking a leading role in seeking a resolution of the Burundi crisis, and advocating increased African political and economic collaboration through multilateral organisations such as the Southern African Development Community (SADC) and the Common Market of Eastern and Southern African States (Comesa).

Nyerere has written several books, including *Uhuru na Umoja* (Freedom and Unity), *Uhuru na Ujamaa* (Freedom and Socialism) and *Uhuru na Maendeleo* (Freedom and Development). He also translated two Shakespeare plays, *The Merchant of Venice* and *Julius Caesar*, into Swahili. The biographical *We Must Run While They Walk: A Portrait of Africa's Julius Nyerere* by William E Smith is a good book to start with for those seeking more detailed information on the statesman's life and philosophy.

the mainland. Over the past three decades, Tanzanians have earned a name for themselves in the region for their moderation and balance. Most observers consider it highly unlikely that the country will disintegrate into the tribal conflicts which have been recently plaguing neighbouring Kenya.

The next presidential and legislative elections are scheduled for late 2000. While President Mkapa receives only muted approval from many Tanzanians on the street, his government has distinguished itself in the international community with its commitment to fight corruption, and with its steps towards financial austerity and reform. There is also no serious contender for Mkapa's seat; the opposition parties are in disarray and none can yet approach the national network or the resources of the CCM. One of Tanzania's political challenges over the next decade will be to overcome the TANU/CCM legacy and to raise awareness among the country's large rural population that they have a choice other than the CCM. This and other necessary adjustments will likely result in some growing pains. Yet, chances are high that this young nation will move smoothly into the 21st century, maintaining the stable and moderate outlook which has characterised Tanzanian development since independence.

GEOGRAPHY

Tanzania is East Africa's largest country. It has a total area of approximately 943,000 sq km, including 2640 sq km belonging to the Zanzibar archipelago. About 6% of mainland Tanzania (59,000 sq km) is covered by inland lakes.

Much of the mainland consists of a central highland plateau averaging between 900 and 1800m in altitude and situated between the eastern and western branches of the geological fault known as the Great Rift Valley (see the boxed text). There is a narrow coastal strip varying in width from about 15 to 65km. In the north-west is the Lake Victoria basin. The main mountain ranges are grouped into a north-eastern section (the

The Great Rift Valley

The Great Rift Valley, which rims and bisects Tanzania's central plateau, is part of the East African rift system, Africa's most distinctive relief feature. This system, which stretches almost 6500km from the Dead Sea in the north to Beira, Mozambique in the south, was formed more than 30 million years ago when the tectonic plates which comprise the African and Eurasian landmasses collided and then diverged again. As the plates moved apart, large blocks of the earth's crust, tens of kilometres wide and hundreds of kilometres long, dropped down between them, similar to the manner in which the keystone of an arch will fall if the walls of the arch move apart. Over the course of millennia, these movements resulted in the escarpments, ravines and flatlands which mark much of Africa's topography today. In some cases the sides of the valleys, created as the earth's crust caved in, consist of dramatically steep walls more than 1000m high. In others, the valley edges are much more gentle, consisting of various tiers.

Many sections of the rift system are marked by volcanoes. In Tanzania, these include Mt Kilimanjaro and Mt Meru, as well as many of the calderas of the Crater Highlands. The volcanoes arose in places where the earth's crust thinned as underlying tectonic plates separated. The thinning then allowed hot molten material from deep within the earth to rise to more shallow depths and, ultimately, to erupt.

Another characteristic of the rift system is its lakes, most of which occur along the course of valley walls. These lakes are generally very deep, with floors well below sea level (even though their surfaces may be several hundred metres above sea level). Two of the deepest lakes of the rift system are lakes Tanganyika and Nyasa.

The Tanzanian rift valley consists of two branches which are formed where the main rift system divides north of Lake Turkana in Kenya. The western branch, or Western Rift Valley, extends past Lake Albert in Uganda through Rwanda and Burundi down to Lake Tanganyika, after which it continues south-east, to Lake Nyasa. Seismic and volcanic disturbances still occur throughout the western branch. The eastern branch, known as the Eastern or Gregory Rift, runs south from Lake Turkana in Kenya past lakes Natron and Manyara. It then joins again with the Western Rift by Lake Nyasa. The lakes of the Eastern Rift are generally smaller than those in the western branch, with some of them only waterless salt beds. The largest are Natron and Manyara. Lake Eyasi is in a side branch off the main rift.

For travellers in Tanzania, the most visually impressive part of the rift valley system is that in the north of the country, near Ngorongoro Crater and Lake Manyara National Park.

Eastern Arc) and a central and southern section (the Southern Highlands or Southern Arc). There is also a belt of volcanic peaks in the centre of the country near the Ngorongoro Crater. Tanzania's (and Africa's) highest mountain is Mt Kilimanjaro (5896m). The lowest point in the country is the floor of Lake Tanganyika, which at 358m below sea level is also the lowest point in Africa.

The largest river is the Rufiji, which drains the Southern Highlands region and much of southern Tanzania. Other major rivers flowing into the Indian Ocean include the Ruvu, the Wami, the Pangani and the Ruvuma. Most of Tanzania's lesser rivers drain into its three major lakes – Victoria, Tanganyika and Nyasa – or into other inland basins.

CLIMATE

Tanzania's climate displays marked regional differences due to the country's widely varying topography. In general, the coolest months are from June to October, and the warmest from December to March.

The climate along the coast and on offshore islands is tropical, with relatively high humidity. Temperatures average between 27 and 29°C, although they are considerably moderated by sea breezes, especially on the islands. On the central plateau, altitude tempers what would otherwise be a tropical climate. Temperatures range from 20 to 27°C during the cooler months of June through August, and reach 30°C and higher between December and March. There are notable variations depending on time of day and altitude, although the country-wide mean monthly temperature variation is less than 5°C. In the mountainous areas of the north-east and south-west, and on the Makonde plateau in the south-east, temperatures occasionally drop below 15°C at night during June and July.

Throughout much of the country, there are two rainy seasons. The long rains fall from mid-March through May, during which time it rains virtually every day, although seldom for the whole day. The short rains fall during

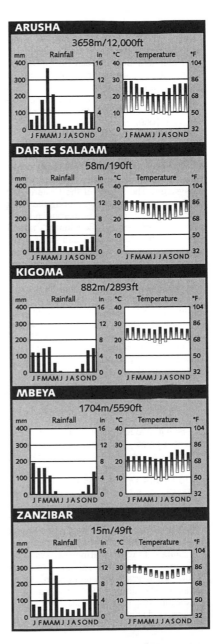

November, December and sometimes into January. Much of central Tanzania is semi-arid, receiving less than 500mm of rain per year, although flooding can be a problem during the rainy season. In contrast, some of the mountainous areas in the north-east and south-west receive over 2000mm of rain annually. Rainfall along the coast ranges between 1000mm and 1900mm annually, with most areas receiving about 1500mm.

ECOLOGY & ENVIRONMENT

Tanzania has exceptionally rich and varied ecosystems. The forests of the Eastern Arc mountain range, which are among the most biodiverse in Africa, host numerous endemic plant and bird species. The country's inland lakes, notably Tanganyika and Nyasa, are also known for their biodiversity. Lake Tanganyika holds over 200 different marine species, including numerous endemic cichlids, molluscs and crustaceans, and Lake Nyasa contains about one-third of the world's known cichlid species. Along the coast and around the offshore islands are pristine coral reefs and a wide diversity of marine life including several rare species. Tanzania's vast plains are home to some of the largest herds of wildlife on the continent.

In order to protect this wealth, the government has set aside about one-fourth of Tanzania's land to protected parks, game and forest reserves, and has recently created its first national marine park. Three of these protected areas – the Ngorongoro Conservation Area, Serengeti National Park and the Selous Game Reserve – have been declared UNESCO World Heritage sites.

Despite these positive steps, significant environmental damage has already occurred in many areas. One of the most serious threats in coastal regions is dynamite fishing. (For more information see the boxed text 'Tanzania's Fragile Marine Ecosystems' later in this chapter.) Inland, concerns include soil degradation and erosion, desertification, and deforestation; according to some estimates, Tanzania loses 3500 sq km of forest land annually due to clearances for agricultural and commercial purposes. In the

national parks, poaching and inappropriate visitor use – especially in the northern circuit – threaten wildlife and ecosystems.

Fortunately, there are a number of dedicated and competent organisations working for environmental conservation in Tanzania, although their effectiveness is often hampered by limited resources and the country's vastness. Following is a list of groups which can provide more in-depth information on environmental issues in the country; all are well worth your support.

Wildlife Conservation Society of Tanzania (WCST)
(☎ 112518, 112496, fax 124572, email wcst@ costech.gn.apc.org, wcst@africaonline.co.tz). WCST is the best place to start. Its small office on Garden St in Dar es Salaam publishes the informative newsletter, *Miombo*, with features on environmental issues throughout the country. There is also a small library which includes information on national parks and game reserves. Staff are dedicated and knowledgeable.

Roots & Shoots
(☎ 0811-334211, or c/o The Goodall Institute at PO Box 727 Dar es Salaam). Roots & Shoots is the educational arm of Jane Goodall's work, and a good contact if you are planning to visit Gombe Stream or Mahale Mountains national parks.

Tanzania Wildlife Protection Fund
(☎ 051-866377 or 0811-325581, fax 051-863496, email selousgamereserve@cats-net .com) PO Box 1994 Dar es Salaam

African Wildlife Foundation
PO Box 48177 Nairobi or 1717 Massachusetts Ave, NW, Washington, DC 20036, USA

Frankfurt Zoological Society
(☎ 49-69-943 4460, fax 943 9348) Alfred-Brehm-Platz 16, 60316 Frankfurt am Main, Germany

Wildlife Conservation Society
(☎ 1-718 220 5100, fax 364 4275, Web site www.wcs.org, Bronx Zoo) 2300 Southern Blvd, Bronx, NY 10460, USA

World Wildlife Fund
(☎ 1-202-293 4800, fax 293 9211, Web site www.worldwildlife.org) 1250 24th St, NW, Washington, DC 20037-1175, USA

Many of the national parks have 'friends' groups which work to promote awareness of issues affecting the individual parks and to channel any available financial resources.

These groups include Friends of Ruaha, Friends of the Serengeti (with their main office located in Switzerland), and Friends of Mikumi. The Wildlife Conservation Society of Tanzania can provide you with updated contact addresses.

The best source of information on the marine resources of the Zanzibar archipelago is the Institute of Marine Sciences in Zanzibar Town on the seafront. For information on environmental issues relating to Lake Victoria, try the National Environmental Management Council in Dar es Salaam (3rd floor, Tancot Bldg, Sokoine Ave, opposite Luther House).

FLORA

Approximately one-third of the Tanzanian mainland, predominantly in the south and west, is covered by miombo woodland. About 13 million hectares have been set aside as permanent forest reserves where small tree plantations have been established. In upland areas, notably in the Eastern Arc

The root-like branches of the baobab tree give it the impression of being 'upside down'.

range, are small but biologically significant areas of tropical rainforest which host most of Tanzania's endemic plant species, including *Celtis africana* (more commonly known as the Usambara or African violet). Much of the dry central plateau is covered with savanna, bushland and thickets, while grasslands cover the Serengeti plain and other areas which lack good drainage. The coastline is broken by extensive mangrove growth, especially at the Rufiji River delta and near the mouths of other major rivers.

Tanzania has a variety of soil, ranging from fertile, volcanic soils in highland areas to the loamy soils of the central plateau, which have moderate to poor fertility.

FAUNA

Tanzania's more than four million wild animals include representatives of 430 species and subspecies. Among the most common are zebra, elephant, wildebeest, buffalo, hippo, giraffe, antelope, dik-dik, gazelle, eland and kudu. There are also many predatory animals, including hyenas, wild dogs, lions and leopards, and bands of chimpanzees in Gombe Stream and Mahale Mountains national parks. (See the colour Safari Guide for descriptions of some of these animals.) In addition, Tanzania has over 60,000 insect species, about 25 types of reptiles or amphibians, including crocodiles, 100 species of snakes and numerous fish species.

The country hosts more than 1000 bird species including a number of endemics, such as the Udzungwa forest partridge, the Pemba green pigeon, the Usambara weaver, the South Pare white eye and the Usambara eagle owl.

Endangered Species

Endangered species include the Uluguru bush shrike; the hawksbill, green, olive ridley, and leatherback turtles; the blue whale; black rhinos; and, the colobus monkey (rare).

Travellers interested in details about the threats faced by any of these species, and measures being implemented to ensure their survival, can contact the Wildlife Conservation Society of Tanzania in Dar es Salaam (see Ecology & Environment, earlier).

NATIONAL PARKS & GAME RESERVES

Tanzania's protected areas include 12 national parks, 14 game reserves and the Ngorongoro Conservation Area. The country's first marine park was recently gazetted, and there are several protected marine reserves. The government has established a college of wildlife management in Mweka, near Moshi, to train conservators, guides and game wardens to work in the parks.

With the exception of Sadani Game Reserve, which has one permanent camp, and the Selous, which has tourist facilities in its northern sector, game reserves countrywide are undeveloped. Among the parks, only those in the north have been extensively developed – in some cases, exploited. In the Serengeti, a moratorium on new lodge development is in effect. The situation in many of the southern parks is the opposite;

NATIONAL PARKS & GAME RESERVES

UGANDA

Lake Victoria

KENYA

◯ NAIROBI

Ibanda Game Reserve

Rumanyika Orugundu Game Reserve

RWANDA

Lake Kivu

Burigi Game Reserve

Rubondo Island National Park

Masai Mara National Reserve

Lake Natron

Tsavo National Park

Serengeti National Park

Olduvai Gorge

Mt Kilimanjaro

Arusha National Park

Galana River

BURUNDI

Biharamulo Game Reserve

Siga Hills

Maswa Game Reserve

Ngorongoro Crater

Mt Meru

MOMBASA

Moyowosi Game Reserve

Kigosi Game Reserve

Ngorongoro Conservation Area

Lake Eyasi

Lake Manyara

Mt Kilimanjaro National Park

Pare Mountains

Mkomazi Game Reserve

Gombe Stream National Park

Lake Manyara National Park

Tarangire National Park

Masai Steppe

Usambara Mountains

Pemba Island

Kitwei Plain

Mahale Mountains National Park

Ugalla River Game Reserve

Nguru Mountains

◯ DODOMA

Sadani Game Reserve

Unguja (Zanzibar Island)

DAR ES SALAAM

Lake Tanganyika

Mala Hills

Kisigo Game Reserve

Rubeho Mountains

Mikumi National Park

Uluguru Mountains

CONGO (ZAÏRE)

Katavi National Park

Uwanda Game Reserve

Rungwa Game Reserve

Lake Rukwa

Ruaha National Park

Udzungwa Mountains National Park

Rufiji River

Mafia Island

Mafia Island Marine Park

Mbeya Range

Poroto Mountains

Kipengere Range

Selous Game Reserve

Lake Mweru

Livingstone Mountains

ZAMBIA

Makonde Plateau

0 100 200 km

MALAWI

Lake Nyasa

Ruvuma River

MOZAMBIQUE

Tanzania's Fragile Marine Ecosystems

For years, Tanzania's rich and extensive marine ecosystems have gone largely ignored and unnoticed by all but a relatively small scientific and research community. While some efforts at protection were initiated as early as the 1970s, they remained largely without practical effect and many detrimental activities continued unabated, including destructive fishing practices, over-fishing, mangrove deforestation, pollution, and unregulated tourism and development. Fortunately, over the past decade the situation has begun to change. Tanzania's first marine park has been gazetted at Mafia island, and several marine conservation projects have been implemented, including those at Chumbe and Misali islands. There are also several private groups now actively working to bring additional marine areas under formal protection. These steps are coming none too soon. Tanzania's coastal resources are valuable not only from an ecological point of view, but also for their many potential economic benefits. Most coastal communities depend on fishing as their main source of income and nutrition. Mangrove forests provide poles and timber for house and boat building, firewood and medicines. Tourism, if properly managed, can contribute to raised living standards for local communities.

One of the most serious threats to marine environments along much of Tanzania's coastline is dynamite fishing, a practice which has been widespread in Tanzania since the 1960s. Using dynamite, fishermen are able to pull in a large catch of fish within a very short time. Yet, in addition to killing all fish within a 15 to 20m radius, a dynamite blast also destroys most of the invertebrates and plankton upon which many fish feed, as well as damaging any hard coral near the area of the blast. As coral cover decreases, so too does the available space for fish to breed, rest and seek shelter from predators. As a result, areas which are subjected to frequent dynamite blasts soon begin to show marked reductions in fish abundance and diversity. The ability of coral reefs to recover from this type of damage is minimal.

In a few areas – for example, that encompassed by Mafia Island Marine Park – increased vigilance has resulted in significant decreases in dynamite fishing. Yet, much of the coastline still goes unpatrolled and unprotected. The problem is made more complex by the fact that in many cases it is not only local fishermen doing the blasting, but also outsiders who have no direct stake in the local environment. A good example of this can be seen in the areas offshore from Kilwa Masoko and around the Songo Songo archipelago, where most dynamite fishing is carried out by fishermen from Dar es Salaam working for businessmen based in the capital. Ultimately, a sustainable solution to the problem will require a combination of measures. In addition to more vigilant patrolling and police enforcement, and intensified community education initiatives, many conservation groups are now calling for more stringent regulation of dynamite supplies, or even the replacement of dynamite with an explosive which would not work in water. Other proposals include increasing accountability on the part of dynamite suppliers by permitting only a small number of companies to import, handle and use explosives; introducing stiff penalties for the unlicensed possession of explosives; and, implementing seize and destroy policies for all boats and equipment of fishermen caught dynamiting.

The Tanzania Coastal Management Partnership (PO Box 71686 Dar es Salaam), which publishes the informative bimonthly *Pwani Yetu* (email gluhikula@epiq.or.tz), can provide you with further information, as can the Wildlife Conservation Society of Tanzania. The major non-governmental organisation working in this area is Frontier Tanzania Marine Research (☎ 051-153053, fax 112752, email frontier@twiga.com, PO Box 9472 Dar es Salaam) or in the UK (☎ 020-7613 2422, fax 7613 2992, 77 Leonard St, London, EC 2A 4QS), a UK-based conservation organisation from whose publications much of this information has been extracted.

utilisation to date has been minimal, and low-impact development is encouraged.

National Parks

The country's national parks are managed by the Tanzania National Parks Authority or TANAPA (☎ 057-2371, 4082, fax 8216, PO Box 3134 Arusha), which is under the Ministry of Natural Resources and Tourism. Gates at all parks are open daily from 6 am to 7 pm. Entry fees must be paid in hard currency, preferably in US dollars cash. While travellers cheques are usually accepted, getting change back in dollars can be difficult.

In general, walking is not prohibited in the national parks, with the notable exceptions of Kilimanjaro, Arusha, Udzungwa Mountains, Mahale Mountains and Gombe Stream. TANAPA has given preliminary approval to a few tour operators to begin multiday walking safaris in some of the other parks including Tarangire and Ruaha; check in Arusha on the current situation. At the time of research, the 'walking safaris' advertised by most operators were short half-day walks. Discussions are also underway to add canoeing or walking safaris around the Momela Lakes in Arusha National Park, and to offer night-time game drives on an expanded basis.

If you are driving your own vehicle, remember that speed limits within the parks are set at a maximum of 50kph, although you will need to go considerably slower than this in order to see wildlife. Honking of horns is prohibited.

All of the parks have camp sites, and usually also simple *bandas* or resthouses. Most also have more comfortable lodges or tented camps. Many in the northern circuit have hostels, although these are generally only for school groups and must be reserved in advance; details can be obtained from the Senior Park Warden at each park.

For a local perspective on some of Tanzania's protected areas, read *A Guide to Tanzania National Parks* by Lilla N Lyogello. TANAPA publishes an informative series of booklets covering many of the parks in-

cluding Arusha, Gombe Stream (including a section on Mahale Mountains), Kilimanjaro, Lake Manyara, Mikumi, Serengeti and Tarangire. There is also a booklet on the Ngorongoro Conservation Area. For details, see the individual park sections in the regional chapters of this book. Each of these booklets also contains a helpful bibliography listing background reading for each of the parks. The booklets are available in bookshops in Dar es Salaam, Arusha and Zanzibar Town for about Tsh3500. In Dar es Salaam, you can also obtain copies at the Wildlife Conservation Society of Tanzania.

Game Reserves

Tanzania's game reserves fall under the jurisdiction of the Wildlife Division of the Ministry of Natural Resources and Tourism (☎ 051-866376, 866064, Ivory Room, Pugu Rd at Changombe Rd, PO Box 25295, Dar es Salaam). As with the national parks, entry fees (generally US$20) should be paid in US dollars. The only reserves relevant for tourists at the time of research were Sadani, the Selous, and possibly Mkomazi. The others have no tourist facilities and access is difficult; large areas of most have been granted to hunting concessions.

Marine Parks & Reserves

The Ministry of Natural Resources & Tourism's Division of Fisheries (☎ 116162, 116159, fax 110352, email fisheries@twiga .com, PO Box 2462 Dar es Salaam) on the 6th floor of Ardhi House at the eastern end of Kivukoni Front in Dar es Salaam, oversees Tanzania's marine park and reserves.

GOVERNMENT & POLITICS

The government of the United Republic of Tanzania can be described as a fledgling multiparty democracy. Executive power rests with the president and the ruling CCM. Both the president and the vice president, as well as members of the unicameral national assembly, are elected by direct popular vote for five-year terms. The prime minister, who functions as the head of the National Assembly, is appointed by the president. Cabinet members are selected by the president from among National Assembly members. Both the prime minister of Tanzania and the president of Zanzibar are vice presidents of the Republic of Tanzania.

Of the 275 seats in the National Assembly, 232 are elected from the mainland and the Zanzibar archipelago. An additional 37 are appointed seats for women, which are divided proportionately among the various political parties based on polling in individual constituencies. The remainder are elected by the Zanzibar House of Representatives. In the 1995 legislative elections, 186 seats went to the CCM, 24 to the main opposition party, the CUF, 16 to the National Convention for Construction and Reform (NCCR), three to Chama Cha Demokrasia Na Maendeleo (CHADEMA) and three to the United Democratic Party.

Under the 1977 constitution, the Union government has jurisdiction over external affairs, defence, and external trade currency, while the Zanzibar government has jurisdiction over all nonunion matters.

The Tanzanian judiciary is divided into five levels – primary courts, district courts, resident magistrate courts, high courts and the Court of Appeals – and combines elements of tribal, Islamic and British common law. Judges of the lower courts are appointed by the Chief Justice, and those for the Court of Appeals and the High Court are appointed by the president. Since the advent of multiparty politics, the judiciary has taken several small but important steps towards increasing its independence from the executive branch. The judicial system on the Zanzibar archipelago is structured in three tiers – a High Court, people's district courts, and Islamic courts (*kadhis*).

Tanzania is divided into 25 administrative regions, including 20 on the mainland, three on Unguja and two on Pemba. Each region is subdivided into districts, with 86 districts for the 20 mainland regions.

Foreign Policy

Since independence, regional and international activism have been hallmarks of Tanzanian foreign policy. During the Nyerere era, the country was a leading member of the Non-Aligned Movement. It has also played and continues to play a prominent role in a variety of other organisations, including the front-line states, the Southern African Development Community Conference (SADC), the Organisation of African Unity (OAU), the Common Market for Eastern and Southern Africa (Comesa) and the United Nations. From the 1960s through the 1980s, Tanzania was in the forefront of African states providing support to regional liberation movements, including those in Mozambique, Angola, South Africa and Rhodesia (Zimbabwe). Although Tanzania has become less activist in recent years, it remains committed to maintaining its alliances and exercising regional influence. A notable example of this can be seen in the country's efforts to play a leading role in resolving the Burundi conflict.

Tanzania enjoys good bilateral relations with Mozambique and Zambia. Relations with Kenya, after being strained for many years in the wake of the break-up of the East African Community, have improved significantly. Relations with Uganda, also strained at several points, including in 1994 by Ugandan support for the Rwandan Patriotic Front's military campaign against the Rwandan government, are also on the upswing. However, relations with Malawi continue to be tense due to the ongoing border dispute over Lake Nyasa. The recent wave of refugees from Congo (Zaïre) is the major factor defining Tanzania's dealings with that country.

Tanzania's border with Burundi has been closed since 1995. Tensions escalated in early 1998 when the Burundian government alleged that refugee camps in north-western Tanzania were being used as training centres for rebel troops. Negotiations between the two countries, facilitated by Julius Nyerere, are ongoing.

For related information on Tanzania's refugee policies, see the boxed text 'Refugees' under Kigoma in the Western Tanzania chapter.

ECONOMY

Agriculture is the mainstay of Tanzania's economy, employing about 80% of the workforce and accounting for about 60% of gross domestic product (GDP). Major commercial crops include coffee, tea, cotton, cashews, sisal and cloves; subsistence crops include rice, cassava, maize, millet and plantains. With the exception of sisal and tea, most agriculture is small-holder cash cropping. Impediments to improved sectoral growth include poor pricing structures, unreliable cash flow to farmers, and an inadequate infrastructure which inhibits large amounts of produce from ever reaching the market.

Tourism, with an annual growth rate of over 8%, is playing an increasingly important role in the economy. According to figures from the Tanzania Tourist Board, 359,096 visitors came to Tanzania in 1997, bringing in revenues of US$392.4 million (about 5% of GDP), this was up from 130,851 visitors and US$31 million a decade earlier. The government hopes to increase tourism revenues to US$500 million by the year 2000. The major constraint to faster growth within this sector is an underdeveloped infrastructure.

Other important sectors include mining, which represents about 7% of GDP, and industry (about 8% of GDP), although in comparison with other countries on the continent the industrial sector is considered weak. Tanzania's widely scattered mineral resources include nickel (in the Kagera region west of Lake Victoria), iron (in the south-west near Chunya and Mbeya), coal (in the south-west in the Mbeya region), gold (in the Lake Victoria region) and gemstones (in the Lake Victoria region, and in the south, near Tunduru); most of these resources are unexploited.

Most outside observers are fairly optimistic about Tanzania's mid-term economic prospects. Economic growth currently averages about 3.5% per year. Inflation, at about 13%, is well down from rates of a few years ago, but not yet at the targeted rate of less than 10%. Throughout much of the 1990s, the government pursued a course of trying to reverse the post-independence socialist policies of the Nyerere era. A major restructuring of state-owned enterprises has begun, including privatization of over 400 parastatals, although progress has been much slower than initially hoped. For travellers, one of the most positive changes has been liberalization of the financial services sector and establishment of open markets in foreign exchange.

Despite these improvements, servicing of Tanzania's US$8 billion external debt (close to half of which is multilateral debt) accounts for more than one-third of government expenditures, and the economy remains heavily dependent on outside donors. While the economic situation in Tanzania is far better than in many of Africa's war-torn or drought-afflicted nations (Tanzania was ranked 149th out of 174 countries on the UNDP Human Development Index in the late 1990s), daily life for many Tanzanians remains a struggle. Annual per capita income is estimated at US$260, although there are wide variations between rural and urban areas, as well as an extensive informal economy which distorts the statistical picture. Unemployment averages about 4%. More of a problem than unemployment is underemployment which, except for a small elite sector, is widespread. Military expenditures account for just over 20% of the overall budget.

Until 1977, Tanzania was a member of the East African Community (EAC), an economic union with Kenya and Uganda which linked the currencies of the three countries and provided for freedom of movement and shared telecommunications and postal facilities. Following the break-up of the EAC due to political differences, Tanzania entered into a long dispute with Kenya, during which the border was closed for six years. Since then relations have improved, and in 1996, the presidents of Tanzania, Kenya and Uganda established the Tripartite Commission for East African Cooperation, which laid the groundwork for re-establishing the old economic and customs union. Unlike the East African Community, which sought to impose supranational control over a variety of areas, the new EAC simply seeks harmonisation of fiscal and other policies. A common passport was adopted at a meeting of the new EAC in 1997 in Arusha, and a joint development strategy was promulgated. The next step on the agenda is political federation, although little concrete progress has been made to date.

POPULATION & PEOPLE

Tanzania's population, estimated at about 31 million, is comprised of about 120 tribal groups. Most of these groups are very small; almost 100 of them combined account for only one-third of the total population. As a result, none have succeeded in dominating politically or culturally, although tribes such as the Chagga and the Haya, which were strongly influenced by Christian missionary work and western education during the pre-independence era, are now disproportionately represented in government and business circles.

About 95% of Tanzanians are of Bantu origin. The largest tribes include the Sukuma (about 13% of overall population), the Nyamwezi, the Makonde, the Haya and the Chagga. The Maasai and several smaller groups including the Arusha and the Samburu are of Nilo-Hamitic (Maasai) or Nilotic origin. The Iraqw, who live in the area around Karatu and north-west of Lake Manyara, are Cushitic, as are the tiny tribes of Gorowa and Burungi; the Sandawe and, more distantly, the Hadzabe, are considered to belong to the Khoisan ethno-linguistic family. There are also small but economically significant Asian and Arabic populations, especially in Dar es Salaam, and a small European community (both expatriate and by descent). For information on the ethnic composition of the Zanzibar archipelago, see Population & People in The Zanzibar Archipelago chapter.

Tanzania is one of the least urbanised countries in sub-Saharan Africa. According to the most recent census (1988), urban dwellers constituted only 11.5% of all mainland Tanzanians, although the urban population is estimated to be growing at an annual average rate of 10%. While average population density country-wide is estimated at about 31 people per sq kilometre, this varies radically from one area to the next. In general, Tanzania is most densely populated around its perimeter, while settlement in the centre of the country is sparse. Major areas of population concentration include the Usambara and Pare mountains, the slopes of Mt Kilimanjaro and Mt Meru, the shores of Lake Victoria, the northern end of Lake Nyasa, and the coastal areas around Tanga and Dar es Salaam. The Zanzibar archipelago is also densely populated. Important determinants of settlement patterns include rainfall and the incidence of the tsetse fly, which causes sleeping sickness in cattle and people, and which thrives in much of north-central and western Tanzania.

Tanzania's largest city is Dar es Salaam, with an estimated population of over two million. The current population of Dodoma, the legislative capital, is estimated to be just under 200,000. Populations of other major towns and average growth rates as per the 1988 census are: Mwanza (pop 223,000, 2.59% average growth rate), Tanga (187,000; 2%), Mbeya (152,800; 3.15%) and Arusha (134,700; 3.9%). Dar es Salaam's growth rate is estimated at over 4%, while the average population growth rate for the Tanzanian mainland is about 3%.

Average life expectancy is 52 years.

EDUCATION

Tanzania's educational system is loosely modelled on that of Great Britain. There are seven years of primary school which, at least in theory, are compulsory, and four years of secondary school with an additional two years required for university entrance. The country has one state-run university (in Dar es Salaam, with an independently administered branch in Morogoro), some trade and technical schools, and several mission-run institutions of higher education. Primary school instruction is in Swahili, while secondary level and university instruction is in English. Although primary school tuition is free, costs for uniforms pose hardships for

Tanzanian Education

Julius Nyerere, who was a teacher himself and is still known throughout the country as *Mwalimu* (Swahili for teacher), was convinced that the key to success for his philosophy of socialism and self-reliance lay in having an educated populace. During the early years of his presidency, he set aside 14% of the national budget for education, offered government assistance to villagers to build their own schools, and made primary education free and compulsory. By the late 1980s, the country's literacy rate had become one of the highest in Africa.

Over the past decade, however, much of this initial momentum has been lost. Only about 50% of children complete primary school, and less than 3% of these go on to complete secondary school. The scenario is particularly bleak for girls, who constitute barely one-fourth of secondary school graduates (a figure which represents less than 5% of all Tanzanian women). Many drop out due to pregnancy; others are needed to work at home. Cost is also a factor, with secondary school tuition rates representing a prohibitive sum for many families. For both girls and boys, language poses additional barriers. Since primary school instruction is in Swahili, many students lack sufficient knowledge of English to carry out their course work at the secondary level. This leads to frustration and exacerbates the already dismal drop-out rate.

Nationally, government spending on education has been steadily declining, and now comprises less than 4% of the total budget. Educational facilities are lacking and morale is low. In many schools there are no lights, no blackboards and no books. Even more serious is the shortage of qualified, committed teachers. Salaries are woefully inadequate, and are often paid months behind schedule, resulting in high rates of teacher absenteeism. It's not uncommon in many areas for teachers to stay away from class during normal school hours, and then – in an effort to compensate for their unpaid salaries – charge students extra for after-hours 'tutoring'. The students are then forced to pay to get the basic course materials required for passing their exams.

To address this situation, the government has again allowed private schools to operate. These are beginning to play a critical role in bridging the enormous gap between the country's

---

many rural families. Secondary school tuition averages between Tsh80,000 and Tsh120,000 per year.

Until independence, most education was affiliated with foreign missions. While the schools were generally of a high standard, there were simply not enough to meet the country's needs. In the wake of the Arusha Declaration, all of the private schools were nationalised. Nyerere strove to 'Africanise' curricula, and implemented a variety of other measures targeted at universalising education and decreasing Tanzania's illiteracy rate (see the boxed text 'Tanzanian Education'). Unfortunately, much of the early progress resulting from these efforts has been halted due to competing priorities for scarce government resources, shortages of

qualified teachers, and insufficient facilities and supplies. Today, the most serious problem lies with secondary education. While close to 70% of children obtain at least some primary schooling, only about 5% enrol at the secondary level. Privately run schools, which have again started operating, are helping, but their geographical distribution is uneven.

ARTS
Dance

The general Swahili term used to refer to dance all along the East African coast, and increasingly in the interior as well, is *ngoma*. As is the case throughout Africa, dance in Tanzania serves as a means of

Tanzanian Education

educational needs and scarce resources, particularly at the secondary level. One of the most notable success stories is St Mary's Secondary School in Mazinde Juu, a tiny village tucked away in the Usambara Mountains near Lushoto, in north-east Tanzania. The area around Mazinde Juu has long been neglected and lags behind much of the rest of the region economically and otherwise. Most local families are small-scale farmers for whom education has traditionally been an unattainable or unnecessary luxury, especially education for girls.

St Mary's was founded in 1989 by an American Benedictine missionary who believes that Tanzania's long-term development can only be achieved through education and empowerment of the country's women. From the outset, the school targeted girls in the Mazinde Juu area who otherwise would have no educational opportunities beyond the primary level. Initially, it had only basic resources and just 42 girls. Today, St Mary's has over 200 students. It is ranked first among the approximately 50 girls' schools in Tanzania, and in the top 20 among about 500 secondary schools country-wide. The school's reputation has spread well beyond the Usambaras; close to 700 girls from all over Tanzania competed in the most recent entrance exam for the 40 places in this year's incoming class, although true to its original mission, the school reserves 50% of the places for applicants from Mazinde Juu.

While St Mary's is still dependent on outside contributions to make ends meet, strong emphasis is placed on achieving sustainability, and in many ways the school can serve as a model for other areas of the country. The headmistress and almost all of the teachers are Tanzanian women. Students are taught ecologically sound farming methods and help out on the school farm, which supplies about 80% of the food needs in the compound. The school grows timber used in construction of new buildings, raises livestock and maintains fruit trees as cash crops.

Although St Mary's is barely a decade old, there is already tangible proof of its success. Several former students are now teaching in primary schools in or near Mazinde Juu. Others are pursuing further professional training, such as nursing or accountancy, and a few are even studying at the university level.

communicating with the ancestors and expressing sentiments such as thanks or praise. Traditionally, it encompasses the entire community in its message. While some of these elements have been lost in modern, tourist-oriented performances, many traditional rhythms and movements have been maintained.

Masked dance is not as widespread in Tanzania as in other parts of sub-Saharan Africa. Among the most significant of those tribes which do practice it are the Makonde and Makua in the south-east, where it plays an important role in coming-out ceremonies for young girls and boys. Chuo cha Sanaa in Bagamoyo is a good place to start for those interested in learning more about dance in Tanzania. (See Things to See & Do under

Bagamoyo in the North-Eastern Tanzania chapter.)

Music

Traditional musical instruments that you are likely to see include the *marimba*, which has metal strips of varying lengths that are plucked with the thumb, and which is particularly popular among the Gogo around Dodoma; *kayamba* (shakers made with grain kernels), and rattles and bells made of wood or iron; xylophones (also sometimes referred to as marimbas); *siwa* (horns), *tari* (tambourines); and *ngoma* (drums), which come in a wide variety of designs. The book, *The Traditional Musical Instruments of Tanzania* by Gareth W Lewis & EG Makala provides a good overview of these and other instruments; examples of some of these instruments are on display at the National Museum in Dar es Salaam.

During the colonial days, German and British military brass bands influenced the development of *beni ngoma* or brass ngoma – dance and music societies combining western-style brass instruments with African drums and other traditional instruments. Later, rhumba-style bands became popular. Some of the better-known ones included Orchestre Makassy, Maquis du Zaïre and Orchestre Super Matimila.

In recent decades, Tanzanian music has been significantly influenced by Zaïrean jazz. One of the country's best-known musicians during the 1980s and 1990s has been the Zaïrean-born Remmy Ongala ('Dr Remmy'), who came to Tanzania in the late 1970s to perform as lead singer with Orchestre Makassy. The dreadlocked Ongala, who is often referred to as the Bob Marley of Tanzania, sings mostly in Swahili, and has been one of the major forces in popularising music from the region beyond Africa's borders. Many of his songs are commentaries on contemporary themes such as AIDS, poverty and hunger.

Literature

Swahili did not become entrenched as a national language in Tanzania until relatively late in the 20th century, and literary development was correspondingly delayed. The most significant author in the 20th century has been Shaaban Robert (1909-62), who was born near Tanga and educated in Dar es Salaam. His extensive writings were a major impetus for establishment of a modern prose style in Swahili. His works include the autobiographical *Maisha yangu*, and several collections of stories told in the form of traditional tales. Other well-known Tanzanian authors of Swahili-language works include Muhammed Said Abdulla and Shafi Adam Shafi (both were born on Zanzibar), Joseph Mbele, and Ebrahim Hussein. Mbele wrote short stories, while Hussein is known primarily for his dramas and theatre pieces.

Contemporary Tanzanian authors of English-language works include Peter Palangyo, William Kamera and Tolowa Marti Mollel. Palangyo, who was born in Arusha in 1939, wrote the novel *Dying in the Sun*, which tells the story of a young Tanzanian who, after questioning his existence, comes to terms with his family and his heritage in rural Tanzania. Kamera (born near Moshi in 1942), wrote several collections of poetry, as well as *Tales of the Wairaqw of Tanzania*, containing stories of the Iraqw people. Mollel has authored numerous short stories. *North of South* by Shiva Narpaul (1979) is an interesting portrayal of Tanzania and Tanzanian life in the 1970s.

Painting

Indigenous painting is relatively undeveloped in Tanzania in comparison with figurative art and other art forms. Stylistic development has been extensively influenced by European painters and by the dictates of the mainly European market. The most well-known school of painting is Tingatinga (see the boxed text).

Those interested in contemporary Tanzanian artists and artwork should stop by the Russian-Tanzanian Cultural Centre in Dar es Salaam, which hosts frequent exhibitions.

Sculpture & Woodcarving

Among the major representatives of Tanzanian figurative art are the Makonde, who are renowned throughout East Africa for their original and often highly fanciful carvings. Authentic Makonde carvings are made from ebony wood. Some of the simpler ones relate to the cult of womanhood and are carried by the male carver as a good luck talisman. More common are those with ujamaa motifs, and those known as *shetani*, which embody images from the spirit world. Ujamaa carvings are frequently designed as a totem pole or 'tree of life' containing from several to many interlaced human and animal figures, each of which is connected with and giving support to all of the others. These carvings often reach several metres in height, and are almost always made from a

Tingatinga Painting

Tanzania's most well-known style of painting was begun in the 1960s by Edward Saidi Tingatinga, after whom it is named. Tingatinga was born in 1932 in southern Tanzania's remote Tunduru district, and had only four years of primary school. In the 1950s, he headed north to Tanga, where he worked on a sisal plantation, and then later to Dar es Salaam, where he worked as domestic help for a British civil servant. During his time in Dar es Salaam, Tingatinga began to seek creative outlets and additional income, first as a member of a musical group, and later as a self-taught artist, painting fanciful and colourful animals on small shingles.

Tingatinga's wife sold his paintings near Morogoro Stores in Dar es Salaam, and his work soon became popular with European tourists. As his success grew, Tingatinga began to attract a small circle of students, with first his relatives and then others learning to imitate his style. Then, one night in 1972, Tingatinga was mistaken for an escaping thief and fatally shot by the police. Following his death, Tingatinga's students organised themselves into the Tingatinga Partnership, which in 1990 was renamed the Tingatinga Arts Cooperative Society. This cooperative, which numbers about 50 members (including two women), is still based near Morogoro Stores in Dar es Salaam, where Tingatinga's works were originally sold. It has received significant support in recent years, including a new building, from Helvetas (the Swiss Association for International Cooperation).

Traditional Tingatinga paintings are composed in a square format, and generally feature colourful animal motifs against a monochrome background. One of the most distinctive characteristics of the style is its use of undiluted and often unmixed enamel and high-gloss paints which give Tingatinga paintings their characteristic glossy appearance.

single piece of wood. Among the most impressive are those designed around a hollow central column. One of the most well known of the original ujamaa-style carvers is Roberto Jacobo. Jacobo traditionally carved only one sculpture each year as inspiration for his students, who would then produce modified versions for commercial sale.

The shetani style, which has become popular in recent years, was first developed by an artist known as Samaki. Carvings with shetani motifs are very abstract, often grotesque, and are designed to challenge the viewer to new interpretations while giving the carver's imagination free reign.

In contrast to the ujamaa and shetani motifs, which are relatively recent, earlier Makonde carvings generally depicted more traditional themes, often relating to various deities or rituals. Even today, the Makonde produce carvings of ordinary household objects such as bowls and walking sticks, although these are seldom seen for sale.

While it can be argued that the extensive commercialisation of Makonde carvings has had a negative impact on artistic and imaginative quality, it has not totally destroyed originality. On the positive side, it has had the effect of securing many carvers a livelihood which they would not have been able to achieve otherwise.

The major centres of Makonde carving in Tanzania are in the south-east on the Makonde plateau, and in Dar es Salaam. Dar es Salaam became a haven for Makonde carvers during the large-scale migrations from Mozambique in the 1950s and 1960s. Many Makonde migrants made their way from Mozambique into southern Tanzania, and from there to the capital, attracted by better employment opportunities and by favourable marketing prospects for their carvings.

Cinema

Tanzania has a tiny indigenous film industry. During the era of British colonial rule, the missionary-initiated Bantu Educational Kinema Experiment (BEKE) produced one feature (*Gumu*), and during WWII, several British comedy films using Tanzanian actors from Chuo cha Sanaa in Bagamoyo were made for propaganda purposes. A series of Swahili-language films was produced during the 1950s with the assistance of South African technical support. Over the next several decades, few films were made. The major post-independence cinematic entity was the government-owned Tanzania Film Company. Some blame video recorders, which have been permitted in Tanzania since the mid-1980s, as a factor in stunting the development of the local film industry.

In July 1998, the first annual Zanzibar International Film Festival was held in Zanzibar Town. Its organisers hope that it will take its place as one of Africa's major film festivals, and together with those in Ouagadougou (Burkina Faso), Carthage (Tunisia) and Harare (Zimbabwe), give an impetus to development of indigenous Tanzanian cinema. One of the films premiered at the festival was *Maangamizi*, which was shot in Tanzania and co-directed by Tanzanian Martin Mhando.

SOCIETY & CONDUCT

Politeness, respect and modesty are highly valued attributes in Tanzania's traditional society. Great emphasis is placed on pleasantries, and people often spend several minutes at the beginning of a conversation simply greeting each other. Try to master *habari gani* and some of the other greetings and responses in Swahili, and use them unsparingly. *Jambo* is usually reserved for foreigners; Tanzanians rarely say it to each other. As a foreigner and guest, you will frequently be greeted, especially by children, with *shikamuu*, the Swahili word used for addressing superiors and for showing respect. The correct reply is *marahaba* (thank you). Other useful words which will help smooth social interactions include *asante* (thank you), *kwaheri* (good bye) or *tutaonana* (we'll see each other), and *karibu* (you are welcome, please come inside).

Along with greetings, handshakes are also an important part of social interactions. People often continue to hold hands for several minutes after meeting, or even throughout an entire conversation. In some areas, particularly in the south-east of Tanzania, you will see people touching their left hand to their right elbow as they shake hands, as a sign of respect.

The elderly, professionals such as doctors, and government officials and other authorities are accorded particular deference in social interactions. In the case of authorities, you will likely have few troubles in Tanzania; most are courteous and even friendly. However, if you do find yourself in an awkward situation, the most important thing is to maintain a polite and composed demeanour. Losing your patience, raising your voice, or otherwise undermining an official's authority will get you nowhere. In contrast, children and women rate very low on the social scale. Children are expected to show deference to adults, and to do what they are told. Particularly in rural areas, women are expected to behave and dress modestly.

For both men and women, dress is important. You will have fewer difficulties, and be met with more respect and openness if you are considerate of local sensibilities and dress modestly, as well as reasonably neatly. Bare-legged or bare-shouldered travellers, or those wearing excessively tatty clothing are often treated with disdain or worse. For women, skirts below the knee or loose-fitting long pants, and modest tops with some sort of sleeve are the best option, and for men, long pants and shirts with sleeves. From a practical point of view, long, loose-fitting clothing also offers better protection from the sun.

Being invited to share a meal with Tanzanians at home is a treat not to be turned down. Before the meal, a bowl and a pitcher of water are often passed around for washing hands. If the bowl is brought to you first as the guest, and you are not sure what to do, indicate that it should be taken to the head of the family, then do what they do. The centre of the meal is usually *ugali* (see the Food section in the Facts for the Visitor chapter) or rice. It is normally taken with the right hand from a communal pot, rolled into balls with the fingers, dipped into some sort of sauce, and eaten. Food is never handled or eaten with the left hand, which is traditionally used for toilet duties. In many areas it is even considered impolite to give someone something with the left hand. At the end of the meal, do not be worried if you are unable to finish what is on your plate, as this shows your hosts that you have been satisfied – though try to avoid being the one who takes the last handful from the communal bowl, as this may leave your hosts worrying they haven't provided enough.

When travelling in remote areas, try to tread lightly and leave as little lasting evidence of your visit as possible. If you are offered a gift, it is fine to accept it, and to reciprocate kindness, though indiscriminate distribution of gifts from outside is inappropriate. Gifts are often received with both hands, particularly in rural areas, or (in the south-east) with the right hand while touching the left hand to your right elbow. Both gestures are ways of expressing gratitude. Spoken thanks are not as common in Tanzania as in the west, so if you give a gift, don't be surprised if the appreciation isn't expressed verbally.

Things which are frowned upon wherever you are in the country include public nudity, immodest attire, public displays of affection (between people of the same or opposite sex), and open anger.

RELIGION

About one-third of Tanzanians are Muslim and about one-third are Christian. The remainder are adherents of traditional religions that centre on ancestor worship, the land and various ritual objects. There are also small communities of Hindus, Sikhs, and Ismaelis.

Muslims have traditionally been concentrated along the coast, as well as in those inland towns which lined the old caravan routes. There are several sects represented, notably the Sunni (Shafi school). One of the areas of highest Christian concentration is in the north-east around Moshi, which has been a centre of missionary activity since the mid-19th century. About two-thirds of Tanzania's Christians are Roman Catholic. Major missionary orders include the Benedictines, the Spiritans and the White Fathers. The Evangelical Lutheran Church in Tanzania (ELCT) is the largest Protestant denomination in the country and the largest Lutheran church in Africa. The other major Christian denomination is Anglican, which has developed in two branches – the Universities' Mission to Central Africa (UMCA) in the south and the Church Missionary Society (CMS) around Dodoma. A small percentage of Tanzanians are adherents of other Christian denominations, including Baptist (with major missions in Mbeya and Kigoma), and Pentecostal.

Following initial friction at independence between Tanzania's Muslim and Christian populations, Nyerere declared that his new government would not tolerate any religious or other discrimination, and even coined a slogan which emphasised that TANU had no religion. This calmed things down, although tensions again flared when Islamic Zanzibar joined the union, and again in 1993 when Zanzibar became a member of the Organisation of the Islamic Conference (OIC). The archipelago has since renounced its membership in the OIC, but tensions continue to simmer, albeit at a low level. Despite all this, religion is not a major factor in the contemporary political life of Tanzania.

Islam

In the early 7th century, in the city of Mecca (in today's Saudi Arabia), the Prophet Mohammed called on the people to turn away from pagan worship and submit to the one true God (Allah). While his teachings appealed to the poorer levels of society, they angered the wealthy merchant class, and by 622 AD Mohammed and his followers were forced to flee to Medina. This migration, the *hijra*, marks the beginning of the Islamic calendar, year 1 AH.

Mohammed died in 632 AD (10 AH) but within about two decades most of Arabia was converted to Islam. Over the following centuries, Islam spread through North and West Africa, down the coast of East Africa, into several parts of southern and eastern Europe and eastward across southern Asia. It has been entrenched along the East African coast since at least the 11th century, and remains the dominant religion on the Zanzibar archipelago and in most areas of coastal Tanzania.

The Five Pillars of Islam Islam is the Arabic word for submission and underlies the duty of all Muslims to submit themselves to Allah. The five pillars of Islam are the basic tenets which guide Muslims in their daily lives:

Shahada (Profession of Faith) 'There is no God but Allah, and Mohammed is his prophet' is the fundamental tenet of Islam.

Salat (Prayer) Muslims must face Mecca and pray five times a day: at dawn, midday, mid-afternoon, sunset and nightfall.

Zakat (Alms) Muslims must give a portion of their income to the poor and needy.

Sawm (Fasting) Ramadan is the month of the Muslim calendar when all Muslims must fast from dawn to dusk.

Haj (Pilgrimage) It is the duty of every Muslim who is fit and can afford it to make the pilgrimage to Mecca at least once.

The Haj All Muslims are supposed to make the *haj*, or pilgrimage to Mecca, at least once in their life if they have good health and the money for the journey. As the cost is typically several thousand dollars, for some this can involve a lifetime of savings, so it's not unusual for families to save up and send one member. Before the advent of air travel, the haj used to involve an overland journey of a year or more, sometimes requiring stops on the way to earn money. Those who complete the pilgrimage receive the honorific title of haj for men, and hajia for women. If you meet someone with this prefix, you can appreciate the honour this bestows on them in the community.

Islamic Holidays The most important Islamic holidays include:

Eid al Kebir (also called *Eid al Haji*) The most important celebration and usually a two day public holiday. Muslims kill a sheep to commemorate the moment when Abraham was about to sacrifice his son in obedience to God's command, only to have God intercede at the last moment and substitute a ram instead. It also coincides with the end of the pilgrimage (haj) to Mecca.

Eid al Fitr The second major Islamic holiday, marking the end of Ramadan.

Eid al Moulid (usually referred to as Maulidi) Marks the birthday of the Prophet Mohammed.

Ramadan (or *ramadhani*) The annual 30 day Muslim fast, when adherents do not eat or drink from sunrise to sunset. Muslims are usually weak during the afternoon and offices can grind to a halt around 1 or 2 pm. The Swahili calendar year is based around Ramadan, with the following months counted as *mfunguo mosi* (first nonfasting month), *mfunguo pili* (second nonfasting month) etc, until *rajabu* and *shabani*, the months preceding Ramadan.

Since the Islamic calendar is based on 12 lunar months, with 354 or 355 days, these holidays are always about 11 days earlier than the previous year. The exact dates depend on the moon and are known for certain only about one or two days in advance. Estimated dates for major Muslim events are:

Event	1999	2000	2001
Ramadan begins	20 Dec	19 Dec	–
Eid al Fitr	20 Jan	19 Jan	–
Eid al Kebir	29 Mar	18 Mar	7 Mar
Eid al Moulid	27 June	16 June	5 June

Tips for the Traveller If you are interested in visiting a mosque, make your request to the mosque elders. Before going inside, take off your shoes. Men and women should be conservatively dressed with most (or all) of their arms and legs covered. Women are also expected to wear a skirt well below the knees (although very loose-fitting trousers often suffice) and to cover their head and shoulders with a scarf. Women are not allowed to enter some mosques if prayers are in progress or if the imam (Islamic leader) is present.

Whether on the mainland or the Zanzibar archipelago, if you have hired a Muslim guide or taxi driver for the day, he will most likely want to say his prayers at the right times. When travelling, three times a day is allowed, so look out for signs indicating he wants a few moments off, particularly around midday, late afternoon and sunset.

Despite the Islamic proscription against alcohol, some Muslims may enjoy a quiet drink. Even so, it's impolite to drink alcohol in their presence unless they show approval.

LANGUAGE

Swahili (KiSwahili) and English are the official languages. As the most important universal language among Tanzania's ethnic groups Swahili has played a major role in unifying the people and solidifying national identity. While English is widely spoken in major towns, in smaller places and rural areas you'll need to know at least a few Swahili phrases. Outside cities and towns, far fewer people speak English than in comparable areas of Kenya. In fact, due to the large number of foreign missionaries and other expatriates in the country who speak Swahili well, rural Tanzanians are often surprised that foreigners do not know their language.

Swahili is grammatically a Bantu language, although it has changed significantly over the centuries as a result of trade and immigration. Its vocabulary includes many words borrowed from Arabic, Persian, Hindi, Portuguese and English.

Swahili has spread from its place of origin along the coast, and is now spoken in much of east and central Africa; it is the lingua

Tanzania's Ethno-Linguistic Composition

Tanzania is the only country in Africa whose indigenous inhabitants include members of each of the continent's four major ethno-linguistic families. The largest of these is the Niger-Congo family, which extends across almost all of sub-Saharan Africa, and which encompasses close to 1000 different languages spoken by more than 300 million people. Of the six different branches of the Niger-Congo family, the most significant is Benue-Congo, to which the Bantu sub-group belongs. Swahili is the most widely spoken Bantu language in Africa.

The Nilo-Saharan family is found primarily around the upper parts of the Chari and Nile rivers, in Uganda, the Sudan, and Kenya, as well as in parts of Mali and Nigeria, although there is some dispute as to the classification of languages belonging to this family. Members of its Nilotic and Nilo-Hamitic sub-groups are found in Tanzania.

The Afro-Asiatic family (also known as Hamito-Semitic) is the major ethno-linguistic grouping in northern Africa. It has more than 200 languages, spoken by close to 200 million people. The most widespread is Arabic, which belongs to the family's Semitic branch. Other branches include Egyptian, Berber, Chadic, Omotic and Cushitic. Other than Arabic, the only significant Afro-Asiatic language now found in Tanzania is Iraqw, which belongs to the Cushitic branch. Cushitic languages once dominated throughout much of Tanzania before being absorbed and replaced during the Bantu expansion in the region.

The smallest of Africa's ethno-linguistic families is Khoisan, which consists of only a few dozen languages. These languages, which are characterised by their use of 'clicks', are spoken primarily in southern Africa, in the area around the Kalahari desert, by hunter-gatherer peoples believed to be descendants of the continent's earliest inhabitants. The most well-known of these people are the San (Bushmen). The two click languages found in Tanzania are Sandawe and, more distantly, Hadza (Hadzabe). These are spoken by small, somewhat scattered and isolated populations in the north-central part of the country who still follow a traditional hunter-gatherer lifestyle.

franca (common language) in Tanzania, Kenya, Uganda and Congo (Zaïre). There are three major Swahili dialects: (Ki)Unguja, or the Swahili of Unguja; (Ki)Mvita, spoken in Mombasa and other areas of Kenya; and (Ki)Amu, spoken on the island of Lamu and in adjacent coastal areas. The most predominant dialect on the Tanzanian mainland is KiUnguja, from which 'standard' Swahili has developed. Due to its status as the standard language the Swahili spoken on Unguja is sometimes said to be of a more pure form than that which you find in other areas of East Africa – many students come to Unguja and Tanzania to study Swahili.

Besides Swahili there are also numerous other African languages spoken in Tanzania, a reflection of the country's ethnic diversity. These local languages are divided into four groups: Bantu, Nilotic, Cushitic and Khoisan. The vast majority (about 95%) of Tanzanians are Bantu-speaking peoples. Bantu languages found in Tanzania include Sukuma, Makonde, Haya, Ha, Gogo, and Yao. The main speakers of the Nilotic languages are the Maasai, while the languages of the tiny Cushitic group are limited to the Iraqw. Khoisan, the most ancient of the language groups, is characterised by 'clicks'; these languages are spoken by the Sandawe and the Hadzabe.

For more information on Swahili and a useful list of words and phrases see the Language chapter at the back of this book.

SAFARI GUIDE

PRIMATES

Bushbabies *Otolemur crassicaudatus (Greater Bushbaby); Galago senegalensis (Lesser Bushbaby); Galago zanibaricus (Zanzibar Lesser Bushbaby)*

Named for their plaintive wailing call, bushbabies are actually primitive primates most similar to Madagascar's lemurs. Heightened night vision and extremely sensitive hearing makes them ideally adapted to their strictly nocturnal way of life. The fruit and sap of trees is the mainstay of their diet, but insects also form an important food source. The lesser bushbaby performs extraordinary leaps from the tips of tree branches to catch flying insects on-the-wing in their dexterous, human-like hands. The bigger greater bushbaby also sometimes preys on lizards, nestlings and eggs. Listen for the 'baby-crying' sound of the greater bushbabys' territorial/alarm call and look for the reddish glow reflected by their huge eyes in torchlight.

Size: greater bushbaby is up to 80cm long, half of which is the distinctive bushy tail, weight 1.5kg; lesser bushbaby is much smaller, 40cm long, weight 150-200g
Distribution: lightly wooded savanna to thickly forested areas. Greater and lesser bushbabies occur throughout the region; the Zanizbar lesser bushbaby is a separate species
Status: common; but hard to see, they're strictly nocturnal

Bushbaby

Vervet Monkey *Cercopithecus aethiops*

The most common monkey of savanna and woodland habitats, vervets are easily recognised by their grizzled, grey, fairly long body hair and black face fringed with white hair. The male has a distinctive bright blue scrotum, an important signal of status in the troop, which may number up to 30 monkeys. Vervet monkeys are diurnal and most active in the early morning and in the evening before sunset when they forage for fruit, seeds, leaves, flowers, invertebrates and the occasional small lizard or nestling. They rapidly learn where easy pickings can be found around lodges and camp sites and become pests when they grow used to being fed. Most park authorities destroy such animals, so avoid feeding them.

Size: up to 130cm long, including a 60cm tail; weight 3.5-8kg
Distribution: all savanna and woodland habitats
Status: very common in parks; easy to see due to their diurnal habits and boldness

Vervet Monkey

JOHN HAY

Blue Monkey

Blue Monkey *Cercopithecus mitis*

Similar to the vervet monkey but slightly larger and much darker. Blue monkeys (also called Samango monkeys) have a grey to black face, black shoulders, limbs and tail, and a reddish-brown or olive-brown back. They are more arboreal than vervet monkeys and generally prefer dense forest and woodland rather than savanna. They feed largely on fruit, bark, gum and leaves. Social groups may be as large as 30 but generally number between four and 12 monkeys. Predators include leopard, pythons and eagles.

Size: 140cm long, 80cm of which is tail; weight 8-10kg
Distribution: throughout most evergreen forests and forest patches
Status: common; active during the day, but often difficult to see among foliage; easy to see in Uganda's Kibale National Park

Eastern Black and White Colobus
Colobus guereza caudatus

The colobus is glossy black with a white face, bushy white tail, and a white fur 'cape' around the back which flows out behind when the monkey moves through the trees. Newborn monkeys are initially white, gaining their adult coat at around six months. The black and white colobus spends most of its time in the forest canopy, satisfying its water needs by drinking from small puddles found in the hollows of branches and trunks. Although locally common, its arboreal habits mean it is easily missed unless you can see into the treetops. Colobus monkeys are usually found in troops of up to 12 animals, consisting of a dominant male, females and young.

Size: up to 140cm long, of which 80cm is the shaggy white tail; weight 10-20kg
Distribution: forests in western Kenya and north-western Tanzania, extending eastwards to Kilimanjaro National Park. The similar Angolan black and white colobus (*C. angolensis*), can be found in Rwanda, eastern Tanzania and south-eastern Kenya.
Status: relatively common within its restricted range

JASON EDWARDS/BIO-IMAGES

Eastern Black and White Colobus

Baboon *Papio cynocephalus*

Baboons are known by different subspecies names in the region but are easily recognised because differences across the species are only superficial. The yellow baboon (*P. c. cynocephalus*) is the most common in the region and is a distinctive yellow-brown colour.

The olive baboon (*P. c. anubis*) has brindled olive-brown hair which grows in a mane around the neck and shoulders, particularly in the males. Baboons live in large troops numbering between eight and 200 animals. Contrary to popular belief, there's no single dominant male in large troops. Social interactions in the troop are extremely complex with males having access to certain females, males forming alliances to dominate other males, and males acting as fathers to unrelated juveniles. Baboons are diurnal, foraging mostly in open savanna and woodland for grasses, tubers, fruits, insects, spiders and occasionally small vertebrates.

They are notorious opportunists and may become pests in tourist areas; those which become dependent on humans for food can be dangerous and often end up being destroyed by park officials, so avoid leaving food in tents and resist the temptation to feed them.

Size: up to 160cm long, height at shoulder 75cm; weight 25-45kg
Distribution: throughout the region
Status: very common in all conservation areas and active during the day; Tanzania's Manyara National Park probably has the highest baboon density of any park in Africa

Baboon near Ngorongoro Crater

Chimpanzee *Pan troglodytes*
Man's closest living relative, chimpanzees are widely recognised. They require a rich year-round food supply, preferring productive, moist forests, but are adaptable and can be found in habitats ranging from dry woodland to arid acacia savanna. Chimpanzees are highly sociable, living in communities numbering up to 120, however all the individuals in a social group rarely congregate and the typical group size is much smaller. Individuals may also spend considerable time alone. Primarily vegetarians, chimps consume fruit, bark, stems and leaves with the occasional meal of insects, nestling birds, eggs and sometimes larger prey.

Size: standing height up to 170cm; weight 40-55kg
Distribution: equatorial forest in western Tanzania, Rwanda, Burundi and eastern Uganda; best seen in Tanzania's Gombe National Park
Status: threatened by habitat destruction, civil unrest and persecution; chimpanzees are endangered and live in small, isolated populations in the region

Infant Chimpanzee

Gorilla *Gorilla gorilla*
The largest primate in the world was made famous by researcher Dian Fossey. Two races occur in the region:

the eastern lowland gorilla (*G. g. graueri*), numbering about 4000 in eastern Zaïre and Rwanda, and the highly endangered mountain gorilla (*G. g. beringei*), in the border region of Congo (Zaïre), Rwanda and Uganda, of which there are probably only 600 to 700 left. Gorillas inhabit humid equatorial rainforest up to 4000m above sea level and can tolerate subzero temperatures. Groups number between two and 20, with one adult male (silverback), though large groups of lowland gorilla may contain up to four silverbacks. Males dominate, making the decisions regarding virtually all aspects of the group's daily life. Despite their fearsome appearance gorillas are vegetarians and eat vines, leaves, shoots, bark and berries. Nonetheless, males are formidable in defence of their family and will die protecting the troop from their only enemy – man.

Size: standing height up to 180cm; weight up to 210kg in the male, females 70-100kg
Distribution: equatorial forest in western Tanzania, Rwanda, Burundi and eastern Uganda
Status: seriously threatened by poaching, habitat destruction and civil unrest, gorillas are highly endangered; best seen in Parc de Volcans and Virunga National Park on the Rwanda-Congo border

LEANNE LOGAN

Gorilla

SCALY ANTEATERS
Manis temminckii

Scaly anteaters, also known as ground pangolins, are covered with large rounded scales over the back and tail, with a sparse covering of hair on the face and underbelly. They subsist entirely on ants and termites which they excavate from termite mounds, rotting wood and dung heaps. Anteaters walk on the outer edges of their paws, with claws pointed inwards, leaving a distinctive track.

Size: 70-100cm long; weight 5-15kg
Distribution: throughout the region
Status: relatively uncommon; nocturnal and difficult to see

MIKE SCOTT

Scaly Anteater

AARDVARK
Orycteropus afer

Looking vaguely pig-like with a long, tubular snout, powerful kangaroo-like tail and large rabbit-like ears, the aardvark resembles no other mammal in Africa. Also known as the antbear, the aardvark has wrinkled pink-grey skin with a sparse covering of stiff greyish

hair to protect it from the bites of its prey· ants and termites. The aardvark forages at night by snuffling along
until it locates a termite or ant nest which it rips open
with powerful front legs ending in large spade-like
nails. Aardvarks dig deep burrows for shelter. They
emerge only at night, but in the morning they may
bask briefly in the sun before retiring underground.

Size: length 140-180cm; weight 40-70kg
Distribution: throughout the region
Status: uncommon; nocturnal, and rarely seen

Aardvark/Antbear

RODENTS

Porcupine *Hystrix africaeaustralis*

This is by far the largest rodent in Africa and, with its
long black-and-white banded quills, cannot be mistak-
en for any other species. A crest of long coarse hair
runs from the head to the shoulders, which it erects
with the quills when alarmed. It is mainly nocturnal
and shelters in caves, burrows or dense vegetation
during the day, emerging at night to forage. Porcu-
pines can occasionally be seen in daylight hours during
winter. Their diet consists mainly of bark, tubers, seeds
and a variety of plants and ground-level foliage.

Size: 75-100cm; weight 10-24kg
Distribution: throughout the region
Status: common; but nocturnal and difficult to see

Porcupine

Springhare *Pedetes capensis*

In spite of its name and large ears, springhares are not
hares, but rodents. With powerful, outsized hind feet
and small forelegs, they resemble small kangaroos and
share a similar hopping motion. Springhares dig extensive burrows, from which they emerge at night to
feed on grass and grass roots. Reflections in their large,
bright eyes often give them away on night safaris.

Size: 75-85cm; weight 2.5-3.8kg
Distribution: extends from southern Kenya into central
Tanzania; generally restricted to grassland habitats
Status: common; but strictly nocturnal

Springhare

DASSIES

Rock Dassie *Procavia capensis*

Although dassies resemble large guinea pigs, they are
more closely related to elephants and dugongs. Three
species occur in East Africa. The most common is the

rock dassie which can be found practically everywhere there are mountains or rocky outcrops. Rock dassies are sociable animals and live in large colonies of up to 60 individuals, spending much of the day sunning themselves on rocks or chasing each other in play. They often live with the bush dassie *(Heterohyrax brucei)* which is smaller, and has white underparts. Rocky outcrops in Tanzania's Serengeti National Park are excellent sites for observing the two species together. The third species, the tree dassie *(Dendrohyrax arboreus)*, has opted for thick forest rather than rocks for refuge. All three species are herbivorous, feeding on leaves, twigs, grass and lichen.

Size: length 60cm; weight up to 5.5kg
Distribution: rock and bush dassies are found throughout the region; tree dassies are restricted to lowland rainforest; best seen in national parks such as Aberdare and Mt Kenya in Kenya and Uganda's Ruwenzori National Park
Status: common; a regular inhabitant of tourist lodges

ANDREW MacCOLL

Rock Dassie

SMALL PREDATORY MAMMALS
Genet *Genetta*

Relatives of mongooses, genets vaguely resemble domestic cats and have a long, slender body and pointed fox-like face. The two species in the region are similar and can best be told apart by their facial markings and tail bands. The small-spotted or common genet *(G. genetta)* has bold black-and-white markings on the face and a white-tipped tail whereas the large-spotted or rusty-spotted genet *(G. tigrina)* has a less marked face and a black-tipped tail. The small-spotted genet also has a prominent crest along the spine which it raises when threatened. All-black individuals of both species may occur, particularly in mountainous regions. Genets live singly and have a wide range of habitats. By day, they sleep in abandoned burrows, rock crevices, hollow trees or on high branches. They are very agile and hunt equally well on land or in trees; their diet consists of small rodents, birds, reptiles, nestlings, eggs, insects and fruit. They sometimes become habitual poultry killers and are persecuted widely by poultry owners.

Size: length 85-110cm; weight 1.5-3.2kg
Distribution: throughout the region
Status: very common, but largely nocturnal; often the most common small carnivore seen on night safari

MICHAEL GORE/WINDRUSH PHOTOS

Small-spotted Genet

African Civet *Civettictis civetta*

Civets have a set of perineal glands that produce a foul-smelling oily substance used to mark their territory. Perfume manufacturers have 'farmed' civets in Africa for thousands of years to harvest this secretion, yet amazingly little is known about the animal in the wild. They are essentially solitary, though pairs may co-inhabit territories. By day they nestle in thickets, tall grass or abandoned burrows, becoming most active after sunset. They have a varied diet consisting of amphibians, birds, rodents, eggs, reptiles, snails, insects, carrion, berries, young shoots and fruit.

African Civet

Size: length 120-140cm of which the tail is 40-50cm; weight 9-15kg
Distribution: wide distribution but shuns very open habitat
Status: common; but mainly nocturnal and difficult to see

Mongooses

Many of the small mammals that dash in front of cars in Africa are mongooses. Most species are solitary, and are usually seen only fleetingly. The most common solitary species is the slender mongoose (*Galerella sanguinea*) quickly recognisable by its black-tipped tail which it holds aloft like a flag when running. A few species are intensely sociable. Tight-knit family groups have the advantage over loners both when raising kittens and confronting threats. Faced with predators many times their size, the entire family bunches together to form a bristling collective to intimidate the enemy. Dwarf (*Helogale parvula*) and banded mongooses (*Mungos mungo*) keep contact while foraging by twittering, and are quick to give alarm calls when in danger. Insects and other invertebrates are their most important prey but amphibians, reptiles, rodents, eggs and occasionally larger prey are also taken.

Dwarf Mongooses

Size: range in size from the dwarf mongoose at 40cm long, weighing 400 grams, to the 150cm long white-tailed mongoose (*Ichneumia albicauda*) weighing up to 5.5kg.
Distribution: throughout the region, but prefer open to closed woodlands and wooded savannas
Status: common where they occur; sociable species are active in the day, solitary species may be diurnal or nocturnal

HYAENA

Spotted Hyaena *Crocuta crocuta*

Widely reviled as a cowardly scavenger, spotted hyaenas are actually very efficient predators with a fas-

TONY WHEELER

Spotted Hyaena

cinating social system. Females are larger and dominant to males and even have male physical characteristics, the most remarkable of which is an erectile clitoris which renders the sexes virtually indistinguishable at a distance. Spotted hyaenas appear distinctly canine, but they are more closely related to cats than to dogs. They can reach speeds of up to 60km/h and a pack of them can easily dispatch adult wildebeest and zebra. The 'ooo-oop' call of spotted hyaena at night is one of the most evocative sounds of the African bush.

Size: height at shoulder 85cm, length 120-180cm; weight up to 80kg
Distribution: throughout the region
Status: very common in protected areas; mainly nocturnal, but also seen during the day

Striped Hyaena *Hyaena hyaena*
Lean long-legged hyaenas whose overall appearance is of a more robust animal due to the long shaggy mane and 'cape' along their backs. Striped Hyaenas subsist largely by scavenging from the kills of other predators and carrying off large parts to cache. They also catch insects and small vertebrates but are poor hunters of larger prey. Striped hyaenas forage alone, but appear to belong to loosely associated clans which cooperate to raise young and defend territories.

Size: height at shoulder 65-80cm; weight 25-45kg
Distribution: extends from central Tanzania into the arid zones of northern Kenya
Status: uncommon, strictly nocturnal

D MASON/WINDRUSH PHOTOS

Striped Hyaena

Aardwolf *Proteles cristatus*
Smallest of the hyaena family, aardwolves subsist almost entirely on harvester termites and, unlike their more predatory relatives, almost never consume meat. Aardwolves superficially resemble the striped hyaena but are considerably smaller. They are not as social as other hyaenas and seem to form loose associations between pairs but spend most of their time foraging alone. They do not form clans or den communally as other hyaena species, but the male assists the female raising the cubs, mostly by baby-sitting at the den while the mother forages.

Size: height at shoulder 40-50cm; weight 8-12 kg, often looks larger due to the fur cape it erects when threatened
Distribution: widespread in savanna and woodland habitats from central Tanzania into the arid north of Kenya
Status: uncommon; nocturnal, seen at dawn and dusk

LUKE HUNTER

Aardwolf

CATS

Cheetah *Acinonyx jubatus*

Occasionally mistaken for a dog due to their long dog-like legs and nonretractile claws, cheetahs are true cats and the world's fastest land mammals. Able to reach speeds of 105km/h, cheetahs approach their prey in a classic feline stalk before unleashing their tremendous acceleration from up to 60m away. The chase can be sustained for only a few hundred metres before the cheetah is exhausted and three out of every four hunts fail. They prey largely on antelopes weighing up to 60kg as well as hares and the young of large herbivores such as wildebeest and zebra. Up to nine cubs may be born in a litter, but in open savanna most are killed by other predators, particularly lions. Female cheetahs may be more successful raising cubs in woodland habitats otherwise considered suboptimal. Young cheetahs disperse from the mother at 18 months old; the males form coalitions while females remain solitary for life.

Size: height at shoulder 85cm, length 180-220cm; weight up to 65kg
Distribution: largely restricted to protected areas or the regions surrounding them; shuns densely forested areas
Status: uncommon, with individuals moving over large areas; active by day and frequently seen in national parks

JOHN HAY

Cheetah

Leopard *Panthera pardus*

The archetypal secretive cat, leopards are heard more often than seen; their rasping territorial call sounds very much like a saw cutting through wood. Leopards are supreme ambush hunters, using infinite patience to stalk to within metres of their prey before attacking in an explosive rush. They eat everything from insects to zebras, but antelopes such as impalas and gazelles are generally their most important prey. Leopards are agile and climb well, spending more time in trees then any other big cat. They also hoist their kills into trees to avoid losing them to lions and hyaenas. The presence of an antelope carcass in the branches often reveals their presence to those on safari. They are solitary animals, pairing up only during the mating season, when the male and female stay in close association for the females' week-long oestrous. A litter of up to three cubs is produced after a gestation period of three months; females raise cubs by themselves.

DAVID WALL

Leopard

Size: height at shoulder 70-80cm, length 160-210cm; weight up to 90kg
Distribution: throughout the region, most abundant in parks, they also persist in human-altered habitats, such as farmland, and even on the outskirts of major cities
Status: common, but mainly nocturnal and very secretive; the most difficult of the large cats to see

Lion *Panthera leo*

Africa's largest cat has a reputation for laziness which it doesn't deserve. People generally see lions during the day when they are inactive, but they spend much of the night hunting, patrolling their territory and playing. Lions live in prides of up to about 30, the core of which is four to 12 related females which remain in the pride for life. Males form coalitions and defend the female groups from foreign males. Lions are strictly territorial, defending ranges of between 50 and 400 sq km, depending on the terrain and the density of prey species. Young males are ousted from the pride at the age of two or three, and enter a period of nomadism which ends at around five years old when they are large enough to take over a pride of their own. Lions hunt as a group but whether they actually cooperate is difficult to determine. They will kill anything, but large herbivores such as wildebeest, zebra and buffalo are the mainstay of their diet. Although they rarely attack unless provoked, lions are extremely dangerous, and do occasionally kill people. Take the warnings seriously, and stay in your vehicle in national parks.

DAVID WALL

Lions mating

Size: height at shoulder 120cm, length 250-300cm; weight up to 240kg males, 160kg females
Distribution: largely confined to protected areas and present in all savanna and woodland parks in the region
Status: common in many of the larger parks; largely nocturnal but conspicuous during the day

African Wild Cat *Felis lybica*

The progenitor of the household tabby, the African wild cat was originally domesticated by the Egyptians. African wild cats differ most obviously from domestic cats in having reddish backs to their ears, proportionally longer legs and a generally leaner appearance. They interbreed freely with domestic cats and this is probably the greatest threat to the integrity of the wild species. The pure wild form can now only be found in very isolated regions. They subsist mainly on small rodents, but also prey on birds, insects and small mammals up to the size of hares. They are solitary

ANDREW MacCOLL

African Wild Cat

animals, only pairing up when mating and when kittens are born.

Size: height at shoulder 35cm, length 85-100cm; weight up to 6kg
Distribution: throughout the region
Status: common; nocturnal, although sometimes spotted at dawn and dusk

Serval *Felis serval*

Tall, slender, long-legged cats, the first impression one gains of servals is that they look like small cheetahs. The tawny to russet-yellow coat has large black spots, forming long bars and blotches on the neck and shoulders. All-black individuals occasionally occur, particularly in the moist, mountainous regions of Kenya. Other distinguishing features include very large upright ears, a long neck and a relatively short tail. Serval are associated with vegetation near water and are most common in flood plain savanna, wetlands and woodlands near streams. They are rodent specialists feeding primarily on mice, vlei rats, cane rats and springhares. Birds, small reptiles and occasionally the young of small antelope are also taken.

Serval

Size: height at shoulder 60cm, length 95-120cm; weight up to 13kg
Distribution: throughout the region
Status: relatively common but mainly nocturnal, sometimes seen in the early morning and late afternoon

Caracal *Felis caracal*

Also called the African lynx due to its long tufted ears, caracals are robust, powerful cats and phenomenal predators for their size. They prey on birds and rodents but are capable of taking down prey many times larger than themselves. Caracals are extraordinarily agile and will leap two metres in the air to catch birds on the wing. They are solitary animals, but male-female pairs spend more time together than other cats. Females give birth to one to three kittens after an 80 day gestation and raise the kittens alone. They are territorial, marking their home range with urine sprays and faeces. Caracals have a wide habitat tolerance but prefer semi-arid regions, dry savanna and hilly country.

Caracal

Size: height at shoulder 40-45cm, length 70-110cm; weight up to 20kg
Distribution: throughout the region
Status: not common; mostly nocturnal, and difficult to see

FOXES & DOGS

Bat-Eared Fox *Otocyon megalotis*

The huge ears of these small foxes look and function like radar dishes. While foraging they listen for the sound of invertebrates below ground. By lowering their head towards the soil, ears pointed, they use their extremely sensitive hearing to get an exact fix on potential food which they then unearth with a burst of frantic digging. The bat-eared fox eats mainly insects, especially termites, but also wild fruit and preys on small vertebrates. Bat-eared foxes are monogamous and pair for life; they are often seen in groups comprising a mated pair and their offspring. Their natural enemies include large birds of prey, spotted hyaenas, caracals and the larger cats. They will bravely attempt to rescue a family member caught by a predator by using distraction techniques and harassment, which extends to nipping much larger enemies on the ankles.

Bat-eared Fox

Size: height at shoulder 35cm, length 75-90cm; weight up to 5kg
Distribution: throughout the region
Status: very common, especially in parks; mainly nocturnal, but often seen in the early morning and late afternoon

Jackal *Canis*

Three species of jackal live in East Africa, all of them similar in behaviour and appearance. The most common is the golden jackal (*C. aureus*), often the most numerous carnivore in open savanna. It is a golden to silvery-grey colour and may be very active in protected areas during the daytime. Also common is the black-backed or silver-backed jackal (*C. mesomelas*). It has a distinctive mantle of silver-grey hair on its otherwise reddish-brown body and tends to predominate as the most common night scavenger. The third species, the side-striped jackal (*C. adustus*) is probably the least common and least studied. At a distance it has a uniform grey appearance but up close, shows a marked light stripe along each side. It has a white-tipped tail which can be used to tell it apart from the black-backed jackal with a black-tipped tail. The three jackals show similar social and feeding behaviour. They form enduring pair bonds which defend a small territory of 1 to 3 sq km. The young of previous litters often stay with the parents and act as helpers in raising new pups, but eventually disperse to find their own range. Jackals gain much of their food by scavenging from the kills of larger predators, which presents excellent opportunities to view them, but they are also efficient hunters, eating insects, rodents, lizards and the young of gazelles and other large herbivores. They also eat some vegetable matter and wild fruit.

Size: three species very similar; height at shoulder 38-50cm, length 95-120cm; weight up to 15kg
Distribution: throughout the region, preferring open plains and woodlands; side-striped jackal is most abundant in well-watered wooded areas
Status: abundant in protected areas; also tolerant of human activity despite intense persecution by farmers

Jackals

Wild Dog *Lycaon pictus*
The wild dog's Latin name means painted wolf, and the blotched black, yellow and white coat, together with its large, round ears, make it unmistakable. Wild dogs are highly sociable, living in packs of up to 40, although packs normally number between 12 and 20. They are efficient predators catching 85% of the animals they chase. Marvellous endurance hunters, they chase prey relentlessly to the point of exhaustion, then the pack cooperates to pull down the quarry. They have been widely reviled for their killing method which involves disembowelment and eating their prey alive, but in fact, this is probably as fast as any of the 'cleaner' methods used by other carnivores. Favoured prey include mid-sized antelope, but they can kill animals as large as buffalo.

Size: height at shoulder 65-80cm, length 105-150cm; weight up to 30kg
Distribution: much reduced by persecution, disease and destruction of habitat, they are now restricted to the largest protected areas in the region; Selous National Park in Tanzania probably has the largest population in East Africa
Status: highly threatened and now absent from many areas of their former distribution except for relict populations; one of Africa's most endangered large carnivores

Wild Dog

OTTERS
Cape Clawless Otter *Aonyx capensis*
Similar to European otters but much larger, Cape clawless otters are a glossy chocolate brown with a white or cream-coloured lower face, throat and neck. Unlike most otters, only the hind feet of Cape clawless otters are webbed, and the front feet end in dexterous, human-like fingers with rudimentary nails. They are active during early morning and evening, though they

ROGER DE LA HARPE/ABPL

Cape Clawless Otter

LORNA STANTON/ABPL

Honey Badger

become nocturnal in areas where they are hunted by humans. Their main foods include fish, crabs and frogs as well as marine molluscs in seashore habitats. Their only known natural enemy is the crocodile.

Size: length 105-160cm of which the tail is 50cm; weight up to 28kg
Distribution: found in large freshwater bodies and along coastlines in the region
Status: locally common; active both day and night but usually seen in the early morning and late afternoon

BADGERS
Ratel *Mellivora capensis*

Also known as honey badgers, ratels are Africa's equivalent of the European badger. They have a reputation for ferocity and a vile temper, and while stories of ratels attacking animals the size of buffalo are folklore, they are relentlessly pugnacious and astonishingly powerful for their size. They have few natural enemies and have even been seen feeding with lions on their kills; nonetheless, they are occasionally killed by the larger carnivores. They are active between dusk and dawn and have a very omnivorous diet, feeding on fish, frogs, scorpions, spiders, reptiles, small mammals, roots, honey, berries and eggs. Ratels have a fascinating relationship with the honeyguide bird (see Birds later) which leads them to bees' nests. Ratels use their prodigious strength to raid the hive for honey and in doing so provides the honeyguide access to its favoured food, beeswax. In some parks, ratels become used to scavenging from bins; this may present the best opportunity for viewing these remarkable animals.

Size: length 90-100cm; weight up to 15kg
Distribution: widespread in the region
Status: generally occurs in low densities though populations are sustainable; mainly nocturnal

ELEPHANT
African Elephant *Loxodonta africana*

The largest land mammal in the world needs little introduction. Elephant live in small family groups of between 10 and 20 which often congregate in much larger herds at a common water or food resource. Elephant society is matriarchal; herds are dominated by senior females, while the bulls live alone or in bachelor groups. Males join the herds when females are in season and a cow may mate with many bulls during her oestrous. Elephant communicate using a range of sounds, including a very deep rumble that is felt as a low vibration by humans. They also produce a high-pitched trumpeting when they're frightened or when threatening a perceived enemy. An adult's average daily food intake is about 250kg of grass, leaves, bark and other vegetation. In drought years, they're capable of destroying dense woodland by felling trees. This has led to them being perceived as a threat to fragile environments, but elephant damage may be necessary in the natural cycle of the savanna. An elephant's life span is about 60 to 70 years, though some individuals may reach 100 or more.

Size: height at shoulder up to 4m in the male; weight 5-6.3 tons
Distribution: widely distributed in the region but large populations only occur in protected areas
Status: parks may be overpopulated by elephants due in part to immigration from areas where they are persecuted

African Elephant

RHINOCEROS
Black Rhinoceros *Diceros bicornis*

Aggressive poaching for rhino horn used in traditional Chinese medicine (though not as an aphrodisiac as is commonly believed) and for dagger handles by Yemeni tribesmen has made black or hook-lipped rhino Africa's most endangered large mammal. In many countries they have been completely exterminated and the white rhino (*Ceratotherium simum*) is now extinct in East Africa (though still very numerous in southern Africa). Black rhino still occur in the region though its numbers have also been drastically reduced. The smaller of the two species, black rhino are more unpredictable and are prone to charging when alarmed or merely uncertain about a possible threat. They are browsers and use their pointed, prehensile lip to feed selectively on branches and foliage. Black rhino are solitary and aggressively territorial, only socialising during the mating season; however, in some areas they seem more tolerant of each other and may form temporary associations.

Size: height at shoulder 160cm; weight 800-1100kg, record horn length 120cm
Distribution: restricted to relict populations in a few reserves; best seen in Tanzania's Ngorongoro Crater and Nairobi National Park in Kenya
Status: highly endangered in the region but easy to see in protected areas; much more numerous in southern Africa

Black Rhinoceros

ZEBRA

Burchell *Equus burchelli* **Grevy** *E. grevyi*

Two zebra species inhabit the region, the most common by far being Burchell's zebra which occur in great numbers in parks and are famous for migrating with huge numbers of wildebeest. Burchell's zebra are boldly marked with broad alternating black and white stripes; faint 'shadow stripes' sometimes occur between each main stripe. Grevy's zebra are marked all over with much finer stripes and lack shadow stripes. Both species are grazers but occasionally browse on leaves and scrub; Grevy's zebra are adapted to arid areas and can subsist on vegetation too tough for cattle. Social systems centre around small groups of related mares over which stallions fight fiercely. Stallions may hold a harem for as long as 15 years but single mares are often lost to younger males as they acquire their own harem. Zebra are preyed upon by all the large carnivores, especially lions.

JULIET COOMBE

Zebras

Size: Burchell's zebra is shorter than Grevy's, but it has a more robust appearance; height at shoulder 140-160cm; weight Burchell's up to 360kg, Grevy's up to 390kg
Distribution: Burchell's zebra occur in parks throughout the region; Grevy's zebra are restricted to northern Kenya
Status: Burchell's zebra are extremely common and very easy to see; Grevy's zebra only occur in significant numbers in Kenya's northern frontier district

WILD PIGS

Bushpig *Potamochoerus porcus*

Hairy bushpigs are similar in many ways to wild boars of Europe. They are sociable, and live in 'sounders' (groups) of up to a dozen animals, which are led by a dominant boar and sow. Boars defend their sounder against the unwanted attentions of interlopers. They eat fallen fruit and root up rhizomes, bulbs and tubers. As a result they are a pest where crops are grown, and are persecuted outside protected areas. Bushpigs are dangerous to humans when cornered or wounded. The forest dwelling bushpig in Uganda, Rwanda and Burundi is a rich rust-red in colour and is known as the red river hog.

ANTHONY BANNISTER/ABPL

Bushpig

Size: height at shoulder 55-88cm; weight up to 115kg but averages 60kg
Distribution: throughout the region from equatorial forest to open woodland
Status: common, but difficult to see in dense vegetation; best chance for viewing is at night at water hole hides

Warthog *Phacochoerus aethiopicus*

The most common pig species in the region, warthogs are abundant in all savanna and woodland habitats in East Africa. Warthogs live in family groups, the core of which is up to four related females accompanied by their dependent young. The males form bachelor groups and only associate with the sows during the breeding season. They grow two sets of tusks: the upper ones curve outwards and upwards and grow as long as 60cm; the lower ones are usually less than 15cm long. The distinctive facial warts giving the animal its name can be used to tell the sexes apart. Females have a single pair of warts under the eyes whereas the males have a second set further down the snout. Warthogs feed mainly on grass, but also eat fruit and bark, and burrow with their snout for roots and bulbs when other food is scarce. They shelter and give birth in abandoned aardvark burrows, or sometimes excavate cavities in abandoned termite mounds.

Warthog

Size: height at shoulder 70cm; weight up to 105kg but averages 50-60kg
Distribution: throughout the region except for dense rainforest and mountains above 3000m
Status: very common; strictly diurnal and easy to see.

HIPPOPOTAMUS
Hippopotamus amphibius

Hippos are always found either close to, or in fresh water. They spend most of the day submerged, feeding on underwater vegetation and emerge at night to graze on land; they can consume 40kg of vegetable matter each evening. They're very gregarious animals and live in large herds, tolerating close contact in the water. However, they forage alone when on land, and cows with young babies are highly aggressive to other hippos. Adult bulls defend their territory from each other very aggressively, though young males are tolerated if they avoid showing an interest in females. Virtually every male hippo bears the scars of territorial conflicts and such marks are often a convenient method of sexing hippos. Hippos are extremely dangerous on land and kill many people in Africa each year, usually when someone inadvertently blocks the animals' retreat to the water. The hippos' only natural predators are lions and crocodiles, which prey on their young.

Hippopotamus

Size: height at shoulder 150cm; weight up to 2 tons, males larger than females
Distribution: restricted to large bodies of fresh water but occur widely throughout the region
Status: common and easy to see

GIRAFFE

Giraffa camelopardalis

Giraffe

The name giraffe is derived from the Arabic *xirapha* (the one who walks quickly). A number of different races are recognised including the reticulated giraffe (*G. c. reticulata*) of northern Kenya, with fine white lines separating large reddish patches, and the more familiar Masai giraffe (*G. c. tippelskirchi*) which is most common in the region. A third race, Rothschild's giraffe (*G. c. rothschildi*), tends to be pale in colour and extends from western Kenya into Uganda. Both sexes have knob-like horns, which are probably vestigial antlers and can be used to tell the sexes apart: males have bald tips to the horns whereas the females have a covering of hair. Despite the giraffe's incredibly long neck, it still has only seven cervical vertebrae – the same number as all mammals, including humans. Giraffe browse on trees, especially acacia species. The juveniles are prone to predation by the major predators and lions will even take down fully grown adults.

Size: up to 5.2m tall; weight 900-1400kg
Distribution: reticulated giraffe occurs in northern Kenya; Masai giraffe very widespread south-west of Nairobi extending into Tanzania; Rothschild's giraffe restricted to Uganda and western Kenya near Lake Barigo
Status: common and easy to see

ANTELOPE

Common Duiker *Sylvicapra grimmia*

One of the most common small antelopes, common or grey duikers are usually solitary, but are sometimes seen in pairs, and prefer areas with good scrub cover. Common duikers are greyish light-brown in colour, with a white belly and a dark brown vertical stripe on the face. Only the males have horns, which are straight and pointed, and grow to 20cm in length. Common duikers are almost exclusively browsers; they often feed on agricultural crops and tend to be persecuted outside conservation areas. They are capable of going without water for long periods.

Common Duiker

Size: height at shoulder 50cm; weight up to 21kg
Distribution: throughout the region
Status: common; active throughout the day

Klipspringer *Oreotragus oreotragus*

Small sturdy antelopes, klipspringers are easily recognised by their curious tip-toe stance; the hooves are adapted for balance and grip on rocky surfaces. The widely spaced 10cm-long horns are present only on the male. Klipspringers normally inhabit rocky outcrops; they also venture into adjacent grasslands, but when alarmed they retreat into the rocks for safety. These amazingly agile and sure-footed creatures are capable of bounding up impossibly rough rock faces.

Size: height at shoulder 60cm; weight up to 13kg
Distribution: on rocky outcrops and mountainous areas throughout the region
Status: common

Klipspringer

Kirk's Dik-Dik *Madoqua kirkii*

Dik-diks are best identified by their miniature size, the pointed flexible snout and a tuft of dark hair on the forehead; only the males have horns. Dik-diks are monogamous and pairs are territorial. They are seen singly, in pairs or in parties of three; their habitat is in woodland, or savanna where there is cover. They feed by browsing on foliage and don't need to drink water.

Size: height at shoulder 43cm; weight up to 5kg
Distribution: throughout the region
Status: common, but shy and easy to miss; active in the morning and afternoon

Kirk's Dik-Dik

Suni *Neotragus moschatus*

These tiny antelopes are best seen from observation hides at water holes, often giving themselves away by the constant flicking of their tails. Suni are monogamous, and use secretions from a large scent gland in front of the eye to mark their territories. They nibble on leaves and fallen fruit. When surprised they will freeze before bounding away making a high-pitched call.

Size: height at shoulder 35cm; weight up to 5kg
Distribution: wooded areas of eastern Kenya and Tanzania; best seen in Kenya at Tana River Primate National Reserve, Mt Kenya or the Aberdares
Status: common, but difficult to see; active in the early morning and late afternoon

Impala *Aepyceros melampus*

Often dismissed because they are so abundant, impalas are a unique antelope with no close relatives. Males have long, lyre-shaped horns averaging 75cm in length. They are gregarious, and males defend harems

Suni

Impala

DEANNA SWANEY
Steenbok

D MASON/WINDRUSH PHOTOS
Thomson's Gazelle

during the rut. Outside the breeding season, males congregate in bachelor groups. Impalas are known for their speed and ability to leap; they can spring as much as 10m in a single bound, or 3m into the air. Impalas are the favoured prey of predators including lions, leopards, cheetahs, wild dogs and spotted hyaenas.

Size: height at shoulder 90cm; weight up to 70kg
Distribution: savanna regions from central Kenya extending south into Tanzania
Status: very common and easy to see

Steenbok *Raphicerus campestris*
Resembles a tall slender duiker; the back and hindquarters range from light reddish brown to dark brown with pale underparts. The nose bears a black, wedge-shaped 'blaze' useful for identification. Males have small, widely separated horns. They're solitary animals, and only have contact with others during mating season. Steenbok are active in the morning and evening.

Size: height at shoulder 50cm; weight up to 11kg
Distribution: restricted to central and northern Kenya
Status: common

Gazelle *Gazella*
One of the most common medium-sized antelope in the region, gazelles are frequently the main prey of many predators. As a result, they are particularly fleet of foot and wary of attack. Three species are common in the region. The pretty Thomson's gazelle (*G. thomsonii*) is the smallest and forms large aggregations on the open plains of the Serengeti and Masai Mara national parks. It is often found with the impala-sized Grant's gazelle (*G. granti*) which lacks the distinctive black side stripe of the 'Thommy'. The third species, the gerenuk (*Litocranius walleri*), is the most distinctive; it's like a miniature giraffe with long limbs and neck. All three species live in herds; the gerenuk in small herds rarely numbering more than 12.

Size: Thomson's gazelle, height at shoulder 70cm, weight up to 29kg; Grant's gazelle, height at shoulder 90cm, weight up to 65kg; gerenuk, height at shoulder 105cm, weight up to 45kg
Distribution: Thomson's and Grant's gazelle are common in savanna and woodland habitats throughout the region; gerenuk inhabit the arid region from northwestern Tanzania extending north into central Kenya
Status: plains species very common; gerenuk less abundant but common in its region; best seen in Kenya's Tsavo and Meru national parks

Blue Wildebeest *Connochaetes taurinus*

Blue wildebeest, also known as brindled gnu, are very gregarious, sometimes forming herds up to tens of thousands strong, often in association with zebra and other herbivores. These huge herds create a cacophony of snorts and low grunts. The wildebeest has been described as ungainly, having the forequarters of an ox, the hindquarters of an antelope and the tail of a horse. Males are territorial, and attempt to lead groups of females. Wildebeest are grazers moving constantly in search of short green grass and water. Because they prefer to drink daily and can survive only five days without water, wildebeest will migrate large distances. During the rainy season they graze haphazardly, but in the dry season they coalesce around water holes. Major predators include lion, hyaena and wild dogs.

Size: height at shoulder 150cm; weight 250kg
Distribution: throughout most parks in the region
Status: common; the largest numbers occur in the Serengeti and Masai Mara national parks in Tanzania and Kenya

Blue Wildebeest

Hartebeest *Alcelaphus buselaphus*

Hartebeest are red to tan coloured, medium-sized antelope easily recognised by their long, narrow face and short horns. Two, very similar subspecies occur in the region, Coke's hartebeest which is slightly darker and larger than the second form, Jackson's hartebeest. In both sexes, the distinctively angular and heavily ridged horns form a heart shape, hence their name which comes from 'heart beast' in Afrikaans. Hartebeest feed exclusively on grass and prefer grassy plains for grazing but are also found in sparsely forested savanna and hills. They're social animals and often mingle with other grazers such as zebra and wildebeest. Predators are mainly hyaena, the large cats and wild dogs.

Size: height at shoulder 125cm; weight 120-150kg
Distribution: wide ranging; Coke's hartebeest (also known by its Swahili name) 'Kongoni' is common in Kenya and Tanzania; Jackson's hartebeest occurs in Uganda
Status: common

Hartebeest

Topi (Tsessebe) *Damaliscus lunatus*

Also known as tsessebe, topi are similar to the hartebeest in appearance but slightly smaller and darker, in some cases appearing almost violet, with dark patches on the legs and face. The horns, carried by both sexes, curve gently up, out and back. A highly gregarious antelope, they live in herds and often

MARK DAFFEY

Topi

JEAN-BERNARD CARILLET

Roan Antelope

MITCH REARDON

Sable

mingle with other grazers. Although topi can live on the dry grasses spurned by other antelope, they prefer flood plains and moist areas that support lush pasture. They are capable of surviving long periods without water as long as sufficient grass is available. They have the characteristic habit of standing on high vantage points such as termite mounds to observe their surroundings.

Size: height at shoulder 120cm; weight 120-150kg
Distribution: widespread throughout all medium length grasslands in the region
Status: common; abundant in Serengeti National Park

Roan Antelope *Hippotragus equinus*

A large, horse-like animal, the roan is one of Africa's rarest large antelope. The coat varies from reddish-fawn to dark reddish-brown, with white underparts and a conspicuous mane of stiff, black-tipped hair stretching from the nape of the neck to the shoulders. The ears are long, narrow and pointed, with a brown tassel at the tip. The face has a distinctive black and white pattern. Both sexes have curving, back-swept horns up to 70cm long. As a grazer, it prefers tall grasses in areas with shade and fresh water but also occupies denser habitats where it supplements its diet with twigs and leaves. For most of the year, roans are in small herds of less than 20 individuals, led by a bull.

Size: height at shoulder 150cm; weight up to 300kg
Distribution: western part of the region, best seen in Tanzania's Ruaha National Park
Status: despite a wide distribution, populations are declining and the species is considered threatened; easy to see where they occur

Sable *Hippotragus niger*

Sable are widely considered the most magnificent of Africa's antelope. They are dark brown to black, with a white belly and face markings; the adult male's coat is a rich glossy black. Both sexes have long sweeping horns, but those of the male are longer and more curved. Sable feed mainly on grass, but foliage accounts for around 10% of their diet. Female and young sable live in herds; males live singly and guard their own territory or form bachelor groups. Like the roan, the sable is a fierce fighter and has been known to kill attacking lions. Other predators include leopards, hyaena and wild dogs.

Size: height at shoulder 135cm; weight up to 270kg
Distribution: Tanzania extending north into Kenya
Status: relatively common

Oryx *Oryx gazella*

Adapted to arid wasteland uninhabitable for most antelope, oryx are a true desert species. Two races occur in the region: the beisa oryx (*O. g. beisa*) and the slightly smaller fringe-eared oryx (*O. g callotis*). Oryx are solid and powerful animals, with impressively long, straight horns; both sexes carry them but they are stouter and shorter in the males. They have a short clipped mane and long horse-like tail. Oryx are principally grazers, but will also browse on thorny shrubs unpalatable to many species. They can survive for long periods without water. Herds vary from five to 40 individuals and have a strict dominance hierarchy.

Size: height at shoulder 150cm; weight up to 300kg
Distribution: beisa oryx can be found in northern Kenya; fringe-eared oryx in southern Kenya extending south into northern Tanzania
Status: relatively common and easy to see, but shy

Oryx

Kudu *Tragelaphus*

The greater kudu (*T. strepsiceros*) is larger than the lesser kudu (*T. imberbis*) and is by far the more spectacular. It is Africa's second tallest antelope and the males carry spiralling horns much sought after by trophy hunters. Both species are light grey in colour with between six and 10 white stripes down the sides and a white chevron between the eyes. Herds are small and are comprised of females and their young. The normally solitary males occasionally band into small bachelor herds and individually seek out females during the breeding season. Kudu are mainly browsers and can eat a variety of leaves, preferring savanna with fairly dense bush cover.

Size: greater kudu, height at shoulder 150cm, weight up to 310kg; lesser kudu, height at shoulder 105cm, weight up to 105kg
Distribution: greater kudu occurs throughout the region, except in the driest areas; lesser kudu prefers the arid regions of Tanzania and northern Kenya
Status: common

Kudu

Bushbuck *Tragelaphus scriptus*

Shy and solitary animals, bushbucks inhabit thick bush close to permanent water. They are chestnut to dark brown in colour and have white vertical stripes on the body between the neck and rump, as well as a number of white spots on the upper thigh and a white splash on the neck. Only the males grow horns, which are straight with gentle spirals and average about 30cm in length. When startled, bushbucks bolt and crash loudly through the undergrowth. They are nocturnal browsers but also active on cool, overcast days. Though shy and elusive, they can be dangerous when cornered. Their main predators are leopard, lion and hyaena, and their young are often taken by pythons.

Size: height at shoulder 80cm; weight up to 45kg
Distribution: throughout the region, favouring denser habitats
Status: relatively common, but difficult to see due to their shy nature and habitat

Eland *Taurotragus oryx*

Africa's largest antelope, the eland resembles an ox. Both sexes have horns about 65cm long, which spiral at the base and sweep straight back. The male has a much hairier head than the female, and its horns are stouter and shorter. Eland prefer savanna scrub, feeding on grass and tree foliage in the early morning and late afternoon into the night. They drink daily, but can go for a month or more without water. Eland live in groups of around six to 12, but herds can contain as many as 50 individuals. A small herd normally has only one male, however in larger herds there may be several.

Size: height at shoulder 170cm; weight up to 900kg in the male
Distribution: patchy distribution in arid zones; best seen in Kenya's Nairobi or Tsavo national parks
Status: naturally low density but relatively common in their range and easy to see

Common Reedbuck *Redunca arundinum*

The dusky brown reedbuck are found on wetlands or around rivers, never straying more than a few kilometres from a permanent water source. Males have distinctive forward-curving horns. The underbelly, inside of the thighs, throat and underside of the bushy tail are white. Reedbuck are usually seen in pairs or small family parties but groups may number up to 20 individuals. Their diet consists primarily of grass with small amounts of leaves and twigs. They give a distinctive shrill whistle when alarmed. Major predators include spotted hyaenas, big cats and wild dogs.

ANDREW MacCOLL

Bushbuck

DAVID WALL

Eland

DENNIS JONES

Common Reedbuck

Size: height at shoulder 95cm; weight up to 70kg
Distribution: southern Tanzania; the very similar bohor reedbuck (*R. redunca*) overlaps in range in southern Tanzania and extends northwards into Kenya
Status: relatively common; easy to see but shy and difficult to approach

Waterbuck *Kobus ellipsiprymnus*

Waterbuck have a distinctive bull's-eye ring around their rump and white markings on the face and throat. They're solid animals with a thick, shaggy, dark brown coat. Only the males have horns, which curve gradually outwards before shooting straight up to a length of about 75cm. The bulk of the waterbuck's diet consists of grass. They never stray far from water and are good swimmers, readily entering the water to escape predators. Herds are small and consist of cows, calves and one mature bull, while younger bulls live in small bachelor groups apart from the herd.

Size: height at shoulder 130cm; weight up to 270kg
Distribution: wet areas throughout the region
Status: common and easy to see

Waterbuck

BUFFALO

African Buffalo *Syncerus caffer*

The only native wild cow of Africa. Both sexes of the African (or cape) buffalo have distinctive curving horns that broaden at the base and meet over the forehead in a 'boss' shape, though those of the female are usually smaller. They have a fairly wide habitat tolerance but prefer areas with abundant grass, water and cover. Although they're generally docile and stay out of humans' way, buffalo can be very dangerous and should be treated with caution. Solitary bulls and females protecting their young are the most aggressive. African buffalo are gregarious and may form herds numbering thousands of animals. Group composition is fluid and smaller herds often break away, sometimes rejoining the original herd later. Buffalo eat at night; they are primarily grazers but also browse on foliage.

Size: height at shoulder 140cm; weight up to 820kg in the bull
Distribution: widespread, but large populations only occur in parks
Status: common, can be approachable in protected areas

African Buffalo

BIRDS

While most people might think of Africa as being remarkable for its large mammals, those who take the time to look at the continent's birdlife will discover this to be equally diverse and spectacular. In a continent rich in birdlife, East Africa is the region with the most diverse bird community of all. Over 1300 bird species have been recorded in East Africa – which represents almost 15% of all the bird species to be found on Earth!

There are a number of reasons for this immense diversity. The tropics are home to a large variety of bird species due to the stable climate and year-round plant growth. East Africa's birdlife, however, is especially diverse because the region lies on a major migration route for birds flying south from Europe to winter in Africa.

The geography of East Africa also supports a wide range of bird habitats with its large surface area, abundant coastline and changes in altitude from the central mountains to the Rift Valley.

Goliath Heron

Bird Habitats

There are seven broad habitat types. Wetlands, lakes and rivers (together with their fringing vegetation) are home to water-loving birds such as ducks, flamingo and other large wading birds. This habitat type, which includes the well-known Rift Valley lakes, supports the greatest diversity of bird species.

The next most important habitat, in terms of bird diversity, is the forests of tall trees with closed canopy which covers much of the Central Highlands, most notably the Aberdare mountains of Kenya and the lower slopes of Mt Kilimanjaro in Tanzania. East Africa's forests are home to turacos, hornbills and parrots.

The cool, high altitude areas above the forest are covered with moorland of stunted grasses and shrubs where many birds of prey can be seen.

Most of East Africa, though, can be classified as savanna and woodland. This habitat is typically African: open woodland with grass-covered ground. Many characteristically African birds can be found here including the secretary bird, guineafowl and rollers.

In contrast, true grassland, where woody plants are either absent or rare, is limited to only a few areas such as Ngorongoro Crater and Serengeti National Park in Tanzania, and the Athi Plains of Kenya. These

BOTH PHOTOS BY DAVID TIPLING

Spoonbill

sweeping grasslands are where whydahs may be seen displaying their magnificent tails.

The arid semi-desert, home to larks and ostriches, is restricted to the north of Kenya.

Finally, the seashore and estuaries provide a habitat for bird species such as gulls, cormorants and migratory shorebirds.

Bird Groups

It is impossible to present details on all of East Africa's bird species here. Rather, some of the most common, unusual or spectacular groups likely to be seen during your trip are briefly noted and illustrated. For more information on bird species see Books on Birdwatching at the end of this section.

Waterfowl This large group includes many species of ducks and geese and, as their collective name suggests, they are almost exclusively associated with water. The distinctive white-faced whistling-duck is one easily identifiable species.

Long-Legged Wading Birds Virtually any waterway will have its complement of herons, egrets, storks, spoonbills and ibis. All have long legs and necks, and bills adapted to feed on specific prey. Members of this group range in size from the tiny, secretive bittern to the enormous goliath heron, which stands 1.4m tall. The ugly marabou stork, which feeds with vultures on carrion, is also a long-legged wader. An unusual looking member of this group is the hamerkop (hammer head). Flamingo are found by the million on the saline lakes of the Rift Valley.

Migratory Shorebirds Every year millions of shorebirds arrive in East Africa on their annual journey south from their breeding grounds in the northern hemisphere. Generally nondescript in their winter plumage, these shorebirds are an identification challenge for the keen birdwatcher. This group includes sandpipers, curlews and small plovers. A number of other species are permanent residents of the region's waterways. These include the boldly marked lapwings, the jacanas and the strange dikkops – cryptic, nocturnal species with weird wailing cries. With few exceptions these birds are found near waterways, feeding along the shores on small creatures or probing intertidal mud for worms.

White-faced Whistling-Duck

Little Egret

Marabou Stork

Blacksmith Plover

African Fish Eagle

Pied Kingfisher

Yellow-billed Hornbill

Goldentailed Woodpecker

Seabirds Lumped into this broad category are a number of birds which share only one common trait: they all feed at sea. This includes the beautiful gannets and boobies, which feed by diving from a great height; the cormorants (shags), which also inhabit brackish and freshwater habitats; and the ubiquitous gulls.

Birds of Prey Hawks, eagles, vultures, falcons and the unique secretary bird all fall under this heading. East Africa is exceptionally rich in birds of prey, which favour savanna and grasslands but may be seen almost everywhere. You will soon notice many species, from soaring flocks of scavenging vultures to the stately bateleur eagle watching for prey. Several have specialised prey or habitat requirements; the striking African fish eagle and the osprey feed almost exclusively on fish.

Kingfishers Colourful and active, kingfishers can be divided into two groups: those which typically dive into water after fish and tadpoles (and as a consequence are found along waterways); and those less dependent on water because they generally prey on lizards and large insects. Of those found around water, the giant kingfisher reaches 46cm in length whereas the jewel-coloured malachite kingfisher is a mere 14cm. The woodland kingfisher is an example of the dry land or forest kingfishers.

Turacos & Louries The beautifully coloured turacos are medium-sized birds of the forest which can be difficult to see because of their habit of hiding in the canopy. In contrast, the related louries ('go-away birds' after their raucous call), birds of savanna and woodland, are duller in colour but more easily seen.

Hornbills Distinctive medium-sized birds which sport massive and brightly coloured down-curved bills. Most species favour forest or woodland, but the yellow-billed hornbill prefers more open country.

Barbets, Woodpeckers & Tinkerbirds Barbets are closely related to woodpeckers but rather than drilling into bark after grubs, they have strong, broad bills adapted to eating fruit and a variety of insects. Barbets are often brightly coloured and perch conspicuously; tinkerbirds are noisy but tiny and sometimes difficult to see.

Honeyguides The cheeky honeyguide displays some of the most remarkable behaviour of any bird. They attract the attention of mammals, such as the ratel (honey badger) or even humans, and then 'guide' them to a beehive by flying a short way ahead of their 'helper' – constantly waiting to see if they are being followed. After its mammal helper has broken open the hive, the honeyguide then feeds on the left-over bees' larvae, eggs and wax.

Ostrich Standing around 2.5m high and weighing as much as 150kg, the instantly identifiable ostrich is the largest living bird. It is widely distributed throughout the savanna plains and can best be seen in the parks and reserves of southern Kenya.

Ostrich

Cranes These graceful, long-legged birds superficially resemble storks and herons, but are typically grassland dwelling birds. In East Africa they are represented by the magnificent crowned crane.

Pigeons & Doves Familiar to city and country dwellers alike, members of this family are found all over the world and have managed to adapt to virtually every habitat. The cosmopolitan 'feral' pigeon and laughing dove are common inhabitants of gardens and human settlements, while the smaller Namaqua dove prefers arid areas.

Crowned Crane

Bee-Eaters & Rollers The various bee-eaters and rollers are colourful and always a delight to watch. Bee-eaters are commonly seen perched on fences and branches, from where they pursue flying insects – particularly, as their name suggests, bees and wasps. They may congregate in thousands, and a flock of the stunning carmine bee-eater is an unforgettable sight. Rollers are not as brightly coloured as bee-eaters, but are still attractive in blues and mauves.

Swifts & Swallows Although unrelated, these two groups are superficially similar and can be seen chasing flying insects just about anywhere. Both groups have long wings and streamlined bodies adapted to their lives in the air; both fly with grace and agility after insects; and both are usually dark in colouration. Swallows, however, differ in one major aspect: they can perch on twigs, fences or even the ground while swifts have weak legs and rarely land except at the nest. In

Whitefronted Bee-eater

Lilacbreasted Roller

Hoopoe

Masked Weaver

fact, swifts are so adapted to life in the air that some are even known to sleep on the wing.

Hoopoe Another attractive bird, the hoopoe is chestnut with a prominent crest and black-and-white patterned wings; it commonly feeds on the ground.

Finches, Weavers & Whydahs This large group includes many small seed-eating species commonly seen in flocks in grassland areas. While some, such as the various finches, are not spectacular, others develop colourful courtship plumage and tail plumes of extraordinary size. Weavers are usually yellow with varying amounts of black in their plumage and, as their name implies, make neatly woven nests of grass. Whydahs are typically shades of brown and grey when not breeding, but males moult into black plumage with red or yellow highlights when courting. The enormous tail of the paradise whydah can be more than twice the bird's body length.

Sunbirds The humming birds of Africa, sunbirds are small, delicate nectar feeders with sharp down-curved bills. The males of most species are brilliantly iridescent while the females are more drab; the malachite sunbird is one striking example of this group.

Starlings & Oxpeckers Africa is the stronghold of the gregarious and intelligent starling and many examples, including the beautiful iridescent glossy starling, may be seen in fast-flying, noisy flocks around the region. The related oxpeckers may often be seen clinging to game, from which they prise parasitic ticks and insects.

Larks & Pipits These drab, brown birds are not spectacular, and their identification may present a real challenge even to expert birdwatchers, but they are numerous and biologically significant to the grassland and semi-desert areas they inhabit.

Where to See East African Birds

With such rich birdlife, birds will be encountered virtually everywhere on your travels in East Africa, but there are obviously a number of sites with particularly abundant or spectacular bird species. Both Kenya and Tanzania are blessed with a number of reserves set up for the protection of wildlife and habitat, and these are good places to concentrate your birdwatching efforts, although some nonprotected areas can also be rewarding. Following are some of the best birdwatching areas in the region.

The freshwater Lake Baringo in western Kenya attracts a very wide range of birds and is a popular stop for birdwatchers.

Lake Nakuru in eastern Kenya is world famous because of the huge numbers of flamingo which congregate there to feed in the shallow soda lake. At one time it was estimated that up to two million birds, including 1.5 million lesser flamingo, could be found at the lake! Unfortunately, recent changes in the water level of the lake have meant that these birds are no longer present in such numbers.

Many flamingo can now be found at other soda lakes, particularly Lake Bogoria in south-western Kenya, where up to one million have been reported at the southern end of the lake, and at Lake Magadi in northern Tanzania's Ngorongoro Crater. The best time of year for flamingo viewing in the region is January and February.

Glossy Starling

The Wembere swamps of western Tanzania have very big breeding colonies of some of the large wading birds, such as herons, ibis and storks. Lake Rukwa, in Tanzania's southern highlands, is situated in a seasonally flooded plain which supports large numbers of birds during the wet season.

The national parks at Kenya's Aberdare mountains, Mount Kenya and Mount Meru, and Tanzania's Mt Kilimanjaro are good for seeing both forest and moorland dwelling bird species.

Sibiloi National Park on the edge of Lake Turkana in northern Kenya provides an example of a semi-arid habitat.

Flamingo

Books on Birdwatching

There are a number of books available which describe East Africa's birds. Some of the most useful for the casual birdwatcher are likely to be:

A Photographic Guide to Birds of East Africa by David Richards, a handy, pocket-sized book. Only some 260 of the region's estimated 1300 bird species are covered, but photographs, text and distribution maps are included for each of these.

Where to Watch Birds in Africa by Nigel Wheatly. It identifies many of the best sites in Africa and provides a bird list for each country.

Sacred Ibis

Facts for the Visitor

HIGHLIGHTS

Among Tanzania's best-known attractions are mighty Mt Kilimanjaro, the world-famous Ngorongoro Crater and the Serengeti, with its annual wildebeest migration. Yet the country has much more to offer. Dar es Salaam is a colourful, bustling place with an interesting history. To the north-east are the cool Usambara Mountains with their winding paths and tiny villages, and the more rugged Pare Mountains which offer good walking and people with an intriguing culture. In the north, in addition to the highlights already mentioned, are several beautiful wildlife areas including Lake Manyara, Tarangire and Arusha national parks, and some good village-based walking trails. Lake Victoria, while not a traditional tourist destination, offers the serene Rubondo Island National Park, and the chance to get acquainted with the Sukuma and the Haya, two of Tanzania's most populous ethnic groups.

In the west of the country are three fascinating parks – the remote and misty Mahale Mountains, beautiful Katavi, and tiny Gombe Stream, world renowned for its primate studies. Tanzania's far south-west corner offers good hiking and beautiful hill scenery around Tukuyu, quiet beaches on northern Lake Nyasa, and a pleasantly cool climate.

Towards the centre of the country are the rugged Ruaha National Park, the easily accessible Mikumi National Park, and Udzungwa Mountains National Park, a hiker's paradise. Travellers with a sense of adventure and plenty of time should not miss Tanzania's remote but spectacular south-east corner, with some of the most attractive shoreline along the East African coast, a wealth of history, and the vast and magnificent Selous Game Reserve.

Finally, the waters edging Tanzania's long coastline offer pristine coral reefs, rich and diverse marine life, and numerous idyllic islands. These include quiet, palm-fringed Mafia, green and mysterious Pemba, and Unguja (Zanzibar island) – East Africa's most famous Swahili city-state, with its mosques, winding alleyways, sultans' palaces and coral-sand beaches.

SUGGESTED ITINERARIES

First-time visitors to Africa and independent travellers usually find Tanzania a relatively easy country to negotiate. However, it's also a very large country; distances are long, and transport infrastructure is poor. Travellers who try to compress too many things into a visit inevitably wind up disappointed and exhausted. Unless you have several months, it's best to choose just one or two regions and concentrate on exploring them well. The following suggestions have been provided to help you get started. Be sure to allow yourself enough travel time, as well as sufficient time to organise things – particularly if you are doing this yourself rather than through a tour operator. As is the case all over Africa, everything always takes longer than you think it will!

If you are planning to go on a wildlife-viewing safari, the general rule is the longer, the better, particularly in vast areas such as Ruaha National Park and the Selous Game Reserve. Much of the safari market focusing on the northern circuit, particularly the Ngorongoro Crater and Serengeti National Park, has degenerated into quick in-and-out trips which – apart from the deleterious environmental effects – turns the whole experience into a bit of a zoo. While it is possible to 'see' plenty of wildlife on a day trip or an overnight excursion, two or three days or more will allow you to experience some of the more subtle attractions of Tanzania's magnificent wilderness areas.

One Week

Assuming that you will be arriving in Dar es Salaam, you could spend a day or two in the capital getting oriented, perhaps a day at

Mikumi National Park, and then the remainder of the week on Unguja, divided between Zanzibar Town and one of the beaches.

Two Weeks

With two weeks, you could expand this base a bit, staying longer on Unguja and adding on a few days hiking in the Usambaras or visiting the Selous Game Reserve or Ruaha National Park. More rugged travellers might prefer to substitute a few days in Udzungwa Mountains National Park. Alternatively, you could head from Dar es Salaam towards Moshi and Arusha, spending a day or two walking in the villages around Marangu and several days visiting one of the northern parks or the Ngorongoro Crater before heading to Unguja.

One Month

Travellers with a month or more will have plenty of time to bring some of Tanzania's more distant attractions into the itinerary. If you're in the area of Lake Victoria, Rubondo Island National Park is well worth a visit. The western parks – Gombe Stream, Mahale Mountains and Katavi – also make good destinations, especially if you are entering Tanzania from Malawi or Zambia. Outdoor fans should not miss at least a few days hiking in the region around Tukuyu and northern Lake Nyasa.

Another option for travellers who have at least a month to spare would be a leisurely trip through the Southern Highlands, between Morogoro and the Mbeya region. Possible stops along the way include Iringa, Ruaha National Park, the Ulugurus, Mbeya and Tukuyu. From Mbeya you could then continue on to Malawi or Zambia. Alternatively, you could head north-west towards Katavi, Mpanda and Tabora and then take the Central Line train back to Dar es Salaam, finishing the trip on the Zanzibar archipelago – although to do this circuit properly you will need closer to six weeks.

Three Months

With three months, you should have plenty of time to explore several regions of the country. A good circular route goes northeast from Dar es Salaam to the Usambara and Pare mountains, then on to Moshi, Arusha and the northern parks. From there, you could make your way south towards Dodoma and Iringa, and then either south-west towards Mbeya, south towards Njombe and Songea, or back east towards Dar es Salaam and the Zanzibar archipelago. The truly rugged could go in the other direction, heading south from Dar es Salaam towards Mtwara with possible stops at Kilwa Masoko and Lindi along the way. After this, if you still have any energy left, you could continue west from Mtwara towards Songea and Njombe, and then back north at a leisurely pace through the Southern Highlands with stops in Iringa and in Ruaha, Udzungwa Mountains or Mikumi national parks. From Morogoro, you could then head north towards the Usambaras, Moshi or Arusha, or else head east towards Unguja and Pemba islands.

No matter which route you take, most travellers find it best to leave the Zanzibar archipelago to the end – you'll be glad of some dust-free relaxation after spending weeks bumping along the roads on the mainland. Many, however, wish that they'd left themselves more time for the offshore islands, so don't cut yourself too short! As for an itinerary, you could easily spend at least two weeks on Zanzibar, and another week or two on Pemba without coming close to exhausting all these places have to offer.

Remember that even with three months, it's difficult to make a full circuit of Tanzania, especially if you're travelling during the rainy season when many roads are closed. Even though it might be tempting to try to 'see' the whole country, it would be far better to concentrate on just a few regions.

PLANNING
When to Go

Weather-wise, the best time to visit Tanzania is between late June and October when the rains have finished and the air is coolest. However, this is also when hotels and park lodges are full and airfares most expensive.

The second-best time is from late December to February or early March, just after the short rains and before the long rains, though temperatures will be higher (see Climate in the Facts about Tanzania chapter for more information). If you plan to spend a lot of time in the Southern Highlands, keep in mind that the short rains last longer here, often well into January.

Budget travellers can save substantially on accommodation costs during the main rainy season from March until June, and you'll have many of the places to yourself. However many secondary roads will be impassable and many areas of the country inaccessible. Some lodges and hotels also close during this period. In the parks, camps are often muddy and messy, although it is also the 'green' season and landscapes can be very attractive.

When calculating lodging costs, remember that most hotels consider the period from June or July until March the high season, and April, May and all or part of June the low season. Upscale places often levy an additional 'ultra high season' charge around the Christmas holidays. Many of those park lodges which do remain open during the low season offer discounts of up to 50% between April and late June, which can translate into substantial savings.

What Kind of Trip

Tanzania's size and diversity make it an ideal country for multiple visits, each one focusing on exploring a different area in depth. (See Suggested Itineraries, earlier, for more on this topic.) Independent travel, involving a combination of public transport, organised safaris and occasional vehicle hire, is generally the most economical option and poses no particular problems in Tanzania other than requiring some time and patience. For those who prefer a more structured trip, or whose time is limited, tour companies abound. With the exception of parts of the south-east and of the Southern Highlands, you can find organised tours to go almost anywhere. This will usually be much more expensive than travelling on your own.

Trips can easily be planned around special interests. For example, you could combine hiking for a week or so in the Usambaras or in the Southern Highlands near Tukuyu with visits to some nearby parks, or combine a dive-based trip with exploration of historical sites on Unguja and Pemba islands.

Maps

Maps of Tanzania are widely available in the USA, Europe and Australia, as well as in bookshops in Dar es Salaam, Arusha and in Zanzibar Town. One of the best is the *Nelles* map (1:1,500,000).

The Map Sales Office at the Surveys and Mapping Division on Kivukoni Front and Luthuli St in Dar es Salaam sells dated but good topographical maps (1:50,000) for mainland Tanzania, though individual sheets covering popular areas are often out of stock. Each sheet costs Tsh2500. Topographical maps of Unguja and Pemba are available in Stone Town (see Orientation under Unguja in The Zanzibar Archipelago chapter).

There is a good series of hand drawn maps by an Italian man named Giovanni Tombazzi and marketed under the name MaCo (PO Box 322, Zanzibar), which cover various areas of the country including Northern Tanzania, Unguja, Ngorongoro Conservation Area, and several of the national parks (including Serengeti, Lake Manyara, Tarangire and Kilimanjaro). They are available in bookshops in Dar es Salaam, Arusha and in Zanzibar Town for Tsh5000.

What to Bring

You can buy almost anything you will need in Dar es Salaam or Arusha, except specialist trekking and sporting equipment. If you plan on doing trekking or a camping safari, you can save money and usually enjoy better quality by bringing your own sleeping bag and tent from home. It's often possible to sell these at the end of your trip to tour operators. Most places, including inexpensive guesthouses, have mosquito nets, but it doesn't hurt to carry your own for those times when none are available. If you plan on staying in budget accommodation, a sleeping sheet is also a good thing to bring along to lay over grubby linen.

In most areas of the country you will need a lightweight jacket in the evenings; in some of the higher elevations along the Southern Highlands, in the Usambara and Pare mountains, and on the rim of Ngorongoro Crater, a jacket or pullover is essential. Trekkers will need a full range of cold-weather clothing, which should be brought from home. There is a helpful section on this topic in Lonely Planet's *Trekking in East Africa*.

In general, the clothing you bring should be lightweight and modest. Women should have at least one pair of slacks or a skirt or other wrap. Both men and women should have shirts with sleeves. A hat and sunglasses are useful during long hikes or drives, or on the beach. Earplugs can be handy as cheap hotels and guesthouses are often very noisy.

Some other items which you may want to consider bringing include: a torchlight/flashlight (essential if you will be in any rural areas), a Swiss army knife, binoculars (if you plan to do birdwatching or game viewing), sun cream/block and lip salve, a small first aid kit, a compass, camera and film, good walking shoes, sandals (for relaxing on the beach), water purification tablets and a sturdy water bottle.

RESPONSIBLE TOURISM

Tourism in Tanzania has had its most obvious detrimental impact on the heavily travelled 'northern circuit', around the wildlife-viewing areas of the Serengeti and Ngorongoro and on Mt Kilimanjaro (see the boxed text 'Tanzania's Overloaded Northern Circuit' in the Northern Tanzania chapter). A few tour operators are making conscious efforts to diversify in an effort to address this problem, but it's slow-going. The best companies are those which have a serious commitment to protecting the fragile ecosystems in these and other areas, and which put at least some portion of profits back into local communities. A few have been highlighted in the listings later in this book. Although tour operators who

place a high priority on environmental conservation, and who collaborate with and assist local communities, are not always the cheapest, the extra money you spend is an important way that you can contribute to the future wellbeing of the people in the areas that you visit.

When evaluating a company based on these criteria, try to distinguish between mere lip service and real action; contact the Wildlife Conservation Society of Tanzania or some of the other agencies listed under Ecology & Environment in the Facts about Tanzania chapter to learn about environmental and tourism-related issues in the areas you wish to visit. Avoiding souvenir shops which stock items made from shells, coral, ivory and turtle shells – the export of which is illegal – is also an important way to contribute to the preservation of Tanzania's ecosystems.

Another dimension of responsible tourism, especially in a country such as Tanzania which sees so many foreign visitors, is the manner and attitude which visitors assume towards locals. Respect is of the utmost importance, both in personal dealings as well as in your overall behaviour and your style of dress. This topic is covered further under Society & Conduct in the Facts about Tanzania chapter.

TOURIST OFFICES
Local Tourist Offices

The Tanzania Tourist Board's main tourist information office is in Dar es Salaam. See that chapter for details. There is also a branch office in Arusha; see the Northern Tanzania chapter for details.

Tourist Offices Abroad

In the UK, the Tanzania Tourist Board is represented by the Tanzania Trade Centre (☎ 020-7407 0566, fax 7403 2003, email director@tanzatrade.co.uk, 80 Borough High St, London, SE1 1LL). In other countries, it is represented by Tanzanian embassies and high commissions (see the listings later in this chapter).

Considerations for Responsible Diving

The popularity of diving is placing immense pressure on many sites. Please consider the following tips in order to help preserve the ecology and beauty of the reefs:

- Do not use anchors on the reef, and take care not to ground boats on coral. Encourage dive operators and regulatory bodies to establish permanent moorings at popular dive sites.
- Avoid touching living marine organisms with your body or dragging equipment across the reef. Polyps can be damaged by even the gentlest contact. Never stand on corals, even if they look solid and robust. If you must hold on to the reef, only touch exposed rock or dead coral.
- Be conscious of your fins. Even without contact the surge from heavy fin strokes near the reef can damage delicate organisms. When treading water in shallow reef areas, take care not to kick up clouds of sand. Settling sand can easily smother the delicate organisms of the reef.
- Practise and maintain proper buoyancy control. Major damage can be done by divers descending too fast and colliding with the reef. Make sure you are correctly weighted and that your weight belt is positioned so that you stay horizontal. If you have not dived for a while, have a practice dive in a pool before taking to the reef. Be aware that buoyancy can change over the period of an extended trip: initially you may breathe harder and need more weight; a few days later you may breathe more easily and need less weight.
- Take great care in underwater caves. Spend as little time in them as possible as your air bubbles may get caught within the roof and thereby leave previously submerged organisms high and dry. Taking turns to inspect the interior of a small cave will lessen the chances of damaging contact.
- Resist the temptation to collect or buy corals or shells. Apart from the ecological damage and the fact that their export is illegal in Tanzania, taking home marine souvenirs depletes the beauty of a site and spoils the enjoyment of others. The same goes for marine archaeological sites (mainly shipwrecks). Respect their integrity; some sites are even protected from looting by law.
- Ensure that you take home all your rubbish and any litter you may find as well. Plastics in particular are a serious threat to marine life. Turtles can mistake plastic for jellyfish and eat it.
- Resist the temptation to feed fish. You may disturb their normal eating habits, encourage aggressive behaviour or feed them food that is detrimental to their health.
- Minimise your disturbance of marine animals. In particular, do not ride on the backs of turtles as this causes them great anxiety.

VISAS & DOCUMENTS
Visas

Visas are required by almost all visitors to Tanzania except nationals of some Commonwealth countries; Canadian and British citizens require visas. The cost of a visa varies between US$10 and US$60 depending on nationality. Tourist visas are usually issued for a maximum of three months, although length of stay is determined at the border – one month is the norm.

It is best to obtain a visa before arrival. If you are unable to do so, visas are usually issued at Dar es Salaam international airport, Kilimanjaro international airport, Zanzibar airport, and at the Kenyan border post of Namanga. Note that entry regulations are constantly changing. It's likely that citizens of several other non-African Commonwealth countries will need visas in the future. For up-to-date information, contact your nearest Tanzanian embassy or high commission.

Visa Extensions Application for a visa extension can be made at the immigration office in any of Tanzania's major towns and cities. There is no charge for an extension, and it will generally be issued the same day; no photos are required. If you have a three month visa, you will be unable to extend without an acceptable reason. In most cases, visitors intending on staying beyond three months must apply for a residency permit. Residency permit applications must be made at the Tanzanian embassy in your home country; you cannot convert from tourist status to resident status while in Tanzania. It is best to apply through your employer or another Tanzanian-based entity as independent applications are discouraged.

Getting Other Visas in Tanzania The visas below can be picked up in Tanzania:

Burundi
Although the Tanzanian-Burundian border is officially closed, visas are being issued. A one-month single entry visa costs US$40 plus two photos and is usually ready the same day if you apply early. The Burundian consulate in Kigoma also issues one-month single entry visas.

Congo (Zaïre)
The consulate in Kigoma issues one-month single entry visas for US$50 plus two photos. It can take from one day to one week or more for processing; one is left with the distinct impression that to get your passport back you will need to give a substantial 'gift' in addition to the visa fee.

Kenya
A one-month single entry visa costs between Tsh15,000 (USA and Australia) to Tsh32,500 (UK), depending on nationality. Visas are issued the same day if you apply early.

Malawi
Citizens of the USA, UK and Germany do not require visas. For other nationalities, visas cost US$40 plus two photos, and are issued within 24 hours, or on the same day if you apply in the morning.

Mozambique
One-month single entry visas costs US$30 plus two photos and are usually ready within two days.

Rwanda
Visas cost Tsh20,000 plus two photos and are ready in 48 to 72 hours.

Uganda
A three-month visa costs US$30 plus three photos, and is usually ready the same day if you apply early.

Zambia
Applications received in the morning will be processed the same day. A one-month single entry visa costs Tsh15,000 for most nationalities, plus two photos.

Zimbabwe
Most nationalities do not need visas. For those who do, one-month single entry visas cost US$45 plus two photos. Allow at least two weeks for processing, as applications must be sent to Harare.

Travel Insurance

A travel insurance policy to cover theft, loss and medical problems is a good idea. Some policies offer lower and higher medical-expense options; the higher ones are chiefly for countries such as the USA that have extremely high medical costs. There are many different types of policies available. Be sure to read the small print before signing.

Many policies specifically exclude 'dangerous activities', which can include scuba diving, motorcycling, and even trekking. A locally acquired motorcycle licence is not valid under some policies.

You may prefer a policy which pays doctors or hospitals directly rather than you having to pay on the spot and claim later. If you have to claim later be sure to keep all documentation. Some policies ask you to call back (reverse charges) to a centre in your home country where an immediate assessment of your problem is made.

Be sure that your policy covers ambulances and an emergency flight home. For additional information on medical evacuations, see the Health section later in this chapter.

Driving Licence & Permits

To drive in Tanzania you will either need to arrange an international driving permit before arrival or get a Tanzanian licence. Tanzanian drivers' licences are available from the traffic police in major towns, and generally cost around Tsh3000 per day. It's less hassle and less expensive – especially if you are planning on a long-term stay – to get an international driving permit before coming to East Africa.

To bring an automobile into Tanzania from a neighbouring country you must have a completed C49 Customs Form (available at border posts), as well as proof of insurance, vehicle registration papers, and a valid international driving permit. Vehicles are admitted into Tanzania for a maximum of three months.

To import a vehicle into Tanzania from a non-neighbouring country you must also have a valid *carnet de passage*; this is available from the Automobile Association of Tanzania (PO Box 3004 Dar es Salaam). Alternatively, contact a motoring organisation in your own country for further information. Without a carnet, you will be required to make a deposit of the import duty payable on the vehicle – usually between one and 1½ times the new value of the vehicle. Trying to get a refund of this deposit can be a time-consuming and frustrating process.

International Health Card
Visitors must have an up-to-date health card showing proof of a yellow fever vaccination.

Photocopies
Before beginning your trip, make copies of your passport, including the Tanzanian visa page, your international health card, airline tickets, travellers cheque serial numbers, and any other essential documents. Leave one set of copies with family or friends and bring a second set with you, stored separately from the originals. Doing this will make replacement much easier should your documents be lost or stolen.

EMBASSIES & CONSULATES
Tanzanian Embassies & Consulates
Tanzania maintains the following embassies in the region and around the world:

Belgium
  (☎ 02-640 6500, fax 646 8026)
  363 Ave Louise, 1050 Brussels

Canada
  (☎ 0613-232 1500, fax 232 5184)
  50 Range Rd, Ottawa, Ontario KIN 8J4
France
  (☎ 33-01-53 70 63 70, fax 01 53 70 63 66)
  13 ave Raymond Poincare, 75116 Paris
Germany
  (☎ 0228-358051, fax 358226)
  Theaterplatz 26, 53177, Bonn
Japan
  (☎ 03-425 4531, fax 425 7844)
  21-9, Kamiyoga 4, Chome Setagaya-Ku, Tokyo 158
Kenya
  (☎ 02-331056, fax 218269)
  Continental House, corner of Uhuru Highway and Harambee Ave, Nairobi
Mozambique
  (☎ 258-1-490110)
  Ujamaa House, PO Box 4515, Maputo
South Africa
  (☎ 012-323 9041, 342 4393 fax 323 9042)
  PO Box 56572, Arcadia 0007, Pretoria
Switzerland
  (☎ 022-731 8920, fax 732 8255)
  47 Ave Blanc, CH-1201, Geneva
Uganda
  (☎ 256-41-256292, 256272, fax 242890)
  6 Kagera Rd, PO Box 5750, Kampala
United Kingdom
  (☎ 020-7499 8951, fax 7491 9321)
  43 Hertford St, London W1Y 8DB
USA
  (☎ 1-202-939 6125, fax 797 7408)
  2139 R St, NW, Washington DC 20008
Zambia
  (☎ 260-1-253320, 227698)
  Ujamaa House, 5200 United Nations Ave, Lusaka

Note that there is no Tanzanian embassy in Malawi.

Tanzania is also represented by either embassies or consulates in the folowing countries: France (Paris), Italy (Rome), the Netherlands (The Hague) and Zimbabwe (Harare).

Embassies & Consulates in Tanzania
Some useful foreign embassies, consulates and high commissions in Dar es Salaam are listed below. For a more complete listing, check the telephone book or alternatively, one of the free tourist magazines available in

Dar es Salaam. Australians needing assistance should contact the Canadian embassy. If you will be spending extended periods in remote areas of Tanzania, it is a good idea to register with your embassy upon arrival in Dar es Salaam.

Belgium
(☎ 112688) 5 Ocean Rd, Upanga
Burundi
(☎ 117615, Kigoma ☎ 0695 2865) Lugalo Rd, Upanga, behind Palm Beach Hotel. Open from 9 am to 3 pm.
Canada
(☎ 112831) 38 Mirambo St
France
(☎ 666021) Bagamoyo Rd
Germany
(☎ 117409) 10th floor, NIC Life House, Samora Ave
India
(☎ 117175) 11th floor, NIC Life House, Samora Ave
Ireland
(☎ 666211, 666348) Msasani St just off Haile Selassie Rd and near the International School
Italy
(☎ 115935) 316 Lugalo Rd, Upanga
Kenya
(☎ 112811) 14th floor, NIC Life House, Samora Ave. Open Monday to Friday from 9 am to 2.30 pm.
Malawi
(☎ 113240) 6th floor, Wing A, NIC Life House Branch, Sokoine Drive. Open Monday to Friday from 8 am to noon and from 2 to 5 pm.
Mozambique
25 Garden Ave. Open weekdays from 8.30 am to 4.30 pm.
Netherlands
(☎ 118593) 2nd floor, ATC House, Ohio St at Garden Ave
Rwanda
(☎ 130119) 32 Ali Hassan Mwinyi Rd, Upanga. Open from 8 am to 3 pm.
Uganda
(☎ 117646) 7th floor, Extelecoms House, Samora Ave
UK
(☎ 112953) Samora Ave at Askari Monument
USA
(☎ 666010)
Zambia
(☎ 118481) 5/9 Sokoine Drive at Ohio St. Open for visa services on Monday, Wednesday and Friday from 9 to 11 am and from 2 to 3 pm.

Zimbabwe
(☎ 116789) 6th floor, Wing C, NIC Life House Branch, Sokoine Drive. Open weekdays 8.30 am to 1 pm and 2 to 4 pm.

CUSTOMS
The export of shells, coral, ivory and turtle shells is illegal.

You are permitted to export a maximum of Tsh2000 without declaration. There is no limit on the importation of foreign currency, although amounts over US$10,000 must be declared.

MONEY
Currency
The unit of currency is the Tanzanian shilling (Tsh). There are bills of Tsh10,000, 5000, 1000, 500, 200 and 100, and coins of Tsh100, 50, 20, 10, five and one shilling(s).

Exchange Rates

country	unit		shilling
Australia	A$1	=	Tsh435
Canada	C$1	=	Tsh445
euro	€1	=	Tsh787
France	1FF	=	Tsh110
Germany	DM1	=	Tsh360
UK	UK£1	=	Tsh1055
USA	US$1	=	Tsh650

Exchanging Money
You can change cash and travellers cheques, usually with a minimum of hassle, at banks or foreign exchange shops in all major towns and cities; rates and commissions vary, so it pays to shop around. Most smaller towns do not have foreign exchange shops; your only option is the bank, which will often change cash only.

Although they are seldom checked, it's a good idea to save at least some of your exchange receipts in order to be able to change any remaining Tanzanian shillings back to hard currency on departure. You can do this at banks or foreign exchange shops in Dar es Salaam and major towns, and at the foreign exchange shops at Dar es Salaam international airport.

Most travellers find they do not need too many shillings. Officially, nonresidents must pay for lodging, park fees, air tickets and similar items with hard currency, although in practice many hotels and some airlines will waive this requirement and convert to Tanzanian shillings at the going rate. For organised treks and safaris you will need US dollars.

Since liberalization of currency laws, there is essentially no black market for foreign currency. You can assume that the frequent offers you'll receive on the street to change at high rates are a setup.

Cash US dollars are the most convenient foreign currency, although other major currencies are accepted in larger towns.

Travellers Cheques Travellers cheques are widely accepted in major towns; exchange rates are generally slightly lower than for cash. If you pay park entry fees with travellers cheques, change is usually given in Tanzanian shillings. In smaller towns, banks often will not exchange travellers cheques; you will need cash.

Credit Cards Credit cards are accepted by many top-end hotels, some tour operators, and increasingly by mid-range establishments. However, most places charge a commission ranging from 5 to 15%. In general, if you pay with a credit card for anything which was not originally priced in US dollars, you will wind up paying between 15 and 20% more, although these additional charges are often disguised.

Dar es Salaam, Unguja and Arusha are the only places in Tanzania where you can get cash advances against Visa or MasterCard. See the relevant regional chapters for details.

Security
The few bills you have stuffed in your back pocket are an enormous sum to many Tanzanians, and pickpocketing is rife in crowded areas such as bus and train stations, and markets. The best way to carry your money is in an inside pocket or pouch, and preferably divided into several smaller stashes stored in various places on your body. Alternatively, leave some of it in your hotel safe. Keep a small amount of cash handy and separate from your other money so that you do not need to pull out a large wad of bills for paying taxi fares or making purchases.

Costs
Local food, accommodation, markets and public transport are inexpensive. A meal of rice and sauce in a local restaurant, usually costs about Tsh500, while budget lodging ranges from Tsh1000 for the most basic fleapit to about Tsh8000 for a simple but fairly comfortable room. If you stay only in budget accommodation, eat local food and travel via public transport, you should have no trouble keeping costs to about US$20 per day or less (not including safaris or other organised activities). In contrast, imported items, organised tours and tourist-class hotels can be very pricey – costs can easily exceed US$200 per person per day on organised safaris. Mid-range travellers seeking a degree of comfort and western-style meals in pleasant surroundings should plan on spending between US$20 and US$60 per day for lodging, and between Tsh6000 and Tsh10,000 for a full-course meal.

There are several ways to economise on costs. Travelling in groups is almost always

Tanzanian Shillings versus US Dollars
The general rule followed in this book is to use local currency whenever possible. Where dollars are listed, it is because prices are quoted in dollars, and/or payment is expected in dollars. Particularly at the lower and middle ranges of the spectrum, however, there is often – though not always – flexibility to convert from dollars and pay in Tanzanian shillings at the going rate of exchange.

cheaper if you are going on an organised trek or safari. Many hotels and park lodges offer discounts of up to 50% in the low season, so travelling then can often result in substantial savings (see When to Go in the Planning section earlier in this chapter). Many travellers try to economise on park fees by entering parks around midday or early afternoon. Since the fees are calculated on a 24 hour basis, you will be able to get in good evening and morning game viewing this way while only paying fees for one day.

Unless otherwise noted, all prices listed in this book are for nonresidents. National parks, museums, ferries, many hotels, and other places often offer resident rates which can be a lot lower (although sometimes 'resident rates' are the same as nonresident rates, just quoted in Tsh). If you have a resident card, always ask if special rates are available. In addition to making you eligible for reduced rates, a resident card also entitles you to pay all fees in Tanzanian shillings.

Tipping & Bargaining

Tipping is generally not practiced in small, local establishments, especially in rural areas. In Dar es Salaam, and in more upscale establishments frequented by tourists, tips may be expected. Some top-end places include a service charge in the bill. Otherwise, 10% is standard, assuming service warrants it. On treks and safaris, it is common practice to tip drivers, guides, porters and other staff if service has been good. For some guidelines on how much to tip see: Tipping under Organised Vehicle Safaris in the Getting Around chapter; the boxed text 'Tipping Guides & Porters on Kilimanjaro' and Guides & Porters under Mt Meru, both in the Trekking chapter.

Bargaining is a way of life in Tanzania, as in many other parts of Africa, and is expected by most sellers, except in a limited number of fixed-price shops. If you pay the first price asked – whether out of ignorance, or due to guilt about how much you have compared with locals – you will likely be considered naive. You'll also be doing fellow travellers a disservice by creating the impression that all foreigners are willing to pay any price named.

There are no set rules, although bargaining should always be conducted in a friendly and spirited manner; it's part of the fun of travel in the region. You will never get anywhere by losing your temper. If the negotiations become exasperating, or begin to seem a waste of time, politely take your leave. Sometimes sellers will call you back if they think their stubbornness has been counterproductive. Very few will pass up the chance of making a sale, however thin the profit.

In any transaction, the vendor's aim is to identify the highest price they are willing to pay, while your aim is to find the price below which the vendor will not sell. The best way to start is to first decide yourself what you want to pay. If you shop around for a while, you will soon get a feel for the 'value' of the item you want. Asking others what they have paid can also be helpful. Many travellers then start at about half of this price and go upwards. Vendors – who may quote an initial price between 50% and more than 200% of what they ultimately hope to receive – may laugh or feign outrage, but the price will quickly drop from the original quote to a more realistic level. When it does, you can begin making better offers until you arrive at a mutually agreeable figure. If the vendor won't come down to a price you feel is fair, it means that they aren't making a profit, or that too many high-rolling foreigners have passed through already.

Taxes

In July 1998, a 20% Value Added Tax (VAT) was introduced on the mainland. While most hotel operators had already made price adjustments by the time this book was researched, many tour companies were still unsure how the new tax would affect them. You should expect that some of the safari prices quoted in later chapters may increase to compensate, although any increase attributable to the VAT should not be more than about 5% since it replaced some existing taxes. Hotel price listings in this book generally include VAT unless otherwise noted.

POST & COMMUNICATIONS
Post
Airmail postage to the USA and Australia costs from Tsh500 (Tsh400 to the UK); postcards cost Tsh400. Allow about two weeks for letters to arrive in Dar es Salaam from abroad, longer for those sent to smaller towns. Sending small parcels (non-valuable items only!) is relatively reliable, although things occasionally go missing.

Poste restante is fairly well organised in Dar es Salaam and in most major towns; there is a charge of Tsh200 per received letter. Most post offices will hold mail indefinitely. Have the sender clearly write your surname in block letters and underline it.

Telephone
You can make domestic and international calls from Tanzania Telecom offices in all major towns; the offices are invariably located near the post office. Local calls average Tsh200 for three minutes, with a three minute minimum charge. Domestic calls start at about Tsh600 for three minutes. International calls are expensive, starting at about US$4 per minute. Outside of major towns, the international exchange is often unreliable. There are now card phones in Dar es Salaam and most major towns, although locals complain that they frequently malfunction. The least expensive phone card costs Tsh5000, which will last less than two minutes for a call to Europe.

There are also private telecommunications centres in the capital and most larger towns which are more expensive, but generally more efficient. When dialling from hotels, expect to pay at least double the Tanzania Telecom rates.

Area codes for major towns in Tanzania are listed below. For smaller towns with just one or two-digit telephone numbers you will need to go through the operator.

Arusha	☎ 057
Bukoba	☎ 066
Dar es Salaam	☎ 051
Dodoma	☎ 061
Iringa	☎ 064
Kigoma	☎ 0695
Lindi	☎ 0525
Masasi	☎ 059
Mbeya	☎ 065
Morogoro	☎ 056
Moshi	☎ 055
Mtwara	☎ 059
Musoma	☎ 068
Mwanza	☎ 068
Njombe	☎ 0632
Pemba Island	☎ 054
Songea	☎ 0635
Sumbawanga	☎ 0637
Tabora	☎ 062
Tanga	☎ 053
Tukuyu	☎ 0658
Unguja	☎ 054

Mobile telephones are very common in Tanzania. The numbers are six digits, preceded by either (0)811 or (0)812. If you are trying to reach a mobile telephone number from outside Tanzania you will need to dial the country code, and then the 811/821 code without the 0. For example, a mobitel number listed as 0812-xxxxxx would be dialled from outside Tanzania as +255-812-xxxxxx. To dial this number from within Tanzania, whether you are in the same city as the number being called or not, you would dial 0812-xxxxxx.

Fax
Faxes can be sent and received from most Tanzania Telecom offices. Rates average about Tsh2700 per minute to Europe and the USA. Private telecommunications and business centres usually charge more. Most tour operators, and mid-range and top-end hotels have faxes. Sending faxes to Tanzania from abroad is generally not a problem.

Email & Internet Access
Tanzania is online. There are several Internet servers in Dar es Salaam and email centres in most major towns (see the listings in the Dar es Salaam and regional chapters). Service is likely to expand rapidly over the next few years. Most places charge about Tsh3000 per half hour to access the Internet, between

Tsh1000 and Tsh2000 to send email messages, and about Tsh500 to receive email.

A growing number of tour operators and hotels now have email addresses as noted throughout this book.

INTERNET RESOURCES

The World Wide Web is a rich resource for travellers. You can research your trip, hunt down bargain airfares, book hotels, check on weather conditions or chat with locals and other travellers about the best places to visit (or avoid).

There is no better place to start your Web explorations for your travels in Tanzania than the Lonely Planet Web site (www .lonelyplanet.com). Here you'll find succinct travel summaries, postcards from other travellers, and the Thorn Tree bulletin board, where you can ask questions before you go or dispense advice when you get back. You can also find travel news and guidebook updates. The subWWWay section links you to the most useful travel resources elsewhere on the Web.

Following are just some of the other Web sites of interest for travellers to Tanzania. This list has intentionally been kept very brief; if you spend some time on the net you should be able to find many more sites.

Africa Online
   www.africaonline.com
Tanzania Tourist Board
   www.tanzania-web.com/home2.htm
University of Pennsylvania
   African Studies Department
   www.sas.upenn.edu

BOOKS

Most books are published in different editions by different publishers in different countries. As a result, a book might be a hardcover rarity in one country while it's readily available in paperback in another. Fortunately, bookshops and libraries search by title or author, so your local bookshop or library is best placed to advise you on the availability of the recommendations following and above.

Lonely Planet

Africa on a shoestring covers more than 50 African countries, concentrating on practical information for budget travellers. If you're intending to combine your visit to Tanzania with travels elsewhere in the region, *East Africa* covers the region in considerably more depth, with information about Kenya, Uganda, Rwanda, Burundi and eastern Congo (Zaïre).

For detailed advice on trekking in the region try *Trekking in East Africa* which is a much expanded version of the Trekking chapter in this book, with all sorts of information on Tanzania and neighbouring countries.

Lonely Planet's *Swahili phrasebook* is a helpful introduction to the language and handy to have in more out-of-the-way areas.

Guidebooks

The *Tourist Guide to Tanzania* (1991) by Gratian Luhikula is one of the better local guides. It's mainly useful for background information on places of interest rather than for practical travel tips.

For guidebooks on Trekking see Maps & Guidebooks in the Trekking chapter later in this book.

History

Tanzania Notes and Records (1993, reprint editions) contain some great period pieces on a wide variety of topics of Tanzanian history and culture. They are sold at the National Museum in Dar es Salaam and at the Arusha Declaration Museum in Arusha (Tsh4500). Older copies (titled *Tanganyika Notes and Records*) are sometimes available at second-hand stalls on the street, although there are not too many left.

The very readable *Memoirs of an Arabian Princess* by Emily Said-Ruete is the autobiography of a Zanzibari princess who elopes with a German to Europe. In recalling her early life, Said-Ruete paints an intriguing historical portrait of Unguja in the days of the sultans.

The White Nile by Alan Moorehead has good descriptions of Zanzibar and inland areas of Tanzania in the last century, and is good reading for those interested in the era of European exploration of East Africa.

Those interested in learning about Dar es Salaam in more depth should get a copy of *Dar es Salaam: A Dozen Drives Around the City* by Laura Sykes & Uma Waide. It's full of interesting tidbits about the city's history and development.

For general historical information on Africa, including Tanzania and East Africa, try one of the following:

- *History of Africa* by Kevin Shillington
- *The Africans* by David Lamb
- *Africa: A Biography of the Continent* by John Reader
- *The Penguin Atlas of African History* by Colin McEvedy

General

To get yourself in the mood for Tanzania and East Africa:

- *The Snows of Kilimanjaro and Other Stories* by Ernest Hemingway
- *Africa Solo: A Journey Across the Sahara, Sahel and the Congo* by Kevin Kertscher
- *In the Shadow of Kilimanjaro: On Foot Across East Africa* by Rick Ridgeway

NEWSPAPERS & MAGAZINES

The *International Herald Tribune* and some international news magazines are available in Dar es Salaam and Arusha.

Tanzanian English-language dailies include the *Guardian* and the *Daily News*. While the major papers are government-owned or aligned, there are a large number of independent publications.

RADIO & TV

Due to Tanzania's vastness, its inadequate infrastructure and its large rural population, most Tanzanians depend on the radio, rather than newspapers, for their news. Radio Tanzania, the national station, is closely aligned with the government and broadcasts in both English and Swahili; Radio Tanzania Zanzibar broadcasts in Swahili only. There are also several private and church-run stations.

Televisions are common in larger towns and cities and almost all top-end hotels have cable TV. Even in fairly remote areas you will usually be able to find at least one TV. Most local programming is in Swahili.

PHOTOGRAPHY & VIDEO
Film & Equipment

Print film is available in major towns, although selection is usually limited. A roll of 100ASA/36 exposures will cost between Tsh2000 and Tsh3000. Faster speed film and slide film are available in Dar es Salaam and in some of the larger towns.

For developing, the Burhani chain is the best. The main shop in Dar es Salaam does very good work. There are also outlets in Dodoma, Mbeya, Kigoma, Tanga, Tabora and Moshi, although quality is not as reliable. The cost of developing a role of 36 exposures ranges from about Tsh5000 upcountry to Tsh8000 in Dar es Salaam.

Serious wildlife photography will require a SLR (single lens reflex) camera which can take long focal-length lenses. Zoom lenses are good as you can frame your shot easily to get the best composition; a 200mm lens is the minimum you will need to get good close-up shots.

Telephoto (fixed focal-length) lenses give better results than zoom lenses, though you will be limited by having to carry a separate lens for various focal lengths. For both zoom and telephoto lenses you will need 200 or 400ASA film.

Whatever equipment you decide to take, be sure that it is in a bag which will protect it from dust and knocks. Also be sure your travel insurance policy covers your camera in the event that it is stolen.

Restrictions

Don't take photos of anything connected with the government or the military, including government offices, post offices, banks, ports, railway stations and airports.

Photographing People

Never snap pictures of people without first asking their permission. In Tanzania, unless you have taken time to build up a relationship first, the answer will often be 'no'. In many places, locals will ask for a fee before allowing you to photograph them, which is fair enough though rates are high these days. In what may appear to you to be the most remote, out-of-the-way area, it's not uncommon to be asked for Tsh1000 or more for a photo!

TIME
Time in Tanzania is GMT/UTC plus three hours. There is no daylight saving.

ELECTRICITY
Tanzania uses 230V, 50 cycles, AC. Surges and troughs are not uncommon. Power cuts also occur with some frequency, particularly outside major towns, though they generally do not last very long.

Plugs and sockets vary but are usually the British three-square-pin or two-round-pin variety. Adaptors are available in Tanzania.

WEIGHTS & MEASURES
Tanzania uses the metric system. Road distances are signposted in kilometres.

LAUNDRY
Local rates are as low as Tsh100 to Tsh200 per piece. Hotels often charge five to 10 times this amount.

TOILETS
Toilets in Tanzania are either 'western' sit-down style or 'eastern' squat style. In some places, the squat toilets are equipped with flush mechanisms, while in others they are simply built over a deep hole in the ground (long drop). You'll also often find western-style toilet seats balanced over a long drop. Cleanliness levels vary; if you go in expecting the worst, you will often be surprised that they're not all that bad. Toilets with running water are a rarity outside major hotels.

HEALTH
Travel health depends on your predeparture preparations, your daily health care while travelling and how you handle any medical problem that does develop. While the potential dangers can seem quite frightening, in reality few travellers experience anything more than an upset stomach.

Before heading to Tanzania, it is well worth considering taking out a membership with the African Medical & Research Foundation (AMREF), which will entitle you to emergency regional evacuation by the Flying Doctors Society of Africa. A two month membership costs US$25. While nonmembers can use AMREF's evacuation services subject to availability of planes and staff, evacuations will be charged at cost. Memberships can be arranged either through AMREF's head office in Nairobi (☎ 254-2-501301) or through their national office in New York (☎ 1-212-768 2440, fax 768 4230). For membership inquiries in Tanzania contact AMREF's Dar es Salaam office (☎ 051-116610, 115832). For evacuations, call AMREF's Nairobi emergency line (☎ 254-2-501280, 501301).

Additional medical resources are listed in the individual towns. The Canadian-based IAMAT (email iamat@sentex.net) provides a list to its members of approved doctors all over the world, including Tanzania.

Pharmacies in Dar es Salaam and major towns are generally well stocked. In villages, selection is limited, although you can get chloroquine and paracetamol almost anywhere. Always check expiry dates when buying medications.

Predeparture Planning
Immunisations Plan ahead for getting your vaccinations: some require more than one injection, and some should not be given together. Note that certain vaccinations should not be given during pregnancy or to people with allergies. Your doctor will be able to advise you on these and related issues.

It is recommended you seek medical advice at least six weeks before travel. Be aware that there is often a greater risk of disease with children and during pregnancy.

Following are descriptions of some vaccinations which you should consider obtaining prior to undertaking travel in Tanzania and East Africa. You should discuss your specific requirements with your doctor. For more details about the diseases themselves, see the individual disease entries later in this section. Carry proof of your vaccinations, especially yellow fever, as this is needed to enter the country.

Diphtheria & Tetanus Vaccinations for these two diseases are usually combined and are recommended for everyone. After an initial course of three injections (usually given in childhood), boosters are necessary every 10 years.

Polio Everyone should keep up to date with this vaccination, which is normally given in childhood. A booster every 10 years maintains immunity.

Hepatitis A Hepatitis A vaccine provides long-term immunity (possibly more than 10 years) after an initial injection and a booster at six to 12 months.

Alternatively, an injection of gamma globulin can provide short-term protection against hepatitis A – two to six months, depending on the dose given. It is not a vaccine, but is a ready-made antibody collected from blood donations. It is reasonably effective and, unlike the vaccine, it is protective immediately, but because it is a blood product, there are current concerns about its long-term safety.

Hepatitis A vaccine is also available in a combined form, with hepatitis B vaccine. Three injections over a six-month period are required, the first two providing substantial protection against hepatitis A.

Hepatitis B Travellers who will be in East Africa for an extended period, or those who are particularly at risk (see Hepatitis under Infectious Diseases, later in this section) should consider vaccination against hepatitis B. Vaccination involves three injections, with a booster at 12 months. More rapid courses are available if necessary.

Typhoid Vaccination against typhoid is often recommended if you are travelling for more than a couple of weeks in the region. Seek specific advice from your doctor. It is available either as an injection or as capsules to be taken orally.

Cholera The current injectable vaccine against cholera is poorly protective and has many side effects, so it is not generally recommended for travellers. All countries and the WHO have dropped the cholera immunisation as a health requirement for entry. While it is rare in East Africa that you will be asked to present a cer-

tificate, it doesn't hurt to have one just in case. You often will not need to actually get the vaccine in order to receive a certificate; in many western countries the certificate simply consists of a statement signed by a doctor stating that the cholera vaccine is medically contraindicated.

Meningococcal Meningitis Vaccination is recommended for travellers to East Africa. A single injection gives good protection against the major epidemic forms of the disease for three years. Protection may be less effective in children under two years.

Yellow Fever Vaccination is needed as yellow fever is a risk in Tanzania. You will need a certificate showing proof of yellow fever vaccination if you are over one-year old, and coming from an infected area.

Rabies Vaccination should be considered if you will be spending a month or longer in the region, especially if you plan to cycle, handle animals, go caving or travel to remote areas. Vaccination should also be considered for children (who may not report a bite). Pretravel rabies vaccination involves having three injections over 21 to 28 days. If someone who has been vaccinated is bitten or scratched by an animal, they will require two booster injections of vaccine; those not vaccinated require more.

Tuberculosis (BCG) Vaccination against TB is recommended for children and young adults living in East Africa for three months or more. In general, the risk of TB to travellers is usually very low, unless you will be living with or closely associated with local people.

Malaria Medication Antimalarial drugs do not prevent you from being infected but kill the malaria parasites during a stage in their development and significantly reduce the risk of becoming very ill or dying. Expert advice on medication should be sought as there are many factors to consider, including the area to be visited, the risk of exposure to malaria-carrying mosquitoes, the side effects of medication, your medical history and whether you are a child or an adult or pregnant. Travellers to isolated areas in high-risk countries may like to carry a treatment dose of medication for use if symptoms occur. See Malaria under the Insect-Borne Diseases section, later.

Health Insurance Make sure that you remember to get adequate health insurance which includes coverage of emergency evacuation costs

Travel Health Guides If you are planning to be away or travelling in remote areas of the country for a long period of time, it may be worth considering taking along a more detailed health guide. Recommendations include the following:

CDC's Complete Guide to Healthy Travel, Open Road Publishing, 1997. Recommendations for international travel from the US Center for Disease Control & Prevention.

Staying Healthy in Asia, Africa & Latin America, Dirk Schroeder, Moon Publications, 1994. Probably the best all-round guide to carry; it's detailed and well organised.

Travellers' Health, Dr Richard Dawood, Oxford University Press, 1995. Comprehensive, easy to read, authoritative and highly recommended, although it's rather large to lug around.

Where There Is No Doctor, David Werner, Macmillan, 1994. A very detailed guide intended for someone, such as a Peace Corps worker, going to work in an underdeveloped country.

Travel with Children, Maureen Wheeler, Lonely Planet Publications, 1995. Includes advice on travel health for younger children.

There are also a number of excellent travel health sites on the Internet. From the Lonely Planet home page there are links at www .lonelyplanet.com/weblinks/wlprep.htm#heal to the World Health Organization and the US Center for Disease Control & Prevention.

Other Preparations Make sure you're healthy before you start travelling. If you are going on a long trip make sure your teeth are OK. If you wear glasses take a spare pair and your prescription. Contact lens wearers may also want to consider bringing a second pair along, especially if you plan on travelling for an extended period.

If you require a particular medication take an adequate supply, as it may not be available locally. Take part of the packaging showing the generic name rather than the brand, which will make getting replacements easier. It's a good idea to have a legible prescription or letter from your doctor to show

that you legally use the medication to avoid any problems.

Basic Rules

Food There is an old colonial adage which says: 'If you can cook it, boil it or peel it you can eat it ... otherwise forget it'. In Tanzania, food is generally well-prepared, vegetables are usually served cooked, and most fruit is of the peelable variety (such as oranges and bananas). Still, it pays to be cautious, especially when eating street food. Vegetables and fruit should be washed with purified water or peeled where possible. Beware of ice cream which is sold in the street or anywhere it might have been melted and refrozen; if there's any doubt (eg a power cut in the last day or two), steer clear. Shellfish such as mussels, oysters and clams should be avoided as well as undercooked meat, particularly in the form of mince. Steaming does not make shellfish safe for eating.

If a place looks clean and well run and the vendor also looks clean and healthy, then the food is probably safe. In general, places that are packed with travellers or locals will be fine, while empty restaurants are questionable. The food in busy restaurants is cooked and eaten quite quickly with little standing around and is probably not reheated.

Water The number one rule is *be careful of the water* and especially ice. If you don't know for certain that the water is safe, assume the worst. Reputable brands of bottled water in Tanzania include Kilimanjaro (the most widely available) and Hemina (one of the least expensive), although there are many others. Bottled water is sold almost everywhere, except in the most remote villages. Although some long term foreign residents say the tap water is fine, it is best to use caution, especially during the rainy season when sewage may overflow into water supplies. Only use water from containers with a serrated seal – not tops or corks, as they may have been refilled with tap water. Soft drinks are generally fine. Take care with fruit juice, particularly if water may have been added. Milk should be treated with suspicion as it is often unpasteurised, though boiled milk is fine if it is kept hygienically. Tea or coffee should also be OK, since the water should have been boiled.

Water Purification The simplest way of purifying water is to boil it thoroughly. Vigorous boiling should be satisfactory; however, at high altitude water boils at a lower temperature, so germs are less likely to be killed. Boil it for longer in these places.

If you cannot boil water it should be treated chemically. Chlorine tablets will kill many pathogens, but not some parasites like giardia and amoebic cysts. Iodine is more effective in purifying water and is available in tablet form. Follow the directions carefully and remember that too much iodine can be harmful.

Consider purchasing a water filter for a long trip. There are two main kinds of filter. Total filters take out all parasites, bacteria and viruses and make water safe to drink. They are often expensive, but they can be more cost effective than buying bottled water. Simple filters (which can even be a nylon-mesh bag) take out dirt and larger foreign bodies from the water so that chemical solutions work much more effectively; if water is dirty, chemical solutions may not work at all. It's very important when buying a filter to read the specifications, so that you know exactly what it removes from the water and what it doesn't. Simple filtering will not remove all dangerous organisms.

Medical Problems & Treatment

Self-diagnosis and treatment can be risky, so you should always seek medical help. Although we do give drug dosages in this section, they are for emergency use only. Correct diagnosis is vital. An embassy, consulate or five-star hotel can usually recommend a local doctor or clinic; there are also some recommendations in the regional chapters of this book.

Antibiotics should ideally be administered only under medical supervision. Take only the recommended dose at the prescribed intervals and use the whole course, even if the illness seems to be cured earlier. Stop immediately if there are any serious reactions and don't use the antibiotic at all if you are unsure that you have the correct one. Some people are allergic to commonly prescribed antibiotics such as penicillin or sulpha drugs; carry this information (eg on a bracelet) when travelling.

Because brand names of drugs vary from place to place, we have given the generic names throughout this section. Ask your pharmacist for brands available locally.

Environmental Hazards

Altitude Sickness Lack of oxygen at high altitudes (over 2500m) affects most people to some extent, and is a concern for trekkers on Tanzania's Mt Kilimanjaro and Mt Meru. The effects may be mild or severe and occur because less oxygen reaches the muscles and the brain at high altitude, requiring the heart and lungs to compensate by working harder. Symptoms of acute mountain sickness (AMS) usually develop during the first 24 hours at altitude but may be delayed up to three weeks. Mild symptoms include headache, lethargy, dizziness, difficulty sleeping and loss of appetite. AMS may become more severe without warning and can be fatal. Severe symptoms include breathlessness, a dry, irritative cough (which may lead to the production of pink, frothy sputum), severe headache, lack of coordination and balance, confusion, irrational behaviour, vomiting, drowsiness and unconsciousness. There is no hard-and-fast rule as to what is too high: AMS has been fatal at 3000m, though 3500 to 4500m is the usual range.

Treat mild symptoms by resting at the same altitude until recovery, usually a day or two. Paracetamol or aspirin can be taken for headaches. If symptoms persist or become worse, however, *immediate descent is necessary*; even 500m can help. Drug treatments should never be used to avoid descent or to enable further ascent.

The drugs acetazolamide (Diamox) and dexamethasone are recommended by some doctors for the prevention of AMS; however, their use is controversial. They can reduce the symptoms, but they may also mask warning signs; severe and fatal AMS has occurred in people taking these drugs. In general we do not recommend them for travellers.

To prevent acute mountain sickness:

- Ascend slowly – have frequent rest days, spending two to three nights at each rise of 1000m. If you reach a high altitude by trekking, acclimatisation takes place gradually and you are less likely to be affected than if you fly directly to high altitude.
- It is always wise to sleep at a lower altitude than the greatest height reached during the day if possible. Also, once above 3000m, care should be taken not to increase the sleeping altitude by more than 300m per day.
- Drink extra fluids. The mountain air is dry and cold and moisture is lost as you breathe. Evaporation of sweat may occur unnoticed and result in dehydration.
- Eat light, high-carbohydrate meals for more energy.
- Avoid alcohol as it may increase the risk of dehydration.
- Avoid sedatives.

Heat Exhaustion Dehydration and salt deficiency can cause heat exhaustion. Take time to acclimatise to high temperatures, drink sufficient liquids and do not do anything too physically demanding.

Salt deficiency is characterised by fatigue, lethargy, headaches, giddiness and muscle cramps; salt tablets may help, but adding extra salt to your food is better.

Anhidrotic heat exhaustion is a rare form of heat exhaustion that is caused by an inability to sweat. It tends to affect people who have been in a hot climate for some time, rather than newcomers. It can progress to heatstroke. Treatment involves removal to a cooler climate.

Heatstroke This serious, occasionally fatal, condition can occur if the body's heat-regulating mechanism breaks down and the body temperature rises to dangerous levels. Long, continuous periods of exposure to high temperatures and insufficient fluids can leave you vulnerable to heatstroke.

The symptoms are feeling unwell, not sweating very much (or at all) and a high body temperature (39 to 41°C or 102 to 106°F). Where sweating has ceased, the skin becomes flushed and red. Severe, throbbing headaches and lack of coordination will also occur, and the sufferer may be confused or aggressive. Eventually the victim will become delirious or convulse. Hospitalisation is essential, but in the interim get victims out of the sun, remove their clothing, cover them with a wet sheet or towel and then fan continually. Give fluids if they are conscious.

Hypothermia Too much cold can be just as dangerous as too much heat. If you are trekking at high altitudes or simply taking a long bus trip over mountains, particularly at night, be prepared. You should always be prepared for cold, wet or windy conditions even if you're just out walking or hitching.

Hypothermia occurs when the body loses heat faster than it can produce it and the core temperature of the body falls. It is surprisingly easy to progress from very cold to dangerously cold due to a combination of wind, wet clothing, fatigue and hunger, even if the temperature is above freezing. It is best to dress in layers; silk, wool and some of the new artificial fibres are all good insulating materials. A hat is important, as a lot of heat is lost through the head. A strong, waterproof outer layer (and a 'space' blanket for emergencies) is essential. Carry basic supplies, including food containing simple sugars to generate heat quickly and fluid to drink.

Symptoms of hypothermia are exhaustion, numb skin (particularly toes and fingers), shivering, slurred speech, irrational or violent behaviour, lethargy, stumbling, dizzy spells, muscle cramps and violent bursts of energy. Irrationality may take the form of sufferers claiming they are warm and trying to take off their clothes.

To treat mild hypothermia, first get the person out of the wind and/or rain, remove their clothing if it's wet and replace it with dry, warm clothing. Give them hot liquids – not alcohol – and some high-kilojoule, easily digestible food. Do not rub victims: instead, allow them to slowly warm themselves. This should be enough to treat the early stages of hypothermia. The early recognition and treatment of mild hypothermia is the only way to prevent severe hypothermia, which is a critical condition.

Jet Lag Jet lag is experienced when a person travels by air across more than three time zones (each time zone usually represents a one-hour time difference). It occurs because many of the functions of the human body (such as temperature, pulse rate and emptying of the bladder and bowels) are regulated by internal 24-hour cycles. When we travel long distances rapidly, our bodies take time to adjust to the 'new time' of our destination, and we may experience fatigue, disorientation, insomnia, anxiety, impaired concentration and loss of appetite. These effects will usually be gone within three days of arrival, but to minimise the impact of jet lag:

- Rest for a couple of days prior to departure.
- Try to select flight schedules that minimise sleep deprivation; arriving late in the day means you can go to sleep soon after you arrive. For very long flights, try to organise a stopover.
- Avoid excessive eating (which bloats the stomach) and alcohol (which causes dehydration) during the flight. Instead, drink plenty of noncarbonated, nonalcoholic drinks such as fruit juice or water.
- Avoid smoking.
- Make yourself comfortable by wearing loose-fitting clothes and perhaps bringing an eye mask and ear plugs to help you sleep.
- Try to sleep at the appropriate time for the time zone you are travelling to.

Motion Sickness Eating lightly before and during a trip will reduce the chances of motion sickness. If you are prone to motion sickness try to find a place that minimises movement – near the wing on aircraft, close to midships on boats, near the centre on buses. Fresh air usually helps; reading and cigarette smoke don't. Commercial motion-sickness preparations, which can cause drowsiness, have to be taken before the trip commences. Ginger (available in capsule form) and peppermint (including mint-flavoured sweets) are natural preventatives.

Prickly Heat Prickly heat is an itchy rash caused by excessive perspiration trapped under the skin. It usually strikes people who have just arrived in a hot climate. Keeping cool, bathing often, drying the skin and using a talcum or prickly heat powder or resorting to air-conditioning may help.

Sunburn In the tropics, at high altitudes or in the desert – the first two conditions are found in Tanzania – you can get sunburnt quickly, even through cloud. Use a sunscreen, a hat, and a barrier cream for your nose and lips. Calamine lotion or aloe vera are good for mild sunburn. Protect your eyes with good quality sunglasses, particularly if you will be near water, sand or snow.

Infectious Diseases

Diarrhoea Simple things like a change of water, food or climate can all cause a mild bout of diarrhoea, but a few rushed toilet trips with no other symptoms is not indicative of a major problem.

Dehydration is the main danger with any diarrhoea, particularly in children or the elderly as dehydration can occur quite quickly. Under all circumstances *fluid replacement* (at least equal to the volume being lost) is the most important thing to remember. Weak black tea with a little sugar, soda water, or soft drinks allowed to go flat and diluted 50% with clean water are all good. With severe diarrhoea a rehydrating solution is preferable to replace minerals and salts lost. Commercially available oral rehydration salts (ORS) are very useful; add them to boiled or bottled water. In an emergency you can make up a solution of six teaspoons of sugar and a half teaspoon of salt to a litre of boiled or bottled water. You need to drink at least the same volume of fluid that you are losing in bowel movements and vomiting. Urine is the best guide to the adequacy of replacement – if you have small amounts of concentrated urine, you need to drink more. Keep drinking small amounts often. Stick to a bland diet as you recover.

Gut-paralysing drugs such as loperamide or diphenoxylate with atropine can be used to bring relief from the symptoms, although they do not actually cure the problem. Only use these drugs if you do not have access to toilets, eg if you *must* travel. Do not use these drugs in children under 12 years or if you have a high fever or are severely dehydrated.

In certain situations antibiotics may be required: diarrhoea with blood or mucus (dysentery), any diarrhoea with fever, profuse watery diarrhoea, persistent diarrhoea not improving after 48 hours and severe diarrhoea. These suggest a more serious cause of diarrhoea and in these situations gut-paralysing drugs should be avoided.

In these situations, a stool test may be necessary to diagnose what bug is causing your diarrhoea, so you should seek medical help urgently. Where this is not possible the recommended drugs for bacterial diarrhoea (the most likely cause of severe diarrhoea in travellers) are norfloxacin 400mg twice daily for three days or ciprofloxacin 500mg twice daily for five days. These are not recommended for children or pregnant women. The drug of choice for children would be co-trimoxazole with dosage dependent on weight. A five-day course is given. Ampicillin or amoxycillin may be given in pregnancy, but medical care is necessary.

Two other causes of persistent diarrhoea in travellers are giardiasis and amoebic dysentery. **Giardiasis** is caused by a common parasite, *Giardia lamblia*. Symptoms include stomach cramps, nausea, a bloated stomach, watery, foul-smelling diarrhoea and frequent gas. Giardiasis can appear several weeks after you have been exposed to the parasite. The symptoms may disappear and then return; this can go on for several weeks. **Amoebic dysentery** caused by the protozoan *Entamoeba histolytica*, is characterised by a gradual onset of low-grade diarrhoea, often with blood and mucus. Cramping abdominal pain and vomiting are less likely than in other types of diarrhoea, and fever may not be present. It will persist until treated and can recur, causing other problems.

You should seek medical advice if you think you have giardiasis or amoebic dysentery, but where this is not possible, tinidazole or metronidazole are the recommended drugs. Treatment is a 2g single dose of tinidazole or 250mg of metronidazole three times daily for five to 10 days.

Fungal Infections Fungal infections occur more commonly in hot weather and are usually found on the scalp, between the toes (athlete's foot) or fingers, in the groin and on the body (ringworm). You get ringworm (which is a fungal infection, not a worm) from infected animals or other people. Moisture encourages these infections.

To prevent fungal infections wear loose, comfortable clothes, avoid artificial fibres, wash frequently and dry yourself carefully. If you do get an infection, wash the infected area at least daily with a disinfectant or medicated soap and water, and rinse and dry well. Apply an antifungal cream or powder. Try to expose the infected area to air or sunlight as much as possible and wash all towels and underwear in hot water, change them often and let them dry in the sun.

Hepatitis Hepatitis is a general term for inflammation of the liver. It is a common disease worldwide. There are several different viruses that cause hepatitis, and they differ in the way that they are transmitted. The symptoms are similar in all forms of the illness, and include fever, chills, headache, fatigue, feelings of weakness and aches and pains, followed by loss of appetite, nausea, vomiting, abdominal pain, dark urine, light-coloured faeces, jaundiced (yellow) skin and yellowing of the whites of the eyes. People who have had hepatitis should avoid alcohol for some time after the illness, as the liver needs time to recover.

Hepatitis A is transmitted by contaminated food and drinking water. You should seek medical advice, but there is not much you can do apart from resting, drinking lots of fluids, eating lightly and avoiding fatty foods. Hepatitis E is transmitted in the same way as hepatitis A; it can be particularly serious in pregnant women.

There are almost 300 million chronic carriers of **Hepatitis B** in the world. It is spread through contact with infected blood, blood products or body fluids, for example through sexual contact, unsterilised needles and blood transfusions, or contact with blood via small breaks in the skin. Other risk situations include having a shave, tattoo or body piercing with contaminated equipment. The symptoms of hepatitis B may be more severe than type A and the disease can lead to long-term problems such as chronic liver damage, liver cancer or a long-term carrier state. Hepatitis C and D are spread in the same way as hepatitis B and can also lead to long-term complications.

There are vaccines against hepatitis A and B, but there are currently no vaccines against the other types of hepatitis. Following the basic rules about food and water (hepatitis A and E) and avoiding risk situations (hepatitis B, C and D) are important preventative measures.

HIV & AIDS Infection with the human immunodeficiency virus (HIV) leads to the acquired immune deficiency syndrome (AIDS), which is a fatal disease. Any exposure to blood, blood products or body fluids may put the individual at risk. The disease is often transmitted through sexual contact or dirty needles – vaccinations, acupuncture, tattooing and body piercing can be potentially as dangerous as intravenous drug use. HIV/AIDS can also be spread through infected blood transfusions. In 1995, 25% of Tanzanian women aged 25 or older tested positive for HIV, and 14% of men. Actual rates of infection are likely to be even higher.

If you do need an injection, ask to see the syringe unwrapped in front of you, or take a needle and syringe pack with you.

Fear of HIV infection should never stop you getting treatment for serious medical conditions.

Intestinal Worms These parasites are most common in rural, tropical areas. The different worms have different ways of infecting people. Some may be ingested on food such as undercooked meat (eg tapeworms) and some enter through your skin (eg hook-

worms). Infestations may not show up for some time, and although they are generally not serious, if left untreated some can cause severe health problems later. Consider having a stool test when you return home to check for these and determine the appropriate treatment.

Meningococcal Meningitis This serious disease can be fatal. A fever, severe headache, sensitivity to light and neck stiffness which prevents forward bending of the head are the first symptoms. There may also be purple patches on the skin. Death can occur within a few hours, so urgent medical treatment is required. Treatment is large doses of penicillin given intravenously, or chloramphenicol injections.

Schistosomiasis Also known as bilharzia, this disease is transmitted by minute worms. They infect certain varieties of freshwater snails found in rivers, streams, lakes and particularly behind dams. The worms multiply and are eventually discharged into the water.

The worm enters through the skin and attaches itself to your intestines or bladder. The first symptom may be a general feeling of being unwell, or a tingling and sometimes a light rash around the area where it entered. Weeks later a high fever may develop. Once the disease is established abdominal pain and blood in the urine are other signs. The infection often causes no symptoms until the disease is well established (several months to years after exposure) and damage to internal organs irreversible.

Prevention is to avoid swimming or bathing in fresh water where bilharzia is present, such as in parts of many of Tanzania's lakes, including certain areas of Lake Nyasa, and around much of the shoreline on Lake Victoria. Always ask long-time foreign residents or locals before swimming. Even deep water can be infected. If you do get wet, dry off quickly and dry your clothes as well.

A blood test is the most reliable way to diagnose the disease, but the test will not show positive until a number of weeks after exposure.

Sexually Transmitted Diseases HIV/AIDS and hepatitis B can be transmitted through sexual contact – see the relevant sections earlier for more details. Other STDs include gonorrhoea, herpes and syphilis; sores, blisters or rashes around the genitals and discharges or pain when urinating are common symptoms. In some STDs, such as wart virus or chlamydia, symptoms may be less marked or not observed at all, especially in women. Syphilis symptoms eventually disappear completely but the disease continues and can cause severe problems in later years. While abstinence from sexual contact is the only 100% effective prevention, using condoms is also effective. The treatment of gonorrhoea and syphilis is with antibiotics. The different sexually transmitted diseases each require specific antibiotics.

Typhoid Typhoid fever is a dangerous gut infection caused by contaminated water and food. Medical help must be sought.

In its early stages sufferers may feel they have a bad cold or flu on the way, as early symptoms are a headache, body aches and a fever which rises a little each day until it is around 40°C (104°F) or more. The victim's pulse is often slow relative to the degree of fever present – unlike a normal fever where the pulse increases. There may also be vomiting, abdominal pain, diarrhoea or constipation.

In the second week the high fever and slow pulse continue and a few pink spots may appear on the body; trembling, delirium, weakness, weight loss and dehydration may occur. Complications such as pneumonia, perforated bowel or meningitis may occur.

Insect-Borne Diseases

Filariasis, leishmaniasis, sleeping sickness, typhus and yellow fever are all insect-borne diseases, but they do not pose a great risk to travellers. For more information on them see Less Common Diseases at the end of this health section.

Malaria This serious and potentially fatal disease, which is endemic in Tanzania and East Africa, is spread by mosquito bites. It is extremely important that travellers to the region avoid mosquito bites and take tablets to prevent this illness. Symptoms range from fever, chills and sweating, headache, diarrhoea and abdominal pains to a vague feeling of ill-health. Seek medical help immediately if malaria is suspected. Without treatment malaria can rapidly become more serious and can be fatal.

If medical care is not available, malaria tablets can be used for treatment. You need to use a malaria tablet which is different from the one you were taking when you contracted malaria. The standard treatment dose of mefloquine is two 250mg tablets and a further two six hours later. For Fansidar, it's a single dose of three tablets. If you were previously taking mefloquine and cannot obtain Fansidar, then other alternatives are Malarone (atovaquone-proguanil; four tablets once daily for three days), halofantrine (three doses of two 250mg tablets every six hours) or quinine sulphate (600mg every six hours). There is a greater risk of side effects with these dosages than in normal use if used with mefloquine, so medical advice is preferable. Be aware also that halofantrine is no longer recommended by the WHO as emergency standby treatment, because of side effects, and should only be used if no other drugs are available.

Travellers are advised to prevent mosquito bites at all times. The main messages are:

• wear light-coloured clothing.
• wear long trousers and long-sleeved shirts.
• use mosquito repellents containing the compound DEET on exposed areas (prolonged overuse of DEET may be harmful, especially to children, but its use is considered preferable to being bitten by disease-transmitting mosquitoes.
• avoid perfumes or aftershave.
• use a mosquito net impregnated with mosquito repellent (permethrin) – it may be worth taking your own.
• impregnating clothes with permethrin effectively deters mosquitoes and other insects.

Dengue Fever This viral disease is transmitted by mosquitoes and is fast becoming one of the top public health problems in the tropical world. Unlike the malaria mosquito, the *Aedes aegypti* mosquito, which transmits the dengue virus, is most active during the day, and is found mainly in urban areas, in and around human dwellings.

Signs and symptoms of dengue fever include a sudden onset of high fever, headache, joint and muscle pains (hence its old name, 'breakbone fever') and nausea and vomiting. A rash of small red spots sometimes appears three to four days after the onset of fever. In the early phase of illness, dengue may be mistaken for other infectious diseases, including malaria and influenza. Minor bleeding such as nose bleeds may occur in the course of the illness, but this does not necessarily mean that you have progressed to the potentially fatal dengue haemorrhagic fever (DHF). This is a severe illness, characterised by heavy bleeding, which is thought to be a result of second infection due to a different strain (there are four major strains) and usually affects residents of the country rather than travellers. Recovery even from simple dengue fever may be prolonged, with tiredness lasting for several weeks.

You should seek medical attention as soon as possible if you think you may be infected. A blood test can exclude malaria and indicate the possibility of dengue fever. There is no specific treatment for dengue. Aspirin should be avoided, as it increases the risk of haemorrhaging. There is no vaccine against dengue fever. The best prevention is to avoid mosquito bites at all times by covering up, using insect repellents containing the compound DEET and mosquito nets – see the Malaria section earlier for more advice on avoiding mosquito bites.

Cuts, Bites & Stings

See Less Common Diseases for details of rabies, which is passed through animal bites.

Cuts & Scratches Wash well and treat any cut with an antiseptic such as povidone-iodine. Where possible avoid bandages and Band-Aids, which can keep wounds wet. Coral cuts are notoriously slow to heal and if they are not adequately cleaned, small pieces of coral can become embedded in the wound.

Bedbugs & Lice Bedbugs live in various places, but particularly in dirty mattresses and bedding, evidenced by spots of blood on bedclothes or on the wall. Bedbugs leave itchy bites in neat rows. Calamine lotion or Stingose spray may help.

All lice cause itching and discomfort. They make themselves at home in your hair (head lice), your clothing (body lice) or in your pubic hair (crabs). You catch lice through direct contact with infected people or by sharing combs, clothing and the like. Powder or shampoo treatment will kill the lice and infected clothing should then be washed in very hot, soapy water and left in the sun to dry.

Bites & Stings Bee and wasp stings are usually painful rather than dangerous. However, in people who are allergic to them severe breathing difficulties may occur and require urgent medical care. Calamine lotion or Stingose spray will give relief and ice packs will reduce the pain and swelling. There are some spiders with dangerous bites but antivenins are usually available. Scorpions often shelter in shoes or clothing and their stings are notoriously painful.

There are various fish and other sea creatures which can sting or bite dangerously or which are dangerous to eat – seek local advice.

Jellyfish Avoid contact with these sea creatures, which have stinging tentacles – seek local advice. Stings from most jellyfish are simply painful, rather than fatal. Dousing in vinegar will de-activate any stingers which have not 'fired'. Calamine lotion, antihistamines and analgesics may reduce the reaction and relieve the pain.

Leeches & Ticks Leeches may be present in damp rainforest conditions; they attach themselves to your skin to suck your blood. Trekkers often get them on their legs or in their boots. Salt or a lighted cigarette end will make them fall off. Do not pull them off, as the bite is then more likely to become infected. Clean and apply pressure if the point of attachment is bleeding. An insect repellent may keep them away.

You should always check all over your body if you have been walking through a potentially tick-infested area as ticks can cause skin infections and other more serious diseases. If a tick is found attached, press down around the tick's head with tweezers, grab the head and gently pull upwards. Avoid pulling the rear of the body as this may squeeze the tick's gut contents through the attached mouth parts into the skin, increasing the risk of infection and disease. Smearing chemicals on the tick will not make it let go and is not recommended.

Snakes To minimise your chances of being bitten always wear boots, socks and long trousers when walking through undergrowth where snakes may be present. Don't put your hands into holes and crevices, and be careful when collecting firewood.

Snake bites do not cause instantaneous death and antivenins are usually available. Immediately wrap the bitten limb tightly, as you would for a sprained ankle, and then attach a splint to immobilise it. Keep the victim still and seek medical help, if possible with the dead snake for identification. Don't attempt to catch the snake if there is a possibility of being bitten again. Tourniquets and sucking out the poison are now comprehensively discredited.

Less Common Diseases

The following diseases pose a small risk to travellers, and so are only mentioned in passing. Seek medical advice if you think you may have any of these diseases.

Cholera This is the worst of the watery diarrhoeas and medical help should be sought. Outbreaks of cholera are generally widely reported, so you can avoid these areas. *Fluid replacement is the most vital treatment* – the risk of dehydration is severe as you may lose up to 20L a day. If there is a delay in getting to hospital, then begin taking tetracycline. The adult dose is 250mg four times daily. It is not recommended for children under nine years nor for pregnant women. Tetracycline may help shorten the illness, but adequate fluids are required to save lives.

Filariasis This is a mosquito-transmitted parasitic infection found in many parts of Africa, including Tanzania. Possible symptoms include fever, pain and swelling of the lymph glands; inflammation of lymph drainage areas; swelling of a limb or the scrotum; skin rashes; and blindness. Treatment is available to eliminate the parasites from the body, but some of the damage already caused may not be reversible. Medical advice should be obtained promptly if the infection is suspected.

Leishmaniasis This is a group of parasitic diseases transmitted by sandflies, which are found in many parts of Africa including Tanzania. Cutaneous leishmaniasis affects the skin tissue causing ulceration and disfigurement, and visceral leishmaniasis affects the internal organs. Seek medical advice, as laboratory testing is required for diagnosis and correct treatment. Avoiding sandfly bites is the best precaution. Bites are usually painless, itchy and yet another reason to cover up and apply repellent.

Rabies This fatal viral infection is found in many countries. Many animals can be infected (such as dogs, cats, bats and monkeys) and it is their saliva which is infectious. Any bite, scratch or even lick from an animal should be cleaned immediately and thoroughly. Scrub with soap and running water, and then apply alcohol or iodine solution. Medical help should be sought promptly to receive a course of injections to prevent the onset of symptoms and death.

Sleeping Sickness In parts of tropical Africa, including Tanzania, tsetse flies can carry trypanosomiasis, or sleeping sickness. The tsetse fly is about twice the size of a housefly and recognisable by the scissor-like way it folds its wings when at rest. Only a small proportion of tsetse flies carry the disease, but it is a serious disease which can be fatal without treatment. No protection is available except avoiding the tsetse fly bites. The flies are attracted to large moving objects such as safari buses, to perfume and aftershave and to colours such as dark blue. Swelling at the site of the bite, five or more days later, is the first sign of infection; this is followed within two to three weeks by fever.

Tetanus This disease is caused by a germ which lives in soil and in the faeces of horses and other animals. It enters the body via breaks in the skin. The first symptom may be discomfort in swallowing, or stiffening of the jaw and neck; this is followed by painful convulsions of the jaw and whole body. The disease can be fatal. It can be prevented by vaccination.

Tuberculosis (TB) TB is a bacterial infection usually transmitted from person to person by coughing but which may be transmitted through consumption of unpasteurised milk. Milk that has been boiled is safe to drink, and the souring of milk to make yoghurt or cheese also kills the bacilli. Travellers are usually not at great risk as close household contact with the infected person is usually required before the disease is passed on. Your doctor may recommend that you need to have a TB test before you travel as this can help diagnose the disease later if you become ill.

Typhus This disease is spread by ticks, mites or lice. It begins with fever, chills, headache and muscle pains followed a few days later by a body rash. There is often a large painful sore at the site of the bite and nearby lymph nodes are swollen and painful. Typhus can be treated under medical supervision. Seek local advice on areas where ticks pose a danger and always check your skin carefully for ticks after walking in a danger area such as a tropical forest. An insect repellent can help, and walkers in tick-infested areas should consider having their boots and trousers impregnated with benzyl benzoate and dibutylphthalate.

Yellow Fever This viral disease is endemic in many parts of Africa, including Tanzania and is transmitted by mosquitoes. The initial symptoms are fever, headache, abdominal pain and vomiting. Seek medical care urgently and drink lots of fluids.

Women's Health

Gynaecological Problems Antibiotic use, synthetic underwear, sweating and contraceptive pills can lead to fungal vaginal infections, especially when travelling in hot climates. Fungal infections are characterised by a rash, itch and discharge and can be treated with a vinegar or lemon-juice douche, or with natural yoghurt. Nystatin, miconazole or clotrimazole pessaries or vaginal cream are the usual treatment. Maintaining good personal hygiene and wearing loose-fitting clothes and cotton underwear may help prevent these infections.

Sexually transmitted diseases are a major cause of vaginal problems. Symptoms include a smelly discharge, painful intercourse and sometimes a burning sensation when urinating. Medical attention should be sought and male sexual partners must also be treated. Remember that in addition to these diseases HIV or hepatitis B may also be acquired during exposure. Besides abstinence, the best thing is to practise safer sex using condoms.

Pregnancy It is not advisable to travel to some places while pregnant as some vaccinations normally used to prevent serious diseases are not advisable during pregnancy (eg yellow fever). In addition, many of the diseases discussed in this section are much more serious for the mother (and may also increase the risk of a stillborn child) in pregnancy (eg malaria).

Most miscarriages occur during the first three months of pregnancy. Miscarriage is not uncommon and can occasionally lead to severe bleeding. The last three months should also be spent within reasonable distance of good medical care. A baby born as early as 24 weeks stands a chance of survival, but only in a good modern hospital. Pregnant women should avoid all unnecessary medication, although vaccinations and malarial prophylactics should still be taken where needed, in consultation with your doctor. Additional care should be taken to prevent illness and particular attention should be paid to diet and nutrition. Alcohol and nicotine, for example, should be avoided.

WOMEN TRAVELLERS

Women travelling alone are often viewed as a curiosity, particularly in rural areas; there is little comprehension of the reasons why you might not have a husband or children, or if you have them, why they are not with you. Otherwise, there are no particular travel hassles worth noting that would distinguish Tanzania from any other part of the world. In general, you'll have a much easier time if you are conservatively dressed – either long pants or skirt, and a modest top with some sort of sleeve.

As when travelling anywhere, avoid isolated or rough areas, especially at night.

GAY & LESBIAN TRAVELLERS

Tanzanian society is conservative, and public displays of affection, whether between people of the same or opposite sex, are frowned upon and show insensitivity to local feelings. Gay sexual relationships are culturally taboo, although some homosexual activity – especially among younger men – does occur. From an official point of view, male homosexuality is illegal in Tanzania, with penalties of up to 14 years imprisonment, although prosecutions rarely, if ever, occur. In general, gay travellers should anticipate no particular difficulties.

The USA-based tour company All Continents Travel (☎ 800-368 6822 or 310-645 7527, fax 645 1071, 5250 West Century Blvd, Suite 626, Los Angeles, CA 90045), which offers specialist tours for gay men and

women in numerous areas of the world, may be a useful source of further information.

DISABLED TRAVELLERS

As in much of Africa, wheelchair facilities, ramps and lifts are virtually nonexistent in Tanzania. It is common for hotels to be multilevel, with most beds on the upper floors; many places, even mid-range establishments, do not have lifts. Bathrooms equipped with grips and railings are not found anywhere, except perhaps in some of the top-end hotels.

This being said, some park lodges are built on ground level (although access paths – in an attempt to maintain a natural environment – are often rough or rocky), and there is no reason why a game-viewing safari could not be custom tailored. While there are no tour operators at present who offer safaris expressly catering to the disabled, hopefully the increasing competition for clients in the region will give impetus to expanded offerings in this area. For additional information, travellers could inquire with some of the upmarket tour operators, or with their national support organisation (preferably with the travel officer, if there is one). In the UK, a useful organisation is RADAR (☎ 020-7250 3222, 250 City Rd, London EC1V 8AS).

SENIOR TRAVELLERS

Tanzania poses no particular difficulties for senior travellers in the major tourist areas. Places like Dar es Salaam, Arusha, Unguja and Mafia island have a good selection of comfortable, upmarket accommodation (on the assumption that you don't want to rough it), western dining options, and direct airport access, and offer a variety of activities (for example, game-viewing safaris) that do not require excessive physical exertion. In other areas of the country, in addition to limited lodging and dining options, one of the major difficulties is transport. Road journeys can be extremely long and taxing even for the most fit travellers, and downright unpleasant for others. Unless you are on an organised tour, or will be met at all your destinations by friends with vehicles, luggage can be another problem for seniors travelling independently; backpacks are in many cases the only practical option. Despite these qualifications, there are many elderly and retired people who have travelled extensively in Tanzania and had a wonderful time, coping with deprivations that may have younger travellers looking for the first flight home. As in life, much comes down to attitude and expectations, rather than to the year listed on your birth certificate.

TRAVEL WITH CHILDREN

Travelling with children presents few problems in Tanzania other than those you would encounter anywhere else in the world. Africans in general are very friendly, helpful and protective towards children and their mothers.

The main concerns would likely be the scarcity of decent medical facilities outside major towns, the length and discomfort involved in many road journeys, and the difficulty of finding clean, decent bathrooms outside of mid-range and top-end hotels. It's also advisable to avoid feeding your children street food. Canned baby foods, powdered milk, disposable nappies and similar items are available in most larger towns, but not elsewhere. Pharmacies in Dar es Salaam and other major towns carry a wide range of medicines, which are sold without a doctor's prescription.

Many places in Tanzania, including the national parks and numerous mid-range and top-end hotels, offer discounts for children on entry fees and accommodation rates. In hotels without special rates, triple rooms are commonly available for not too much more than a double room.

For more information and hints on travelling with children, Lonely Planet's *Travel with Children* by Maureen Wheeler is highly recommended.

DANGERS & ANNOYANCES

In general, Tanzania is a safe, hassle-free country. The main danger for most travellers is road accidents, particularly involving

buses. See the Getting Around chapter for more on this. In terms of muggings and robberies, Tanzania is no worse than most other places, and can be a relief if you've recently been somewhere like Nairobi.

There have been sporadic occurrences of organised crime in some of the more remote areas near the Kenyan border. It's best to follow the advice of your embassy and tour operator when planning travel to this region. If you visit some of these border areas on your own, travel in a convoy if possible.

See Dangers and Annoyances in The Zanzibar Archipelago and the Dar es Salaam chapters for more information.

BUSINESS HOURS

Government offices are open from 7.30 am to 3.30 pm, Monday to Friday. Business hours are from 8 am to 5 pm, Monday to Friday and from 8.30 am to 1 pm on Saturday; many shops close for an hour between noon and 2 pm, and on Friday afternoons for mosque services.

PUBLIC HOLIDAYS & SPECIAL EVENTS

Public holidays in Tanzania:

New Year's Day	1 January
Zanzibar Revolution Day	12 January
CCM Foundation Day	5 February
Eid al Fitr (end of Ramadan)	
Eid al Kebir (also called Eid al Haji) (celebration of the sacrifice of Ismail, and an important time for pilgrimages to Mecca)	
Good Friday	
Easter Monday	
Union Day	26 April
Labour Day	1 May
Maulidi (Mohammed's Birthday)	
Saba Saba (Peasants' Day)	7 July
Nane Nane (Farmers' Day)	8 August
Independence Day	9 December
Christmas	25 December
Boxing Day	26 December

The dates of Muslim holidays are based on the Islamic lunar calendar and are not fixed.

In general, they fall about 11 days earlier each year

ACTIVITIES
Safaris
Many travellers come to Tanzania to visit its national parks and game reserves, all of which offer an exceptional diversity of wildlife in spectacular natural settings. See the Safaris section in the Getting Around chapter for more information on different types of Safaris and how to go about organising them.

Cycling
Tanzania is too large to make cycling an option for most travellers, although there are a fair number of cyclists who cover one or more sections of the country as part of a regional or trans-continental tour. In rural areas away from the mountain regions, cycling is one of the best ways of getting to know Tanzania. If you do plan on cycling, it is best to bring your own bicycle into the country; only occasionally are good second-hand bikes available from resident expatriates in Dar es Salaam or other major towns. You will also need to carry all your own spare parts. Distances are very long, usually away from the main roads and there are many stretches without even a village, so you will need to plan your food, water and lodging needs fairly carefully.

Hiking & Trekking
There is excellent hiking in the Usambara and Pare mountains in the north-east and in the area around Tukuyu in the south-west. Udzungwa Mountains and Mahale Mountains national parks also offer good hiking, as do the Uluguru mountains near Morogoro and the lower slopes of Mt Kilimanjaro near Marangu. The main trekking destinations are Mt Kilimanjaro, Mt Meru and the Crater Highlands. For more information see the individual chapters covering these areas, and the Trekking chapter.

Diving & Snorkelling
Tanzania's coast – particularly around the islands of Unguja, Pemba and Mafia – is edged with spectacular coral reefs which offer superb diving and snorkelling opportunities. Charges are reasonable in comparison with many other places in the world. For information on dive outfitters see the Diving sections in the Dar es Salaam and The Zanzibar Archipelago chapters. See also the boxed text 'Considerations for Responsible Diving' earlier in this chapter.

Comprehensive literature on Tanzanian dive sites is scarce. *Dive Sites of Kenya & Tanzania* by Anton Koornhof is a decent introduction, but omits many of the dive sites north of Dar es Salaam.

COURSES
Visitors interested in studying Swahili can contact the following:

ELCT Language & Orientation School
(☎/fax 056-3173, PO Box 740 Morogoro) c/o Lutheran Junior Seminary
Institute of Swahili & Foreign Languages
(☎ 054-30724, PO Box 882 Zanzibar, attn: Department of Swahili for Foreigners)
KIU Ltd
(☎ 051-851509 or 0812-781160, fax 051-850503, email kiu@raha.com, PO Box 2345 Dar es Salaam) c/o Salvation Army Hostel, Dar es Salaam
Maryknoll Language School
(PO Box 298, Musoma)
Nyumba ya Sanaa
(☎ 051-133960, Ohio St) next to the Sheraton Hotel in Dar es Salaam; courses offered together with KIU, above.

Swahili: A Complete Course for Beginners by DV Perrott is a good start for those who want to study Swahili on their own. This and several other introductory Swahili books, and some English-Swahili dictionaries are available at bookshops in Dar es Salaam, Arusha and in Zanzibar Town.

ACCOMMODATION
Camping
All of the national parks have established camp sites. There are two types. 'Ordinary' camp sites have basic facilities including toilets, fireplaces and often (though not always) a water source. Many of those in the

crowded northern circuit parks are in poor condition, while those in the less visited parks can be quite pleasant. 'Special' camp sites are generally smaller than ordinary sites and usually have no facilities other than pit toilets. Unlike ordinary camp sites, they must be booked in advance. For either type of camp site you will need to bring everything, including drinking water. Although you can purify water in some places, it's best not to count on this, particularly in the Serengeti where the sources in many camp sites are very dirty.

If you will be camping as part of an organised trek or safari you can cut costs by bringing your own sleeping bag; rentals through tour operators cost as much as US$5 per night or more, and the bags are often not in good condition. Many travellers succeed in selling their bags to a safari company at the end of their trip.

Outside of the national parks, camping possibilities are limited. While there are camping grounds in or near most major towns, some of the sites leave a lot to be desired. There are, however, an increasing number of good private camp sites opening up in areas near national parks or along major overland routes. Costs average US$3 to US$5 per person per night.

Guesthouses & Hostels

Almost every Tanzanian town of any size has at least one (usually very basic) guesthouse. Larger towns will have several to choose from. Rates average from Tsh2000 to Tsh3000 per night. For those who like their peace and quiet, guesthouses without bars are usually the best choice. Most guesthouses offer shared facilities only, though some have rooms with a private bathroom; these will cost an additional Tsh1000 to Tsh2000. In many towns, water can be a problem during the dry season, particularly at less expensive guesthouses and hotels. Note that in Swahili, the word *hotel* (or *hoteli*) does not mean lodging, but rather food and drink only. The more common term used if you are seeking accommodation is *guesti* or 'guesthouse'.

There are mission hostels and guesthouses all over Tanzania. While these are primarily for missionaries and aid organisation staff, they often have extra room available for independent travellers. In most cases, they are clean, safe, and very good value.

Hotels

All major towns have at least one mid-range hotel. Dar es Salaam, Arusha, Unguja, and several other centres also offer a good selection of top-end accommodation. Most mid-range places have rooms with bathroom, and often also with air-con. Facilities are invariably somewhat faded but adequate. Prices range from US$20 to US$60 per person per night.

Top-end hotels offer all the amenities you would expect for the price you will be paying – from US$60 to US$300 or more per person per night.

FOOD

In Dar es Salaam and other major towns, there is a good selection of places to eat, ranging from local food stalls to western-style restaurants. The choice is much more limited in smaller towns and villages. In remote areas, you often have no choice at all. The main meal is at midday; many places are closed in the evening.

Local Food

One of the most common local dishes is *ugali*, a staple made from maize or cassava flour and eaten with a sauce usually containing meat, fish, beans and/or greens. Good ugali is neither too dry nor too sticky; ask locals where to find the best. Rice and cooked plantains are also served frequently as staples; chips are ubiquitous in larger towns. Also very popular and available almost everywhere is *nyama choma* (grilled meat). On the coast and in the Zanzibar archipelago you'll find a wide range of traditional Swahili dishes based on seafood cooked in coconut.

Early in the mornings in Zanzibar Town and in many parts of the mainland, vendors sell *uji*, a thin, sweet porridge made from bean flour, as well as bread and hard-boiled eggs. Many regions of Tanzania, notably in the north-east around Tanga and near Lake Victoria, have fresh *mtindi* (also called *mtindi wa maziwa*), a cultured milk product similar to yoghurt.

There is not much that is specifically billed as 'vegetarian', but there are many options and you can almost always find a basic beans and rice dish. In the capital and larger towns, the Indian restaurants are good places to try for vegetarian meals. Some tour operators are willing to cater to special dietary requests such as vegetarian, kosher or halaal. Most food on safaris tends to be halaal anyway, as many commercial sellers follow the halaal ritual.

To learn more about local ingredients, skim the book, *Tanzania Traditional Cookery* by Amir A Mohammed. It contains a selection of recipes, with emphasis on Zanzibari dishes, and is available in Dar es Salaam and Zanzibar Town.

Some useful Swahili words at mealtimes include *maharage* (beans), *kuku* (chicken) and *mbuzi* (goat). The Language chapter at the end of this book includes a list of Swahili words and their English translation, which may come in handy for trying to decipher menus when ordering meals.

Self-Catering
In general, a wide range of imported products is available in major towns, though the items are often expensive. Locally produced items, including dairy products, are very inexpensive.

In Dar es Salaam, there is a large western-style supermarket stocking almost any product you could want. In Arusha, Mwanza, and Zanzibar Town, there are numerous smaller grocery stores that sell a decent range of imported products such as processed cheese, peanut butter, crackers, cereals, and similar items.

DRINKS
Nonalcoholic Drinks
Sodas are available everywhere, usually cold. They cost about Tsh200 on the street.

Fresh juices, including pineapple, sugar cane and orange are also widely available and inexpensive.

Alcoholic Drinks
Mbege or banana beer is a speciality of the Kilimanjaro area. In cashew growing areas, you will sometimes note a strong alcohol smell when passing through villages; it's usually from *gongo* (sometimes also called *nipa*), a distilled cashew drink which is illegal. The brewed version, *uraka*, is legal as is *konyagi*, the general term for local liquor. Local brews made from pawpaws are also common.

Safari and Kilimanjaro are the local beers. Kenyan, South African and German beers are also available. Beers cost between Tsh450 and Tsh600.

ENTERTAINMENT
Every town has a bar, except small places along the heavily Muslim coast. Dar es Salaam and Arusha have the best selection of nightclubs.

In Dar es Salaam, good-quality western films are shown at some of the cultural centres. Otherwise, at most theatres throughout the country you will find only B-grade westerns or Indian films.

In towns which see a lot of tourists there are often performances of traditional dancing or drumming. Many hotels offer live music, generally on weekends.

SPECTATOR SPORTS
Soccer is the main spectator sport; no matter where you find yourself on a Sunday afternoon, you are sure to find a match to watch.

SHOPPING
Tanzania has a good selection of local crafts, ranging from basketry and wood-carving to textiles and paintings. Craft centres and artists cooperatives in the capital and major towns often have good buys and prices are generally very reasonable. Things to look for include Makonde carvings (best purchased in Mtwara or in

Dar es Salaam), Tingatinga paintings (the best buys are in Dar es Salaam); Singida baskets (the best are found in the villages around Singida, but these are difficult to reach, so try craft shops in Dar es Salaam and Arusha); Gogo woodcarvings (sold in Dodoma), including carved gourds, called *vibuyu*; and textiles (Zanzibar Town has some great buys), including the *kanga*, the traditional cloth garment worn by many Tanzanian women.

If you want to be able to cook coconut dishes like those you eat on the Zanzibar archipelago and along the coast, you'll need a *mbuzi* (literally, a 'goat') – the small wooden stool with a metal tongue for shredding coconut. They're available at markets throughout the country.

Getting There & Away

For information about organised tours, see the Safaris section in the Getting Around chapter.

AIR
Airports & Airlines
International flights to and from Tanzania are handled by Dar es Salaam international airport, Kilimanjaro international airport (KIA, situated midway between Arusha and Moshi) and Zanzibar airport. The airport in Mwanza handles some regional flights.

Regional and international carriers servicing Tanzania include Air India, Air Tanzania, Air Zimbabwe, British Airways, EgyptAir, Ethiopian Airlines, Gulf Air, Kenya Airways, KLM and Swissair. Most of these airlines as well as Air France, Lufthansa and others also fly to Nairobi, from where there are daily connections to Dar es Salaam. In Dar es Salaam, you may see advertisements for Alliance Air, a joint venture established in 1994 between Air Tanzania, South African Airways and Uganda Airlines with the goal of improving direct connections between Tanzania and various destinations in Europe, Africa and Asia. Following a mid-1998 announcement that Air Tanzania was pulling out, flight schedules and the airline's future remain uncertain.

Buying Tickets
Tickets can be purchased through a travel agent or directly from the airlines. The cost will be the same, but the travel agencies can probably give you a better overview of scheduling options. While most of the major international carriers accept credit cards for tickets purchased abroad, many accept cash only for bookings made in Tanzania.

Full-fare economy tickets, which are usually valid for 12 months, offer the maximum amount of flexibility. Students and those under age 26 are often eligible for discounted tickets; the best places to check out are student travel bureaus.

Another option is an advance-purchase ticket, which is usually between 30 and 40% cheaper than the full economy fare, but with restrictions. These include advance purchase requirements (usually 21 days), as well as minimum and maximum stay limitations (usually two weeks and three months, respectively). Penalties are often levied if you change your dates of travel or destination.

Stand-by fares – under which some airlines will let you travel at the last minute if there are seats available just before departure – are another option. These tickets cost less than the economy fare but are usually not as cheap as advance-purchase fares.

Departure Tax
The departure tax for regional and international flights is US$20, payable in US dollars. This is often included in the ticket price for international flights.

The USA & Canada
Most flights from North America are via Europe; there are few bargain deals. Expect

to pay anywhere between US$1500 and US$2500 depending on the season. Good places to look for whatever deals there may be around include the Sunday travel sections in the major newspapers, such as the *Los Angeles Times* or *San Francisco Examiner-Chronicle* on the west coast and the *New York Times* on the east coast. The student travel bureaus are also worth trying – STA Travel or Council Travel. If you are really interested in cutting costs, your best option is to buy an inexpensive ticket to London and then purchase an onward ticket to Africa when you get there.

Travel agents handling flights to East Africa include the following. This list has been provided to help you get started. Please remember that they are suggestions only, and not necessarily recommended. Before booking, shop around and gather as much information as you can. If possible, talk with others who have used the services of the agent you plan to use.

AdventureWomen Inc
(☎ 800-804-8686 or 406-587-3883, fax 587-9449) 15033 Kelly Canyon Rd, Bozeman, MT 59715 (tours for women)
African Adventures
(☎ 800-927-4641 or 803-559-2300, fax 559-2325, email warthogs@charleston.net) 1618 Regimental Lane, Johns Island, SC 29455
Baobab Safari Company
(☎ 800-835-3692, email info@baobabsafaris .com) 210 Post Street, Suite 911, San Francisco CA USA 94108
Himalayan Travel, Inc
(☎ 800-225-2380 or 203-359-3711, fax 359-3669, email worldadv@netaxis.com) 110 Prospect Street, Stamford, CT 06901 (for Kilimanjaro treks)
Rafiki Safaris
(☎ 207-236-4244, fax 236-6253, email rafiki @midcoast.com) 45 Rawson Ave, Camden, ME 04843
The Legendary Adventure Company
(☎ 800-324-9081 or 713-744-5244, fax 895-8753, email legendary@tfcomp.com) 13201 NW Freeway, Ste 800, Houston, TX 77040
Thomson Family Adventures
(☎ 800-262-6255 or 617-864-4803, fax 497-3911, email info@familyadventures.com) 347 Broadway, Cambridge, MA 02139 (family oriented tours)

Voyagers International
(☎ 607-273-4321, fax 3873, email explore @voyagers.com) PO Box 915, Ithaca, NY 14851

Australia & New Zealand

There are no direct flights from Australia or New Zealand to Tanzania or anywhere else in East Africa. Qantas and South African Airways have flights to Harare (Zimbabwe) and Johannesburg (South Africa), from where you can connect direct to Dar es Salaam. Expect to pay between A$1700 and A$2000 for the intercontinental leg of the trip. Other options would be routings via Cairo, via Singapore and the United Arab Emirates, via Mumbai (Bombay), or a round-the-world ticket, all of which usually average between A$1700 and A$2500. A good place to start your search for a ticket is the travel section of the Saturday issue of either the *Sydney Morning Herald* or the *Age*, or alternatively by visiting a student travel bureau.

African flight specialists include:

Africa Travel Centre
(☎ 02-9267 3048) Level 11, 456 Kent St, Sydney, NSW 2000, Australia
African Wildlife Safaris
(☎ 03-9696 2889) 1st floor, 259 Coventry St, South Melbourne, VIC 3205, Australia
Africa Travel Shop
(☎ 09-520 2000) 21 Remuera Rd, Newmarket, Auckland, New Zealand

The UK & Continental Europe

The least expensive round-trip ticket between London and Dar es Salaam costs about US$900 during the high season, with prices averaging about US$1100. From continental Europe fares are similar or slightly higher. Flights between Europe and Dar es Salaam are often heavily booked between June and August, so try to reserve well in advance. There are often better deals available to Nairobi than to Dar es Salaam, so it's worth checking these out as well. Aeroflot flies between Moscow and Nairobi once weekly or twice monthly depending on the season for about $US650 round-trip.

Air Travel Glossary

Baggage Allowance This will be written on your ticket and usually includes one 20kg item to go in the hold, plus one item of hand luggage.

Bucket Shops These are unbonded travel agencies specialising in discounted airline tickets.

Bumped Just because you have a confirmed seat doesn't mean you're going to get on the plane (see Overbooking).

Cancellation Penalties If you have to cancel or change a discounted ticket, there are often heavy penalties involved; insurance can sometimes be taken out against these penalties. Some airlines impose penalties on regular tickets as well, particularly against 'no-show' passengers.

Check-In Airlines ask you to check-in a certain time ahead of the flight departure (usually one to two hours on international flights). If you fail to check-in on time and the flight is over-booked, the airline can cancel your booking and give your seat to somebody else.

Confirmation Having a ticket written out with the flight and date you want doesn't mean you have a seat until the agent has checked with the airline that your status is 'OK' or confirmed. Meanwhile you could just be 'on request'.

Courier Fares Businesses often need to send urgent documents or freight securely and quickly. Courier companies hire people to accompany the package through customs and, in return, offer a discount ticket which is sometimes a phenomenal bargain. In effect, what the companies do is ship their freight as your luggage on regular commercial flights. This is a legitimate operation, but there are two shortcomings – the short turnaround time of the ticket (usually not longer than a month) and the limitation on your luggage allowance. You may have to surrender all your allowance and take only carry-on luggage.

Full Fares Airlines traditionally offer 1st class (coded F), business class (coded J) and economy class (coded Y) tickets. These days there are so many promotional and discounted fares available that few passengers pay full economy fare.

ITX An ITX, or 'independent inclusive tour excursion', is often available on tickets to popular holiday destinations. Officially it's a package deal combined with hotel accommodation, but many agents will sell you one of these for the flight only and give you phoney hotel vouchers in the unlikely event that you're challenged at the airport.

Lost Tickets If you lose your airline ticket an airline will usually treat it like a travellers cheque and, after inquiries, issue you with another one. Legally, however, an airline is entitled to treat it like cash and if you lose it then it's gone forever. Take good care of your tickets.

MCO An MCO, or 'miscellaneous charge order', is a voucher that looks like an airline ticket but carries no destination or date. It can be exchanged through any International Association of Travel Agents (IATA) airline for a ticket on a specific flight. It's a useful alternative to an onward ticket in those countries that demand one, and is more flexible than an ordinary ticket if you're unsure of your route.

No-Shows No-shows are passengers who fail to show up for their flight. Full-fare passengers who fail to turn up are sometimes entitled to travel on a later flight. The rest are penalised (see Cancellation Penalties).

Air Travel Glossary

On Request This is an unconfirmed booking for a flight.

Onward Tickets An entry requirement for many countries is that you have a ticket out of the country. If you're unsure of your next move, the easiest solution is to buy the cheapest onward ticket to a neighbouring country or a ticket from a reliable airline which can later be refunded if you do not use it.

Open Jaw Tickets These are return tickets where you fly out to one place but return from another. If available, these can save you backtracking to your arrival point.

Overbooking Airlines hate to fly empty seats and since every flight has some passengers who fail to show up, airlines often book more passengers than they have seats. Usually excess passengers make up for the no-shows, but occasionally somebody gets 'bumped' onto the next available flight. Overbooking is par for the course on many airlines within Tanzania and East Africa. Passengers who check in late are those most likely to get bumped.

Point-to-Point Tickets These are discount tickets that can be bought on some routes in return for passengers waiving their rights to a stopover.

Promotional Fares These are officially discounted fares, available from travel agencies or direct from the airline.

Reconfirmation If you don't reconfirm your flight at least 72 hours prior to departure, the airline may delete your name from the passenger list. Almost all flights within and to/from Tanzania and East Africa require confirmation.

Restrictions Discounted tickets often have various restrictions on them – such as needing to be paid for in advance and incurring a penalty to be altered. Others are restrictions on the minimum and maximum period you can be away, such as a minimum of 14 days or a maximum of one year.

Round-the-World Tickets RTW tickets give you a limited period (usually a year) in which to circumnavigate the globe. You can go anywhere the carrying airlines go, as long as you don't backtrack. The number of stopovers or total number of separate flights is decided before you set off and usually cost a bit more than a basic return flight.

Stand-By This is a discounted ticket where you only fly if there is a seat free at the last moment.

Transferred Tickets Airline tickets cannot be transferred from one person to another. Travellers sometimes try to sell the return half of their ticket, but officials can ask you to prove that you are the person named on the ticket. This is less likely to happen on domestic flights, but on an international flight tickets are compared with passports.

Travel Agencies Travel agencies vary widely and you should choose one that suits your needs. Some simply handle tours, while full-service agencies handle everything from tours and tickets to car rental and hotel bookings. If all you want is a ticket at the lowest possible price, then go to an agency specialising in discounted fares.

Travel Periods Ticket prices vary with the time of year. There is a low (off-peak) season and a high (peak) season, and often a low-shoulder season and a high-shoulder season as well. Usually the fare depends on your outward flight – if you depart in the high season and return in the low season, you pay the high-season fare.

UK-based travel agencies specialising in East Africa include:

Africa Travel Centre
  (☎ 020-7387 1211) 21 Leigh St, London WC1H 9QX
African Travel Specialists
  (☎ 020-7630 5434) Glen House, Stag Place, Victoria, London SW1E 5AG
Council Travel
  (☎ 020-7437 7767) 28A Poland St, London W1V 3DB
Footloose Adventure Travel
  (☎ 01943-604030) 105 Leeds Rd, Ilkley, West Yorkshire LS29 8EG
STA Travel
  (☎ 020-7581 4132) 86 Old Brompton Rd, London SW7 3LQ; offices also in Manchester, Bristol and elsewhere
Trailfinders
  (☎ 020-7938 3939) 42-50 Earls Court Rd, London W8 6FT; and (☎ 020-7938 3366) 194 Kensington High St, London W8 7RG; there are also offices in Manchester, Bristol and other towns
USIT Travel
  (☎ 01-679 8833) 19 Aston Quay, Dublin, Ireland

Africa

In West Africa, the best connections are from Abidjan via Addis Ababa on Ethiopian Airways or via Addis and Nairobi on Ethiopian Airways and Kenya Airways. A round-trip ticket will cost about US$1100 to US$1500.

From southern Africa, there are connections two or three times weekly between Dar es Salaam and Johannesburg on South African Airways and Air Tanzania for about US$500. Air Tanzania flies once or twice weekly between Dar es Salaam and Lilongwe (US$195) and Blantyre (US$240), and twice weekly between Dar es Salaam and Lusaka (US$290). Air Zimbabwe and Air Tanzania fly four times weekly between Dar es Salaam and Harare for about US$330. There is also a small private plane which flies weekly between Pemba in northern Mozambique and Mtwara in south-eastern Tanzania (US$150). See the Mtwara section in the South-Eastern Tanzania chapter for more details.

From East Africa, there are daily flights between Nairobi and Dar es Salaam on Kenya Airways and Air Tanzania (US$150), twice weekly between Nairobi and Mwanza on RenAir/SkyLink, twice weekly on Air Tanzania between Mombasa and Dar es Salaam (US$75), and five times weekly between Mombasa/Nairobi and Unguja on Air Kenya and sometimes on Air Tanzania (US$59 for Mombasa and US$136 for Nairobi). There are also sporadic flights on Air Tanzania and Precision Air between Nairobi and Arusha. Ethiopian Airlines flies twice weekly between Dar es Salaam and Addis via Entebbe and Kilimanjaro international airport or via Entebbe and Kigali for US$290/531, one way/round trip. There are flights about three times weekly on Air Tanzania and Alliance Air between Dar es Salaam and Entebbe (US$225), and weekly on Air Tanzania between Dar es Salaam and Kigali (US$220). Many of these regional flights also include stops at Kilimanjaro international airport and occasionally at Mwanza in their routings. There are usually many cancellations or changes to Air Tanzania's regional flight schedule depending on demand and season, so get up-to-date information before setting your plans. All international flights on Air Tanzania must be paid for in US dollars (or the Tanzanian shilling equivalent, converted at the going bank rate). Much cheaper fares are often available for round-trip journeys.

Asia

Connections from Asia are via Singapore and the United Arab Emirates, or via Mumbai (Bombay), from where there are flights twice weekly to Dar es Salaam and more frequently to Nairobi. Fares between Dar es Salaam and Mumbai average about US$500.

LAND
Border Crossings

Burundi The border between Tanzania and Burundi has been officially closed since 1995. However, crossing is generally allowed at the Kobero bridge border post between Ngara (Tanzania) and Muyinga (Burundi). The region of Tanzania near the Burundian border is not considered safe for independent travellers at present. If you plan on coming here, get an update on the situation first from your embassy or from other knowledgeable sources.

Kenya The main route between Tanzania and Kenya is the tarmac road connecting Arusha and Nairobi via the border post at Namanga. There are also border crossings at Horohoro, north of Tanga, at Taveta, east of Moshi, at Illassit, north-east of Moshi, at Bologonya in the northern Serengeti and at Isebania, north of Musoma.

Malawi The only crossing is at the Songwe river bridge, south-east of Mbeya.

Mozambique The main crossing is at Kilambo, south of Mtwara. There is another border post further west between Masuguru (Tanzania) and Negomane (Mozambique), but this puts you in the middle of nowhere on the Mozambique side.

Rwanda The main crossing is at Rusumu falls, south-west of Bukoba.

Uganda The most commonly used post is at Mutukula, north-west of Bukoba. There is also a crossing at Nkurungu, to the west of Mutukula, but the road is bad and little transport passes this way.

Zambia The main crossing is at Tunduma, south-west of Mbeya. There is also a crossing between Isopa (Tanzania) and Mbala (Zambia).

Burundi

Private vehicles can generally cross without problem at Kobero bridge (see Burundi Border Crossings earlier). While nongovernmental organisation, and other official, vehicles do this frequently, independent travellers should first get a thorough security briefing before setting out for this region. Due to security considerations, public trans-

port is not a feasible option at the moment. The road between Ngara in Tanzania and Bujumbura is tarmac the entire way.

Kenya

Masai Mara There is no public transport along the route linking the northern Serengeti with Kenya's Masai Mara Game Reserve. Private vehicles are permitted to cross assuming you have the appropriate vehicle documentation. See under Driving Licence & Permits in the Visa & Documents section in the Facts for the Visitor chapter for details. Remember that you will have to pay park fees on both sides, and will need to arrange your visas in advance.

Mombasa Tawfiq/Takrim runs daily buses (several times weekly during the low season) between Dar es Salaam and Mombasa (Tsh9000, 10 to 11 hours). Departures from Dar es Salaam are usually at 8.30 am (arriving between 6 and 7 pm) and 2.30 pm (arriving early the next morning). There are also daily buses between Tanga and Mombasa (Tsh3500, six hours plus time for border formalities). The road is good tarmac between Dar es Salaam and Tanga, deteriorated between Tanga and the border at Horohoro, and in good condition from there to Mombasa.

A 'tourist shuttle' links Mombasa and Diani with Moshi and Arusha. Departures are Monday, Wednesday and Friday from Diani at 9 am, from Mombasa at 10.30 am, from Voi at 12.30 pm and from Moshi at 4 pm, arriving in Arusha about 6 pm. Going in the other direction, departures are Tuesday, Thursday and Saturday at 8 am from Arusha, at 10 am from Moshi, at 1.30 pm from Voi, and at 3.30 pm from Mombasa, arriving Diani at 5 pm. Tickets cost US$40/60/70 between Arusha and Voi/Mombasa/Diani and US$20/40/50 between Moshi and Voi/Mombasa/Diani. In Moshi, book at Mauly Tours & Travel or at the Moshi Hotel. The pick-up/drop-off point is at the post office. In Arusha, booking and pick-up/drop-off are at the Hotel Equator. You can also book tickets at Adventure Tours on

Goliondoi Rd. In Mombasa, the contact point is the BP petrol station opposite the railway. In Voi, the contact point is also the BP petrol station.

Nairobi Direct buses link Dar es Salaam with Nairobi most days. The journey takes about 12 hours or a bit more and costs about Tsh15,000. Departures from Dar es Salaam are about 7 am. Try to avoid changing money at the border as the rates are poor.

Buses link Arusha and Nairobi daily (Tsh6000); delays at the border often make the journey very long. There are also shared taxis from Arusha bus station to the border (about Tsh2500). You'll have to walk a few hundred metres across the border and then pick up another vehicle on the other side (about US$6 to Nairobi).

The best option, and that used by most travellers, is one of the daily shuttles which run between Nairobi and Arusha with connections to Moshi. These are comfortable 20-seater buses which cover the route in about five hours, including about half an hour to cross the border. They are also generally the safest road transport option. The one-way fare on all the buses between Arusha and Nairobi is US$25 (Tsh8000 for residents) and US$35 (Tsh13,000) between Moshi and Nairobi. With a little prodding, all the companies seem prepared to sell tickets to nonresidents for resident prices as long as you purchase the ticket directly with them rather than through a tour operator. If you do not have a visa, you will need to bring additional money (US dollars) to purchase one at the border. Shuttle bus companies include:

Davanu
   Departures daily at 8 am and 2 pm in each direction between Nairobi and Arusha with connections to Moshi. The Arusha booking office is at the Novotel. The Davanu office in Moshi (☎ 055-53416 or 057-53749) is on the ground floor of Kahawa House on the clock tower roundabout. Departures from Moshi are daily at 11.30 am. Davanu's headquarters in Nairobi (☎ 254-2-222002, fax 216475) are on the 4th floor of Windsor House, University Way, PO Box 9081.

Riverside
   Departures daily at 8 am and 2 pm in each direction and at 10.30 pm from Moshi. In Arusha, book tickets at Riverside's office (☎ 057-2639, 3916) near the Chinese restaurant on Sokoine Rd. Pick-up/drop-off points are at the Riverside office and at the Novotel. In Moshi, the booking office and pick-up/drop-off point is at the Moshi Hotel. In Nairobi (☎ 254-2-33 55 61) book at 4th floor, Room 1, Pan African House, Kenyatta Ave. The pick-up/drop-off point is at the New Stanley Hotel. Many travellers have complained that Riverside promises to drop them at their hotels in Nairobi, but then on arrival just takes everyone to the New Stanley.

There are often touts at Jomo Kenyatta airport in Nairobi advertising 'direct' shuttle bus service from the airport to Arusha for about US$30. They generally just bring you into Nairobi to one of the regular shuttles where you will join other passengers who are paying the standard shuttle fare.

Voi There are daily minibuses between Moshi and Holili on the border. From there you can walk a few kilometres to Taveta in Kenya, from where there are daily *matatus* (Kenyan minivans) to Voi.

There is also a 'tourist shuttle' several times a week linking Voi with Moshi and Arusha; see the earlier Mombasa section.

Train There is no longer any passenger train service between Tanzania and Kenya.

Malawi
Direct buses run two to three times weekly between Mbeya and Mzuzu (Tsh10,000) and Lilongwe (Tsh17,000). See the Mbeya Getting There & Away section in The Southern Highlands chapter for departure details. There are also occasional direct minibuses between Mbeya and the border, but you'll need to verify that they really go all the way to the border, as many that say they do only go to Ibanda junction, 7km before the border. Going in the other direction, you can sometimes find minibuses direct from the border all the way to Dar es Salaam (Tsh10,000), although it's far more

comfortable to just go to Mbeya and then get an express bus from there.

If you want to do the trip in stages, take one of the minibuses (there are several daily) which run between Mbeya and Kyela and get out about 5km before Kyela at the Ibanda junction. From here it's another 7km to the border. As there is no regular public transport on this stretch you will either have to hitch (usually no problem as there is frequent through traffic), walk, or get a ride on a bicycle (also not a problem, as there are boys there waiting for you; they'll charge about Tsh500). Once at the border, you'll need to walk a few hundred metres across the bridge. On the Malawian side, several minibuses a day run between the border and Karonga (about US$1). There are also many trucks along the route between Mbeya and Karonga so it is usually easy to find a direct lift between the two towns.

Between Dar es Salaam and Lilongwe there is direct weekly service on the Twiga bus line (on Sunday) and the Matema Beach line (twice weekly, on Tuesday and Friday), departing Dar es Salaam's Mnazi Mmoja station at 5 am and arriving in Lilongwe about 27 hours later (Tsh25,000 on Twiga, Tsh20,000 on Matema Beach). Twiga is the more reliable of the two companies. The fare between Dar es Salaam and Mzuzu is about Tsh16,000.

The border closes at 6 pm; remember that there is a one hour time difference between Tanzania and Malawi (Malawi is GMT +2). The border crossing is hassle free. If you are coming from Malawi into Tanzania, have your visa arranged in advance. There is no Tanzanian embassy in Malawi, and visas are not issued at the border. The road from Mbeya to Karonga is good tarmac. From Karonga south towards Chiweta it is badly deteriorated.

Mozambique

There is usually at least one pick-up a day between Mtwara and the Tanzanian border post at Kilambo. From Kilambo, you will have to walk about 5km to the Ruvuma river, which is bridged only by dugout canoe. Crossing can take over half an hour if the river is high, and just a few minutes during the dry season. Once on the Mozambique side of the river, you will have to walk another 45 minutes or so on a sandy track to the Mozambique customs post, from where you can get transport to Palma and on to Moçimboa da Praia and further south. Going in the other direction, there is usually at least one pick-up every morning from Moçimboa da Praia up to Palma (about four hours) and the border post. There is basic accommodation in Palma and in Moçimboa da Praia.

The other border crossing at Masuguru is reached via Masasi and Mangomba; there is only very sporadic transport on the Tanzanian side. On the Mozambican side, you will find yourself in the middle of nowhere. The nearest major town is Mueda, 150km away.

Rwanda

The main junction on the Tanzanian side is Ngara, from where there is daily transport to the border at Rusumu falls. For details of air and road connections to Ngara, see the Mwanza and Bukoba sections in the Lake Victoria chapter. At the border, you will need to change to Rwandan cars to Kibungo and on to Kigali. Samma bus line has twice weekly direct service between Mwanza and Kigali (Tsh15,000).

South Africa

Twiga bus line runs occasional direct buses between Dar es Salaam and Johannesburg, depending on demand (US$150). However, it's about US$50 cheaper to take a bus from Dar es Salaam to Lilongwe, then get transport from Lilongwe to Johannesburg. If Twiga isn't running any buses, try checking with the Monorama line which also has occasional direct service between Dar es Salaam and Johannesburg.

Uganda

Tawfiq/Takrim runs a direct bus twice weekly between Dar es Salaam and Kampala via Nairobi (Tsh36,000, 24 hours). Departures from Dar es Salaam are at 6.30 am, usually on Thursday and Saturday.

Tawfiq also runs buses three times weekly between Bukoba and Kampala, departing Bukoba at 7 am Tuesday, Thursday and Saturday and arriving in Kampala about 3 pm the next day (Tsh10,000). There are also minibuses most days between Bukoba and Mutukula on the Ugandan border (three to four hours), from where you just need to walk a short distance over the border to catch Ugandan transport to Kyotera and Masaka. From Masaka there is frequent transport to Kampala; plan on spending the night in Masaka.

The border crossing is not usually problematic. There is not much traffic along this route, although it is used by many overland companies.

Zambia

Bus Twiga bus line runs twice weekly (usually Monday and Wednesday) between Dar es Salaam and Lusaka (Tsh25,000 or US$40, 24 hours). Departures from Dar es Salaam's Mnazi Mmoja station are about 5 am. The border closes at 6 pm, so if your bus hasn't left Dar es Salaam by about 5 am, you will likely wind up sleeping in Tunduma.

Buses also run three or four times weekly between Mbeya and Lusaka (Tsh17,500). Otherwise, there are minibuses daily between Mbeya and Tunduma on the border (Tsh1500, two hours) where you can change to Zambian transport. From the border to Lusaka costs between ZK40,000 and ZK45,000.

Train The Tanzania-Zambia (TAZARA) rail line links Dar es Salaam with New Kapiri Mposhi in Zambia via Mbeya and Tunduma. There are express and ordinary trains, but only express trains cross the border into Zambia. Express trains depart Dar es Salaam on Tuesday and Friday at 5.34 pm, and Mbeya at 1.30 pm on Wednesday and Saturday, arriving in New Kapiri Mposhi at 8.40 am on Thursday and Sunday (Tsh42,400/27,700/16,600; 1st/2nd/3rd class). Departures from New Kapiri Mposhi are on Thursday and Sunday at 2.27 pm, arriving in Mbeya at 11.51 am on Friday and Monday,

and in Dar es Salaam at 8.30 am on Saturday and Tuesday. You will need a Tanzanian visa before boarding the train in Zambia.

There are also ordinary trains to New Kapiri Mposhi from Nakonde on the Zambian border which are less expensive, but slower. Plans have been announced to build an additional line linking Tanzania with the Zambian port of Mpulungu on Lake Tanganyika, although nothing concrete had happened at the time of research.

SEA & LAKE
Departure Tax
For all boat and ferry services from Tanzanian ports there is a US$5 port tax (Tsh500 for residents).

Burundi
At the time of research, there was no ferry service between Tanzania and Burundi. Previously, the MV *Liemba* connected Kigoma with Bujumbura weekly; US$30/25/20 1st/2nd/3rd class.

Congo (Zaïre)
There is no longer any regular passenger service between Congo (Zaïre) and Tanzania on Lake Tanganyika. The *Mwongozo* is running between the two ports, but is only for refugee transport. Previously, the MV *Liemba* connected Kigoma with Kalemie weekly (US$25/20/15 for 1st/2nd/3rd class).

Kenya
Mega-Speed's MS *Sepideh* connects Dar es Salaam, Unguja and Tanga weekly with Mombasa. Departures are on Saturday at 8 am from Dar es Salaam, at 10.15 am from Unguja, at 1 pm from Pemba and at 2.45 pm from Tanga, arriving in Mombasa about 5.30 pm. Going in the other direction, departures are on Sunday at 8 am from Mombasa, at 10.45 am from Tanga, at 1 pm from Pemba and at 4 pm from Unguja, reaching Dar es Salaam at 5.45 pm. Fares are US$75/60/40/30 between Mombasa and Dar es Salaam/Unguja/Pemba/Tanga. See the Getting There & Away section in the Dar es Salaam chapter for Mega-Speed's booking contacts.

At the time of research there was no ferry service on Lake Victoria between Mwanza and Kisumu (Kenya).

Dhows sail sporadically between Mombasa and Unguja or Pemba. Journeys can be risky, very uncomfortable, and often wind up taking far longer than planned. You will need to bring all your own food and drink if you travel this way. Ask at the port in Zanzibar Town, or in Mkoani or Wete on Pemba for information about sailings.

Malawi

Nkhata Bay in Malawi is connected with Mbamba Bay in Tanzania via the Tanzanian ferry *Iringa* and the Malawian boat *Ilala*. The Tanzanian MV *Songea* normally does the route instead of the *Iringa*, but it was out of service at the time of research.

The *Iringa* departs Nkhata Bay weekly on Friday late afternoon or evening, arriving at Mbamba Bay about four or five hours later – sometime in the middle of the night. From Mbamba Bay, it continues up to Itungi port. Going in the other direction, the *Iringa* departs Itungi on Thursday morning, arriving in Mbamba Bay around noon on Friday and in Nkhata Bay by late Friday afternoon. Tickets between Nkhata Bay and Mbamba Bay cost Tsh1340 (deck seating). There is a Malawi immigration office at Nkhata Bay.

The *Ilala*, which runs up and down the Malawian side of Lake Nyasa, connects Nkhata Bay with Mbamba Bay once or twice weekly, usually on Tuesday and/or Sunday though the schedule is very erratic. Tickets cost US$16/10/2 for cabin/1st class deck/3rd class deck.

Mozambique

There is a small motorboat which sails several times a month between Mtwara and Moçimboa da Praia. Inquire at the port for details. Otherwise, the only option is local boats, which sporadically join the two towns. These trips can be very long and are often very risky. Depending on weather conditions, the trip can take anywhere between 12 and 30 hours.

Uganda

There is no longer any ferry service on Lake Victoria connecting Tanzanian and Ugandan ports. Before the sinking of the MV *Bukoba*, Port Bell (Kampala) was connected with Mwanza in Tanzania twice weekly for US$35/25/20, 1st/2nd/3rd class.

Zambia

The MV *Liemba* connects Kigoma with Mpulungu in Zambia weekly. Departures from Kigoma are Wednesday at 4 pm, arriving in Mpulungu on Friday morning. From Mpulungu, departures are Friday at 4 pm, arriving in Kigoma on Sunday anywhere between 10 am and 6 pm. Fares are US$55/45/40 for 1st/2nd/3rd class. Food is available on board, but it's best to bring some supplements, as well as your own water. First class is relatively comfortable, with two reasonably clean bunks and a window. Second class cabins (four bunks) and 3rd class seating, however, are both poorly ventilated and uncomfortable. If you are going to travel 3rd class, it's much better to find yourself deck space than to sit in the 3rd class seating section. Be sure to keep watch over your luggage, especially with deck seating.

Getting Around

AIR
Domestic Air Services
There are two noncharter airlines operating domestic flights within Tanzania. Air Tanzania is the national carrier. Service varies from prompt and pleasant to hopelessly delayed and chaotic. Cancellations and delays are frequent, particularly during low season when there are often not enough passengers to fill up the planes. The airline is scheduled to be privatised soon, which hopefully will improve its performance.

The major private carrier is Precision Air. Their record for punctuality and reliability is also spotty.

Nonresidents can pay for Air Tanzania flights in US dollars, Tanzanian shillings or with major credit cards (charged in US dollars at the current bank rate), except in Moshi where the Air Tanzania office requires foreigners to pay in hard currency. Precision Air accepts $US cash only. Both Air Tanzania and Precision Air have offices in Dar es Salaam and other major towns. Getting refunds from either airline for cancelled flights is possible, though time consuming. All tickets must be reconfirmed.

Given the unreliability and gaps in regularly scheduled air services, charter airlines are commonly used for domestic and regional travel; prices can be reasonable if you have a group large enough to fill the plane.

Scheduled Services The state-owned Air Tanzania operates flights between Dar es Salaam and Kilimanjaro international airport (Tsh51,000, daily), Mwanza (Tsh80,500, daily), Mtwara (Tsh49,500, three times weekly) and Unguja (Tsh22,500, five times weekly), and between Kilimanjaro international airport (midway between Arusha and Moshi) and Unguja (Tsh49,000, three times weekly) and Mwanza (Tsh55,000, twice weekly).

The privately operated Precision Air concentrates on routes not serviced by Air Tanzania. There are flights several times weekly between Dar es Salaam and Arusha (US$146) and between Arusha and Mwanza (US$145), daily flights between Arusha and Unguja (US$175) and between Mwanza and Bukoba (US$65), twice weekly flights between Mwanza and Ngara (US$65) and weekly flights between Arusha and Shinyanga (US$120). Precision Air's resident rates are generally considerably lower than their nonresident tariffs. The company is planning on expanding service to Mbeya, Kigoma, Musoma, Tabora and possibly also to Mafia Island sometime in the near future, so it is worth inquiring at their offices in Dar es Salaam or other major towns to see if these flights have started running.

Air Charters Air charter operators fly to all areas of Tanzania. Most towns have an airstrip capable of handling small planes, at least during the dry season. Charter companies based in Dar es Salaam include the following operators. See the Getting There & Away section of The Zanzibar Archipelago chapter for additional listings.

Coastal Travels
 (☎ 117959, fax 118647, email coastal@twiga .com) office on Ali Hassan Mwinyi Rd
Dar Aviation
 (☎ 844168) office at the airport at Terminal 1
Tanzanair
 (☎ 113151/2, ext 7884 or 0811-406407, fax 112946, email joanna@tanzanair@raha.com) office at the Sheraton

Domestic Departure Tax
Domestic departure tax is Tsh2000; it is generally included in the ticket price.

BUS
Road accidents are probably your biggest safety risk while travelling in Tanzania, with speeding buses being among the worst offenders. Road conditions are poor and driving often very substandard. The situa-

tion is generally even worse where road conditions are good, as buses and minibuses move along at dizzying speeds. The Dar es Salaam to Arusha highway is one of the most notorious stretches. In the wake of several fatal bus accidents in recent years, stricter speed controls have been introduced on some of the main roads and several bus companies have begun working to build a reputation for safety through speed moderation and vehicle maintenance, although there is still a lot of room for improvement. On the northern routes (Dar es Salaam to Moshi and Arusha), Fresh ya Shamba is considered to be the best line. On the southern routes (Dar es Salaam to Iringa and Mbeya), the best is Scandinavian. Ask locals which bus lines they recommend for other areas, or if any competitors have started on these routes.

For the major long-distance routes you generally have a choice of buses ranging from express to ordinary. Express buses are only marginally more expensive than ordinary buses, but are more comfortable, less crowded, and do not make as many stops en route. Other than on heavily travelled routes, it's generally not necessary to book in advance. Exceptions to this have been noted in the regional chapters. Each bus line will have its own booking office at or near the bus station. Most express buses depart on or close to schedule, so arrive in time to get your seat. Ordinary buses depart when full; no advance reservation is required although it's usually best to arrive well before departure if there will only be one bus going that day, in order to get a seat.

Buses are not permitted to drive at night in Tanzania. Although this rule is sometimes ignored, the last departure on any particular route will generally be timed so that the bus reaches its destination by evening (assuming that all goes well!). For cross-border routes, departures are usually timed so that night driving will be done once outside of Tanzania.

For shorter trips away from the main routes, the choice is generally between ordinary buses and *dalla-dallas* (minivans, equivalent to Kenyan *matatus*); both options

are uncomfortable, slow and often dangerous (see Local Transport later in this chapter). If you want to go only a short stretch along a main route, the express buses will generally drop you, but you'll usually be required to pay the full fare to the next major destination. Shared taxis are relatively rare, except in northern Tanzania. Like ordinary buses, dalla-dallas and shared taxis leave when full; fares are fixed and journeys are almost always slow and uncomfortable.

Most express buses have a compartment underneath for luggage. Otherwise, stow your backpack under your seat or in the front of the bus, near the driver. Putting it on the roof is the least secure option.

Prices are based on both distance and road conditions. They are more or less fixed, although for heavily travelled routes buses trying to fill up their seats will often undercut their competitors. If you do feel that you haven't been quoted the correct price, ask to see the ticket seller's receipt book.

TRAIN

Due to the high rate of road accidents, many travellers prefer to take trains, especially on the Dar es Salaam to Mbeya route, even though travel time is significantly longer. Tanzania has two rail lines, which operate on different gauges: the TAZARA line links Dar es Salaam with New Kapiri Mposhi in Zambia via Mbeya and Tunduma; the Tanzanian Railway Corporation's Central Line links Dar es Salaam with Kigoma and Mwanza via Morogoro, Dodoma and Tabora. A branch of the Central Line links Tabora with Mpanda; there also may be a passenger service on the spur between Dodoma and Singida. Train service to Moshi and Tanga has been indefinitely suspended. TAZARA is the more comfortable and efficient of the two lines. The Central Line is in the midst of being modernised, but much of the system remains in poor condition and cancellations and delays are frequent.

While most travellers do not have any troubles, as with travel anywhere in the region, it's best to keep an eye on your gear at all times, particularly in 3rd class. Even in 1st and 2nd class, make sure that the window is jammed shut at night to avoid the possibility of someone entering when the train stops at stations. There is usually a piece of wood provided for this purpose, as the window locks often don't work.

Classes

There are three train classes: 1st class (two or four-bed compartments); 2nd class sleeping (six-bed compartments); and 3rd class (varies from very crowded and basic to tolerable, depending on the train). Some trains also have a 2nd class sitting section, slightly cheaper than 2nd class sleeping, with comfortable seats, one seat per person. Men and women can only travel together in the sleeping sections if they book the entire compartment. Food is available on the trains (meals average about Tsh2500) and from vendors at the stations.

Reservations

Tickets for 1st and 2nd class should be reserved at least several days in advance – even a week is not too soon – although very occasionally you will be able to get a seat on the day of travel. Waits of three to five days are common. It is not unheard of for railway staff to tell you all seats are full just to get a bribe from you. Depending on how good your interpersonal skills are and how badly you want the seat, you may have to arrange a small 'gift'.

Schedules & Costs

TAZARA The TAZARA line runs both express and ordinary trains. Express trains depart Dar es Salaam on Tuesday and Friday at 5.34 pm, arriving in Mbeya the following day at 1.10 pm. Ordinary trains depart Dar es Salaam on Monday, Thursday and Saturday at 11.25 am and arrive in Mbeya at 12.24 pm the next day. In the other direction, express trains depart Mbeya on Wednesday and Saturday at 12.11 pm, arriving in Dar es Salaam at 8.30 am the next day. Ordinary trains depart Mbeya on Tuesday, Friday and Sunday at 5 pm, arriving in Dar es Salaam about 6 pm the next day.

Fares to travel between Dar es Salaam and Mbeya are:

	1st	2nd	3rd
express	Tsh19,400	Tsh12,700	Tsh7600
ordinary	Tsh16,700	Tsh11,100	Tsh6700

For fares and schedules to and from New Kapiri Mposhi, see the Zambia section in the Getting There & Away chapter.

Central Line Central Line trains from Dar es Salaam to Kigoma and Mwanza depart on Tuesday, Friday and Sunday at 5 pm. The journey to both destinations normally takes between 36 and 40 hours, although it can sometimes take 50 hours or more. Trains from Mwanza to Dar es Salaam depart on Tuesday, Thursday and Sunday at about 8 am; departures from Kigoma leave on the same days at 7 am. If you are travelling between Mwanza and Kigoma, you will need to spend at least one night in Tabora waiting for the connection. A section of the Central Line between Morogoro and Dodoma was washed out by unusually heavy rains in 1997 which resulted in curtailed services and schedule changes. Full service from Dar es Salaam has since resumed and it is possible that schedules may be altered again to reflect this, so be sure to check departure days and times in advance if you are planning to travel on any of the Central Line routes.

The Central Line has a helpful Information Centre (☎ 117833) at the TRC Building at the corner of Railway St and Sokoine Dr in Dar es Salaam. It's open from 8 am to 1 pm and 2 to 5 pm weekdays, and from 8 am to 1 pm on weekends and holidays.

CAR & MOTORCYCLE

About 20% of Tanzania's road network is paved. Many secondary roads are in poor condition at best and impassable during the rainy season. For most trips outside major towns you will need a 4WD; inquire with locals about road conditions before setting out.

While road accidents are probably your biggest safety risk travelling in Tanzania, you can possibly minimise the risks by being in your own vehicle or with a competent driver so speed can be controlled.

Road Rules

Tanzania follows the British keep-left traffic system. At roundabouts, traffic in the roundabout has the right of way. Avoid driving at night if possible. If you're not used to driving in Africa, watch out for pedestrians, children and animals on the road. Especially in rural areas remember that many people have never driven themselves and are not aware of the necessary braking distances and similar concepts; moderate your speed accordingly.

Rental

Dar es Salaam There are numerous car rental agencies in Dar es Salaam, some of which are listed below. Most charge approximately the same prices, although the local companies tend to be slightly cheaper than the international agencies. For self-drive vehicles, daily rates start at about US$40 plus US$30 to US$40 for insurance, not including fuel. Land Cruisers range from US$80 to US$130 per day plus driver fees (US$15 to US$30 per day) and fuel. Most companies do not permit self-drive outside of Dar es Salaam and none are presently offering unlimited kilometres for trips outside Dar es Salaam. Avis, and perhaps some of the other companies, offer a special business drive package within Dar es Salaam; see Car & Motorcycle in that chapter for details. All the car rental agencies accept major credit cards.

Petrol costs about Tsh480 per litre in Dar es Salaam (Tsh380 for diesel), more inland and in remote areas.

Avis
  (☎ 861214/6, 0812-780981, fax 861212, email avis@raha.com). The efficiently managed office is on Pugu Rd at FK Motors, near the airport.
Business Rent-a-Car
  (☎ 666693, email business@raha.com). Office at Oysterbay Shopping Centre, Toure Drive, Msasani Peninsula; saloon cars and vans, town rentals only.
Europcar/InterRent
  (☎ 0811-786000, 325990, fax 326770, email europcar@raha.com). The office is at 2 Nelson Mandela Rd.

Evergreen Car Rentals
  (☎ 182107, fax 183348, email evergreen@raha .com). Office on Nyerere (Pugu) Rd, near Nkrumah St.
Hertz
  (☎/fax 117753, email savtour@twiga.com). Main office at the Sheraton, with a branch at the Kilimanjaro Hotel.
Tanzania Car Rentals
  (☎ 843036, 0811-601726, fax 844320). Main office at the New Africa Hotel, with a branch office at the airport.

Outside Dar es Salaam Elsewhere in Tanzania, you can rent vehicles in Arusha and Mwanza, although self-drive is generally not permitted. In other places, including Unguja, rentals with or without driver can often be arranged privately or through a travel agency or hotel. If you do rent in this manner, be sure to determine before setting out who bears responsibility for any repairs that might be necessary. See the individual town listings for further information. Motorcycle rental is fairly common on Unguja. See Car & Motorcycle in the Getting Around section of The Zanzibar Archipelago chapter.

BICYCLE

Main roads are not good for cycling: there is often no shoulder and traffic moves dangerously fast. Many of Tanzania's secondary roads, however, are ideal, though distances are long enough that you'll have to plan your food and water needs in advance and carry supplies. You will need to be self-sufficient with repairs and spare parts, including inner tubes. Mountain bikes are most suitable for Tanzania's terrain, although standard touring bicycles are fine for many areas.

You can transport your bicycle on minibuses and ordinary large buses. There is no problem and no additional cost to bring your bike on the Dar es Salaam to Unguja ferries or any of the lake ferries.

See Other Safaris later, for organisations to contact regarding cycling trips in Tanzania.

HITCHING

In many of Tanzania's more remote areas your only transport option, unless you have your own vehicle, will be hitching a lift with truck drivers. Payment is generally expected, usually equivalent to or a bit less than what you would pay on a bus for the same journey, but it's best to clarify before getting in. A ride in the cab usually costs about double the price of a lift on top of the load. To flag a vehicle down on the road, hold out your hand at about waist level and wave it up and down; the common western gesture of holding out one's thumb is not used in Tanzania. Good places for trying to arrange truck lifts in advance are around ports or markets.

Expatriate workers or well-off locals may also offer you a ride. While payment is generally not expected, you should still offer some token of thanks such as picking up a meal tab, or making a contribution for petrol on longer journeys.

Remember that as in any other part of the world, hitching is never entirely safe, and we don't recommend it. Travellers who decide to hitch should understand that they are taking a perhaps small but potentially serious risk. Hitching in pairs is obviously safer; hitching through less salubrious suburbs, especially at night, is asking for trouble.

BOAT
Ferry

Ferries operate on Lake Victoria, Lake Tanganyika and Lake Nyasa. See below, and the regional sections for further details. In general, the ferries tend to be tolerable or even comfortable in 1st class, and overcrowded and uncomfortable in 2nd and 3rd class. As with ferries anywhere, especially in countries like Tanzania where overcrowding and less than optimal maintenance standards are often issues, there is always a safety risk, particularly on the smaller boats. This being said, countless Tanzanians as well as foreign travellers use the ferries without mishap, and they can be a pleasant (and perhaps safer) alternative to road travel. Since the sinking of the MV *Bukoba* on Lake Victoria in 1996, in which several hundred passengers died, at least lip service has been paid to reducing overcrowding and improving safety standards.

Lake Victoria There are four ferries operating on Lake Victoria, although only two were running as this book was being researched. See Getting There & Away in the Mwanza section of the Lake Victoria chapter for schedule and fare information.

Lake Tanganyika The MV *Liemba* is the only passenger ferry now operating on Lake Tanganyika. See Getting There & Away in the Kigoma section in the Western Tanzania chapter for details.

Lake Nyasa There is only one ferry now operating on the Tanzanian side of Lake Nyasa. Two ferries connect Mbamba Bay in Tanzania with Nkhata Bay in Malawi. See the Itungi section of The Southern Highlands chapter, and Malawi in the Sea & Lake section of the Getting There & Away chapter for details.

Offshore Islands & South-Eastern Coast See Boat in the Getting There & Away section of The Zanzibar Archipelago chapter for information on ferry connections between Dar es Salaam, Unguja and Pemba. See Rufiji River Ferries under Getting There & Away in the Mtwara section, and Boat under Getting There & Away in the Mafia section of the South-Eastern Tanzania chapter for details of boats between Mtwara, Mafia and Dar es Salaam.

Dhows

Dhows have sailed the coastal waters of Tanzania and East Africa for centuries. Main routes include those connecting Unguja and Pemba with Dar es Salaam, Tanga, Bagamoyo and Mombasa, and those connecting Kilwa Masoko, Lindi and Mtwara with other coastal towns. Though now overshadowed by more modern ships, they still play an important role in local commerce. Many dhows are motorised, but it's still possible to find those which rely entirely on sail. They are dependent on wind and tide, and travel only when these variables are favourable.

Despite their romantic image, dhow journeys can be long, uncomfortable and risky.

Following several accidents involving tourists, the Tanzanian government now prohibits foreigners on non-motorised dhows, and on any dhows between Dar es Salaam and Unguja. As a result, boat captains are often unwilling to take you. If you do find one who is amenable, you will need to bring all the food and water you will require. Journeys often last much longer than originally anticipated. Stories abound of trips that were supposed to take less than a day but which turned into two or three day ordeals.

LOCAL TRANSPORT
Dalla-Dalla
Local routes are serviced by ordinary buses and, more commonly, by pick-ups and minivans (generally referred to as dalla-dallas or, occasionally, matatus). Prices are fixed and very inexpensive. The vehicles make many stops and are invariably extremely overcrowded. Accidents are frequent, particularly in dalla-dallas. Many are caused when the drivers race each other to an upcoming station in order to get first dibs on new passengers. For many Tanzanians, especially in rural areas, they are the only transport option.

Taxi
Taxis can be hired in all major towns and cities. The base rate is generally Tsh1000, more for longer trips. Shared taxis of the type found in many areas of West Africa are relatively rare, except in the north near Arusha.

SAFARIS
Organised Vehicle Safaris
Many travellers to Tanzania use tour companies for assistance with all or some of their travel arrangements. While this often makes things easier and can be the best option if your time is limited, it usually works out to be more expensive than if you arrange things yourself.

There are close to 200 registered tour companies in Tanzania. Almost half of these are based in Arusha, with many of the rest in Dar es Salaam and Moshi. Most of the less expensive companies are generalist outfits which simply put together standard packages

for the most common tourist sites. Specialist companies are usually more expensive, but are willing to customise your itinerary. The best operators are experts themselves in a particular area or activity, such as trekking, birdwatching, bicycling, etc. Try to find out whether you're dealing with an agent; it's often, although not always, cheaper to deal directly with the operating company. Many of the top end companies also have branches or agents abroad which can assist in arranging all or part of your trip before you arrive in Tanzania.

If you are already in Tanzania and decide to book through a tour operator, especially one you don't know, it's usually best to just do local bookings with them. For example, don't book your itinerary on Unguja with a tour operator in Moshi, unless you are sure they are reliable. Rather, wait until you get to Unguja to book. That way if something goes wrong, you will be able to track the company down and attempt to find a resolution – not so easy if they are in a distant city. In general, it's probably best to book Kilimanjaro or Meru treks, and visits to the northern parks, in Arusha or Moshi, and visits to the Selous Game Reserve, to Mikumi National Park, or Mafia island in Dar es Salaam. Unless you book in Kigoma itself, excursions to Gombe Stream and Mahale Mountains national parks will probably be subcontracted to a local agent anyway.

If you're travelling alone or with just a few others, be aware that budget companies will often combine groups. While this will definitely save you money, you may not know the people who will be on your safari with you.

Most Tanzanian-based companies can organise safaris very quickly; you should not have to wait more than two or three days at most, and can often leave the next day.

Costs The general rule is that you get what you pay for. Companies in this book have been classed into three categories: budget, mid-range and top end. For budget companies, expect to pay between US$85 and US$100 per person per day for organised vehicle safaris. These prices will often not be all inclusive. If camping is involved, you can expect barely adequate equipment; meals will be no-frills and chances are that the vehicle will break down at least once. Mid-range companies average between US$120 and US$200 per person per day. Standards at these prices should be higher, including better equipment, better vehicles, and more specialised knowledge. Prices are often all-inclusive, though you should always verify this at the outset. Top end companies aim to offer comfortable, luxury tours, generally individually tailored; prices are from US$200 per person per day and up and are generally all-inclusive although, again, it's best to confirm this. There are of course exceptions where you will get very good service from a budget or mid-range company, and mediocre service from a top end outfit, but as a rule, price is a good gauge.

One variable which significantly affects overall tour price is accommodation. Camping safaris will be the least expensive, while those including accommodation in luxury lodges or luxury tented camps will cost much more. Group size is another important variable. Almost all operators charge a supplement for single-room accommodation, ranging from 20 to 50% of the shared-room rate. The larger your group, the lower will be your per person vehicle costs.

Tipping It is common practice to tip drivers, guides and (on treks) porters if service has been good, and you should calculate these costs into your overall trip budget. Tipping guidelines for treks on Mt Meru are given in Guides & Porters in the Mt Meru section of the Trekking chapter. For vehicle safaris, there are no set rates. Staff of top end companies will likely be accustomed to (and expect) better tips than those working for budget outfits. A rough guideline is to give an additional 10% of wages per day, or an additional day's wage for every five days worked. Exceptional service deserves a higher than average tip, while substandard service would call for a lower tip or, in some cases, no tip at all.

Choosing a Company A selection of safari and tour operators have been listed in the regional chapters – check the Travel Agencies sections of Arusha and Moshi in the Northern Tanzania chapter, and the Travel Agencies section of the Dar es Salaam chapter. There are many other reputable companies which could not be listed in this book due to space limitations, and many companies based abroad in places like London or New York. See the regional listings of travel agents in the Getting There & Away chapter.

When choosing a company, try to talk with others who have used the same operator before finalising your arrangements. Some issues to be aware of are highlighted under Travel Agencies in the Arusha section

---

WARNING

! Tourism in Tanzania has developed rapidly in recent years. With this development has come competition among tour operators for clients, and the resultant shortcuts and cost-cutting associated with this. At Lonely Planet we receive letters extolling the virtues of some companies and lamenting the lack of them in others. Unfortunately, in such a changing industry, the practices of tour operators can vary widely in a relatively short period of time. Companies mentioned in this book (see listings under Arusha and Moshi in the Northern Tanzania chapter, the listings in the Dar es Salaam and The Zanzibar Archipelago chapters) enjoyed a good reputation at the time of research. However, we cannot emphasise enough the need to check on the current situation with all of the listed companies and any others you may hear about. The Tanzania Tourist Board's Tourist Information Centre in Arusha maintains a black list of tour operators, as well as a listing of all registered companies. An excellent source of advice is other travellers – those you meet on the road will always be the most reliable source of up to date and impartial information.

of the Northern Tanzania chapter. Many of the considerations discussed in the boxed text 'Choosing a Trekking Company' in the Trekking chapter also apply to safari tour operators.

It is important before finalising your arrangements to verify exactly what will be included in the price, and what costs you must pay separately during your trip. If you are booking with a shoestring company, quoted prices will often not include park fees or – in the case of camping safaris – equipment rental. With top end companies, prices are frequently all-inclusive – often covering accommodation costs before and after your trip, airfield transfers, if applicable, and all meals and park fees.

Other Safaris

There are a variety of options for those who do not want to tour the country in a vehicle on an organised tour. An increasing number of mid-range and top end companies are offering **walking safaris**, if not in the national parks themselves, then in bordering areas. North of Arusha, you can go on **camel safaris**, organised within the framework of the SNV (Netherlands Development Organisation) Cultural Tourism Program. See Around Arusha in the Northern Tanzania chapter for further details. Those interested in organised **cycling trips** can contact Bicycle Africa Tours (www.ibike.org/bikeafrica). For information about cycling in Tanzania try Guide to Bicycle Touring in Africa (www.ibike.org/africaguide) and see also Bicycle earlier in this chapter.

For those wanting to arrange their own vehicle safari, keep in mind that in most parks, fees for foreign-registered vehicles are US$30 per day (Tsh1000 per day for local registration).

Dar es Salaam

'… This was my first glimpse of Dar es Salaam … a vast rippling blue-black lagoon and all around the rim of the lagoon there were pale-yellow sandy beaches, almost white, and breakers were running up on to the sand, and coconut palms with their little green leafy hats were growing on the beaches, and there were casuarina trees, immensely tall and breathtakingly beautiful … And then behind the casuarinas was what seemed to me like a jungle, a great tangle of tremendous dark-green trees that were full of shadows and almost certainly teeming … with rhinos and lions and all manner of vicious beasts. Over to one side lay the tiny town of Dar es Salaam, the houses white and yellow and pink, and among the houses I could see a narrow church steeple and a domed mosque and along the waterfront there was a line of acacia trees splashed with scarlet flowers … '

(from *Going Solo* by Roald Dahl)

Dar es Salaam has come a long way since the late 1930s when Roald Dahl first glimpsed it. With a population of over two million and an area of more than 1350 sq km, it is Tanzania's major city, capital in everything but name, and one of the least likely places in the country for sighting rhino or lion.

However, despite its size, Dar is a pleasant city with a picturesque seaport, a vaguely oriental feel, and much of its colonial character still intact. While there's not too much to actually do, there are enough historical buildings, attractive nearby beaches, shops, and good restaurants – especially on the fast-developing Msasani peninsula – to keep most visitors busy for at least several days.

History

Until the mid-19th century, what is now Dar es Salaam was just a humble fishing village, one of many along the East African coast. In the 1860s, Sultan Sayyid Majid of Zanzibar decided to develop the area's inland harbour into a port and trading centre, and named the site Dar es Salaam (Haven of Peace). No sooner had development of the harbour

- **Central Dar** – strolling through the streets and enjoying the bustling harbour, colourful vending stalls and vibrant street life
- **Msasani Peninsula** – spending an afternoon on Coco beach or exploring other areas of the peninsula
- **Markets** – visiting Dar's many markets and craft shops

begun, however, than the sultan died and the town sunk again into anonymity, overshadowed by Bagamoyo, an important dhow port to the north. It wasn't until the 1880s that Dar assumed new significance, first as a station for Christian missionaries making their way from Unguja to the interior of the mainland, and then as a seat for the German colonial government, which viewed Dar's protected harbour as a better alternative for steamships than the dhow port in Bagamoyo. In 1891, the colonial administration was officially moved to Dar from Bagamoyo. Since then the city has remained Tanzania's undisputed political and economic capital, although the legislature and official seat of government were transferred to Dodoma in 1973.

Orientation

The city centre runs along Samora Ave from the clock tower to the Askari Monument. This is a bustling, congested section with

GREATER DAR ES SALAAM

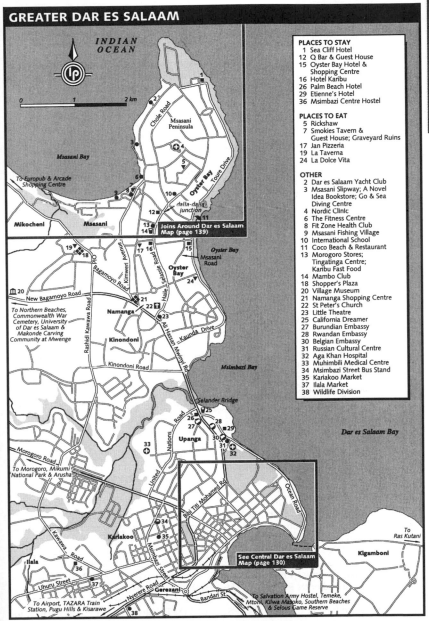

INDIAN OCEAN

Msasani Peninsula

Msasani Bay

To Europub & Arcade Shopping Centre

Mikocheni   Msasani

Chole Road

Toure Drive

Oyster Bay

dalla-dalla junction

Joins Around Dar es Salaam Map (page 139)

Oyster Bay

Oyster Bay

Msasani Road

Bagamoyo Road

Kimweri Avenue

Haile Selassie Road

New Bagamoyo Road

To Northern Beaches, Commonwealth War Cemetery, University of Dar es Salaam & Makonde Carving Community at Mwenge

Rashidi Kawawa Road

Namanga

Kinondoni

Ali Hassan Mwinyi Rd

Kaunda Drive

Kinondoni Road

Msimbazi Bay

Selander Bridge

United Nations Road

Upanga

Dar es Salaam Bay

To Morogoro, Mikumi National Park & Arusha

Morogoro Road

Bibi Titi Mohamed Rd

Ocean Road

To Ras Kutani

Kigamboni

Kariakoo

See Central Dar es Salaam Map (page 130)

Kawawa Road

Ilala

Mchikichi Street

Uhuru Street

Nyerere Road

Gerezani

Bandari St

To Airport, TAZARA Train Station, Pugu Hills & Kisarawe

To Salvation Army Hostel, Temeke, Mtoni, Kilwa Masoko, Southern Beaches & Selous Game Reserve

PLACES TO STAY
1 Sea Cliff Hotel
12 Q Bar & Guest House
15 Oyster Bay Hotel & Shopping Centre
16 Hotel Karibu
26 Palm Beach Hotel
29 Etienne's Hotel
36 Msimbazi Centre Hostel

PLACES TO EAT
5 Rickshaw
7 Smokies Tavern & Guest House; Graveyard Ruins
17 Jan Pizzeria
19 La Taverna
24 La Dolce Vita

OTHER
2 Dar es Salaam Yacht Club
3 Msasani Slipway; A Novel Idea Bookstore; Go & Sea Diving Centre
4 Nordic Clinic
6 The Fitness Centre
8 Fit Zone Health Club
9 Msasani Fishing Village
10 International School
11 Coco Beach & Restaurant
13 Morogoro Stores; Tingatinga Centre; Karibu Fast Food
14 Mambo Club
18 Shopper's Plaza
20 Village Museum
21 Namanga Shopping Centre
22 St Peter's Church
23 Little Theatre
25 California Dreamer
27 Burundian Embassy
28 Rwandan Embassy
30 Belgian Embassy
31 Russian Cultural Centre
32 Aga Khan Hospital
33 Muhimbili Medical Centre
34 Msimbazi Street Bus Stand
35 Kariakoo Market
37 Ilala Market
38 Wildlife Division

0   1   2 km

many banks, foreign exchange bureaus, vendors and shops. North-west of Samora Ave, around India and Jamhuri Sts, is the Asian quarter, with many Indian merchants and traders. West of Mnazi Mmoja Park are the colourful areas of Kariakoo and Ilala.

On the other side of town, to the northeast of Askari Monument, is a quiet area of tree-lined streets where you'll find the National Museum, Botanical Gardens and State House. Proceeding north from here along the coast, you first reach the upper-middle class section of Upanga and then, after crossing Selander Bridge, the fast developing diplomatic and upscale residential areas of Oyster Bay and Msasani.

Maps The most widely available is the tiny *Dar es Salaam City Map* (1:25,000) sold for Tsh1500 at many kiosks around town.

Better is the *Dar es Salaam Visitors Map* put out by the British Council together with the University of Dar es Salaam's Department of Geography (1:15,000, 1995); it's available from the British Council.

The Surveys and Mapping Division publishes a fairly good street map (*Dar es Salaam City Map and Guide*, 1:20,000) although few features are marked on it. It's available from the Map Sales Office at the Surveys & Mapping Division at Kivukoni Front and Luthuli St (Tsh5000). The office is open from 7.30 am to 3.30 pm, Monday to Friday.

Information

Tourist Offices The Tanzania Tourist Board Information Centre (☎ 120373, 123491) is on Samora Ave just west of Zanaki St. It's open from 8 am to 4 pm Monday to Friday and from 8.30 am to 12.30 pm on Saturday. The office has free tourist maps of Tanzania, photocopied maps of Dar es Salaam and Zanzibar Town and a few interesting leaflets.

The Tanzania Tourist Board (☎ 111244, 110812, fax 116420, email ttb@unidar.gn .apc.org or md@ttb.ud.or.tz, PO Box 2485) has its marketing and policy-making headquarters on the 3rd floor of the high-rise IPS building just south of the post office on Maktaba St; it is of interest primarily to those doing tourism related work in Tanzania.

Local Guides The free bimonthly *Dar es Salaam Guide* contains a variety of useful information including a listing of diplomatic missions, hotel and restaurant advertisements, tide tables and airline schedules. The monthly *What's Happening in Dar es Salaam* is similar, although without the tide tables. Both are available from the Tourist Information Centre and from numerous hotels, restaurants, travel agencies and shops around town.

Immigration The Immigration Office is on Ghana Ave west of Ohio St, and marked only in Swahili (*Wizara ya mambo ya ndani*). It's open from 8 am to 1 pm Monday to Friday.

Money Banking hours are 8.30 am to 3 pm Monday to Friday and 8.30 am to noon on Saturday. Major banks which offer foreign exchange include the National Bank of Commerce (NBC) on the corner of Azikiwe St and Sokoine Dr, CRDB on Azikiwe St opposite the main post office, and Greenland Bank, near the Askari Monument at Indira Ghandi and Azikiwe Sts.

In addition to the banks, there are many foreign exchange (forex) bureaus scattered around the centre of Dar, with many on or near Samora Ave. They are generally open between 8 am and 5 pm Monday to Friday and on Saturday mornings. Rates are usually better at foreign exchange bureaus than at banks, especially for travellers cheques. While there is not much variation between individual foreign exchange bureau rates, banks often vary considerably in commissions. The exchange bureau at the Sheraton offers lower rates, but is open longer hours (8 am to 8 pm Monday to Saturday and 10 am to 1 pm on Sunday and holidays).

You can withdraw cash (in Tanzanian shillings) against a Visa or MasterCard at two places in Dar. Coastal Travels on Upanga Rd charges US$5 for telex fees and there's a withdrawal limit of US$500 per week. The office is open for credit card transactions from 9 am to 4 pm Monday to Friday and 9 am to noon on Saturday. Galaxy Bureau de Change at the airport has similar rates and fees.

American Express is represented by Rickshaw Travels (☎ 115110), with offices at the Sheraton and on Upanga Rd. It does not give cash advances but issues US dollar travellers cheques against an American Express card.

Post The main post office on Maktaba St is open from 8 am to 4.30 pm weekdays, and 9 am to noon on Saturday. Poste restante charges Tsh200 per letter and will hold mail for one month.

Telephone & Fax The cheapest place to make an international telephone call is at the Extelecoms House on Samora Ave (entrance on Bridge St). It is open from 7.30 am to midnight Monday to Friday, and from 8.30 am to midnight on weekends and holidays. Charges are Tsh2600 per minute to most international destinations outside Africa.

There are also private telecommunications bureaus throughout town which charge higher fees. Calls from hotel switchboards are usually at least twice as costly as Extelecom rates. Card phones have been installed at many places in Dar, and phone cards, available at the Extelecoms House and the post office, can be used for international calls.

Faxes can be sent from the Extelecoms House (Tsh2725 per minute to all international numbers), or from the EMS building next to the main post office (rate depends on destination). You can receive faxes at the Extelecoms House (fax 112752, 112754, Tsh300 per page); incoming faxes are held indefinitely. Most private telecommunications bureaus also offer fax services.

Email & Internet Access Communication centres offering email services and Internet access are springing up all over Dar. A selection of places, together with prices for email services follows, although there are likely to be many more options by the time this book is published. Internet access usually costs Tsh3000 to Tsh4000 per hour. For computer supplies or repair try Imagination Computer Centre (☎ 124232) in Sukari House on Ohio St.

Allyvay Secretarial Bureau
Upanga Rd in the YMCA compound; one of the cheapest places, charging just Tsh600 per email message, but you cannot type yourself.
CyberTwiga
Upange Rd above Coastal Travels; Tsh2000 per half hour.
Java Internet Cafe
Opposite Hard Rock Cafe on Indira Ghandi Rd; Tsh3000 per hour.
Luther House Secretarial Services
Opposite Luther House Hostel; Tsh1000 per message, they type for you.
Management & Secretarial Services
At the Sheraton; Tsh2000 per message or per 15 minutes computer time.
Raminklal Chatrabhuj Ltd Internet Cafe
On the corner of Zanaki and Libya Sts near the roundabout; Tsh2000 per hour.
The Work Station Computer & Email Centre
Lehman Bldg, on Mission St just south of Samora Ave; Tsh1500 per half hour.

Travel Agencies Travel agencies and tour operators in Dar es Salaam include:

Coastal Travels
(☎ 117959, fax 118647, email coastal@twiga.com, PO Box 3052) Upanga Rd. Covers the whole country but specialises in the southern circuit parks, Unguja and Mafia island.
Emslies Travel
(☎ 114065, fax 113972, email emslies@raha.com, PO Box 6684) Upanga Rd, near Citibank. Offers airline bookings and hotel reservations only.
Gogo Safaris
(☎ 114719, fax 113619, PO Box 7064) Mkwepu St near Samora Ave. Budget tour operator to the northern circuit, Selous Game Reserve and Zanzibar.
Hippo Tours & Safaris
(☎ 71610 or 0811-320849, fax 75165, email hippo@twiga.com, PO Box 13894) Kilimanjaro Hotel. Specialises in the southern circuit parks, Unguja and Mafia island.
Hit Holidays Travel & Tours
(☎ 119024 or 0611-324552, fax 112376, email hittrvls@intafrica.com, PO Box 6666) corner of Ali Hassan Mwinyi and Bibi Titi Mohamed

DAR ES SALAAM

Rds near UNICEF. Specialises in the northern circuit, Kilimanjaro and Marangu (including village to village hikes around the lower slopes of Kilimanjaro).

Rickshaw Travels
(☎ 115620 at Sheraton Hotel) main office is on Upanga Rd next to Citibank; branch offices at the Sheraton, the Sea Cliff Hotel and in Arusha. Offers country-wide tours.

Savannah Tours
(☎ 117753, fax 117321, email savtour@twiga.com, PO Box 20517) Sheraton Hotel. Specialises in the northern and southern circuit parks.

Southern Tanganyika Game Safaris & Tours
(☎ 0812-786679, fax 116413, 647583, email stgs@twiga.com, PO Box 2341) between Upanga Rd and Ohio St. Specialises in the southern circuit parks.

See also the boxed text 'Warning' under Choosing a Company in the Getting Around chapter.

Bookshops Bookshops in Dar es Salaam have a decent selection of books on Tanzanian and Zanzibari history, and numerous publications on the country's parks and wildlife. They also stock a variety of travel guides. Except for locally published books, prices are significantly higher than in the US, Europe or Australia. There are many second-hand bookstalls on the street in Dar es Salaam, although selection is fairly limited.

A Novel Idea at Msasani Slipway has an excellent selection of books, ranging from literature classics to modern fiction novels to travel guides and maps. It's open from 10 am to 7 pm Monday to Saturday and from noon to 6 pm on Sunday.

For older books, try some of the second-hand street stalls on and near Samora Ave. One of the best is on the corner of Sokoine Drive and Pamba Rd, opposite Luther House.

International newspapers and magazines are available from the Sheraton Hotel, and occasionally at news stands downtown.

Libraries The Central Library, corner of Maktaba St and Bibi Titi Mohamed Rd, is primarily of interest for those wanting to do research. It has an extensive selection of old materials on Tanzanian history and culture. Access to the reference room and card catalogues can be arranged with the supervisor; browsing in the stacks is not permitted.

Universities The University of Dar es Salaam is Tanzania's only public university, although branches for agriculture (Sokoine University in Morogoro) and business are now separate entities and independently administered. It was established in the early 1960s as part of the University of East Africa, and in 1970 as the University of Dar es Salaam. The main campus is at Observation Hill about 15km from town off New Bagamoyo Rd.

Cultural Centres Cultural centres in Dar include the following:

Alliance Française
(☎ 119415) Azikiwe St opposite the post office
American Cultural Center
(☎ 117174) Bibi Titi Mohamed Rd
British Council
(☎ 116574) Ohio St
Russian Cultural Centre
(☎ 136578) corner of Ufukoni and Ocean Rds

Photography Burhani at Shopper's Plaza in Msasani does good quality developing. They also have a branch at Oyster Bay Shopping Centre. Rates are between Tsh6000 and Tsh7700 for a roll of 36 exposures.

Medical Services For medical emergencies try the Nordic Clinic (☎ 601650 or 0811-325569 for the 24-hour emergency line) in the Valhalla compound on the Msasani peninsula.

Dar's two main hospitals are the Aga Khan Hospital (☎ 114096), on the corner of Ocean Rd and Ufukoni Rd, and Muhimbili Medical Centre (☎ 151351) – the country's teaching hospital – off United Nations Rd. While both have some well-qualified staff, medication and equipment are often in short supply and many foreign residents prefer to be treated in Nairobi.

For emergency evacuations contact the Flying Doctors (☎ 116610, 115832 in Dar for membership information and 254-2-501280 or 501301 in Nairobi for evacuations). For further information see the Health section in the Facts for the Visitor chapter.

Emergency The central police station (☎ 115507) and traffic police headquarters (☎ 111747) are on Sokoine Drive near the Tanzania Railways Corporation Central Line office. For the Msasani peninsula, use the Oyster Bay Police (☎ 667332).

Dangers & Annoyances Dar is considered to be much safer than many other places in the region, notably Nairobi. However, muggings and thefts do occur and visitors should take the usual precautions. The main danger during the day is pickpocketing which is rife, particularly at crowded markets and bus and train stations. If you go out at night, take a taxi rather than a dalla-dalla and try to avoid travelling alone.

Walking or jogging alone along the path paralleling Ocean Rd is not recommended.

National Museum
The National Museum (☎ 112030), open daily from 9.30 am to 6 pm, is next to the Botanical Gardens between Samora Ave and Sokoine Drive. It houses some important archaeological pieces, notably the fossil discoveries of *Zinjanthropus* from Olduvai Gorge, as well as small and somewhat scattered displays on a variety of other topics including the Shirazi civilisation of Kilwa, the Zanzibar slave trade and the German and British colonial periods. Entry costs Tsh1800.

Village Museum
The open-air Village Museum (☎ 700437, email staff@twiga.com), open daily from 9 am to 6 pm, is 10km from the city centre along the New Bagamoyo Rd. It consists of a collection of authentically constructed dwellings from various parts of Tanzania, although unfortunately it has suffered from neglect and rain damage and is therefore fairly empty these days. Entry costs Tsh2000 (plus an additional Tsh2400 if you want to take pictures). *Ngoma* (drumming) shows

are sometimes held here on weekends from 4 to 6 pm, and other cultural events are occasionally scheduled. Contact the Village Museum, the Tourist Information Centre or the National Museum for details about upcoming programmes. To get here with public transport, take the Mwenge dalla-dalla from the New Posta transport stand and get off at Mikocheni by Makaburi St, near the Commonwealth War Cemetery (Tsh150).

Markets
Kariakoo market between Mkunguni and Tandamuti Sts, is a bustling place with a large variety of fruit, fish, spices and vegetables. Watch your wallet here as there are frequent reports of pickpocketing and bag slashing.

Ilala market, with a good selection of everything from fresh produce to cloths and pots and pans, is favoured by locals as one of Dar's best.

The colourful **fish market** on Ocean Rd near Kivukoni Front is best visited in the early morning, when it is at its busiest. All sorts of fish are sold here, including shark and barracuda.

Msasani
On the western side of the Msasani peninsula, on the site of one of the oldest Arabic settlements along the Swahili coast, is the picturesque Msasani **fishing village**. Nearby, next to Smokies Tavern & Guesthouse, are **ruins** of what is said to be Dar's oldest graveyard, dating back to the 17th century.

Bird Walks
The Wildlife Conservation Society of Tanzania (☎ 112518) on Garden Ave has weekly bird walks to various places in and around Dar es Salaam. The walks are free and usually last between two and three hours.

Beaches
The best beach in Dar es Salaam proper is at Oyster Bay, more commonly known as **Coco Beach**. It's popular with locals on weekends, but you can only swim at high tide so check the tide tables (published in the *Dar es Salaam Guide*) before coming out. To

Dar es Salaam Walking Tour

While central Dar es Salaam does not have any 'sights' as such, it is full of historical buildings, interesting architecture and atmosphere. It's well worth setting aside half a day to explore the area on foot. The best times are Saturday afternoon or Sunday when traffic is less heavy.

The **Askari Monument** at the intersection of Samora Ave and Azikiwe St is a good place to begin. This bronze statue is dedicated to the Africans who fell in WWI. From the monument, head north-east along Samora Ave, crossing Pamba Rd, Ohio St and Mirambo St. Immediately after the next intersection (Shaban Robert St) and to the left on Samora Ave are the small and somewhat run-down **Botanical Gardens**. To the south, down Shaban Robert St, is the **National Museum**. Continue eastwards along Samora Ave past the botanical gardens for another half a block. On the right is **Karimjee Hall** where Julius Nyerere was sworn in as president. This was the former house of parliament before the legislature was relocated to Dodoma. Now it is used for parliamentary committee meetings and various political functions. Continue eastwards along Samora Ave to Luthuli St. To the north-east is the **Ocean Road Hospital** which is no longer operational, but nevertheless interesting architecturally. It was built in 1897 and combines both Arabic and German influences. Before reaching the hospital, you will see a small, white, domed building. It was here that Robert Koch carried out his pioneering research on malaria and tuberculosis around the turn of the century.

From Ocean Road Hospital you can head south either along Ocean Rd, or along Luthuli St. If you're alone, it's best to take Luthuli St as this section of Ocean Rd is usually deserted. To your right (or to your left if you are on Luthuli St) are the State House grounds. The **State House**, which sits in their centre, was originally built by the Germans and rebuilt after WWI by the British. To the south-east of the State House on the seafront is the **Tanganyika Beach Club** where you can use the beach and swim in dubiously clean ocean water for Tsh300 per day (Tsh2000 per month). This is a popular spot early in the day with Dar's Indian residents. Just beyond the beach club is the colourful **fish market**, at its bustling best in the morning.

From the fish market, head westwards along Kivukoni Front (sometimes also called Azania

---

get here by public transport, take the Masaki dalla-dalla from the New Posta transport stand in front of the main post office and get off at Msasani Rd. From there, it's a 500m walk back. Taxis from the centre of town charge Tsh2000; to find a taxi back to town, walk to the dalla-dalla junction at Haile Selassie and Msasani Rds. There is parking at Coco Beach for those coming with their own vehicles. On weekends, refreshments and food are available at the Coco Beach Restaurant. Be careful when walking around in the evenings or on weekdays when there aren't too many people about, as several muggings have been reported here.

Across the harbour from the fish market near Kivukoni Front is the **Kigamboni** peninsula and beach, although not too many tourists visit as muggings are frequent. The ferry to Kigamboni leaves throughout the day from next to the fish market and costs Tsh50.

For information on the beaches north and south of Dar es Salaam, see the Around Dar es Salaam section at the end of this chapter.

Diving

The only diving centre within Dar is Go & Sea Diving Centre (☎ 0812-784925), 200m south of the Msasani Slipway. They offer excursions to the various dive sites near the city at prices comparable to the dive centres based at the northern beaches (see the Around Dar es Salaam section at the end of this chapter).

Blue Chip Dive Shop at Sea Cliff Hotel stocks some diving equipment and supplies.

Dar es Salaam Walking Tour

Front), which meets up again with Luthuli St. Soon you'll see a row of government buildings on your right, including the Ministry of Foreign Affairs, the Ministry of Justice and the Bureau of Statistics, all dating from the German era. To your left is the seafront, which is usually filled with boats and lined with vendors. Past the government buildings is the old **Kilimanjaro Hotel**, whose rooftop restaurant was long a popular gathering spot before being closed recently for renovations. Just after the Kilimanjaro Hotel is the **Hotel Tourism & Training Institute** (Forodhani's), which enjoyed its heyday during the British era as the Dar es Salaam Club.

The next important building you will reach is the striking **Azania Front Lutheran Church**, one of Dar's major landmarks. The church was built at the turn of the century by German missionaries, and is still used for services. Diagonally opposite the church is the enormous headquarters of the National Bank of Commerce. Shortly after passing the bank (and continuing south-west along the waterfront) you will reach **St Joseph's Cathedral**, another of Dar's famous landmarks. The cathedral was built at the same time as the Lutheran church, also by German missionaries, and still contains many of the original German inscriptions and artwork. Directly opposite the cathedral are the Zanzibar ferry terminals. From St Joseph's, if you still have energy left, continue a few blocks further to the old German boma (which now houses UN and other offices). It is on Sokoine Drive, west of Morogoro Rd. The Central Line railway station is just beyond the boma at the corner of Sokoine Drive and Railway St. To finish up, walk one block north to Samora Ave, which you can then follow eastwards, past numerous small shops and foreign exchange bureaus back to the Askari Monument.

During the walk, it's interesting to note the street names you are passing, as they provide a good overview of Tanzanian history. Luthuli St, for example, is named after Albert Luthuli, the former South African ANC president. Shaban Robert St honours one of Tanzania's most famous writers, while Sokoine Drive is named after Edward Moringe Sokoine, who served as prime minister and was considered to be Julius Nyerere's most likely successor until he was killed in a car crash in 1984.

Places to Stay

Almost all budget lodging is downtown, between Morogoro Rd and Mnazi Mmoja Park. The popular places tend to fill up quickly, so it's best to arrive early or to make a reservation.

The situation with upmarket accommodation in Dar has improved markedly over the past few years, and now travellers willing to spend a bit more have plenty of choices. Advance bookings are recommended, particularly during the high season travel months of June through August.

Places to Stay – Budget
Camping There is nowhere to camp in Dar itself. The closest places are at Rungwe and Silver Sands, about 25km north of the city.

See the Around Dar es Salaam section at the end of this chapter.

Hostels & Guesthouses All of the following offer decent, reasonably clean budget accommodation. Breakfast is included in room prices.

The cheapest place to stay is the *YWCA* (☎ 122439) on Maktaba St near the post office, with simple singles/doubles for Tsh4000/6000 (Tsh10,000 for a double with bathroom); women and couples are accepted. The nearby *YMCA* (☎ 110833) on Upanga Rd has more expensive rooms with nets for US$13/15. The YMCA takes both men and women. Both Ys have canteens. The main drawback at both places is that some of the rooms get a lot of street noise.

DAR ES SALAAM

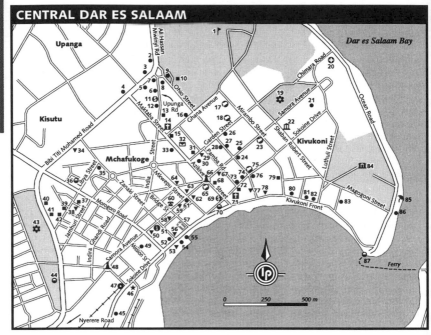

CENTRAL DAR ES SALAAM

Luther House Hostel (☎ *120734*) near the junction of Sokoine Drive and Kivukoni Front has clean rooms with bathroom for Tsh12,000/15,000.

South of town on Kilwa Rd near the stadium is the *Salvation Army Hostel* (☎ *851509*) with two-bed bungalows for Tsh4000 per bed. The availability of running water is sometimes a problem but staff will be happy to arrange a bucket. To get here take the Temeke or Mtoni dalla-dalla from the New Posta transport stand (Tsh150) and ask to be dropped near the 'Jeshi'. There are several Temeke routes, so be sure the dalla-dalla is going via Kilwa Rd. A taxi from the centre will cost Tsh1500.

Msimbazi Centre Hostel (☎ *863508*), west of town on Kawawa Rd, is run by the Archdiocese of Dar es Salaam. It has small but spotlessly clean singles with bathroom for Tsh7800, and doubles from Tsh6400

(Tsh8200 with bathroom). To get here, take the Buguruni dalla-dalla from the Old Posta transport stand (Tsh150) and ask them to drop you at Msimbazi Centre. Taxis cost Tsh1500, more at night.

New Dar Guesthouse is a good place conveniently located on Chagga St near the intersection of Morogoro Rd and Libya St. Basic but spacious rooms are Tsh4500/5000 with fans and shared baths.

Q Bar & Guest House (☎ *0811-322119, 335374*) in Msasani just off Haile Selassie Rd has a six-bed 'backpacker room' with bathroom for US$15 per bed. Singles/doubles with bathroom and refrigerator are US$45/55. All rooms have air-con.

Hotels There are several decent hotels frequented by budget travellers near the Kisutu and Mnazi Mmoja bus stands. Room prices include continental breakfast.

CENTRAL DAR ES SALAAM

PLACES TO STAY
10 Sheraton Hotel
13 YMCA; Allyvay Secretarial Bureau
15 YWCA
31 Embassy Hotel
37 New Dar Guesthouse
39 Econo-Lodge; Safari Inn
40 Peacock Hotel
41 Hotel Starlight
42 Jambo Inn
68 New Africa Hotel; Shuttle Bus to Northern Beaches
72 Luther House Hostel & Secretarial Services; Swiss Air
79 Kilimanjaro Hotel

PLACES TO EAT
29 Street Food Vendors
34 The Cedars
38 Chef's Pride; Imran Restaurant
50 Fosters
53 Street Food Vendors
56 Blue Marlin
58 Sno-Cream
59 The Alcove; Gully's Fast Food; Caffee Espresso
62 Salamander Coffee House
63 Burger Bite
64 Hard Rock Cafe; Club Bilicanas; Java Internet Cafe
67 She Supermarket
77 Chinese Take-Away; NIC Life House Branch Building
78 Hotel & Tourism Training Institute

OTHER
1 Golf Course; Gymkhana Club
2 Hit Holidays Travel & Tours; UNICEF
3 Air India

4 Central Library
5 American Cultural Center
6 Air France; KLM; Kenya Airways
7 Raha Towers; Gulf Air; Alliance Air
8 Ethiopian Airlines; Southern Tanganyika Game Safaris & Tours
9 Nyumba ya Sanaa
11 Citibank; City Restaurant; Rickshaw Travels; Emslies Travel; American Airlines; Jet Air
12 Coastal Travels; CyberTwiga
14 St Alban's Anglican Church
16 Immigration
17 Canadian Embassy
18 Mozambican Embassy
19 Botanical Gardens
20 Ocean Road Hospital (closed)
21 Karimjee Hall
22 National Museum
23 NIC Life House (Main Building); Embassies of Germany, Kenya, Malawi & India
24 British Council
25 Aeroflot
26 Wildlife Conservation Society of Tanzania
27 Precision Air
28 Air Tanzania; Netherlands Embassy
30 Tanzania Tourist Board; IPS Building
32 Main Post Office; EMS Building; New Posta Local Transport Stand
33 Alliance Française
35 Raminklal Chatrabhuj Ltd Internet Cafe

36 Kisutu Bus Stand
43 Mnazi Mmoja Park
44 Mnazi Mmoja Bus Stand
45 Traffic Police Headquarters
46 Central Police Station
47 Central Line Train Station
48 Clock Tower; Local Transport Stand
49 The Work Station Computer & Email Centre
51 Tanzania Tourist Board Information Centre
52 National Shipping Agencies
54 Flying Horse Ferry Booking Office
55 Zanzibar Ferries; Booking Offices
57 St Joseph's Cathedral
60 Extelecoms House; Ugandan Embassy
61 Gogo Safaris
65 British High Commission
66 Askari Monument
69 National Bank of Commerce
70 Old Posta Local Transport Stand
71 Azania Front Lutheran Church
73 Second-Hand Book Vendors
74 Tancot Building
75 Zambian High Commission
76 Imagination Computer Centre; Sukari House
80 Ministry of Foreign Affairs; Ministry of Justice
81 Bureau of Statistics
82 Surveys & Mapping Division; Map Sales Office
83 Ardhi House; Division of Fisheries
84 State House
85 Tanganyika Beach Club
86 Fish Market
87 Ferry to Kigamboni

Econo-Lodge (☎ 116048, fax 116053), on Band St, and just off Libya St, has singles/doubles/triples with bathroom for Tsh10,000/15,000/18,000 (Tsh22,000 for a double with air-con).

Jambo Inn (☎ 114293) on Libya St has good-value rooms with bathroom for Tsh6000/11,000 (Tsh18,000 for a double with air-con).

Safari Inn (☎ 138101, 119104, fax 116550) around the corner is similar but slightly cheaper. Rooms with bathroom cost Tsh6000/9600.

Well out of the centre, less than 1km south-west of Selander Bridge on Ocean Rd, is the pleasantly dilapidated **Etienne's Hotel**, with rooms for Tsh8000/10,000 (Tsh12,000 for a double with bathroom). All rooms are on the ground floor and have nets and fans.

Places to Stay – Mid-Range

City Centre The following hotels are often frequented by local businessmen or by travellers seeking a bit of luxury but not wanting to pay top-end prices. Most of the places in this category, while fairly comfortable, tend to be dark, drab and overpriced.

The faded and somewhat dingy *Embassy Hotel* (☎ *117084*), on Garden Ave in the busy downtown area, has singles/doubles for US$71/80 (US$80/90 with TV) including breakfast.

Peacock Hotel (☎ *114071, 115568*), opposite Mnazi Mmoja Park on busy Bibi Titi Mohamed Rd, has rooms with TV, air-con and continental breakfast for US$60/70/105; credit cards are not accepted.

A few doors down is the similar *Hotel Starlight* (☎ *119387*). Singles/doubles with air-con, TV and continental breakfast cost Tsh25,200/30,000.

The government-run *Kilimanjaro Hotel* (☎ *0811-332100*) off Kivukoni Front has been taken over by private owners and is due to be temporarily closed for rehabilitation. Pre-renovation prices were US$50/60 a single/double.

Upanga & Msasani Peninsula The mid-range accommodation situation improves markedly once you leave the city centre.

The *Palm Beach Hotel* (☎ *122931*) on Ali Hassan Mwinyi Rd is popular and has clean singles/doubles for Tsh11,000/16,000 (Tsh19,500/26,000 with bathroom) including continental breakfast. There's a nice restaurant here. It's a 25 minute walk from the city centre or Tsh1500 in a taxi.

Hotel Karibu (☎ *667761, fax 668254*) just off Haile Selassie Rd is a popular place with a swimming pool and rooms from US$80/90 including taxes and breakfast; credit cards are accepted.

For business travellers seeking an alternative to hotels, *Smokies Tavern & Guest House* (☎ *0811-337346 or 0812-780567, fax 601077, email smokies@twiga.com*) on

the western edge of Msasani peninsula has rooms for US$70/90 including full breakfast and taxes. Rooms in the smaller Kaburini annex across the street are US$45/65. Discounts are available for longer stays; advance bookings are recommended.

Places to Stay – Top End

City Centre Dar's most expensive hotel is the *Sheraton* (☎ *112416, fax 113981*), on Ohio St adjacent to the golf course and Gymkhana Club. Rooms start at $230 ($260 with breakfast), including a swimming pool and fitness and business centres.

The only other top-end hotel downtown is the recently rebuilt and now privately owned *New Africa Hotel* (☎ *117050, 117051*), with comfortable rooms from US$162/192 including breakfast buffet and all the amenities. It's on Azikiwe St, just south of Askari Monument. The rooms are better value than at the Sheraton and many foreigners on business or travel in Dar use this place.

Msasani Peninsula The new *Sea Cliff Hotel* (☎ *600380, fax 600476, email seacliff@tztechno.com*), overlooking the ocean at the tip of Msasani peninsula, has well-equipped singles/doubles from US$155/185 including breakfast and use of the fitness centre and swimming pool.

Oyster Bay Hotel (☎ *668062, fax 668631, email oysterbay-hotel@twiga.com*), on Toure Drive opposite Oyster Bay beach, has rooms from US$120/150 including continental breakfast. While standards are fine, the place seems to be permanently under construction and has a somewhat dusty atmosphere.

All top-end hotels accept credit cards.

Places to Eat

Good places for street food include the stalls on Garden Ave diagonally opposite the Embassy Hotel, and the stalls along Kivukoni Front by the harbour.

For self-caterers, the best-stocked supermarket, with a large selection of imported items, is at Shopper's Plaza in Msasani (open 8.30 am to 8.30 pm Monday to Saturday and 10 am to 4 pm on Sunday). Downtown, the only option is *She Supermarket* on Samora Ave, with a much smaller selection.

The *Melela Bustani* outlet at the Msasani Slipway sells expensive but delectable home-made cheeses, cakes, breads and other items. It's open 10 am to 6.30 pm (3 pm on Saturdays), except on Wednesday and Sunday, when it is closed.

For home-made wheat breads, the best place is *Fast Food Corner* at Oyster Bay Shopping Centre (closed Sunday). They also have a good selection of cheese and home-made jams.

For good hard-scoop ice cream, try *Fairy Delights*, with branches at Shopper's Plaza, Oyster Bay, and the Msasani Slipway. For soft ice cream, the most popular place is *Sno-Cream*, near Samora Ave on Mansfield St.

Places to Eat – Budget

City Centre Unless you will be dining at your hotel, keep in mind that most places in downtown Dar are closed on Sunday. The few that are open are noted.

There are many small restaurants and canteens in the city centre where you can buy a traditional African meal or Indian food for as little as Tsh600. The area south of Morogoro Rd and Mosque St is particularly good for inexpensive Indian food and takeaways.

The tiny *City Restaurant*, tucked away next to Citibank on Upanga Rd, has good local food at midday for between Tsh700 and Tsh1000. It's closed evenings and Sundays.

Moving up a step, there are many inexpensive places along and near Samora Ave with chicken and chips, burgers and other fast food for between Tsh1000 and Tsh2500. One of the most popular is *Salamander Coffee House*, on the corner of Samora Ave and Mkwepu St, where you can eat on the veranda. They have a good menu selection which sometimes includes fresh yoghurt.

Opposite is *Burger Bite* with inexpensive pizzas, burgers, chicken and curries. This is one of the few places downtown which is open on Sundays. *Fosters* nearby has all the standard dishes, plus ice cream.

Closer to the Askari Monument and also on Samora Ave is the spotlessly clean

Gully's Fast Food (☎ 113944), which serves pizzas, curries, burgers and omelettes. *Caffee Espresso* a few doors away has a smaller selection from Tsh1000.

A good place near the ferry terminals is the clean and air-conditioned *Blue Marlin* (☎ 0812-787712), on Zanaki St near Sokoine Drive, with a good selection of very reasonably priced chicken dishes, pizzas, omelettes and snacks. Takeaway service is also available. It's open from 7 am to 11 pm Monday to Saturday.

Chef's Pride on Chagga St opposite the New Dar Guesthouse has good local food at very reasonable prices, and is also open on Sunday. *Imram Restaurant* next door has inexpensive Indian and local dishes.

The best Chinese restaurant downtown is the *Chinese Take-Away* (☎ 134397), just off Kivukoni Front on Ohio St on the ground floor of the NIC Life House Branch building. They also have sit-down meals; the food is good and service is fast. Prices average about Tsh2000 per meal. It's open from 9 am to 8 pm weekdays (3 pm on Saturday).

The Cedars on Bibi Titi Mohamed Rd has snacks and good Lebanese food.

The *Hotel Tourism and Training Institute*, previously Forodhani's, on Kivukoni Front has a daily set western menu for about Tsh4000. Next door, local dishes are available for about Tsh1000.

Msasani Peninsula The selection of budget options on Msasani peninsula is much more limited. For street food, the best places are in Masaki village or, on weekends, from vendors at Coco Beach. There are also several local food places in Namanga, at the southern end of the peninsula. Otherwise, *Karibu Fast Food* on Haile Selassie Rd near Morogoro Stores has good snacks and inexpensive fast food.

Places to Eat – Mid-Range & Top End

City Centre *The Alcove* (☎ 137444) on Samora Ave is a bit dark but it has a good selection of Indian vegetarian dishes from about Tsh3200 plus 20% tax. If you're

DAR ES SALAAM

coming with your own vehicle, parking here can be difficult. The restaurant is closed on Sunday.

Hard Rock Cafe, off Jamhuri St, serves burgers and the standard Hard Rock menu including a few vegetarian specials, but the place is pricey, usually empty, and nothing special. Meals cost Tsh4000 to Tsh5000.

Both the *New Africa Hotel* and the *Sheraton* have good midday buffets on weekdays (Tsh9500 at the New Africa, and Tsh12,000 at the Sheraton). Both hotels also have good à la carte restaurants (the *Bandari Grill* and *Sawasdee Thai* restaurants at the New Africa, and the *Serengeti* and *Raj* restaurants at the Sheraton).

Msasani Peninsula *Smokies Tavern & Guest House* has a popular buffet dinner on its rooftop terrace (see Entertainment).

For Italian food, try *La Dolce Vita* (☎ 668896) on Toure Drive south of Oyster Bay Hotel. It has a pleasant setting and good Italian food and pizzas (closed Monday lunch).

Jan Pizzeria (☎ 0811-325420) near Kimweri Rd also has good pizzas and take-away service.

The Europub (☎ 0811-326969), to the west of Msasani peninsula about 1km off Old Bagamoyo Rd, has good food, including Mexican dishes, seafood and steaks. Most meals range from Tsh4000 to Tsh8000.

La Taverna (☎ 667146), also west of the peninsula just beyond Shopper's Plaza on Old Bagamoyo Rd has Italian food, as well as some Chinese dishes.

Rickshaw (☎ 601111) off Haile Selassie Rd is good for Chinese food.

Amadeus Cafe at Oyster Bay Shopping Centre has good crepes and other light meals.

For Ethiopian food, try *Addis* in Dar, signposted off Old Bagamoyo Rd near the British Club.

Azuma (☎ 600893 or 0811-341345) is a good Japanese restaurant at the Msasani Slipway. It's closed Monday.

Dhow Restaurant at the Sea Cliff Hotel has expensive but good seafood and Indian meals. Reservations are required (see Places to Stay).

Entertainment

Bars & Nightclubs The rooftop terrace at *Smokies Tavern & Guest House* on Msasani peninsula is the place to go on Thursday evenings if you want to meet other foreigners. There's a happy hour, a buffet dinner from 8 pm (Tsh8000 or Tsh6000 for residents of Smokies) and live music.

The nearby *Q Bar* (just off Haile Selassie Rd to the north of the Karibu Hotel) is also popular, particularly on Friday and Saturday evenings. Happy hour is from 5 to 7 pm.

Popular western-style places for dancing include *Club Bilicanas* (Tsh2000 admission during the week, Tsh2500 on weekends), downtown adjoining the Hard Rock Cafe, and *California Dreamer* (Tsh5000 admission), on Ali Hassan Mwinyi Rd opposite the Palm Beach Hotel. The *New Silent Club*, 10km out of town on Sam Nujoma Rd in Mwenge, is favoured by locals.

The *Mambo Club* on Haile Selassie Rd near Karibu Hotel is popular on weekends.

The free bimonthly *Dar es Salaam Guide* has an up-to-date listing of other nightspots.

Traditional Music & Dance In town, *Nyumba ya Sanaa* (see Shopping) often has traditional dance performances on Friday evenings.

The *Village Museum* also has traditional drumming and dance performances. See the Village Museum listing earlier in this chapter for further details.

Cinemas The British Council has free films on Wednesday evenings at 6.30 pm (general admission). The US Embassy Marine House shows free films on Tuesday evenings beginning about 7.30 pm (passport or photo identification required). There are also films on Tuesday evenings at the Msasani Slipway (Tsh1500).

Local theatres include the Avalon on Zanaki St and the Empire on Azikiwe St. They generally show Indian or B-grade western films.

Art The Russian Cultural Centre has frequent showings of Tanzanian artwork. Upcoming exhibitions are usually advertised in the *Dar es Salaam Guide*.

Fitness Centres The Fitness Centre (☎ 600786) just south of the Msasani Slipway has a weights room and aerobics sessions. Day passes are available for Tsh2500. It's open 9 am to 8 pm on weekdays (6 pm on Saturday).

The weights room at the nearby Fit Zone Health Club (☎ 602696) is better; there are also aerobics classes. Daily memberships are not available – the minimum is one month (Tsh60,000). It's signposted just off Kimweri Ave and is open 8 am to 9 pm weekdays (6 pm on Saturday) and 9 am to 5 pm on Sunday.

Shopping

Shopping Centres For upmarket, western mall-style shopping try Shopper's Plaza on Old Bagamoyo Rd; Oyster Bay Shopping Centre at Oyster Bay Hotel on Toure Drive; The Arcade on Old Bagamoyo Rd; or the Msasani Slipway on the west side of the Msasani peninsula. All these places cater to Dar's large expat population; you may have trouble remembering you are in Tanzania.

Crafts & Souvenirs There are numerous curio shops scattered throughout central Dar selling woodcarvings, batiks and other crafts. Galleries selling more expensive works include Gallery Acacia at Oyster Bay Shopping Centre and the small shop at the airport in the far corner of the international departures lounge.

For Tingatinga motifs, try the *Tingatinga Centre* (☎ 668075) at Morogoro Stores on Haile Selassie Rd. It's open daily from 7 am to 6 pm and you can watch the artists at work. There are also some Tingatinga artists at the Msasani Slipway, in the area between the shops and the boatyard.

Nyumba ya Sanaa (*House of Art*) (☎ 133960) is a conglomeration of nonprofit artists' cooperatives aimed at supporting young talent. You can watch local artists at work here and buy crafts from all over Tanzania. It's next to the Sheraton at the junction of Ohio St, Ali Hassan Mwinyi Rd and Bibi Titi Mohamed Rd. Operating hours are from 8 am to 5 pm weekdays and 10 am to 4 pm on weekends.

For woodcarvings, one of the best places is *Mwenge*, a Makonde carving community. It's a few kilometres past the Village Museum off the Bagamoyo road and is a good place to pick up Makonde carvings at very reasonable prices. To get there, take the Mwenge dalla-dalla from the New Posta transport stand.

Getting There & Away

Air Dar es Salaam is the major international arrival point for flights from overseas and the main hub for domestic service. See the Getting There & Away and the Getting Around chapters for details of international and domestic flights – except those connecting Unguja with Dar, which can be found in the The Zanzibar Archipelago chapter.

The Dar es Salaam airport has two terminals. Most regularly scheduled domestic flights and all international flights depart from Terminal Two (new terminal), while all flights on small planes and all air charters depart from Terminal One (old terminal) about 700m down the road past Terminal Two. Verify your departure terminal when purchasing your ticket.

Airlines with offices in Dar es Salaam include the following:

Aeroflot
 (☎ 113332) Samora Ave, near Ohio St
Air France
 (☎ 116443) corner of Ali Hassan Mwinyi Rd and Bibi Titi Mohamed Rd, near Citibank
Air India
 (☎ 152642) corner of Ali Hassan Mwinyi Rd and Bibi Titi Mohamed Rd
Air Tanzania
 (☎ 110273, 110245) ATC Bldg, Ohio St and Garden Ave
Alliance Air
 (also handling South African Airways)
 (☎ 117044) Raha Towers, on the corner of Bibi Titi Mohamed Rd and Upanga St

American Airlines & Jet Air
  (☎ 138798) Upanga Rd next to Citibank
British Airways
  (☎ 113820) at the Sheraton Hotel on Ohio St
Dar Aviation
  (☎ 844158, 844168) Terminal One at the airport
Ethiopian Airlines
  (☎ 117063) corner of Ohio St and Upanga Rd
Gulf Air
  (☎ 137856) Raha Towers, on the corner of Bibi
  Titi Mohamed Upanga Rds
Kenya Airways
  (☎ 119376) in the same building as KLM
KLM
  (☎ 113336) Upanga Rd near Citibank
Precision Air
  (☎ 113036, 130800) Ohio St opposite Air
  Tanzania
Swissair
  (☎ 118870) Luther House, Sokoine Drive

Bus There's no central bus station in Dar es Salaam; buses to various parts of the country leave from different bus stands as follows:

Msimbazi St Bus Stand
  (between Kariakoo market and Msimbazi St)
  Buses for Bagamoyo, Morogoro, Dodoma,
  Singida, Shinyanga, Mwanza
Mnazi Mmoja Bus Stand
  (on Bibi Titi Mohamed Rd near Uhuru and
  Lindi Sts, along the south-east side of Mnazi
  Mmoja Park) Buses for Tanga, Lushoto,
  Mombasa (Kenya), Iringa, Mbeya, Songea,
  Lake Nyasa, Malawi, Zambia and South Africa
Kisutu Bus Stand
  (near Morogoro Rd and Libya St) Buses for
  Moshi, Arusha, Nairobi (Kenya), Uganda,
  Lindi and Mtwara
Temeke Bus Stand
  (about 5km south-west of the centre, just off
  Nelson Mandela Rd) Minibuses to Kilwa
  Masoko and Mloka (for Selous Game Reserve)

See individual town entries for details of fares and journey times. For information about direct buses between Dar es Salaam and destinations in Kenya, Uganda, Zambia, Malawi and South Africa, see the individual country headings in the Getting There & Away chapter.

Train For information about the TAZARA line between Dar es Salaam and New Kapiri Mposhi in Zambia, see the Getting There &

Away chapter. Alternatively, for details of Central Line trains between Dar es Salaam and Kigoma or Mwanza, see the Getting Around chapter.

The TAZARA train station in Dar (☎ 860344) is located several kilometres from the centre at the corner of Nyerere and Nelson Mandela Rds. The Tanzanian Railways Corporation (Central Line) office (☎ 117833) is not far from the port at the corner of Railway St and Sokoine Drive.

Boat Dar is connected with Unguja, Tanga, Mombasa (Kenya), Mafia island and Mtwara by boat. For details of boat connections between Dar and Unguja (including Pemba), see the Getting There & Away section in The Zanzibar Archipelago chapter. Booking offices for all ferries are on the seafront opposite St Joseph's cathedral unless otherwise noted. Contact numbers include the following:

Azam Marine (☎ 134012, 123324)
Canadian Spirit (c/o Adecon Marine, ☎ 120856)
Flying Horse (☎ 124507) 200m beyond (south-
  east) of the main row of ferry offices
Maendeleo (☎ 115176) in a container behind the
  Flying Horse office
Mega-Speed Liners (☎ 110807 or 0811-326414)
Sea Express (☎ 114026)

Mega-Speed has a weekly service on the MS *Sepideh* between Dar, Tanga and Mombasa via Unguja and Pemba islands. Departures from Dar are at 8 am on Saturday, arriving in Tanga at 2.45 pm and in Mombasa about 5.45 pm. Going in the other direction, the boat departs on Sunday at 8 am from Mombasa and at 10.45 am from Tanga, reaching Dar about 5.45 pm. Fares are US$45/65 1st/2nd class between Dar and Tanga, and US$75/90 between Dar and Mombasa, including the US$5 port tax.

The *Canadian Spirit* and the MV *Maendeleo* connect Dar es Salaam with Mtwara. The *Canadian Spirit* usually also stops at Mafia Island en route to and from Dar. See the Mtwara Getting There & Away section in the South-Eastern Tanzania chapter for further details.

Getting Around

To/From the Airport Dar es Salaam airport is about 15km from the city centre. Dalla-dallas (marked U/Ndege) go there from the New Posta transport stand and from Kariakoo (Tsh150); in heavy traffic it can take over an hour from either point.

Taxis to or from the airport cost Tsh5000 (more at night), although first quotes and citations of the 'official price' are often as high as Tsh10,000.

From the airport to town there is a 'shuttle' which meets most daytime arrivals, and will drop you at most hotels (Tsh1000). Check first to be sure the driver is going near your hotel.

Bus Local buses (dalla-dallas) usually have their first and last stops indicated in the front window. Fares for all destinations are between Tsh100 and Tsh200. All buses are very crowded and difficult to board with a large rucksack or luggage. The main terminals are:

New Posta Transport Stand
In front of the main post office on Maktaba St
Old Posta Transport Stand
On Sokoine Drive opposite the Lutheran church
Stesheni Transport Stand
Near the clock tower

Dalla-dallas to the Temeke bus stand (Tsh150) leave from near the Central Line railway station; ask for *Temeke Mwisho*. For the TAZARA train station, take any dalla-dalla from either the New Posta or Old Posta transport stands heading to Vigunguti, U/Ndege (the airport) or Buguruni.

Car & Motorcycle Most of the car rental agencies listed in the main Getting Around chapter have packages for self-drive rentals within Dar. Avis also offers a special business drive package; a car with driver for 10 hours per day costs US$65 including fuel, insurance and 100 free kilometres.

Taxi Taxis have no meters and charge a standard TSh1000 per journey inside the city centre. Slightly outside this area, they'll charge TSh1500, and to Oyster Bay between TSh2000 and TSh2500. To the TAZARA railway station, a taxi will cost between TSh2000 and Tsh3000.

Good places to find taxis in town include Kivukoni Front near Mirambo St and around the Askari Monument. On Msasani peninsula the best place is the intersection of Msasani and Haile Selassie Rds.

Bicycle Dar's roads are too heavily travelled and too narrow to make cycling safe or enjoyable. If you have come on a bicycle and need parts, you can try some of the shopping malls to see if any bike shops have opened. While there are many bike shops downtown on or near Samora Ave, few sell components for western-made bikes.

Around Dar es Salaam

PUGU HILLS

The Pugu Hills area, about 40km south-west of Dar near Kisarawe, has some attractive forests which host a variety of animal and bird life including leopard, bush babies, civets, and crowned eagles. It makes a pleasant day-excursion from Dar for those with their own vehicles; there is also a resthouse. Part of the area has been gazetted as a forest reserve, and efforts at reforestation and enhanced environmental protection are under way. For further information contact the Wildlife Conservation Society of Tanzania.

OFFSHORE ISLANDS

The islands of Bongoyo, Mbudya, Pangavini and Fungu Yasini off the coast of Dar were gazetted in 1975 as part of the Dar es Salaam Marine Reserve System. Although there is a high diversity of fish in the islands' waters, many of the surrounding coral reefs have been damaged by dynamite fishing and the commercial removal of coral. Despite this damage the islands and surrounding reefs are popular diving and snorkelling sites, particularly Bongoyo and Mbudya islands. See the Diving section earlier in this

The Zaramo

The Zaramo, a Bantu-speaking people who live in the area around Dar es Salaam between Bagamoyo to the north and Kisarawe to the south-west, are the area's original inhabitants and still comprise one of its largest population groups. Most Zaramo are subsistence farmers; they are also skilled woodcarvers and make many of the musical instruments and other carved objects found at craft shops in Dar es Salaam.

Thanks to their coastal location, the Zaramo have been influenced by centuries of contact with the outside world, and today their culture incorporates elements from diverse backgrounds. Among the most obvious of these influences has been Islam, to which the majority of modern-day Zaramo adhere. Another is Swahili which is now spoken by most Zaramo as a mother tongue, although their indigenous language (Ki)Zaramo is still used in rural areas, among older generations, and in certain traditional ceremonies and rituals.

Despite these outside influences and increasing urbanisation, the Zaramo have succeeded in maintaining many of their traditions. Among the most fascinating are their beliefs associated with creation. According to these beliefs, all Zaramo trace their origins back to *Nyalutanga*, the common mother from whom comes all life and knowledge. Nyalutanga had no creator and no husband but rather emerged from the earth (which is seen as a female element) and brought forth a line of daughters, from whom all Zaramo are descended. The Zaramo's present-day matrilineal clan structure is a direct outgrowth of this perception of the female as the creative power. However, in contrast to many other matrilineal societies in which men are regarded merely as a labour force or as begetters of children, Zaramo society also incorporates a strong bilinear element. Zaramo men play an essential role as nourishers of female creative power and as the source of the cultural qualities which complement women's biological contribution. Thus, while family lines are continued through the mother, Zaramo children take the name of their father's mother's clan and are considered to inherit the cultural qualities of their father.

Also interesting are Zaramo beliefs relating to life and death. The Zaramo believe that all life arises from death. Death is seen as part of the natural continuum of life, as a transition rather than a transformation. The rituals that mark this transition extend into many areas. For example, Zaramo traditional healers often place newly procured medicinal plants on compost heaps for a few days, in order that they gain potency. As the plants wither they take on new power, and a place connected with death and decay (the compost heap) assumes the symbolism of a place of regeneration.

A good source of more detailed information on the Zaramo people of the greater Dar es Salaam area is *Blood, Milk and Death: Body Symbols and the Power of Regeneration Among the Zaramo of Tanzania* by Marja-Liisa Swantz with Salome Mjema and Zenya Wild, from which most of this section was extracted.

---

chapter and The Northern Beaches section, following, for the names of dive companies which organise excursions.

Bongoyo Island

Bongoyo Island Marine Reserve, located about 7km north of Dar es Salaam, has a nice beach, some short walking trails, and makes a pleasant day excursion. You can arrange a seafood meal with locals on the beach but you'll need to bring your own drinks. There is a boat to the island from the Msasani Slipway departing daily at 9.30 and 11.30 am and 1.30 and 3.30 pm, returning at 10.30 am and 12.30, 2.30 and 5 pm (Tsh5000 round-trip); swimming here is not tide dependent like it is on the mainland beaches.

Mbudya Island

Mbudya island, about 4km north of Bongoyo, is best reached from the beaches north of Dar es Salaam. There is good swimming and snorkelling here. You will have to bring whatever food and drink you need. White Sands Hotel, Silver Sands Hotel or Jangwani Sea Breeze Lodge (see The Northern Beaches, below) can assist with arranging boat rentals and excursions.

THE NORTHERN BEACHES

The beaches about 25km north of Dar es Salaam and east of the Bagamoyo road are lined with resorts and are popular weekend getaways for Dar's resident foreigners.

Ruins

In between The Haven at Kunduchi and Silver Sands Hotel, about 1km from the now-closed Kunduchi Beach Hotel are the **Kunduchi ruins**. They include the remnants of a mosque dating from the late 15th century as well as Arabic graves from the 18th or 19th century. It is not considered safe to walk to the ruins; numerous muggings have been reported.

Several kilometres north of the beach hotel turn-offs, and about 5km off the road to Bagamoyo down a sandy path at **Mbweni**, are said to be more ruins of an old Arabic cemetery. Mbweni is signposted from the main road.

Diving & Snorkelling

The dive centres at the northern beach hotels primarily organise trips to Dar es Salaam's offshore islands, though most can also arrange excursions further afield including to Mafia island. All have diving and snorkelling equipment for hire. While prices may vary slightly among the different dive centres, expect to pay approximately US$35 for a single dive (less with your own equipment), US$50 to US$60 for a double dive, US$230 to US$250 for a 10 dive package,

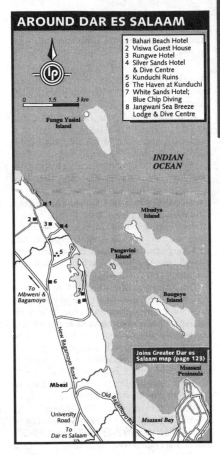

AROUND DAR ES SALAAM

1 Bahari Beach Hotel
2 Visiwa Guest House
3 Rungwe Hotel
4 Silver Sands Hotel & Dive Centre
5 Kunduchi Ruins
6 The Haven at Kunduchi
7 White Sands Hotel; Blue Chip Diving
8 Jangwani Sea Breeze Lodge & Dive Centre

and US$300 to US$350 for a four day certification course.

Blue Chip Diving
(☎ 0811-325483 or 0812-784408, PO Box 32185 Dar es Salaam) at White Sands Hotel
Sea Breeze Dive Centre
(☎ 0812-783241, fax 0811-320714, PO Box 934 Dar es Salaam) at Jangwani Sea Breeze Lodge – same management as Silver Sands Dive Centre
Silver Sands Dive Centre
(☎ 650567, fax 0811-320545, PO Box 9314 Dar es Salaam) at Silver Sands Hotel

Places to Stay

Camping There is camping at Silver Sands Hotel and at Rungwe Hotel. See below for details.

Hotels Lodging is listed from south to north. All prices include breakfast unless otherwise noted.

Jangwani Sea Breeze Lodge (☎ 647215 or 0811-325908, fax 0811-320714) is a pleasant place with singles/doubles from US$88/108 plus 20% tax. There is a dive centre here and they can arrange charters to offshore islands, including Mafia island.

Just next door is *White Sands Hotel* (☎ 116483, fax 118483, email wsandshtl @intafrica.com), also with a dive centre. Rooms cost US$118/174; special weekend rates are also available. Both White Sands and Jangwani Sea Breeze Lodge are signposted on the same turn-off from the Bagamoyo road.

The Haven at Kunduchi (☎ 650276 or 0812-786165) is a small lodge modelled after an English country house. It's a bit inland so those who want to swim must use the hotel's private beach at Bahari, a few kilometres up the road; transport is provided. Rooms cost US$130/150. The hotel is signposted from the Bagamoyo road shortly after the turn-off for Jangwani Sea Breeze Lodge and White Sands Hotel.

About 3km north of The Haven is the South African-run *Silver Sands Hotel* (☎ 650231 or 0812-781602, fax 650428, email silversands@africaonline.com.tz) a popular place with budget travellers. Camping costs US$3 per night; you must have your own tent. There are also rooms with fan for US$31/48 (US$35/54 with aircon) and suites for US$34/86. Children with their parents stay free. The daily buffet dinner costs Tsh4000. The owners are actively involved in protecting the offshore reefs. There is also a dive centre here, as well as a Marine Action Conservation Tanzania office which sponsors events aimed at teaching local children about the environment and promoting the appreciation of marine life.

A bit further up the coast road is the dilapidated *Rungwe Hotel* (☎ 650295), with camping for Tsh1000 per person and accommodation in basic bungalows for Tsh10,000 per bungalow.

The northernmost place is the *Bahari Beach Hotel* (☎ 650352, fax 650351), with rooms for US$90. Credit cards are not accepted. For diving you will have to go to Silver Sands Hotel.

In between Bahari Beach Hotel and Rungwe Hotel is the very basic *Visiwa Guest House* with rooms for Tsh2000 (Tsh3000 with bathroom). This place is not recommended unless you're on a strict budget and don't want to camp. There is no food; you will have to bring some supplies or try to arrange something with locals.

Getting There & Away

If you don't have your own vehicle the best way to get to the northern beaches is via the shuttle bus which runs three times a day between the New Africa Hotel in Dar and the Silver Sands and Bahari Beach hotels. Departures from the New Africa are at 9 am, 2 pm and 5 pm. The trip takes about an hour and costs Tsh2000 one way. If you are driving, just follow the Bagamoyo road north. All the hotels are signposted to the right, beginning about 25km north of central Dar.

Dalla-dallas go throughout the day from Dar towards Bagamoyo. However, if you take these you will have to walk between 2 and 4km as most of the hotels are set well east of the main road.

Taxis from Dar to the northern beaches cost about Tsh10,000.

THE SOUTHERN BEACHES

The coastline south of Dar es Salaam is attractive but for the most part undeveloped and difficult to access. For this reason it makes a pleasant alternative to the more crowded northern beaches. There are two resorts. *Ras Kutani*, about 30km south of Dar, has cottage-style luxury accommodation for US$140 per person, full board, plus 20% VAT. Windsurfing, snorkelling and sailing can be arranged. Book through Selous Safari Co (☎ 051-34802, fax 112794, email selous@twiga.com, PO Box 1192 Dar es Salaam). Most guests fly in via charter aircraft (approximately US$150 plus tax one way from Dar for a three-seater plane). You can also reach the resort by 4WD via Mijimwema and Mbwamaji; the road is in rough condition.

The newer Amani Beach Club (☎ 051-600020, 601721, fax 602131, email abc@wilken-dsm.com, PO Box 1547) also around 30km south of Dar es Salaam, has accommodation in 10 luxury cottages overlooking the ocean for US$290 per person including full board. Access is via charter plane or 4WD. Diving and game fishing excursions can be arranged.

The Zanzibar Archipelago

The lure of the 'spice islands' is legendary. From exotic Stone Town with its fascinating labyrinth of narrow streets, to palm fringed beaches and pristine coral reefs, the archipelago is a complete change of pace from the mainland with which it is linked as part of the United Republic of Tanzania.

While Unguja (also called Zanzibar island) gets most of the attention, the archipelago is also made up of Pemba to the north, plus numerous smaller islands and islets offshore. Each of the main islands has its own distinct character. Unguja's main attraction is Stone Town, with its whitewashed, coral-rag houses, quaint shops, bazaars, mosques, courtyards and squares. Another draw is its spectacular turquoise sea, abounding in marine life and beautiful coral formations and edged by fine, white sand beaches. Although many places have become very developed, there are still some quiet and unspoiled spots left.

Pemba, in contrast, is seldom visited and one of the most laid-back places you will find in East Africa. In addition to its attractive, hilly terrain, the island offers some beautiful beaches and offshore islands, a fascinating, largely undiscovered culture, and some of the best diving in the world.

HISTORY

The Zanzibar archipelago is believed to have been inhabited for well over 2000 years. Its earliest residents were most likely Bantu-speaking peoples who made their way over from the mainland. The islands had also been visited at a very early date by traders and sailors from Arabia; there is evidence of Arabic trade relationships with various portions of the East African coast, possibly also including Zanzibar, as early as 700 BC. The *Periplus of the Erythraean Sea*, a travel guide for sailors written about 60 AD by a Greek merchant, documents that Arabic trading settlements along the coast were already well established by the 1st century,

Highlights

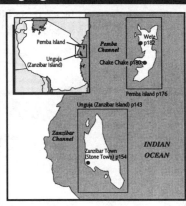

Wete p182
Pemba Channel
Pemba Island
Chake Chake p180
Unguja (Zanzibar Island)
Pemba Island p176
Unguja (Zanzibar Island) p143
Zanzibar Channel
INDIAN OCEAN
Zanzibar Town (Stone Town) p154

- **Stone Town** – ancient rhythms, exotic atmosphere and fascinating architecture
- **Coastal Life** – enticing beaches, rich marine life and superb diving and snorkelling
- **Pemba Island** – discovering the unknown corners and culture of this unique island
- **Experiencing Zanzibar** – enjoying a *taarab* concert or one of the archipelago's colourful festivals

and makes reference to the island of Menouthias, which many historians believe to be Unguja. Whether these trade settlements were permanent is not clear, nor is there much information about the next few centuries other than that trade between Arabia and East Africa was ongoing. Shirazi traders from Persia also began to make their way to East Africa and by the 10th century or earlier had established settlements at several places in the region, including Pemba and perhaps also Unguja, near Unguja Ukuu.

UNGUJA (ZANZIBAR ISLAND)

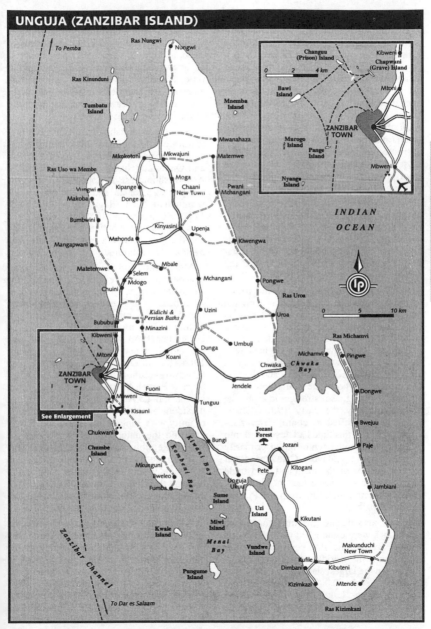

Over the next several centuries, trade with Arabia and the Persian Gulf grew and flourished, reaching its pinnacle between the 12th and 15th centuries. Zanzibar became a powerful city-state with trade links as far away as India and Asia, supplying these places with slaves, gold, ivory and wood. In exchange, the eastern traders imported spices, glass, textiles and many other items. With the trade from the east also came Islam, and the Arabic architecture that still characterises Zanzibar today. One of the most well known archaeological remnants from this era is the mosque at Kizimkazi, which dates from the early 12th century.

While trade westwards with the mainland during this period paled in comparison with eastward activity, links did exist and intermarriages with Bantu peoples on the islands as well as on the mainland laid the foundation for today's ethnic milieu on the archipelago.

In the early 16th century, with the arrival of the Portuguese, this golden age on the archipelago came to an end as first Unguja and then Pemba fell under Portuguese control. The era of Portuguese dominance did not last long, however. It was challenged first by the British who were using Unguja as a way station en route to India, and then by Omani Arabs who in the mid-16th century attacked Portuguese strongholds on the archipelago. By the early 19th century, Oman had solidified its control over Zanzibar, which by this time had developed into a major commercial centre based primarily on trade in slaves and ivory. Caravans set out for the interior of the mainland, and trade reached such a pinnacle that the Sultan of Oman relocated his court from the Persian Gulf to Zanzibar.

It was also during this time that clove plantations were established on Unguja and Pemba. By the mid-19th century, Zanzibar had become the world's largest producer of cloves and the largest slaving entrepôt along the coast. Nearly 50,000 slaves, drawn from as far away as Lake Tanganyika, passed through its market every year. Many were used as labour on the plantations. Others

were shipped to places like Réunion, Mauritius and the Dutch East Indies. The advent of steamships gave an additional impetus to trade, and cloves were soon being exported as far away as India and Europe. During this time, Zanzibar also became an important gateway for European missionaries to the mainland, many drawn to Zanzibar by stories of the horrors of the slave trade.

With the establishment of European protectorates in the late 18th century, the situation began to change. In 1798, Britain and Oman concluded a commercial treaty. As British interests in Zanzibar grew, so too did pressure for an end to the slave trade which had been illegal in Britain since 1772. Beginning in 1845, the slave trade was limited to that between the archipelago and the mainland, and from 1873, all trade by sea was prohibited.

Meanwhile, Omani rule over Zanzibar was beginning to weaken and, in 1862, the sultanate was formally partitioned. Zanzibar became independent from Oman with Omani sultans ruling under a British protectorate. This arrangement lasted until 10 December 1963 when independence was granted. Just one month later, in January 1964, the sultans were overthrown in a bloody revolution instigated by the Afro-Shirazi Party (ASP), which then assumed power. On 12 April 1964, Abeid Karume, president of the ASP, signed a declaration of unity with Tanganyika (mainland Tanzania) and the union became known as the United Republic of Tanzania. In 1977, the ASP merged with the Tanzanian African National Union (TANU) on the mainland to become the Chama Cha Mapinduzi (CCM, or Party of the Revolution), which still officially holds the majority today.

Following Karume's assassination in 1972, Aboud Jumbe assumed the presidency of Zanzibar (and a vice-presidency of the Tanzania Union) until resigning in 1984 in the face of growing discontent over union with the mainland. Ali Hassan Mwinyi succeeded Jumbe and ruled until becoming president of Tanzania in 1985. Mwinyi was followed by Abdul Wakil, whose unpopular

ar es Salaam **Top to Bottom Right:** This Azania-front Lutheran church was built between 1898 d 1901 by German missionaries; kangas, colourful cloth garments worn by many Tanzanian omen; Dar is full of architectural reminders of the colonial era, such as this building on Samora Ave.

MARY FITZPATRICK

Beautiful Nungwi beach is an important dhow-building centre on Unguja.

CHRISTINE OSBORNE

Bikes are a common method of transport for many Tanzanians, such as this man on Unguja.

term ended in 1990, when Salmin Amour, the current president, was elected.

Since the 1995 elections, friction between the CCM and the opposition CUF (Civic United Front), and between the isles and the mainland, has been ongoing. Residents of Pemba, from where the CUF draws its primary support, remain bitter. Ethnic cleansing carried out in the wake of the elections removed most Pembans from Unguja and exacerbated Pemba's marginalisation. Since then, discontent and calls for Amour's removal have increased. The general disregard displayed by the Unguja government towards the mainland has further clouded the atmosphere. While most observers do not believe the situation will deteriorate into outright violence, secessionist sentiment is strong and the union is fragile enough that its durability is being questioned. No matter how the assessment is drawn, lasting stability will only be achieved if some of these outstanding issues are resolved.

GEOGRAPHY & GEOLOGY

Both Unguja and Pemba are coral islands. Unguja, which lies about 40km offshore from the mainland north-west of Bagamoyo, measures about 110km in length and about 40km at its widest point. It is predominantly flat, with some low ridges in the west and centre. The highest point on the island is 117m. Pemba, which lies about 50km east of the mainland and about 50km north of Unguja, measures about 67km long and 22km wide. It is hillier and more fertile than Unguja, particularly on its western shore, where there are numerous small, steep hills separated by deep valleys. Much of the island is now used for small-scale agriculture, with crops including cassava rice, mangoes, bananas and papaya. Pemba's highest point is 93m; the eastern side of the island is flatter and more arid. In contrast to Unguja, Pemba has an irregular coastline with many deep inlets. While Unguja is connected to the mainland by a shallow, submerged shelf, Pemba is actually separated by a channel exceeding 1000m in depth.

CLIMATE

As on the mainland, the long rains are between March and May, and the short rains between October and December. Rainfall averages 1500mm on Unguja and about 1800mm on Pemba. Short rain showers are also common during the dry seasons on both islands, especially on their western sides.

Temperatures on the archipelago are fairly constant year-round, averaging between 24 and 29°C, though they are considerably moderated by sea breezes. See Climate in the Facts about Tanzania chapter for a climate chart of Zanzibar.

ECOLOGY & ENVIRONMENT

Both Unguja and Pemba were originally covered by tropical high forest, except in the shallow-soiled coral rag areas where low scrub grew. Today, about 95% of the original forest cover on the archipelago is gone. The only areas remaining are the forests at Jozani on Unguja, and Ngezi and Msitu Mkuu on Pemba, all of which are protected reserves. There are also patches of primary forest on some of the islands offshore from Pemba. With the collapse of the clove market, many former plantation areas on Pemba are becoming dominated by secondary forest cover.

Both Unguja and Pemba host several rare or endemic species, notably the red colobus monkey on Unguja and the Pemba flying fox bat on Pemba.

Those interested in learning about Zanzibar's marine environment can read the *Marine Green Book* by Antje Förstle & Rainer Vierkötter, a small pocket encyclopedia of marine life and activities on the Zanzibar archipelago. A more detailed work is *A Guide to the Seashores of Eastern Africa*, edited by Matthew D Richmond.

Both are available in bookshops in Zanzibar Town. The University of Dar es Salaam's Institute of Marine Sciences on the waterfront is a useful stop for those wanting to do research on the archipelago.

GOVERNMENT & POLITICS

Zanzibar shares foreign and monetary policy, postal and telecommunications systems, and defence policy with the mainland. Education, infrastructure and numerous other areas are the responsibility of the local government, although distinctions between the two spheres are often blurred.

The two major parties are the ruling CCM and the opposition CUF, with the CUF drawing much of its support from Pemba. There is considerable friction between the two parties, with tensions peaking following the 1995 elections.

POPULATION & PEOPLE

The three indigenous ethnic groups on the islands are the Hadimu, the Tumbatu and the Pemba. The Hadimu are of mixed origin, stemming from different parts of the mainland, although all originally professed loyalty to a single chief, known as the *Mwinyi Mkuu*. The Tumbatu live primarily on Tumbatu island and in the northern part of Unguja, while the Pemba are on the island of Pemba. Members of the non-African population are primarily Shirazi and consider themselves descendants of immigrants from Shiraz in Persia (Iran), although many show evidence of mixed descent.

The archipelago's population is estimated at just over 813,000, with about a third of this number on Pemba.

SOCIETY & CONDUCT

Zanzibar is a conservative, Muslim society. You will gain more respect and have fewer hassles if you respect local customs. Dressing modestly is important; many Zanzibaris take offence at scantily-clad westerners. For women, this means no sleeveless tops, and preferably slacks, skirts or at least knee-length shorts. For men, it means shirts and slacks or knee-length shorts. During Ramadan you can respect local sensibilities by not eating or drinking in the street.

RELIGION

Most Zanzibaris are Sunni Muslims. Zanzibaris claiming direct descent from Omanis follow Ibadhism. Christians comprise barely 1% of the population. There is also a small Hindu community.

VISAS & DOCUMENTS

You must have a valid Tanzanian visa to visit the archipelago. If you are coming from the mainland, you will need to take care of immigration formalities again when you arrive in Zanzibar. It's no cause to take offence – Zanzibar is proud of its semi-autonomous status and guards it jealously. Length of stay is determined on arrival; tourists are generally given one month.

In addition to a visa, you will also be required to show proof of yellow fever vaccination.

PUBLIC HOLIDAYS & SPECIAL EVENTS

For a listing of public holidays see the Holidays & Special Events section in the Facts for the Visitor chapter. Muslim holidays are celebrated in a big way on Unguja and can be an interesting time to be on the island, although many restaurants may be closed during the day. See Islam under Religion in the Facts about Tanzania chapter for more information about Muslim holidays. Other festivals include the Zanzibar Cultural Festival (held annually in mid-July), the Zanzibar International Film Festival (held annually in July, since 1998), and Mwaka Kogwa (marking the Shirazi New Year or *Nairuzim*). For information about the cultural festival, check with the Zanzibar Cultural Centre at the Old Fort. For scheduling and other information about the film festival, contact the organisers via email (ziff@zanzibar.org) or check their Web site, www.zanzibar.org/ziff. Mwaka Kogwa is held in late July, though the exact date varies. It will be on or about 24 July from 2000 to 2003. The best place to watch it is Makunduchi in the south-easternmost corner of Unguja.

ACTIVITIES
Diving & Snorkelling

The waters of the archipelago offer some excellent diving and snorkelling, with dive sites for all levels of ability. Pemba, in particular, is considered to have some of the best and most varied dive sites in the world although most are accessible only via charter trips. In addition to steep wall dives, drift dives and world-class coral formations, one of the highlights of diving near Pemba are large schools of hammerhead sharks, manta rays and big fish. Pemba's east coast tends to be better for big fish, while coral formations tend to be better to the west. Visibility at some locations around Pemba can exceed well over 25m at certain times of year.

In general, diving sites near Zanzibar Town and at Nungwi (at the northern tip of Unguja) are considered ideal for all beginner and intermediate divers, although there are some challenging advanced dives further off-shore near Leven Bank. The best sites are considered to be near Nungwi in the north, and off the east coast, especially near Mnemba island. Most dives off Pemba are for experienced divers, though there are also protected anchorages and snorkelling opportunities for novices, and some of the dive outfits may be able to provide instruction.

The *Zanzibar at Sea* map put out by MaCo (1996) and on sale at shops around Zanzibar Town provides a good overview of diving and snorkelling sites around Unguja. Dive operators can give you more specific information.

Some of the major dive companies based on Unguja are listed below. Except at Cat-Diving (see details following), prices for standard (noncustomised) packages off Unguja average US$35 for a single dive to about US$230 for a 10 dive package, including equipment. Night dives cost about US$45. Four-day certification courses cost about US$300. Most places give a discount of approximately 10% if you have your own equipment. Most also offer snorkelling trips and can arrange other water sports including water-skiing, wake boards and knee boards.

Cat-Diving Ltd
(☎ 0812-781376 or 054-31040, in Germany 49-5130-790326, email a.martinkat@t-online.de, PO Box 3203 Zanzibar). A quality outfitter, and the only operation specialising in Pemba. Trips are customised, and based aboard a 24m catamaran. Three-day all-inclusive packages off Pemba cost around US$490 per person (US$980 for a seven day trip). There's also a 10 day standard package for US$1400 which

circles the island, encompassing a full range of dive sites. Groups of between four and 10 people can be accommodated.

Dive Africa Water Sports/Indian Ocean
(☎ 0811-323096, 338351, fax 054-30267, email zanzibar@diveafrica.com, PO Box 2370). In Zanzibar Town on Mizingani Rd; other branches at Paradise Beach Club in Nungwi (☎ 0811-326574, 338351) and at Ras Nungwi Beach Hotel (☎ 33767, fax 33098, email rasnungwi@zanzibar.net, for hotel guests only); payments via credit card or travellers cheque incur an additional 5% charge.

Pre-Dive Safety Guidelines

Before embarking on a scuba diving, skin diving or snorkelling trip, careful consideration should be given to a safe as well as an enjoyable experience. You should:

- Possess a current diving certification card from a recognised scuba diving instructional agency (if scuba diving).

- Be sure you are healthy and feel comfortable diving.

- Obtain reliable information about physical and environmental conditions at the dive site (eg from a reputable local dive operation).

- Be aware of local laws, regulations, and etiquette about marine life and the environment.

- Dive at sites within your experience level; if available, engage the services of a competent, professionally trained dive instructor or dive master.

- Be aware that underwater conditions vary significantly from one region, or even site, to another. Seasonal changes can significantly alter any site and dive conditions. These differences influence the way divers dress for a dive and what diving techniques they use.

- Ask about the environmental characteristics that can affect your diving and how local, trained divers deal with these considerations.

East African Diving & Water Sports
(☎/fax 0811-337453, 327747, email cadc @sbc.zenj.glcom.com, PO Box 2750). Based at Amaan Bungalows in Nungwi; also at Amaan Annex at Kendwa (☎ 0811-335090); in addition to dives off Unguja also runs charters to Pemba.

One Ocean/The Zanzibar Dive Centre
(☎ 0811-328206, ☎/fax 0811-323091, PO Box 608 Zanzibar). Located under Africa House on the sea in Zanzibar Town.

Scuba Diving Adventure Afloat
(☎ 0811-336454, fax 054-33080, email mcc @cctz.com, PO Box 3419). Located at Mtoni Marine Centre (2km outside of Zanzibar Town); a good outfit, somewhat less expensive than the other places.

Zanzibar Dive Adventures
(☎/fax 32503, PO Box 2282). Based at Matemwe Bungalows (see Matemwe under Beaches later in this chapter).

In addition to the above listings, diving on Pemba can also be arranged through Manta Reef Lodge in the far north of Pemba on Kigomasha peninsula. See Kigomasha Peninsula in the Pemba section later in this chapter for more information. Kiweni Marine Resort off Pemba's south-east coast is also due to start its dive operations soon. See Kiweni Island in the Pemba section later in this chapter.

Fishing
There is good deep sea and game fishing off Zanzibar, especially in the Pemba channel. The *Zanzibar at Sea* map (see Diving & Snorkelling earlier in this section) provides an overview of sites. Some of the dive centres listed earlier, notably East African Diving & Water Sports, also arrange charter fishing excursions. Otherwise, try contacting Mtoni Marine Centre; see Places to Stay, Outside Zanzibar Town, in the Unguja (Zanzibar Island) section. Prices average about US$25 per person per hour with a minimum of two people.

LANGUAGE COURSES
The Institute of Swahili and Foreign Languages (see Courses in Facts for the Visitor) is on Vuga Rd. Rates are US$4 per hour or US$80 per week; books cost an extra US$4.

Unguja (Zanzibar Island)

ORIENTATION
Zanzibar Town, on the western side of the island, is the main settlement and the first stop for most travellers. The most well known section is the old Stone Town, surrounded on three sides by the sea. Directly east of Stone Town is the much less picturesque, but bustling and growing section of Ng'ambo. To the north of Zanzibar Town are some beaches, though once you get past Bububu most towns do not have tourist accommodation. At the northern tip of Unguja is Nungwi, until recently a quiet fishing village and dhow building centre, now a major tourist destination. Unguja's best beaches stretch along its eastern side, including at Matemwe, Uroa, Bwejuu, Paje and Jambiani. The main village in the far south-east is Makunduchi, and in the south-west it is Kizimkazi, known for its dolphins.

Maps
Dated but detailed topographical maps of Unguja (five-sheet series, 1:50,000, Tsh1000 per sheet) and Zanzibar Town (two sheet series, 1:5000, Tsh2000 per sheet) are available from the Commission for Lands & Environment (commonly referred to as the 'Planning Office') near the People's Bank of Zanzibar.

The best commercially available map is that put out by MaCo (1996, Tsh3000). On one side is a detailed map of Stone Town and on the other, Unguja; it's on sale in many shops in Zanzibar Town.

The Zanzibar Tourist Corporation also puts out a decent map on sale at many shops around town for Tsh1500 to Tsh2000.

INFORMATION
Tourist Offices
The Zanzibar Tourist Corporation or ZTC (☎ 31341) is located at Livingstone House, north of town on the Bububu road. There's also a more convenient office on Creek Rd in Malindi. Its selection of tourist informa-

tion is sparse, although there is a helpful map of Stone Town (Tsh2000). It also handles reservations for the government-run guesthouses in Bwejuu and Jambiani.

The Zanzibar Commission for Tourism (☎ 33485, fax 33448, PO Box 1410) is the entity responsible for tourism development and planning. They are located in the Sebleni section of Mikunguni, east of town near Amani Stadium. Take the 'A' *dalla-dalla* and ask them to drop you in Sebleni.

Tourist Information

The free bimonthly *Recommended in Zanzibar* has updated information on cultural events, transport time tables, tide tables, etc. It's available at restaurants, hotels and shops around Zanzibar Town.

The Gallery (email gallery@swahilicoast .com, PO Box 3181) on Gizenga St offers a tourist information service where you can stop by daily except Sunday between 10 am and 12.30 pm. Travellers staying for an extended period can arrange post office box service with them as well.

Those with a serious interest in Zanzibari history and culture can contact John da Silva (☎ 32123), an artist and local historian who sometimes is available for tours in his spare time. Prices vary, but usually average about US$20 for two people and US$10 for each additional person; group size is limited.

Money

There are many foreign exchange bureaus where you can change cash and travellers cheques with a minimum of hassle. The National Bank of Commerce (NBC) near the tunnel at the end of Shangani St also changes travellers cheques.

Mtoni Marine is the agent for Visa and MasterCard. Their branch office next to the Zanzibar Serena Inn gives cash (Tanzanian shillings only) against these credit cards, as well as Eurocard, at a rate of US$1 to Tsh610 plus a Tsh4000 telex charge. There is a US$600 per day withdrawal limit.

The VAT tax had not yet been introduced on Zanzibar when this book was researched and there was still uncertainty as to if and

when it would be. Keep this in mind when calculating costs: if the VAT is introduced many of the prices quoted in this chapter may increase, though the overall increase should not be much more than 5% since the VAT would replace several existing sales taxes.

Officially, accommodation must be paid for in US dollars on Unguja. While this holds true in practice at most mid-range and top-end hotels, almost all of the budget accommodation options will accept payment in Tanzanian shillings, converted at the current rate of exchange.

Post

The main post office with poste restante is west of the centre near Amani Stadium. For posting letters, there is a more convenient branch on Kenyatta Rd in Shangani.

Telephone & Fax

Telephone calls can be made from the Shangani post office or from the card telephones outside. There are also many efficient private telecommunications offices around Zanzibar Town (see listings under Email & Internet Access, following).

Email & Internet Access

Email and internet access places are popping up all around Zanzibar Town. Most also offer general computer and telecommunications services in addition to email. Some convenient ones include:

Asko
    Shangani St next to the post office; Tsh1500/ 500 per page to send/receive email, open 8.30 am to 8.30 pm daily
Institute for Computer Technology
    Hurumzi St, Tsh1500/500 per page to send/ receive, open weekdays until 10 pm
Internet Zanzibar
    Just off Vuga Rd in the ZAMEDIC building; Tsh2000 per half hour; 8.30 am to 5.30 pm weekdays and 8 am to 1 pm Saturday

Travel Agencies

There are numerous travel agencies in Zanzibar Town which can help in arranging excursions on the island. They include the following:

Chemah Brothers' Tours & Safaris
(☎/fax 33385 or 0812-750158, email emah
@zanzinet.com) office on Kenyatta Rd near
the High Court

Eco Tours & Travel
(☎ 30514, fax 33476, PO Box 2731) office off
Vuga Rd

Madeira Tours & Safaris
(☎/fax 30406, email madeira@zanzinet.com,
PO Box 251) office opposite Baghani House
Hotel

Maha Travel & Tours Safaris
(☎ 30029, 31729, fax 30016, email mahatravel
@zanzinet.com, PO Box 1511) office on Vuga
Rd

Marlin Tours & Safaris
(☎/fax 32378, email marlin@zanzinet.com, PO
Box 3435) office in Shangani on Kenyatta Rd

Sama Tours
(☎ 33543, fax 33020, email step@www
.intafrica.com) office on Gizenga St

Shangani Tours & Travel
(☎ 31660, fax 33688, PO Box 4222) office at
Shangani Hotel on Kenyatta Rd

Tropical Tours
(☎/fax 30868 or 0811-339302, PO Box 325)
office on Kenyatta Rd opposite Mazson's
Hotel. A friendly and helpful place ideal for
budget travellers; also good for Pemba island.

Zan Tours
(☎ 33116, 33042 or 0811-335832, fax 33116)
office on Malawi Rd opposite Ciné Afrique;
focuses on upmarket, quality tours

Bookshops & Libraries

The best selection of books is at The Gallery
on Gizenga St, which has a wide selection of
books ranging from travel guides to historical books and more.

Masumo bookshop opposite Shamshu
Pharmacy near the market sells international magazines such as *Time* and *Newsweek*.

Historians or others interested in delving
deeper into Zanzibari history should stop by
the Archives just off the airport road in the
Kilimani section of town. It contains a
wealth of information, and staff are helpful.
To get here, turn left off the airport road at
the prison, then make an immediate right;
the Archives are up on the hill.

Photography

The Burhani chain plans to establish a branch
in Zanzibar Town on Gizenga St opposite
The Gallery in 1999. When it opens, this
would be the best place on the island for film
processing. Film is available in many shops
on Unguja though selection is often limited.

Medical Services

Dr Mario Mariani (☎ 33113 or 0812-
750040 for the 24-hour emergency line) at
the Zanzibar Medical & Diagnostic Centre
(ZAMEDIC) comes highly recommended.
His well-equipped office, including a small
laboratory, is just off Vuga Rd near the Air
Tanzania office.

Shamshu Pharmacy (☎/fax 32641) near
the market is well stocked.

Dangers & Annoyances

While Unguja remains a relatively safe
place, reports of robberies, muggings and
other security incidents are increasing, especially within Zanzibar Town and along
the beaches, and police follow-up is often
lackadaisical.

Follow the normal precautions: avoid isolated areas, especially isolated stretches of
beach, and keep your valuables out of view.
Women can minimise hassles and worse by
dressing appropriately. For all travellers, if
you go out at night in Zanzibar Town it's
best to take a taxi or walk in a group. As a
rule, it's best to leave your valuables in a
hotel safe, although it's not unheard of at
some of the less reputable hotels for things
from the safe to go missing as well. Should
your passport be stolen, get a written report
from the police. Upon presentation of this
report, immigration will issue you a travel
document which will get you back to the
mainland, and sometimes even further.

In Zanzibar Town, you will without doubt
come into contact with street touts (*papaasi*
in Swahili). These guides are not registered
with the ZTC; while some can be helpful,
others can be aggressive and irritating. There
are also a small number who are involved
with Unguja's increasing drug trade; arranging a tour with them is not recommended. A
polite but firm approach usually works best
if you're being hassled. One thing to remember when you're trying to decide

whether to use the services of the papaasi is that you have a better chance of getting a discount on your hotel room if you arrive alone (ie, without papaasi), since the hotel can then give you the discount that would have been paid to the touts as commission.

STONE TOWN

The old Stone Town of Unguja is a fascinating place to wander around and get lost in, though you can't really get lost for too long because, sooner or later, you will end up either on the seafront or on Creek Rd. Nevertheless, every twist and turn of the narrow alleyways will present you with something of interest – be it a school full of children chanting verses from the Quran, a beautiful old mansion with overhanging verandas, a shady square studded with huge old trees, a collection of quaint little hole-in-the-wall shops, or a gaggle of women in *bui bui* (veils) sharing a joke and some local gossip.

Much of the fabric of this historic place has fallen into disrepair and you'll see a lot of crumbled and crumbling buildings as you walk around. Fortunately, a determined effort is now being made to restore some of Stone Town's more important architecture, see The Conservation of Stone Town colour section for more details. Those concerned about the preservation of Zanzibar Town's old buildings should skim a copy of *Zanzibar: A Plan for the Historic Stone Town* by Francesco Siravo (Agha Khan Trust for Culture, 1996), or read *The History and Conservation of Zanzibar Stone Town* edited by Abdul Sheriff (1995).

While a large part of the attraction of Stone Town is walking around and simply letting it unfold before you, it's worth putting in the effort to see some of its major features, which are described following.

Beit el Ajaib (House of Wonders)

One of the most prominent buildings in the old Stone Town is the Beit el Ajaib, or House of Wonders, formerly a palace for the sultan and one of the largest structures in Zanzibar. It was built in 1883 by Sultan Barghash

Muslim women stroll past a lattice veranda, typical of Zanzibar Town's Arab architecture.

(1870-88), and is an elegant multistorey structure surrounded by wide verandas. In 1896 it was the target of a British naval bombardment, the object of which was to force Khalid bin Barghash, who had tried to seize the throne after the death of Sultan Hamad (1893-96) to abdicate in favour of a British nominee. After it was rebuilt, Sultan Hamoud (1902-11) used the upper floor as a residential palace until his death. Later, it was used as the local political headquarters of the CCM. Recently it has been partially rehabilitated.

Beit al Sahel
(The Palace Museum)

This palace, on Mizingani Rd just north of the Beit el Ajaib, served as the Sultan's residence until 1964 when the dynasty was overthrown. After being closed to the public after the revolution, it reopened several years ago as a museum devoted to the era of the Zanzibar sultanate.

The ground floor displays details of the formative period of the sultanate from 1828 to 1870, during which commercial treaties were signed between Zanzibar and the USA (1833), Britain (1839), France (1844) and the Hanseatic Republics (1859). There is also memorabilia of Princess Salme.

The exhibits on the 2nd floor focus on the period of affluence from 1870 to 1896 during which modern amenities such as piped water and electricity were introduced to Zanzibar under Sultan Barghash.

The 3rd floor consists of the modest living quarters of the last sultan, Khalifa bin Haroub (1911-60), and his two wives, both of whom clearly had very different tastes in furniture.

Outside is the Makusurani graveyard where some of the sultans are buried.

Entry to the museum costs Tsh2000. It's open from 9 am to 6 pm Tuesday to Saturday and from 9 am to 3 pm on Sunday, Monday and public holidays.

Old Fort

Just south of the Beit el Ajaib is the Old Fort, a massive, bastioned structure originally built around 1700 on the site of a Portuguese chapel by Omani Arabs as a defence against the Portuguese. In recent years, it has been partially renovated to house the Zanzibar Cultural Centre. Inside is an open-air theatre that hosts frequent performances of local

Zanzibar's Slave Trade

While slavery has been practised in Africa throughout recorded history, its most significant expansion in East Africa came with the rise of Islam, which prohibits the enslavement of Muslims. Demands of European – primarily French – plantation holders on the islands of Réunion and Mauritius also contributed significantly to the trade, particularly during the second half of the 18th century.

Initially, slaves were taken from coastal regions, and then shipped to Arabia, Persia and the Indian Ocean islands. Many were shipped via Kilwa Kisiwani, which was one of the most important slave exporting towns in East Africa. As demand increased, traders made their way further inland, so that during the 18th and 19th centuries, slaves were being brought from as far away as Malawi and the Congo. By the 19th century, with the rise of the Omani Arabs, Zanzibar had eclipsed Kilwa Kisiwani as the major slave trading depot. According to some estimates, by the 1860s between 10,000 and 30,000 slaves were passing through Zanzibar's market each year. Overall, close to 600,000 slaves were sold through Zanzibar between 1830 and 1873, when a treaty with the British abolished the slave trade in the sultan's territories and closed down the Zanzibar slave market. While many of these slaves were shipped to Oman and elsewhere in the Middle East, others were kept to work on clove plantations in the Zanzibar archipelago.

music and dance. There is also a small tourist information centre that has scheduling information for the performances, some craft shops, an art gallery, and the pleasant Neem Tree Café (see Places to Eat).

Anglican Cathedral & Old Slave Market

The Anglican cathedral, which was constructed in the 1870s by the Universities' Mission to Central Africa (UMCA), was the first Anglican cathedral in East Africa. It was built on the site of the old slave market, alongside Creek Rd, although nothing remains of the slave market today other than some holding cells under St Monica's Hostel next door. Services are still held at the cathedral on Sundays; for those wanting to visit during the week there is a nominal admission fee which includes a visit to the slave chambers.

St Joseph's Cathedral

The spires of St Joseph's Roman Catholic cathedral are one of the first sights travellers see when arriving at Unguja via ferry. Yet, the church is deceptively hard to find in the narrow confines of the adjacent streets. (If you get lost, the best thing to do is follow signs for Chit Chat restaurant, which is fairly well-marked. The cathedral is opposite the restaurant.) The cathedral, which was designed by the French architect Beranger and built by French missionaries, celebrated its 100th centenary in 1998. There is a brief summary of the mission's history just inside the entrance. Much of the cathedral's artwork is beginning to deteriorate; plans for renovations are under way assuming adequate funding can be found. The church is still in active use by Unguja's tiny Catholic community. If the front gate is closed, there is a second entrance via the small courtyard to the back.

Mosques

Unguja is a strongly Muslim society, and there are mosques scattered all around Zanzibar Town. The oldest one is the **Msikiti wa Balnara** (Malindi Minaret Mosque), originally built in 1831, enlarged in 1841 and extended again by Seyyid Ali bin Said in 1890. Others include the **Aga Khan Mosque** and the impressive **Ijumaa Mosque**. It is generally not permitted to enter any of the mosques because they are all in active use,

Zanzibar's Slave Trade

Apart from the human horrors, the slave trade had significant effects on local life on the mainland. In some areas, particularly the sparsely populated and politically decentralised south, it led to increased inter-clan warfare as ruthless entrepreneurs from one tribe began to raid neighbouring tribes for slaves. In others, particularly in northern and central Tanzania, the slave trade contributed to increased stratification of local society, and resulted in altered settlement patterns. Some tribes, for example, began to build fortified towns encircled by trenches, while others – notably the Nyamwezi and other central Tanzanian peoples – began to concentrate their populations in towns as a defence against the increased inter-clan warfare. Another fundamental societal change was the gradual shift in the nature of chieftainship from a religiously based position to one resting on military power or wealth – both of which could be obtained through trade in slaves and other goods.

From a European perspective, the slave trade served as a major impetus for the initiation of missionary activity in East Africa, prompting the establishment of the first mission stations, as well as missionary penetration of the interior. After slavery was ended on Zanzibar, the Universities' Mission to Central Africa (UMCA) took over the slave market, and built the Anglican cathedral which still stands on the site today.

THE ZANZIBAR ARCHIPELAGO

ZANZIBAR TOWN (STONE TOWN)

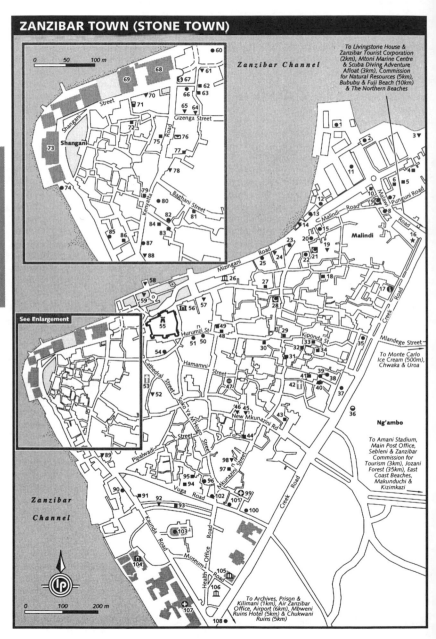

Zanzibar Channel

To Livingstone House &
Zanzibar Tourist Corporation
(2km), Mtoni Marine Centre
& Scuba Diving Adventure
Afloat (3km), Commission
for Natural Resources (5km),
Bububu & Fuji Beach (10km)
& The Northern Beaches

0   50   100 m

Shangani Street

Shangani

Gizenga Street

Kenyatta Road

Baghani Street

Malindi

Malindi Road

Malawi Road

Pungumi Road

Creek Road

Mizingani Road

See Enlargement

Hurumzi St

Cathedral Street

Hamamni Street

Soko ya Mhogo Street

New Mkunazini Rd

Mkunazini Street

Pipalwadi

Vuga Road

Kaunda Road

Pipalwadi Street

Ng'ambo

Mlandege Street

To Monte Carlo
Ice Cream (500m),
Chwaka & Uroa

To Amani Stadium,
Main Post Office,
Sebleni & Zanzibar
Commission for
Tourism (3km), Jozani
Forest (35km), East
Coast Beaches,
Makunduchi &
Kizimkazi

Zanzibar
Channel

Museum Office Road

Health Road

To Archives, Prison &
Kilimani (1km), Air Zanzibar
Office, Airport (6km), Mbweni
Ruins Hotel (5km) & Chukwani
Ruins (5km)

0   100   200 m

ZANZIBAR TOWN (STONE TOWN)

PLACES TO STAY
4 Malindi Guest House
5 Malindi Lodge; Malindi Annex
6 Warere Guest House
10 Hotel Marine
18 Pyramid Hotel
27 Kiponda Hotel
29 Spice Inn
30 Emerson's &
   Green (Hurumzi)
31 Emerson's House (Mkunazini)
32 Hotel International
33 House of Spices; Zee Pizza
34 Hotel International
41 Riverman Hotel
43 St Monica's Hostel;
   Old Slave Chambers
44 Jambo Guest House
48 Bottoms Up Guest House
   & Bar
49 Hotel Clove
62 Karibu Inn
63 Coco de Mer Hotel
69 Tembo House Hotel
72 Shangani House
73 Zanzibar Serena Inn
75 Shangani Hotel;
   Shangani Tours & Travel
77 Blue Ocean Hotel
79 Mazsons Hotel
81 Chavda Hotel
83 Baghani House Hotel
   & Livingstone Bar
84 Dhow Palace Hotel
86 Africa House Hotel;
   New Happy Lodge
91 Garden Lodge
93 Victoria Guest House
94 Florida Guest House &
   Culture Musical Club
95 Haven Guest House; Manch
   Lodge; Nyumbani Restaurant
97 Flamingo Guest House

PLACES TO EAT
3 Pagoda Chinese Restaurant
14 Pichy's Pizza
19 Bopa Bakery

24 Sea View Indian Restaurant;
   Dive Africa Watersports
   (Indian Ocean)
45 Baobab Restaurant
46 Omy's Ice Cream Parlour
52 Chit Chat Restaurant
57 1001 Nights Cafe
58 Blue's Restaurant
59 Forodhani Gardens;
   Food & Craft Vendors
61 Radha Food House
64 Luis Yoghurt Parlour
65 Luna Mare Restaurant
70 Fisherman Restaurant
78 Dolphin Restaurant
88 Camlurs Restaurant
89 Maharaja Restaurant
92 Sambusa Two Tables
   Restaurant
98 Green Garden Restaurant

OTHER
1 Customs & Immigration
2 Boat Company Ticket Offices
7 Ciné Afrique
8 Zan Air & Zan Tours
9 Malindi Minaret Mosque
11 Boat Company Ticket Offices
12 Tickets for Mapinduzi Ferry
13 Institute of Marine Sciences
15 Old Dispensary
16 Traffic Police; Greenland Bank
17 Zanzibar Tourist Corporation
   Branch Office
20 Gulf Air
21 Ijumaa Mosque
22 Kenya Airways; Mega-Speed
   Office; Oman Air
23 The Big Tree
25 Old Customs House
26 Beit al Sahel (Palace
   Museum) & Makusurani
   Graveyard (Visa
   & MasterCard Agent)
28 Aga Khan Mosque
35 Markets
36 Bus Station
37 Darajani Market

38 Fruit Market
39 Shamshu Pharmacy
40 Masumo Bookshop
42 Anglican Cathedral;
   Old Slave Market
47 Hamamni Persian Baths
50 Institute for Computer
   Technology
51 Sama Tours
53 St Joseph's Cathedral
54 The Gallery
55 Old Fort, Zanzibar Cultural
   Centre; Neem Tree Cafe
56 Beit el Ajaib (House of
   Wonders)
60 Orphanage
66 Commission for Lands &
   Environment; People's Bank
   of Zanzibar
67 NBC Bank
68 The First British Consulate
71 The Garage Club
74 Mtoni Marine
   Branch Office
76 Post Office; Telephones;
   Asko Communications Centre
80 Tropical Tours
82 Madeira Tours & Safaris
85 One Ocean/The Zanzibar
   Dive Centre
87 Marlin Tours & Safaris
90 Chemah Brothers'
   Tours & Safaris; High Court
96 Eco Tours & Travel
99 ZAMEDIC (Zanzibar Medical
   & Diagnostic Centre);
   Internet Zanzibar
100 Institute of Swahili
   & Foreign Languages
101 Air Tanzania Booking Office
102 Maha Travel & Tours Safaris
103 Victoria Hall; Victoria Gardens
104 State House
105 Peace Memorial Museum
106 Peace Memorial Museum
107 Mnazi Mmoja Hospital
108 Mnazi Mmoja
   Cricket Grounds

although exceptions may be made if you are appropriately dressed.

Hamamni Persian Baths

The baths were built by Sultan Barghash in the late 19th century, and were the first public baths on Unguja. Although they are no longer functioning and there is no water inside, you can still visit them. To get in, you'll need to ask the caretaker across the alley to unlock the gate; there is a nominal entrance charge.

Peace Memorial Museum (Beit el Amani or Beit el Salaam)

The larger of the two buildings that make up this museum presents a catalogued history of the island from its early days up until independence. It contains Livingstone memorabilia, artefacts from the days of the Omani sultans and the British colonial period, as well as drums used by the sultans, and a priceless collection of old lithographs, maps and photographs dating from the 19th and early 20th centuries. There are also stamp and coin displays. The smaller building houses a decaying natural history collection specialising in butterflies, fish, small mammals, snakes and shells.

The museum is located at the junction of Kaunda and Creek Rds. It's open daily except Sunday; entry costs Tsh1000.

Livingstone House

Livingstone House, just north of town along the Bububu road, was built around 1860 and was used as a base by many of the European missionaries and explorers before they started on their journey for the mainland. Missionary-explorer David Livingstone stayed here before setting off on his last expedition. Now it houses the main office of the Zanzibar Tourist Corporation. You can walk from town, or take a 'B' dalla-dalla.

Old Dispensary

The Old Dispensary, on Mizingani Rd near the port, was built at the turn of the century by a wealthy Indian merchant. It has been recently renovated by the Agha Khan Charitable Trust, and now houses some boutiques and craft shops and a few small bookshops.

Other Sights

The bustling **market** off Creek Rd has a wide assortment of items and is worth a visit.

Forodhani Gardens (also called Jamituri Gardens) are located along the seafront opposite the Old Fort. They are a popular gathering spot for locals in the evenings and a good place for inexpensive street food.

Shortly before the cricket grounds after the hospital on Kaunda Rd, is Victoria Hall which used to house the Legislative Council during the British era. The hall is not open to the public, but you can walk in the surrounding **gardens**. Opposite is the State House (closed to the public).

PLACES TO STAY
Places to Stay – Budget

There is a wide selection of good-value budget lodging in Zanzibar Town. Following are some of the more popular places listed in approximately ascending order of price. All room rates include breakfast.

Bottoms Up Guest House, off Hurumzi St, has basic rooms with shared facilities for US$10/20 single/double and a noisy bar downstairs.

New Happy Lodge (☎ 31543) around the corner from Africa House Hotel also has a noisy bar, and rooms with shared facilities for US$10/20.

Flamingo Guest House (☎ 32850) off New Mkunazini Rd is very average but it's quieter and the price is right. Rooms with shared facilities cost US$8/16.

Manch Lodge (☎ 31918) in Vuga has simple but adequate rooms for US$10/20 (US$24 for a double with bathroom).

Haven Guest House nearby is simple but fine, with rooms for US$10/20 (US$25 for a double with bathroom).

Jambo Guest House (☎ 33779) near Mkunazini St has rooms for US$10 per person. They will provide free transport from the port if you call to arrange this in advance.

Florida Guest House (☎ 33136, fax 31828) on Vuga Rd is a friendly place with a variety of rooms ranging from US$8 to $15 per person.

Warere Guest House near the port gets good reviews from budget travellers. Rooms with fan, net and shared facilities cost US$8/16.

Riverman Hotel (☎/fax 33188) not far from the Anglican cathedral has well maintained rooms with shared facilities for US$10 per person; there's a nice breakfast room on the adjoining porch.

Garden Lodge (☎ 33298, fax 31619) on Kaunda Rd diagonally opposite the High

Court has a tiny garden and small but good rooms for US$10 per person.

Victoria Guest House *(☎ 32861)* nearby is in a pleasant part of town off Kaunda Rd. Large, airy rooms cost US$10 per person.

Pyramid Hotel *(☎ 33000, fax 30045)* on Kokoni St near the seafront is recommended by many travellers. Clean rooms cost US$10 per person; there's also cable TV.

St Monica's Hostel *(☎ 32484)* near the Anglican cathedral has large rooms with shared facilities for US$12/24 (US$28 for a single with bathroom and US$32 for a double with air-con).

Kiponda Hotel *(☎ 33052)* near the waterfront is a pleasant place with a reasonably priced rooftop restaurant and singles/doubles/triples for US$18/35/45 (US$45/55 for doubles/triples with bathroom).

Karibu Inn *(☎ 33058)* near Coco de Mer Hotel in Shangani has singles/doubles for US$15/25 (US$20/30 with bathroom and US$30/40 with air-con), plus dormitory-style rooms with four, six and seven beds for US$10 per bed.

Hotel Clove *(☎ 32560)* near the Old Fort has rooms with refrigerator, bathroom and fan from US$20/25.

Malindi Lodge *(☎ 32359)*, just around the corner from and not related to Malindi Guest House (see listing later in this section), has good value rooms for US$10/20/30. The lodge also runs the nearby ***Malindi Annex***, which has somewhat more basic accommodation for the same price.

The government-run ***Zanzibar Hotel*** near Africa House Hotel has interesting architecture but run-down rooms, overpriced at US$15/20 single/double.

Malindi Guest House *(☎ 30165, fax 33030, email jinjahotels@zanzinet.com, PO Box 609)*, near the port in Malindi, is an attractive, well-maintained place with very good value singles/doubles/triples for US$15/30/45 (US$40 for a double with bathroom). Low-season rates are US$15/25/35 (US$35 with bathroom). Credit cards are accepted, with a 5% surcharge. It's best to make advance reservations as this place is heavily booked.

Africa House Hotel between Kenyatta Rd and the sea is also government run. It has a good setting on the water, but facilities are very run-down. Singles/doubles cost US$20/25 (US$20 for a double with shared bath).

Blue Ocean *(☎ 33566)* in a small courtyard off Kenyatta Rd has overpriced rooms with air-con for US$20/40.

Spice Inn near Hurumzi St has a lot of character including a great veranda, but declining facilities. Decent sized but fairly run-down singles/doubles with net and fan cost US$28/46 (US$25/31 with shared bathroom). The cafe on the porch downstairs is a popular place for yoghurt, shakes and other snacks.

Coco de Mer Hotel *(☎ 30852)* in Shangani has a pleasant atmosphere and clean but cramped singles/doubles for US$35/50.

Places to Stay – Mid-Range & Top End

All the following offer comfortable accommodation. Prices include breakfast.

Baghani House Hotel *(☎ 0811-321058, fax 054-33030, email jinjahotels@zanzinet .com)* just off Kenyatta Rd is a well-managed place with a lot of character. Spacious, good value singles/doubles/suites cost US$45/50 /55 (US$30/40/45 in the low season). Credit cards are accepted for an additional 5% charge. Advance bookings are recommended. Downstairs is the popular Livingstone Bar.

House of Spices *(☎ 31264, fax 33520)*, a popular restaurant on Kiponda St, has a few comfortable rooms for US$30/60 (US$75 for a double with bathroom). In addition to the restaurant, they also have a breezy bar and tiny second-hand book collection, and a gift shop selling all sorts of spices.

Shangani Hotel *(☎/fax 33688, 33524)* on Kenyatta Rd opposite Shangani post office has doubles/triples with TV, refrigerator, fan and air-con for US$55/65 (US$40 with common bathroom), plus a US$5 per person per day tax. Credit cards incur an additional 10% charge. There's also a rooftop restaurant.

Hotel Marine *(☎ 32088, fax 32598)* diagonally opposite the port entrance is a new place with comfortable, well-equipped singles/doubles for US$65/70.

Mazson's Hotel (☎ 33694, fax 33695, email mazson@zanzinet.com) on Kenyatta Rd has comfortable but slightly stuffy rooms from US$45/60/80 and a restaurant.

Hotel International (☎ 33182, fax 30052) near Kiponda St and behind the House of Spices has comfortable rooms with TV and refrigerator from US$50. The hotel can organise excursions, and there is a bureau de change in the lobby.

Chavda Hotel (☎ 32115, fax 31931, email chavda@zanzinet.com) on Baghani St has comfortable rooms with air-con, TV and telephone for US$70/90 single/double. There's a rooftop bar and a good restaurant at ground level.

Emerson's House (☎ 30609, 32153, fax 33135, email emerson@zanzibar.org) in Mkunazini is a well-established place full of character. The rooms are beautifully decorated to give you an idea of what Unguja must have been like in its heyday. There's also a very good rooftop restaurant. Singles cost from US$50 to US$75, and doubles from US$60 to US$85. The hotel closes in May.

Emerson's & Green (☎ 30171, 30609, fax 31038, email emegre@zanzibar.org, 236 Hurumzi St), in a late 19th century building, is under the same management as Emerson's House. Each room has its own decor, and all are priced at US$125 per room. The hotel is open year-round. There is a teahouse/restaurant on the roof with excellent meals and superb views of the harbour and town. See Places to Eat.

Dhow Palace, under the same management as the Tembo House Hotel, is a well-appointed place decorated in old Unguja style. Singles/doubles cost US$50/80; guests can use the pool at the Tembo House Hotel for no additional charge. The Dhow Palace is next door to Baghani House Hotel, just off Kenyatta Rd.

Tembo House Hotel (☎ 33005, fax 33777, email tembo@raha.com), in an attractive setting on the seafront at the end of Shangani St, has rooms in both a new and an old wing. All are priced at US$75/85 a single/double; most have a TV and refrigerator, and all have air-con. There's also a pool, and a restaurant overlooking the water. No alcohol is served here. The Tembo is frequently used by tour groups.

Zanzibar Serena Inn (☎ 33470, 31015, fax 33019, email zserena@cctz.com) is the most expensive hotel in Zanzibar Town. It's in the old Extelecoms House and has a beautiful setting on the water. Comfortable rooms with all the amenities cost from US$185/280 single/double including full board; low-season rates are also available. Bookings can be made locally or through Serena Hotels (☎ 057-4158, 4153, fax 4155, email serena@yako.habari.co.tz).

Private Residences

For groups seeking nontraditional accommodation, private homes are sometimes available to let. Remember that these places are not hotels and while very comfortable, do not provide hotel service. The minimum rental period is normally one week.

Shangani House, a restored building with a lot of character and a rooftop teahouse, can accommodate up to eight persons. It's off Kenyatta Rd in Shangani and costs US$250 per day for the entire house; special arrangements are available for long-term rentals. Book through Emerson's House (see earlier).

The decadently luxurious *Salome's Garden*, set in large gardens about 10km north of town in Bububu, is a rehabilitated plantation house which once belonged to the Omani royal family. It can accommodate up to 10 persons. Price depends on the season, but averages between US$2500 to US$3500 per week for the entire house. Book through ☎ 0812-750557 (ask for Nicole) or 39-51-234 974.

Outside Zanzibar Town

Just outside Zanzibar Town are a few other places worthy of mention.

Mtoni Marine Centre (☎/fax 32540 or 0811-323226, email mmc@twiga.com), about 3km north of town just off the Bububu road, is a relaxing place with attractive beachfront grounds. Comfortable air-con rooms cost US$30 for a 'standard double' and from US$60 for suites or cottage-style accommodation including continental breakfast. There's a dive shop here which also offers snorkelling and can arrange excursions to Bawi and Prison islands. The hotel can assist with flight booking and other services.

Mbweni Ruins Hotel (☎ 31832 or 0811-320855, fax 30536, email mbweni-ruins@twiga.com) is attractively set in large gardens on the water about 5km south of town near the airport. Comfortable accommodation costs US$90/180 single/double with breakfast (US$145/210 including full board). There is swimming here at high tide, and the hotel can arrange excursions to nearby islands. A hotel shuttle runs several times daily to the Old Fort in town; schedules are posted at the fort. The Mbweni ruins are on the grounds of the hotel.

PLACES TO EAT

The best place for cheap street food in the evenings is *Forodhani Gardens*, where you can eat well for about Tsh500. In the mornings, you'll find women on street corners selling piping hot *uji* (bean flour porridge).

For fresh, warm bread try the Greek-owned *Bopa Bakery*, tucked away in a courtyard behind the Ijumaa mosque opposite Kenya Airways.

Dolphin Restaurant near the post office on Kenyatta Rd is popular with budget travellers. Service is slow, but prices are very reasonable.

Baobab Restaurant on New Mkunazini Rd has shady outdoor tables and inexpensive local dishes from Tsh2000.

Green Garden Restaurant near Jambo Guest House has a nice outdoor setting and inexpensive snacks and meals. It is closed Friday lunch.

Radha Food House has thalis and other vegetarian dishes for very reasonable prices. It's on the small street just before the tunnel at the end of Shangani St.

1001 Nights Cafe near the Old Fort is usually deserted but the garden is pleasant. Good curries and similar fare cost from Tsh3500 to Tsh4500.

Luis Yoghurt Parlour, just off Kenyatta Rd, is a very pleasant place offering several freshly made menus of the day for about Tsh4000 plus excellent yoghurt, shakes and other light meals.

Luna Mare on the same street has seafood, Indian and Chinese dishes for about Tsh3000.

For good Goan cuisine, the best places are *Chit Chat* (☎ 32548) on Cathedral St (evenings only, closed Monday) and *Camlur's* on Kenyatta Rd.

The French Alsatian-run *Fisherman Restaurant* opposite the Tembo House Hotel has a pleasant atmosphere and a good selection of seafood dishes from Tsh4000.

Maharaja Restaurant (☎ 30359 or 0811-328243) on Kenyatta Rd not far from the High Court has good northern and southern Indian cuisine.

Sea View Indian Restaurant (☎ 33081) is less expensive and also good. It's on the waterfront next to Dive Africa Water Sports/Indian Ocean, on the 1st floor.

Pagoda (☎ 31758) is considered to be Zanzibar Town's best Chinese restaurant. It's near Bwawani Plaza and open evenings only.

Neem Tree Café at the Old Fort (Zanzibar Cultural Centre) has good meals for about Tsh4500, as well as yoghurt. It is open daily from 8 am.

Pichy's Pizza (☎ 0812-750244) has good pizzas from Tsh3000 and live music on weekends. It's on the waterfront just down from Forodhani Gardens. Take-away service is also available.

One of the best places to try authentic Zanzibari dishes is *Sambusa Two Tables Restaurant* (☎ 31979, 31929), off Kaunda Rd near Victoria Gardens. You must make reservations in advance.

Nyumbani Restaurant opposite Haven Guest House in Vuga is another place to try local cuisine. They have a set menu featuring various Zanzibari dishes for Tsh5000 per person. It's open evenings only (and closed on Sunday); you will need to let them know in the morning that you will be coming.

The Italian-run *Zee Pizza* at the House of Spices (see listing under Places to Stay) is a very good restaurant with pizzas from Tsh3500, pasta dishes from Tsh4000 and fish and other grills for about Tsh5000. They also serve breakfast and lunch. The restaurant is upstairs, with pleasant views; there's also a nice bar and sitting area on the porch.

Blues (☎ 0812-750339), part of the South African chain, has a good setting on the water at Forodhani Gardens, but the food is often very mediocre. Pizzas start at Tsh2800; pasta, seafood and grills from about Tsh4000.

Zanzibar Serena Inn (☎ 31015 for reservations) has a good Sunday brunch between 10 am and 3 pm for Tsh7000.

Dinner at the rooftop restaurant at *Emerson's & Green* (see listing under Places to Stay) is an experience not to be missed. The views over Stone Town at sunset are superb, and on Fridays there are often traditional drumming and dancing performances. The fixed menu costs Tsh12,000; reservations are essential (see Places to Stay). There is a similarly good rooftop restaurant at *Emerson's House* in Mkunazini (see Places to Stay).

The best place for ice cream is *Omy's Ice Cream Parlour* next to Baobab Restaurant, on New Mkunazini St. For sundaes and soft ice cream try *Monte Carlo* on Mlandege St.

ENTERTAINMENT
Bars & Nightclubs
One of the more popular, quality bars is *Livingstone Bar* at Baghani House Hotel. The bar at *Africa House Hotel* has a good setting overlooking the sea, but is fairly dilapidated.

For nightclubs and dancing try *The Garage Club* (☎ 33592) on Shangani St diagonally opposite the Tembo House Hotel. It's open Wednesday through Sunday; Thursday and Sunday are ladies' nights. Beers cost Tsh700.

Traditional Music & Dance
Taarab is Zanzibar's most well-known form of traditional music. See the black & white Taarab Music section for details.

On Tuesday, Thursday and Saturday evenings from 7 pm, there are traditional dance and drumming performances at the Old Fort. It costs Tsh3000 for the performance, or Tsh6000 for the performance and dinner.

Emerson's & Green has traditional drumming and dancing on Friday evenings. See the listing under Places to Eat, earlier.

SPECTATOR SPORTS
South of the centre of Stone Town along Kaunda Rd and just after the hospital are the Mnazi Mmoja Cricket Grounds. On Sunday afternoons they're filled with locals playing or watching soccer matches. It's a good place to come to escape the tourist crush in town.

SHOPPING
There are craft dealers all over Zanzibar Town. A good place to start is Gizenga St, where you will find all sorts of shops lining the road. *The Gallery* (☎/fax 32244) has the widest selection.

The shop at the *orphanage* on the waterfront at the tunnel near Forodhani Gardens sells local crafts and textiles; profits go to support the children. At the same end of Forodhani Gardens are numerous vendors selling woodcarvings and other crafts.

Mlandege St is a good place to look for cheap *kangas* (the colourful cloths worn by many women); you can often find them for as little as Tsh1200.

There are craft shops at the Old Fort and vendors at the House of Wonders.

GETTING THERE & AWAY
Air
Unguja is connected with both Dar es Salaam and Arusha by several flights daily. There are also frequent connections with Mombasa and Nairobi, and occasional connections with some of the mainland game parks.

Air Tanzania flies five times weekly between Unguja and Dar es Salaam, and once weekly from Unguja to Arusha. There are also scheduled weekly flights to Mombasa (US$59) and to Nairobi (US$136), although these are usually cancelled. In general, flights from Unguja on Air Tanzania are often overbooked, delayed or cancelled.

THE CONSERVATION OF STONE TOWN

 Much of Stone Town was built in the 19th century by Indian and Arab traders. However, unlike the older sections of many other towns and cities around the world, Stone Town is still the heart of surrounding Zanzibar Town, and the focus of commercial activity on Unguja island. In addition to being home for about 16,000 Zanzibaris, it contains an important post office branch, the main market and almost all of Unguja's administrative services.

Stone Town's Architecture

For visitors, one of the most striking aspects of a visit to Stone Town is its fascinating architecture, which consists of a hybrid mixture displaying Arabic, Indian, European and African characteristics. Arabic buildings are often square, with two to three storeys, and have rooms lining the outer walls, allowing space for an inner courtyard and verandas. Indian buildings, also several storeys high, generally include a shop on the ground floor and living quarters above, with exposed and ornate facades decorated with railings and lacework balconies. The *baraza* – a stone bench facing into the street that serves as a focal point around which townspeople meet and chat – is a common feature of many houses.

The majority of Stone Town's buildings were constructed by merchants from ancient trading nations who used a technique in which chunks of coral limestone were bound together with a mixture of lime and *laterite* (red soil produced by rock decay). In addition to relying on materials which were readily available, this technique also permitted the construction of multistorey buildings.

Top: Hotel Tembo

Bottom: The architectural blend characteristic of Stone Town is evident in the street facade at the old dhow harbour, where wooden dhows from the mainland and Kenya unload their goods.

Zanzibari Doors Another fascinating feature of Zanzibari architecture is the carved wooden door. There are over 500 remaining today in Stone Town, many of which are older than the houses in which they are set. The door, which was often the first part of a house to be built, served as a symbol of the wealth and status of a household. While older doors generally have a square frame with a geometrical shape, 'newer' doors – many of which were built towards the end of the 19th century and incorporate Indian influences – often have semi-circular tops and intricate floral decorations. Many doors are decorated with carvings of passages from the Quran. Other commonly seen motifs include images representing things desired in the household, such as a fish (expressing a hope for many children) or chains (displaying the owner's wish for security). Some doors have large brass spikes, which are a tradition from India, where spikes protected doors from being battered down by elephants.

Architectural Threats

Despite Stone Town's integral role in Zanzibari life, and the beauty and historical value of its architecture, many of its buildings have been allowed to disintegrate or become severely dilapidated. One of the major contributing factors is water, which has been quietly and efficiently destroying Stone Town's buildings by eroding their limestone foundations. Damp-proofing, which would have protected the foundations, was a technique either unknown or unused 200 years ago when the buildings were originally constructed. Another culprit has been inherent design flaws, particularly flaws in roof design. Most original roofs in Stone Town are flat – a design which works well in drier Arab countries such as Oman. On Unguja, however, it is unsuitable due to the much heavier rainfall. The flat roofs trap water, and exacerbate problems with dampness. While many flat roofs have since been replaced with angled ones, this has often been done at the expense of preserving the adornments which traditionally decorated many of the buildings.

The unique architectural blend of Stone Town is also being disrupted by the collapse of damp-affected buildings because replacement structures are not made to fit the thread-like contour of winding alleyways.

Middle: The intricately carved doors in Stone Town once indicated the wealth and societal status of a household.

Conservation Efforts

In 1982, following several deaths resulting from collapsed structures, the United Nations Center for Human Settlements (the Habitat Fund) developed a plan focused on the preservation of Stone Town's architecture. The Stone Town Conservation and Development Authority (STCDA) was also created and given the responsibility for restoring the town to its former glory. Following the creation of the STCDA, the government, which owned many of the buildings most in need of repair, began selling these properties to their occupants and then channelling the proceeds into architectural restoration. By the end of 1998, about 300 buildings had been sold.

One of the major international entities involved in Stone Town's restoration is the Agha Khan Trust for Culture, which was established to preserve buildings in historic Islamic societies. Other important donors include the European Union and SIDA (a Swiss development agency). The German and Finnish governments are helping to renew sewerage and water systems – a particularly critical aspect in halting water-induced erosion of limestone foundations. After almost two decades of work, progress is now clearly visible, with about 600 buildings restored by early 1999. Stone Town has also recently been proposed as a possible contender for World Heritage status which – if granted – would enhance future architectural preservation efforts.

What You Can Do

Top: Angled roofs such as these have replaced the traditional flat roofs which were the cause of damp problems in many buildings, often contributing to their collapse.

Raising awareness of some of the above issues is one of the most important tasks for the future. Other steps which you, as a visitor, can take include the following:

• Remember that Stone Town is a living town, and not a tourist show piece. Treat residents and their homes with respect.

CHRISTINE OSBORNE

- Be aware that you are in a traditional, Islamic society and behave accordingly. See Tips for Travellers under Religion in the Facts about Tanzania chapter for advice. If visitors show respect for culture and architecture, local appreciation can also be enhanced.
- For further information, or to make a financial contribution, contact one of the international agencies mentioned earlier.

Left: The High Court is another good example of the architectural mix that is found all over Stone Town.

Even those holding confirmed reservations often get bumped, so keep this in mind if you have a connecting flight from the mainland.

Precision Air flies daily between Unguja and both Dar es Salaam (US$55) and Arusha (US$165).

Air Zanzibar has one flight daily between Unguja and Dar es Salaam (US$55) and Unguja and Arusha (US$175).

Coastal Travels has daily flights to Dar es Salaam (US$55) and Arusha (US$175) as well as daily connections to Selous Game Reserve given sufficient demand (US$120), and three-times weekly connections with Ruaha National Park (US$300).

Kenya Airways flies five times weekly between Unguja, Mombasa and Nairobi (US$59 to Mombasa and US$136 to Nairobi).

Spot Tours (☎ 0811-333725 or 0812-750206) is the booking agent for a government Fokker 50 which flies every two weeks between Unguja and the Comoros islands (US$210/285 one way/return). The office is on Creek Rd near the Zanzibar Tourist Corporation branch office.

In addition to these regional connections, Gulf Air flies three times weekly between Unguja and Muscat via Dar es Salaam (US$512/745 one way/round trip).

Airline offices on Unguja include:

Air Tanzania
 (☎ 30297, 30213) office on Vuga Rd
Air Zanzibar
 (☎ 32512) office on the airport road, near Unicef
Coastal Travels
 (☎ 33112 or 0811-324378) representative at the airport; main office in Dar es Salaam
Gulf Air
 (☎ 32824) office off Mizingani Rd
Kenya Airways
 (☎ 32041) office opposite Ijumaa mosque
Oman Air
 (☎ 32043) office behind Kenya Airways, in the same building. This is a booking office only for onward flights from Muscat; Gulf Air handles all travel between Unguja and Muscat.

Air Charter If you are in a group it can be fairly reasonable to charter a flight. Prices between Dar es Salaam and Unguja for a five seater are about US$300 one way. Charter operators include:

Air Zanzibar
 (☎ 32512, 33098, fax 32512, email air@zanzibar .net) office on the airport road
Coastal Travels
 (☎/fax 33112) representative at the airport, otherwise office in Dar es Salaam
Zan Air
 (☎ 33670, 33678 or 0811-321061; at the airport 32993 or 0812-750476) office opposite Ciné Afrique

Train
Riverman Hotel is the TAZARA agent; a small section of seats is reserved for passengers booking in Unguja.

Boat
To/From Unguja Several ferries daily connect Dar es Salaam and Unguja. Most take about 90 minutes, though a few take much longer. In Dar es Salaam, all ferry offices are on the waterfront opposite St Joseph's cathedral. See the Getting There & Away information in the Dar es Salaam chapter for telephone contact information. In Unguja, all ferry offices are at or near the port.

For all boats, there is a US$5 port tax in addition to the fares quoted below. This is normally collected at the same time you purchase your ticket.

Flying Horse This is the cheapest regularly scheduled ferry. Departures from Unguja are at 10 pm, arriving at Dar es Salaam about 6 am. Tickets cost US$10 one way. From Dar es Salaam, departures are at 12.30 pm, arriving at Unguja about four hours later. The Flying Horse office (☎ 33031) is at the port.

Maendeleo The MV *Maendeleo* (see the Mtwara Getting There & Away section in the South-Eastern Tanzania chapter) runs sporadically between Dar es Salaam and Unguja and is theoretically the least expensive (less than US$5). However trying to get accurate information about departures is almost impossible. Inquire at the port.

THE ZANZIBAR ARCHIPELAGO

ZANZIBAR'S TAARAB MUSIC

Taarab, Zanzibar's most popular form of music, combines African, Arabic and Indian influences. It is viewed by many Zanzibaris as a unifying force which has fostered a degree of harmony among the island's many different cultures. Taarab is traditionally played by an orchestra consisting of several dozen musicians using both western and traditional instruments, including the violin, the *kanun* (similar to a zither), the accordion, the *nay* (an Arabian flute) and drums. There is also always a singer involved. The individual songs and pieces can be quite varied, some incorporating strong Arabic elements, others displaying more Indian or African influence. Themes usually centre around love, with many puns and double-meanings interwoven. Taarab is generally played without written music, and traditions are passed down from musician to musician.

Taarab-style music was played in Zanzibar as early as the 1820s at the Sultan's palace, where it had been introduced from Arabia. However, it was not until the 1900s – when Sultan Seyyid Hamoud bin Muhammed encouraged formation of the first taarab clubs – that it became more formalised. Hamoud, who had travelled in the Middle East, was impressed by the game and music clubs he had seen there and tried to introduce a similar concept on the island. One of the first clubs founded was Akhwan Safaa, established in 1905 in Zanzibar Town. Since then, numerous other clubs have sprung up, including the well-known Culture Musical Club and the smaller, more traditional Twinkling Stars who are an offshoot from Akhwan Safaa. Many of the newer clubs have begun to abandon the traditional acoustic style in favour of

Top: The pitch of the *tama* drum changes according to the pressure applied when squeezed under the musician's arm

Bottom: To raise the tone of a particular string on the *kanun*, a skilful player will apply one finger of the left hand to the string, with deliberate, uniform pressure, while plucking it with fingers of the right hand.

electronic equipment, although older musicians tend to look down on this as an adulterated form of taarab. Taarab's popularity now extends well beyond Zanzibar, along much of the East African coast and into Burundi, Congo (Zaïre), and even the Comoros islands.

For an introduction to taarab music you can stop by the Zanzibar Serena Inn, where the Twinkling Stars play on Wednesday and Friday evenings on the veranda from about 6 to 8 pm. To experience more of the classic club atmosphere, try the Culture Musical Club on Vuga Rd, which has rehearsals most evenings from about 7 pm (closed Sunday and Monday, entry Tsh1000, sometimes free). Akhwan Safaa also has rehearsals several times a week from about 9.30 pm. They are located in Malindi between Greenland Bank and the market off Creek Rd; locals can point you in the right direction. The performances themselves are quite an event. In the more traditional clubs, men and women still sit separately, with all – especially the women – sporting their finest outfits and elaborate hairstyles. There is a lot of audience participation, and listeners frequently go up to the stage to give money to the singer. A particularly good time to see taarab performances is during Zanzibar's annual cultural festival in July.

Top: The *nay* usually has one finger hole underneath and six on the front. The tone depends on the length of the pipe, and by combining the angle of the head and lips with the opening and closing of finger holes while blowing, a range of notes is produced.

Bottom: Arabs often call the *ud* 'the Sultan of the musical instruments'. In the 9th century it changed from a four to a five stringed instrument.

Mega-Speed Liners Mega-Speed's MS *Sepideh* goes daily except Sunday between Dar es Salaam and Unguja, departing Dar es Salaam at 8 am and arriving at Zanzibar Town at 9.45 am. The boat then continues on to Pemba, departing Unguja at 10.15 am and arriving at Mkoani on Pemba at 12.45 pm. Going in the other direction, departures from Pemba are daily except Saturday at 1 pm, reaching Unguja at 3.30 pm and Dar es Salaam at 5.45 pm. Fares are US$30 between Dar es Salaam and Unguja, US$40 between Dar es Salaam and Pemba, and US$35 between Unguja and Pemba.

On Saturdays, the *Sepideh* departs Unguja at 10.15 am and Pemba at 1 pm, reaching Tanga at 2.45 pm and Mombasa at about 5.30 pm. The return trip is on Sunday, departing Mombasa at 8 am, Tanga at 10.45 am and Pemba at 1 pm, reaching Unguja at 3.30 pm and Dar es Salaam at 5.45 pm. It costs US$30 between Pemba and Tanga, and US$40 between Pemba and Mombasa. The fare is US$40 between Unguja and Tanga, and US$60 between Unguja and Mombasa.

There are two classes of ticket for the *Sepideh*, although the boat is comfortable and there is no need to buy 1st class. All prices listed here are for the standard 'saloon' class. First class tickets cost from US$5 to US$20 more, depending on the route. Mega-Speed's booking office in Unguja (☎ 0811-326413, 333171 or 32423) is in the same building as Kenya Airways, just off Mizingani Rd near the seafront.

Azam Marine Azam Marine has regular service on the *Sea Bus*, the *Kondor* and the *Kondor 7*, and sporadic connections on the *Mungano*.

The *Sea Bus* departs Dar es Salaam at 8.15 am and 1.15 and 4 pm daily and reaches Unguja about 90 minutes later. Tickets cost US$35/30 for 1st/2nd class. The *Kondor* departs Dar es Salaam at 11.15 am daily, arriving in Unguja about two hours later; tickets cost US$20. The newer *Kondor 7* departs daily about 10 am and takes about 75 minutes. Tickets cost US$35/30 for 1st/2nd class. The *Mungano* departs several times

weekly at 11.15 am, arriving between three and four hours later. Tickets are US$15. Days of departure vary; inquire at the port for scheduling information.

The Azam Marine office (☎ 33046 or 0811-334347) is at the port.

Sea Express Sea Express (☎ 33002 or 0811-326413), located at the port, has departures from Dar es Salaam at 8 and 10 am and noon and 3.15 pm; departures from Unguja are at 7 and 10 am and noon and 3.30 pm. The trip takes 90 minutes and costs US$35/30 1st/2nd class.

To/From Pemba There are connections between Unguja and Pemba on Mega-Speed's *Sepideh*, on the *Mapinduzi*, and on Azam Marine's *Serengeti*. See Getting There & Away in the Pemba section later in this chapter for information. Mega-Speed's office is in the Kenya Airways building just off Mizingani Rd. You can buy tickets for the *Mapinduzi* on Mizingani Rd just after the Marine Institute; look for an unmarked hole in the wall. Azam Marine's Zanzibar Town office is at the port.

Dhow

Dhows still run fairly often linking Unguja and Pemba with Dar es Salaam, Tanga, Bagamoyo and Mombasa (Kenya). For more information, see Dhows in the Getting Around chapter. Foreigners are not permitted on dhows between Dar es Salaam and Zanzibar. If you want to try out one of the other routes, inquire at the port in Zanzibar Town or in Mkoani or Wete on Pemba. Allow anywhere between 12 and 48 hours or more for dhow trips between the archipelago and the mainland. You will need to bring all your own food and water.

GETTING AROUND
To/From the Airport

The U bus line connects Zanzibar Town with the airport (Tsh200). U buses depart from the corner opposite Mnazi Mmoja Hospital, and from Darjani bus stand on Creek Rd. Taxis cost about Tsh5000 to/from the airport.

Bus & Taxi

Converted pick-ups (dalla-dallas or *matatus*) link all major towns on the island. They are either lettered (for destinations around Zanzibar Town) or numbered (for destinations elsewhere on the island). Prices for town journeys are between Tsh100 and Tsh200. The maximum fare for destinations elsewhere on the island is Tsh1500; most routes cost about Tsh500. Most numbered buses run only once a day, departing Zanzibar Town around noon and then returning early the next morning. Allow a lot of time when taking public transport. All transport leaves from Darajani bus stand on Creek Rd, or from the market. Routes include the following:

A	Amani Stadium
B	Bububu
J	Jangombe
M	Magomeni
U	airport
1	Mkokotoni and sometimes on to Nungwi (Tsh1000)
1A	Mkwajuni and sometimes on to Nungwi (not daily)
2	Mangapwani and Bumbwini
3	Kizimbani
4	Mchangani
5	Ndagaa
6	Chwaka (Tsh500) and sometimes to Uroa
7	Fumba
8	Unguja Ukuu (Tsh1500)
9	Paje, and sometimes Jambiani and Bwejuu
10	Jozani (Tsh500), transfer junction for Kizimkazi, and Makunduchi
11	Fuoni
16	Nungwi (Tsh600)
17	Kiwengwa (Tsh500)

Taxis do not have meters; you will need to agree on a price with the driver before getting into the car. Trips within town cost Tsh1000.

Car & Motorcycle

Many travellers rent cars, mopeds or motorcycles on Unguja. In general, prices are reasonable and there are few hassles, although breakdowns are fairly common, as are moped accidents.

Before renting, you must have either an international driver's licence, or a licence from Zanzibar, Kenya, Uganda or South Africa. Zanzibari licences can be obtained at the traffic police office in Malindi on the corner near Greenland Bank. They cost Tsh3000 per day and are issued on the spot. If you rent through a tour company they will usually assist you with getting the necessary papers. If you do not have an international licence and have not arranged a Zanzibari licence, you will almost certainly wind up paying a fine or being at least temporarily detained.

Daily rates average about US$20 for a moped, US$25 for a motorcycle, and US$40 to US$50 for a Suzuki 4WD. You can rent through any of the tour companies, or else arrange rentals on your own by the market (this is where many of the tour companies come anyway). The quality of the vehicles is often dubious. If you're not mechanically minded, bring someone along with you who can be sure the motorbike or vehicle you're renting is in reasonable condition, and try to take a test drive before renting.

You are normally required to pay in full at the time of delivery for the number of days you will be keeping the vehicle. Do not pay any advance deposits before delivery of the vehicle.

Hired Vans

Private minivans run daily to Nungwi and to the east coast beaches. Book through any travel agent the day before you want to travel. The vans will pick you up at your hotel in Zanzibar Town between 8 and 9 am. It costs Tsh3000 and takes about 1½ hours to either destination. For the return trip drivers often want an additional Tsh500 or more; don't pay drivers for the return trip in advance as you will likely see neither the driver nor your money again.

Bicycle

You can rent bicycles through some tour companies, and by the market for between US$5 and US$7 per day. Most are in substandard condition.

Around Zanzibar Town

RUINS

There are a number of historical sites around Zanzibar Town. Many are included in Spice Tours (see Spice Tours).

Mbweni & Chukwani

Mbweni is about 5km south of Zanzibar Town off the airport road. In the late 19th century, the land here was owned by the Universities' Mission to Central Africa (UMCA) and used as a settlement for freed slaves. On the grounds of the Mbweni Ruins Hotel are the ruins of the UMCA's St Mary's School for Girls. About 5km further south are the remains of Chukwani palace, built in the late 19th century. Although marked on many maps, the Chukwani ruins are not open to the public.

Maruhubi Palace

The Maruhubi palace, around 4km north of Zanzibar Town and signposted off the Bububu road, was constructed by Sultan Barghash in 1882 to house his harem. In 1899 it was almost destroyed by fire. The columns which remain once supported a large upper-floor balcony as well as an overhead aqueduct.

Mtoni Palace

The ruins of Mtoni palace, built in the early 19th century, lie just north-east of Maruhubi. You can get an idea of how the palace must have looked by reading Emily Said-Reute's *Memoirs of an Arabian Princess*; see Books in the Facts for the Visitor chapter.

The Persian Baths

The Persian Baths, about 15km north-east of Zanzibar Town near Kidichi, were built in 1850 by Sultan Seyyid Said for his Persian wife at the highest point on the island. You can still see the baths, though they are in poor condition. To get here, take the 'B' dalla-dalla to Bububu, from where it's about 5km east down an unpaved road.

Mangapwani Caves

The Mangapwani caves are located about 20km north of Zanzibar Town along the coast and are best visited in conjunction with a Spice Tour (see below). It is believed that they were used by slave traders to hide slaves after the legal trade was abolished in the late 19th century. The village of Mangapwani itself is a pleasant place which sees few tourists, and is worth a couple of hours. If you decide to come up here via public transport you will likely wind up having to hitch back.

SPICE TOURS

While spices no longer dominate Zanzibar's economy as they once did, there are still numerous plantations in the centre of the island which make an interesting visit if you've never seen cloves, vanilla or other spices in the wild. Most tour operators in Zanzibar Town organise 'spice tours' which take in some plantations, as well as some of the ruins described above and other sights of historical interest. Along the way you'll be invited to taste many of the spices, herbs and fruits which the island produces, including cloves, black pepper, cardamom, cinnamon, nutmeg, breadfruit, jackfruit, vanilla and lemongrass.

Among the best tours are those given by the well-known Mr Mitu who, contrary to what you may be told by the papaasi on the street, is alive and well. His office is signposted off Malawi Rd near Ciné Afrique. A full day tour costs US$10 per person in a group of about 15, including a lunch of local food and an hour or two on Mangapwani beach at the end of the afternoon. Tours generally depart about 9.30 am and return by 6 pm. It's best to book a day in advance, though it's usually no trouble to just show up in the morning.

Piles of cloves are spread out by children to dry in the sun just outside Zanzibar Town. The Zanzibar archipelago was the world's largest producer of cloves in the mid-19th century.

BEACHES

There are some superb beaches around Unguja, although many unfortunately are getting overcrowded and built-up, especially in parts of the east and north. Still, there are a few quiet spots left, and all of the beaches offer a wonderful respite if you've been bumping along dusty roads on the mainland for any length of time. All are protected by coral reefs offshore and have fine, white coral sand. Depending on the season, they may also have a lot of seaweed. Locals harvest the seaweed for export; you'll see it drying in the sun in many villages. Except for Nungwi, swimming at all of the beaches is tide dependent.

Bububu (Fuji Beach)

Fuji beach, 10km north of town in Bububu ('B' dalla-dalla), is the closest place to Zanzibar Town for swimming. It's located a few hundred metres off the main road down the dirt track heading west from the Bububu police station. Budget travellers can try the *Bububu Beach Guest House* (☎/fax 31110) which has simple accommodation for US$10 per person. Otherwise, there is the *Imani Beach Club* (☎ 0811-333731, fax 33939, PO Box 3248)*, a small, Italian-run place directly on the beach with comfortable air-con singles/doubles for US$60/120; low-season rates are also available. The good Arabic-style restaurant serves Italian-Arabic dishes.

About 10km north of Fuji beach is *Mawimbini Venta Club*, an Italian-run package tour resort with accommodation starting at about US$120 per person. Book through Venta Club in Kiwengwa or through any tour operator in Zanzibar Town.

There is no tourist lodging in Mangapwani, Bumbwini or the other villages to the north.

Nungwi

Nungwi is a large village at the northernmost tip of Unguja, and an important dhow building centre. It has also become completely overrun with tourists in recent years, although you can still find a few quiet sections to the south-west and south-east of the main hotel area.

Other than diving, snorkelling and relaxing on the beach, you can watch the dhow builders, which is fascinating, or visit the **Mnarani Aquarium**, which houses a few hawksbill turtles. It's near the lighthouse at

Tides

Most of Unguja's beaches are subject to large tidal fluctuations and are swimmable only at high tide. At low tide, you may have to walk more than 20 minutes just to reach wading depth. An exception to this is Nungwi, where the tidal variations are not as great. Tide tables are published in the free listings booklet *Recommended in Zanzibar*. Otherwise, they're sometimes available from the Institute of Marine Sciences on the waterfront in Zanzibar Town.

the northernmost tip of Ras Nungwi, and about a 15 minute walk from the Paradise Beach Club. Entry costs Tsh500.

Places to Stay & Eat There is a decent choice of both budget and upmarket accommodation at Nungwi. Places on the northern and western edges of the cape tend to attract a younger clientele who are interested in diving; they are fairly hectic and crowded. The beaches on the eastern edge are quieter and more attractive, though lodging is generally more expensive.

In Nungwi village itself are two basic guesthouses. *Morning Star Guest House* offers no-frills accommodation in a private home for US$8 per person including mosquito net. The similar *Ikibala Guest House* nearby also charges US$8 per person. Neither place is anything special, except that here you'll be mostly with locals rather than with the tourist herds on the beach.

Ruma Guest House is on the edge of Nungwi village, and also inland from the beach. It's fairly unattractive with basic, undistinguished rooms built around a concrete courtyard for US$10 per person.

Most travellers stay in one of the more upmarket places directly on the beach. They are listed here from west to east.

Amaan Bungalows (☎ 0811-327747, ☎/fax 337453), run by East Africa Diving & Water Sports, has pleasant cottages with fans and screens for US$20/25/36 single/double/

triple (US$25/35/50 with bathroom). There is a restaurant, and you can also rent bicycles (US$10 per day) as well as a full range of diving equipment. Most guests are here to do diving, and the atmosphere is fairly hectic.

Even more hectic is *Paradise Beach Club* (☎ 0811-338351, fax 30267, email zanzibar @diveafrica.com), which is run by Dive Africa. Singles/doubles/triples are US$36/ 36/45; discounts are available in the low season and a full range of equipment rental is available. This is definitely not the place to come if you want a quiet, secluded beach holiday. Next door to Paradise Beach Club is *Eddie's Bungalows* which has been recommended by some travellers. Simple accommodation costs about US$6 per night.

Just up from Paradise Beach Club is the calmer *Baraka Bungalows*. Singles with shared facilities cost US$15 and doubles/ triples with bathroom cost US$45/55. Snorkelling equipment can be rented here.

All of these seaside places have restaurants; meals cost from Tsh3000. For less expensive food try *Gossip Restaurant* between Amaan Bungalows and Paradise Beach Club.

On the quieter and more attractive eastern edge of the cape, the first place you reach coming from the north is *Mnarani Beach Cottages* (☎/fax 33440 or 081-334062, email mnarani@cctz.com). Accommodation in pleasant bungalows costs US$50/70 single/double including breakfast; half and full-board options are also available and credit cards are accepted.

Next is *Saheles*, a pleasant place with doubles (no singles) from US$30 (US$45 with bathroom). There are also simple *bandas* (thatched huts) overlooking the sea for US$8 per person, including rope beds and a common shower. Saheles is also building bungalows which will be priced at US$45 per double. There's no telephone here, but you can book through Tabasam Arts & Crafts on Cathedral St in Zanzibar Town, just a few doors away from Chit Chat restaurant.

Ras Nungwi Beach Hotel (☎ 33767, fax 33098, email rasnungwi@zanzibar.net) is next door to Saheles. It's a luxury lodge with comfortable accommodation from US$80 per person sharing, including full board (US$115 in a chalet with sea views). Low-season rates are also available; there is a 'very high season' supplement of US$20 per person per night from mid-December to early January. Credit card payments are charged an additional 10%.

A branch of Dive Africa is located at Ras Nungwi for hotel clients.

Kendwa About 3km south-west of Nungwi along the beach is tiny Kendwa village, which is good for budget travellers wanting somewhere quieter than Nungwi. There are reefs for snorkelling, and you still have some beach at high tide – unlike at Nungwi, where it essentially disappears. You can walk to Kendwa from Nungwi at low tide in about 25 to 30 minutes. Alternatively, there is a boat taxi from Amaan Bungalows (see earlier) about four times daily depending on demand (Tsh1000 per person with a minimum of five people). To reach here by vehicle, take the unmarked, rough dirt road cutting sharply south-west off the main road into Nungwi; allow about 40 minutes.

Places to Stay & Eat There are three accommodation options at Kendwa, listed here from north to south. The first is *White Sands*, with simple bandas for US$8 per person. *Kendwa Rocks* is next, with bandas for US$9 per person, as well as a few bungalows for US$35 per double. *Amaan Annex* (*☎/fax 0811-337543, 335090*), south of Kendwa Rocks, is run by Amaan Bungalows at Nungwi. All accommodation here is en suite, and is priced the same as en suite accommodation at Amaan Bungalows. There is a small dive centre, and live music on Wednesday and Saturday evenings.

Meals are available at all three of these places.

Getting There & Away To get to Nungwi from Zanzibar Town, take bus No 16 (Tsh600, four to six hours), which departs around 11 am from the market. Alternative-

ly, minivans arranged by tour operators come here daily (Tsh3000, 1½ to two hours). If you are driving on your own, it's faster to take the tarmac route from Mahonda via Kinyasini (to the east), rather than the deteriorated road from Mahonda due north via Dongwe and Mkokotoni.

Matemwe

Matemwe is a beautiful and quiet beach with some of the finest sand on Unguja. It's about 25km south-east of Nungwi, and reached via an unpaved road branching east off the main road by Mkwajuni.

The place to stay here is the wonderfully relaxing *Matemwe Bungalows* (*☎ 33789, fax 31342, PO Box 3275 Zanzibar*) with simple but comfortable singles/doubles for US$80/130 (US$110/160 with bathroom), including full board; there is no electricity. The owners have made great efforts to reduce the impact of their establishment on the local community, and have set up a variety of small scale conservation projects aimed at building community support for and collaboration in conservation. Matemwe Bungalows has very good cuisine, made primarily with local ingredients and produce. Their booking office is just a few kilometres north of Zanzibar Town, signposted off the Bububu road. Diving and snorkelling excursions can be arranged at Matemwe through Zanzibar Dive Adventures (*☎/fax 32503, PO Box 2282*).

Some travellers have written about a place called the *H-Beach Village Resort*, about 2km south of Matemwe, with accommodation for US$15 per person and a simple restaurant.

Kiwengwa

Kiwengwa is set on a beautiful, long beach, much of which is occupied by Italian-run resort hotels. The village itself is divided into three parts: Cairo to the north, Kiwengwa proper in the centre and just east of the main junction, and Kumba Urembo to the south. Public transport will drop you in Kiwengwa proper unless you pay the driver extra to take you further.

Places to Stay & Eat The most laid-back place to stay is the relaxing *Reef View (PO Box 3215)*, in the Kumba Urembo section of Kiwengwa. It's run by a British-Zanzibari couple, and is primarily for those who have at least several nights to spend. Accommodation in simple bandas costs US$10 per person including breakfast. The owners are also building bungalows to be priced about US$30 per double, as well as a restaurant and bar. Good meals, including good vegetarian selections, are available for about Tsh3000. Other special dietary requests, such as kosher, will also be entertained given sufficient notice. There is a boat and snorkelling equipment for rent, and a small book exchange. To get here, you can either take the No 17 bus to Kiwengwa centre and then walk about 20 minutes, or pay the driver about Tsh1000 extra to be dropped off at Reef View. From the main junction to Reef View is 1.5km. At low tide you can walk along the beach. If you have trouble finding it, just ask locals to point the way to 'Haroub and Helen's place'.

Other budget options include *Paradise Restaurant* just north of Francorosso (see listing following), which has simple bandas for about US$12 per person, and the *Family Beach Resort*, just south of Vera Club (see listing following), with one or two rooms for US$15 per person.

North of the main junction are a string of upmarket resorts catering to Italian package tourists. All can be booked through tour operators in Zanzibar Town. They include the *Bravo Club* (☎ 0811-339961, fax 333729), with full-board accommodation from US$140 per person, the *Vera Club*, *Kiwengwa Club Village – Francorosso* and *Venta Club*.

Further north is *The Shooting Star Restaurant & Lodge* (☎ 0811-335835) which is known for its good food and cosy atmosphere. There are some inexpensive bandas for rent, and cottage-style accommodation from about US$50 per person.

Between Kiwengwa and Pwani Mchangani to the north are the *Mapenzi Beach Resort*, with luxury accommodation from US$120 per person including full board, and the *Hotel Coral Reef Village*, with equally comfortable accommodation from US$100 per person. Both cater to the Italian package tourist market; bookings can be made through tour operators in Zanzibar Town.

Getting There & Away Bus No 17 runs once daily between Zanzibar Town and Kiwengwa (Tsh500).

Uroa

Uroa is set on an attractive beach north of Chwaka. Places to stay here include the upmarket *Uroa Bay Hotel & Fishing Club* (☎ 33552), with comfortable bungalow-style accommodation from about US$120 per person full board, or the less expensive but pleasant *Tamarind Beach Hotel* (☎ 33941, 51859 or 0811-323556), with accommodation from US$100 per person including breakfast.

The best access is from the south, via Chwaka. The road to the north between Uroa and Kiwengwa is passable in a 4WD. In a conventional car, there is one very rocky area that you may not be able to get around without causing some damage to the undercarriage.

Chwaka

Chwaka, a lively fishing village on Chwaka Bay almost due east of Zanzibar Town, is seldom visited by tourists. Much of the bay is very shallow, and suitable only for small boats. For accommodation try the *Chwaka Bay Beach Hotel* with rooms from about US$25 per person, and a restaurant.

Bwejuu to Pingwe

Bwejuu is about 3km north of Paje along a sand track. The tarmac road bypasses Bwejuu; you must take the sand track. To get here from Zanzibar Town, take bus No 9 from the market to Paje, from where you will have to walk or hitch a ride.

The *ZTC resthouse* is basic but decent, with lodging for US$10 per double or US$20 for the whole bungalow which can accommodate between one and five persons. You must book in advance through the tourist office at Livingstone House in Zanzibar Town, where you will be given a permit to show to the caretaker in Bwejuu. There are some pans if you want to cook; supplies can be purchased in the village. Alternatively, the caretaker can shop and/or cook for you for a fee.

Just next door is the busy *Bwejuu Dere Beach Resort* (☎ *31047, 31017)* with rooms for US$8 per person (US$10 with bathroom). Meals can be arranged on request.

Heading further north, *Seven Seas Bungalows & Restaurant* has simple but clean rooms for US$10 per person including bathroom. There is also a restaurant.

Next up is *Palm Beach Inn* (☎ *32733 or 0811-338553, fax 33886)*, with good rooms for US$15/30 including bathroom and nets, and a restaurant. The nearby *Jamal's Restaurant* has good, inexpensive meals.

Kibuda Family Guest House is just a bit further up. It's somewhat inland and on the opposite side of the road, but cheaper, with rooms for about US$7 per person; meals can be arranged.

Beyond here is *Evergreen Bwejuu* with accommodation for US$10 per person. There is also camping for US$5 per person including shower, but security is questionable and this place isn't recommended.

Continuing northwards towards Dongwe are *Twisted Palm* with accommodation for US$10 per person, and *Hammond's Guest House*, a family-style place about 2km from Bwejuu and set back from the beach with basic lodging for about US$7.

From here north to Pingwe, the only accommodation options are upmarket. The first that you will reach is the attractive Belgian-German managed *Sunrise Hotel & Restaurant* (☎/fax *0811-320206)* with comfortable bungalow-style accommodation for US$60/70 single/double and a highly recommended restaurant. It's about 3km north of Bwejuu.

Next up is the ritzy *Breezes Beach Club* (☎ *0811-326595, fax 333151, email breezes @zanzinet.com)*, which bills itself as the island's only five-star accommodation out-

side of Zanzibar Town. Rooms start at about US$90 per person sharing including half board. Low-season rates are also available. Breezes is still marked on some maps as the Alpha Project.

Towards the end of the peninsula are *Dongwe Blue Marlin*, another upmarket place, and *Karafuu Hotel Beach Resort* (☎ *0811-325157, fax 325670)* with accommodation from US$160 per person. All can be booked through tour operators in Zanzibar Town.

To reach these northern places there is a new, tarmac road running from Paje up to the Karafuu Hotel. You can also take the sand track along the beach, although it deteriorates to the north. There is no public transport on this stretch north of Bwejuu, and only sporadic transport on the new road. Local boats to Chwaka run from Michamvi, on the western tip of the peninsula opposite the Karafuu Hotel.

Paje

Paje is the tiny village at the junction where the coastal road north to Bwejuu and south to Jambiani joins with the road from Zanzibar Town.

Paje Ndame Village (☎ *0811-329535)* has doubles with bathroom from US$25. They rent snorkelling equipment (US$15 including boat transport) and can arrange diving excursions (US$65 for a double dive including equipment rental).

Paradise Beach Bungalows (fax *32327)* is also a pleasant place, with rooms for US$16/27 including bathroom and net. They rent snorkelling equipment (Tsh500 for a mask, Tsh1500 for fins, Tsh2000 per person for boat transport with a minimum of five people) and bicycles (Tsh2500 per day).

Jambiani

Jambiani is an attractive beach stretching for several kilometres down the coast. It's popular with budget travellers as there are numerous inexpensive accommodation options here, although there are some upscale places, too. To get to Jambiani, take bus No 9 from the market. The trip takes about three hours. Alternatively, take one of the daily minivans organised by tour operators in Zanzibar Town (Tsh3000, 1½ to two hours). The places described below are listed in order from north to south.

The **ZTC resthouse** is set directly on the beach. Accommodation rates and booking information are the same as for the ZTC resthouse in Bwejuu. It's a good deal at US$20 for up to five people.

Annex of Imani Beach Lodge (*π/fax 33476*), which has no relation to Imani Beach Lodge north of Zanzibar Town, is a tiny family-style place on the beach with simple but decent accommodation for US$10 per person (US$30 for a double with bathroom), and a restaurant.

Oyster Hotel (*π 32150 or 0811-333215*) has very mediocre singles/doubles, all with fans and nets, from US$20/30 (US$30/40 with bathroom). Hot water is also supposedly available.

Oasis Inn has simple but acceptable rooms for US$7/16, including nets, and common facilities.

East Coast Visitor's Inn (*π 0811-333964, 331258*) is also not bad, and is popular with travellers. Singles/doubles are US$20/30 (US$40 for a double with bathroom).

Jambiani Beach Hotel has a concrete-block atmosphere, but the rooms are not bad, and it's popular with travellers. Singles/doubles with bathroom are US$10/20. You can book through Suna Tours in Zanzibar Town (*π 33597*). They also have a restaurant and offer bike rental (Tsh500 per hour or Tsh3000 per day).

The upscale **Sau Inn Hotel** (*π 0811-340039, π/fax 337440, email sau-inn @cats-net.com or in Zanzibar Town c/o Zenith Tours π 32320, fax 33973*) has comfortable bungalow-style accommodation for US$50/60 including breakfast. Half and full-board arrangements can be made, and fax and email services are available.

Many travellers have written to recommend **Shehe Guest House**, towards the southern end of Jambiani beach. Tiny but clean rooms with nets cost about US$10 per person; meals are available, and they are sometimes willing to provide transport from Zanzibar Town.

OFFSHORE ISLANDS
Changuu (Prison) Island
Changuu island lies north-west of Zanzibar Town. It was originally used to detain 're-calcitrant slaves' and later as a quarantine station. Today the island makes a pleasant day excursion from Unguja; the nearby reef is good for novice snorkelling. Changuu is also known for its large family of giant tortoises, which are believed to have been brought here from Aldabra in the Seychelles around the turn of the century.

Changuu is run by the Zanzibar Tourist Corporation, and there is a US$4 entry charge, though if you are spending the night on the island you do not need to pay this fee.

Accommodation in basic bungalows costs US$12/20/24 for a single/double/triple; book in advance through the ZTC's office at Livingstone House in Zanzibar Town. There is also a restaurant in the former house of the British governor, General Lloyd Matthews; meals cost about Tsh2500. At the time this book was being researched, the house and restaurant were being renovated and the bungalows were temporarily closed; inquire in Zanzibar Town to see if they have re-opened. The rental of snorkel equipment on Changuu costs Tsh1000 per day.

Any of the Zanzibar Town tour operators can arrange an excursion. Alternatively, fishing boats can be hired from the beach by the Tembo House Hotel or near Pichy's Pizza. It costs between Tsh12,000 and Tsh15,000 for a day trip.

Bawi Island
Tiny Bawi lies about 7km west of Zanzibar Town and several kilometres south-west of Changuu. There is no village on the island, but it offers a nice beach and good snorkelling. You will need to bring equipment with you or hire it in Zanzibar Town or on Changuu island. Fishing boats can be hired from Zanzibar Town near the Tembo House Hotel or near Pichy's Pizza for about Tsh15,000; the trip takes about 40 minutes.

Camping is not considered safe, according to the Zanzibar Tourist Corporation. Various tour operators run day trips to Bawi with a stop en route at Changuu. Prices range from Tsh12,000 to Tsh25,000 per person, usually including lunch.

Chapwani (Grave) Island

This tiny, privately owned island is about 4km north of Zanzibar Town. There is a cemetery here, a small beach and a few bungalows for overnight lodging. Inquire at tour operators in Zanzibar Town for details.

Tumbatu Island

The large island of Tumbatu lies off the north-west coast of Unguja. It is populated by the Tumbatu people, one of the three original ethnic groups on the archipelago. At the southern tip of the island are the ruins of a mosque, possibly dating from the early 11th century. As recently as the last century, there were no water sources on Tumbatu and villagers had to come over to the mainland for supplies.

To get here, you can arrange transport with local fishing boats from Mkokotoni, opposite Tumbatu on the main island, or from Nungwi. There is no accommodation on Tumbatu.

Mnemba Island

Tiny Mnemba island, just off the east coast of Unguja and north-east of Matemwe, is surrounded by a coral reef hosting a large variety of marine life, including tuna, barracuda, moray eel and reef shark. The island is privately owned. The only hotel is the exclusive *Mnemba Island Lodge* run by Conservation Corporation Africa with booking offices in Kenya (☎ 254-2-441001, 746707, fax 750512, email conscorp@users .africaonline.co.ke, PO Box 74957 Nairobi), Dar es Salaam (☎ 051-750298, fax 746826) and Unguja (☎ 33110). Accommodation is in 10 luxury cottages and costs US$400 per person per day, all-inclusive, with boat transfer from Unguja. The lodge is closed during April and May. Access to Mnemba is restricted to hotel guests, although diving is permitted on the surrounding reef. Visibility is said to average about 25m.

Chumbe Island

Chumbe is an uninhabited island located 12km south of Zanzibar Town and 6km south-west of Chukwani. It measures just over 1km long and about 300m wide and is composed of coral rag and surrounded by coral reef, with an exceptional shallow-water coral reef along its western shore noted for its diversity of corals and fish life. The reef is in excellent condition, thanks largely to the fact that since the 1960s Chumbe was part of a military zone and off-limits to locals and visitors. Since 1992, the coral rag forest and western fringing reef have been under protection. In 1994, Chumbe Island Coral Park (CHICOP) was created, making the island Zanzibar's first marine sanctuary. In addition to nearly 200 species of coral, the surrounding waters host about 350 species of fish; groups of dolphins pass by to feed on the abundant fish life. The island also provides a haven for hawksbill turtles, and has diverse bird life with over 50 species recorded to date, including the endangered roseate tern. In addition to its marine life, there are three historical buildings on the island: a lighthouse and a small mosque dating from the early 1900s, and the former warden's house.

Apart from protection of Chumbe's reef and ecosystems, one of the main goals of the island's development has been the education of local school children, and an environmental education centre has been built especially targeting this group. There are also forest and marine nature trails.

While you can visit Chumbe as a day trip (US$50 all-inclusive, book through Mbweni Ruins Hotel), overnighting is encouraged in order to facilitate maintenance of and appreciation for its environment. Comfortable accommodation in attractive bungalows built with environmental conservation in mind costs from US$100 per person including full board. Bookings can be made through CHICOP (☎/fax 31040, email chumbe .island@raha.com, PO Box 3203 Zanzibar) or the Mbweni Ruins Hotel.

Other Islets

Just offshore from Zanzibar Town are several tiny islets, many ringed by coral reefs. These include Nyange, Pange and Murogo, which are simply sand banks and partially disappear at high tide although they offer good snorkelling and diving.

OTHER ATTRACTIONS
Kizimkazi

Kizimkazi is the site of a Shirazi mosque dating from the early 12th century and considered to be one of the oldest Islamic buildings on the East African coast, although much of what you see today is restorations carried out in the 1770s. The Quran verses inscribed in its *mihrab* (the prayer niche showing the direction to Mecca) date to 1107 and are among the oldest known examples of Swahili writing.

Kizimkazi is also known for its dolphins, and many travellers come here to see them, although with the large numbers of visitors it is getting a bit overdone these days. You can either arrange trips with tour operators in Zanzibar Town, or in Kizimkazi with local fishermen.

Most travellers come here as a day trip from Zanzibar Town. There is basic accommodation in Kizimkazi if you want to spend the night.

To get here take the No 10 bus towards Makunduchi (Tsh700), then transfer at Kufile to cars for Kizimkazi, or walk (5km). The mosque is actually about 2km north of the main section of town in Dimbani village.

Jozani Forest

Jozani forest, located about 35km south-east of Zanzibar Town off the road to Paje, is the largest area of mature forest left on Unguja. For the past several years it has been part of the Jozani-Chwaka Bay Conservation Area (see the boxed text). The forest hosts populations of the rare red colobus monkey, as well as Sykes monkeys, bushbabies, Ader's duikers, hyraxes, over 50 species of butterflies, about 40 species of birds and several

---

Jozani-Chwaka Bay Conservation Area

Jozani forest forms the core of the Jozani-Chwaka Bay Conservation Area (JCBCA), which covers about 44 sq km of Unguja, from Uzi Bay in the south-west to Chwaka Bay in the north-east. In addition to the forest, the JCBCA encompasses a wide variety of ecosystems, and protects several rare and endemic species.

In contrast to some other areas of Tanzania, where local human populations have been excluded from their home areas in the name of conservation, the JCBCA is notable for the extent to which communities living within and near its boundaries are being incorporated into environmental activities. Good examples of this collaboration are the Natural Resource Committees which have been established in numerous villages. These committees work to encourage support for conservation measures, provide a forum for the exchange of ideas between villagers and forestry staff members, and ensure that forest conservation is balanced with community needs.

JCBCA's collaborative approach has already yielded results. Programmes under way which are benefiting local communities and the forest, and which are promoting a sustainable relationship between the two, include establishment of tree nurseries, community education activities, forest guide training, and local involvement in tourism development.

Additional information on the JCBCA can be obtained from the Commission for Natural Resources (☎/fax 31252, edgznz@twiga.com, PO Box 3950 Zanzibar), or the forest officer (see the contact information under Jozani Forest). At present, the major funding for JCBCA activities comes from the government of Austria through the nongovernmental organisation CARE.

other animals. There is a nature trail in the forest, which takes about 45 minutes to walk. Guides are available at the information centre by the entrance gate. Entry (including a guide) costs US$10. Those with a scientific or research interest in Jozani can contact the forest officer (☎ 31252, email edgznz @twiga.com, PO Box 3526). Despite what many tour operators say, when observing the monkeys it's important not to get too close – park staff recommend no closer than 3m. This is both for your safety and the safety of the animals. In addition to there being a risk of being bitten by the monkeys, there is considerable concern that if the monkeys were to catch a human illness it could possibly spread and rapidly wipe out the already threatened population.

You can reach Jozani via bus No 9 or 10 (Tsh500), via chartered taxi, or with an organised tour from Zanzibar Town. The forest entrance is on the main road, and signposted; the bus will drop you at the entrance.

Clove plants have been Pemba's economic mainstay for hundreds of years.

Pemba

For much of its history, Pemba has been overshadowed by Unguja, its larger, more visible and more politically powerful neighbour to the south. Although the islands are only separated by about 50km of water, relatively few tourists make their way across the channel for a visit. The adventurous travellers who do, however, are seldom disappointed.

Unlike Unguja, which is flat and sandy, Pemba's terrain is hilly, fertile and heavily vegetated. In the old days of the Arab traders it was even referred to as *al khuthera* or 'the green island'. Throughout much of the period when the sultans of Zanzibar held sway over the East African coast, it was Pemba, with its extensive clove plantations and agricultural base, that provided the economic foundation for the archipelago's dominance. Even today, cloves continue to be the mainstay of the island's economy, with between 75 and 80% of overall clove production on the archipelago coming from Pemba. Earnings from the clove crop are buttressed by other agricultural products, by

cattle raising, and by fishing, which is an important source of livelihood.

Pemba has also been long renowned for its voodoo and traditional healers. Even today, people come from throughout East Africa either seeking cures or to learn the skills of the trade from practitioners on Pemba.

In addition to its rich history and traditions, Pemba is of interest to tourists for its wealth of natural resources ranging from beaches to mangrove ecosystems to natural forests. The coral reefs surrounding the island shelter a multitude of marine species and offer some of the best diving in the world. While much of the coast is lined with mangrove swamps, there are a few good stretches of shoreline and enough attractive offshore islands with good beaches and interesting bird life to keep visitors busy for awhile. There are 27 mammalian species on the island, several endemic bird species, and 13 bat species, including the endemic Pemba flying fox which is considered to be endangered.

The tourism industry on Pemba is in its infancy and infrastructure is for the most

---

Pesky Mangroves?

There are about 18,000 hectares of mangrove forests along Unguja's coasts and inlets; even more of Pemba's coastline is 'overgrown' with mangroves. From a traveller's point of view it may seem that they just take up what otherwise would be prime beach space. However, mangroves play an important role in coastal ecosystems by anchoring shifting mud and sands and thereby curbing erosion. The trees, which are resistant to insects, are also important links in the food chain, enriching both inter-tidal zones as well as the open sea with organic nutrients. Locals use mangroves for making boats and dhows, and as building material. In the old days of trade between Arabia and the East African coast, mangrove wood was a coveted barter item.

---

part fairly basic, although this is slowly beginning to change. The main requirement for exploring the island is time, as there is little regular transport off the main routes.

HISTORY

Pemba is geologically much older than Unguja and is believed to have been settled at an earlier date, although little is known about its original inhabitants. According to an ancient legend, the island was once peopled by giants known as the Magenge. More certain is that Pemba's first inhabitants migrated from the mainland, perhaps as early as several thousand years ago. The Shirazi presence on Pemba is believed to date from the 9th or 10th century, although a recent report claiming the discovery of remnants of a 6th century mosque near Chake Chake may push this date back even further. Some 12th century Shirazi ruins at Ras Mkumbuu, north-west of Chake Chake, indicate that settlements were well established on Pemba by that point. The Portuguese attacked Pemba in the early 16th century and sought to subjugate its inhabitants by ravaging many towns and demanding tributes. As a result, many

Pembans fled to Mombasa. By the late 17th century, the Busaidi family of Omani Arabs had taken over the island and driven away the last remaining Portuguese. Before long, however, the Mazrui, a rival group of Omanis based in Mombasa, gained the upper hand on Pemba and governed the island until 1822. In 1890, Pemba, together with Unguja, became a British protectorate.

Following the Zanzibar revolution in 1964, President Karume closed Pemba to foreigners in an effort to contain strong anti-government sentiment on the island. Pemba

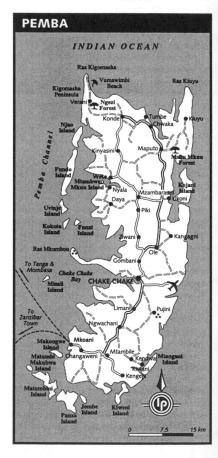

PEMBA

INDIAN OCEAN

Ras Kigomasha

Vumawimbi Beach

Kigomasha Peninsula

Ras Kiuyu

Verani

Ngezi Forest

Njao Island

Konde

Tumbe

Chwaka

Kiuyu

Kinyasini

Maputo

Msitu Mkuu Forest

Fundo Island

Wete

Mtambwe Mkuu Island

Nyala

Kojani Island

Uvinje Island

Daya

Mzambarauni

Likoni

Piki

Kokota Island

Funzi Island

Ziwani

Kangagni

Ras Mkumbuu

Gombani

Ole

To Tanga & Mombasa

Chake Chake Bay

CHAKE CHAKE

Misali Island

Limani

Pujini

To Zanzibar Town

Ngwachani

Makongwe Island

Mkoani

Matumbi Makubwa Island

Changaweni

Mtambile

Kendwa

Mtangani Island

Kiweni

Kengeja

Matumbini Island

Jombe Island

Kiweni Island

Panza Island

0   7.5   15 km

Pemba Channel

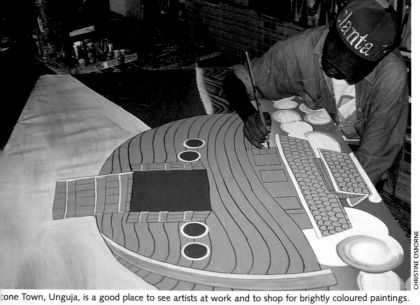

:one Town, Unguja, is a good place to see artists at work and to shop for brightly coloured paintings.

Unguja's main market is still in Stone Town, which continues to be the trading hub of the archipelago

Stone Town architecture, Unguja

Chicken market, Stone Town, Unguja

House of Wonders, Stone Town, Unguja

remained closed until the 1980s, although even then the situation remained strained. Tensions peaked during the 1995 elections, and relations have steadily deteriorated since then with Pembans feeling increasingly marginalised and frustrated. Away from main towns, illiteracy rates are as high as 95% in some areas and roads and other infrastructure badly neglected, particularly in the island's forgotten south-eastern and north-eastern corners.

ORIENTATION
Maps
The only map of Pemba available on the island is the one put out by the Commission for Lands & Environment (1:100,000). The best place to look for it is at the tourist office in Chake Chake. The Commission also has a good two-sheet topographical series for Pemba (1:50,000, 1986, Tsh1000 per sheet), as well as individual sheets for the island's major towns (1:10,000); see Maps in the Unguja (Zanzibar Island) section.

INFORMATION
Tourist Offices
The Zanzibar Tourist Corporation's Pemba branch (☎ 054-52121) is located in Chake Chake next to the Hoteli ya Chake. It is worth stopping by to ask if any new hotels have opened, or for information about Pemba's sights. The office can also assist in arranging car hire. Sometimes they have maps of Pemba for sale.

Money
There are foreign exchange bureaus in Chake Chake and Wete where you can change cash or travellers cheques.

Post & Communications
The postal service is fairly efficient. It takes about two weeks for a letter between the island and Europe or Australia.

You can make telephone calls to the mainland or abroad from the post office or from card phones in the major towns. Rates for the card phones range from Tsh1000 for a 10 unit card to Tsh32,000 for a 2000 unit card.

Travel Agencies
The best travel agency on the island is Partnership Travel & Tours. Their main office is in Chake Chake. Guesthouses in Chake Chake and Wete can also be helpful in arranging visits to various places on the island.

If you are making arrangements to visit Pemba from Zanzibar Town, Eco Tours & Travel is good for assisting with excursions to Misali island and Tropical Tours is good for general information on Pemba. See Travel Agencies in the Unguja (Zanzibar Island) section earlier in this chapter.

Libraries & Newspapers
There are no bookshops on Pemba, but there is a good library in Chake Chake thanks to the British Council and the work of VSO volunteers.

Same-day English language newspapers from the mainland are available in Chake Chake.

Medical Services
For dire emergencies, the Chinese-run government hospital in Mkoani is probably your best bet, although standards leave much to be desired.

Chloroquine (for malaria) is available in major towns.

Accommodation
There is no accommodation outside the main towns other than a few new tourist resorts. In Chake Chake, Wete and Mkoani there are government hotels and basic guesthouses, although all are expensive for what you get in comparison to elsewhere in Tanzania, unless you are eligible for resident rates; budget at least US$10 to US$15 per night. Pemba has its own generator and main towns have electricity most days, though there are usually two or three days a month when it is down.

Food & Drink
The food situation on Pemba is fairly bleak, although there are plenty of fruits in the markets. Wete is the best place for vegetables from the mainland. Guesthouses in the main

THE ZANZIBAR ARCHIPELAGO

towns prepare good meals, but you usually need to organise this well in advance.

Other than local brews (the most common of which is *nazi*, a fermented coconut wine), there is little alcohol available on the island. The best places to try for a beer are the government hotels or the police canteens in the main towns. If you try the nazi, be sure it's fresh (made within the past 24 hours), otherwise it goes bad.

GETTING THERE & AWAY
Air
There is currently no commercial air service to Pemba. However, there are plans to rehabilitate the airport so it is worth inquiring to see if regular flights from Unguja or Dar es Salaam have begun.

Charter flights from Unguja cost between US$450 and US$500 one way for a five seater plane. A one-way charter between Pemba and Dar es Salaam costs about US$700. For further details, contact Zan Air or other air charter operators (see Air Charter under Getting There & Away in the Unguja (Zanzibar Island) section earlier in this chapter).

If you're travelling alone or in a small group, it's often worth checking to see if there are any charter flights with spare seats. The best source of information is the control tower at the airport in Chake Chake (☎ 52238). Extra seats on chartered flights between Pemba and Unguja are usually sold for between Tsh20,000 and Tsh25,000.

Boat
The best connections are on Mega-Speed's efficiently run MS *Sepideh*, which sails six days weekly between Dar es Salaam and Pemba via Unguja, and once weekly between Pemba, Tanga and Mombasa. For schedule and price information, see Getting There & Away under the Unguja (Zanzibar Island) section earlier in this chapter. Mega-Speed (☎ 56100 on Pemba) has booking offices in Mkoani, Chake Chake, and Wete.

The next best option is the *Mapinduzi*, though it's far inferior to the *Sepideh*. It departs Unguja every Friday at 9 pm, arriv-

ing at Pemba about 6 am the next morning. The return trip is on Sunday, departing Pemba about 9 am and arriving Unguja sometime during the afternoon. It costs Tsh8000/6500/4000, 1st/2nd/3rd class plus US$5 port tax. On the *Mapinduzi*, it's well worth buying 1st class if you can afford it; deck seating is crowded and uncomfortable. You can arrange tickets at the port in Mkoani, or with travel agents in Chake Chake and Wete.

The third option is Azam Marine's *Serengeti*, which travels irregularly between Unguja and Pemba. Comfort (or discomfort) levels are slightly better than those on the *Mapinduzi*. Departures from Unguja are usually about 10 pm, arriving early the next morning at Pemba. The return trip from Pemba usually departs about 11 am, arriving in Unguja between four and five hours later. Tickets cost US$15 plus US$5 port tax. Inquire at the port at Mkoani or with travel agents in Chake Chake or Wete for schedule details. If you take this boat at night, try to get to the port early to get one of their '1st class' couches; there's no extra charge, but they're more comfortable than the other seating.

While dhows ply between Pemba and the mainland, notably between Wete and Tanga, the journey is risky, and captains are usually unwilling to take foreigners. If you want to travel this way anyway, inquire near the port in Mkoani or Wete.

GETTING AROUND
Pemba is a small place and getting around is not too difficult provided that you have lots of time and patience. Bus drivers are usually willing to take you to destinations off the main routes for an additional fee. Otherwise, cars and motorbikes can be hired in Chake Chake and sometimes in Wete, and the entire island is great for cycling.

Road conditions in Pemba are not bad at all in comparison with mainland Tanzania, although all secondary routes are unpaved. Between Mkoani and Chake Chake the road is deteriorated tarmac. Between Chake Chake and Wete via Ziwani (the 'old' road) is tarmac but deteriorated in places; from Wete on to Konde is in poor condition. The route from Chake Chake north to Konde via Ole (the 'new' road) is in good condition. From Konde north to the Kigomasha peninsula is a sandy track. In the south, the road from Mtambile to Kengeja is in poor condition.

To/From Mkoani Port

Mega-Speed runs a shuttle bus from Wete (Tsh1000) and Chake Chake (Tsh500) to Mkoani connecting with all the *Sepideh* departures. The buses leave from Wete about three hours before the *Sepideh's* scheduled departure time, and from Chake Chake approximately two hours before. It's best to book a place in advance when buying your boat ticket, as the bus is often very crowded. In Wete, the main pick-up point is at Raha Tours, around the corner from the post office, though it's worth finding out where the bus will stop before Raha because by the time it reaches Raha most of the good seats are taken. In Chake Chake the pick-up point is in front of the Mega-Speed office at Partnership Travel & Tours.

For departures on the *Mapinduzi* or *Serengeti* you will have to take local transport to the port or hire a car in Chake Chake.

Bus

Pemba's three major towns and several of the smaller ones are connected throughout the day by local buses. Prices for all destinations are about Tsh400 to Tsh500. The main lines are as follows:

No 3 connects Mkoani with Chake Chake.
No 6 connects Chake Chake with Wete via the 'old' road.
No 24 connects Wete with Konde.
No 34 connects Chake Chake with Wete via the 'new' (eastern) road.
No 35 connects Chake Chake with Konde via the 'new' (eastern) road (Tsh500).

To reach towns off these main routes via public transport, take one of the above buses to the nearest intersection, from where you will either have to walk or rely on sporadic pick-ups or other local transport. Bus drivers are often willing to make detours to drop you for an additional fee.

Taxi & Car Rental

Pemba's taxi industry is in its infancy and there are few vehicles. However, in Chake Chake (and sometimes in Wete), you can arrange to hire a car, minivan or motorbike for the day. Rates average from US$40 per day for a small Suzuki 4WD with driver, and about US$25 per day for motorbikes. Both Partnership Travel & Tours and the tourist office in Chake Chake can assist with rentals.

Bicycle

Cycling is an excellent way to get around Pemba, although you'll need to bring your own bicycle unless you're content with one of the single-speeds available locally. Distances are relatively short and roads are not as heavily travelled as on the mainland. You'll need to come equipped with any spare parts you may need.

CHAKE CHAKE

Lively Chake Chake is Pemba's main town. Although it has been occupied for centuries, there is little architectural evidence remaining from its past other than the ruins of an 18th century fort near the hospital, and some 12th century ruins at nearby Ras Mkumbuu. As this book was being researched, there were also reports that remnants of a 6th century mosque had been found near Chake Chake.

The town is set on a ridge overlooking Chake Chake Bay, and there is a small dhow port and fish market along the water.

While there isn't much of interest in Chake Chake itself, the town makes a good base for visiting **Misali island** (see the boxed text later), and for exploring Pemba.

Information

The Pemba bureau de change opposite the tourist information office changes cash and travellers cheques. Rates are roughly equivalent to or slightly lower than what you can get on Unguja. If they are closed or out of money, try the small electrical shop next door; otherwise there's a branch of the People's Bank of Zanzibar just up the street.

Partnership Travel & Tours at the main intersection is the agent for Mega-Speed.

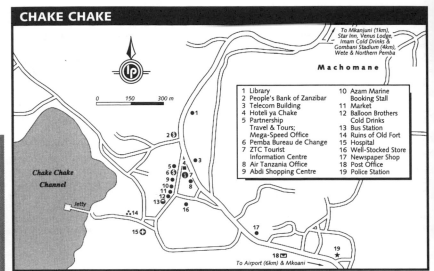

CHAKE CHAKE

To Mkanjuni (1km), Star Inn, Venus Lodge, Imam Cold Drinks & Gombani Stadium (4km), Wete & Northern Pemba

Machomane

0   150   300 m

Chake Chake Channel

Jetty

1	Library	
2	People's Bank of Zanzibar	
3	Telecom Building	
4	Hoteli ya Chake	
5	Partnership Travel & Tours; Mega-Speed Office	
6	Pemba Bureau de Change	
7	ZTC Tourist Information Centre	
8	Air Tanzania Office	
9	Abdi Shopping Centre	
10	Azam Marine Booking Stall	
11	Market	
12	Balloon Brothers Cold Drinks	
13	Bus Station	
14	Ruins of Old Fort	
15	Hospital	
16	Well-Stocked Store	
17	Newspaper Shop	
18	Post Office	
19	Police Station	

To Airport (6km) & Mkoani

Car hire (with driver) can be arranged by asking around at the main junction between the tourist office and the foreign exchange bureau. Look for minivans or smaller vehicles saying 'private hire'. You can sometimes find motorbikes here for rent as well. Partnership Travel & Tours and the tourist office can also assist.

Places to Stay & Eat

The only place to stay in the centre of town is the **Hoteli ya Chake** (☎ 054-52069), with singles/doubles for US$15/25 (despite the sign at reception quoting higher rates). It's fairly bleak, though the rooms are large and reasonably clean, and the place overall is not as bad as its reputation would suggest. If you stay, you'll probably be the only one here.

About 4km north of town in Gombani are two decent guesthouses. Prices at both include breakfast. To get to Gombani, take any dalla-dalla going north and ask them to drop you by the stadium.

Star Inn (☎ 56042) opposite Gombani Stadium has clean singles/doubles with share bath from US$15/30, and a good restaurant.

About 300m down the road heading back towards Chake Chake is **Venus Lodge** (☎ 52294) with rooms for US$20 with common bathroom. You can get meals here with a lot of advance notice – at least half a day.

Apart from the restaurants at the Star Inn and Venus Lodge, there are several local food stalls in town. For drinks, try **Balloon Brothers Cold Drinks** near the market.

The tiny **Imam Cold Drinks** kiosk immediately to the north of Star Inn has good, fresh yoghurt (*mtindi*) and, sometimes, grilled meat.

Most shops sell only basic supplies, but there are a few which have tinned cheese and peanut butter.

Getting There & Away

Air Chake Chake's Karume airport is Pemba's only airfield. It's signposted from Chake Chake, about 6km east of town. There is no regular bus service to the airport. You will have to arrange a ride, or walk.

Bus See the Pemba Getting Around section for information on local bus routes.

THE ZANZIBAR ARCHIPELAGO

Misali Island

Tiny Misali island, rumoured to be the site where the infamous Captain Kidd hid some of his treasure in the late 17th century, lies offshore from Chake Chake. It's about 1km long, up to 500m wide, partly forest-covered and surrounded by extensive coral reefs. In addition to offering attractive beaches, the island hosts rich inter-tidal ecosystems, abundant fish and bird life, and provides a sea turtle nesting area. The beaches on its western side are set aside for nesting turtles and breeding sea birds. Also on its western side are reefs offering very good snorkelling. On the eastern side is a mangrove forest. Misali's lack of fresh water has limited the development of permanent settlements. However, the surrounding waters are favoured by local fishermen and there are several fishing camps.

In 1998, the island and surrounding coral reef were gazetted as the Misali Island Marine Conservation Area, within which the island's ecosystems are to be preserved in harmony with ongoing use by local fishermen. There are both underwater and terrestrial nature trails at Misali. If you're interested in more detailed information on the Misali project, contact the Zanzibar Protected Areas Project at the Commission for Natural Resources (☎/fax 31252, email edgznz@twiga.com, PO Box 3950 Zanzibar), located about 5km north of Zanzibar Town on the Bububu road. There is also a project manager for Misali based at the Commission for Natural Resources office in Wete (☎ 54126), signposted about 2km north-east of the Hoteli ya Wete.

Camping is permitted on Misali, but you will have to bring all your own supplies, food and water and check in first with the Commission for Natural Resources in either Zanzibar Town or Wete. There is a US$10 per day conservation and community development fee.

Fishing boats can be hired to go over to Misali from the coast in the Mkanjuni area, about 1km north of Chake Chake on the Wete road. Expect to pay about Tsh35,000 for a return day trip. It takes about 1½ hours on a local boat; seas can be rough. Eco Tours & Travel in Zanzibar Town is knowledgeable about the island and can organise excursions including boat transport, a guide and food. Three-day, two-night packages from Zanzibar Town, including one day on Misali and one day on Pemba cost about US$200 per person, all-inclusive.

THE ZANZIBAR ARCHIPELAGO

MKOANI

Mkoani is the southernmost of Pemba's main towns and its most important port, where ships from Unguja or elsewhere usually arrive. There is little to see in Mkoani. Most travellers stop here only briefly en route to or from Kiweni, Chake Chake or beyond.

Information

There's no bureau de change in Mkoani (despite the signs you will see on the road). You must go to Chake Chake to change money.

Car hire is also difficult to arrange here; it's best to take a public bus to Chake Chake and arrange onward transport there.

The Mega-Speed ferry booking office is opposite the port. Immigration is next door.

Places to Stay & Eat

The best place to stay in Mkoani is *Mkoani Guest House* (☎ 56102), just to the northeast of the port. Singles/doubles with common bathroom are US$10/20. The restaurant here is the best place in town for meals. The other option is the usually empty government-run *Hoteli ya Mkoani*, with singles/doubles for US$15/25. It is worth checking to see if *Jondeni Guest House* has reopened; previously it was Mkoani's best lodging option.

For a cheap meal while waiting for the ferry, try *Salsad Café,* next to the Mega-Speed office at the port. There are numerous street food stands in town and by the port; one speciality is *pwezu* (grilled octopus).

Getting There & Away

See the Pemba Getting Around section for details of local transport. The bus station is about 200m east of the port, up the hill and just off the main road.

WETE

Wete is a pleasant town and a good base for exploring northern Pemba. It has the island's second most important port, through which much of its clove crop is exported. The road leading from Chake Chake to Wete via Ziwani is very pretty, with hills, villages and lots of banana trees.

Information

You can change cash or travellers cheques at the Wete bureau de change on the main road.

Mega-Speed has at least three booking offices in town for the *Sepideh*. The main one is at Raha Tours & Travel (☎ 54228) just off the main road. There's also one at Sunda House on the main road and a small stall near the market.

You can occasionally find motorbikes for rent in Wete.

Places to Stay & Eat

Hoteli ya Wete just off the main road near the junction is similar to the government hotels in Chake Chake and in Mkoani, and charges the same prices.

Sharouk Guest House (☎ 54386) at the western end of town is a good place with singles/doubles for US$10/20 (US$25 for a double with bathroom). Meals can be arranged with advance notice. The owner is knowledgeable about Wete and the surrounding area and can help you arrange excursions to Ngezi forest, Vumawimbi beach and other nearby destinations. He's also building a second guesthouse, *Sharouk II*, on the beach, which may be open by the time this book is published. Rooms will likely be priced mid-range.

Diagonally opposite Sharouk's is the government-owned *Bomani Guest House* which looks okay from the outside, but hadn't opened at the time of research.

Just south of the main road as you come into town is the friendly *Super Guest House* (☎ 54062) with singles/doubles from US$8/18.

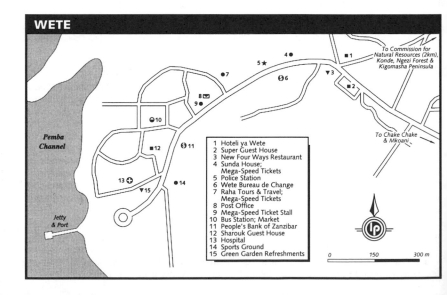

WETE

Pemba Channel

Jetty & Port

To Commission for Natural Resources (2km), Konde, Ngezi Forest & Kigomasha Peninsula

To Chake Chake & Mkoani

1 Hoteli ya Wete
2 Super Guest House
3 New Four Ways Restaurant
4 Sunda House; Mega-Speed Tickets
5 Police Station
6 Wete Bureau de Change
7 Raha Tours & Travel; Mega-Speed Tickets
8 Post Office
9 Mega-Speed Ticket Stall
10 Bus Station; Market
11 People's Bank of Zanzibar
12 Sharouk Guest House
13 Hospital
14 Sports Ground
15 Green Garden Refreshments

0   150   300 m

THE ZANZIBAR ARCHIPELAGO

For budget accommodation, there are a few local guesthouses which charge about Tsh1500 to Tsh2000 for basic rooms, but they are generally unwilling to take foreigners. If you are planning on staying in Wete for an extended period, they may be worth looking into.

For food, try *Green Garden Refreshments* at the western edge of Wete, which has a few outdoor tables on a tiny patio.

New Four Ways just off the main road near the entrance of town also has inexpensive meals, though it's not as good as the Green Garden.

There are a number of places where you can find street food; one place to look is by the market.

Getting There & Away
For information on local bus routes see the Pemba Getting Around section.

Dhows sail frequently between Tanga and Wete for about Tsh4000, but most captains will not take foreigners.

OTHER DESTINATIONS
Following are descriptions of some areas of interest around Pemba island and outside the main towns. Much of the island is relatively 'undiscovered'; for those with an adventurous spirit and lots of time, there are many more scenic and laid-back spots well worth exploring.

Kigomasha Peninsula
The Kigomasha peninsula in Pemba's northwest corner has several attractive beaches and a diving resort. It's also the site of the Ngezi forest (see Ngezi Forest, later in this chapter).

The nicest beach is **Vumawimbi** on the east coast of the peninsula. There is nothing here, and only the most basic provisions are available at the nearby village, so you'll have to bring your own food and drink. To get here you can bike or try to hitch a ride from Manta Reef Lodge, to the west. There's a daily water truck which goes from the lodge towards Konde and can drop you by Vumawimbi. Alternatively, Konde bus drivers

are usually willing to take you out for an extra fee, although you'll need to make arrangements for the return. Car hire for the day from Chake Chake will cost from about Tsh35,000.

On the western side of the peninsula is **Verani beach** and the relaxing *Manta Reef Lodge* which has its own generator and comfortable cottage-style accommodation for US$120 per person per night full board. Significant discounts of 50% and more are often available during the low season, or for bed and breakfast only arrangements. It's primarily a diving operation, and is run out of Kenya. Dive prices are comparable to those offered by outfitters on Unguja. Book through Partnership Travel & Tours in Chake Chake, or Zanzibar Town tour operators. The lodge often closes for periods during the off season, so check first in Chake Chake before making your way up here. If you book in advance, you can request the lodge to pick you up at the ferry in Mkoani. Otherwise, take the No 35 bus to Konde, from where you'll have to arrange with the driver to take you onwards to Manta Reef. Expect to pay about an additional Tsh5000.

Kiweni Island
Kiweni, shown as Shamiani island on some maps, lies just off the south-east coast of Pemba. Together with sections of the northeast, it's one of Pemba's more remote areas, neglected by the government and overlooked by most visitors. However, it's also one of Pemba's most beautiful corners, and an ideal place for relaxing and doing nothing.

The island hosts a very rich variety of birdlife (five of Pemba's six endemic species have been sighted here), and provides a nesting ground for some sea turtle colonies. It also offers some good snorkelling and diving, with one side of the island protected by the reef, and drop-off diving on the other side.

Near Kiweni, in the area around Kengeja (as well as at various other spots on Pemba) you will occasionally come across lighthearted '**bull fights**', said to date back to the days of Portuguese influence on the island.

Places to Stay & Eat The only place to stay on Kiweni is the wonderfully laid-back *Kiweni Marine Resort*, which was just about ready to open when this book was being researched. Visitors have a choice of comfortable tented accommodation (US$50 per person) or bungalow-style lodging on the beach (US$150); all prices include full board. The hotel has its own garden and is about 80% self-supporting; a percentage of profits are channelled back into the nearby community through the local women's group. Once the hotel is fully operational, a full range of water sports is also planned including diving, windsurfing and fishing. Although most of the diving in the area is advanced, there will be a dive master at Kiweni, and certification courses will be offered. There is also good snorkelling. The hotel is closed from mid-April to mid-June. For reservations or further information, write to PO Box 215 Chake Chake, or call ☎ 051-600901 in Dar es Salaam and ask for Liria.

Getting There & Away To get here, take any bus along the Mkoani-Chake Chake road to Mtambile junction. From Mtambile, you can find pick-ups or other transport to Kengeja, from where you will have to walk a few kilometres to the water and then take a boat over to Kiweni (Tsh2000). It costs about Tsh10,000 to hire a car from Chake Chake to Kengeja.

Ngezi Forest

The small, dense forest at Ngezi is part of the much larger natural forest which once covered large areas of Pemba. It is notable in that it resembles the highland rainforests of East Africa more than the lowland forests found on Unguja. Ngezi is also important as the home of *Pteropus voeltzkowi* or the Pemba flying fox, a bat endemic to the island, and the only fully endemic mammalian species known on Pemba. The forest is now a protected area and there is a small information centre, a short nature trail, and a US$5 entry fee.

Ngezi is north of Wete between Konde and Tondooni and makes a pleasant excursion

from Wete. To get here via public transport, take the bus to Konde, from where it is about a 3 to 4km walk. Bus drivers are sometimes willing to drop you at the information centre for an additional Tsh1000 to Tsh2000. You can easily combine Ngezi with a visit to Vumawimbi beach, either by walking (less than one hour) or by arranging a vehicle to wait while you visit the forest before going on to the beach.

Pujini Ruins

About 10km south-east of Chake Chake at Pujini are ruins of a town dating from about the 14th century. This was the seat of the infamous Mohammed bin Abdul Rahman who ruled on Pemba around the 15th century, prior to the arrival of the Portuguese. Locally, Rahman is known as *Mkame Ndume*, or 'milker of men'. For Pemba residents, his name is synonymous with cruelty due to the harsh punishments he meted out to his people. The ruins are in poor condition, and there is not too much to see now.

There is no regular public transport to Pujini. The best way to get here is by bicycle. Car hire from Chake Chake costs about Tsh10,000 round-trip.

Ras Mkumbuu

Ras Mkumbuu is the cape jutting out into the sea to the north-west of Chake Chake. It is the site of ruins of a mosque, some tombs and houses estimated to date from around the 14th or 15th century, possibly earlier. The settlement is thought to have been built by a group of Shirazis, although this too is uncertain. Although little is known about the early settlement on Ras Mkumbuu, it is believed to have been one of the major towns along the East African coast, with links to places as distant as Kilwa, although evidence for this is scanty. There is nothing at the ruins now except for a tiny fishing camp. For those interested in more details, there is an interesting article on the Ras Mkumbuu excavations in the History volume of *Tanzania Notes & Records* (1993 reprints edition).

The best way to visit the ruins (which are also referred to by locals as Ndagoni or Makutani) is by boat from Chake Chake, although this can be expensive. If you go via road, you will have at least an hour's walk at the end; one section of the path often becomes submerged at high tide, so plan accordingly.

Tumbe

Tumbe is a picturesque village and Pemba's major fishing centre. It's also the home of a significant lobster fisheries project which exports to Unguja and beyond. There is no accommodation, but the town makes a pleasant excursion from Wete or an interesting detour if you are heading north towards Vumawimbi. It's best to set out early from Wete so you can see the colourful fish market at its busiest. Offshore are some pleasant islets. About 2km south-east from Tumbe at

Chwaka are the overgrown ruins of a mosque, and a fort from the 18th century.

To get to Tumbe, take the No 35 bus and ask the driver to drop you at the junction, from where you can walk.

Other Islands

There are tiny islets dotted all along the coast of Pemba, most of which have nothing on them, but which make pleasant excursions. If you have any ideas of camping, keep in mind that many of the islands off Pemba's western coast are badly rat infested.

Some that are said to make good destinations include the tiny fishing islands offshore from Tumbe village, Mtambwe Mkuu island south-west of Wete, and the much larger Kojani island in the north-east, with areas of protected forest.

North-Eastern Tanzania

North-Eastern Tanzania is one of the country's most enticing regions for travellers and one of its most diverse. Inland are the lush, forested Usambara and Pare mountains which offer great hiking, beautiful scenery and – particularly in the Pares – some fascinating culture. Along the coast are attractive beaches and Sadani, Tanzania's only seaside game reserve. For history buffs there is the former colonial capital of Bagamoyo and enough ruins to occupy several days.

The north-east has lured foreign visitors for many years, at least in part due to its pleasant climate and varied topography. Since the mid-19th century it has been an important centre for missionary activity of a variety of denominations, first in Bagamoyo and later in the Usambaras, and numerous churches still have bases here. There are also a large number of development projects, many focusing on erosion control and environmental conservation. If you do any hiking, you are certain to come across some of these.

The region plays an important role in Tanzania's economy. Tanga has one of East Africa's largest ports and is a major industrial and sisal-producing centre. Other agricultural products from the area include tea, coffee, cardamom and fruit.

Most places are easily accessible from both Dar es Salaam and Arusha. While many secondary roads are in less than optimal condition, distances are not great and the local transport network is fairly good. If you have time to visit only one part of the country, the north-east would be a good choice.

Highlights

North-Eastern Tanzania p187
KENYA

● Lushoto p198
Tanga p193 ●

INDIAN
OCEAN

- **Usambara & Pare Mountains** – striking landscapes and intriguing cultures
- **Sadani** – Tanzania's only coastal game reserve
- **Bagamoyo & Pangani** – historic ports
- **Amani** – cool forests and a very rich ecosystem

BAGAMOYO

Bagamoyo was once one of the most important dhow ports along the East African coast and the terminus of the trade caravan route linking Lake Tanganyika with the sea. Slaves, ivory, salt and copra were unloaded here before being shipped to Unguja (Zanzibar island) and elsewhere. In 1868, French missionaries established Freedom Village at Bagamoyo as a shelter for ransomed slaves, and for the remainder of the century the town served as an important way station for missionaries travelling from Unguja to the interior. Many of the European explorers, including Burton, Stanley and Livingstone, also began and ended their trips here.

From 1887 to 1891 Bagamoyo was the capital of German East Africa, and in 1888 it was the site of the first major uprising against the colonial government. When the capital was transferred to Dar es Salaam in 1891, the town rapidly faded into anonymity. Today, Bagamoyo is a sleepy place and most of its buildings are in an advanced stage of decay. The beaches are attractive, though, and enough interest remains to

NORTH-EASTERN TANZANIA

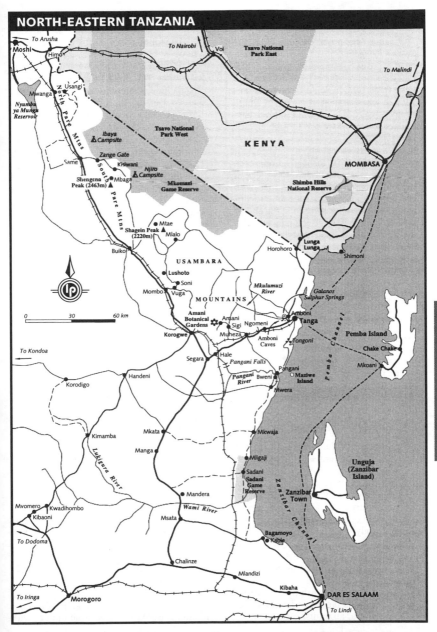

Bagamoyo

The name Bagamoyo, deriving from the Swahili *bwagamoyo* or 'throw down your heart', is usually interpreted as a reminder that the town was once the terminus of the slave trade caravan route from Lake Tanganyika and the point of no return where captives were loaded onto dhows and shipped to Unguja for sale to Arab buyers. However, earlier on it seems the town's name was associated with a happier definition, 'throw off melancholy' – a reference to the fact that Bagamoyo was the end point for thousands of caravan porters who had been marching for days from the hinterland and were finally nearing the end of their arduous journey. It was only with the rise of the slave trade that Bagamoyo's name took on its new, sadder meaning.

make the town a good overnight excursion from Dar es Salaam.

Things to See & Do

Bagamoyo is a centre for dhow building; you can watch the **boat builders** at work near the port. There is also a colourful **fish market** here with auctions most afternoons.

The small **museum** (☎ 440063, open daily) at the Catholic mission north of town is well worth a visit. It has interesting displays on the history of Bagamoyo and a section on some of the European explorers. If you are on good terms with the museum curator he will register your name in his 'friends book' (now in its 35th volume) and give you a card with your 'friend number', to be used in any future correspondence. On the same compound is the chapel where Livingstone's body was laid before being taken to Zanzibar Town en route to Westminster Abbey. The mission itself dates from the 1868 establishment of Freedom Village and is the oldest in Tanzania.

Scattered around town are some **carved doors** and various buildings from the German colonial era, all in disrepair.

About 500m south of Bagamoyo along the road to Dar es Salaam is **Chuo cha Sanaa**, a well-known theatre and arts college. When school is in session there are sometimes performances of traditional dancing or drumming. You can also arrange drumming lessons here. Inquire at the school or at the Badeco Beach Hotel for information or, during school holidays, ask in town whether any of the teachers are around.

Still further south, about 5km from the centre along the beach, are the **Kaole ruins** which include the remains of a mosque from the 13th century and some gravestones estimated to date from the 15th century. The mosque is one of the oldest on mainland Tanzania. It was built when Kaole was an important Arabic trading post, long before Bagamoyo had assumed any significance. Today, the ruins are overgrown and deserted. If you are on foot (and especially if you plan on walking on the beach), it's best to go in a group; don't bring any valuables.

Places to Stay

Other than in the top-end places, be prepared for an erratic water supply at many of Bagamoyo's hotels and guesthouses during the dry season.

In the centre of town are several very cheap and grubby guesthouses, most of which are not recommended. The best is *Azania Guest House* on Majengo Rd, with basic but acceptable rooms for Tsh1500. Closer to the market on the same road is the *Azania Guest House Annex* which is similar, though not quite as good.

Most of the beach hotels are strung out along the 2km stretch of road leading north from the Catholic mission. The first one you come to is the laid-back *Bagamoyo Beach Resort* (☎ 440083), with decent singles/doubles for Tsh10,000/16,000 (Tsh16,000/22,000 with air-con and Tsh17,000/24,000 with air-con and bathroom) and bungalows for Tsh5000 per person. Prices include breakfast; half-board and full-board options are also available.

Next up is *Travellers Lodge* (☎ 440077). It's the least-expensive seaside option, with cottage-style accommodation for Tsh5000/ 7000 a single/double (Tsh14,000/22,000 with bathroom and Tsh22,000/24,000 with air-con). You can also camp here for Tsh1000 per person. Room prices include continental breakfast.

Paradise Holiday Resort (☎ *440136, email paradise@raha.com*), a few hundred metres further north, has comfortable accommodation and a decent sized pool. Singles/doubles are US$48/60; credit cards are not accepted.

Just next door to the north, and about 2km from the centre of town, is the luxurious, Italian-run *Livingstone Club* (☎ *440080, fax 440059, email pshark@intafrica.com*) which has singles/doubles/triples for US$110/150/ 210 including breakfast. Full-board rates are also available.

The German-owned *Badeco Beach Hotel* (☎ *440018, email 02132-70010@t-online .de*) is also on the beach, but at the southern end of town next to the German cemetery. It has comfortable rooms (all doubles) with bathroom for Tsh16,000/ 24,000 fan/air-con. There is also a double with shared bath for Tsh10,000, and a triple with fan for Tsh20,000. Near the entrance to the hotel is a small monument marking the spot where the 'rebellious Africans' who led the 1888 uprising against the German colonial government were hanged.

The *Kasiki Marine Club* (☎/*fax 324707*) is set on its own several kilometres from the centre of town. Bungalow-style accommodation costs Tsh12,000 per person including breakfast (Tsh25,000 per person with full board). There is a 20% reduction for weekday rentals and reductions on the full-board price for groups of four or more. Camping is permitted, and tented accommodation is available for Tsh8000. Kasiki is inland, overlooking the beach but separated from it by a large mangrove swamp. As you approach Bagamoyo from the south, take the signposted road heading to Mbegani Fisheries and then follow signs for Kasiki. If you are on public transport, have the bus drop you at the Fisheries junction; from there it is a 2 to 3km walk.

Places to Eat

The best place for local food is the small *canteen* near the museum. Plates of rice, meat and greens cost Tsh500. Look for the thatched *bandas*, or ask at the museum.

Otherwise, all of the hotels listed above have restaurants.

Getting There & Away

Minibuses run throughout the day between Bagamoyo and Dar es Salaam (Tsh1000, three hours). In Dar es Salaam, departures are from Msimbazi St, opposite the petrol station.

If you have your own vehicle, the best route from Dar es Salaam is via New Bagamoyo Rd (which soon joins Old Bagamoyo Rd, and is potholed or sand most of the way). With a 4WD, you can also reach Bagamoyo from the Dar es Salaam-Tanga highway. The signposted turn-off is at Msata; the 65km stretch from the turn-off to Bagamoyo is in rough condition.

Dhows sail between Bagamoyo and Unguja, but safety is an issue and most captains will not take foreigners anyway.

SADANI GAME RESERVE

Sadani Game Reserve is on the coast about 70km north of Bagamoyo. It's a laid-back and wonderfully relaxing place where you can enjoy the beach and a good diversity of animals at the same time. The reserve is particularly noted for its birdlife. Species you may see include fish eagles and lesser flamingos. Sadani's many animals include giraffe, buffalo, wildebeest, elephant, crocodile and hippo.

The reserve was recently enlarged to about 1000 sq km. It is slated to be gazetted soon as Tanzania's newest national park.

Information

Entry to the reserve costs US$20 per day. In addition to relaxing on the beach and observing bird life, the main activities are walking safaris and game drives. Boat trips on the river can be arranged with the camp (see Places to Stay) or with residents of nearby Sadani village.

NORTH-EASTERN TANZANIA

Sadani is under the jurisdiction of the Wildlife Division of the Ministry of Natural Resources & Tourism (☎ 866376, 866064, Ivory Room, Pugu Rd at Changombe Rd, PO Box 25295, Dar es Salaam).

Places to Stay

The best place and the only permanent camp is *A Tent with a View*. Comfortable accommodation in tented en suite bandas along the beach costs US$85 per person including full board. There's a treehouse at the camp that is good for bird and game viewing at the nearby water hole. Bookings can be made through Safaris Ltd (☎ 0811-323318, fax 051-151106, email tentview@intafrica.com, PO Box 40525, Dar es Salaam). Walking safaris cost US$12 per person (US$5 per person in a group of six); half-day game drives cost US$40.

Getting There & Away

Air The easiest access to Sadani is via charter fight from Dar es Salaam or Unguja. A five-seater plane from Unguja costs about US$200 one way. If you're travelling alone, it's worth checking with A Tent With a View to see if they have any charter flights scheduled with extra seats; if so, you may be able to arrange transport very cheaply or even for free.

Road To reach Sadani from Pangani, you need to first cross the Pangani River by ferry, then continue south along a very rough road via Mkwaja to the reserve's north gate at Mligaji. This route is only possible during the dry season, and even then you will need a 4WD and lots of time. There is also road access via Mandera village, about 55km north of Chalinze. The road is rough, and often impassable during the rainy season. The road just west of Bagamoyo which heads north to Sadani is not a feasible option as the Wami River ferry is almost always out of service.

Boat Local fishing boats sail regularly between Sadani and Unguja, although safety is a concern and captains are not always willing to take foreigners. If you want to try this way, ask the fishermen at the beach near the Tembo House Hotel in Zanzibar Town. Alternatively, motorised boats can be chartered from Unguja or from Pangani. From Pangani, it's about a seven hour trip.

PANGANI

Pangani is a small village about 55km south of Tanga on an attractive stretch of beach. Its early history is undistinguished; the town is believed to have been just one of many dhow ports along the coast. During the Shirazi era, settlements at or near the site of present-day Pangani began to increase in significance and the Pangani River assumed an important role as a transport channel to the interior. By the late 19th century, Pangani had become a terminus of the caravan route from Lake Tanganyika, a major export point for slaves and ivory, and one of the largest ports between Bagamoyo and Mombasa. Numerous sisal and copra plantations were established in the area, and several European missions and exploratory journeys to the interior began from here. By the turn of the century focus had shifted to Tanga and Dar es Salaam and Pangani rapidly declined. Today, while there are still a few carved doorways and buildings from the German colonial era to be seen, the town is primarily of interest to those with plenty of time who are seeking somewhere to relax, and as a base for trips along the river or to nearby islands.

Orientation

The centre of Pangani is set on the corner of land where the Pangani River meets the sea. About 2km north of here is the main junction where the road from Muheza joins the coastal road. The market and transport stand are in the town centre, while the most popular hotels are north of the main junction.

Things to See & Do

About 10km offshore from Pangani is **Maziwe island**, a sand island and nature reserve offering good snorkelling around the surrounding coral reef. The diving is also said to be good, but you will need to bring your own equipment. Visits to Maziwe are only possible at low tide. Excursions can be arranged through the Tinga Tinga Resort (Tsh60,000 for a boat with a capacity of about 10 to 12 passengers). Alternatively, you can arrange transport with local dhow captains. There is no village on the island so bring whatever food and drink you will need.

The scenic **Pangani River** hosts rich bird life, as well as populations of crocodiles and other animals. The best way to explore it is on one of the sunset cruises arranged by the Tinga Tinga Resort (Tsh5000 per person, five passengers minimum).

About 12km south-east of Hale along a good tarmac road are the **Pangani Falls**. The turn-off is marked on the main road to Muheza. If you want to visit you will need your own vehicle, and you must arrange a permit in advance from the TANESCO office on the main road in Hale, at the eastern end of town.

When exploring Pangani, it's best not to walk alone on the beaches as several muggings have been reported.

Places to Stay

The best lodging in the centre is at *The New River View Inn Restaurant & Lodge*, a simple but clean place on the riverfront with singles/doubles for Tsh2000/4000. Despite the name, there is no food here.

Most travellers stay north of town, where there are several comfortable hotels. The most popular is the *Tinga Tinga Resort* (☎ Pangani 22 or 79, email habari@kiboko .com), which has doubles (no singles) for Tsh18,000 (Tsh5000 for each additional person) not including breakfast. Accommodation is in bungalows; rooms are large, with three beds. It's signposted just beyond the main junction on the coastal road, and about 2km north of the centre of town. The owner can assist with organising snorkelling trips, river excursions, walking tours of Pangani and other activities.

Just south of the Tinga Tinga Resort on the coastal road is the pleasant *Pangani Beach Resort* (☎ Pangani 88), with air-con singles/ doubles (no fan) for Tsh18,000/24,000;

breakfast is available for an additional Tsh1500/2000, continental/full.

About 3km beyond these two places along the coastal road is the run-down *YMCA* with bleak rooms for Tsh5000 and no locks on the doors. The place is not recommended.

On the south side of the Pangani River on a high bluff overlooking the sea is *Mashado Pangani River Lodge* (☎ 0811-440044, fax 440045, email mashado@habari.co.tz), one of Tanzania's most exclusive hotels. Rooms cost US$180/270 a single/double including all the amenities. The hotel has its own airstrip, and most clients arrive by charter flight (approximately US$500 plus tax one-way from Dar es Salaam for a three-seater plane). Hotel bookings can also be made through Rickshaw Travels in Dar es Salaam.

Several mid to upper range hotels are being planned or constructed along the beach south of Pangani. Inquire at travel agents in Dar es Salaam or Arusha for further details.

Places to Eat

For inexpensive local food try *Central Restaurant* near the main square, or *Pangadeco Bar & Lodge* at the beach end of the main street, about 50m through the coconut palms.

The *Tinga Tinga Resort* has a good restaurant specialising in seafood meals.

Getting There & Away

Public transport stops at the main junction and in the town centre. If you are going to the Tinga Tinga Resort, the Pangani Beach Resort or the YMCA, get out at the junction. Otherwise, stay on until the centre.

Minibuses go several times daily between Pangani and Muheza (Tsh500) along a rough but passable dirt road, from where you can get onward transport north-east to Tanga or west towards Korogwe and Lushoto. There is also usually a daily direct bus between Tanga and Pangani via Muheza (Tsh800, four to five hours). It's not feasible to plan on doing Pangani as a day trip from Tanga using public transport since the bus from Tanga to Pangani is the same one that runs from Pangani to Tanga – you would only have an hour or two in town. In the dry season there

NORTH-EASTERN TANZANIA

is occasional transport from Pangani to Tanga along the coastal road (Tsh800).

There is a sporadic car ferry from Pangani across the river to Bweni, though the road on the southern side is only passable in the dry season, and then only with difficulty. Those without a car can take this ferry (Tsh100) or the more frequent local boats (Tsh200).

If you are driving, the best way between Pangani and Tanga is via Muheza; allow about 1½ hours. The coastal road is in poor condition and often impassable; the Muheza route, although lengthier, will be at least as fast if not faster.

Getting Around
A bike is a good thing to have in Pangani, particularly if you are staying at one of the hotels north of the junction. Rentals can be arranged in town for Tsh1000 per day. Alternatively, minibuses run every few hours from the centre up to the junction.

If you want to explore the river via local boat the best place to look is by the small dhow port near the customs building on the river, to the west of The New River View Inn Restaurant & Lodge.

TANGA
Tanga is Tanzania's second largest seaport, and its third largest town behind Dar es Salaam and Mwanza. Despite its size, it's a pleasant place with a sleepy, semi-colonial atmosphere and makes a good stop for those en route to or from Mombasa. There are several interesting excursions in the nearby area, including to the Amani botanical gardens (see the Around Tanga section, later in this chapter).

In its early days, Tanga was a starting point for trade caravans to the interior. It was built up by the Germans in the late 19th century in connection with the construction of a rail line linking Moshi and the Kilimanjaro region with the sea. The town's protected harbour was also expanded during this era. Today, one of the main industries in the area is sisal, with Tanga's port serving as the main export channel for the crop. The plants were originally introduced by the Germans and

plantations now stretch from Tanga westward along the plains edging the Usambara mountains. West of town in Ngomeni is one of the world's largest sisal spinning mills.

Orientation
The town centre lies along the waterfront and is easily covered on foot. The main streets, with the post office, the market, and many shops, are Independence Ave and Sokoine St (also called Market St), both running parallel to the water. To the east of town well past the harbour is the upper-class Ras Kazone section, with several swimming clubs and some good hotels. In between Ras Kazone and town is the Bombo area, with Bombo hospital. South of the railroad tracks is the dusty and bustling Ngamiani quarter with the bus station and lots of local commerce.

Information
There are no foreign exchange bureaus in Tanga. The NBC bank at Sokoine and Bank Sts changes travellers cheques with a minimum of hassle.

Things to See & Do
Tanga has several **parks**, including Jamhuri Park overlooking the harbour, and the park and cemetery surrounding the Askari Monument at the end of Sokoine St. Directly offshore is **Toten island** which has ruins of a mosque and some gravestones. There are fishing boats on the western side of the harbour which can take you over.

Places to Stay – Budget
The *Bandarini Hotel* (☎ 46674), overlooking the harbour on Independence Ave, has a lot of character and is fairly well maintained. Basic singles/doubles with bathroom (bucket showers) and breakfast are Tsh4000/5000 (Tsh3500 for a single with common bath).

The rambling *Planters Hotel* (☎ 47819) on Sokoine St also has appealing architecture including a good balcony, but there's frequently no running water, the communal bathrooms are dirty, and most travellers who stay here move out after the first night.

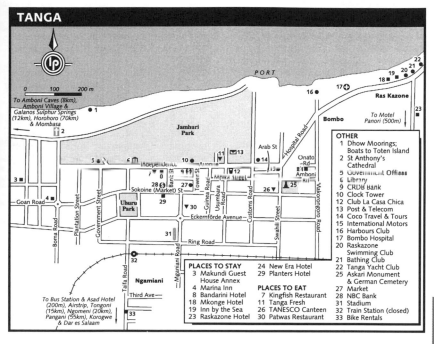

TANGA

P O R T

Ras Kazone

Bombo

To Amboni Caves (8km),
Amboni Village &
Galanos Sulphur Springs
(12km), Horohoro (70km)
& Mombasa

To Motel
Panori (500m)

Jamhuri
Park

Arab St

Onato
-Rd-

Independence

Avenue

Tower St

Amboni
Rd

Sokoine (Market) St

Uhuru
Park

Eckernförde Avenue

Ring Road

To Bus Station & Asad Hotel
(200m), Airstrip, Tongoni
(15km), Ngomeni (20km),
Pangani (55km), Korogwe
& Dar es Salaam

Ngamiani

Third Ave

Goan Road

Boma Road

Plantation Street

Government Street

Guinea Road

Usumbara
Road

Customs Road

Swahili Street

Makorongoro Road

Hospital Road

Mganiani Road

Taifa Road

OTHER
1 Dhow Moorings;
   Boats to Toten Island
2 St Anthony's
   Cathedral
5 Government Offices
6 Library
9 CRDB Bank
10 Clock Tower
12 Club La Casa Chica
13 Post & Telecom
14 Coco Travel & Tours
15 International Motors
16 Harbours Club
17 Bombo Hospital
20 Raskazone
   Swimming Club
21 Bathing Club
22 Tanga Yacht Club
25 Askari Monument
   & German Cemetery
27 Market
28 NBC Bank
31 Stadium
32 Train Station (closed)
33 Bike Rentals

PLACES TO STAY
3 Makundi Guest
   House Annex
4 Marina Inn
8 Bandarini Hotel
18 Mkonge Hotel
19 Inn by the Sea
23 Raskazone Hotel
24 New Era Hotel
29 Planters Hotel

PLACES TO EAT
7 Kingfish Restaurant
11 Tanga Fresh
26 TANESCO Canteen
30 Patwas Restaurant

0   100   200 m

Grubby singles/doubles cost Tsh2000/3000 (Tsh4000 for a double with bathroom); downstairs are a restaurant and bar.

If you are on a tight budget, one of the cheapest places is the *New Era Hotel* on Amboni Rd just off Makorongoro Rd. Grubby rooms are Tsh2500 for a single with shared bath and Tsh5000 for a double with private bathroom; the owner is often willing to negotiate. Camping is permitted, although the grounds are cramped.

Asad Hotel is the best place near the bus station; it's directly north of the station and the only high-rise building. Doubles (no singles) are Tsh6000 (Tsh8000 with air-con).

At the same end of town but north of the railroad tracks and about 1.5km north-west of the bus station is *Makundi Guest House Annex*. Clean rooms with fan and net are Tsh3000/3500 single/double (Tsh4000 for a double with bathroom).

Places to Stay – Mid-Range & Top End

The most convenient mid-range option is *Marina Inn* (☎ 44362) to the west of town on Goan Rd. It's a dark but decently maintained place with its own bar and restaurant. Air-con doubles (no singles) cost Tsh8100 including continental breakfast.

On the eastern extension of Hospital Rd and overlooking the sea is *Mkonge Hotel* (☎ 44542), with comfortable doubles (no singles) for US$50 including full breakfast.

Just beyond the Mkonge on the same road is *Inn by the Sea* (☎ 44614), also with an attractive waterside setting. Good value air-con rooms facing the sea are Tsh10,000, while rooms with fan and no sea view are Tsh7000. Prices include continental breakfast.

At the far eastern end of town and a few hundred metres inland is the popular *Raskazone Hotel* (☎/fax 43897), with comfortable singles for US$15/20 (US$30 for a double with air-con), including full breakfast. The owner is willing to negotiate special 'backpacker' rates; camping can also be arranged. The hotel can assist with excursions to Amboni caves and other nearby attractions.

Half a kilometre further inland is *Motel Panori* (☎ 46044, fax 47425), which is frequented by local businessmen. Doubles (no singles) are Tsh20,400 including continental breakfast.

Places to Eat

Kingfish Restaurant on Independence Ave is a good place for inexpensive meals. It's open from 8 am until late evening.

Other budget places include the clean, good and cheap *TANESCO Canteen* on Sokoine St, which is open for breakfast, lunch and dinner, and the pricier *Food Palace,* also on Sokoine St (closed Monday evenings). The curries at *Patwas Restaurant* opposite the market are said to be good.

The restaurant at *Marina Inn* has decent meals for between Tsh1500 and Tsh2500.

Several travellers have reported that there are good Indian meals available in the evening at the *Raskazone Swimming Club* (see Entertainment, following).

For fresh milk and yoghurt, try the *Tanga Fresh* outlet near the post office.

Entertainment

Club La Casa Chica on the top floor of the old Twiga Hotel building on Independence Ave has a disco on Wednesday, Friday, Saturday and Sunday. Admission is about Tsh2000.

East of town along the water and off Hospital Rd is *Raskazone Swimming Club* which charges Tsh500 per person for a swim at their small 'beach' and access to showers and changing rooms. The *Bathing Club* next door is similar but not as nice.

Getting There & Away

Air There is no commercial air service to Tanga. The airstrip for charter flights is several kilometres west of town along the road to Korogwe.

Bus & Car Buses or minibuses run daily between Tanga and Dar es Salaam (Tsh3500, five hours), Lushoto (Tsh2500, three hours), Mombasa (Tsh3500, six hours plus border crossing time), Moshi (Tsh4200, five hours), Muheza (Tsh300, 45 minutes), and Pangani (Tsh800, four to five hours). The road to Horohoro at the Kenyan border is unpaved and potholed.

Segara is where the roads to Tanga and Moshi/Arusha split. Chalinze is the junction town where the highway from Tanga meets the Dar es Salaam-Morogoro highway. From Chalinze it is 245km to Tanga. There is no good accommodation in Chalinze, just some grubby guesthouses.

Train There is no longer any passenger train service to Tanga.

Boat Mega-Speed's MS *Sepideh* stops at Tanga weekly en route to and from Mombasa, Pemba, Zanzibar Town and Dar es Salaam. Departures from Tanga are Saturday about 3.30 pm, arriving in Mombasa about 5.30 pm. Going in the other direction, the *Sepideh* departs Tanga Sunday at 10.45 am, arriving in Pemba at 12.30 pm, in Zanzibar Town at 3.30 pm, and in Dar es Salaam at 5.45 pm. Fares are US$30 to both Mombasa and Pemba, US$40 to Zanzibar Town and US$45 to Dar es Salaam, plus the US$5 port tax and a Tsh300 embarkation fee. Coco Travel & Tours (☎ 44131, 44332, fax 44132, email cocotravel@cats-net.com) in the Bandari building on Independence Ave is the Mega-Speed agent.

Getting Around

There are bicycles for rent on the island in the middle of Taifa Rd, in the section between the bus stand and the train station. Rates are about Tsh100 to Tsh200 per hour. You can also sometimes find bikes for rent opposite the post office.

AROUND TANGA
Amani Botanical Gardens

Amani is located west of Tanga in the heart of the eastern Usambara mountains (see the

Usambara Mountains section later in this chapter). The botanical gardens began at the turn of the century as part of a biological research station established by the Germans. Large areas of forest were cleared and numerous new species introduced. Within a few years the gardens were the largest in Africa, totalling 304 hectares and containing between 600 and 1000 different species including numerous endemics. Soon thereafter, exploitation of the surrounding forest began. A sawmill was set up and a railway link was built connecting Sigi, about 10km below Amani, with the main Tanga-Moshi line in order to facilitate transport of timber to the coast. The gardens began to decline.

During the British era, biological research was shifted from Amani to Nairobi and the railway was taken up and replaced by a road linking Amani with Muheza. Many of the facilities at Amani were taken over by the nearby government-run malaria research centre, and the gardens fell into neglect.

Today the gardens – now managed somewhat unenthusiastically from Lushoto by the Tanzania Forestry Research Institute (TAFORI) – are largely overgrown, but the area is still beautiful. The real work at Amani is being undertaken within the framework of the East Usambara Catchment Forest Project. In 1997, the area was gazetted as a nature reserve and rehabilitation work is under way.

Amani is a peaceful place and well worth a detour if you are travelling in the region. There are some good walks in the surrounding forest and in the near future an extended series of guided trails around both Amani and Sigi are planned. In addition to the large variety of plants, you may see several endemic bird species including the Nduk eagle owl, the Uluguru violet-backed, Amani and banded green sunbirds, and the green-headed oriole.

Information The best source of information on Amani and on the status of the nature reserve is the East Usambara Catchment Forest Project office (☎ 053-43820, 46721, 43453) at the Finnida compound in Tanga.

It's on the main Korogwe road, after the Total station as you leave town. The TAFORI office in Lushoto, about 1km above town on the road to Mtae and Mlalo (and signposted as the Silvicultural Research Centre), has a few bits of random information about plant species to be found in the gardens but is not particularly helpful. There are also information centres at both Amani and Sigi.

Islands in the Clouds by Graham Mercer is a small booklet full of interesting historical and cultural tidbits for those interested in more detailed information on Amani and the eastern Usambaras. It's available through the Finnida Office, and at the information centres at Amani and Sigi. The information centre at Amani also has a helpful booklet describing some of the nearby trails.

Places to Stay & Eat There are two *resthouses* at Amani. Lodging costs between Tsh6000 and Tsh10,000 per person; meals can be arranged with the caretaker. A six-room *resthouse* is also being rehabilitated at Sigi and should be open by the time this book is published.

Getting There & Away Amani is about 30km north-west of Muheza. Minibuses run several times daily between Muheza and Amani, stopping at Sigi en route. The road is very muddy in parts, and slow going during the rainy season; allow at least three hours for the trip. If you're driving yourself you'll need a 4WD during most of the year; the trip takes between one and two hours in a private vehicle.

Amboni Caves

These limestone caves are variously estimated to extend from about 30 to 200km or more, although visitors can only see a small part of them. They are said to have been used by the Kenyan Mau Mau during the 1950s as a hide-out from the British.

The caves are located about 8km northwest of Tanga off the Horohoro/Mombasa road. The best way to reach them is by bicycle. Otherwise charter a taxi, or take a dalla-dalla heading to Amboni village and have the driver drop you at the turn-off for the caves (Tsh200). From here, it's about 2km on foot to Kiomoni village; the caves are nearby on the Mkulumuzi River. There is a Tsh1000 entry fee (Tsh500 for children).

The Raskazone Hotel in Tanga can help organise a trip, though it's easy enough to do on your own. Guides can be arranged either through the Raskazone Hotel or locally.

Galanos Sulphur Springs

About 4km north of the Amboni caves along the Tanga-Mombasa road at Amboni village are some sulphur springs. The area is attractive, but the springs aren't suitable for bathing. They're best reached by bicycle; otherwise dalla-dallas run to Amboni village from Tanga several times daily (Tsh400).

Tongoni Ruins

About 15km south of Tanga along the coastal road are the Tongoni ruins. These include the remains of a mosque and some graves estimated to date from the 14th or 15th century when Tongoni was a significant coastal trading port. There is no admission charge, although the caretaker appreciates a small donation.

MUHEZA

Muheza is a junction town where the roads to Amani botanical gardens and to Pangani branch off the main Tanga highway. If you need to stay here, there are some local guesthouses in town. The *Hotel Ambassador* on the main road has basic singles/doubles for Tsh1800/2200 (Tsh3000/3600 with bathroom), and a *restaurant*. It's mostly a truck stop and the bar can be noisy at night.

KOROGWE

Korogwe's primary importance for travellers is as a transport junction. In the western part of town, known as New Korogwe, are the bus stand and several accommodation options. To the east is Old Korogwe with the train station (no passenger service).

If you need a place to stay, the *Travellers Inn* opposite the bus stand has clean doubles

(no singles) with enormous bathtubs for Tsh5000. There is also a *restaurant*. Otherwise try the slightly more expensive *Korogwe Transit Hotel* about 500m up the road towards Arusha.

MKOMAZI GAME RESERVE

Mkomazi Game Reserve, located north and east of the Pare mountains on the Kenyan border, is contiguous with Tsavo National Park in Kenya. In contrast to the moist forests of the nearby Pare mountains, Mkomazi's terrain is predominantly dry savanna land. The reserve, which has essentially no tourist facilities, is known for its black rhino which were introduced into the area from South Africa for breeding. Other animals include elephant, giraffe, zebra, antelope and numerous snakes. There is also a good diversity of bird life. The reserve was initially earmarked for environmental development as a link between Tanzania's northern parks circuit, the Usambara and Pare mountains and the coast. In addition to the rhinos, wild dogs were also reintroduced into the area, and a research station was established.

Information

At the time of research, the reserve had been temporarily closed to tourists in favour of hunting concessions. Check at the Zange Gate, or at the Wildlife Conservation Society of Tanzania in Dar es Salaam for updated information.

The roads in and around Mkomazi can become impassable during the rainy season. Walking tours in the reserve require an armed guide and can be arranged at Zange Gate.

Fees Entry costs US$20 per day; camping costs US$20 per person. To visit the black rhino breeding area at Kisima you will need to get a special permit. These are issued at Zange Gate, the main entrance to the reserve, about 5km east of Same.

Places to Stay

There are three camp sites in the reserve, at Ibaya, Kisima and Njiro. Ibaya, at the northwestern end of the reserve, is the closest to

Same (about 15km). Njiro is just south of Kisiwani village, near the road running along the reserve's south-western border. You will need to bring all your own provisions.

Usambara Mountains

The cool and beautiful Usambaras, part of the ancient Eastern Arc chain, are divided into two ranges separated by a 4km-wide valley. The western Usambaras, around Lushoto, are the most accessible to travellers and have the better road network. The eastern Usambaras, around Amani, are less developed. Both ranges are densely populated, with an average of more than 300 persons per square kilometre.

The Usambaras have one of the highest degrees of biodiversity on the African continent. One of their most well known plants is the Usambara or African violet (*Celtis africana*), which is endemic to the region.

The Eastern Arc Mountains

The Eastern Arc mountains, which stretch in a crescent shape from the Taita Hills in southern Kenya down to Morogoro and the Southern Highlands, are one of Africa's most fascinating geological features. They are estimated to be at least 100 million years old, with the stones forming them even older – perhaps as old as 600 million years. Thanks to their climatic isolation and stability, which has offered plant species a chance to develop during all these years, the mountains have an exceptional degree of biological diversity. They contain about one-third of Tanzania's flora and fauna species, including numerous endemics. Of the more than 2000 plant species which have been identified in the mountains, about one-quarter are endemic. The degree of endemism is particularly remarkable in the eastern Usambara region of the Eastern Arc chain, due to its proximity to the Indian Ocean and the resulting moist climate. This region, which averages 2000mm of rainfall per year, harbours more than a dozen unique tree species, as well as a number of endemic molluscs, amphibians and reptiles. Several areas of the eastern Usambaras, as well as of the Pare mountains to the north-west, are also renowned for their wealth of medicinal plants.

Over the past century, with the growth of logging interests, increasing population density, and a corresponding increase in the clearance of forest areas for small-scale farm plots, forest depletion has become a serious problem throughout the Eastern Arc. One of the most obvious and deleterious effects of this deforestation is erosion, which became so bad in parts of the western Usambara region in the early 1990s that entire villages had to be shifted to lower areas. Another less noticeable but just as serious concern is contamination of water resources. Villages in the Eastern Arc mountains, as well as those in lower-lying coastal areas depend on the maintenance of watershed areas for good quality water supplies. Diminished vegetation and forest cover at higher altitudes affect both rainfall levels and ground water supplies, which in turn affect river flows and water quality and supply at lower levels.

There are numerous sources of additional information on environmental issues in the Eastern Arc. In Dar es Salaam, the best contact is the Wildlife Conservation Society of Tanzania (see the listing under Ecology & Environment in the Facts about Tanzania chapter). For information on the eastern Usambara section of the mountains, contact the East Usambara Catchment Forest Project office (see the listing under Information in the Amani Botanical Gardens section). The tourist information centre in Lushoto can provide names of some of the organisations working in the western Usambaras.

The wild date palm (*Phoenix reclinata*) is also found here. In addition to their diverse plant life, the Usambaras host a number of endemic and rare bird species including the Usambara eagle owl, Kenrick's starling and the Usambara warbler.

The main ethnic groups in the mountains are the Sambaa, the Kilindi, the Zigua and the Mbugu. There are many development projects under way working to preserve the natural forest cover and assist local populations in developing sources of livelihood that do not deplete or destroy the mountains' delicate ecosystems.

The Usambaras offer superb hiking and birdwatching and striking vistas. The climate is comfortable year-round, but during the rainy season paths become muddy. The best time to visit is from July to October, after the rains and when the air is at its clearest.

LUSHOTO

Lushoto is an attractive town set in a valley at about 1200m. It's the centre of the western Usambaras and makes an excellent base for hikes into the surrounding hills.

During the German era, Lushoto (or Wilhelmstal as it was then known) was a favoured vacation spot for colonial administrators and an important regional centre. It was even slated at one point to become the colonial capital. Lushoto was also an important mission station during this time, and today numerous churches are based here. Its temperate climate is favourable to many fruit trees, and today the area produces much of Tanzania's pear and plum crops.

Due in part to the high population density of the area around Lushoto and the resulting deforestation, erosion has long been a serious environmental concern. Erosion control efforts were first initiated during the British era. Today, you will see numerous such projects as you hike in the area, many now supported by German and Dutch government funding.

Information

There's a good Tourist Information Centre (☎ Lushoto 132, PO Box 151) next to the

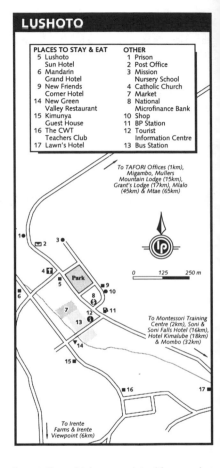

LUSHOTO

PLACES TO STAY & EAT
5 Lushoto Sun Hotel
6 Mandarin Grand Hotel
9 New Friends Corner Hotel
14 New Green Valley Restaurant
15 Kimunya Guest House
16 The CWT Teachers Club
17 Lawn's Hotel

OTHER
1 Prison
2 Post Office
3 Mission Nursery School
4 Catholic Church
7 Market
8 National Microfinance Bank
10 Shop
11 BP Station
12 Tourist Information Centre
13 Bus Station

To TAFORI Offices (1km), Migambo, Mullers Mountain Lodge (15km), Grant's Lodge (17km), Mlalo (45km) & Mtae (65km)

0   125   250 m

To Montessori Training Centre (2km), Soni & Soni Falls Hotel (16km), Hotel Kimalube (18km) & Mombo (32km)

To Irente Farms & Irente Viewpoint (6km)

bus station which can assist with arranging excursions and guides. Rates are Tsh6000 per group or tour plus a Tsh1500 per person per day village development fee. For overnight trips, there is an additional Tsh4000 fee per group for the guide plus a Tsh2000 camping fee. You'll need to bring your own tent. SNV (the Netherlands Development Organisation) and local residents have been working together to develop sources of livelihood that do not deplete the natural resources of the mountains. The fees you pay for excursions go to support these efforts.

Hiking without a guide is not recommended as several muggings of lone travellers have been reported. When arranging a guide be sure the one you hire is really from the information centre.

The National Microfinance Bank will change cash and travellers cheques; it's open weekdays from 8 am to 3 pm.

Things to See & Do

The main activity in Lushoto is hiking. There are numerous routes which make good day trips from town. The most popular is to **Irente Viewpoint**, approximately an hour's walk from Lushoto, which offers good views over the surrounding hills. En route and shortly before the viewpoint is the pleasant Irente Farm (see Places to Eat). Camping is possible at the viewpoint.

The tourist office can offer suggestions for other hikes. Some destinations are also described in the Around Lushoto section.

Places to Stay – Budget

There are numerous guesthouses in town, all basic. One of the better ones is *The CWT Teachers Club* at the southern edge of town. Singles/doubles with common bath are Tsh1500/2500. From the bus station, cross the small footbridge over the creek and follow the dirt road to the left (southeast) for about 700m.

Kimunya Guest House, closer to the centre on the same road leading south-east from the footbridge, has relatively clean rooms for Tsh1000/2000.

Lushoto Sun Hotel, opposite the park on the main road, is a big step up, with clean, comfortable doubles for Tsh5000 (Tsh8000 for a double with bathroom) including breakfast and hot water in the showers.

On the other side of the park is *New Friends Corner Hotel* with singles/doubles for Tsh3000/5000 (Tsh6000 for a double with bathroom). The rooms are quite clean, but there is no food and the bar can be noisy.

Places to Stay – Mid-Range

The faded *Lawn's Hotel* at the entrance to town as you approach from Soni has spacious, rustic rooms for Tsh8000/10,000 (Tsh14,000/18,000 with bathroom) including full breakfast. You can camp here for Tsh2000 per person including a hot shower and bathroom facilities.

Mandarin Grand Hotel, behind the Catholic church on the hill, has singles/doubles/triples for Tsh6000/7500/10,000 including breakfast. To get here, turn left at the church and follow the signs up the hill. It's about a seven minute walk from the centre. The hotel seems to be permanently under construction, but the rooms are large and fairly clean.

The best places are around 15km outside Lushoto in the hilly area near Migambo village. The relaxing *Grant's Lodge* (☎ c/o 053-42491, fax 43628, email tanga4@twiga .com or email grants@tt.sasa.unep.no) is a rehabilitated colonial era farmhouse with home-grown fruit and vegies and comfortable singles/doubles/triples for Tsh30,000/ 60,000/80,000 including fullboard. There are discounts for children.

The similar *Mullers Mountain Lodge* (☎ Lushoto 134, PO Box 34) is set in attractive gardens and offers comfortable, good value accommodation in the main house or in self-contained cottages for Tsh14,000 per person including breakfast. Lunch and dinner are an additional Tsh5000 each. Discounts are available for stays during the week (Monday to Thursday). If you are already in Lushoto you can book or obtain further information from the BP petrol station in town.

Both Mullers and Grant's are ideal bases for walking and relaxing. To get to either from Lushoto, take the road heading up to Magamba, turn right at the signposted junction and continue for about 7km to Migambo. You will see signs for both places; Grant's is about 2km after Mullers.

Both Grant's and Mullers can also be reached via public transport. Take a dalla-dalla heading to Mkuzi and ask them to drop you at the lodge turn-offs. Transport from Lushoto towards Mkuzi is in the afternoon; returning from the lodges, transport is in the mornings only.

Places to Eat
New Green Valley Restaurant near the bus stand has good, cheap local food.

The restaurant at *Lushoto Sun Hotel* also has good meals for between Tsh600 and Tsh2500; locals recommend the *ugali* here.

There are several places near Lushoto to buy fresh cheese. The closest to town is the *Montessori Training Centre* which sells excellent home-made cheeses as well as a variety of home-made jams and the regional Dochi banana wine. It's about 2km outside town off the road to Soni, down the hill to the right.

You can also get fresh cheese, as well as jams, home-made bread, and other delicacies at *Irente Farm*, en route to Irente Viewpoint.

Getting There & Away
Buses run throughout the day between Lushoto and Mombo, on the main Dar es Salaam-Arusha highway (Tsh500, one hour). There is also at least one minibus daily from Lushoto to Dar es Salaam (Tsh4000, departing about 7.30 am and sometimes taking up to nine hours), and from Lushoto to Moshi (Tsh3000). To both Dar es Salaam and Moshi it's faster and more comfortable to take a minibus to Mombo and then get one of the larger buses running along the main highway, though the big buses are often full so you may have to stand for most of the ride.

Getting Around
Lawn's Hotel rents bikes for about Tsh2000 per day.

AROUND LUSHOTO
Mlalo
Mlalo, 45km north-east of Lushoto, is an attractive town with a bustling market. The town is in a valley but there are good hikes and wide views from the surrounding hills.

The best place to stay is *Silver Dollar Guest House* with basic rooms for about Tsh2500. If you are coming on public transport you will need to sleep here as buses generally only depart for Mlalo from Lushoto in the afternoon, returning the next morning (Tsh1000). Sometimes there is also

a bus from Mlalo direct to Dar es Salaam, departing Mlalo about 5 am.

Mtae
Mtae is a good destination if you only have time to visit one village from Lushoto. It is set on a cliff about 20km beyond Mlalo and 65km north-west of Lushoto and offers spectacular views over the surrounding area. On clear days you may even be able to see Mt Kilimanjaro. Just to the south-east of Mtae is Shagein peak (2220m), one of the highest in the Usambaras. In addition to its many hiking paths, the area around Mtae is also known for its traditional healers. Visits can be organised through the tourist information centre in Lushoto.

Places to Stay & Eat The *Muvano 2 Guest House* near the bus stand has simple but adequate rooms for about Tsh2500. *Kuma Maneno Guest House* has similar rooms for the same price.

Getting There & Away If you are travelling by public transport you will need to spend at least one night in Mtae as buses from Lushoto (Tsh1000) go only in the afternoons, departing Lushoto about 2 pm. The return buses from Mtae leave very early (often around 5 am), as many continue on to Dar es Salaam.

Soni
Tiny Soni lies about half-way along the Mombo-Lushoto road. From town, you can walk to the nearby Soni falls or, in about 30 minutes, to the top of Kwa Mungu peak which offers some nice views and is known for its butterflies.

The best place to stay is the *Soni Falls Hotel* (☎ Soni 74, *but the phone is often broken*), a rustic place with good atmosphere about 1km south-west of town. Double rooms (no singles) cost Tsh9000 including breakfast. It's on a small side road on the side of the valley opposite the main road; ask locals to point the way.

If it's full, which is frequently the case, the next best place is the small *Hotel Kimalube*,

Chief Kimweri

Kimweri, chief of the powerful Kilindi (Shambaa) kingdom during the first half of the 19th century, is one of the Usambara region's most legendary figures. From his capital at Vuga, which lies on the main road between Mombo and Lushoto, he ruled over an area stretching from Kilimanjaro in the north to the Indian Ocean in the east, levying tributes on towns as distant as Pangani. The extent of his domination in the coastal regions soon brought him into conflict with Sultan Seyyid Said of Zanzibar, who also claimed sovereignty over the same areas. Ultimately, the two leaders reached an agreement for joint governance of the north-eastern coast. This arrangement lasted until Kimweri's death in 1869, after which the sultan assumed full authority.

According to tradition, Kimweri is believed to have had magical powers, including control of the rain and the ability to call down famines upon his enemies. His kingdom was highly organised, divided into sub chiefdoms ruled by his sons, and districts with governors, prime ministers and local army commanders. It was Kimweri to whom the missionary Johann Ludwig Krapf went to request land to build his first church for the Anglican Church Missionary Society.

Following Kimweri's death, inter-clan rivalries caused the kingdom to break up. Fighting over succession to his throne continued until the Germans arrived in the region.

about 2km south-west of Soni on the main road and about 500m before the Vuga Printing Press. Simple but clean singles/doubles with nets, common bath and breakfast cost Tsh2000/3500. There is a car park for those with their own vehicles.

Transport (usually minivans) from Soni to both Lushoto and Mombo costs Tsh300.

Mombo

Mombo is the junction town at the foot of the Usambaras where the road to Lushoto branches off the main Dar es Salaam-Arusha highway. Try to arrange your travel to avoid overnighting here. If you get stuck, then the best option is *Midway Express* at the main junction, with pretty basic but clean singles/doubles for Tsh1500/2000 and a *restaurant*.

Buses go throughout the day from Mombo to Lushoto (Tsh500), 32km away on a good, sealed road. Dar es Salaam-Arusha buses will drop you at the junction, though boarding these buses in Mombo can be difficult as they are almost always full. There are local minibuses which go several times daily to both Moshi and Dar es Salaam.

Pare Mountains

The Pare mountains, just to the north-west of the Usambaras, are also part of the Eastern Arc chain, and like the Usambaras they are divided into two ranges – north and south. The main ethnic group in the area are the Pare, also called the Asu. While there are some historical and linguistic differences among various Pare groups, socially they are considered to be a single ethnic entity.

The Pare mountains are not as accessible or developed for tourism as the Usambaras, although this is gradually changing. Due to their relative inaccessibility, the mountains have remained fairly isolated and over the years have seldom been visited by outsiders other than missionaries. As a result, the rich traditions and folklore of the Pare remain largely untouched and make the region a fascinating one to explore.

The Pares offer very good village-based hiking and good birdwatching. Unlike the Usambaras, however, there is no major base with developed infrastructure from which a series of hikes can be undertaken. The best way to explore the mountains is to spend a

The Pare

The Pare people are part of the larger Shambaa cluster of peoples who inhabit the northern and southern Pare mountains. They come originally from the Taita Hills area of southern Kenya, where they were herdsmen, hunters and farmers. According to tradition, the Pare were pursued into the mountains by the Maasai, who began to capture and steal their cattle. Over the years, they adapted their lifestyle to the more rugged mountain terrain. Today they are known principally as farmers, cultivating well-organised plots of vegetables, maize, bananas, cassava and cardamom. Thanks to significant missionary activity, the Pare are among Tanzania's most educated groups. During the 1940s, they formed the Wapare Union which played an important role in the drive for independence. While many Pare are now Christian or Muslim, traditional beliefs are still strong.

The Pare language (also called KiPare or Chasu) belongs to the Bantu family; the dialect spoken in the north Pares is closely related to that spoken over the border in the Taita Hills. Although recent figures are not available, the Pare population is estimated to number between 200,000 and 300,000.

Traditional Pare society is patrilineal. Fathers are considered to have great authority during their lifetime as well as after death, and all those descended from a single man through male links share a sense of common fate. Once a man dies, it is believed that his ghost has influence over all male descendants for as long as the ghost's name is remembered. After this, the dead man's spirit joins a collectively influential body of ancestors. Daughters are also dependent on the goodwill of their father. Yet, since property and status are transmitted through the male line, a father's ghost only has influence over his daughter's descendants until her death.

Because of the great powers which deceased persons are believed to possess, the Pare have developed elaborate rituals centring on the dead. Near most villages are sacred areas in which skulls of tribal chiefs are kept. When people die, they are believed to inhabit a netherworld between the land of the living and the spirit world. If they are allowed to remain in this state, ill fate will befall their descendants. The prescribed rituals allowing the deceased to pass into the world of the ancestors are thus of great importance. Old beliefs also hold that when an adult male dies, others in his lineage will die as well until the cause of his death has been found and 'appeased'. As the personal effects of the deceased are believed to carry some of the moral personality of their owner with them, the lineage member who inherits these personal effects is believed to be in the greatest danger. As a result, great emphasis has been traditionally placed on determining why someone has died. Many of the possible reasons have to do with disturbances in moral relations within the lineage or in the village, or with sorcery.

Two very worthwhile books for those interested in learning more about Pare customs, culture and legends are *The Shambaa Kingdom* by S Feierman (1974), from which some of this section was based; and, *Lute – The Curse and the Blessing* by Jakob Janssen Dannholz (revised translated edition 1989).

night at Mwanga or Same getting organised, and then head up to either Usangi or Mbaga. From each of these places there are several good hikes, ranging from half a day to three days or more in length. Alternatively, you could arrange an organised trip through an Arusha-based travel agency.

Information

Lodging and food in the Pares are for the most part very basic. With the exception of Hill-Top Tona Lodge (see Mbaga, later) most accommodation options are with villagers. Camping is also possible, though you will need your own equipment. For all destinations except Mbaga and Usangi, it's also a good idea to bring a portable stove.

In Usangi and some other places, 'house-sitting' situations can sometimes be arranged with village elders in which visitors interested in staying in the region for a week or more can stay in the house of local businessmen or others who are away on travel. These houses are usually fairly comfortable; prices average about Tsh2000 per night or less.

Guide fees for hikes from either Mbaga or Usangi are Tsh4000 per group per day or Tsh2000 for half a day, plus an overnight fee of Tsh2000 per group per day. There is an additional village development fee of Tsh2000 per person per day. Porters can be arranged for Tsh2000 per group per day. Camping in forest areas around the villages costs Tsh2500 per person.

More detailed information on tourism activities in the Pares is available from the SNV (Netherlands Development Organisation) Cultural Tourism Program (☎/fax 057-7515, email tourinfo@habari.co.tz, AICC/Serengeti Wing, Room 643, PO Box 10455 Arusha).

The best time to visit the Pares is between July and November, although hikes are possible through January and February. During the long rains from March to June, paths become too muddy.

SAME

Same (SAH-may) is the main town in the southern Pares. Unlike Lushoto in the Usambaras, there is little tourist infrastructure here, and the town is more suitable as a starting point for excursions into the Pares than as a base. If you do want to stay a few days before heading into the villages, there are several walks into the hills behind town, though for most of the better destinations you will need to take local transport at least part of the way.

The main hiking area reached from Same is Mbaga.

Places to Stay & Eat

The best place to stay in Same is the *Amani Lutheran Centre* near the market. Clean,

good value rooms are Tsh2000/3000 (Tsh3500 with bathroom); there's also a *restaurant*.

Otherwise, for budget accommodation try the far inferior *Tukutane Guest House* with basic but relatively clean rooms for Tsh1500/2000. It's on the same street as the Catholic church, but a bit further down. The equally basic *Kambeni Guest House* opposite the bus stand has rooms for Tsh2000/2500 (Tsh3500 with bathroom).

For more upmarket accommodation, your only option is *Elephant Motel*, approximately 1km south-east of town on the main Dar es Salaam-Arusha highway. Comfortable singles/doubles are Tsh12,000/18,000 including breakfast. There's also a *restaurant* and a TV.

Getting There & Away

Minibuses go several times a day between Same and Dar es Salaam (Tsh5000), Moshi (Tsh1000) and Mombo (Tsh1500), from where you can get transport to Lushoto. There is also daily local transport to Kisiwani, and on most days to Mbaga and other nearby hill villages.

MBAGA

Mbaga, about 30km south-east of Same next to the Mkomazi Game Reserve, is a good base for hikes deeper into the surrounding southern Pare hills and villages. You can also trek from here in two or three days to the top of Shengena peak (2463m), the highest in the Pares. Mbaga has traditionally been an influential town due to its location near the centre of the Pare mountains and even today is in many respects a more important local centre than Same.

Places to Stay & Eat

Hill-Top Tona Lodge (☎ 600158, 601630, PO Box 32 Mbaga-Same or PO Box 1592 Dar es Salaam) is the place to stay in Mbaga. It offers simple but good accommodation for US$10 per person. Lunch and dinner can be arranged with advance notice for an extra Tsh2500 each. Camping costs US$5 per person. It's a very good idea to bring water

NORTH-EASTERN TANZANIA

purification tablets. You can get information about the lodge and transport options at the Sasa Kazi hotel near the bus station in Same.

Getting There & Away

There is transport most days from Same to Mbaga (about Tsh1000) via Kisiwani; the last bus departs Same about 2 pm. For those driving their own vehicle, there is an alternative route via Mwembe, reached by following the Dar es Salaam-Arusha highway 5km south to the dirt road leading off to the left.

MWANGA

Mwanga, about 50km north of Same on the Dar es Salaam-Arusha highway, is a good starting point for excursions into the northern Pares.

The best place to stay is the **Rhino Hotel**, signposted about 2km out of town off the road to Usangi. Simple but decent rooms are Tsh5000.

There is daily transport linking Mwanga with Arusha, Moshi, Same and Usangi.

USANGI

Usangi, in the hills east of Mwanga, is the centre of the northern Pares and the best base for hiking in this area.

The main point of interest in town as far as hiking is concerned is **Lomwe Secondary School**, which has been designated as a centre to assist tourists with finding guides and accommodation. There is also a camping ground here with water, and a hostel when school is not in session. It costs Tsh2000 per person for either option. If you can't find anyone at the school, ask for Mr Kangero or Mr Mashauri. Other than Lomwe, accommodation options include home stays in the village (generally in houses near the school), or the **guesthouse** in town near the Jumaa mosque. Basic rooms here are about Tsh3500, and there is also a **restaurant**.

A good source of information on Pare culture is Mr Fundi Semvua. He lives just outside Usangi in Mbale village, about 15 minutes on foot.

Getting There & Away

There are several minibuses or pick-ups daily between Mwanga and Usangi; the road is in decent condition during the dry season. From Arusha, there is a minibus most days from the central bus station, departing in the morning (Tsh2500). Drivers on both routes will drop you at Lomwe Secondary School. Start your travels early as it can take a while to get up here. Budget at least two days for an excursion to Usangi.

Northern Tanzania

There are few areas of the continent which attract as much tourist attention as northern Tanzania. With mighty, snow-capped Mt Kilimanjaro, the wildlife-packed Ngorongoro Crater and the vast plains of the Serengeti, the region embodies what is for many quintessential Africa. While these places are certainly well worth visiting, the north also holds many other fascinating attractions. The area around Marangu, for example, offers good village to village walking and numerous opportunities for getting to know the local culture. North of Arusha are small villages where you can experience the Maasai way of life. The remote Crater Highlands have some of Tanzania's most rugged and striking scenery and hold excellent hiking possibilities for the more adventurous. There are also some lesser known national parks that are just as spectacular as the Serengeti, including the serene Lake Manyara; Tarangire, with its varied topography and high concentration of wildlife; and the tiny but beautiful Arusha National Park.

Northern Tanzania is an accessible region and fairly easy to explore. Its larger towns offer a range of accommodation and dining options, and main roads are in good condition. There is also direct air access from Europe and elsewhere in East Africa via Kilimanjaro international airport.

MOSHI

Moshi is a bustling town at the foot of Mt Kilimanjaro, lying at an altitude of about 800m. It's the home of the Chagga people and centre of one of Tanzania's major coffee growing regions. It's also a regional capital and an important educational centre, with one of the highest per capita concentrations of secondary schools in the country. Moshi has traditionally been an important base for missionary activity and the Chagga now comprise one of the largest Christian communities in Tanzania, about evenly split among Lutherans and Catholics.

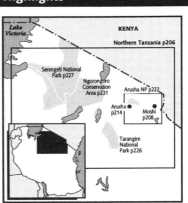

Highlights

- **Wildlife Viewing** – superb opportunities in one of the region's many national parks and protected areas
- **Spectacular Topography** – Serengeti plains, the rugged Crater Highlands, and magnificent Mt Kilimanjaro and Mt Meru
- **Colourful Tribal Groups** – including the Maasai and the Chagga
- **Village-based Walking** – around Arusha, Moshi and Marangu

Most visitors use the town as a starting point for climbing Mt Kilimanjaro, although it's a pleasant place in its own right to relax for a couple of days. It also tends to be less expensive than nearby Arusha.

Information

Immigration The Moshi immigration office is in Kibo House near the clock tower. It's open Monday to Friday from 7.30 am to 3.30 pm. Visa extensions are usually handled while you wait.

NORTHERN TANZANIA

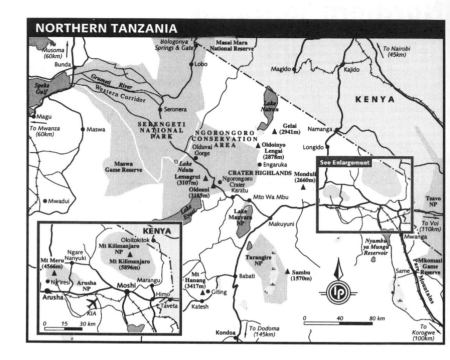

Tourist Information The small Moshi Guide contains helpful information for those planning to stay for an extended period. It is available for Tsh2000 at The Coffee Shop, Abbas Ali's Hot Bread Shop & Patisserie and other places around town.

Money There are several foreign exchange bureaus on Boma Rd. Try Key's Bureau de Change (open weekdays until 4.30 pm) and Executive Bureau de Change (open weekdays until 5 pm and Saturday until 2 pm).

The NBC and CRDB banks are both located on the main circle by the clock tower; both exchange travellers cheques.

Post, Telephone & Fax You can make telephone calls and send and receive faxes (fax 51113, Tsh300 per page to receive) at the Telecom building near the clock tower. There is also a disorganised poste restante here.

Email & Internet Access At the time of research the only place with email facilities was Kilimanjaro Information Technology (☎/fax 54182) in Technology House on Ghalla St, north-east of the clock tower roundabout. Rates were Tsh2000 per page to send and Tsh1000 per page to receive. By now, several other places will most likely have opened.

Travel Agencies There are many travel agencies and tour operators based in Moshi who can assist with arranging climbs of Mt Kilimanjaro and excursions to the nearby national parks. The atmosphere isn't quite as cut-throat as in Arusha, although you will still be frequently approached by street touts. Some of the better agencies are listed on the following page. For more information on travel agencies see the boxed text 'Warning' under Choosing a Company in the Getting Around chapter.

The Chagga

The Chagga people, who live on the slopes of Mt Kilimanjaro in and around Moshi, are one of Tanzania's largest ethnic groups. For much of their early history, they were subdivided into numerous small, independent chiefdoms which were often at war with each other and with their neighbours, each seeking control over caravan trade with the coast. During the colonial era, in the early 20th century, the Germans succeeded in overpowering the Chagga and ruling them; largely through a system of deposing resisters and appointing more pliable chiefs in their stead. It was during this time that a common cultural Chagga identity began to develop.

The Chagga, who are patrilineal, were traditionally small-scale banana farmers, and even today are known for their *mbege* or banana beer. During the colonial and post-colonial periods, coffee came to replace bananas as the most economically important crop. Together with British colonial administrators, the Chagga formed a successful sales cooperative early in the 20th century for marketing the coffee crop. With the increased revenues earned in the coffee industry, more and more Chagga were able to receive formal education, and today the Chagga are one of the most modernised and prosperous ethnic groups in Tanzania.

While most Chagga are Christian, animistic beliefs continue to play an important role in daily life. The Chagga maintain close links with the spirit world and rituals and traditional practices are common.

The Chagga settlements containing traditional thatched houses usually have a large network of hidden passageways and caverns underneath.

Key's Hotel
(☎ 52250, fax 50073, email keys@form-net .com, PO Box 933) mid-range; standard Kilimanjaro packages

Kilimanjaro Crown Birds
(☎ 51162, fax 52038, PO Box 9519) at New Kindoroko Hotel; mid-range; standard Kilimanjaro packages

Mauly Tours & Safaris
(☎ 50730, fax 53330, email mauly@africaon line.co.tz, PO Box 1315) on Mawenzi Rd between the clock tower and the bus station; budget to mid-range; standard Kilimanjaro packages

Samjoe Tours & Travels
(☎ 51468, fax 52136, PO Box 1467) located on the ground floor of the KNCU Building; budget to mid-range; standard Kilimanjaro packages and safaris to Tanzania's northern parks

Shah Tours
(☎ 52370, 52998, fax 51449, email kilimanjaro @eoltz.com, PO Box 1812) on Mawenzi Rd; mid-range to top end; quality standard and customised packages for Kilimanjaro and Mt Meru as well as wildlife safaris

Zara Tanzania Adventures
(☎ 54240, 50808, fax 53105, email zara @form-net.com, PO Box 1990) on Rindi Lane behind Moshi Hotel; budget to mid-range; standard Kilimanjaro packages

Medical Services In an emergency you could try the Kilimanjaro Christian Medical Centre (☎ 54377), about 3km from town on Sokoine Rd, although many foreign residents in Moshi prefer to go to Nairobi for treatment.

Photography The best place to get film developed is Burhani Colour Lab on the corner of Hill and Selous Sts. Same-day service costs Tsh90 per print plus a Tsh500 fee; the lab is also open Sunday mornings. Burhani's sells slide and print film for about Tsh5000 per roll.

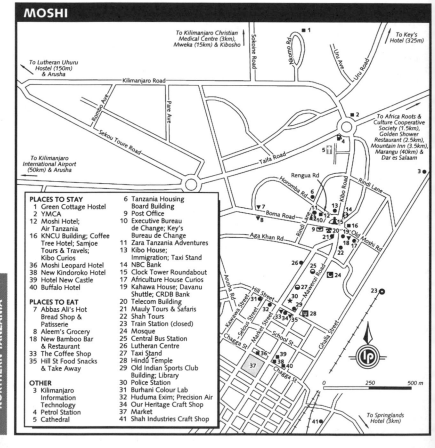

MOSHI

To Kilimanjaro Christian Medical Centre (3km), Mweka (15km) & Kibosho

To Key's Hotel (325m)

To Lutheran Uhuru Hostel (150m) & Arusha

Kilimanjaro Road

Sokoine Road

Nkomo Rd

Uru Ave

Uru Road

Rombo Ave

Pare Ave

To Africa Roots & Culture Cooperative Society (1.5km), Golden Shower Restaurant (2.5km), Mountain Inn (3.5km), Marangu (40km) & Dar es Salaam

Sekou Toure Road

To Kilimanjaro International Airport (50km) & Arusha

Taifa Road

Rengua Rd

Kibo Road

Rindi Lane

Horomba Rd

Boma Road

Aga Khan Rd

Rindi Lane

Old Moshi Rd

Arusha Rd

Hill Street

Mawenzi Road

Kawawa Street

Selous Street

Market Street

School St

Challa Street

Chagga St

Chagga St

To Springlands Hotel (3km)

0   250   500 m

PLACES TO STAY
1 Green Cottage Hostel
2 YMCA
12 Moshi Hotel; Air Tanzania
16 KNCU Building; Coffee Tree Hotel; Samjoe Tours & Travels; Kibo Curios
36 Moshi Leopard Hotel
38 New Kindoroko Hotel
39 Hotel New Castle
40 Buffalo Hotel

PLACES TO EAT
7 Abbas Ali's Hot Bread Shop & Patisserie
8 Aleem's Grocery
18 New Bamboo Bar & Restaurant
33 The Coffee Shop
35 Hill St Food Snacks & Take Away

OTHER
3 Kilimanjaro Information Technology
4 Petrol Station
5 Cathedral
6 Tanzania Housing Board Building
9 Post Office
10 Executive Bureau de Change; Key's Bureau de Change
11 Zara Tanzania Adventures
13 Kibo House; Immigration; Taxi Stand
14 NBC Bank
15 Clock Tower Roundabout
17 Africulture House Curios
19 Kahawa House; Davanu Shuttle; CRDB Bank
20 Telecom Building
21 Mauly Tours & Safaris
22 Shah Tours
23 Train Station (closed)
24 Mosque
25 Central Bus Station
26 Lutheran Centre
27 Taxi Stand
28 Hindu Temple
29 Old Indian Sports Club Building; Library
30 Police Station
31 Burhani Colour Lab
32 Huduma Exim; Precision Air
34 Our Heritage Craft Shop
37 Market
41 Shah Industries Craft Shop

The Kaole ruins near Bagamoyo include one of the oldest mosques on the Tanzanian mainland.

Approaching the summit of Mt Kilimanjaro. Use of wood for fuel on treks is causing serious environmental damage on the mountain, particularly along the heavily travelled Marangu Route.

CHRISTINE OSBORNE

GREG ELMS

DAVID WALL

MARK DAFFEY

GREG ELMS

Top Left & Right: Bright, bold jewellery and clothing are a sign of wealth for the colourful Maasai.
Bottom: Young Maasai warriors, near Arusha, look startling with their painted faces.

Tanzania's Coffee Industry

Coffee has played a major role in Tanzania's economy since the 1960s when it replaced sisal as the country's chief export crop. While coffee is said to have originated in south-western Ethiopia, it was not until the turn of the century that it was planted in Tanzania, after being introduced by Jesuit missionaries from Réunion island. The industry began to flourish during the British colonial era in the early 20th century, with the formation of successful coffee marketing cooperatives among the Chagga.

There are two types of coffee. *Coffea arabica*, which accounts for just under 75% of Tanzanian coffee exports, is used to make higher quality speciality coffees, and is grown around Mt Kilimanjaro, Mt Meru and in the Southern Highlands. *Coffea robusta*, more neutral in taste and used to make less expensive blends and soluble coffees, is grown around western Lake Victoria. Over 90% of Tanzanian coffee is grown on tiny smallholder farms, with the rest coming from cooperatives and private estates.

After rapid expansion during the 1970s and 1980s due to favourable world prices, Tanzanian coffee production has declined dramatically in recent years. In 1997 the yield on smallholder farms fell to an average of only 170kg of coffee per hectare, compared with close to 700kg per hectare in the early 1970s. Quality has also diminished, with less than 25% of coffee exports qualifying in the top eight grades, compared to close to 50% two decades ago. This decline has mainly resulted from adverse weather conditions, the industry's difficult transition away from a state-controlled system, and fluctuations in international commodities prices. The El Nino floods of 1998, which devastated the coffee crop in much of northern Tanzania, were also a severe blow.

In response to concerns that the coffee sector might disappear altogether, numerous measures are now being implemented, including the large-scale distribution of coffee seedlings and the introduction of revised payment schemes for farmers.

Business Hours In addition to regular weekday hours, many tourism-related businesses in Moshi, such as trek and safari outfitters, are also open on Sunday mornings.

Things to See & Do

Downtown Moshi makes an interesting walk. The area around the market and Mawenzi Rd has a vaguely Asian flavour, with a Hindu temple, several mosques and many Indian traders.

A dip in the 25m pool at the YMCA makes a refreshing break. It costs Tsh2000 for nonhostel residents.

About 15km north of Moshi in Mweka is the College of African Wildlife Management where many of the elite guides for Kilimanjaro and other national parks are trained.

Machame, Umbwe and other towns above Moshi on Kilimanjaro's lower slopes are all linked by easy-to-follow footpaths offering good walks through attractive terrain.

Places to Stay – Budget

Golden Shower Restaurant (☎/fax 51990), north-east of the centre on Taifa Rd, allows camping for US$3 per person.

One of the most popular places is the *YMCA (☎ 51754, 52923)* north of the clock tower on the roundabout between Kibo and Taifa Rds. It has simple but clean singles/doubles for US$13/15 with shared facilities and there is a nice pool, a dining room and a coffee bar.

KNCU Coffee Tree Hotel (☎ 55040) just east of the clock tower has basic rooms for Tsh4000/6000 (Tsh3000 for a single with shared facilities); suites cost Tsh12,000. There's also an inexpensive restaurant here and good views from the top of the building.

The rather faded, state-run *Moshi Hotel (☎ 55212, fax 53105)*, just to the west of the clock tower, has rooms for US$10/15 (US$35 with bathroom), including breakfast.

Green Cottage Hostel is a private house about 1.5km north of the centre on Nkomo Rd. Small rooms are US$10/15 (US$20 for a double with bathroom); there is no food here.

In the busy downtown area near the market and bus stand are several popular places. The *New Kindoroko Hotel (☎ 54054, fax 54062)* on Mawenzi Rd does a brisk business with tourists and locals. Rooms with bathroom and breakfast cost Tsh6000/12,000 (Tsh18,000 for a suite). There is also a restaurant with a few vegetarian selections.

Hotel New Castle (☎ 53203) is in the same area on Mawenzi Rd but it's not as good. Rooms are US$10/15 (US$15/20 with bathroom), including breakfast and hot water. The rooms on the upper floors tend to get a lot of noise from the rooftop bar.

Buffalo Hotel, on Chagga St south-east of the Hotel New Castle, has doubles for US$10; breakfast is extra.

Places to Stay – Mid-Range & Top End

The best value in this category is *Lutheran Uhuru Hostel (☎ 54084)* north-west of the centre on the road to Arusha, with spotless rooms in beautiful, quiet grounds from US$30/45 including a buffet breakfast. There is also a good restaurant with meals for between Tsh3000 and Tsh5000. The only disadvantage is its location 3km from the centre. It's on the Kibosha dalla-dalla route (Tsh200); otherwise, taxis from the hostel into town cost Tsh1000 (Tsh2000 for the hostel taxi).

Key's Hotel (☎ 52250, fax 50073, email keys@form-net.com), on Uru Rd north-east of the clock tower, has been popular with travellers for years. Comfortable rooms cost US$40/50 single/double (US$50/60 with air-con). There is a substantial discount on room prices for guests who book a Kilimanjaro trek with the hotel. Downstairs is a restaurant and a popular bar.

Moshi Leopard Hotel (☎ 50884, fax 51261), on a busy section of Market St near the bus stand, is a modern place with rooms for US$30/40 including continental breakfast. Nonresidents must pay in hard currency.

About 4km from town on the Marangu road is *Mountain Inn*, with a nice garden and rooms for US$35/45 including breakfast. It's run by Shah Tours and discounts on the rooms are available for their trekking

and safari clients. There is a restaurant here and a mountain-climbing equipment shop.

About 3km south-east of the centre on Ruaha St in the Pasna section of town is *Springlands Hotel (☎ 53581)*, with rooms for US$25/35 including breakfast. Bookings can be made directly or through Zara Tanzania Adventures.

Places to Eat

Abbas Ali's Hot Bread Shop & Patisserie, on Boma Rd, is open from 6.30 am to 6 pm weekdays and until 5 pm on Saturday. It has good wholegrain breads, cheese and other home-made products.

The *Green Bamboo Restaurant* at the Lutheran Uhuru Hostel has good nyama choma and other grills for about Tsh2000. Several other places to stay have restaurants (see earlier).

For inexpensive local food try *New Bamboo Bar & Restaurant* opposite the KNCU building or *Hill Street Food Snacks & Take Away* on Hill St.

The Coffee Shop on Hill St one block west of Mawenzi Rd is a great place with good coffee, home-made breads, cakes and light meals. Proceeds go to a church project. It's open from 8 am to 5.30 pm weekdays and until 4.30 pm on Saturday.

For a splurge, try the *Golden Shower Restaurant* (see Places to Stay) which has a pleasant garden setting and good meals from about Tsh3000.

Shopping

There are craft shops dotted throughout town. Try Africulture House Curios south-east of the KNCU building; Kibo Curios, in the central courtyard of KNCU; Our Heritage on Hill St; or Africa Roots & Culture Cooperative Society on the right side of the Marangu road, 500m after the last major roundabout. For pricier leatherwork and other crafts, try the Shah Industries craft shop, south of town over the train tracks.

Getting There & Away

Air Moshi is served by Kilimanjaro international airport, about 50km west of town off the main Moshi-Arusha road. For details of flight schedules and prices see the Arusha Getting There & Away section.

Air Tanzania's Moshi office (☎ 55205) is next to the Moshi Hotel. Unlike Air Tanzania elsewhere in the country, the Moshi office generally requires nonresidents to pay for tickets in hard currency.

The Precision Air representative in Moshi is Huduma Exim (☎ 53495) on Hill St.

Bus Most of the minibus shuttles which service the Nairobi-Arusha sector also continue on from Arusha to Moshi, though most of the normal buses do not. The principal minibus shuttle company is Davanu. Its Moshi office (☎ 53416) is in Kahawa House near the CRDB bank by the clock tower. Departures from Moshi are daily at 11.30 am from Kahawa House, arriving 7 pm in Nairobi. It costs US$35 plus visa fees at the border; advance bookings are required.

The thrice-weekly 'tourist shuttle' between Arusha and Mombasa (Kenya) also stops in Moshi. It departs from Moshi on Tuesday, Thursday and Saturday at 10 am, arriving Mombasa at 3.30 pm. Tickets between Moshi and Mombasa are US$40; the booking contact in Moshi is Mauly Tours & Safaris. See Land in the Getting There & Away chapter for details on both shuttles.

Minibuses to Marangu (Tsh500, one hour) and Arusha (Tsh1000, one to 1½ hours) leave throughout the day from the central bus station. Large buses also service Arusha (Tsh1000, one hour).

Getting Around
To/From the Airport Air Tanzania runs a shuttle bus between Moshi and Kilimanjaro international airport connecting with most arriving and departing flights. It costs Tsh3000 (unless you are the only passenger, in which case it costs Tsh12,000) and leaves from the Air Tanzania office about two hours before scheduled flight departure time.

Taxi & Dalla-Dalla Good places to catch a taxi include Kibo House by the clock tower and Market St, near the police station.

Most dalla-dallas leave from the central bus station which is between Market St and Mawenzi Rd.

MARANGU
Marangu is a small, attractive town on the slopes of Mt Kilimanjaro about 40km northeast of Moshi. In addition to serving as a convenient overnight stop for those trekking on the Marangu Route, it also makes a good base for day and overnight hikes on Kilimanjaro's lower slopes. For details of the Marangu Route see the Trekking chapter.

Travel Agencies
Most of the hotels in Marangu organise Kilimanjaro treks; some of the better ones are listed following. For hotel addresses and telephone numbers see under Places to Stay. For an explanation of price categories see Costs in the Money section of the Facts for the Visitor chapter.

Alpine Tours at Coffee Tree Camp Site
    Budget Kilimanjaro packages; village hiking around Marangu.
Babylon Lodge
    Budget to mid-range Kilimanjaro packages.
Capricorn Hotel
    Upmarket Kilimanjaro packages.
Marangu Hotel
    Mid-range to more expensive; focus is on quality treks on Kilimanjaro. The hotel also offers a special no-frills 'hard way' option for travellers interested in cutting costs as much as possible. For US$170 plus park fees for a five-day Marangu climb, the hotel will take care of hut reservations and provide a guide with porter; you must provide food and equipment.

For village hiking in the Marangu area, the best source of information and assistance is Alpine Tours at Coffee Tree Camp site. They can arrange day or overnight excursions in the surrounding area. If you are trying to make arrangements for this from Dar es Salaam, contact their partner there, Hit Holidays Travel & Tours (see the listing under Travel Agencies in the Dar es Salaam chapter). Possibilities for excursions include day hikes to Mandara Hut and walks to nearby villages, markets and waterfalls.

Places to Stay

Coming from Moshi, the first hotel you reach is the good-value **Marangu Hotel** (☎ *51307, fax 50639, email marangu@africaonline .co.ke, PO Box 40 Moshi)*, with comfortable singles/doubles for US$70/100 including breakfast and dinner, and camping for US$3 per person including hot showers. Room and camping prices are discounted if you join one of the hotel's fully equipped treks.

About 1.5km west of the main junction is **Kibo Hotel** (☎/fax 51308, email kibohotel @form-net.com)* with rooms for US$37/54 including breakfast. Camping costs US$6 per person with shower. The atmosphere is good but the rooms are overpriced.

About 500m east of the main junction is **Babylon Lodge** (☎ Marangu 5, fax 055-51315, PO Box 227)* with simple but clean rooms for US$25/40 including breakfast. Another 3km further down the same road is **Ashanti Lodge** (☎ Marangu 206, fax 057-8204, PO Box 339)* with singles/doubles/triples for US$20/40/50 including breakfast. Camping is possible here for US$5 per person or free if you arrange your trek through Ashanti. The place is pleasant enough with a nice garden but not really worth the hike from town.

North of the main junction on the road to the national park gate is the drab **Bismarck Hut Lodge** with very basic rooms for Tsh5000/6000 with common facilities; at the time of writing much of the building was still under construction.

Further north, about 3km from the junction, is the upmarket **Capricorn Hotel** (☎/fax 055-51309, PO Box 938)* with comfortable rooms for US$55 per person including breakfast.

Just beyond the Capricorn is the signposted turn-off for **Coffee Tree Camp site** (☎ 50656, fax 50096, PO Box 835)*; it's about 700m east of the main road down a steep hill. There are actually two access roads. The steeper, signposted one is just north of the Top-Kibo Grocery. An unmarked dirt road closer to the Capricorn Hotel also leads to the camp site. Camping costs US$5 per person per night including hot and cold water and

cooking facilities (fireplaces); you'll need to bring your own tent and food. The owner, who also runs Alpine Tours, is knowledgeable about the Marangu area and committed to introducing visitors to the region and helping them get acquainted with local customs. For reasonable prices he can organise a variety of hikes in the surrounding area. He also has experience in arranging mountain hikes for international student groups. There is no accommodation near the park gate.

Getting There & Away

Minibuses run throughout the day between Marangu and Moshi (Tsh500). In Marangu they drop you at the main junction from where you can sometimes get a pick-up to the park gate (Tsh200) or to the various hotels to the north and east.

ARUSHA

Arusha is one of Tanzania's most developed and fastest growing towns. It was the headquarters of the East African Community in the days when Tanzania, Kenya and Uganda were members of this economic and customs union. Today, Arusha is headquarters of the Tripartite Commission for East African Cooperation – a revived attempt at regional collaboration. It is also the site for the Tanzanian-moderated negotiations on Burundi, and for the Rwanda genocide tribunal.

The town sits in lush countryside near the foot of Mt Meru (4566m) and enjoys a temperate climate throughout the year. Surrounding it are many coffee, wheat and maize estates tended by the Arusha and Meru people, whom you may see in the market area of town.

Arusha is the gateway to Serengeti, Lake Manyara, Tarangire and Arusha national parks. As such, it is the safari capital of Tanzania. It is also an excellent base for exploring the Crater Highlands and the Ngorongoro Conservation Area; for details of trekking in these areas and climbing Mt Meru see the Trekking chapter.

About 250km south-west of Arusha is Mt Hanang (3417m), Tanzania's fourth highest mountain and a good trekking destination for rugged travellers. For more details see later in this chapter.

Orientation

Arusha is divided into two sections by the small Naura River Valley. To the east of the valley are most of the top-range hotels, the post office, immigration, government buildings, safari companies, airline offices, craft shops and the Arusha International Conference Centre (AICC). Across the valley to the west are the commercial and industrial areas, the market, budget hotels and the bus station.

The AICC, where many tour companies cited in this section are located, is divided into three wings – the Serengeti Wing to the west, the Kilimanjaro Wing in the centre and the Ngorongoro Wing to the east.

Maps MaCo is planning to put out a new business map of Arusha sometime in 1999, costing about Tsh5000. Otherwise, there are some old photocopied town maps available from the tourist information centre and tour operators.

Information

Immigration The immigration office on Simeon Rd near the junction with Makongoro Rd is open from 7.30 am to 3.30 pm Monday to Friday. Visa extensions are normally processed while you wait.

National Parks & Game Reserves Offices The Tanzania National Parks (TANAPA) headquarters (☎ 057-8040, PO Box 3134) is located on the 6th floor of the Kilimanjaro Wing of the AICC building. It stocks booklets on some of the national parks but is primarily of interest for tour operators or those needing specialised information on the parks.

The Wildlife Division, which manages Tanzania's game reserves, has a small office near the AICC but for more substantial information you will have to go to their main office in Dar es Salaam.

Tourist Information The Tanzania Tourist Board has a Tourist Information Centre

(☎ 3842, 3843, fax 8256, PO Box 2348) on Boma Rd just up from the post office. It's open 8 am to 4 pm weekdays and 8.30 am to 1 pm on Saturdays. They do not assist with bookings or reservations but have some helpful information on Arusha, the nearby parks and other tourist sites in Tanzania. They also have copies of a 'blacklist' of tour operators as well as a list of registered tour companies.

There are good travellers' bulletin boards at the Hot Bread Shop, The Outpost hotel and Mambo Jazz Cafe.

Money There are several foreign exchange bureaus. The best is Northern Bureau de Change on Joel Maeda St, which changes both cash and travellers cheques. Most are open 9 am to 5 pm weekdays and on Saturday mornings. Banks in Arusha also change cash and travellers cheques.

You can get cash advances against Visa or MasterCard from the bureau de change at the Impala Hotel. There are also several other shops which offer this service, though not all are reliable. One of the better ones is Renada Minerals Corporation next to the Modern Refrigeration Company on Goliondoi Rd.

American Express is represented by Rickshaw Travels (☎ 6655) at the east end of Sokoine Rd but their Arusha office cannot issue travellers cheques.

Post, Telephone & Fax The main post office is on Boma Rd near the clock tower; it has a fairly organised poste restante.

The telephone exchange, in the Telecom building, is also on Boma Rd. It's open for domestic and international calls from 8 am to 10 pm Monday through Saturday and from 9 am to 8 pm on Sunday and holidays. You can also send and receive faxes here (Tsh300 per page to receive, fax 057-8360).

Alternatively, there are several business centres offering efficient telephone and fax services at rates somewhat higher than those at the telephone exchange. One of the better ones is Multilink (☎/fax 4228, 8115, email link@yako.habari.co.tz) behind the Mambo Jazz Cafe on Old Moshi Rd.

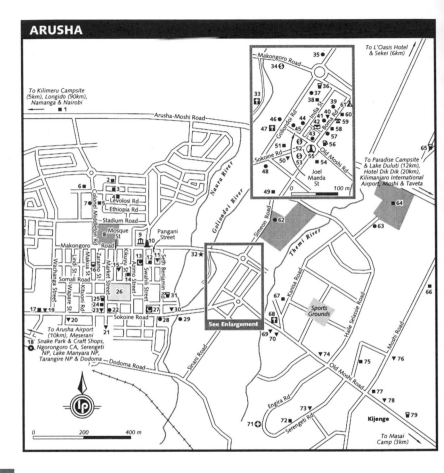

ARUSHA

Email & Internet Access Email and internet service providers in Arusha include:

A&A Computers
(☎ 8306, 7708) Goliondoi Rd; Tsh5000 per hour for internet access or email; off-line typing/send later option costs Tsh3000 per hour
Chemichem
Boma Rd at Chemichem Creative Arts Centre; Tsh500/2000 per page to receive/send email
CyberNet
India St in Arusha Art Shop; Tsh1800/3600 per half hour/hour for internet access; Tsh500/1800 per page to receive/send email

Modern Robots
New Arusha Hotel lobby; Tsh1800/2400 per page to receive/send email

Travel Agencies Arusha has close to one hundred registered tour operators as well as many unregistered ones. Only a small number of the reliable agents can be listed here. If you have doubts about a particular company, check before finalising your arrangements to see if they have an original licence (not a photocopy) from the Tourist Agents Licensing Authority (TALA).

ARUSHA

PLACES TO STAY		
1	Eland Motel	
2	Mashele Guest House; Mashele Guest House Annex; Twins Guest House; Pizzarusha	
3	Levolosi Guest House	
4	Monjes Guest House	
5	Palm Inn	
6	Golden Rose Hotel	
12	Arusha Centre Inn	
14	Robannyson Motel	
17	Meru House Inn	
24	Hotel Pallson's	
38	YMCA Youth Hostel	
49	Arusha Resort Centre	
51	Naaz Hotel	
54	New Arusha Hotel; Modern Robots Business Centre	
58	Lutheran Centre; Cafe, Bamboo & Kase Bookstore; Chemichem; Creative Arts Centre	
60	Hotel Equator	
61	Vision Campsite	
64	Novotel Mt Meru	
66	Hotel 77	
67	Centre House Hostel	
72	The Outpost	
75	Le Jacaranda	
77	Impala Hotel	

PLACES TO EAT	
11	Best in Town Grills
15	Khan's
19	Tandoor
20	Shanghai Chinese Restaurant; Meru Post Office
21	Amar Cuisine
23	McMoody's
30	Arusha Chinese Restaurant; Riverside Shuttle Office
40	Jambo Snacks & Bar
50	Hot Bread Shop
69	Roaster's Garden
70	Everest Chinese Restaurant
73	The Mandarin
74	Mambo Jazz Cafe; Multilink
76	Mezza Luna
78	Spices & Herbs Ethiopian Restaurant

OTHER	
7	Sunny Safaris
8	Stadium
9	Arusha Declaration Museum
10	Uhuru Monument
13	Mosque
16	Central Bus Station
18	Train Station
22	Bike Rentals
25	The Cavern
26	Market
27	Mosque
28	Metropole Cinema
29	Moona's Pharmacy
31	Crystal Club
32	Police
33	Catholic Church
34	Central Bank of Tanzania; Ngorongoro Conservation Area Authority
35	Immigration; Wildlife Division
36	Barracuda Bar
37	Renada Minerals Corporation
39	Ethiopian Air
41	Tanzanian Tourist Board
42	Post Office
43	Craft Shops
44	CyberNet; Arusha Art Shop
45	Kase Bookstore; KAM Real Art Centre
46	A&A Computers
47	Lutheran Church
48	Rickshaw Travels
52	Northern Bureau de Change
53	National Microfinance Bank
55	Clock Tower
56	Petrol Station
57	Air Tanzania
59	Telecom Building
62	Arusha International Conference Centre (AICC)
63	Arusha Gymkhana Club
65	The Big Y Club
68	Anglican Church
71	Trinity Medical Diagnostic Clinic
79	Mawingu Club

The best information often comes from other travellers; try to talk with others who have used the company that you are considering. Problems can come up in any trip; the important factor is whether the tour operator is willing to deal with such situations and to refund where necessary. Be wary of sham operators trading under the same names as the following companies. See the boxed text 'Warning' in the Getting Around chapter.

Adventure Tours & Safaris
(☎ 7600, fax 8195, PO Box 1014) on Goliondoi Rd. Mid-range; offers standard treks and safaris.

Bobby Tours & Safaris
(☎ 3490, fax 8176, email bobbytours@yako .habari.co.tz, PO Box 2169) on Goliondoi Rd.

Mid-range to top end; offers standard treks and northern circuit safaris.

Corto Safaris
(☎ 4213 or 0811-510056, fax 4393, PO Box 12267) at Le Jacaranda Hotel. Mid-range; offers treks and northern circuit safaris. Private camp site for safari and trekking clients, about 7km outside of Arusha in Moivaro.

Equatorial Safaris
(☎ 3302 or 0811-510731, fax 2617, email equatorial@form-net.com, PO Box 2156) Rm 460, Serengeti Wing, AICC. Budget to mid-range; offers standard Kilimanjaro packages and can also arrange trips to the Pare mountains.

Hoopoe Adventure Tours
(☎ 7011, 7541, fax 8226, email hoopoesafari @cybernet.co.tz, PO Box 2047) on India St. Mid-range to top end; a well-established, high quality operator organising wildlife safaris in all

the northern parks, with specialised knowledge of Tarangire National Park. They also arrange treks on Mt Kilimanjaro, Mt Meru and in the Crater Highlands, and can customise trips to a variety of destinations.

IntoAfrica (☎ 44-114-255 5610 or 254-2-350978, email enquiry@intoafrica.co.uk, 59 Langdon St, Sheffield, S118BH). Although not based in Arusha (offices in London and Nairobi), IntoAfrica is listed here as they run many tours in northern Tanzania, and are one of few tour operators truly committed to the principles of responsible eco-travel. Mid-range; organises safaris and treks, with a focus on providing travellers in-depth insights into Tanzanian life. Geared more for those seeking insights into Tanzanian life, rather than luxury lodge style travel. A portion of profits directly benefits local communities.

Let's Go Travel (☎ 7111, fax 4199, email letsgotravel@cybernet .co.tz, PO Box 12799) on Goliondoi Rd. Mid-range to more expensive; offers standard and customised safaris to the northern parks, and treks on Mt Meru and Mt Kilimanjaro. Specialises in walking and mountain bike safaris in the Tarangire Wildlife Conservation Area.

Nature Discovery (☎ 4063 or 0811-336949, fax 8406, email naturediscovery@eoltz.com, PO Box 10574) in Sakina, about 5km from the clock tower. Mid-range to top-end; focusing on ecologically sound safaris on the northern circuit including Crater Highlands and Lake Eyasi, as well as excursions to the Usambara mountains.

Nyika Treks & Safaris (☎/fax 4588, fax 3384, email nyikatreks@arusha .com, PO Box 13077) Rm 213, Serengeti Wing, AICC. Budget to mid-range; very knowledgeable about hiking in the Pare mountains.

Roy Safaris (☎ 2115, 8010, fax 8892, email roysafaris @intafrica.com, PO Box 50) just off Sokoine Rd. Well-established, reliable and efficiently managed tour operator offering standard mid-range wildlife safaris and Kilimanjaro trekking packages.

Scan-Tan Tours (☎ 8170, fax 6375, email scantan@yako.habari .co.tz, PO Box 2611) 3rd floor, Serengeti Wing, AICC. A mid-range to more expensive general safari operator; specialising in birding safaris and excursions to the Usambara mountains.

Silver Spear Safaris & Tours (☎/fax 8885, PO Box 1115) on Boma Rd opposite the Telecom building. Offers no-frills, bare-bones budget treks on Mt Kilimanjaro.

This outfit had some difficulties earlier but seems to be working hard to clean up its act. If it has, it may be a good bet for those on a tight budget. Just to be sure, check with other travellers before booking.

Sunny Safaris (☎ 7145, fax 8094, email sunny@arusha.com, PO Box 7267) on Colonel Middleton Rd north-west of the stadium. Budget to mid-range Kilimanjaro and Meru treks; popular with shoestring travellers.

Tanganyika Film & Safari Outfitters (☎ 2713, fax 8547, email jones@yako.habari .co.tz, PO Box 49) on Boma Rd. Top-end safari operators offering customised, longer expeditions and walking safaris.

Tropical Africa Trails (☎/fax 8299 or 0811-510669, email mike_ brydon@africaonline.co.ke, PO Box 6130) at Masai Camp on the edge of Arusha (see Places to Stay). Mid-range to top end, though will also cater to budget travellers. Specialises in treks and walking safaris on Kilimanjaro, Meru and the Crater Highlands; recommended for those who want customised Kilimanjaro treks away from the standard routes. Also willing to cater to groups with special requests, including kosher treks. A portion of profits goes to support education projects in Maasai schools.

Tropical Tours (☎ 8353, fax 8907, email tropical-tours @cybernet.co.tz, PO Box 727) on Joel Maeda St. Well-respected specialist trekking company offering a variety of mid-range to more expensive treks and safaris by foot or vehicle; includes routes on Mt Kilimanjaro, Mt Meru, the Crater Highlands and the Monduli mountains. If you are unable to reach Tropical Tours at the above numbers, try contacting them through Hoopoe Adventure Tours.

Bookshops The selection in Arusha pales in comparison with Nairobi, or even Dar es Salaam. The best are the Kase Bookstores opposite the post office and on Joel Maeda St. Both outlets have a decent selection of books about Tanzania's national parks. The bookshop in the New Arusha Hotel also has a good selection of books on the national parks, including the TANAPA booklet series.

Medical Services For medical care try the excellent Trinity Medical Diagnostic Clinic (☎ 4401, fax 4392, email kfg@yako.habari .co.tz) at 35 Engira Rd, south-west of Old

Moshi Rd. They have after-hours access for emergencies.

Moona's pharmacy (☎ 0811-510590) on Sokoine Rd is well stocked.

Dangers & Annoyances Arusha is the worst place in Tanzania for street touts and slick tour operators. Such people prey on the gullibility of newly arrived travellers by offering them safaris and Kilimanjaro treks at ridiculously low prices. Among the worst places for touts are in and around the AICC building and along Boma and Goliondoi Rds. Be sure that any tour company you sign up with is properly registered; ideally, get recommendations from other travellers, and check the current 'blacklist' at the Tourist Information Centre on Boma Rd. For a list of reputable operators, see the Travel Agencies section earlier in this chapter.

Numerous muggings have been reported in the area between the Novotel and the AICC building; take a taxi for this section.

Things to See & Do

The small **Arusha Declaration Museum** near the Uhuru Monument on Makongoro Rd has a moderately interesting display on post-colonial Tanzanian history. It's affiliated with the National Museum in Dar es Salaam. The Natural History Museum in the old German boma is closed for renovations.

Other diversions include the colourful **market** and the **swimming pool** at the Novotel (Tsh1500 for nonguests).

About 20km west of Arusha along the Dodoma road is the **Meserani Snake Park**; admission costs US$5. There are several well-stocked but very commercialised **craft shops** along the main road near the snake park including Cultural Heritage, the Tinga Tinga Art Gallery and the Oldonyo Orok Arts Gallery.

Places to Stay – Budget

Camping The best place is *Masai Camp*, about 3km from the centre of Old Moshi Rd. It costs US$3 per person including hot showers. There's also a restaurant and a bar.

The main drawback here is that the site is sometimes inundated with overland trucks.

Vision Camp site on Boma Rd is conveniently located but is nowhere near as nice as Masai Camp. Security can be a problem and the camp site is often noisy during weekend days due to a nearby children's disco. Camping costs Tsh1000 per person.

Kilimeru Camp site about 5km from town on the Arusha-Moshi (Nairobi) road, is scheduled to open in 1999. Camping rates are US$5 per night; tent and sleeping bag rental can be arranged for an extra US$7.

Paradise Camp site by Lake Duluti has a good setting, but is run-down. It is on the Arusha-Moshi road, around 12km east of the town .

Guesthouses & Hotels There is a good choice of budget hotels in Arusha. The least expensive ones are concentrated in the area east of Colonel Middleton Rd and north of the stadium. Most of these places rent by the hour but there are a few decent ones. The most popular with budget travellers is *Mashele Guest House* with singles/doubles/triples for Tsh2000/3000/6000; breakfast is available for an additional Tsh1000/1500 continental/full, and there is a restaurant. Rooms with windows opening onto the patio can be noisy.

Next door is the quieter *Mashele Guest House Annex* with rooms for Tsh4000.

Other acceptable places include *Twins Guest House* with rooms for Tsh2000/3000, and *Levolosi* and *Monjes Guesthouses*, each with rooms for Tsh3000/3500. All have shared facilities.

Several blocks west of this area is *Palm Inn* (☎ 7430) which has clean, good value doubles with insect nets for Tsh6000.

There are also many budget places closer to the central bus station. The *Robbanyson Motel* on Kikuyu St has decent rooms for Tsh5000 per person with bathroom, and a good restaurant with meals for under Tsh1500. The building is under construction and may not look like much from the outside, but once inside, the rooms are fine for the price.

Arusha Centre Inn off Pangani St has reasonably clean rooms with bathroom for US$15/20.

Meru House Inn (☎ 7803, fax 8220) at the west end of Sokoine Rd has clean rooms for Tsh3500/4500 (Tsh7500 for a double with bathroom) and is popular with budget travellers. For some peace and quiet try to get a room on one of the upper levels facing away from the noisy inner courtyard.

Several other budget places are located in the east end of town around the clock tower and Boma Rd. The *Naaz Hotel (☎/fax 2087)* on Sokoine Rd has sterile but decent rooms for US$10/20 (US$20/25 with bathroom). There's a self-service snack bar downstairs for breakfast and lunch.

The *YMCA Youth Hostel (☎ 6907)* on India St has tolerable rooms with shared facilities for US$13/15.

The *Lutheran Centre (☎ 8855)* on Boma Rd near the post office has clean rooms for Tsh10,000/15,000.

Centre House Hostel on the grounds of Sekei Secondary School on Kanisa Rd is run by the Catholic diocese. Simple but clean rooms with shared facilities cost Tsh4000/8000 including breakfast.

Places to Stay – Mid-Range

The best in this price range, and one of the most pleasant hotels in Arusha, is *Le Jacaranda (☎ 6529, 4624, fax 8585, email jacaranda@cybernet.co.tz)* or in France *(☎ 33-660 21 20 51)*. It's a small place reminiscent of a French country home with singles/doubles for US$40/45 (US$50/55 with bathroom) including breakfast. Half-board and full-board options are also available; the restaurant here is very good. Camping can sometimes be arranged for US$3 per person including shower. It's about 100m north of Old Moshi Rd. There's also a small bookshop, and a boutique with unusual local products and hand-made crafts. Groups can arrange to rent out the entire place.

Another good option nearby is *The Outpost (☎ 3908)*, about 1km south-east of the clock tower, on Serengeti Rd. It's an old house with rooms in the main building as

well as small bungalows in the garden. Rooms cost US$24/30. There are also beds in a five-bed room for US$13 each. The garden restaurant has a good buffet dinner for Tsh3700.

The sprawling *Hotel 77 (☎ 3802, 8054)*, known locally by its Swahili name 'Hotel Saba Saba', has small but decent rooms for US$30/40. It's on the Moshi Rd about 400m north of the Impala Hotel.

Mezza Luna (see Places to Eat), just south of Hotel 77 on Moshi Rd, has a few rooms for US$35/45.

A good option in the busy downtown area near the market is *Hotel Pallson's (☎ 6411)*. Singles/doubles/triples with TV cost US$30/40/50 including continental breakfast. Bills must be paid in foreign currency; credit card payments are charged an additional 10%.

The *Golden Rose Hotel (☎ 7959, fax 8862)* nearby has overpriced rooms for US$36/48/60 plus 20% VAT, and a good restaurant with inexpensive local dishes. Credit card payments are charged an additional 10%.

Hotel Equator on Boma Road has acceptable rooms for US$40/50 including breakfast. There is live music here most nights so rooms can be noisy. Credit card payments are charged an additional 5%.

In the north-west of the town on the Arusha-Moshi (Nairobi) road is *Eland Motel (☎ 6892)* with comfortable rooms for US$40/50 including breakfast.

Places to Stay – Top End

Novotel Mt Meru (☎ 2711, 8804, fax 8503, email tahifin@yako.habari.co.tz, PO Box 877 Arusha) is the only luxury hotel in central Arusha. Rooms are US$116/145 including breakfast, use of the pool and all amenities. It's north-east of the centre off the Arusha-Moshi road.

Impala Hotel (☎ 2962, 7083, fax 8220) at the junction of Moshi and Old Moshi Rds has comfortable rooms for US$65/78 including breakfast.

New Arusha Hotel (☎ 8541, 3244, fax 8085) near the clock tower doesn't look like much from the outside but the rooms are OK and there are attractive surrounding gardens. Rooms with breakfast cost US$65/75.

The Swiss-owned **Hotel Dik Dik** (☎/fax 8110) is well east of town on the lower slopes of Mt Meru and has well-appointed bungalow-style accommodation for US$141/212 including breakfast. It's signposted north of the Moshi road.

L'Oasis (☎/fax 7089 or 0811-510531), about 7km north-east of the centre in Sekei, has comfortable rooms set in nice gardens for US$65/90 including breakfast. They also have a good restaurant. It's signposted about 1km off the main Moshi to Nairobi Rd; the turn-off is diagonally opposite the Novotel.

Places to Eat – Budget

For inexpensive fast food near the market, **McMoody's** (open from 10 am to 10 pm daily except Monday) has burgers, pizzas and similar fare for between Tsh1300 and Tsh3000.

Chick-King on the ground floor of the Serengeti Wing, AICC, also has inexpensive fast food; outside there's a patio grill serving nyama choma.

Khan's is an auto spares store by day and a very popular barbecue by night. It's on Mosque St next to Music Land Restaurant.

Nearby on Pangani St is **Best in Town Grills** (☎ 6905). They have sandwiches and standard fare for between Tsh1500 and Tsh2500.

Pizzarusha opposite Mashele Guest House has inexpensive meals and is popular with budget travellers.

There are several good places near the clock tower. The **Hot Bread Shop** on Sokoine Rd is a great place to meet other travellers. Coffee, soup, sandwiches and light meals are available at reasonable prices.

Another good establishment to try is **Cafe Bamboo** (☎ 6451) on Boma Rd, with sandwiches, coffee, home-made cakes and other snacks at reasonable prices. It is open from 8 am to 5 pm on weekdays and until 3 pm on Saturday.

Across the road is **Jambo Snacks & Bar** with filling meals for less than Tsh2000.

Places to Eat – Mid-Range & Top End

Amar Cuisine (☎ 3463) off Sokoine Rd has a good variety of tandoori dishes for Tsh3500 or less, including a selection of vegetarian meals.

Arusha Chinese Restaurant (☎ 7860) on Sokoine Rd is inexpensive but very mediocre. The menu is a mixture of local and Chinese dishes; most meals are between Tsh2000 and Tsh2500.

The best Chinese food can be had at **Everest Chinese Restaurant** (☎ 8419) on Old Moshi Rd, which has pleasant garden seating, good food and good service. Meals range from Tsh1600 to Tsh4800.

Mambo Jazz Cafe (☎ 6995) on Old Moshi Rd has an all-day breakfast for Tsh3800, and a good lunch buffet from Tsh2800.

The Mandarin (☎ 7844) south-east of the centre on Serengeti Rd, near The Outpost Hotel, has a variety of Thai and Chinese dishes from Tsh3500 to Tsh6700.

Mezza Luna (☎ 4381) on Moshi Rd has a large Italian selection and outdoor seating.

Spices & Herbs on Old Moshi Rd, around the corner from the Impala Hotel, has a good selection of reasonably priced Ethiopian dishes and a pleasant atmosphere.

Roaster's Garden, next to Everest Chinese Restaurant on Old Moshi Rd, has nyama choma and rice for Tsh3000; it's not a bad place although service is slow.

Shanghai Chinese Restaurant (☎ 3224) at the western end of Sokoine Rd, behind the Meru Post Office, has very good food; meals are expensive, starting at Tsh4500 plus tax.

Tandoor (☎ 0811-510895) on Sokoine Rd has a good selection of Mughlai cuisine from Tsh3000; it's closed for Sunday lunch and all day Monday.

Entertainment

A popular nightspot and good place to meet locals is **The Big Y Club**, about 1km off the main Moshi-Arusha (Nairobi) road; the turn-off is diagonally opposite the Novotel. There is a breezy terrace upstairs and live African music most evenings. Admission costs Tsh1000.

Popular clubs include the *Mawingu Club* on Old Moshi Rd in Kijenge; *Crystal Club* on Seth Benjamin Rd north of the Metropole Cinema, and the disco at *Hotel 77*. Admission charges are between Tsh1000 and Tsh1500; these places get going after 10 pm.

In town is *The Cavern*, with pool table, TV and a bar. It's open from 7 pm Tuesday to Friday and from 2 pm on weekends.

Several readers have recommended the open-air *Barracuda Bar* on Makongoro Rd between Goliondoi Rd and India St.

The *Hotel Equator* has live music most evenings; admission is Tsh1000.

There are movies one evening a month at *Le Jacaranda*, usually in French with English subtitles.

Shopping

The small alley opposite Northern Bureau de Change and just off Joel Maeda St is full of craft dealers. A place to try for batiks is KAM Real Art Centre on Joel Maeda St.

Getting There & Away

Air Arusha is serviced by two airports. Most flights use Kilimanjaro international airport, about halfway between Moshi and Arusha off the main highway. Many charters and some regularly scheduled routes use Arusha airport, about 10km from town on the Dodoma road. Verify which airport your flight will be using when buying your ticket.

Arusha is connected by scheduled flights with:

Dar es Salaam
   daily; Tsh51,000/95,000/114,000; Air Tanzania, Coastal Travels, Precision Air
Mombasa
   irregular; US$147; Precision Air
Mwanza
   five times weekly; Tsh55,000/95,000; Air Tanzania, Precision Air
Nairobi
   irregular; US$150; Air Tanzania, Precision Air
Seronera (Serengeti National Park)
   irregular; US$135; Precision Air
Unguja
   three times weekly; approximately Tsh110,000; Air Tanzania, Air Zanzibar, Coastal Travels, Precision Air

Charter flights can be arranged between Arusha and Seronera (in Serengeti National Park), as well as to some of the other surrounding parks. Inquire with tour operators in Arusha or Dar es Salaam, or with air charter companies (see the listing in the Dar es Salaam chapter) for details. Precision Air has a scheduled flight between Arusha and Seronera (US$135) twice weekly, though it is often cancelled.

Airlines with offices in Arusha include:

Air Tanzania
   (☎ 3201, 7957) Boma Rd opposite the post office
Ethiopian Air
   (☎ 2013) Old Moshi Rd near the clock tower
Gulf Air
   (☎ 4152) Old Moshi Rd near the clock tower
Precision Air
   (☎ 2818) Ground floor, Ngorongoro Wing, AICC

Bus Arusha is well connected by road in all directions. The Arusha central bus station has a reputation for being particularly chaotic, so watch your luggage here.

Dar es Salaam
   Buses depart daily between 6 am and noon and cost from Tsh7800 for local buses which stop everywhere to Tsh12,500 for large express buses. The trip takes about nine hours along a good tarmac road. Better bus lines include Fresh ya Shamba and Tawfiq/Takrim.
Dodoma
   Most transport to Dodoma goes via Chalinze (Tsh10,700). If you want to go via Kondoa, you'll need to take a bus first to Babati (Tsh5000), then find onward transport from there. The road is in poor condition.
Mombasa (Kenya)
   There is a tourist shuttle linking Arusha with Mombasa, see the Getting There & Away chapter for more details.
Moshi
   Buses and minibuses run throughout the day between Arusha and Moshi (Tsh1000, one hour).
Mwanza & Musoma
   The most common route to Mwanza is via Nairobi; buses depart Arusha daily in the afternoon (Tsh19,000, 20 to 24 hours). To Musoma via Nairobi costs Tsh17,500.
   Alternatively, during the dry season there is a bus once or twice a week through the

Serengeti via Seronera and Ikoma Gate (Tsh25,000 plus park fees for Serengeti National Park and Ngorongoro Crater).

The third possibility is to go via Singida and Shinyanga in a big south-western loop (once or twice weekly in the dry season, Tsh18,000), but the road is in very bad shape and the trip can take up to three days or more.

Buses also go occasionally from Arusha to Musoma through the Serengeti's Western Corridor via Seronera and Ndabaka Gate (Tsh19,000 plus park fees).

Nairobi (Kenya)
Between Arusha and Nairobi there is a choice of normal buses and minibus shuttles; all go through the border posts without a change. Normal buses are cheaper but slower; they cost Tsh5000 and take about six to seven hours. For further information on minibus services see the main Getting There & Away chapter.

Tanga
There is usually at least one bus daily direct to Tanga (Tsh5200).

Getting Around
To/From Kilimanjaro International Airport
Air Tanzania has a shuttle connecting with all their arriving and departing flights. It costs Tsh3000 per person and departs from the Air Tanzania office on Boma Rd about two hours before flights leave.

Taxis from town cost between Tsh15,000 and Tsh20,000, more at night.

To/From Arusha Airport
Any dalla-dalla heading out along the Dodoma road can drop you at the junction, from where you'll have to walk. Taxis from town charge between Tsh5000 and Tsh6000.

Precision Air runs a shuttle from its office at the AICC to Arusha airport, departing AICC about 1½ hours before scheduled flight departures. It costs Tsh1000 one way.

Taxi Stands are opposite the Metropole Cinema and around the central bus station.

Bicycle Bicycles can be rented on Market St, near the market and opposite McMoody's.

AROUND ARUSHA
Outside town are some good hikes which offer views over Arusha and of Mt Kili-

manjaro and Mt Meru. Sunny Safaris can provide guides for day hikes to local Maasai villages for about US$15 per person for groups of four or more.

Several villages outside Arusha are sites for cultural tourism programmes sponsored by the SNV (Netherlands Development Organisation). At **Ng'iresi village**, about 7km north of Arusha on the slopes of Mt Meru, you can visit local irrigation projects, enjoy some light hiking and visit a local farm. **Longido**, about 90km north of Arusha, is the site of a weekly Maasai cattle market and the starting point for hikes to the top of Longido mountain. The Maasai graze their cattle on the slopes of this mountain; it's about a four hour walk to the summit. In **Mkuru**, near the Momela Gate of Arusha National Park, is a camel camp. You can take camel safaris ranging from half a day to a week, or climb nearby Oldoinyo Landaree mountain; it's about two hours to the summit. For further information contact SNV (☎/fax 057-7515, email tourinfo@habari.co.tz, Rm 643, Serengeti Wing, AICC, PO Box 10455 Arusha).

The volcanic **Mt Hanang** is 200km south-west of Arusha off the Arusha-Dodoma Rd. Although it's a bit time-consuming to reach, its summit makes a good day or overnight trek. From Arusha there is transport most days to Babati (Tsh5000, 5 to 8 hours), 160km south-west on the Dodoma road. From here you can find pick-ups to Giting to the north of Mt Hanang or Katesh to the south; the trek can be started from either point. You'll need to be completely self-sufficient, including carrying your own water supplies. Lonely Planet's *Trekking in East Africa* contains a detailed description of the trekking route from Katesh. IntoAfrica (see listing under Arusha Travel Agencies, or check their website at www.intoafrica.co.uk) may also be able to assist with arranging treks on Mt Hanang.

ARUSHA NATIONAL PARK
Arusha National Park, although one of Tanzania's smallest parks, is one of its most beautiful and topographically varied. Its main features are Ngurdoto Crater (often

NORTHERN TANZANIA

dubbed Little Ngorongoro), the Momela Lakes, and rugged Mt Meru (4566m), Tanzania's second highest peak. The park's altitude, which varies from 1500m to over 4500m, has a variety of vegetation zones supporting numerous animal species.

The **Ngurdoto Crater** is surrounded by forest, while the actual crater floor is a swamp. To the west lies Serengeti Ndogo (Little Serengeti), an extensive area of open grassland and the only place in the park where herds of Burchell's zebra can be found.

The **Momela Lakes**, like many in the Rift Valley, are shallow and alkaline and attract a wide variety of wader birds, particularly flamingos. The lakes are fed largely by underground streams; due to their varying mineral content each lake supports a different type of algal growth which gives them each a different colour. Bird life also varies quite distinctly from one lake to another, even where the lakes are only separated by a narrow strip of land.

Mt Meru is a mixture of lush forest and bare rock with a spectacular crater. For further information on Mt Meru see the Trekking chapter.

Animal life in the park is abundant. You can be fairly certain of sighting zebra, waterbuck, reedbuck, klipspringer, hippopotamus, buffalo, elephant, hyena, mongoose, dik-dik, warthog, baboon, and vervet and colobus monkeys, although there is dense vegetation in some areas. You may even catch sight of the occasional leopard. There are no lions however, and no rhinos due to poaching.

While it's possible to see much of the park in a day, to appreciate the wildlife or do a walking safari you'll need to stay at least a night or two.

Information

Park entry fees for Arusha National Park and Tanzania's other northern parks are US$25 per person per day (US$5 for children between five and 16, free for children under five). Camping costs US$20 per night at public camp sites and US$40 per night at special camp sites. There is a US$30 per day vehicle fee for the parks, and a US$20 rescue fee per person per trip for hikes on Mt Meru and Mt Kilimanjaro.

For advice on minimising your expenses in Arusha and other national parks, see

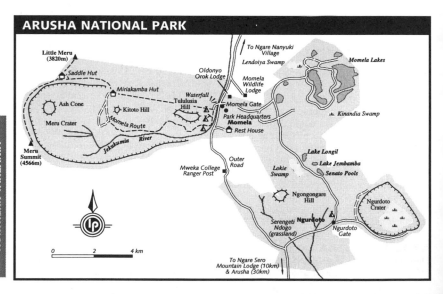

ARUSHA NATIONAL PARK

Costs under Money in the Facts for the Visitor chapter.

To walk in Arusha National Park you must be accompanied by an armed ranger (US$10, or US$15 for hikes on Mt Meru). While you can drive or walk around the Ngurdoto Crater rim, you are not allowed to walk down to the crater floor.

Park headquarters are by Momela Gate, on the northern side of the park. There is a second entrance at Ngurdoto Gate, on the south-east edge of the park. For information, camp site reservations or to arrange a guide, contact the senior park warden at park headquarters or through PO Box 3134 Arusha.

The booklet *Arusha National Park* put out by TANAPA contains a good summary of the history and geology of the area including descriptions of the many animals, birds and plants found in the park. It's available at bookshops in Arusha and Dar es Salaam or from TANAPA headquarters in Arusha.

The MaCo series contains a good map of the park, including trekking routes on Mt Meru. It's available in bookshops in Dar es Salaam and Arusha for Tsh5000.

See the Trekking chapter for information about treks on Mt Meru.

Places to Stay

There are *camp sites* at Momela, close to park headquarters, and at Ngurdoto; you will need to bring all your own provisions. There's also a self-help *resthouse* near the Momela Gate which accommodates up to five people (US$30 per person); book through the senior park warden.

Just outside the park and north-east of Momela Gate is the pleasant *Momela Wildlife Lodge* (☎ 057-6426, 8104, fax 8264, PO Box 999 Arusha). Bed and breakfast costs US$55/75 for singles/doubles in the low season, more during the high season. Half-board rates are also available and lunch boxes can be arranged if ordered in advance. The lodge has good views of Mt Meru and Mt Kilimanjaro.

The nearby *Oldonyo Orok Lodge* has accommodation for US$115 per person (US$85 in the low season) including full board. Book through Multilink (☎/fax 057-8115, 4228, 45 Old Moshi Rd in the Mambo Jazz Cafe building, PO Box 14991 Arusha).

Ngare Sero Mountain Lodge (☎ Usa River 38, 057-8689, 3629, fax 8690, PO Box 425 Arusha), at the foot of Mt Meru and 20km from Arusha on the Arusha-Moshi road, is also comfortable. Accommodation costs US$150 per person, including full board; there is trout fishing in the nearby lake. To get here turn north off the Arusha-Moshi road at the sign for the Dik Dik Hotel, then follow signs for Ngare Sero.

Getting There & Away

The Arusha National Park gate is about 35km from Arusha and can be reached by turning off the main Arusha to Moshi road at the signpost for the national park and Ngare Nanyuki. For information about other access options, including public transport, see Access under the Mt Meru section in the Trekking chapter.

There's a good series of gravel roads and tracks within s park which will take you to all the main features and viewing points. Most are suitable for all vehicles, though some of the tracks get slippery in the rainy season; a few tracks are only suitable for 4WDs.

MT KILIMANJARO NATIONAL PARK

At 5896m, snowcapped Mt Kilimanjaro is the highest peak in Africa and one of the continent's magnificent sights. It's also one of the highest volcanoes, and one of the highest freestanding mountains in the world.

From cultivated farmlands on the lower levels, Kilimanjaro rises through lush rainforest to alpine meadows and finally across a barren lunar landscape to the twin summits of Kibo and Mawenzi. The rainforest is home to many animals including buffalo, leopard and monkey. You may encounter herds of eland on the saddle between Mawenzi and Kibo.

Information

For park fees, see Information under Arusha National Park. Huts cost US$40 per person.

Park headquarters are located in Marangu (☎ Marangu 50, PO Box 96 Marangu).

The booklet *Kilimanjaro National Park* has interesting information on Kilimanjaro's history, flora and fauna. It's available in bookshops in Arusha, Dar es Salaam and Unguja, and from TANAPA headquarters in Arusha for about Tsh3000.

Getting There & Away
From Moshi there are dalla-dallas throughout the day to Marangu, from where you can sometimes find local transport to the park gate. Otherwise, it's a 5km walk from the main junction in Marangu.

There are also several minibuses a day from Moshi to Mweka, Umbwe and Machame, although transport to these villages is almost always included in trekking packages.

LAKE MANYARA NATIONAL PARK
The serene and beautiful Lake Manyara National Park is often underrated in tourist literature; many visitors are surprised by how nice the park really is. In addition to its peaceful setting, Manyara's main attractions are its rich bird life, its tree-climbing lions and its hippos, which you can see at closer range here than at most other places. There are also a fair number of elephants although the population has been declining in recent years. The park, which lies between 900m and 1800m above sea level, is bordered to the west by the dramatic western escarpment of the Rift Valley. To the east is the alkaline Lake Manyara which at certain times of year hosts thousands of flamingos, as well as a diversity of other bird life and a substantial hippo population. Depending on the season, about two-thirds of the park's total 330 sq km area is covered by the lake. Although Manyara is one of the smallest parks, its vegetation is diverse, ranging from savanna to marshes and acacia woodland, enabling it to support a variety of wildlife habitats.

Information
See Information under Arusha National Park for details of park fees. For booking camp sites or for further information contact the senior park warden (☎ 12 Mto Wa Mbu, PO Box 12 Mto Wa Mbu).

Lake Manyara National Park is a dated but useful booklet published by TANAPA; it's available in bookshops in Dar es Salaam, Unguja and Arusha.

MaCo produce a good map of the park; it's available at bookshops in Dar es Salaam and Arusha for Tsh5000.

Places to Stay
There are camp sites and some simple bandas by the park entrance. You will need to bring all your own provisions, although there is a good selection of basic foodstuffs available in Mto Wa Mbu village, about 3km east of the park gate on the main road to Arusha.

There are also several tented camps and luxury lodges. The best is *Kirurumu Luxury Tented Camp*, set on the escarpment about 12km from the park gate. It's a small, relaxing place with views of Lake Manyara in the distance. Its 20 tents are arranged so that you may feel as if you are the only one there. Accommodation costs about US$100 per person including full board. The camp is noted for its cuisine; low season rates are also available. Book through Hoopoe Adventure Tours (☎ 057-7011, 7541, fax 8226, email hoopoesafari@cybernet.co.tz, PO Box 2047 Arusha, or in London at ☎ 44-020-8428 8221, fax 8421 1396).

To the south-west of Kirurumu, and also on the escarpment overlooking the Rift Valley, is the much larger *Lake Manyara Serena Lodge*. Rates are US$183/280 for luxury accommodation including full board and use of all the amenities (US$138/210 between 1 April and 30 June). Bookings can be made through Serena Hotels (☎ 057-4158, 4153, fax 4155, email serena@yako .habari.co.tz, 6th floor, Ngorongoro Wing, AICC, PO Box 2551 Arusha). *Lake Manyara Lodge* (☎ 057-4292, fax 8071, 8502, email tahi@yako.habari.co.tz) also has an attractive setting on the escarpment and luxury accommodation for US$135/186 per person including half board.

Maji Moto Luxury Camp is run by Conservation Corporation Africa (☎ 254-2-441001, fax 750512, email conscorp@users.africaonline.co.ke, PO Box 74957 Nairobi, Kenya) and is 17km south-west of the park gate on the main road. Upmarket accommodation in one of 10 luxury cottages costs US$275 per person including full board; the camp is closed during April and May.

Migunga Forest Camp, 3km outside the park border, has much simpler but still decent tented accommodation for US$35 per person including half board. Book through The Safari Company (☎ 057-3935, fax 8272, email sengo@habari.co.tz, PO Box 207 Arusha).

Mto Wa Mbu Village

Mto Wa Mbu (River of Mosquitoes) is just north of Lake Manyara and makes a good base for visiting the park. It has a colourful though somewhat touristy market and there are some good walks in the surrounding area. With the assistance of SNV the villagers have organised a cultural tours programme formalising several of the better routes. You can get information from SNV (☎/fax 057-7515, email tourinfo@habari.co.tz, Rm 643, Serengeti Wing, AICC, PO Box 10455 Arusha) or at the Red Banana Cafe on the main road in Mto Wa Mbu. Rates are Tsh5000 per person per tour plus a Tsh1000 village development fee.

The river running through town feeds into Lake Manyara. Minibuses run daily between Mto Wa Mbu and Arusha.

Places to Stay & Eat The *Twiga Camp site & Lodge* (☎ *Mto Wa Mbu 1*) or book through Parrot Tours (☎ 057-7850, 4th floor, Serengeti Wing, AICC) has camping for US$5 per person, and double rooms with bathroom and breakfast for US$20. There is hot and cold water, cooking facilities and a restaurant. You can arrange car hire here to visit Lake Manyara and Ngorongoro Conservation Area, although it's expensive at about US$120/150 for a half/full day. Twiga Camp sites is at the Arusha end of town, signposted just off the main road.

Jambo Camp site & Lodge is slightly cheaper though not quite as nice. It's also signposted off the main road at the Arusha end of town.

Manyara Guest House, just of the main road to the right as you come into town from Arusha, has simple rooms with shared facilities for Tsh2000.

Red Banana Cafe has a few grubby rooms for Tsh1200/2400; food is available. It's on the main road diagonally opposite the market on the left when coming from Arusha.

Camp Vision, despite its name, has no camping; rooms are about Tsh6000. It's signposted to the south of the main road.

For more upmarket lodging the best option is *Holiday Fig Resort (☎ Mto Wa Mbu 2)* with rooms for US$15/30; breakfast is extra. Camping costs US$5, including showers. There's also a small pool and nice grounds. It's signposted just to the north of the main road.

Getting There & Away

There is an airstrip just north of Lake Manyara for charter flights. Coastal Travels also runs occasional flights between Arusha and Lake Manyara (US$50 one way), connecting with flights from Dar es Salaam or Unguja. Bookings should be made through Coastal Travels' Dar es Salaam office.

The only road to Lake Manyara is to the north of the park, near Mto Wa Mbu. Most visitors come as part of an organised safari or with their own vehicles. While Mto Wa Mbu can be easily reached on public transport, hitching within the park is generally not feasible. There are vehicles for hire in Mto Wa Mbu (see Twiga Camp sites & Lodge under Places to Stay & Eat), but unless you are travelling in a group, this often works out to be just as expensive as an organised safari.

TARANGIRE NATIONAL PARK

Tarangire is a beautiful area stretching south-east of Lake Manyara around the Tarangire River. During the dry season, particularly between August and October, it has one of the highest concentrations of wildlife

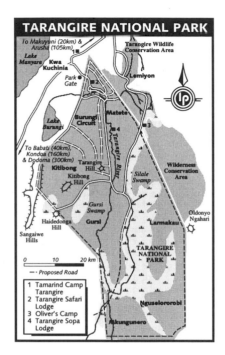

TARANGIRE NATIONAL PARK

To Makuyuni (20km) & Arusha (105km)
Lake Manyara   Kwa Kuchinia
Tarangire Wildlife Conservation Area
Park Gate
Lemiyon
Lake Burungi
Burungi Circuit
Matete
To Babati (40km), Kondoa (160km) & Dodoma (300km)
Tarangire River
Kitibong Hill
Tarangire Hill
Kitibong Hill
Silale Swamp
Wilderness Conservation Area
Gursi Swamp
Haidedonga Hill
Sangaiwe Hills
Gursi
Oldonyo Ngahari
Larmakau
TARANGIRE NATIONAL PARK
0   10   20 km
-·- Proposed Road
Nguselororobi
Akungunero

1 Tamarind Camp Tarangire
2 Tarangire Safari Lodge
3 Oliver's Camp
4 Tarangire Sopa Lodge

Information

See Information under the earlier Arusha National Park section for details of park fees. The senior park warden can be contacted at PO Box 3134 Arusha.

The TANAPA booklet *Tarangire National Park* has detailed information on Tarangire's flora, fauna and history. It's available at bookshops in Dar es Salaam, Arusha and Unguja. MaCo puts out a Tarangire map available in Dar es Salaam and Arusha bookshops as well as some of the lodges in the park.

For information on the Tarangire Wildlife Conservation Area, contact the Tarangire Conservation Company (☎ 057-2814, fax 4199, PO Box 1215 Arusha).

Places to Stay & Eat

There are two public *camp sites* and six *special camp sites*. You will need to bring all your own provisions including water.

Otherwise, there are several comfortable lodges and luxury camps. *Tarangire Sopa Lodge* has accommodation for US$135 per person including half board (US$55/110 single/double during the low season). Book through Sopa (☎ 057-6886, fax 8245, email sopa@africaonline.co.tz, PO Box 1823 Arusha).

Tarangire Safari Lodge run by Serengeti Select Safaris (☎ 057-7182, PO Box 2703 Arusha), set on a bluff overlooking the Tarangire River, has luxury tented accommodation from US$60.

The exclusive *Oliver's Camp* (☎ 057-4116, fax 8548, email olivers@habari.co.tz, PO Box 425 Arusha), just outside the park to the east in the wilderness conservation area, has all-inclusive luxury tented accommodation from US$300 per person. It's closed from 1 November to mid-December and from March through May.

Tamarind Camp Tarangire, just outside the north-west corner of the park and about 20km from Makuyuni, has comfortable tented accommodation in a 'rustic classic' style with full board for US$98/155 plus 20% tax. Bookings can be made through Hoopoe Adventure Tours (☎ 057-7011, 7541, fax

of any of the country's parks. Large herds of zebra, wildebeest, hartebeest and elephant can be found here until October when the short wet season allows them to move on to lush new grasslands. Eland, lesser kudu, gazelle, giraffe, waterbuck, impala, and the occasional leopard or rhino can be seen at Tarangire year-round. The park is also very good for birdwatching, with over three hundred different species recorded. For ornithologists and birdwatchers, the best time to visit is between October and May.

Bordering Tarangire to the north-east is the Tarangire Wildlife Conservation Area, which was created to address the varying needs of local communities, outside visitors and wildlife conservation projects in the area. Visitors can enjoy walking safaris here, while local villagers – who have set aside some of their land for the project – benefit directly from tourist revenue and remain involved in management of the conservation area.

8226, email hoopoesafari@cybernet.co.tz, PO Box 2047 Arusha).

Getting There & Away

To visit Tarangire you will need to join an organised tour or use your own vehicle. The main gate is in the north-west corner of the park 5km south-east of Kwa Kuchinia.

SERENGETI NATIONAL PARK

Serengeti, which covers 14,763 sq km and is contiguous with the Masai Mara Nation-

al Reserve in Kenya, is Tanzania's largest and most famous national park. On its vast, treeless plains are several million hoofed animals, constantly on the move in search of fresh grassland. The wildebeest, of which there are up to two million, is the chief herbivore and also the main prey of large carnivores such as lion and hyena.

One of the Serengeti's biggest attractions is the annual migration of wildebeest herds in search of better grazing. During the rainy season between March and May the herds

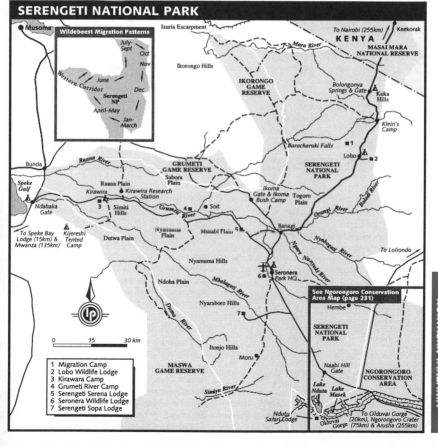

SERENGETI NATIONAL PARK

Wildebeest Migration Patterns

1 Migration Camp
2 Lobo Wildlife Lodge
3 Kirawara Camp
4 Grumeti River Camp
5 Serengeti Serena Lodge
6 Seronera Wildlife Lodge
7 Serengeti Sopa Lodge

NORTHERN TANZANIA

Tanzania's Overloaded Northern Circuit

According to the Tanzania Tourist Board, well over 100,000 people visit Serengeti National Park annually. The numbers are similar for Ngorongoro Crater. As these figures illustrate, tourism is big business in the north. Unfortunately, it has become such big business that the parks are beginning to suffer serious environmental damage.

Some of the problems arise from the sheer volume: with such large numbers of visitors, the parks are bound to suffer negative effects no matter what controls are implemented. Another aspect however, is the manner in which the parks are visited. 'Low impact tourism' is a meaningless term in these parts. Tour operators – scrambling for money – aim to attract as many clients as possible, and high-impact, quick in-and-out trips are standard practice in most of the northern parks. While many companies pay lip service to 'eco-friendly' tours, there are few who actually take the extra steps necessary to ensure that their safaris contribute to the wellbeing of the environment and of local communities.

If you decide to visit northern Tanzania's popular attractions, there are some steps you can take to ensure you will not be part of the problem. One of the most important is to thoroughly research tour operators and patronise only those that make environmental conservation a priority in fact as well as in word, and who collaborate with and assist local communities. Structuring your trip so that you have the time and opportunity to get to know the locals who live in or near the areas you are visiting is another step. Trekking and walking safaris are ideal in this respect. On treks and camping safaris, ensure that your rubbish is properly disposed of; keep water sources clean; use camping stoves rather than wood fires; stay on established roads and paths; and only patronise companies which make these measures a priority. Practising respect in your behaviour and dress is also an important way of indicating that you value both the areas that you visit and their inhabitants, and can contribute to an overall atmosphere which encourages respect for environment and culture.

are widely scattered over the southern section of the Serengeti and the Nogorogoro Conservation Area. As these areas have few large rivers and streams they dry out quickly when the rains cease. When this happens, the wildebeest concentrate on the few remaining green areas, forming large herds which move north and west in search of food. The wildebeest spend the dry season in the these parts of the Serengeti, only moving back east in anticipation of the rains.

The best time to see the wildebeest migration in the Western Corridor of the Serengeti is between May and July, although the actual viewing window can be quite short.

The Serengeti is also famous for its lions, many of which have collars fitted with transmitters so their movements can be studied

and their location tracked. It's also known for its cheetah and large herds of giraffe.

Information

See Information under the earlier Arusha National Park section for details of park fees. Headquarters are located at Seronera, in the centre of the park. Camp sites can be reserved by contacting the senior park warden (☎ 622852 for Seronera or 622029 for Ikoma, PO Box 3134 Arusha).

The booklet *Serengeti National Park* put out by TANAPA has interesting information on the history and ecology of the park. It's available at bookshops in Arusha and Dar es Salaam, as well as TANAPA headquarters in Arusha. MaCo has a good map on the Serengeti, available in Arusha and Dar es Salaam and in some of the park lodges.

Those with a scientific interest in the Serengeti can contact the Serengeti Wildlife Research Institute (☎ 057-7677, PO Box 661 Arusha) in the Njiro Hill area of Arusha.

Activities

In addition to vehicle safari, you can also see the Serengeti via **balloon safari**. Hot air balloons take off daily at dawn from Seronera, accommodating up to 24 passengers. The cost is US$375 per person, including a champagne breakfast after the two hour flight. Book through Serengeti Balloon Safaris (☎ 057-8578, fax 8997, PO Box 12116, Goliondoi Rd, Arusha). Bookings must be made in advance. Credit cards attract no additional charge if you book in Arusha; through one of the lodges at Seronera you'll be charged an additional 6%.

Places to Stay & Eat

Camping There are numerous *public camp sites* (US$20 per person) in the park, including at Seronera, Kirawira, Ndabaka and Lobo. Facilities are minimal and some don't even have water, so you'll need to bring everything with you.

There are also several *special camp sites* (US$ 40 per person) at Seronera, Kirawira, Lobo and Bologonya.

Lodges In addition to Ndutu Safari Lodge (see Olduvai Gorge), there are four other lodges within the Serengeti, all with varying degrees of luxury accommodation.

Serengeti Serena Lodge in the centre of the park has singles/doubles for US$183/280 including full board (US$138/210 between 1 April and 30 June). Book through Serena Hotels (☎ 057-4158, 4153, fax 4155, email serena@yako.habari.co.tz, 6th floor, Ngorongoro Wing, AICC, PO Box 2551 Arusha).

Rates at the *Serengeti Sopa Lodge* are US$135 per person including half board (US$55/110 in the low season including half board/full board). Book through Sopa (☎ 057-6886, fax 8245, email sopa@africaonline .co.tz, PO Box 1823 Arusha).

The *Seronera Wildlife Lodge* in the centre of Serengeti and the *Lobo Wildlife*

Lodge in the north-east have rooms for US$135/186 including half board. Book through Accor/Tahi (☎ 057-4292, fax 8071, 8502, email tahi@yako.habari.co.tz).

About 15km west of the Ndabaka Gate on the park's far western border is the comfortable and reasonably priced *Speke Bay Lodge* (see Places to Stay in the Mwanza section of the Lake Victoria chapter).

Tented Camps All of the following offer tented accommodation in attractive settings.

Migration Camp (☎ 057-2814 or 051-114914, fax 057-8997 or 051-112987, PO Box 12095 Arusha) is near Lobo by a good game-viewing area overlooking the Grumeti River. It costs US$228 per person for all-inclusive luxury accommodation. The camp can accommodate 32 people.

Kirawira Camp, about 90km west of Seronera near the Grumeti River, is the most expensive option. Accommodation 'with a classic Victorian atmosphere' costs US$425/677. Book through Serena Hotels (see details under Serengeti Serena Lodge, earlier). It's closed from mid-April to the end of May.

Conservation Corporation Africa (☎ 254-2-441001, fax 750512, email conscorp@users .africaonline.co.ke, PO Box 74957 Nairobi, Kenya) run *Grumeti River Camp*. Accommodation in luxury tents costs US$275 per person, full board (US$325 all-inclusive); it's closed April and May.

Ikoma Bush Camp, 3km from Ikoma Gate near the Western Corridor, has simpler but decent facilities for US$55 per person, half board plus a US$10 per person village levy. Book through The Safari Company (☎ 057-3935, fax 8272, email sengo@habari .co.tz, PO Box 207 Arusha).

Kijereshi Tented Camp (☎ 40139, 41068, PO Box 190 Mwanza) is in the Western Corridor about 15km east of the road between Mwanza and Musoma near Ramadi. Simple but decent accommodation costs US$30 per person including continental breakfast.

Getting There & Away

Air There is an airstrip at Seronera and frequent charter flights. Precision Air has a scheduled flight between Arusha and Seronera (US$135) twice a week, though it is often cancelled.

Land Most vehicles enter at Naabi Hill Gate at the south-eastern edge of the park on the road that runs through the Ngorongoro Conservation Area. From the gate, it's 75km to Seronera.

Alternatively, you can enter through the Western Corridor at Ndabaka Gate, about 140km north-east of Mwanza and just south of the Western Corridor boundary, or at Ikoma Gate ('Fort Ikoma'), about 30km north of Seronera and accessed by a rough road running east of Bunda off the Mwanza-Musoma road. Both of these routes are often impassable in the rainy season. Bolongoya Gate, 5km from the Kenyan border, leads into the Masai Mara National Reserve. This route is also in poor condition. If you intend to cross the border you will need to arrange visas in advance. See Visas & Documents in the Facts for the Visitor chapter.

The majority of travellers visit the Serengeti with an organised safari or with their own vehicle. For budget travellers the only other option for trying to get a glimpse of the animals is to take a bus or truck travelling between Arusha and Mwanza or Musoma via the Western Corridor route, although you will still need to pay park fees. However, this is only possible in the dry season and you will not be able to stop at will to observe the wildlife. Although it's fairly easy to get to Ndabaka Gate or Seronera by truck or public transport, efforts to hitch a lift from one of the lodges or camp sites inside the park are generally futile.

Ngorongoro Conservation Area

The Ngorongoro Crater is just one part of a much larger area of interrelated ecosystems consisting of the Crater Highlands (to which the Ngorongoro Crater belongs) together with vast stretches of plains, bush and woodland. The entire Ngorongoro Conservation Area (NCA) covers about 8300 sq km. Near its centre is Olduvai Gorge where many famous fossils have been unearthed. To the west are the alkaline Ndutu and Masek lakes, although Ndutu is actually just over the border in the Serengeti. Both lakes are particularly good areas for wildlife viewing during the rainy season from March to May. In the east of the conservation area are a string of volcanoes and craters (collapsed volcanoes, often referred to as calderas); most, but not all, are inactive. Further east, just outside the NCA's boundaries, is the archaeologically important Engaruka. Along the NCA's southern border is Lake Eyasi, a salt lake around which the Hadzabe people live. They are believed to be descendants of one of Tanzania's original ethnic groups. To the north-east of the NCA on the Kenyan border is the beautiful Lake Natron.

Information

The NCA is under the jurisdiction of the Ngorongoro Conservation Area Authority (NCAA), which has its headquarters at Park Village at Ngorongoro Crater (☎ Ngorongoro Crater 6 or 7, PO Box 1 Ngorongoro Crater). The NCAA also has a branch office in Arusha near the Central Bank (☎ 057-6091, fax 3339, PO Box 776 Arusha).

There is a petrol station at NCAA headquarters. You can also arrange guides and vehicle hire here for Ngorongoro Crater and other areas of the NCA. Car hire costs about US$90/130 for a half/full day.

For activities within the NCA you must pay the standard park fees. For details see Information under the earlier Arusha National Park section. There is an additional 'crater service' fee of US$10 to drive down into the Ngorongoro Crater. Guides cost US$20 per day.

The two official entry points to the NCA are Lodoare Gate just south of Ngorongoro Crater and Naabi Hill Gate to the west in Serengeti National Park. If you intend to use any other access routes you will need to get permission from the NCAA.

The booklet *Ngorongoro Conservation Area* put out by the Wildlife Conservation

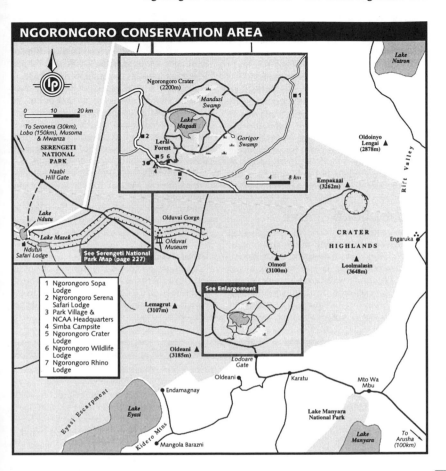

NGORONGORO CONSERVATION AREA

Lake Natron

Ngorongoro Crater (2200m)

Mandusi Swamp

Lake Magadi

Lerai Forest

Gorigor Swamp

0   10   20 km

To Seronera (30km), Lobo (150km), Musoma & Mwanza

SERENGETI NATIONAL PARK

Naabi Hill Gate

Lake Ndutu

Lake Masek

Ndutui Safari Lodge

See Serengeti National Park Map (page 227)

Olduvai Gorge

Olduvai Museum

Oldoinyo Lengai (2878m)

Empakaai (3262m)

CRATER HIGHLANDS

Engaruka

Rift Valley

Olmoti (3100m)

Loolmalasin (3648m)

See Enlargement

Lemagrut (3107m)

Oldeani (3185m)

Lodoare Gate

Oldeani

Karatu

Mto Wa Mbu

Eyasi Escarpment

Endamagnay

Lake Eyasi

Kidero Mtns

Mangola Barazni

Lake Manyara National Park

Lake Manyara

To Arusha (100km)

1 Ngorongoro Sopa Lodge
2 Ngrorongoro Serena Safari Lodge
3 Park Village & NCAA Headquarters
4 Simba Campsite
5 Ngorongoro Crater Lodge
6 Ngorongoro Wildlife Lodge
7 Ngorongoro Rhino Lodge

Society of Tanzania has detailed information about the different geographical zones within the NCA, plus sections on ecology and history. It's available at bookshops in Arusha and Dar es Salaam for about Tsh3000. Also of interest is the NCAA series on Ngorongoro covering topics such as animal life and geology.

MaCo puts out a good map of the Ngorongoro Conservation Area, available in Dar es Salaam and Arusha bookshops, and usually at the Lodoare Gate.

THE CRATER HIGHLANDS

The Crater Highlands consist of an elevated range of volcanoes and collapsed volcanoes which rises from the side of the Great Rift Valley and runs along the eastern edge of the NCA. The peaks include Oldeani (3185m), Lemagrut (3107m), Olmoti (3100m), Loolmalasin (3648m), Empakaai (3262m, also spelled Embagai), the still active Oldoinyo Lengai (2878m) and of course, Ngorongoro (2200m). The area is remote and seldom visited but offers some of Tanzania's most rugged and unusual scenery as well as superb hiking. See the Trekking chapter for further information.

It's also possible to arrange a vehicle safari to the highlands through one of the Arusha-based tour operators although you'll miss much of the area's essence by not exploring on foot. If you want to use your own vehicle, keep in mind that there is essentially no infrastructure and roads can be very isolated. You will also need to get permission and a guide from the NCAA. There are no lodges in the highlands apart from the facilities at Ngorongoro Crater.

NGORONGORO CRATER

Ngorongoro Crater is one of Africa's best known wildlife-viewing areas and one of Tanzania's most visited. At about 20km wide it is also one of the largest calderas in the world. Within its walls are a variety of animals and vegetation, including grasslands, swamps, forests, salt pans and a freshwater lake. You are likely to see lion, elephant, rhino, buffalo and many of the plains herbivores such as wildebeest, Thomson's gazelle, zebra and reedbuck, as well as thousands of flamingos wading in the shallows of Lake Magadi, the soda lake at the crater's base.

Despite its steep walls, there's considerable movement of animals in and out of the crater – mostly to the Serengeti, since the land between the crater and Lake Manyara is intensively farmed. Yet it remains a favoured spot for wildlife because there's permanent water and grassland on the crater floor.

The animals don't have the crater to themselves. Local Maasai tribes have grazing rights and you may come across them tending their cattle. During the German colonial era there were two settlers' farms in the crater; you can still see one of the huts.

Information

For details on fees see Information under the earlier Arusha National Park section. If you intend to do commercial filming in the crater, there is an additional US$100 fee per person per day.

The Maasai

Travellers in northern Tanzania are almost certain to meet some Maasai, one of the region's most colourful tribes. The Maasai are pastoral nomads who have actively resisted change, and today still follow the same lifestyle that they have for centuries. Their culture centres around their cattle, which provide many of their needs – milk, blood and meat for their diet, and hides and skins for clothing – although sheep and goats also play an important dietary role, especially during the dry season. The land, cattle and all elements related to cattle are considered sacred.

Maasai society is patriarchal and highly decentralised. Elders meet to decide on general issues but ultimately it is the lives of the cattle which dominate proceedings. One of the most important features of Maasai society is its system of social stratification based on age. Maasai boys pass through a number of transitions throughout life, the first of which is marked by the circumcision rite. Successive stages include junior warriors, senior warriors, junior elders and senior elders; each level is distinguished by its own unique rights, responsibilities and dress. Junior elders, for example, are expected to marry and settle down – somewhere between the ages of 30 and 40. Senior elders assume the responsibility of making both wise and moderate decisions for the community. The most important group is that of the newly initiated warriors, *moran*, who are charged with defending the cattle herds.

Maasai women play a markedly subservient role and have no inheritance rights. Polygyny is widespread and marriages are arranged by the elders, without consulting the bride or her mother. Since most women are significantly younger than men at the time of marriage, they often become widows; remarriage is rare.

You can visit Ngorongoro at any time of the year, but during the months of April and May it can be extremely wet and the roads difficult to negotiate. Access to the crater floor may be restricted at this time.

Places to Stay & Eat

Camping There are no longer any camp sites inside the crater. On the crater rim there is *Simba Camp site*, which is dirty and in bad condition. There are also nine *special camp sites* scattered throughout the park. No advance booking is necessary for Simba; the special camp sites should be booked in advance through NCAA. It can get very cold camping on the crater rim due to its altitude, so bring enough protective gear. See also the Karatu section later for more information.

Lodges There are five lodges on or near the rim of the crater. The least expensive is the NCAA-run *Ngorongoro Rhino Lodge* (☎ *Ngorongoro Crater 21 or 057-4619, fax 3339, PO Box 16 Ngorongoro Crater)*. There are no views of the crater but the rooms are simple and clean. Singles/doubles cost US$45/70 (US$26/42 between 1 April and 30 June) including breakfast; half-board and full-board arrangements are also available.

The *Ngorongoro Wildlife Lodge* is on the edge of the crater rim with good views. Singles/doubles cost US$135/186 half board. Book through Accor/Tahi (☎ 057 4292, fax 8071, 8502, email tahi@yako.habari.co.tz).

The *Ngorongoro Crater Lodge* also has views of the crater and very upmarket accommodation for US$325 per person including your own butler. It's run by the

Maasai Land Issues

Although the Maasai have grazed cattle for many centuries in the Serengeti, the Crater Highlands and in surrounding parts of the Great Rift Valley, over the last three decades they have been forcibly excluded from much of their traditional homelands. This is due to wildlife conservation – it has long been believed by some conservationists that the Maasai cattle compete with wild animals for grazing and water, and their large herds contribute to soil erosion.

Conservationists who take a broader view hold that the needs of indigenous people must be included in any plan to conserve wildlife or natural resources, not simply for humanitarian reasons but because without the full support of local people any conservation project is ultimately doomed to failure. This subject is discussed in the excellent book *No Man's Land* by George Monbiot, in which the author – a highly respected investigative journalist – points out that in the name of conservation the Maasai have been excluded completely from Serengeti National Park and Mkomazi Game Reserve simply because 'tourists did not like to see them there'. The Maasai were forced onto private farmland on the edge of these areas and became 'trespassers' unable to return to their traditional grazing lands. Of those Maasai who dared enter the protected areas, many were fined and imprisoned. Those who stayed outside, and managed to avoid trespassing on farmland, were safe – however, cut off from essential migration routes and grazing lands, their cattle died of starvation. Meanwhile, the Maasai have seen new roads and hotels built for tourists. This has led many to feel that they are seen as less important than wildlife or tourists, and has fostered resentment. Many have turned to poaching – some simply for meat because their cattle have died, others for ivory and rhino horn. The Maasai and wildlife have coexisted for hundreds of years, but Monbiot says conservation has forced the Maasai to become enemies of nature: 'Conservation has done as much as anything to destroy the East African environment'.

Of course, there are those who argue against George Monbiot's assertions but most of the Maasai would probably agree with him. Reading *No Man's Land* before you visit Tanzania will increase your awareness of these issues and add another dimension to your travels.

David Else

Conservation Corporation Africa (☎ 254-2-441001, fax 750512, email conscorp@users.africaonline.co.ke, PO Box 74957 Nairobi, Kenya).

On the eastern rim of the crater is the attractive *Ngorongoro Sopa Lodge*, with luxury accommodation for US$135 per person including half board. There are also low season rates of US$55/110 single/double. Book through Sopa (☎ 057-6886, fax 8245, email sopa@africaonline.co.tz, PO Box 1823 Arusha).

Ngorongoro Serena Safari Lodge, on the western rim, has luxury accommodation for US$183/280 including full board (US$138/210 between 1 April and 30 June). Bookings can be made through Serena Hotels (☎ 057-4158, 4153, fax 4155, email serena@yako.habari.co.tz, 6th floor, Ngorongoro Wing, AICC, PO Box 2551).

Karatu In addition to the lodges at the crater, there are several less expensive options outside the NCA in the nearby town of Karatu, about 20km east of Lodoare Gate. Many camping safaris out of Arusha use this place as an overnight stop in order to economise on park entry fees for Ngorongoro. There is a post office here and a branch of the National Microfinance Bank which will exchange cash.

The *Ngorongoro Safari Resort (☎ 59 Karatu or 057-7102)* is a good place, signposted on the main road in the middle of Karatu. It has camping for US$3 per person. Tents can be rented for an additional Tsh1000; sleeping bags are also available. There is hot and cold water, a well-stocked store, cooking facilities and a restaurant. If this place is full, there are several other camp sites signposted off the main road.

If you don't want to camp, the best choice is the *ECLT Lutheran Centre Hostel (☎ Karatu 55)* which has rooms for about Tsh12,000. It's just west of Ngorongoro Safari Resort, along the main road.

For upmarket accomodation, the best option is the long-established *Gibbs Farm (☎ 057-6702, 8930 or Karatu 25, email ndutugibbs@marie.sasa.unep.no, PO Box 6084 Arusha or PO Box 2 Karatu)*, with comfortable lodging for US$90/110. Good meals made with home-grown produce are available. It's signposted off the main road and closed during April and May.

Another good place is *Kifaru Lodge (☎ Karatu 20 or ☎/fax 057-8908, PO Box 1187 Arusha)*, in a former farmhouse. Rooms cost US$90/112 including breakfast. It's about a 10 minute drive from Karatu.

Getting There & Away

The cheapest way to visit the crater is to take the Ngorongoro Crater bus from the central bus station in Arusha. It's a large white bus marked 'Ngorongoro Crater' and leaves daily at about 9 am, reaching park headquarters at about 3 pm (Tsh3500). Ask the driver to drop you at Ngorongoro Rhino Lodge, from where you can arrange vehicle rental with park headquarters (see Information under Ngorongoro Conservation Area). You can also rent vehicles from the lodges around the crater rim or in Karatu, although rates are generally more expensive. Returning to Arusha, the bus departs from park headquarters at about 6.30 am; ask staff at the Rhino Lodge to show you the pick-up point.

If you are coming with your own vehicle, remember that only 4WDs are allowed down into the crater, except at certain times during the dry season when the authorities *may* allow conventional vehicles to enter. All roads into the crater, except the road from Sopa Lodge on the eastern side, are very steep, so if you are driving your own vehicle, make sure it can handle them.

Whether you are driving on your own or are part of an organised tour, you must take a park ranger with you (US$20 per day) and also pay the US$10 per vehicle crater access fee.

OLDUVAI GORGE

The Olduvai Gorge is a canyon about 50km long and up to 90m deep which runs to the north-west of Ngorongoro Crater. Thanks to its unique geological history, in which layer upon layer of volcanic deposits were laid down in orderly sequence over a period of almost two million years, it provides remarkable documentation of ancient life.

The most famous of Olduvai's fossils is the 1.8 million-year-old ape-like skull known as *Australopithecus boisei* which was discovered by Mary Leakey in 1959 and which gave rise to a heated debate about human evolution. The skull is also often referred to as *zinjanthropus*, which means 'nutcracker man', referring to its large molars. In 1972, hominid (human-like) footprints estimated to be 3.7 million years old were discovered at Laetoli, about 45km south of the Olduvai Gorge. Based on these findings as well as other ancient fossils excavated in Kenya and Ethiopia, it has been posited that there were at least three hominid species in the region about two million years ago, including *Australopithecus boisei*, *Homo habilis* and *Homo erectus*. While *Australopithecus boisei* and *Homo habilis* appear to have died out (or in the case of *Homo habilis*, been absorbed by or evolved into *Homo erectus*), it is theorised that *Homo erectus* continued and evolved into *Homo sapiens*, or modern man. Other lesser known but significant fossils excavated from the upper layers of Olduvai provide some of the oldest evidence of *Homo sapiens* in the area.

There is now a small museum on the site, which is mainly of interest to those who are archaeologically inclined. It's about 45km from park headquarters off the road to Serengeti. The museum closes at 3 pm and in the rainy season is often not open at all. It's possible to go down into the gorge at certain times of the year to view the excavation sites. You must be accompanied by a guide, which can be arranged at the museum.

Information

As well as standard fees applying to the Ngorongoro Conservation Area, there is an additional US$2 per person per day fee to visit the Olduvai Gorge.

Places to Stay

There is nowhere to stay at Olduvai but at the western end of the gorge, where the creek which flows through it empties into Lake Ndutu, is *Ndutu Safari Lodge* (☎ 057-6702, 8930, PO Box 6084 Arusha) on the border of Serengeti National Park. Comfortable bed and breakfast accommodation costs US$104/127 (US$65/86 in the low season). There is also a good restaurant; the lodge is open year-round.

ENGARUKA

Dusty Engaruka, on the eastern edge of the Ngorongoro Conservation Area near the foot of Empakaai, is a small village famous for its extensive ruins of a complex irrigation system with terraced stone housing sites estimated to be at least 500 years old. Scientists are still not sure of the origin of the ruins; some speculate they were built by ancestors of the Iraqw (Mbulu) people who live in the area today, while others suggest that the site was built by the Sonjo, a Bantu-speaking people. Those interested in Engaruka can read more about the site in the first chapter of Henry Forsbroke's *The Eighth Wonder*. The ruins are best viewed from the air, although archaeology buffs will probably find that the site itself is more interesting.

There are two camp sites at Engaruka, one in Engaruka village and the other just after the river, on the left before you reach the village. The village often levies a 'visitor's fee' on tourists, ranging from US$5 to US$20.

Road access to Engaruka is via the village of Mto Wa Mbu along the Arusha road. From Mto Wa Mbu, it's another 60km further north along an unpaved road. Alternatively, you can hike from the Empakaai Crater but you will need a guide from the NCAA.

LAKE NATRON

Lake Natron, 25km north of Oldoinyo Lengai on the Kenyan border, is a 60km long alkaline lake known for the huge flocks of flamingos that gather at certain parts of the lake at the end of the rainy season. Lake Natron has no outlet so its size varies dramatically between seasons. The swampy marshes around the banks make access difficult during much of the year. To visit the lake you will need a 4WD.

Due to a spate of recent attacks on tourist vehicles in the vicinity of the lake, few tour operators were venturing up to Lake Natron at the time this book was researched, though many were planning to start again soon. Inquire in Arusha about the current situation.

If you go to the lake in your own vehicle, be sure that you are self-sufficient; take extra supplies of petrol and water as there is none to be found along the way. Also, don't be surprised if the nearby villages ask for a 'visitors fee'. This can sometimes be as high as US$30 per vehicle but is usually closer to US$10.

The only camp site is *Lake Natron Camp* at the south-west corner of the lake near the lake flats. It costs US$50 per person; you must bring all your own provisions and book in advance (The Safari Company, ☎ 057-3935, fax 8272, email sengo@habari.co.tz, PO Box 207 Arusha).

LAKE EYASI

Lake Eyasi is a salt lake lying at about 1000m between the Eyasi escarpment in the north (an ancient fault line that is part of the Rift Valley system) and the Kidero mountains in the south. It's a hot, dry area, around which live the Hadzabe (also known as Hadzapi or Tindiga) people who are believed to have lived here for nearly 10,000 years. Today there are only a few hundred left. Their language is characterised by clicks and may be distantly related to that of the San (Bushmen) of southern Africa, although it shows only a few connections to Sandawe, the other click language spoken in Tanzania. The lifestyle of the Hadzabe still centres around hunting and gathering traditions. Also in the area are the Iraqw (Mbulu), a people of Cushitic origin who arrived about 2000 years ago, as well as Maasai (of Nilotic origin) and various Bantu groups.

Access to the lake is difficult and only feasible on foot. Arusha-based tour operators can arrange treks from Oldeani or other areas on the escarpment down to Lake Eyasi.

Trekking

Tanzania offers some of the finest trekking in Africa. The biggest attraction is, of course, Kilimanjaro, the highest mountain in Tanzania and indeed the whole of Africa, with several spectacular trekking routes up to the top of the famous snowcapped summit dome. Tanzania's other major trekking areas include Mt Meru, the country's second-highest peak, and the rolling hills and volcanic cones of the Crater Highlands, rising above the Great Rift Valley.

WHEN TO GO

The main mountains of Tanzania are in the north of the country and, as with safaris, the best time to go trekking is in the dry season, from late June to October when the rains have finished and from late December to February or early March, just after the short rains and before the long rains. (For more details see When to Go under Planning in the Facts for the Visitor chapter.)

In the rainy season, the rain can make trekking on the lower slopes a somewhat damp affair, and on the higher slopes the rain turns to snow or ice which can make routes impassible or treacherous. It is important to note, however, that even during the dry season the chance of rain is still quite high. It generally only falls for a few hours a day (usually in the late afternoon and sometimes at night) so it doesn't affect trekking too much.

Mt Kilimanjaro

Kilimanjaro's huge snowcapped summit dome, towering high above the surrounding savanna, often with a giraffe conveniently posing in the foreground, is one of Africa's all-time classic images. It is the highest mountain in Africa, and one of the highest volcanoes in the world. The lure is irresistible, and a trek up 'Kili' is a popular aspect of many people's visit to Tanzania. The trek is even more attractive because,

with the right preparation, you can walk all the way to the summit without the need of ropes or technical climbing experience.

GEOGRAPHY

The Kilimanjaro massif has an oval base about 40 to 60km across, and rises almost 5000m above the surrounding plains. The two main peak areas are Kibo, the dome at the centre of the massif which dips inwards to form a crater that can't be seen from below, and Mawenzi, a group of jagged pinnacles on the eastern side. A third peak, Shira, on the west end of the massif, is lower and less distinctive than Kibo and Mawenzi.

The highest point on Kibo is Uhuru peak (5896m), and this is the goal for most trekkers. The highest point on Mawenzi is Hans Meyer Point (5149m), but this cannot be reached by trekkers, and is only rarely visited by mountaineers.

TREKKING INFORMATION
Route Standard & Duration

Kilimanjaro is surrounded by dense forest, so to get to the higher moorlands and main peaks you have to follow an established route. There are at least 10 trekking routes that begin on the lower slopes but only three continue to the summit. Of these, the **Marangu Route** is the easiest and by far the most popular. A trek on this route usually takes five days (four nights) for the round

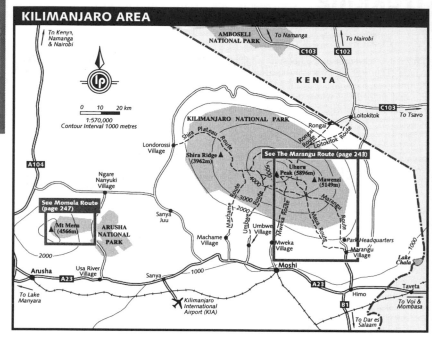

KILIMANJARO AREA

trip, although an extra night is recommended to help acclimatisation. This route is described later in this chapter.

Other routes on Kili are more serious undertakings, usually taking six days (which costs more, but helps acclimatisation) and passing through a much wider range of scenic areas than the Marangu Route, although trekkers must use tents as huts along the way are in very poor condition. The **Machame Route** has a gradual ascent, including a spectacular day contouring the southern slopes, and then approaches the summit via the top section of the Mweka Route. The **Umbwe Route** is much steeper with a more direct way to the summit – very enjoyable if you can resist the temptation to gain height too quickly. Unfortunately, some trekking companies now offer five-day options on the Umbwe Route, but because the top section of this route (called the Western

Breach or Arrow Glacier Route) is a serious undertaking – steep, and often covered with snow and ice – trekkers are sometimes forced to turn back. Very few people who rush this route make it to Uhuru peak.

Trekkers on the Machame and Umbwe routes come down from the summit by the Marangu Route or the **Mweka Route** which is for descent only. Some Marangu treks also descend on the Mweka Route.

Costs

Independent trekking is not allowed on Kilimanjaro, and all treks must be organised through a tour company. Companies organising treks are listed in the Moshi and Arusha sections of the Northern Tanzania chapter. Before arranging anything, however, see the boxed text 'Choosing a Trekking Company'. Standard five-day (four-night) treks up the Marangu Route start from US$350 to

The Importance of Acclimatisation

The number of days quoted for a trek on each of the routes is the usual number most trekkers take. If you can spend an extra night on any of the routes, at about halfway, this will help acclimatisation and will also give you time to see some other parts of the mountain. It will also greatly increase your chances of actually getting to the top.

Although many hundreds of trekkers reach Uhuru peak every year without any real difficulty, many thousands more don't make it because they suffer terribly from altitude sickness, having ascended too quickly. Part of the fault lies with some trekking companies who run quick up-and-down trips, although they are only responding to demand. The real fault lies with trekkers who overestimate their own ability or who don't appreciate the serious nature of trekking at altitude and the importance of acclimatisation. There have been too many sad cases of trekkers who went too high too quickly on Kili. At best, they felt ill and went down; at worst, they became so sick they had to be carried down. Every year a few unlucky/unprepared trekkers die.

Most people seem to forget that Uhuru peak, at 5896m, is 500m *higher* than Everest Base Camp in the Nepal Himalaya, which trekkers often take at least two weeks to reach from Kathmandu. All trekkers should read and observe the advice on Altitude Sickness in the Health section of the Facts for the Visitor chapter.

David Else

US$450, but at the absolute bottom end of this price range don't be surprised if your hut is double booked, meals are on the small side and porters are desperate for tips. For budget treks of six days on the Machame Route you should expect to pay around US$650 to US$750. Better quality trips on the Marangu Route go from US$500, while they start at US$850 on the Machame Route.

Whatever you pay for your trek, remember that between US$300 and US$500 of this goes on park fees. The rest of the money covers food, tents (if required), guides, porters and transport to and from the start of the trek. With these figures in mind, we honestly can't see how some of the budget outfits make a legal profit.

Park Fees

The area above about 2700m is Kilimanjaro National Park, and fees must be paid to enter. Although you organise your trek through a company, you may have to pay fees separately at the park gates. Some companies quote a price that includes park fees and make the payments on your behalf. It is therefore very important when arranging your trek to check whether park fees are included. Fees are listed in Information under Arusha National Park in the Northern Tanzania chapter. For an adult trekker, they come to a total of US$305 for a standard five-day Marangu trip and US$370 for six days on another route. Guides and porters also pay fees, but this is handled directly by your trekking company.

Guides & Porters

Guides, and at least one porter (for the guide), are obligatory and are provided by your trekking company. You can carry your own gear on the Marangu Route, although porters are generally used, but one or two porters per trekker are essential on all other routes.

All guides must be registered with the national park authorities. If in doubt, check your guide's permit is up to date. On Kili, the guide's job is to show you the way, and that's it. Only the best guides, working for reputable companies, will be able to tell you about wildlife, flowers or other features on the mountain.

Porters will carry bags weighing up to 15kg (not including their own food and

TREKKING

Choosing a Trekking Company

If you are arranging things on the spot, choosing the right company to organise your trek on Kilimanjaro (or anywhere else) is very important. This is especially true for budget travellers, as a lack of money and an eagerness to save every last dollar often seems to cloud the judgement. At Lonely Planet we get endless letters from backpackers who have arrived in Arusha or Moshi, arranged a trek with the first company they come across, and ended up having a bad time. Touts patrol the budget hotels promising great things for ridiculously low sums, and it's amazing how many people fall for it. What sounds like a dream bargain turns into a nightmare as food runs out, huts are not booked and porters go on strike.

We frequently hear from travellers who end up camping in substandard tents even though their company assures them they have hut bookings. The park runs a wait-list system and huts become overbooked. Ask to see proof of your company's *confirmed* hut booking (unless of course you're happy to camp). We also hear from people who pay for five nights on the Marangu Route, so as to have an extra night's acclimatisation at Horombo, but only the usual four nights actually get paid for at the gate, so they find themselves being forced on up to Kibo instead of having a nice rest day.

Another common trick is for the company to 'run out' of money at the gate and travellers having to pay a contribution to the entrance fees. Promises of refunds when the group returns from the trek are of course forgotten or flatly denied back in Arusha. We've even heard of travellers having to pay park fees virtually at gunpoint, after their tour company told them these fees were already included in the price.

One of the worst scams of all involves travellers being promised a bargain deal by a tout, but to seal it payment must be made on the spot for which, 'of course sir', a receipt will be issued. Next day, the promised transport to Kilimanjaro doesn't show at their hotel, the receipt turns out to be for a bogus company, and the tout (now renamed 'thief') is never seen again. What's even worse is sometimes the tout *is* seen again, casually strolling the streets, but naturally he denies everything and there's nothing anyone can do.

So if you're fresh off the plane or the bus in Moshi or Arusha, don't rush into any deals however good they sound. Take the time to shop around the reliable outfits and see what's on offer. Never give money to anyone who doesn't work out of an office. This applies when you're arranging general safaris too, to places like the Serengeti. By far the best way to get the low-down is by talking to travellers who have returned from a trek. Personal recommendations of companies and guides can generally be relied upon. Anybody who's had a raw deal will be more than happy to stop the company conning anyone else!

David Else

clothing, which they strap to the outside of your bag). Heavier bags will be carried for a negotiable extra fee.

The staff provided by some cheaper trekking outfits leave a lot to be desired. If you're a hardy traveller you might not worry about basic meals and substandard tents, but you might be more concerned about incompetent guides or dishonest porters. We've heard stories about guides who leave the last

hut deliberately late on the summit day, to avoid going all the way to the top. But if you make sure you know about all aspects of the route – and are polite but firm with your guide – you should avoid problems like this.

Maps & Guidebooks

The *Map & Guide to Kilimanjaro* by Andrew Wielochowski is a 1:75,000 topo map with detailed insert maps of Kibo and

The Usambara mountains, a lush and frequently cloudy range of hills rising above the dry savanna.

Pondering the ascent – hikers at the base of Mt Lengai.

Trekkers camp behind Mt Kilimanjaro.

Melting snow and ice form spectacular shapes on Mt Kilimanjaro.

Flamingos wading in the shallows of Lake Magadi, Ngorongoro Crater.

Tipping Guides & Porters on Kilimanjaro

Most guides and porters are honest and hard working, so you will probably want to give them a tip after your trek. Over the years, some high-rolling trekkers on Kili have tipped very generously, causing the local guys to expect large bonuses at the end of every trek. This situation is understandable. The porters know that you have just paid anything from US$300 to US$1000 for the trek. Even if you think of yourself as a budget traveller, they will regard you as a wealthy tourist with a lot of spare cash to throw around. So don't plead poverty. If the service has been good, pay a fair tip.

As a guideline, a tip could be around 10% of the total bill paid for the trek (or the trekking section of the tour, if it also includes other items such as transport or hotels) divided between the guides and porters. Some guides and porters may imply that official 'tipping rates' are set by the park authorities, but this is not true.

As a guide, for example, if each member of a group paid US$450 for a short trek, everyone could pay around US$40 into a tips 'kitty', to be divided between the guide and porters. Generally for a trip up the Marangu Route guides get about US$30 (more with a large group, especially if they've also done the cooking) and porters around US$10. For longer treks, guides usually get around US$50 and porters around US$15. US dollars or local currency is accepted. Of course, you can pay more if you're particularly impressed, and less if you're not. But explain why you're doing this – it will help porters and future trekkers if it's understood that tips are not automatic. Note that any gifts you may leave for guides and porters (old boots, clothing, food, etc) will not be regarded as part of (or accepted instead of) a hard cash tip.

David Else

Mawenzi. The similar-looking *Kilimanjaro Map & Guide* by Mark Savage at 1:50,000 should make map-reading easier, but it contains less information. The back of both sheets contain brief information on access and equipment, plus lots of other tips.

In a different style is the beautiful hand-drawn full-colour *New Map of the Kilimanjaro National Park* by Giovanni Tombazzi (MaCo); not so good for detailed route finding (although the back of the sheet has a topo map of the summit area and some useful gradient profiles) but much nicer to hang on your wall as a souvenir.

If you want to do something other than the Marangu Route, then Lonely Planet's *Trekking in East Africa* is highly recommended. It contains detailed directions for the Umbwe and Machame routes, and outlines several other routes on Kili, plus lots of general information on matters such as equipment, mountain health, wildlife and vegetation.

The *Guide to Mount Kenya & Kilimanjaro*, published by the Mountain Club of Kenya, is mainly for technical mountaineers, with detailed descriptions of rock and ice routes on Kibo and Mawenzi. Beware of old copies of this book; many of the huts (and even a few of the glaciers!) have disappeared since they were printed.

PLACES TO STAY

For details of hotels at the 'base towns' of Moshi and Marangu see those sections in the Northern Tanzania chapter. Accommodation on the Marangu Route consists of three 'huts' (actually groups of bunkhouses) spaced a day's walk apart. These are administered by the national park and you pay overnight fees with your entrance fees. You can also camp on this route but you still have to pay the same overnight fees. Other routes have small metal huts which are all in very bad condition, and used by only guides and porters, so trekkers must camp. In the future all the small metal huts on Kili may be removed by the park authorities.

THE MARANGU ROUTE

Distance 64km
Duration 5 days (minimum)
Start & Finish Marangu Gate
Highest Point Uhuru Peak (5896m)
Overall Altitude Gain 3916m

Access

The Marangu Route starts at Marangu Gate, near Marangu village, on the south-east side of Kilimanjaro, about 40km by road from Moshi. Most trekking companies provide transport to the gate. If you are taking public transport, the bus between Moshi and Marangu runs several times each day however it only goes as far as Marangu village. Marangu Gate is a further 5km up the hill. You may be lucky and hitch a ride, otherwise you'll have to walk – look on it as a good warm up!

Stage 1: Marangu Gate to Mandara Hut

7km, 4-5 hours, 700m ascent

From Marangu Gate (1980m) the path is wide and clear, passing through a beautiful section of forest. A short distance from the gate the path divides: the right fork is the main route; the left fork is a slightly longer alternative designed to give you more opportunity to enjoy the forest and observe the birds and monkeys. The paths rejoin after about two hours, and again after 2½ hours. From this final junction it's another one to 1½ hours to Mandara Hut (2700m) – with beds for about 80 people.

From Mandara Hut you can visit nearby Maundi Crater, a small mound to the north. It's a two-hour return walk and the path is clearly signposted. Views from the top of the crater, over the forest up to the main peaks of Kibo and Mawenzi, provide plenty of inspiration for the trek to come.

Stage 2: Mandara Hut to Horombo Hut

11km, 5-7 hours, 1000m ascent

From Mandara Hut two paths run roughly parallel through the forest and then a zone of giant heather, meeting near the start of the moorland. The eastern path is slightly longer but more pleasant. As you leave the forest you'll get your first clear view of the top of the Kibo dome. To the right are the jagged peaks of Mawenzi, looking higher than Kibo from this angle. The path, although undulating and steep in places, is easy to follow all the way up to Horombo Hut (3700m) – a large group of bunkhouses sleeping about 120 people.

If you've got time you may prefer to spend two nights at Horombo to help acclimatisation. A good rest-day walk is up to The Saddle and the lower slopes of Mawenzi.

Stage 3: Horombo Hut to Kibo Hut

10km, 5-7 hours, 1000m ascent

After Horombo Hut the path divides. The western path is more popular; it gradually

THE MARANGU ROUTE

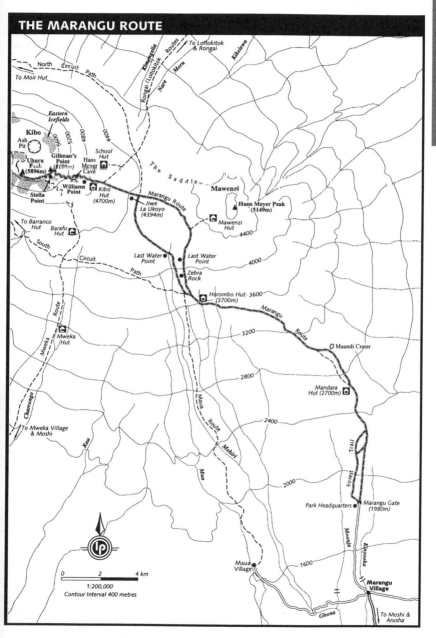

North Circuit Path

To Moir Hut

To Loitokitok & Rongai

Rongai / Loitokitok Routes

Kikelewa

Nare

Moru

Eastern Icefields

Kibo

Ash Pit

Uhuru Peak (5896m)

Gillman's Point (5700m)

Stella Point

Williams Point

Kibo Hut (4700m)

School Hut

Hans Meyer Cave

The Saddle

Mawenzi

Hans Meyer Peak (5149m)

Marangu Route

Jiwe La Ukoyo (4394m)

Mawenzi Hut

4400

To Barranco Hut

Barafu Hut

South Circuit Path

Last Water Point

Last Water Point

Zebra Rock

4000

Horombo Hut - 3600 (3700m)

Marangu Route

3200

Maundi Crater

Mweka Route

Mweka Hut

2800

Mandara Hut (2700m)

Charrongo

Kau

To Mweka Village & Moshi

2400

Maua Route

Mahiri

Mua

2000

Forest Trail

Park Headquarters

Marangu Gate (1980m)

Moonja

Kisiyoka

Maua Village

1600

Marangu Village

Ghona

To Moshi & Arusha

0   2   4 km

1:200,000
Contour Interval 400 metres

gains height, passing the landmark Last Water point, and crossing The Saddle. The eastern path (reached by forking right after Horombo) is steep and rough, passing the black-and-white striped Zebra Rock and another Last Water point. It is not used much but is worth considering if you want to escape the crowds plodding along the western path. The two paths meet at *Jiwe La Ukoyo* (pointed rocks), at 4394m. From here to Kibo Hut takes one to 1½ hours.

Kibo Hut (4700m) is more basic than Horombo and Mandara, with space for about 60 people. There is no reliable water supply. All water must be carried from Horombo or one of the Last Water points. At busy times, the huts are often over-full, with people sleeping two to a bunk and on the floor, so the next day's early start usually comes as a relief.

Stage 4: Kibo Hut to Uhuru Peak; plus descent to Horombo Hut
4km, 7-8½ hours, 1200m ascent; plus 14km, 4½-7 hours, 2200m descent
This stage of the trek can involve up to 16 hours of very strenuous walking, although it's easy to bail out at any point and return the way you've come. It's usual to start very early in the morning, to see the sunrise from the crater rim, and to give you more chance of avoiding the mist. Also, the scree slope up to Gillman's Point, and the snow on the path to Uhuru peak, will still be frozen, which will make the walking safer and less tiring. Sunrise is around 6 am, and you should allow five to six hours to get from Kibo Hut to Gillman's Point plus another two hours to reach Uhuru peak. This normally means leaving Kibo Hut between midnight and 1 am.

If you're only going to Gillman's, it is important not to arrive too early, as this will mean waiting for sunrise, sometimes in extremely cold conditions. Experienced guides will assess your abilities and pace the walk to arrive on the rim at exactly the right time.

Ascent Route From Kibo Hut, the path is easy to follow as it zigzags up the scree.

After Hans Meyer Cave (5182m) the gradient gets steeper and the walk becomes, without doubt, a slog. It seems endless but when you finally get to the rim at Gillman's Point (5680m), it's all worthwhile. You can see down into the snow-filled crater, across to the spectacular cliffs of the Eastern Icefields, back down to The Saddle with the dark bulk of Mawenzi behind, and along the edge of the rim to Uhuru peak.

Most people are happy with reaching Gillman's Point, especially when they see how much further it is to Uhuru, but if you're feeling good and there's still time, it's well worth carrying on to the summit. The walk around the crater rim, with the steep drop into the crater on one side and the smooth snow-covered outer slopes of the dome on the other, is one of the most spectacular in Africa. From Gillman's to Uhuru takes another two to 2½ hours.

At Uhuru peak (5896m) there's a flag pole, a plaque inscribed with a quote of President Nyerere, and a sign to say you've reached the highest point in Africa. If the weather's good you might want to revel in your success and take in the views. If the weather is bad you'll probably take a quick photo and hightail it down again.

Descent Route The return from Uhuru to Gillman's takes about one to 1½ hours. You should aim to be back at Gillman's about three hours after sunrise, as after this time the top layer of snow becomes wet and much harder for walking.

From Gillman's back down to Kibo Hut the scree is blissfully easy-going compared with the slog up. An easy walk takes about two hours. If you've got strong knees and nerves of steel you can run down the scree and be back at Kibo Hut in less than an hour. From here, retrace the path to Horombo Hut – another two to three hours.

Stage 5: Horombo Hut to Marangu Gate
18km, 5-7 hours, 1900m descent
On the last day, retrace the route, following the clearly marked path down to Marangu

Gate. Mandara Hut is about halfway down – a good place for a break.

Mt Meru

At 4566m Mt Meru is the second-highest mountain in Tanzania. Although it is frequently overlooked by trekkers it is a spectacular volcanic cone, and well worth a visit. A trek to the summit takes you through grassland and lush forest on the mountain's lower slopes, followed by a dramatic and exhilarating walk along the knife edge of the crater rim.

GEOGRAPHY

Mt Meru has a circular base some 20km across at 2000m, where it rises steeply above the plains as an almost perfect cone with an internal crater surrounded by a steep wall of cliffs. At about 2500m the wall has broken away so the top half of the mountain is shaped like a giant horseshoe. The cliffs of the inner wall below the summit are over 1500m high which makes them among the tallest in Africa. Inside the crater recent volcanic eruptions have created a subsidiary peak called the Ash Cone.

TREKKING INFORMATION
Route Standard Duration

Despite its attractions Meru still remains a relatively obscure mountain completely overshadowed by its more famous neighbour, Kilimanjaro, whose lower slopes are only 40km away. For trekkers this obscurity is an advantage: you'll meet few other people and for much of the time have the place completely to yourself.

The Momela Route is the only route up Meru. It starts at Momela Gate on the eastern side of the mountain and goes to the summit along the northern arm of the horseshoe crater. The route is steep but can be done comfortably in four days (three nights), although trekkers often do it in three days by combining Stages 3 and 4.

Although Meru appears small compared with Kilimanjaro, don't think that condi-

tions won't be serious. It's still high enough to make the effects of altitude felt, so you shouldn't try to rush up Meru if you are not properly acclimatised.

If you've got the time and money for two treks, a visit to Meru is a great way to prepare for Kilimanjaro. It helps you build up acclimatisation and the views across the plains to Kili's great dome rising above the clouds provide plenty of inspiration for the major trek to come.

Costs

Organised treks on Mt Meru can be arranged with many of the companies listed in the Arusha and Moshi sections of the Northern Tanzania chapter. Rates for a four day trip range from US$250 to US$500, and the considerations outlined in the boxed text 'Choosing a Trekking Company' earlier in this chapter also apply here.

Organised treks are not obligatory, and you can do things quite easily on your own. Costs for an independent trek are mostly park entrance and hut fees. Guides, provided by the park, are obligatory and also have to be paid for. Porters are optional. The cost of getting there is also important to consider. All these items are detailed separately below.

Park Fees & Regulations

Mt Meru is in Arusha National Park; see the Information section under Arusha National Park in the Northern Tanzania chapter for fee details.

All fees are payable at Momela Gate. If you enter the park at Ngurdoto Gate you must pay your entrance fees there, but your mountain fees at Momela. As in all Tanzania's parks, a 'day' is a 24-hour period. Entry permits are marked with the time of entry. If you enter at noon on Monday morning and leave before noon on Wednesday you should only need to pay two days' fees, although this might be a difficult point to agree upon with the rangers at the gate.

Guides & Porters

A guide is mandatory and can be arranged at Momela Gate. The fee of US$15 per day is paid to the national park (not to the guide himself). Unlike on Kilimanjaro, guides on Meru are rangers armed in case you meet some of the park's buffalo or elephant, rather than to show you the way (although they do know the route). It is unlikely that an animal will have to be shot, but you should not underestimate the danger and walk too far away from your guide.

Most trekkers go up Mt Meru with only a guide, but if you want porters they are also available at Momela Gate for US$6 per porter per day. They come from nearby villages and are not park employees. This fee is paid at the gate and given to the porters after the trip. You also have to pay park entrance and hut fees for porters (US$3 per day, US$1.50 per night). Porters carry rucksacks weighing up to 15kg (not including their own food and clothing).

Generally the guides and porters on Mt Meru are hard-working and reliable. They do not expect the huge tips sometimes demanded by their counterparts on Kilimanjaro. For a standard trek reasonable tips might be US$10 to US$15 for the guide and around US$5 for each porter.

Maps & Guidebooks

The only dedicated map of Mt Meru is on the back of *Arusha National Park*, one of the ever-growing series of maps by Giovanni Tombazzi (MaCo), which also contains details on vegetation and gradient profiles. The booklet Arusha National Park, edited by Deborah Snellson and published by TANAPA, is very helpful. It has a section on Mt Meru, with a small map, plus good information on animals and birds, vegetation, geology and so on. Both are available in Arusha and Dar es Salaam. See also Information under Arusha National Park in the Northern Tanzania chapter.

PLACES TO STAY

The town nearest Mt Meru is Arusha (see that section in the Northern Tanzania chapter). There are also a couple of options in Arusha National Park (see that section also in the Northern Tanzania chapter), including camp sites and lodging near the Momela Gate.

On Mt Meru the Momela Route has two large well-maintained bunkhouses, conveniently spaced for a three or four day trek, so a tent is not usually necessary, and camping won't save you money anyway. If you coincide with a large group of trekkers, the huts may be full, but this is unlikely. Check at the gate before starting. Each bunkhouse has a cooking and eating area, and some kerosene stoves for public use, although you must bring your own fuel. There's a separate dormitory for guides and porters, and outside toilets – beware of meeting local wildlife if you go out in the middle of the night!

THE MOMELA ROUTE

Distance 33km
Duration 3 or 4 days
Start & Finish Momela Gate
Highest Point Meru Summit (4566m)
Overall Altitude Gain 3066m

Access

Arusha National Park consists of two main areas: Ngurdoto Crater and Momela Lakes on the east side, and Mt Meru in the west, joined by a narrow strip of land with Momela Gate at its centre. Organised treks provide transport to the gate, but if you're going independently take any bus between Arusha and Moshi, and get off at the park junction, 1km east of a village called Usa River. The fare is about Tsh1000. From Usa River there are local pick-ups which run most days through the park carrying goods and passengers (the fare is about Tsh2000) to the village of Ngare Nanyuki, 10km beyond Momela Gate. There are two roads through the park: on the Outer Road fees are not required for transit traffic; however on the Park Road (which goes through the park proper) fees are required. This is no problem if you intend to start your trek up Meru on the same day, as fees have to be paid at Momela Gate anyway. The roads rejoin at Momela Gate.

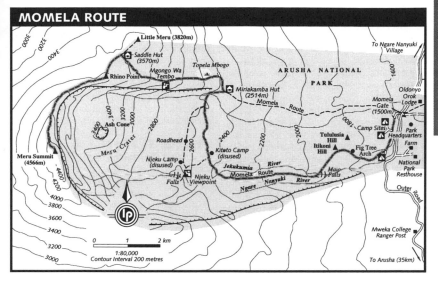

MOMELA ROUTE

Little Meru (3820m)
Saddle Hut (3570m)
Mgongo Wa Tembo
Topela Mbogo
Rhino Point
To Ngare Nanyuki Village
ARUSHA NATIONAL
Miriakamba Hut (2514m)
Momela Route
PARK
Oldonyo Orok Lodge
Momela Gate (1500m)
Ash Cone
Camp Sites
Park Headquarters
Meru Crater
Roadhead
Kitoto Camp (disused)
Tululusia Hill
Itikoni Hill
Fig Tree Arch
Farm
Meru Summit (4566m)
Njeku Camp (disused)
Jekukumia River
Momela Route
National Park Resthouse
Njeku Falls
Njeku Viewpoint
Momela Route
Ngare Nanyuki River
Majo Falls
Outer Road

Mweka College Ranger Post

0   1   2 km
1:80,000
Contour Interval 200 metres
To Arusha (35km)

Your other options are to hitch or walk the 24km from Usa River to Momela Gate along the Outer Road, which takes between six and eight hours. Many local people walk this way. The track rises very gently for the first 10km, passing through farmland and coffee plantations, to reach the fork at a place called Serengeti Ndogo, where the Outer and Park roads divide. Keep left here. On the final 8km, the dirt road becomes rougher and steeper as it climbs towards the gate.

If you don't fancy walking or public transport, guests at Momela Wildlife Lodge (see Places to Stay under Arusha National Park in the Northern Tanzania chapter) can sometimes arrange transport in the minibus which brings staff from Arusha. Alternatively, tour companies can provide transport to Momela Gate (for around US$100 per vehicle, divided between up to five passengers), or you can arrange a one-day safari to Arusha National Park (for slightly more) which drops you at Momela Gate at the end.

Paying park fees and arranging guides and porters at Momela Gate can take a couple of hours. You can save time by making arrangements the night before. The

park office officially opens at 6 am, but delays may occur.

Stage 1: Momela Gate to Miriakamba Hut
10km, 4-5 hours, 1000m ascent

Two routes are available from Momela Gate. The first is a track that goes through the forest towards the crater floor, and then steeply up to Miriakamba Hut. The second is a path that climbs gradually through the grassland direct to Miriakamba. The first option is more interesting and is described here. The second option is shorter and makes a suitable descent route. Some guides prefer to go up and down the short route, and may take some persuading to take the forest route.

From Momela Gate, cross the Ngare Nanyuki River and follow the track into the forest. The track winds uphill, to reach Fig Tree Arch about one hour from the gate. This parasitic wild fig originally grew around two other trees, eventually strangling them. Now only the fig tree remains, with its distinctive arch big enough to drive a car through.

The track continues to climb, reaching Itikoni Clearing on the left side of the track, after another 15 minutes. From a small hill on the right, you can often see buffalo grazing. Half an hour further on, the track crosses a large stream just above the Maio Falls. Continue for another hour to reach Kitoto Camp, with excellent views over the Momela Lakes and out to Kilimanjaro in the distance.

Continue following the track, to reach a junction after half an hour. (The left track leads to the floor of Meru Crater.) Take the right track, over flat ground, to cross a rocky stream bed (usually dry) and descend slightly through trees, ignoring the path that comes in from the left, to reach Miriakamba Hut (2514m), one hour from Kitoto Camp.

From Miriakamba you can walk to Meru Crater floor (a two to three hour return trip) either in the afternoon of Stage 1, or before Stage 2. The path across the floor leads to Njeku Camp (an old forest station) and Njeku Viewpoint, on a high cliff overlooking a waterfall, with excellent views of the Ash Cone and the whole extent of the crater.

Stage 2: Miriakamba Hut to Saddle Hut

4km, 2-3 hours, 1050m ascent

From Miriakamba the path climbs steeply up through pleasant glades between the trees, to reach Topela Mbogo (Buffalo Swamp) after 45 minutes and Mgongo Wa Tembo (Elephant Ridge) after another half an hour. From the top of Mgongo Wa Tembo there are great views down into the crater and up to the main cliffs below the summit. Continue through some open grassy clearings and over several stream beds (usually dry) to Saddle Hut (3570m).

From Saddle Hut you can walk up to the summit of **Little Meru** (3820m) in about an hour on a clear path. From the top you'll get impressive views of Meru Summit, the horseshoe crater, the top of the Ash Cone, and the sheer cliffs of the crater's inner wall. In the other direction, across the top of the clouds, you can see the great dome of Kilimanjaro. As the sun sets behind Meru, casting huge jagged shadows across the clouds, the snows on Kili turn orange, then

pink, as the light fades. Allow 45 minutes to get back to Saddle Hut.

Alternatively, you can go to **Rhino Point** (about two hours return from Saddle Hut), from where the views of Kili are similarly stunning and you can also see down to the base of the Ash Cone and across the crater floor. You'll pass this point on your way up and back from the summit, but the views are so impressive it's worth going at least twice.

Stage 3: Saddle Hut to Meru Summit & return

5km, 4-5 hours, 1000m ascent;
plus 5km, 2-3 hours, 1000m descent

This stage, along a very narrow ridge between the outer slopes of the mountain and the sheer cliffs of the inner crater, is one of the most dramatic and exhilarating sections of trekking anywhere in East Africa. Some trekkers leave Saddle Hut early in the morning (2 to 3 am) to reach the summit in time to see the sun rising from behind Kilimanjaro, and to stand a chance of avoiding the late morning mist, although others find this section too exposed for comfort, especially when done in the dark, or find the altitude makes the going beyond Saddle Hut a bit tough. If the sunrise is your main point of interest, there's no need to go to the top. It's just as impressive from Rhino Point (about an hour from Saddle Hut), or even more so because you also see the main cliffs of the inner wall of the crater being illuminated by the rising sun. The ideal combination is sunrise at Rhino Point, then up to the summit for the views (depending on the mist). If you spend two nights at Saddle Hut you can still see the sunrise at Rhino Point, then trek up to the summit and back in daylight. Many trekkers combine Stages 3 and 4, but this doesn't leave a margin for delays.

If you decide to go for the summit, take plenty of water. Even though it can be below freezing just before dawn, as soon as the sun rises the going becomes hot and hard. During the rainy season, ice and snow can occur on this section of the route, so take care.

Ascent Route Take the path from behind Saddle Hut, across a flat area, then steeply up through bushes. After an hour the vegetation gives way to bare rock and ash. Rhino Point is marked by a cairn and a pile of bones (presumably rhino, but what was it doing up here?).

From Rhino Point the path drops slightly then rises again to climb steeply around the edge of the rim over ash scree and bare rock patches. Continue for three to four hours to reach Meru Summit (4566m). The views are, of course, spectacular. To the west, if it's clear, you can see towards the Rift Valley, and the volcanoes of Kitumbeini and Lengai, while down below you can see the town of Arusha, and the plains of the Maasai Steppe beyond.

Descent Route To descend from the summit, simply retrace the route around the rim, back to Saddle Hut (two to three hours).

Stage 4: Saddle Hut to Momela Gate
9km, 3-5½ hours, 2000m descent
From Saddle Hut, retrace the Stage 2 route to Miriakamba (1½ to 2½ hours). From Miriakamba, you can either return through the forest (2½ to three hours), or take a shorter route down the ridge which leads directly to Momela Gate (1½ to 2½ hours). This direct route goes through forest for some of the way, then through open grassland, where giraffe and zebra are often seen.

The Crater Highlands

The Crater Highlands lie to the west of Mounts Meru and Kilimanjaro and overlook the savanna plains of the Serengeti, while to the east the land drops to the floor of the Great Rift Valley. Peter Matthiessen, in his classic book *The Tree Where Man Was Born*, called it 'the strangest and most beautiful of all regions that I have come across in Africa'.

For most people, a visit to the Crater Highlands means a day of wildlife viewing in Ngorongoro Crater – one of the best-known wildlife reserves in Tanzania. Its

fame is undeniably justified but beyond Ngorongoro are several more craters, with impressive peaks, steep escarpments, dense forests, grassy ridges, lakes, streams and waterfalls. There's even Oldoinyo Lengai – an active volcano. The area is also home to the Maasai people who have grazed cattle here for hundreds of years. This all adds up to an excellent trekking area, but most of the Crater Highlands remain very seldom visited.

The Crater Highlands are shown on the regional map of Northern Tanzania in the chapter of the same name.

GEOGRAPHY
The Crater Highlands measure about 80 by 40km, rising steeply from the plains at about 1500m to heights of between 2500 and 3500m. They are volcanic in origin although the different peaks were created over many millions of years by a series of eruptions connected with the birth of the Great Rift Valley. The older volcanoes have collapsed to form the craters which give the range its name.

TREKKING INFORMATION
Route Standard Duration
Due to the rugged terrain, and the presence of some fairly rugged animals, unaccompanied trekking in the Crater Highlands is not allowed. A vehicle, local guide and armed park ranger are essential, as are donkeys to carry supplies and water, and Maasai men to look after the donkeys. Organised treks can be arranged though a tour company – these are listed in the Arusha section of the Northern Tanzania chapter – and usually include a visit by vehicle to Ngorongoro.

Trekking in the Crater Highlands is not as strenuous as on Kilimanjaro and Meru. You generally follow paths, although some sections cross trackless grassland, and conditions underfoot are generally good.

Most treks start just north of Ngorongoro Crater and cross the Highlands to finish at Ngare Sero near Lake Natron. This normally takes four days, but can be cut to three by starting at Nainokanoka. An extra day is required for the ascent of Oldoinyo Lengai (2878m).

Costs

The cost of an organised trek depends on the standard of guides, vehicles and equipment, and the number of people in your group. Rates start at about US$70 per day, but for more quality you should expect to pay over US$100. This includes entrance fees for the Ngorongoro Conservation Area, which are on a par with the rates charged at Mt Meru. As an example, we heard from two travellers who arranged a seven-day trek, including an ascent of Oldoinyo Lengai and two days game viewing at Ngorongoro, for US$750 each, all-inclusive.

Maps & Guidebooks

Maps of the Crater Highlands are limited to *Ngorongoro Conservation Area*, one of the best in the series of colour maps by Giovanni Tombazzi (MaCo), covering the area from Lake Eyasi to Oldoinyo Lengai. The *Ngorongoro Conservation Area* booklet by Jeannette Hanby and David Bygott also has a map, plus some good information about the wildlife, vegetation, ecology, geography and history. You will find both available in Arusha.

For full details on trekking options in the Crater Highlands and surroundings, Lonely Planet's *Trekking in East Africa* contains a comprehensive chapter on this area, including maps.

Lake Victoria

With an area of 68,800 sq km, Lake Victoria is the largest lake in Africa and the second largest freshwater lake in the world; about half of it lies in Tanzania. The surrounding region, while lagging behind many other areas of the country in terms of transportation and telecommunications, is one of Tanzania's fastest growing and most populous areas.

Fishing has traditionally been the economic mainstay of most lakeside towns, but industry is playing an increasingly important role, particularly in Mwanza. Agriculture is also important, with a large percentage of Tanzania's coffee production coming from around Bukoba. Cotton is also a major crop. To the south of the lake near Shinyanga and Geita are gold and mineral mining areas.

Historically, the region – specifically, the area west of Lake Victoria near Bukoba – was home to numerous small but powerful kingdoms that appear to have been among the most highly developed early societies on the continent.

One of the main tourist attractions of Lake Victoria is the serene and beautiful Rubondo Island National Park, an excellent place for birdwatching and relaxing.

MWANZA

Mwanza is one of Tanzania's largest towns and the economic centre of the lake region. It has numerous industries and a busy port which handles much of the cotton, tea and coffee grown in the fertile western part of the country. The Sukuma people who live in the area are Tanzania's largest tribe.

Although very dusty in the dry season and very muddy during the rains, Mwanza is a fairly attractive place set among hills strewn with enormous boulders. It makes a good base for a visit to Rubondo Island National Park, and in the dry season is a convenient starting point for a trip through the western Serengeti. It's also the major regional transit point for those travelling between other areas of Tanzania and Rwanda or Uganda.

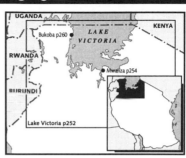

Highlights

- **Rubondo Island National Park** – serene, beautiful and rich in birdlife
- **Bukoba** – small, attractive and bustling town, worth an overnight stop
- **Mwanza** – capital of the Lake region, and a centre of Sukuma culture

Orientation

Central Mwanza is large, although it can be covered on foot. To the west are the ferry docks, the clock tower, the local bus stand for transport to the airport, and several banks and shops. In the centre are most shops, guesthouses, and mosques. On the eastern side of town are the market and the main bus stand. The train tracks skirt the town to the south-west.

Central Mwanza has a vaguely oriental feel due to its various mosques and Hindu temples and is well worth a stroll, particularly the area around Temple St. Some of the hills and boulders around Mwanza offer good views over the town and lake.

Information

Money In addition to the banks, there are several foreign exchange bureaus including

251

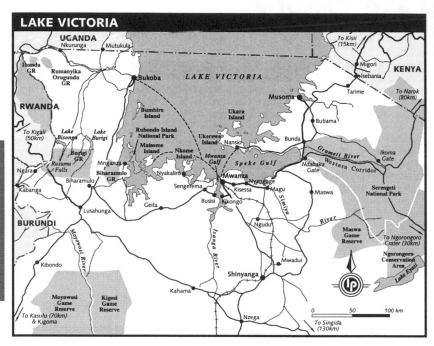

LAKE VICTORIA

UGANDA
Nkrunga   Mutukula
Ibanda GR
Rumanyika Orugundu GR
Bukoba
LAKE VICTORIA
To Kisii (15km)
Migori
Isebania
KENYA
Musoma
Tarime
To Narok (80km)
RWANDA
To Kigali (50km)
Lake Bisongu
Lake Burigi
Bumbire Island
Ukara Island
Butiama
Rubondo Island National Park
Maisome Island
Ukerewe Island
Nansio
Bunda
Burigi GR
Biharamulo GR
Mnganza
Nkome Island
Mwanza Gulf
Speke Gulf
Grumeti River
Western Corridor
Ikoma Gate
Ngara
Rusumu Falls
Nyakaliro
Mwanza
Ndabaka Gate
Serengeti National Park
Kabanga
Biharamulo
Sengerema
Kisessa
Nyanguge
Magu
Maswa
Lusahunga
Geita
Busisi
Kikongo
BURUNDI
Moyowosi River
Isanga River
Simiyu River
Ngudu
River
Maswa Game Reserve
To Ngorongoro Crater (30km)
Kibondo
Mwadui
Ngorongoro Conservation Area
Lake Eyasi
Moyowosi Game Reserve
Kigosi Game Reserve
Shinyanga
To Kasulu (70km) & Kigoma
Kahama
Nzega
To Singida (130km)
0   50   100 km
To Singida (130km)

DBK Bureau de Change at Serengeti Services & Tours (see Travel Agencies).

Post & Communications Mwanza's post office has a semi-organised poste restante (Tsh200 per letter). Incoming faxes (fax 068-500676) cost Tsh300 and are held indefinitely.

The Internet Cafe (☎ 500241, email cbcs @raha.com) at Computer Bureau & Commercial Services on Bantu St charges Tsh1500/500 to send/receive an email. Internet links cost Tsh3000/5000 for 30 minutes/ one hour.

Travel Agencies There are two good travel agencies in town; both can assist with trips to Rubondo Island National Park, the western Serengeti and other destinations. They can also arrange car hire (Tsh15,000, plus Tsh400 per kilometre, including fuel). Four-

ways Travel Service (☎ 502620, 502273, fax 502502, email vinaysapra@hotmail.com, PO Box 990) is on Station Rd near the junction with Kenyatta Rd. Serengeti Services & Tours (☎ 500061, 41666, fax 500446, email serengeti@mbio.net, PO Box 308) is on Post St opposite the telecom building.

Around Mwanza

The islands of Ukerewe, Maisome and Nkome are all said to offer decent hiking, although we weren't able to verify this. If you try it, let us know how it is! Ukerewe and Maisome are reached by ferry from Mwanza. To Nkome there are sporadic local boats from Mwanza and from Nyakaliro village, opposite the island on the western side of the Mwanza Gulf.

Sukuma Museum The open-air Sukuma Museum (also referred to as the Bujora

Museum) is about 20km from Mwanza on the Musoma road near Kisessa. It was originally established by a Quebecois missionary and focuses on the culture and traditions of the Sukuma tribe. The museum also puts on occasional performances of traditional dance; inquire at travel agents in town for schedule information. To get there, take a

The Sukuma

The Sukuma (people of the north) are Tanzania's largest ethnic group, comprising close to 15% of the country's total population. They live in the area around Mwanza and the southern Lake Victoria region. For much of their history the Sukuma were loosely organised into numerous Bantu-speaking subgroups; it is only recently that they have come to view themselves as a single entity. Their ancestors are believed to have migrated into Tanzania from present day Uganda, beginning in about the 17th century. The Sukuma are closely related to the Nyamwezi, Tanzania's second largest ethnic group, centred in the Tabora region.

Most Sukuma are farmers and their lands comprise one of Tanzania's most important agricultural areas, producing the majority of the country's cotton as well as other crops. Cattle are also an important source of livelihood. The Sukuma have traditionally had a highly developed and structured form of village organisation in which each settlement is subdivided into chiefdoms ruled by a chief, or ntemi, in collaboration with a council of elders. Divisions of land and labour are made by village committees consisting of similarly aged members from each family in the village. These age-based groups, each with their own leader, perform numerous roles ranging from assisting with the building of new houses to farming and other community-oriented work. This system gives most families at least a representational role in many village activities. As a result, houses and land are often viewed as communal property among the Sukuma.

dalla-dalla from the market or from the stand near the Aga Khan Hospital to Kisessa, from where it's about a 15 minute walk. There is a nominal entry fee.

Saa Nane Game Reserve The Saa Nane Game Reserve is on a tiny island just off Capri Point. There's a ranger and a small zoo, but no food or lodging on the island. A boat departs daily at 11 am and 1, 3 and 5 pm from next to the Tilapia Hotel (Tsh700, 15 minutes). For information, visit the reserve's office on Capri Point Rd, about 500m from the Tilapia Hotel.

Places to Stay – Budget & Mid-Range

Camping You can camp on the pleasant grounds of the *Sukuma Museum* (see earlier). There are cooking facilities and two-bed bandas if you have no tent. Unfortunately it's located well out of Mwanza along a rough road.

Hotels For inexpensive lodging in the centre try *Kishamapanda Guest House* (☎ 42523) at Uhuru and Kishamapanda Sts. Clean singles and en suite doubles with fan and mosquito net cost Tsh2500/4000. Adjoining is the slightly cheaper but much grubbier *Geita Guest House*. The entrance and reception for both places is at Geita Guest House.

Pamba Hostel (☎ 502697) on Station Rd has fairly clean singles/doubles with common bath for Tsh3600/5400 including continental breakfast. The only problem with this place is that the gate to the floors is kept locked; if you want to depart at an odd hour, you'll need to make advance arrangements with the staff.

North of the bus station across Nyerere Rd and over a footbridge is *Majukano Hotel*. Singles/doubles with mosquito nets and bathroom are Tsh4800/6000; breakfast is available (extra). It's a bit away from the centre and quieter than some of the other budget options, but it's nothing special.

Hotel Deluxe (☎ 500831) opposite Kishamapanda Guest House is nicer. Clean

LAKE VICTORIA

LAKE VICTORIA

MWANZA

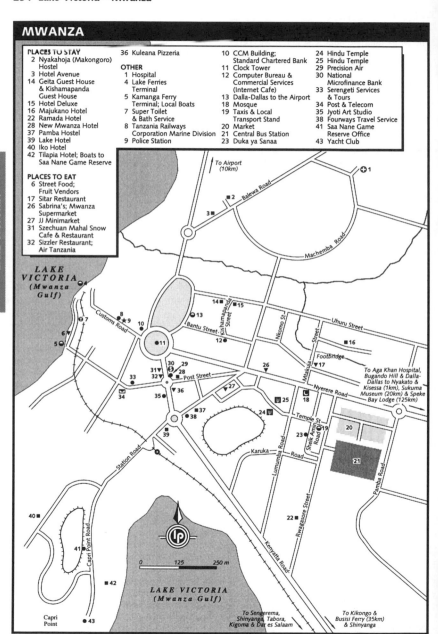

PLACES TO STAY
2 Nyakahoja (Makongoro) Hostel
3 Hotel Avenue
14 Geita Guest House & Kishamapanda Guest House
15 Hotel Deluxe
16 Majukano Hotel
22 Ramada Hotel
28 New Mwanza Hotel
37 Pamba Hostel
39 Lake Hotel
40 Iko Hotel
42 Tilapia Hotel; Boats to Saa Nane Game Reserve

PLACES TO EAT
6 Street Food; Fruit Vendors
17 Sitar Restaurant
26 Sabrina's; Mwanza Supermarket
27 JJ Minimarket
31 Szechuan Mahal Snow Cafe & Restaurant
32 Sizzler Restaurant; Air Tanzania

36 Kuleana Pizzeria

OTHER
1 Hospital
4 Lake Ferries Terminal
5 Kamanga Ferry Terminal; Local Boats
7 Super Toilet & Bath Service
8 Tanzania Railways Corporation Marine Division
9 Police Station

10 CCM Building; Standard Chartered Bank
11 Clock Tower
12 Computer Bureau & Commercial Services (Internet Cafe)
13 Dalla-Dallas to the Airport
18 Mosque
19 Taxis & Local Transport Stand
20 Market
21 Central Bus Station
23 Duka ya Sanaa

24 Hindu Temple
25 Hindu Temple
29 Precision Air
30 National Microfinance Bank
33 Serengeti Services & Tours
34 Post & Telecom
35 Jyoti Art Studio
38 Fourways Travel Service
41 Saa Nane Game Reserve Office
43 Yacht Club

singles/doubles with bathroom cost Tsh6000/7200, including continental breakfast.

Hotel Avenue about 1km from the clock tower on Balewa Rd has clean, good value doubles for Tsh6000 with common bath.

A few doors further down is the *Nyaka-hoja (Makongoro) Hostel* with doubles (only) for Tsh4000, including mosquito nets and common bath. It's primarily for missionaries but sometimes has space available for other travellers. Breakfast is an additional Tsh1000.

Lake Hotel (☎ 500658) near the junction of Station and Kenyatta Rds has singles/doubles from Tsh7200/8400 with bathroom and continental breakfast.

Modern *Ramada Hotel* (☎ 40237), not far from the bus stand on Rwagasore St, has clean, good value rooms with bathroom for Tsh7800/9600 including breakfast.

If you have your own vehicle, try *Speke Bay Lodge* (radio frequency 4490.0 USB from 9.30 to 10.30 am, PO Box 953 Mwanza, or book through a travel agency). It's on the lake, about 125km north of Mwanza off the Musoma road, and about 15km from the Serengeti's Ndabaka Gate. Comfortable tents cost US$19/28 single/double, while luxury bungalows are US$65/80/105; camping facilities are also available.

Places to Stay – Top End

Mwanza's most luxurious option is *Tilapia Hotel* (☎ 500517) on the east side of Capri Point. Doubles cost from US$70 including continental breakfast and most amenities;

Tanzania's Street Children

In Tanzania, as in so many other places in the world, there are distressingly high numbers of children and youth – particularly boys – on the streets. Although some are orphans, often due to AIDS, this is relatively rare as these children are usually absorbed by extended families. In most cases, the children are fleeing violence or stressful living situations in the home, do not have access to education, or have dropped out of school and turned to the street as an alternative.

While there are few accurate statistics, the scope of the problem is hinted at by the large numbers of children who seek help at outreach programs which have been set up in some of the larger towns. One of the most well known of these is the Kuleana Centre for Children's Rights in Mwanza, which was established in 1992 as a private initiative. Since then it has become the major youth centre in the Lake Victoria region and the leading children's rights organisation in the country. The main goal of the Kuleana program, which attracts youth from Mwanza, as well as from a much larger surrounding area, is community reintegration. In addition to its street work and outreach activities, the centre offers residential, health and counselling programs, as well as a basic education component aimed at getting children back into their local primary schools. A limited number of scholarships are also available to help keep children who live in difficult circumstances off the streets.

Most of the youths who come to Kuleana are boys aged between 10 and 13 years; about 20% are girls. The centre has about 70 children at any one time, and assists about 300 to 400 per year, plus many more in its outreach activities. The Kuleana Pizzeria (see the Mwanza Places to Eat section) is staffed entirely by youth from the centre, giving them practical skills and invaluable work experience.

The children's rights arm of Kuleana does advocacy work on a variety of issues including popularising the United Nations Convention on the Rights of the Child; seeking to end corporal punishment in schools, and the practice of expelling pregnant girls; and formulating fair employment standards for Tanzania's youth.

air-con suites cost US$100. There's a pool (Tsh4000 for nonresidents) and a small business centre with email services, and the hotel can assist with car rentals.

On the west side of Capri Point, *Iko Hotel* (☎ 40900) has doubles from Tsh15,000 (Tsh45,000 with air-con) including continental breakfast. There are no singles.

In town, *New Mwanza Hotel* (☎ 501070) at the intersection of Post St and Kenyatta Rd has doubles for US$48 (no singles) including continental breakfast.

Places to Eat

Good places for street food are the *stalls* opposite the post office, the area along the train tracks near the ferry terminals, and the ladies near the train station who sell whole fried fish for Tsh800.

You can also get good, cheap local food at *Hotel Deluxe*, *Snow Café & Restaurant* (next to Szechuan Mahal on Kenyatta Rd) and the canteen at *Pamba Hostel*.

The best food in town is at *Kuleana Pizzeria* across the street from the New Mwanza Hotel. It's open from 10 am to 8 pm Monday to Saturday. In addition to good pizzas (Tsh1000 to Tsh3000), they have salads, sandwiches, desserts and other dishes at very reasonable prices. Service is prompt and the atmosphere is excellent. The pizzeria serves as a vocational training centre run by the Kuleana Centre for Childrens's Rights and profits go to benefit the centre.

Sizzler Restaurant nearby has good value Chinese and Indian dishes between Tsh2400 and Tsh4000. Portions are large and service is fast. It's also open for breakfast.

Szechuan Mahal Restaurant (☎ 0811-530786) just a few doors down has good Chinese meals averaging about Tsh3500.

Tilapia Hotel has a nice terrace barbecue which is popular on weekends; meals average about Tsh3000. There is also a more expensive restaurant at the hotel with dishes from Tsh5000 to Tsh6000.

Sitar Restaurant north of Nyerere Rd near the footbridge is overpriced and not very good, but is convenient if you're staying at the Majukano Hotel.

Self-Catering Well-stocked supermarkets for self-caterers include *Sabrina's* on Nyerere Rd, *Mwanza Supermarket* next door (both open 9 am to 9 pm daily), and *JJ Minimarket* on the extension of Station Rd.

Shopping

Duka ya Sanaa near the market has a small selection of leatherwork and other crafts from various regions of Tanzania. It's closed on Sunday.

Getting There & Away

Air Air Tanzania (☎ 40413/4) flies between Mwanza and Dar es Salaam (Tsh80,500, three times weekly direct, otherwise via Arusha), Arusha (Tsh55,000, four times weekly), Kigali in Rwanda (US$123, weekly), Lubumbashi in Congo (Zaïre) (US$275, weekly), and Entebbe in Uganda (US$124, weekly). Their office is on Kenyatta Rd next to Sizzler Restaurant. Eagle Air also flies weekly between Mwanza and Entebbe (US$100); book at any Mwanza travel agency. (Air Tanzania is the only airline that accepts credit cards.)

Precision Air (☎ 41688), across the street from Air Tanzania, flies between Mwanza and Dar es Salaam (Tsh83,000, three times weekly), Bukoba (Tsh43,000, daily), Arusha (Tsh95,000, five times weekly), Unguja (Tsh83,000, five times weekly), Ngara (Tsh46,000, twice weekly) and Shinyanga (Tsh28,000, twice weekly; four times weekly *from* Shinyanga).

The privately owned RenAir/SkyLink (☎ 562069, fax 560403) runs reliable flights twice weekly connecting Mwanza with Nairobi and Kigoma. The journey between Mwanza and Kigoma costs US$175/340 one way/round trip. A US$20 airport tax (rather than the normal Tsh2000 domestic flight tax) is imposed on each leg of this trip since the flight originates in Kenya. Plans were underway to expand this schedule, so check with a travel agent for the latest details. RenAir has an office at the airport, but flights can be booked through Serengeti Services & Tours or Fourways Travel. See Travel Agencies earlier in this chapter.

Western Airways is due to restart flights between Mwanza and Nairobi in the near future.

Bus Buses between Mwanza and Musoma run daily, throughout the day (Tsh2500, six hours). The first bus in either direction departs about 7 am. From Mwanza to the Kenyan border costs Tsh3000.

There is a daily bus to Geita (Tsh2000) and on to Biharamulo (Tsh4500). From Biharamulo, there are daily connections to Bukoba, Lusahunga and on to Ngara on the Rwanda/Burundi borders. There is sporadic direct service between Mwanza and Bukoba, but it's better to do the trip in stages.

The Samma and Lake Transport lines run twice weekly buses direct from Mwanza to Ngara (Tsh7000), and to Rulenge (Tsh8000).

To Tabora, it's far preferable to go via train. If you want to go by road, take any bus heading to Nzega (Tsh6000). From Nzega, Landrovers run to Tabora (Tsh2000).

To Shinyanga, there are daily buses (Tsh3500, five to six hours).

There are three routes from Mwanza to Arusha/Moshi and Dar es Salaam. The best is via Nairobi (Tsh25,000, approximately 30 hours to Dar es Salaam). Alternatively, there is a bus twice weekly during the dry season from Mwanza via the Ndabaka Gate and through the Serengeti to Moshi (Tsh19,000 to Moshi plus park fees for the Serengeti and for Ngorongoro Crater). At Moshi you must change buses for Dar es Salaam. Depending on road conditions, some buses may alternatively go from Mwanza via Bunda to the Fort Ikoma Gate, and then into the Serengeti from there. For information on the Serengeti routes, check with the Tanganyika Bus Service office at the central bus station in Mwanza.

Trucks ply the western corridor route fairly regularly; ask around in Mwanza near the port if you want to find a ride this way. The most unpleasant way to get to Dar es Salaam with the bus is via Singida (Tsh19,000); allow at least three days.

The Saratoga line runs weekly between Mwanza and Kigoma (Tsh12,000) via Ka-hama and Shinyanga, departing about 5 am and arriving the next day if you're lucky. To go to Kigoma via Biharamulo (Tsh12,000), your only option is Lake Transport, which has a weekly bus on Friday, departing about 5 am. Service is frequently interrupted or cancelled, especially during the rainy season.

To Kigali, there are buses twice weekly (Tsh15,000). See the Uganda section in the Getting There & Away chapter for further details.

Road From Mwanza north-east to Musoma, the road is in very poor condition for about the first 35km to Nyanguge, and good tarmac from there to Musoma and over the border into Kenya. From Mwanza south to Shinyanga, the road is under rehabilitation; it's about a four hour drive in a private vehicle. The stretch from Shinyanga to Nzega is in poor condition. From Nzega north-west towards Kabanga on the Burundi border, the road is good, while from Nzega south-east to Singida is rough. On the western side of the Mwanza Gulf, the road between Sengerema and Bukoba via Geita is in bad condition, particularly the stretch between Sengerema and Geita.

Train Mwanza is the terminus of a branch of the Central Line from Dar es Salaam. Trains depart Mwanza three times weekly for Tabora (Tsh11,700/7100/5300, 12 hours) and Dar es Salaam (Tsh29,800/17,700/12,300, 36 to 40 hours). If you are heading to Kigoma you must change trains at Tabora. Tickets for 1st and 2nd class should be booked at least several days in advance.

Boat Two ferries ply the Mwanza Gulf, connecting Mwanza and Sengerema/ Geita. The northernmost (or Kamanga) ferry docks at Mwanza port and is the more reliable of the two. It stops running at 6 pm. The more southerly Busisi ferry operates until 10 pm but is not reliable. Its eastern terminus is at Kikongo, about 25km south of Mwanza.

Mwanza is also connected by ferry to Bukoba and to numerous islands in Lake

LAKE VICTORIA

Victoria, including Ukerewe and Maisome. All ferries (four in total) are operated by the Tanzania Railways Corporation Marine Division. Their office is next to the police station at the harbour, and tickets and schedule information can be obtained there or at the port entrance gate.

The two main ferries are the MV *Serengeti* and the MV *Victoria*. The *Victoria*, which is the larger of the two ferries, is indefinitely out of commission and as a result, the ferry schedules have been cut back. If service is resumed current schedules may be altered or expanded.

The MV *Serengeti* sails from Mwanza to Bukoba on Tuesday, Thursday and Sunday at 3 pm, arriving early the next morning in Bukoba. Prices are Tsh9390/6000/4600 for 1st/2nd/3rd class plus port tax (US$5 for nonresidents, Tsh500 for residents). There are three 1st class cabins, and a restaurant on board. Transporting a vehicle costs Tsh29,330; arrangements should be made at the cargo office at the port.

Should service on the faster *Victoria* resume, departures from Mwanza would be around 9 pm, arriving in Bukoba early the next morning.

The *Butiama*, a small boat with deck class only, sails to Maisome Island on Wednesdays at about 3 pm (Tsh2800). From Maisome you can continue to Rubondo Island (see Rubondo Island National Park, later).

The larger *Clias* was under repair at the time of research, but targeted to be back in service soon. It normally goes daily to Nansio on Ukerewe (Tsh2500/2000, 2nd/3rd class; no 1st class). Until the *Clias* is back in service, the daily Ukerewe trips are being done by the *Butiama* for the same price.

If you are feeling grubby after a long boat ride, the Super Toilet & Bath Service, about 300m along the waterfront to the right as you exit the ferry port, has fairly clean showers for Tsh200.

Getting Around

To/From the Airport Mwanza's airport is about 10km north of town. Taxis ask Tsh5000, but you can usually find one for

Tsh3000 to Tsh4000, especially coming from the airport into town.

Both Air Tanzania and Fourways Travel run a shuttle bus which meets most incoming flights (Tsh1500). Fourways also runs a shuttle to the airport for some departures; inquire at their office for details.

Dalla-dallas to the airport (Tsh200) leave from the local bus station near the clock tower. Allow an hour. The airport road is in bad condition, particularly during the rainy season.

Bus & Taxi Local transport to towns north of Mwanza leaves from the bus stand near the clock tower. Transport to Nyakato, Kisessa and other destinations along the Musoma road leaves from the Bugando Hill stand near Aga Khan Hospital, south-east of the market. There are also local taxis and dalla-dallas to these and other destinations at the stand opposite the market.

BUKOBA

Bukoba is Tanzania's second largest port on Lake Victoria and a fairly popular overnight stop for travellers en route to/from Uganda or Rwanda. It's a small but bustling town with an attractive waterside setting.

The main ethnic group in Bukoba are the Haya. The area around Bukoba is believed to have been inhabited by one of the most prosperous and highly developed early societies known. Artefacts discovered in the region, including remnants of kilns estimated to be close to 2000 years old, indicate that steel production was already well developed in the region long before equivalent techniques were known in Europe. Although there's nothing in Bukoba now relating to these archaeological excavations, there is a small display on Iron Age findings from the region at the National Museum in Dar es Salaam.

Information

There are no foreign exchange bureaus in Bukoba. Travellers cheques can be changed at the NBC and sometimes at the CRDB. Merchants in town are also sometimes willing to change cheques or cash.

The Haya

The Haya, who live in the region west of Lake Victoria around Bukoba, are one of Tanzania's largest ethnic groups. They are related linguistically to both the Bantu and Nilotic families. The Haya had one of the most highly developed early societies on the continent. By the 18th or 19th century they were organised into eight different states or kingdoms, each headed by a powerful and often despotic *mukama* who ruled in part by divine right. It was the mukama who controlled all trade and who at least nominally owned all property, while land usage was shared among small, patrilineal communes. Order was maintained through a system of appointed chiefs and officials, assisted by an age group-based army. With the arrival of the colonial authorities, this political organisation began to erode. The various Haya groups splintered and many chiefs were replaced by persons considered more malleable and sympathetic to colonial interests.

In the 1920s, in the wake of growing resentment of these propped-up leaders and of the colonial government, the Haya began to regroup and in 1924 founded the Bukoba Bahaya Union. This association was initially directed towards local political reform but soon developed into the more influential and broad-based African Association. Together with similar groups established elsewhere in the country – notably in the Kilimanjaro region and in Dar es Salaam – it constituted one of Tanzania's earliest political movements and was an important force in the drive towards independence.

Telephone calls can be made at the telecom building between 7.30 am and 9 pm weekdays (shorter hours on weekends).

Places to Stay

Bukoba has a number of good budget accommodation options. One of the cheapest places is *Nyumba ya Vijana* south-east of the telecom building, with basic but decent doubles for Tsh3000 with common bath. No food is available.

Kahawa Guest House, a few blocks north of Jamhuri Rd, is even cheaper, with doubles for Tsh2500 (Tsh3500 with bathroom).

Across the street, *Kolping House* (☎ 21289) has a spotless six-bed room for Tsh1400 per bed. Church workers have priority, and if you stay you will have to abide by house rules.

Bishop Hirth Youth Centre, run by the Catholic diocese, has tiny but clean rooms from Tsh2000 (Tsh4500 with bathroom); many have only small windows. It's down a dirt road opposite the telecom building.

The *ELCT Lutheran Centre* (☎ 23121) on the airport road is very good value. Clean, comfortable singles/doubles are Tsh6000/10,800. Breakfast is extra.

New Banana Hotel (☎ 20861), on Zamzam St not far from the bus station, has decent singles/doubles for Tsh6500/7500 including bathroom and breakfast, although there is sometimes no running water.

The faded *Coffee Tree Hotel* (☎ 20412) on the road leading to the lake has singles/doubles for Tsh3600/4200 (Tsh7200 for a double with bathroom), including continental breakfast.

Lake Hotel (☎ 20237), at the edge of town overlooking the lake, is Bukoba's luxury option. Somewhat dilapidated but comfortable singles/doubles with bathroom are Tsh6500/8500 (Tsh4500 for a double with shared facilities), including continental breakfast. Camping is permitted for Tsh2500 per person including shower facilities.

Places to Eat

Corner Cafe not far from the bus stand and *Bishop Hirth Youth Centre* are both good for inexpensive local dishes and snacks.

Near the market is *Pizzeria Snacks*, also with inexpensive food.

New Banana Hotel has a decent restaurant with reasonably priced local dishes.

For self-caterers, there are a few supermarkets with decent selections on Jamhuri Rd; the best two are *Zain Supermarket* and

LAKE VICTORIA

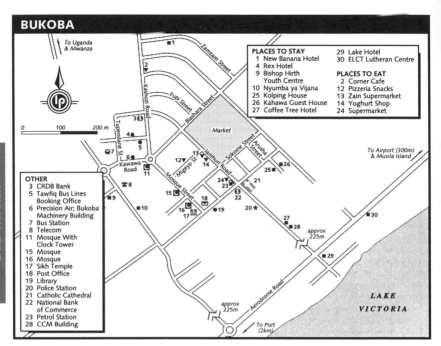

BUKOBA

PLACES TO STAY
1 New Banana Hotel
4 Rex Hotel
9 Bishop Hirth
  Youth Centre
10 Nyumba ya Vijana
25 Kolping House
26 Kahawa Guest House
27 Coffee Tree Hotel
29 Lake Hotel
30 ELCT Lutheran Centre

PLACES TO EAT
2 Corner Cafe
12 Pizzeria Snacks
13 Zain Supermarket
14 Yoghurt Shop
24 Supermarket

OTHER
3 CRDB Bank
5 Tawfiq Bus Lines
  Booking Office
6 Precision Air; Bukoba
  Machinery Building
7 Bus Station
8 Telecom
11 Mosque With
   Clock Tower
15 Mosque
16 Mosque
17 Sikh Temple
18 Post Office
19 Library
20 Police Station
21 Catholic Cathedral
22 National Bank
   of Commerce
23 Petrol Station
28 CCM Building

To Uganda & Mwanza

To Airport (300m) & Musila Island

LAKE VICTORIA

To Port (2km)

the unnamed supermarket near the petrol station. Next door to Zain's is a small *shop* selling *mtindi* (a cultured milk product similar to yoghurt).

Getting There & Away

Air Precision Air flies daily between Mwanza and Bukoba (US$65). Their office in Bukoba (☎ 20545) is located in the Bukoba Machinery building on Kawawa Rd. From Bukoba to Dar es Salaam costs US$270, via Mwanza and/or Arusha.

Bus Roads in almost all directions from Bukoba are in poor condition and most buses are in rough shape. Allow plenty of time for journeys.

Buses go several times weekly to Biharamulo (Tsh4000), an important junction for regional travel. From Biharamulo, you can catch onward transport to Lusahunga (Tsh1000), and from there on to Ngara and the Rwandan and Burundi borders. Alternatively, Vislam runs a direct bus from Bukoba to Ngara once or twice weekly (Tsh6000, at least eight hours).

Vislam also goes weekly via Kibondo to Kasulu (Tsh7500), from where you can get transport to Kigoma. The road between Lusahunga and Kasulu is very bad; the trip can take several days. For schedule information, check at the Vislam office off Kashozi Rd past Zamzam Rd.

Lake Transport goes twice weekly (Tuesday and Saturday) from Bukoba via Biharamulo to Mwanza (Tsh8000), though service is frequently interrupted; it's better to do the trip in stages.

There are occasional buses to Singida and Dodoma via Biharamulo, Kahama and Nzega (Tsh20,000). This is a very long and rough journey.

To Uganda and Kenya, Tawfiq runs buses three times weekly, departing Bukoba at 7 am Tuesday, Thursday and Saturday and arriving in Kampala about 3 pm the next day (Tsh10,000). From Kampala, there are onward connections to Nairobi (Tsh20,000 direct fare from Bukoba). There are also minibuses most days between Bukoba and Mutukula on the Ugandan border (about three hours), where you can catch Ugandan transport to Kampala.

Tawfiq also runs a direct bus three times weekly from Bukoba to Dar es Salaam (Tsh34,000) via Nairobi and Arusha. The Tawfiq booking office is a block away from the bus station opposite the Rex Hotel. It's best to book a day in advance.

Boat The only ferry destination from Bukoba is Mwanza. Departures from Bukoba are every Monday, Wednesday and Friday at 6 pm, arriving in Mwanza the next morning. Tickets cost Tsh10,000/6000/4600 for 1st/2nd/3rd class plus US$5 port tax (Tsh500 for residents). See the Mwanza Getting There & Away section for additional information.

On tiny Musila Island, directly offshore from the airport, there is nothing except a small fishing camp. Fishing boats go there from the small port just north of the airport.

MUSOMA
Musoma is a quiet, pleasant town on the eastern shore of Lake Victoria and the capital of the surrounding Mara region. Its port has become clogged in recent years and is no longer used by the lake ferries. About 45km south of Musoma is Butiama, the home town of Julius Nyerere.

Places to Stay & Eat
For budget travellers, the unfortunately named *Stigma Hotel* in the centre near the market has rooms for about Tsh5000.

Hotel Orange Tree, near the lake on Kawawa St off Iringa St, has decent rooms from about Tsh8000.

The *Peninsula Hotel*, though a bit faded, is Musoma's luxury lodging, with rooms for

approximately Tsh25,000. It's about 2km from the centre on the Makoko road.

All of these places have restaurants.

Getting There & Away
There are occasional air charters to Musoma that may have an empty seat available. Inquire in town for details.

Buses run throughout the day between Musoma and Mwanza (Tsh2500, six hours). The first bus departs in each direction at 7 am, the last about 3 pm. There are also frequent minibuses to the border (Tsh1000) where you can change to Kenyan transport. The road from Musoma to the border and into Kenya is good tarmac the entire way.

There are no ferry connections from Musoma. To Mwanza, your only option is via road.

RUBONDO ISLAND NATIONAL PARK
Rubondo Island National Park, in the southwest corner of the lake, encompasses Rubondo Island as well as several smaller islands nearby. It was gazetted in 1977 with a total area of 460 sq km, about 240 sq km of which is land. Rubondo's main attraction is its rich and diverse bird life. Close to 400 species have been identified including fish eagle, heron, stork, ibises and cormorant. In addition to all the birds, there are many different types of butterflies, as well as populations of chimpanzee, hippo, crocodile, giraffe and even elephant (the latter were introduced several decades ago). The island is also one of the few places in East Africa where you can observe sitatunga, an amphibious antelope that likes to hide among the marshes and reeds along the shoreline.

Rubondo is a beautiful, quiet place, ideal for those seeking relaxation. It is a complete change of pace from Tanzania's other parks and is well worth a visit.

Information
The park is open year-round, but the best time to visit is from June through early November, before the heavy rains set in. Entry fees are US$15 per person per day (US$5

for children between the ages of five and 16). Camping fees are US$20 (US$5 for children). For booking camp sites or obtaining further information contact the Senior Park Warden (PO Box 111 Geita).

Activities in the park include boat trips (approximately US$50 per boat for a half-day trip), forest walks (US$15 ranger fee for half a day), birdwatching, and fishing. The park levies a fee of US$50 per day for sport fishing.

Places to Stay

There is a camp site on Rubondo, and some basic bandas; you'll need to book these in advance through the park warden and bring all your own provisions.

The pleasant **Rubondo Island Camp** overlooking the lake offers comfortable luxury tented accommodation for US$160 per person sharing with full board. Prices are reduced by half during the low season, and there are also significant discounts available for children. Bookings can be made through Flycatcher Safaris Ltd (☎ 057-6963, fax 8261, email flycat@swissonline.ch, Haile Selassie Rd 50, PO Box 591, Arusha), or in Switzerland (☎ 41-32-392 5450, fax 392 5451, PO Box 20, CH-3283 Kallnach).

Getting There & Away

Air Most guests staying at Rubondo Island Camp arrive via chartered flight which is arranged through the camp. It costs around US$100 per person one way for a group of five people (US$520 if you want an entire five-seater plane).

Boat The *Butiama* ferry sails weekly from Mwanza to Maisome Island just east of Rubondo. (See the Mwanza Getting There & Away section for details.) From Maisome you can arrange a pick-up with park headquarters or Rubondo Island Camp (US$60 and US$250 depending on the pick-up point and size of the boat).

Local boats also go to Rubondo from Maisome, and from Mnganza, which can be reached by road from Biharamulo or Geita. (You can't bring your own vehicle onto the island.) If you plan to arrive this way, be sure to radio the park in advance so that someone is there to meet you. Fourways Travel in Mwanza can assist with this and all other arrangements for a visit to Rubondo.

SHINYANGA

Shinyanga lies south of the lake region in a traditional gold mining area. You will only need to come through here if you are travelling between Mwanza and Tabora or Dodoma by road. There are several local guesthouses in the centre of town, although none are outstanding. About 45km north-east of Shinyanga near Mwadui is the Williamson diamond mine. The Mwadui pipe covers an area of 146 hectares and is the world's largest, although production at the mine has been erratic over the past decade and its resources are believed to be almost depleted.

Western Tanzania

Western Tanzania, while remote from Dar es Salaam and lacking any sort of developed transport infrastructure, has numerous sites of interest for travellers. The seldom visited but beautiful Katavi and Mahale Mountains national parks are here, as is Jane Goodall's world-renowned chimpanzee research station at Gombe Stream National Park. Tiny Ujiji was the terminus of one of East Africa's most important caravan routes linking Lake Tanganyika with Bagamoyo and the sea. It is also an important dhow-building centre and served as a way station for several European exploratory expeditions. Lake Tanganyika itself – the world's longest and second deepest freshwater lake – is a useful transport route for those heading to or from northern Zambia. Its shores, though only sparsely populated, provide a respite for road-weary travellers. The lake also has a high degree of biodiversity, with numerous endemic species of cichlids, crustaceans and molluscs.

KIGOMA

Kigoma is a regional capital and the most important Tanzanian port on Lake Tanganyika. For much of its history it remained overshadowed by Ujiji to the south. It was only with the building of the Central Line railway terminus that the town gained regional significance. In recent years, with the upheavals in nearby Congo (Zaïre), Rwanda and Burundi, the area around Kigoma has also become a major refugee centre and numerous international aid organisations have offices in or near the town.

While there's little of interest in Kigoma itself, it's a pleasant place and a good base for visits to Gombe Stream and Mahale Mountains national parks.

Information

Immigration An immigration officer is posted at the port on Wednesdays to take care of immigration formalities for travellers departing for Zambia on the MV *Liemba*.

Highlights

![Map of Western Tanzania showing Burundi, Kigoma p266, Tabora p272, Congo (Zaïre), Lake Tanganyika, Lake Rukwa, Zambia, and reference to Western Tanzania p264]

- **Gombe Stream National Park** – observe the chimpanzees at close range
- **Ujiji** – while away some time in this laid-back village
- **Lake Tanganyika** – relax on its tranquil shores
- **Mahale Mountains National Park** – visit this remote and rugged area, or beautiful Katavi National Park

Otherwise, the immigration office is on the main road towards Ujiji, near the hospital.

Money There are no foreign exchange bureaus in Kigoma. The NBC bank near the bus stand accepts travellers cheques.

Post & Communications You can make telephone calls at the Telecom building near the post office, or more efficiently and only slightly more expensively at Nguza Communications Centre, opposite the market.

Travel Agent The long-established Sunset Tours at Aqua Lodge (☎ 2586, fax 3707, PO

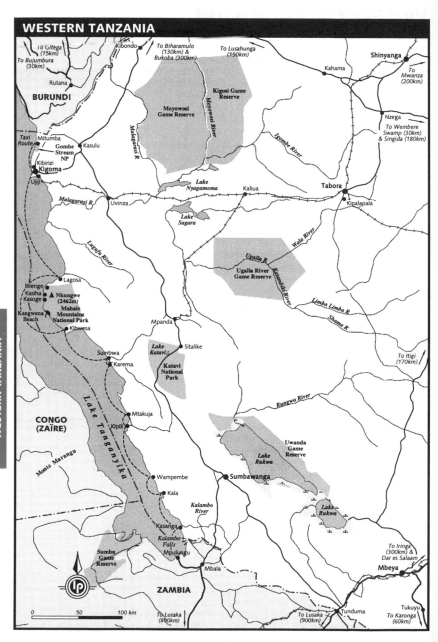

WESTERN TANZANIA

To Uitega (15km)
To Bujumbura (30km)

Rutana

BURUNDI

Kibondo

To Biharamulo (130km) & Bukoba (300km)

To Lusahunga (150km)

Kahama

Shinyanga

To Mwanza (200km)

Moyowosi Game Reserve

Kigosi Game Reserve

Moyowosi River

Nzega

To Wembere Swamp (30km) & Singida (180km)

Taxi Route
Mitumba
Gombe Stream NP
Kasulu
Kibirizi
Kigoma
Ujiji

Malagarasi R

Lake Nyagamoma

Kaliua

Tabora

Kipalapala

Malagarasi R.
Uvinza

Lake Sagara

Igombe River

Ugufu River

Lake Tanganyika

Lagosa
Bilenge
Kasiha
Kasoge
Kangwena Beach
▲ Nkungwe (2462m)
Mahale Mountains National Park
Kibwesa

Mpanda

Ugalla R
Ugalla River Game Reserve

Wala River

Kalambiki River

Limba Limba R.

Shama R.

To Itigi (170km)

Sumbwa
Karema

Lake Katavi
Sitalike
Katavi National Park

Rungwa River

CONGO (ZAÏRE)

Kipili
Mtakuja

Monts Marangu

Wampembe
Kala

Lake Rukwa

Uwanda Game Reserve

Sumbawanga

Kalambo River

Kasanga
Kalambo Falls
Mpulungu

Lake Rukwa

To Iringa (300km) & Dar es Salaam

Mbeya

Sumbu Game Reserve

Mbala

ZAMBIA

0   50   100 km

To Lusaka (800km)

To Lusaka (900km)

Tunduma

Tukuyu
To Karonga (60km)

WESTERN TANZANIA

Refugees

For much of its post-independence history, Tanzania has distinguished itself in Africa and in the world for its willingness to take in large numbers of refugees. Julius Nyerere saw accepting refugees as a means of supporting regional liberation movements and as an act of political solidarity with oppressed Africans. As a result, thousands of people from Mozambique, South Africa, Rwanda, Burundi and Congo (Zaïre) found safe haven in Tanzania during the 1970s and 80s. In keeping with the *ujamaa* philosophy (see Socialist Tanzania under History in the Facts about Tanzania chapter), Nyerere also went to extraordinary lengths to provide refugees a dignified existence, in many cases offering land, housing and even citizenship. In 1983, Nyerere was honoured with the UNHCR's Nansen medal for these outstanding contributions.

During the 1990s, the massive influxes of Rwandans fleeing the 1994 genocide in their country, the resulting deteriorating security and environmental situations along Tanzania's western border, and changing political and economic trends (notably Tanzania's move to multi-party politics), led to a shift in the country's asylum policy. In 1995 Tanzania closed its border with Burundi and announced that while it would continue to honour its humanitarian obligations it would not tolerate insecurity along its borders, nor the extensive environmental damage resulting from the new influxes. Today, despite this shift, Tanzania continues to host about 300,000 Burundian and Congolese (Zaïrean) refugees – the largest refugee concentration of any East African country. Most are in the Kigoma region, with a significant number near Ngara in the Kagera region.

In the south-west of the country at Mishamo and Katumba, north of Mpanda in the Rukwa region, are two other very large groups of Burundian refugees who came to Tanzania in 1972. These sites are not camps, but enormous villages. Both were initially established during the ujamaa days in the spirit of promoting self-sufficiency among the refugees. In the early 1980s, Nyerere offered all of these Burundians citizenship, although only a few thousand accepted the offer. Today, while most of the residents of these villages are officially still Burundian, and still refugees, they are for the most part completely integrated linguistically and otherwise into Tanzanian society. Both Mishamo and Katumba are now under the jurisdiction of the Tanzanian Ministry of Home Affairs.

Box 34, Kigoma) rent boats and can arrange visits to both Gombe Stream and Mahale Mountains national parks.

Medical Services If you fall ill, the best hospital is the mission-run Kigoma Baptist Hospital (☎ 2241) near the airport.

Things to See & Do

South of town in Katonga is a **chimpanzee centre** for orphaned chimps, run by the Jane Goodall Institute. One of its goals is to give the chimps a home until a better sanctuary can be arranged. There are usually several in residence, many of whom have been recap-

tured from illegal traffickers (see the boxed text 'Chimpanzees' later). To get here, take a dalla-dalla to Katonga and then ask locals to show you the way to the centre.

Also near Katonga is the small but popular **Jacobsen's Beach**. It costs Tsh2000 per day; the lake here is believed to be free of bilharzia (see Health in the Facts for the Visitor chapter). To get here, take a dalla-dalla from the Tanzanian Revenue Authority roundabout to Katonga (about a 30 minute ride) and ask the driver to drop you at the turn-off for 'wazungo beach'. From there it's about a 15 minute walk; you'll need to ask locals for directions. If you are driving, Katonga is to the right at the fork after the Kigoma Hilltop Hotel.

Places to Stay

The cheapest place is the **Community Centre** near the post office run by the Kigoma diocese. It has grubby rooms and grubbier shared baths for Tsh1500/2000 a single/double. The only advantage, besides the price, is that the linen is clean and it's quiet.

Kigoma Hotel on the main street is even grubbier, and also noisy. Singles/doubles cost Tsh2200/2400. Diagonally opposite is the similarly depressing **Lake View Hotel**, with rooms for about the same price. The bathrooms are filthy and the place has nothing to recommend it except the price.

About 2km from the centre, up the hill in the Mwanga section of town, are numerous local guesthouses. The best one is **Zanzibar Lodge** on the main road. It has clean singles/doubles from Tsh3000/4000 (Tsh5000 for a double with bath); the rooms facing the main street are noisy.

For mid-range accommodation, there are two choices. **Aqua Lodge** (☎ 2586) at the western edge of town has comfortable doubles (no singles) for Tsh18,000, including continental breakfast. The only disadvantage is its location opposite the loud TANESCO generator.

Another 300m back towards town, and just off the same road, is the slightly faded but very pleasant **Tanganyika Beach Hotel** (☎ 2694) (formerly the Railway Hotel), with an attractive lakeside setting. Rooms are Tsh12,000/18,000 including a continental breakfast. The lawn sloping down to the lake is a popular spot in the evenings and on weekends for a drink. On Saturday evenings there is a popular disco.

For luxury, the **Kigoma Hilltop Hotel** (☎ 0695-4435, fax 4434, email kht@raha .com) has accommodation in individual cottages with TVs and all amenities from US$51/72 plus 20% VAT, including continental breakfast. The hotel is set atop a hill overlooking the lake at the western end of town, and has a pool (Tsh2000 for nonresidents), a good restaurant, and numerous other facilities. It can also organise waterskiing and parasailing on the lake, and trips

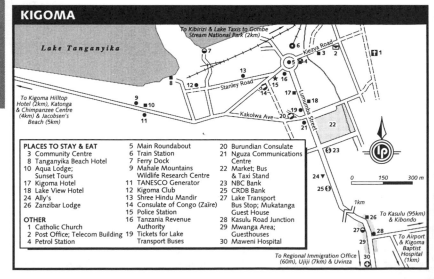

KIGOMA

Lake Tanganyika

To Kibirizi & Lake Taxis to Gombe Stream National Park (2km)

Kierzu Road

Stanley Road

To Kigoma Hilltop Hotel (2km), Katonga & Chimpanzee Centre (4km) & Jacobsen's Beach (5km)

Lumumba Street

Kakolwa Ave

0   150   300 m

1km

To Kasulu (95km) & Kibondo

To Airport & Kigoma Baptist Hospital (1km)

To Regional Immigration Office (60m), Ujiji (7km) & Uvinza

PLACES TO STAY & EAT	5 Main Roundabout	20 Burundian Consulate
3 Community Centre	6 Train Station	21 Nguza Communications
8 Tanganyika Beach Hotel	7 Ferry Dock	Centre
10 Aqua Lodge;	9 Mahale Mountains	22 Market; Bus
Sunset Tours	Wildlife Research Centre	& Taxi Stand
17 Kigoma Hotel	11 TANESCO Generator	23 NBC Bank
18 Lake View Hotel	12 Kigoma Club	25 CRDB Bank
24 Ally's	13 Shree Hindu Mandir	27 Lake Transport
26 Zanzibar Lodge	14 Consulate of Congo (Zaïre)	Bus Stop; Mukatanga
	15 Police Station	Guest House
OTHER	16 Tanzania Revenue	28 Kasulu Road Junction
1 Catholic Church	Authority	29 Mwanga Area;
2 Post Office; Telecom Building	19 Tickets for Lake	Guesthouses
4 Petrol Station	Transport Buses	30 Maweni Hospital

to Gombe Stream and Mahale Mountains national parks.

Places to Eat

The best place for inexpensive local food is *Ally's* on the main street.

The restaurant at the *Aqua Lodge* is good; you must order in advance. *Tanganyika Beach Hotel* also has good meals though service is slow. The restaurant at *Kigoma Hilltop Hotel* is expensive, but has a wide selection of western dishes.

Getting There & Away

Air The only commercial service is the twice weekly flight (Monday and Friday) of RenAir/SkyLink linking Kigoma with Mwanza and Nairobi. See the Mwanza Getting There & Away section in the Lake Victoria chapter for details. Air Tanzania has indefinitely suspended service to Kigoma.

Although there is usually at least one taxi meeting the RenAir flights, it's best to arrange a ride in advance or with another passenger if you can. The airport is about 5km from the centre of town.

Bus Roads from Kigoma in all directions are in very rough condition. To Mwanza, the best option is the Saratoga line, which has a direct bus every Tuesday from Ujiji (Tsh12,000, at least 36 hours). For information and bookings contact Khalfan Sood (☎ 3450) in Ujiji. If you're in Ujiji, it's the only two-storey building in town. Departures are about 5.30 am. To pick up the bus in Kigoma, stand at the Kasulu road junction off the main road to Kigoma. The route is via Kahama and Shinyanga (not via Biharamulo). The fare to Shinyanga is Tsh10,000.

To go to Mwanza via Biharamulo, your only option is Lake Transport, which has a weekly bus on Friday (Tsh12,000 to Mwanza, Tsh8500 to Biharamulo, or Tsh7500 to Lusahunga). Buses depart at about 5 am from the Mukatanga Guest House in the Mwanga section of Kigoma not far from Zanzibar Lodge, or from the Kasulu road junction. Lake Transport can be booked at their 'office' opposite the market.

For Bukoba, you will need to change buses at Lusahunga, or else travel to Kasulu and wait for the weekly Vislam bus (Tsh7500 from Kasulu to Bukoba). Allow several days for the trip, although it is sometimes faster.

Local buses go daily to Kasulu (Tsh1500) and Kibondo (Tsh3000).

Train The train departs Kigoma three times weekly for Tabora (Tsh12,600/10,600/5700, 1st/2nd/3rd class, 12 hours) and Dar es Salaam (Tsh30,200/24,200/18,000/12,500, 36 to 40 hours). If you are going north to Mwanza or south to Mpanda, you will need to change trains in Tabora (or else in Kaliua for Mpanda). First and 2nd class tickets should be booked at least several days in advance.

Lake Ferries The two ferries operating from Kigoma are the MV *Liemba* and the MV *Mwongozo*. The only one relevant for travellers is the *Liemba* which services ports on the Tanzanian lake shore down to Mpulungu in Zambia. The smaller *Mwongozo* is used for refugee transport from Congo (Zaïre). At the time of research there was no service between Kigoma and Burundi.

The *Liemba* departs on Wednesday at 4 pm, arriving in Mpulungu at about 8 am on Friday morning. An immigration officer is at Kigoma port for all arrivals and departures to/from Zambia. See Zambia in the Getting There & Away chapter for further details.

Lake Taxis Lake taxis are small, wooden boats, usually overcrowded with people and produce, which connect villages along the lake shore. They are very inexpensive, but offer no creature comforts and usually no shade either. The taxis don't stop at Kigoma itself, but at Kibirizi village, just a few kilometres north of Kigoma along the train tracks. See Getting There & Away under Gombe Stream National Park, later in this chapter. They run daily except Sunday.

AROUND KIGOMA
Ujiji

Ujiji, one of Africa's oldest market villages, was the main settlement in the region until the building of the Central Line railway terminus at Kigoma. Burton and Speke stopped here in 1858 before setting out to explore Lake Tanganyika. It's a laid-back, pleasant place and well worth a visit.

Ujiji is also where the famous words, 'Dr Livingstone, I presume', were spoken by the explorer and journalist Henry Morton Stanley in 1871. The site where Stanley's encounter with Livingstone allegedly occurred is set in a walled compound near an attractive garden. There's the inevitable plaque, as well as two mango trees which are said to have been grafted from the original tree growing there when the two men met. There is also a bleak museum housing a few pictures by local artists of Livingstone's time here. Entry is free, but a small donation is welcome. The caretaker's historical presentation about Livingstone is not to be missed! The site is signposted to the right of the main road (when coming from Kigoma), down the side street next to the Bin Tunia Restaurant – just ask for Livingstone and the bus driver will make sure you get off at the right place.

About 500m past the compound along the same street is Ujiji's picturesque beach and dhow port, with many local boat builders. It's a thriving local industry, and fascinating to watch. The best day is Sunday when most boats are brought ashore for repairs. No power tools are used, and construction methods are the same as they were generations ago.

Places to Stay & Eat If you want to sleep in Ujiji, your only option is the *Matunda Guest House* on the main road, a basic but friendly place with fairly clean singles/doubles with mosquito net and common bath for Tsh700/1000. Your only options for food are a few undistinguished local eateries along the main street.

Getting There & Away Ujiji is about 8km south of Kigoma centre. Dalla-dallas run between the two towns throughout the day (Tsh200).

GOMBE STREAM NATIONAL PARK

With an area of only 52 sq km, Gombe Stream is Tanzania's smallest national park. It is also the site of the longest-running study of any wild animal population in the world and, for those interested in primates, a fascinating place.

The Gombe Stream area was gazetted as a game reserve in 1943. In 1960, the British researcher, Jane Goodall, arrived to begin a study of wild chimpanzees, and in 1968 Gombe was designated as a national park. Goodall's study is now in its fourth decade.

Chimpanzees

The natural habitat of Tanzania's chimpanzees (*Pan troglodytes schweinfurthii*) once extended along much of the western border of the country, throughout the Kigoma and Rukwa regions and into Burundi, Rwanda, Uganda and Congo (Zaïre). Deforestation and human population pressures have greatly reduced these areas, and today the chimps are found mainly in Gombe Stream National Park, and in and around Mahale Mountains National Park.

In addition to deforestation, the main threat to Tanzania's remaining populations is illegal chimp trafficking. Chimpanzees, which are coveted as pets, sought for medical research, and wanted for commercial zoos, command high prices on the black market. Yet, to capture a baby chimpanzee, all nearby adults must be killed. The result is many dead chimps, and many orphans. For young chimps which are recaptured from illegal traffickers, there is also the problem of reintegration. With few exceptions, chimps cannot be reintroduced to the wild in an area where there are other chimps already living. While there are numerous groups working hard to halt illegal trafficking, the networks are entrenched, and it is an uphill task requiring constant vigilance. The chimpanzee centre in Katonga, south of Kigoma, is a good source of more detailed information on these issues.

There are approximately 150 chimps in Gombe. They are well habituated, and you can sometimes get to within 5m of them. In addition to observing the chimps, visitors can swim in the lake or hike in Gombe's forest. Other animals you may see in the park include colobus and vervet monkey, bushbuck, baboon, bushpig, and a variety of birdlife.

Gombe Stream is located on the eastern shore of Lake Tanganyika, about 20km north of Kigoma.

Information

In an effort to moderate the number of visitors to Gombe, entry fees have been set high, at US$100 per person per day (US$20 for those between the ages of five and 16). Accommodation at the park hostel costs US$10, and camping US$20 per person per night. Guides cost US$20 per group.

The park can be visited year-round. Bookings for the hostel should be made through Sunset Tours in Kigoma or through the senior park warden (PO Box 185 Kigoma). Park headquarters are at Mitumba, at the northern end of the park.

There are plans to open a visitors centre for Gombe in Kigoma; you can inquire at the Mahale Mountains Wildlife Research Centre (☎ 2072, PO Box 1053 Kigoma) as to the current status.

The booklet *Gombe Stream National Park* put out by TANAPA is useful for those seeking more detailed information on the park. It's available in bookshops in Arusha and Dar es Salaam or from TANAPA headquarters in Arusha for about Tsh3000.

Places to Stay

The main place to stay is the resthouse near park headquarters. You can also camp on the beach. For either option you will need to be self-sufficient, bringing all your own provisions from Kigoma.

Getting There & Away

The only way to reach Gombe is via boat. Budget travellers should take a dalla-dalla from Kigoma to Kibirizi, a few kilometres north of Kigoma (Tsh200). If you prefer to walk, follow the train tracks past the BP petrol station. From Kibirizi, small, motorised lake taxis go to Gombe daily except Sunday (Tsh1000); it takes about three hours. When leaving Gombe, park staff can help you wave down a boat. Alternatively, you can arrange with a local fisherman to charter out a whole boat for yourself, although this will be expensive.

Boats can also be arranged through Sunset Tours or Kigoma Hilltop Hotel. Sunset Tours charges US$165 round-trip per boat with a maximum of 15 passengers, plus a waiting fee of US$83 if you stay in Gombe overnight. For two or more nights, transport fees total US$330. Kigoma Hilltop Hotel charges US$300 per boat (10 passengers maximum) for a one-night/two-day visit to the park.

MAHALE MOUNTAINS NATIONAL PARK

Mahale is one of Tanzania's most remote parks and one of its most attractive. It is situated directly on Lake Tanganyika, with the misty and rugged Mahale mountain range running down its centre. Like Gombe Stream to the north, Mahale is primarily a chimpanzee sanctuary, with a population of approximately 700 chimpanzees inside its boundaries. There are also a variety of other animals to be seen including elephant, giraffe, zebra, buffalo and even some lions. The area has been the site of an ongoing Japanese-sponsored primate research project since 1965. It was gazetted as a national park in 1980 with an area of close to 1600 sq km. The park's highest peak is Mt Nkungwe (2462m), first climbed in 1939.

Information

Entry fees are US$50 per person (US$20 for those between the ages of five and 16 and free for children under five). Camping costs US$20 per person per night and should be booked through the senior park warden (PO Box 1374 Kigoma), or through Sunset Tours in Kigoma. Sunset Tours can also assist with a radio call to park headquarters to let them know of your arrival. Guide fees are US$20 per group (maximum six).

There are no roads in Mahale. The main way of exploring the park is by foot; boat trips along the lake shore can also be arranged with park headquarters. In Kigoma, you can obtain further information about the park through the Mahale Mountains Wildlife Research Centre (☎ 2072, PO Box 1053 Kigoma), located in an unmarked white house opposite the TANESCO generator and next door to the Aqua Lodge. The booklet *Gombe Stream National Park* published by TANAPA also contains a small section on Mahale. *The Chimpanzees of the Mahale Mountains: Sexual and Life History Strategies* has a wealth of detailed scientific information, as well as a brief history of the Kyoto University Africa Primatological Expedition which started the initial research in the park.

Places to Stay

There is a camp site near park headquarters and a basic resthouse with cooking facilities in the park north of Kasiha. For both you will need to be self-sufficient and bring all your own provisions from Kigoma.

Alternatively, there is the *Mahale Mountains Tented Camp* on Kangwena Beach to the south of park headquarters. Comfortable accommodation is US$295 per person, all-inclusive. Book through Greystoke Safaris (☎ 057-3629, fax 2123, PO Box 425 Arusha) or in Kenya (☎ 254-2-502491, fax 502739, email bushhome@africaonline .co.ke, PO Box 56923 Nairobi). The camp is open between June and mid-October and from mid-December to mid-February.

Getting There & Away

The only way to reach Mahale is via charter aircraft, or by boat.

Boat Mahale lies directly on Lake Tanganyika, about 130km south of Kigoma. The MV *Liemba* stops at Lagosa (also called Mugambo), north of Mahale and outside the park border. The trip takes 10 to 12 hours from Kigoma (Tsh7400/5400/2900 for

1st/2nd/3rd class). From Lagosa, you can either arrange for a local (motorised) boat to take you to park headquarters about two hours further south, or arrange a pick-up in advance with park headquarters (US$50 per person one way). Sometimes, you may be lucky enough to find park staff already at Lagosa who may be willing to give you a lift to the park in their boat for a reduced fee.

Alternatively, you can hire a boat through Sunset Tours in Kigoma (US$800 round-trip including two to three nights in the park).

Local boats depart Ujiji twice a week (usually Tuesday and Friday) and sail down the coast towards Lagosa. The trip, which costs about Tsh3000, is very long and uncomfortable; allow about 24 hours, as the local boats stop everywhere. They have no facilities, shade or amenities; bring whatever food and water you may need.

UVINZA

Salt production has been the most important industry in Uvinza for at least several hundred years and today the town remains Tanzania's major salt producing area. In order to visit the Uvinza salt factory, which has been running since the 1920s, you'll need to arrange a permit at the entry gate. This is usually no problem – as so few travellers pass this way, they will be happy to see you. For lodging try the *Sibuondo Guest House* in the centre of town.

Uvinza lies about two hours south-east of Kigoma via the Central Line train. Road access to and from the town is difficult. To Kigoma, head north-west along a rough, sparsely travelled road towards Kasulu. About 10km before Kasulu, branch west towards Kigoma. There is no regular public transport. Trucks will charge you about Tsh2000 for a lift as far as Kasulu, from where there are daily minibuses to Kigoma (Tsh1500). Between Uvinza and Mpanda there are trucks a few times a week during the dry season. They will usually charge you about Tsh4000 for a lift. The trip takes between one and two days. There is very little traffic on this road, and little available en route. Along the way you will pass the

Mishamo refugee settlement (see the boxed text 'Refugees' earlier in this chapter).

TABORA

Tabora was once one of the most significant trading centres along the old caravan route connecting Lake Tanganyika and Central Africa with Bagamoyo and the sea, and centre of the infamous slave trader Tippu Tib's empire. After the Central Line railway was constructed, it became the largest town in German East Africa.

Tabora hosted some of the European explorers including Stanley and Livingstone. By the turn of the century it had also become an important mission station. It has traditionally been a regional centre for education and Julius Nyerere attended school here.

Tippu Tib

Tippu Tib, whose real name was Hamed bin Mohamed el Murjebi, was one of East Africa's most infamous slave traders, notorious for his ruthless cruelty.

Tippu Tib was born around 1830 in Zanzibar. His father was a wealthy plantation holder from Tabora. When he was still young, Tippu Tib began to assist his father with trade and soon came to dominate an extensive area around Lake Tanganyika that stretched well into present-day Congo (Zaïre). At the height of his power in the late 19th century he had trading stations strung out across eastern Congo and Tanzania, with Tabora an important centre. Tippu Tib knew some of the European explorers and assisted Livingstone and Stanley with their expeditions. In 1887, Stanley managed to persuade him to become governor of the eastern region of the Congo although the undertaking was short-lived. In 1890, Tippu Tib left his base in the Congo for Zanzibar, where he died in 1905. His house still stands in Zanzibar Town near the Africa House Hotel, although it is privately occupied and not open to visitors. Tippu Tib wrote an autobiography which has been published in Swahili, English and German.

Today, although Tabora gives the initial impression of being a bit of a dusty backwater, it still plays an important role as a transport junction where the Central Line branches for Mwanza and Kigoma. There are a few old houses in town dating back to Tippu Tib's era.

Things to See

About 6km from town along the Kipalapala road is a house where Livingstone lived, in which there's a tiny museum containing some of his letters, diary and other items. Entry is free, but a small donation is appreciated. Any dalla-dalla heading that way can drop you, or you can walk.

Places to Stay & Eat

The **Moravian Hostel** is probably the best budget lodging. Doubles with mosquito nets are Tsh2000. It's north-west of the centre, about 2.5km from the train station and past the market. There are no meals available.

As far as hotels go, the **Golden Eagle**, in a convenient central location near the market, and **Hotel Wilca**, a bit away from the centre off Boma Rd, have acceptable, reasonably priced rooms.

Top of the line is the **Tabora Hotel** (☎ 4566) at the junction of Boma and Station Rds. Formerly the Railway Hotel, it was originally built by a German baron as a hunting lodge but was later rehabilitated. It has a nice veranda overlooking the gardens and offers singles/doubles with bathroom and mosquito nets for TSh6000/9000. They also have a good restaurant and satellite TV.

If you are travelling via train from Mpanda, you will arrive in Tabora about 3 am. Many of the guesthouses and hotels will not admit you at that hour. One which will is Tabora Hotel.

The best place to eat is **Mayor's Restaurant & Ice Cream Parlour**, just south of School St, which has good, inexpensive meals, fresh pineapple juice, and ice cream.

For self-caterers, a good place is **Mr Sudra's store**, off Lumumba St close to the junction with Market St. Mr Sudra is also a good source of information on Tabora and

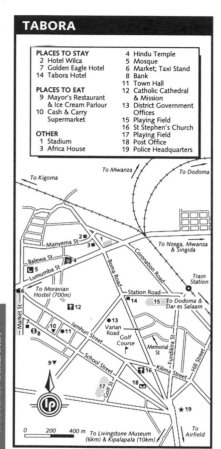

TABORA

PLACES TO STAY
2 Hotel Wilca
7 Golden Eagle Hotel
14 Tabora Hotel

PLACES TO EAT
9 Mayor's Restaurant & Ice Cream Parlour
10 Cash & Carry Supermarket

OTHER
1 Stadium
3 Africa House
4 Hindu Temple
5 Mosque
6 Market; Taxi Stand
8 Bank
11 Town Hall
12 Catholic Cathedral & Mission
13 District Government Offices
15 Playing Field
16 St Stephen's Church
17 Playing Field
18 Post Office
19 Police Headquarters

To Kigoma
To Mwanza
To Dodoma
Manyema St
Balewa St
Lumumba St
To Moravian Hostel (700m)
Market St
Boma Road
Coronation Road
To Nzega, Mwanza & Singida
Train Station
Station Road
To Dodoma & Dar es Salaam
Jamhuri Street
Varian Road
Golf Course
School Street
Golf St
Memorial St
Kilima Street
Fundikira St
Hill Street
0   200   400 m
To Livingstone Museum (6km) & Kipalapala (10km)
To Airfield

WESTERN TANZANIA

the surrounding area. *Cash & Carry Supermarket* on School St also has a decent selection.

Getting There & Away

Road The road network around Tabora is in poor condition. Landrovers go most days north to Nzega from where you can get onward transport to Mwanza (see the Mwanza Getting There & Away section in the Lake Victoria chapter) or to Singida and on to Dodoma or Arusha. Allow several days for these journeys. Stretches of the routes are often impassable, particularly during the rainy season; inquire locally before setting out and have extra food, water and petrol with you if you are driving your own vehicle. To go to Kigoma, your only option is via train.

Train Tabora is the main junction along the Central Line for trains going north to Mwanza, west to Kigoma, or south to Mpanda. Trains depart Tabora three times weekly for Mwanza (Tsh11,700/7100/5300 for 1st/2nd/3rd class, 12 hours), Kigoma (Tsh12,600/10,600/5700, 12 hours), Mpanda (Tsh7200/4100/2800, 14 hours) and Dar es Salaam (Tsh21,800/13,100/9200, 24 to 28 hours). You will need to spend at least one night in Tabora waiting for most connections.

Getting Around

Most of the taxis are opposite the market at the junction of Lumumba and Market Sts.

Taxis meet all train arrivals, including the 3 am train from Mpanda. Expect to pay about Tsh1000 from the station into the town centre.

MPANDA

Mpanda is of interest mainly as a starting point for visits to Katavi National Park. It's also the terminus of a branch of the Central Line railway.

Most travellers stay at *Super City* in the centre of town; it's a bit of a brothel, but tolerable. Clean doubles with mosquito nets and bathroom cost Tsh4000. To get here from the train station, follow the tracks south to their end, then take the first left. There's also a newer, nameless *hotel* directly behind Super City, with clean en suite rooms for about Tsh6000.

Some travellers have written to recommend the basic but secure *Moravian Hostel*, just north-east of the centre. They will bring you a bucket of hot water to bathe and food is available.

Super City is the main place in town to eat; the food is OK, but service is slow.

Top Left: Repairing a dhow in Ujiji; the town was historically an important dhow-building centre, and the craft continues to be a thriving local industry. **Top Right:** Boisterous children in Ujiji.
Bottom: Roadside tailors, like this one near Kigoma, do a roaring trade.

CHRISTINE OSBORNE

DAVID WALL

BETHUNE CARMICHAEL

Meeting children is one of the delights of travelling in Tanzania.

Getting There & Away

Bus Local buses to Katavi National Park and Sumbawanga (Tsh5000, six to seven hours) depart from just in front of Super City. There is very little traffic on the road towards Uvinza.

Train If you are heading from Mpanda to Kigoma, the train is the best option. Mpanda is linked with the main Kigoma to Dar es Salaam line by a train that runs three times weekly between Mpanda and Tabora via Kaliua. You can get out and wait for the connection at Kaliua, however as there are few guesthouses and little to do, most travellers continue on until Tabora and wait there. Between Mpanda and Kigoma there is not an immediate connection; you will have to spend at least one night in either Kaliua or Tabora.

Departures from Mpanda are Tuesday, Thursday and Saturday at 1 pm, reaching Kaliua around 10.30 pm and Tabora around 3 am. Going in the other direction, the train departs Tabora Monday, Wednesday and Friday about 9 pm, arriving in Kaliua after midnight, and in Mpanda sometime the next morning. Fares from Mpanda direct to Dar es Salaam are Tsh29,000/17,200/12,000.

KATAVI NATIONAL PARK

Katavi, about 35km south-west of Mpanda, is one of Tanzania's most unspoiled and beautiful parks. You will likely have the place to yourself, and are almost guaranteed to see animals, particularly around Lake Katavi and Lake Chada. Because so few visitors come here, park staff are exceptionally welcoming and helpful.

Katavi was originally gazetted in 1974 with an area of 2253 sq km. In mid-1998 its area was approximately doubled and the park now encompasses about 4500 sq km. Katavi is noted for its buffalo herds that are said to be among the largest in Tanzania. Other animals you are likely to see include zebra, giraffe, antelope, leopard, crocodile, elephant, lion and hippo. The park is also an excellent place for birdwatching, particularly around its two lakes.

Information

The entry fee is US$15 per person (US$5 for children between the ages of five and 16). Camping costs US$20 per person per night (US$5 for children); guide fees are US$10. There is a US$30 per day vehicle fee. The park is best visited in the dry season, between June and October. In general, the best viewing tends to be off the main road and near the lakes. On the lakeside road you will need to be accompanied by an armed ranger.

Fuel at the park costs Tsh500 per litre, so you will need to budget between Tsh15,000 and Tsh20,000 for an excursion around Lake Katavi, more for a drive to Lake Chada.

Park headquarters are near Sitalike, on the north-eastern edge of the park. For hut bookings or information, contact the senior park warden (PO Box 89 Mpanda).

Places to Stay

Thanks to the fact that it has not been overrun with visitors, Katavi's Chief Nsalambo camp site is in good condition and pleasant. For those without a tent, there is also a well-situated resthouse. You will need to bring all your own provisions, including food and water (or purifying tablets).

Otherwise, there is the *Katavi Tented Camp*, a luxury camp operated by Greystoke Safaris (☎ 057-3629, 2420, fax 2123, 8126, PO Box 425 Arusha) or in Kenya (☎ 254-2-502491, 571647, fax 502739, 571665, email bushhome@africaonline.co.ke, PO Box 56923 Nairobi). The camp is closed between mid-October and mid-December, and from mid-February until early June.

There is no lodging in Sitalike village just outside the park gate, although park staff allow you to come and go to get food and supplies.

Getting There & Away

Bus From Mpanda, take any local bus heading towards Sumbawanga and get off at the gate. Alternatively, it is sometimes possible to find a lift with one of the park vehicles which come frequently to Mpanda for supplies.

From Sumbawanga there is transport most days towards Mpanda along a rough road. It's best to get out at the north gate, near park headquarters.

Boat The MV *Liemba* stops at Sumbwa or Karema, from where you can find transport to Mpanda and Katavi, though you may have to wait for a while. The road is in poor condition.

SUMBAWANGA

Sumbawanga, capital of the Rukwa region and centre of an important agricultural area, is a useful stopping point for those travelling between Zambia and Mpanda or Katavi National Park. Despite the fact that the surrounding area is quite underdeveloped, particularly the transport infrastructure, Sumbawanga is a peppy, pleasant place with a well-stocked market and friendly people.

South-west of Sumbawanga on the Zambian border is **Kalambo Falls**; with a drop of close to 250m, it is the highest waterfall in Africa. The main access route to the falls is from Zambia, via Mbala. You will need your own vehicle. Some travellers have walked to the falls and back in around three or four days.

For lodging in Sumbawanga, try *Upendo View Hotel* on Kiwelu Rd near the market. Basic but clean doubles cost about Tsh5000. You can also get meals here, or at *Sim's Restaurant*, opposite.

Gloria's on Maendeleo St just off Kiwelu Rd also has good meals.

There is at least one bus daily between Sumbawanga and Mpanda (Tsh5000, six to seven hours), as well as occasional Land-rovers. Buses also go several times weekly directly to Mbeya (Tsh8000, at least 10 hours); otherwise, you will need to transfer at Tunduma.

The Southern Highlands

The Southern Highlands (also known as the Southern Arc mountains) stretch from Morogoro in the east to Lake Nyasa and the Zambian border in the west. It's one of Tanzania's most pleasant and scenic regions, offering beautiful hill panoramas, good hiking, and a generally temperate climate.

The region is also one of the country's most important agricultural areas, producing a large percentage of Tanzania's maize, as well as some of its best coffee, tea and numerous other crops. Markets in most towns tend to be abundant and colourful.

On the northern edge of the highlands is Dodoma, Tanzania's official capital and seat of the ruling CCM party. To the east, between Morogoro and Iringa, is Mikumi National Park, one of Tanzania's most accessible protected areas, and Udzungwa Mountains National Park, a paradise for hikers and birdwatchers. The scenic Uluguru mountains near Morogoro also offer good hiking, and host an exceptional number of endemic plant and bird species. Further west, past Iringa, is the beautiful and unspoiled Ruaha National Park, which is home to one of Africa's largest elephant populations. The Mbeya and Kipengere mountain ranges near Lake Nyasa offer good scenery and hiking, as do the Livingstone mountains on the lake's eastern shore. Most of the tiny lake shore villages are very relaxing, though undeveloped and rarely visited other than by those affiliated with missions in the area.

While many travellers pass through the Southern Highlands en route to or from Malawi or Zambia, few stop along the way although there is much of interest. Facilities in most places are more than adequate and main routes are in generally good condition. For those seeking opportunities to hike, bike or just relax, the area is ideal.

DODOMA

Dodoma lies in the geographic centre of the country at a height of about 1100m. Al-

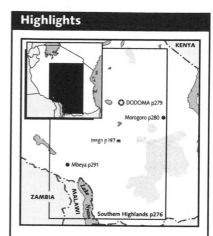

Highlights

- **Ruaha National Park** – explore the vast and beautiful territory which hosts one of the largest elephant populations in Africa

- **Udzungwa Mountains National Park** – hike in one of Tanzania's most beautiful wilderness areas

- **Iringa & Songea** – hunt for bargains in the colourful, abundant markets

- **Around Lake Nyasa** – enjoy good walking in the hill country around the lake

though the town was located along the old caravan route which connected Lake Tanganyika and Central Africa with the sea, it did not take on significance until the construction of the Central Line railway just after the turn of the century. Since 1973, Dodoma has been Tanzania's official capital and headquarters of the ruling CCM party. According to the original plan, the entire government was to move to Dodoma by the mid-1980s, and the town was to be expanded to ultimately encompass more than

THE SOUTHERN HIGHLANDS

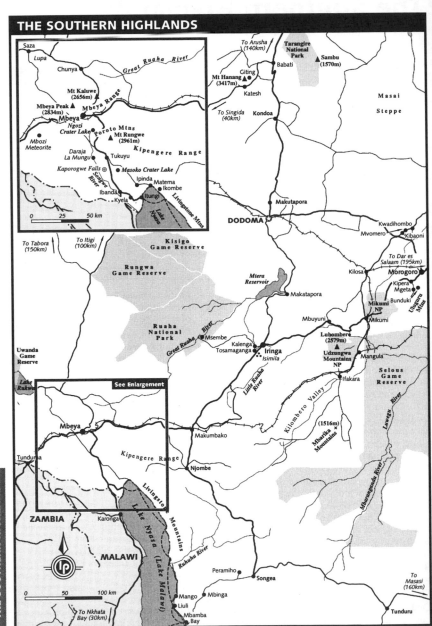

300,000 residents, all living in smaller independent communities set up along the lines of the *ujamaa* (familyhood) village. The plans proved unrealistic for a variety of reasons, including lack of any sort of viable economic base and an insufficient water supply, and have therefore been abandoned. Today, although the legislature meets in Dodoma, the economic and political centre of the country remains in Dar es Salaam.

With the advent of the railway, Dodoma also became an important mission centre and today the town is notable for its many different churches

There is not much reason for travellers to come to Dodoma. However, if you find yourself in the region, the town's agreeable climate and relaxed, friendly atmosphere make it a pleasant place to spend a few days.

Information

Dodoma is the headquarters of Mission Aviation Fellowship (☎ 354036), at the air-field. In the case of a serious medical emergency, they may be able to offer evacuation assistance.

Water supply can be a problem in Dodoma, particularly during the dry season and especially at some of the cheaper hotels.

Dangers & Annoyances

Exercise caution if using a camera in and around Dodoma. Many of the buildings are considered government buildings, and photography is prohibited in most areas.

Things to See & Do

Lion Rock, overlooking Dodoma from the north-east, offers good views and makes a pleasant hike. Don't take any valuables up with you and go in a group if possible, as muggings are not uncommon. It's about a 45 minute walk to the top. To get to Lion Rock, ask any dalla-dalla heading out the Arusha road to drop you nearby, or else take a taxi. Don't leave your vehicle unattended at the

The Kolo Rock Paintings

Ancient rock paintings have been found at several sites in Tanzania including near Masasi in the south-east, near Dodoma and Singida on the central plateau, and in the Lake Victoria region. One of the most well known and extensive sites is that near Kolo, just north of Kondoa and about 180km north of Dodoma.

Little is known about either the artists or the age of the Kolo paintings (also referred to as the Kondoa rock paintings). One theory maintains that they were made by the Sandawe, who are distantly related linguistically to South Africa's San (Bushmen), a group also known for their rock art. Others say that the paintings, particularly some of the more recent ones, were done by various Bantu-speaking peoples who moved into the area at a later date. Some of the paintings are believed to date back more than 3000 years, while others are much more recent, probably not more than a few hundred years old.

Many of the paintings, which range in colour from white to shades of red, orange and brown, are simplified portrayals of human beings, often pursuing activities such as hunting or playing musical instruments. Others are of various animals, notably giraffe and antelope. Still others are unintelligible forms, perhaps early attempts at abstract art. It is assumed that the paintings were made at least in part using the hands and fingers, as well as perhaps brushes made of reeds or sticks. Some of the colours were probably made by mixing various pigments with animal fat to form crayons.

Those interested in a detailed analysis of the paintings can read the article *Some Common Aspects of the Rock Paintings of Kondoa and Singida* printed in *Tanzania Notes and Records* (1976, volumes 77 and 78), from which much of this information was extracted.

base. Although it's also enticing, the hill to the south-west of town near the prison is off-limits for hiking.

Near the Dodoma Hotel is a small geological **museum**, although it's in very substandard condition these days.

The area around Kolo, 180km north of Dodoma and just north of Kondoa, is known for its centuries-old rock paintings. See the boxed text on the previous page.

Places to Stay

For those on a tight budget, the *Saxon Guest House* not far from the train station has basic but acceptable singles/doubles for Tsh2000/2500.

In the centre of town on the grounds of the Anglican church is the *Christian Council of Tanzania (CCT) Compound*, with basic singles/doubles for Tsh5500/9000.

Dodoma Hotel (Railway Hotel) near the train station has faded singles/doubles for Tsh12,000/18,000.

Tanzania's Wine Industry

Dodoma is the centre of Tanzania's tiny wine industry, and one of the few wine-producing areas in Africa south of Morocco and Algeria and north of South Africa. There are vineyards throughout the surrounding area.

Dodoma's vineyards were first started by Italian missionaries earlier in this century. Many are still run by the missions, and much of the wine produced is for church use. However, over the years there has been enough sold by the state-run wine company to make the industry an economically significant one for the region.

The quality of the commercially produced wine has traditionally been decidedly inferior, although it has improved significantly in recent years. If you are interested in visiting one of the wine cellars, a good place to start is the Tanganyika Vineyards Company, just out of town to the south of the Dar es Salaam road.

The best place to stay in Dodoma is the *Vocational Training Centre* (☎ 324154). Comfortable singles/doubles are Tsh10,000/14,000 with fans, bathroom and breakfast. It's several kilometres south-east of town, to the south of the Dar es Salaam road.

Nam Hotel in Area C is a step down, but has decent singles/doubles for Tsh9000/12,000, and a more luxurious suite for Tsh24,000. To get here, take the second right after the airfield and follow the signs. It's a 30 minute walk from the centre on foot.

Also in Area C is the *Tiger Hotel & Restaurant* with acceptable singles/doubles for Tsh6600/15,000 including breakfast, though it's a bit of a brothel. To get here, turn right immediately after the airfield, then left at the sign for the hotel.

Places to Eat

All of the places listed in the previous Places to Stay section have restaurants. By far the best is the restaurant at the *Vocational Training Centre*, where good meals average Tsh4000; there is also a bar with TV.

The next best is probably the restaurant at *Nam Hotel*. It's slightly cheaper, although neither the food nor service are as good as at the Vocational Training Centre.

If you eat at *Tiger Hotel* allow plenty of time; meals take at least an hour to arrive.

Aladdin's, in the centre of town just next to the Esso station on the main roundabout, is the place to go for soft ice cream. It's closed on Monday.

Entertainment

Climax Swimming Club has Dodoma's only pool, as well as a squash court, sauna, dartboard, bar and TV. Day membership costs Tsh1500. It's a few kilometres to the west of town past the prison.

Tiger Restaurant has a large courtyard bar area with TV that is popular in the evenings.

Shopping

There are some good crafts available in Dodoma, notably *marimbas* (musical instruments played with the thumb), *vibuyu* (carved gourds), wooden stools, and other

items made by the local Gogo people. Good quality sisal crafts are available from the prison to the west of town, although you generally have to place an order in advance.

Getting There & Away

Air There are no scheduled commercial flights to Dodoma. There is an airstrip for charter flights.

Bus There are daily buses connecting Dodoma with Morogoro (Tsh3000, five to seven hours) and Dar es Salaam (Tsh4500, seven to nine hours). For Dar es Salaam, the last bus in either direction leaves around 11 am.

Buses run several times a week between Dodoma and Iringa via Makatapora. See the Iringa Getting There & Away section for more information.

There are also buses a few times a week from Dodoma to Singida and north to Arusha via Kondoa. Both roads are long and rough. If you need accommodation in **Singida**, there are several local guesthouses in the centre of town. Otherwise, try the more comfortable *Legho Hotel* on the edge

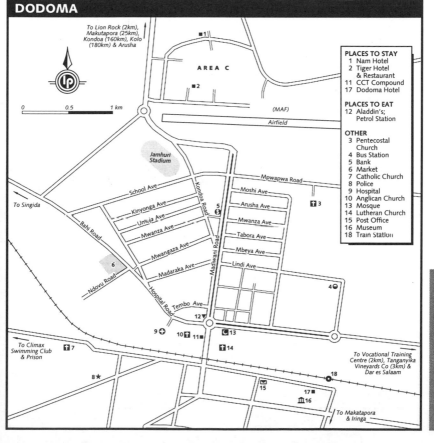

DODOMA

To Lion Rock (2km),
Makutapora (25km),
Kondoa (160km), Kolo
(180km) & Arusha

AREA C

(MAF)

Airfield

Jamhuri
Stadium

To Singida

School Ave

Kinyonga Ave

Umoja Ave

Mwanza Ave

Mwangaza Ave

Madaraka Ave

Ndovu Road

Bahi Road

Hospital Road

Tembo Ave

Kondoa Road

Madiwani Road

Mpwapwa Road

Moshi Ave

Arusha Ave

Mwanza Ave

Tabora Ave

Mbeya Ave

Lindi Ave

To Climax
Swimming Club
& Prison

To Vocational Training
Centre (2km), Tanganyika
Vineyards Co (3km) &
Dar es Salaam

To Makatapora
& Iringa

PLACES TO STAY
1 Nam Hotel
2 Tiger Hotel
  & Restaurant
11 CCT Compound
17 Dodoma Hotel

PLACES TO EAT
12 Aladdin's;
   Petrol Station

OTHER
3 Pentecostal
  Church
4 Bus Station
5 Bank
6 Market
7 Catholic Church
8 Police
9 Hospital
10 Anglican Church
13 Mosque
14 Lutheran Church
15 Post Office
16 Museum
18 Train Station

0   0.5   1 km

THE SOUTHERN HIGHLANDS

of town, which has nice gardens and decent rooms for about Tsh10,000.

Train Dodoma lies along the Central Line railway connecting Dar es Salaam with Kigoma and Mwanza. Fares between Dodoma and Dar es Salaam are Tsh13,900/11,500/6200 for 1st/2nd/3rd class. See the Getting Around chapter for further details.

Getting Around

Taxis charge about Tsh1000 for rides within Dodoma, including to Area C.

MOROGORO

Morogoro is an attractive town set at the foot of the Uluguru mountains. It is one of Tanzania's most important agricultural areas, and if you venture up into the hills you will see numerous farm plots with all sorts of fruit and vegetables, as well as coffee and other crops. Morogoro is also an important educational and mission station. Sokoine University, Tanzania's major agricultural institute, as well as several church seminaries are located here.

Information

There are no foreign exchange bureaus. Both the CRDB and the National Microfinance Bank change travellers cheques, though you may be required to show your purchase receipt.

Telephone calls can be made at the telecom building next to the post office; fax services are also available. Card phones are located by the post office, the Morogoro and Hilux hotels and near the bus stand. There were no online services available when this book was being researched, but one is scheduled to open near the CRDB bank; ask at the Sheriff Q Kays shop for information.

For medical attention, your best bet is to go to Dar es Salaam. The pharmacy opposite Lukanda Family Lodging & Hotel is well-stocked.

The Morogoro Art Gallery & Gift Shop on Machupa Rd has a small, fairly pricey selection of crafts.

Things to See & Do

Other than hiking (see the following section), there is not too much to do within

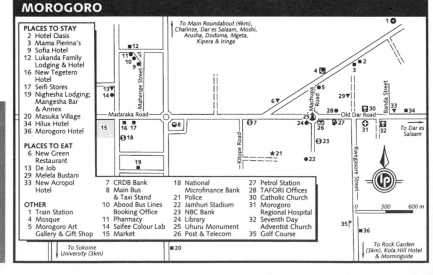

MOROGORO

PLACES TO STAY
2 Hotel Oasis
3 Mama Pierina's
9 Sofia Hotel
12 Lukanda Family Lodging & Hotel
16 New Tegetero Hotel
17 Seifi Stores
19 Nighesha Lodging; Mangesha Bar & Annex
20 Masuka Village
34 Hilux Hotel
36 Morogoro Hotel

PLACES TO EAT
6 New Green Restaurant
13 De Job
29 Melela Bustani
33 New Acropol Hotel

OTHER
1 Train Station
4 Mosque
5 Morogoro Art Gallery & Gift Shop
7 CRDB Bank
8 Main Bus & Taxi Stand
10 Abood Bus Lines Booking Office
11 Pharmacy
14 Saifee Colour Lab
15 Market
18 National Microfinance Bank
21 Police
22 Jamhuri Stadium
23 NBC Bank
24 Library
25 Uhuru Monument
26 Post & Telecom
27 Petrol Station
28 TAFORI Offices
30 Catholic Church
31 Morogoro Regional Hospital
32 Seventh Day Adventist Church
35 Golf Course

To Main Roundabout (4km), Chalinze, Dar es Salaam, Moshi, Arusha, Dodoma, Mgeta, Kipera & Iringa

Mahenge Street
Machupa Road
Banda Street
Madaraka Road
Kitope Road
Rwegasore Street
Old Dar Road

To Dar es Salaam

To Sokoine University (3km)

To Rock Garden (3km), Kola Hill Hotel & Morningside

0   300   600 m

Morogoro itself unless you like golf; the course opposite the Morogoro Hotel is considered to be good. The nonmember green fee is Tsh6000, plus Tsh1000 for a caddy for nine holes. The **rock garden** (Tsh500 admission fee), about 3km south of the main road, is not worth visiting, although the surrounding area is attractive. The market sometimes has good buys on textiles.

Morogoro is a good base for excursions to Mikumi National Park, although you'll need to have your own vehicle or arrange to hire one in Dar es Salaam. See the Mikumi National Park section later in this chapter.

Hiking There are many good hikes in the hills surrounding Morogoro. One of the more popular ones is to **Morningside**, an old German mountain hut to the south of town. It takes between one and two hours to reach the hut. The Morogoro Hotel can help you arrange a guide, although you don't need one; just follow the road. Staying overnight at the hut is no longer possible. The radio station further up the mountain is off-limits.

The **Uluguru mountains** (see the boxed text) offer some very good hiking, although tourist infrastructure is essentially nonexistent. A good starting point is Mgeta, about 25km south of the Iringa road. From here, you can hike north-east towards Bunduki (about 10km), further north towards Mzumbe, back near the main highway, or to any of the many nearby villages. Some of the views along the way are superb. Guides can be hired locally. There are a few basic guesthouses in Mgeta, and a simple but comfortable resthouse in Nyandira village, about 4km beyond Mgeta, run by Sokoine University in Morogoro. If you want to stay at the resthouse, stop first at the university to make arrangements. Basic food supplies are available in Mgeta.

To get to Mgeta from Morogoro via public transport, take a dalla-dalla to Kipera on the main road, from where there is sporadic transport to Mgeta and Nyandira. If you're driving your own vehicle you will need a 4WD; allow about three hours for the trip. Hiking is only feasible during the dry season.

The Uluguru Mountains

The Uluguru mountains to the south-east of Morogoro are part of the Eastern Arc chain which runs up to the Taita Hills in Kenya. (See the boxed text 'The Eastern Arc Mountains' in the North-East Tanzania chapter.) They contain some of the oldest original forest in Africa; parts are estimated to be about 25 million years old. The forest provides shelter for a rich variety of bird, plant and insect life with a high degree of endemism. In addition to numerous endemic plants, endemic bird species which have been identified here include the Uluguru bushshrike and Loveridge's sunbird. The only comparable mountain forest area in East Africa, as far as age and endemism are concerned, is the Usambaras in north-east Tanzania.

The Ulugurus, which reach to more than 2500m, are also the source of the Ruvu river which supplies Dar es Salaam with drinking water and – together with the Pangani river – with much of its hydroelectric supply. You cross the Ruvu on the main road towards Morogoro between Dar es Salaam and Chalinze.

The main ethnic group in the mountains are the matrilineal Luguru, who earn their living primarily through subsistence agriculture. Due to the relatively high population density in the Ulugurus, most of the original forest cover has been depleted – you'll see this right away on the hillsides – with only a few small protected patches remaining. Accompanying the deforestation has come severe erosion.

The Wildlife Conservation Society of Tanzania in Dar es Salaam is a good source of information on the Ulugurus, as is Sokoine University in Morogoro. The university can also assist with information about the resthouse in Nyandira.

Places to Stay

For those on a tight budget, the best place is the basic but friendly *Lukanda Family Lodging & Hotel* just around the corner from the Abood Bus Lines booking office. Doubles with common bathroom are Tsh2500. In a ground floor annex are singles with bathroom for Tsh3500. No meals are available, but there are several local food stalls nearby.

Other places to try are *Nighesha Lodging* a few blocks south of the market and bus station with basic singles for Tsh1500, and *Mangesha Bar & Annex* next door with small but clean doubles with net and fan for Tsh3000 (Tsh3500 with bathroom). The only drawback to the latter place is its noisy bar.

New Tegetero Hotel, on the main road near the bus stand, is a step up though rooms are noisy. Singles/doubles are Tsh4800/6000 (Tsh5400/6600 with bathroom), including continental breakfast.

In the mid-range, *Mama Pierina's* (☎ 4640) off Machupa Rd has deteriorated somewhat but is still decent value. Singles/doubles with mosquito nets, fan and bathroom are Tsh6000/7200 including breakfast.

Masuka Village (☎ 4774) is in a leafy area about 1km south of the main road. Its rooms are good value at Tsh7200 for a double with bathroom.

Sofia Hotel (☎ 4847) near the bus stand on Mahenge St has singles/doubles for Tsh6000/7000 including breakfast (Tsh9000/10,000 with bathroom).

Two places used frequently by business travellers are *Hotel Oasis* (☎ 3535) with comfortable singles/doubles for Tsh25,000/30,000 including breakfast, and *Hilux Hotel* (☎ 3066, 3946), with rooms from Tsh18,000 (Tsh22,000 in the new wing). The Oasis is next door to Mama Pierina's; the Hilux is on Old Dar Rd, 300m past the Catholic church.

Several readers have written to recommend the *Kola Hill Hotel* off the main road not far from the Rock Garden with comfortable, good value doubles for about Tsh12,000 (Tsh18,000 with air-con).

The most expensive option is *Morogoro Hotel* (☎ 3270, 4001) opposite the golf course, with comfortable but overpriced bungalows for US$60/65/85 a single/double/triple including full breakfast for residents. The hotel is frequently used for receptions

and other functions, so if you want to be assured of peace and quiet check before booking that nothing is scheduled.

Places to Eat

Melela Bustani has an excellent, upscale gourmet shop with ice cream, cakes, wine, breads, and other delicacies, all home-made. It's on a small path behind the Catholic church, and is open from 10 am to 5.30 pm Tuesday to Friday and from 10 am to 1 pm on Saturday.

For inexpensive food, try the restaurant at *New Tegetero Hotel*, or the tiny *De Job* food stall near Lukanda Family Lodging and just down from Saifee Colour Lab.

Masuka Village also has a pleasant restaurant, though it's a bit on the expensive side. *Mama Pierina's* does a mixture of Italian and local dishes. Portions are large, but the food is very average.

New Green Restaurant does good Indian dishes and other food for between Tsh2500 and Tsh5000.

The recently renovated *New Acropol Hotel* (☎ 3403) next to Hilux Hotel is a pricey but good restaurant favoured by resident expatriates. Meals are about Tsh5000 or more.

Entertainment

New Acropol Hotel and *Hilux* have popular bars. There is a disco on many weekends at *Morogoro Hotel*.

Getting There & Away

Bus Buses go throughout the day to Dar es Salaam (Tsh1000 to Tsh1500, 3½ hours) from 5.45 am. The best lines are Saddiq or Islam; buy tickets at the bus stand. The Abood line has the most frequent buses, but they have a reputation for high speed and unsafe driving. Their ticket office is around the corner from Sofia Hotel. Minibuses also run throughout the day, but are slower and much more crowded.

There's at least one bus daily to Moshi and Arusha via Chalinze (Tsh4000, eight hours to Moshi, nine to 10 hours to Arusha), usually departing about 8 am.

To Dodoma, there are daily minibuses (Tsh3000, six to seven hours), and a large bus (Mbaraka line) every other day; departures are at 7 am. Otherwise, you can go up to the main roundabout (known locally as the 'Msamvu keep-left'), about 5km from the centre and try to catch one of the Dar es Salaam to Dodoma buses there, though they are often full so you will probably have to stand. The buses stop about 200m down from the roundabout on the Dodoma Rd, usually arriving from Dar es Salaam between 8.30 and 9.30 am, daily.

Train Morogoro lies on the Central Line connecting Dar es Salaam with Mwanza and Kigoma. To Dar es Salaam, it's several hours faster to travel by bus.

MIKUMI NATIONAL PARK

Mikumi is Tanzania's third largest national park and the most accessible from Dar es Salaam. It's an ideal place for those who do not have a lot of time, but want to see a large variety of wildlife. Within its 3230 sq km set between the Uluguru mountains to the north and the Lumango mountains to the south-east, Mikumi hosts populations of buffalo, giraffe, elephant, lion, zebra, leopard, crocodile and many others. It is likely that you'll see at least some of these within just a short time of entering the park. Although Mikumi receives comparatively few visitors, those who do come rarely leave disappointed. In the section of the park to the west of the main road, there is a hippo pool which provides an excellent opportunity to watch the animals at close range. This is also a good place for observing varied water birds.

Mikumi is a significant educational and research centre. Among the various projects being carried out is an ongoing field study of yellow baboons, which are numerous here. It's one of just a handful of such long-term primate studies on the continent.

To the west of Mikumi, around Mbuyuni, is an enormous and striking collection of baobab trees stretching along the side of the main road.

Information

The entry fee to Mikumi is US$15 per person per day (US$5 for children between five and 16 years old, free for those under five), plus a US$30 per day vehicle fee. Camping costs US$20 per person per night (US$5 for children).

The park can be visited year-round. The best animal viewing is in the western section. For information or camp site bookings, contact the Senior Park Warden, PO Box 62 Mikumi. Those with research interests can contact the Animal Behavioural Research Unit at Mikumi.

The booklet *Mikumi National Park*, edited by Deborah Snellson and published by TANAPA is somewhat dated, but nevertheless well worth reading by those interested in more detailed information on the park. It's available at bookshops in Dar es Salaam and Arusha for about Tsh3000.

Places to Stay

The most popular place to stay is *Mikumi Wildlife Camp*, with comfortable cottage-style accommodation for US$100 per person sharing with full-board. There is also dormitory accommodation for US$50/37/30/25 per person in groups of two/three/four/five people not including meals. Book through Oyster Bay Hotel (☎ 051-668062, fax 668631, email oysterbay-hotel@twiga.com, PO Box 2261 Dar es Salaam). Accommodation can be paid for with credit card in advance at the Oyster Bay Hotel; no credit cards are accepted at the camp itself. The camp is just west of the main road, near the park entrance.

The other accommodation in the park, *Mikumi Wildlife Lodge*, is somewhat cheaper, with rooms from about US$45, but more run-down. Book through park headquarters or any Dar es Salaam travel agent. The lodge is in the southern half of the park, about 3km east of the main road.

Also inside the park are several camp sites; you will need to bring a tent and all provisions.

In Mikumi town, *Genesis Motel*, about 1.5km from the main junction on the Dar es

Salaam road, has simple but clean and inexpensive rooms. There are also decent rooms available for about Tsh6000 at the *guesthouse* behind Mikumi hospital.

About 55km west of Mikumi and 20km east of Mbuyuni is *Baobab Valley Campground* (☎ 0812-785296, email snail79 @hotmail.com), a pleasant riverside place offering both catered and self-catered camping. They have horses, kayaking, guided mountain hikes, fishing and other activities. There are self-contained chalets for those without tents. Overland groups are welcome. The camp site is signposted, about 1km off the main road. To reach here via public transport take any local bus heading between Iringa and Mikumi.

Getting There & Away

Although getting to the gate of Mikumi is easy via public transport (take any of the buses running along the Morogoro-Iringa highway), there is no vehicle rental at the park. Efforts to hitch a ride are generally futile, so you'll need your own car.

Vehicle rental and tours of Mikumi are best arranged with any of the Dar es Salaam rental agencies or tour operators. Coastal Travels has minivan service to Mikumi. A one-night, two-day safari costs Tsh200,000 for a group of up to seven, excluding accommodation, food and park fees. Allow about four hours driving time from Dar es Salaam. The road is good tarmac the entire way. If you are driving your own vehicle, remember that speed limits on the section of main highway inside the park are controlled.

The train tracks running through the west of the park link the Central Line with TAZARA; there is no passenger service on this route.

UDZUNGWA MOUNTAINS NATIONAL PARK

Udzungwa Mountains National Park is a paradise for hikers and one of Tanzania's most beautiful wilderness areas. Its most striking feature, apart from its mountainous terrain, is its pristine and biologically diverse forest which hosts a variety of animal and plant species not found anywhere else in the world. Among its residents are six species of primates, including the rare Iringa red colobus and the Sange crested mangabey monkeys, as well as populations of elephant, buffalo, leopard, and a rich variety of birdlife. The rare Udzungwa partridge is endemic to the area and has been sighted near the park's boundaries.

The high degree of endemism and biodiversity that characterises Udzungwa is due mainly to the area's constant climate over millions of years, which has given species a chance to evolve. Another factor is Udzungwa's altitudinal range. From the low-lying Kilombero Valley south-west of Udzungwa (at approximately 200m) to Luhombero peak (2579m), there is essentially continuous forest. The area is one of the few places in Africa with continuous rainforest over such a great span.

There are no roads in Udzungwa; instead, there are about four major and several lesser hiking paths winding through various sections of the park. Popular hikes include a short but steep half-day hike to Sange waterfalls, and a two day climb to the top of Luhombero, Udzungwa's highest peak.

Udzungwa, which has an area of 1900 sq km, was gazetted in 1992 and is Tanzania's newest national park.

Information

Entry costs US$15 per person per day (US$5 for children between five and 16 years old, and free for children under five). It's US$20 per person per night for camping (US$5 for children), and US$10 for a guide.

The park is best visited between July and October. Hikes can be steep in parts and you must be accompanied by a guide. Both day and overnight hikes are possible; to visit the plateau where the best animal viewing is you should allow two to three days. A book detailing species of birds would be a good thing to bring along as none are available at the park.

Headquarters are located in Mang'ula, 60km south of Mikumi town. For information, you need to contact the Senior Park

Warden (☎ Ifakara 24), Udzungwa Mountains National Park, PO Box 99 Mang'ula. Those with a serious research or scientific interest in Udzungwa can contact the Udzungwa Mountains National Park Monitoring Program (email bios@hotmail.com).

Places to Stay & Eat

There are three camp sites inside the park with fireplaces and a nearby stream. You will need to bring a tent and all your own supplies with you.

Just outside the park in Mang'ula is *Twiga Guesthouse* (☎ *Mang'ula 31 or 056-3357)*, with simple but decent singles/doubles with nets for Tsh2500/3500. It's a five minute walk from Twiga to park headquarters.

Another five minute walk down the road is *Udzungwa Mountain View Hotel*, with somewhat more luxurious rooms for Tsh9000 per person. You can also camp here for Tsh2000 per person.

Both hotels serve simple meals. Basic supplies are available at Mwaya village, about 25 minutes on foot from park headquarters. Twiga Guesthouse also has a small shop stocking some basics, including mineral water. If you'll be staying for a while, it's not a bad idea to bring a supply of dried fruit and nuts with you as the diet available in Mang'ula is not particularly varied or vitamin-rich.

Getting There & Away

Bus To reach Udzungwa via public transport, take any bus or dalla-dalla to Mikumi town, on the Morogoro to Iringa road. From the Mikumi junction, there are pick-ups and minibuses which run several times a day south to Mang'ula (Tsh700 to Tsh1000, three hours), on the Ifakara road.

Train For budget travellers, the easiest way to reach Udzungwa is via the TAZARA line to Mang'ula station, from where park headquarters is about a 30 minute walk. Note that express trains do not stop in Mang'ula; you will have to catch an ordinary train. The train from Dar es Salaam arrives in Mang'ula about 8 pm.

IRINGA

Iringa is an attractive town set on a 1600m bluff overlooking the valley of the Little Ruaha river. The town was initially built up by the Germans at the turn of the century as bastion against the Hehe, the major ethnic group in the surrounding area. Now Iringa is a district capital, and the centre of an important agricultural region. With its picturesque setting and pleasantly cool climate, Iringa makes a good base for exploring the surrounding region.

Things to See & Do

Iringa has a well stocked **market** with all sorts of fruits and vegetables, as well as large, locally made **Iringa baskets**. Nearby, in front of the police station, is a **monument** to the Africans who fell during the Maji Maji uprising between 1905 and 1907.

The hills surrounding Iringa are ideal for **walking**. To the north-east of town is **Gangilonga Rock**, where Chief Mkwawa often used to go to meditate, and where he learned that the Germans were after him (see the boxed text 'Chief Mkwawa'). Gangilonga, which means 'talking stone' in Hehe, offers good views over Iringa. It's just a few minutes walk to the top.

Places to Stay

Camping Some distance outside Iringa are two good camping options. *Kisolanza Farm* charges US$3 per person, including a hot shower. You'll need to bring your own food, though you can often buy vegetables there. Overland groups are welcome. It's about 50km south-west of Iringa and about 1km off the main road to Mbeya. There are also rooms in the farmhouse or in cottages for US$50 per person including breakfast.

About 50km north-east of Iringa, and about 2km off the main road towards Morogoro is *Riverside Camp site*. It charges the same rates, has hot showers and also welcomes overland groups. You'll need to bring your own food.

Hotels & Guesthouses The best budget accommodation option in Iringa is at the

Chief Mkwawa

Mkwawa, chief of the Hehe and one of German colonialism's most vociferous resistors, is a legendary figure in Tanzanian history. He is particularly revered in Iringa, near which he had his headquarters.

Under Mkwawa's leadership during the second half of the 19th century, the Hehe became one of the most powerful tribes in central Tanzania. They overpowered one group after another until by the late 1880s they were threatening trade traffic along the caravan route from western Tanzania to Bagamoyo. In 1891, after several attempts by Mkwawa to negotiate with the Germans were rejected, his men trounced the colonial troops in the infamous battle of Lugalo, just outside Iringa on the Mikumi road. The next year, Mkwawa's troops launched a damaging attack on a German fort at Kilosa, further to the east. The Germans placed a bounty on his head and, once they had regrouped, initiated a counter attack in which Mkwawa's headquarters at Kalenga were taken. Mkwawa escaped, but later, in 1898, committed suicide rather than surrender to a contingent that had been sent after him. His head was cut off and the skull sent to Germany where it sat almost forgotten (though not by the Hehe) until it was returned to Kalenga in 1954. The return of Mkwawa's remains was due in large part to the efforts of Sir Edward Twining, then the British governor of colonial Tanganyika.

Today, the skull of Mkwawa and some old weapons are on display at the Kalenga museum.

Lutheran Centre (☎ 2286), which has basic but clean singles/doubles from Tsh1700/2500 (Tsh3000 for a single with bathroom). It's at the end of Kawawa Rd.

If they are full, there are numerous local guesthouses throughout town, most of which are very seamy. Two of the better ones are *Taj Lodge* (☎ 2332) on the main road, with rooms for Tsh2500/3000, and *Santiago Lodge & Pub* on Kawawa Rd, with rooms from Tsh2000/2500.

A step up is *Ruaha International Lodge* (☎ 2746) on the corner of Kawawa Rd and Titi St, with singles/doubles for Tsh2500/4000 (Tsh3500/4500 with bathroom). There is a disco here on Friday and Saturday nights.

Iringa has several good mid-range options. One of the nicest places is the *Huruma Baptist Conference Centre* (☎ 2579), set on large grounds about 3km from the centre down Mkwawa Rd near the Danish School. It has comfortable, quiet singles/doubles/triples with bathroom for Tsh8500/12,000/15,000, including breakfast; good lunches and dinners can be arranged on request. You can also camp for Tsh4200 per person including use of showers. If you are without your own vehicle, dalla-dallas run every hour or so from the nearby intersection to the bus station beginning from about 7 am.

Isimila Hotel, at the northern end of town on the main road, has comfortable singles/doubles for Tsh6000/8000 including continental breakfast.

Iringa Hotel (formerly the Railway Hotel), one block north-east of the main road and one block south-east of Kawawa Rd, has doubles (only) for Tsh10,000. There's no train in Iringa: the hotel was built and optimistically named when the routing of the TAZARA line was still in the planning stages. The rail line was ultimately routed south-east of Iringa by Ifakara.

In the centre of town on Mkwawa Rd next to the bus stand is the pleasant and modern *MR Hotel* (☎ 2006, fax 2661) with clean, good value rooms with TV from Tsh15,000/18,000 and a restaurant with a good selection of meals.

Hasty Tasty Too (see Places to Eat following) is planning to open an inexpensive guesthouse. Inquire at the restaurant to see whether it's operating yet.

Places to Eat

There are many good places to eat in Iringa. For inexpensive local food, try the pleasant *Staff Inn* (☎ 2586) near the market,

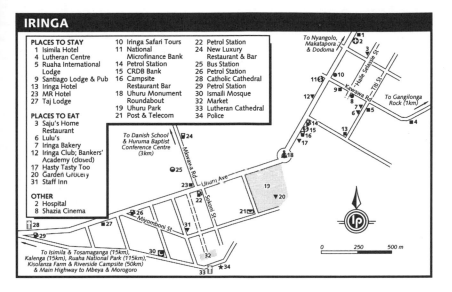

IRINGA

PLACES TO STAY
1 Isimila Hotel
4 Lutheran Centre
5 Ruaha International Lodge
9 Santiago Lodge & Pub
13 Iringa Hotel
23 MR Hotel
27 Taj Lodge

PLACES TO EAT
3 Saju's Home Restaurant
6 Lulu's
7 Iringa Bakery
12 Iringa Club; Bankers' Academy (closed)
17 Hasty Tasty Too
20 Garden Grocery
31 Staff Inn

OTHER
2 Hospital
8 Shazia Cinema
10 Iringa Safari Tours
11 National Microfinance Bank
14 Petrol Station
15 CRDB Bank
16 Campsite Restaurant Bar
18 Uhuru Monument Roundabout
19 Uhuru Park
21 Post & Telecom
22 Petrol Station
24 New Luxury Restaurant & Bar
25 Bus Station
26 Petrol Station
28 Catholic Cathedral
29 Petrol Station
30 Ismaili Mosque
32 Market
33 Lutheran Cathedral
34 Police

Garden Grocery in Uhuru Park or *Saju's Home Restaurant*, on Haile Selassie St at the north end of town.

For western dishes in a pleasant atmosphere, the two best places are Hasty Tasty Too and Lulu's. *Hasty Tasty Too* (☎ 2061), on Uhuru Ave and open from 7.30 am to 8 pm daily, has good breakfasts, yoghurt, shakes, and a variety of reasonably priced main dishes. It's *the* place to meet people in Iringa. The owners, Shaffin and his father Karim, are a good source of information on Iringa and the surrounding area and can assist in arranging excursions. They can also arrange food if you are planning to camp in Ruaha National Park. Hasty Tasty also runs the *Iringa Club* behind the old Bankers' Academy. It's open for evening meals only from 6 to 10 pm.

The Greek-owned *Lulu's* (☎ 2122) is a quiet and friendly place with a pleasant dining area and a varied menu selection, including soft-serve ice cream. There's a small boutique in the restaurant selling good quality crafts from various areas of Tanzania. The restaurant is open from 8.30 am to 3 pm

and 6.30 to 9 pm Monday to Saturday. It's one block south-east of the main road near Kawawa Rd.

Next to Lulu's is the *Iringa Bakery* with fresh rolls and bread.

Iringa Hotel has a decent restaurant, though it's more expensive.

Entertainment

Shazia Cinema near Santiago Lodge & Pub shows films most evenings and at weekend matinees (Tsh200, generally B-grade Indian or karate flicks).

Ruaha International Lodge has a popular disco on Friday and Saturday nights (Tsh500/1000 admission for women/men on Fridays, Tsh1000/1500 on Saturdays). It usually gets going around midnight.

Campsite Restaurant near Hasty Tasty Too has a popular bar with dancing on weekends. *New Luxury Restaurant & Bar* on Mkwawa Rd is popular with locals.

Getting There & Away

Buses go every morning to Morogoro (Tsh3500), Dar es Salaam (Tsh5000) and

Mbeya (Tsh4000). The best line is Scandinavian; book tickets a day in advance.

To Dodoma, there is a bus several times a week via Nyangolo and Makatapora (Tsh4000, nine to 12 hours). However, the road is unpaved and in poor condition, particularly between Makatapora and Dodoma, and most travellers go via Morogoro. If you are heading to Dodoma via Makatapora in a private car allow about six hours.

For those driving their own vehicle the Morogoro to Mbeya highway bypasses Iringa town to the south-east of the city.

Getting Around

Bus & Taxi The main dalla-dalla stands are at the bus station and near Uhuru Park; the main taxi stand is opposite the bus station near the market. Buses continuing on to Morogoro or Mbeya will generally drop you at the bus stand along the main highway at the base of the cliff, about 4km from the centre. Taxis between here and town charge Tsh1000.

Car Iringa Safari Tours (☎ 2718) can assist with arranging car rental to Ruaha National Park, but it is expensive (US$220 for one day, US$300 for two days, one night).

Bicycle You can rent bicycles by the market – standard Chinese-made one-speeds and good mountain bikes. Before renting, check the brakes and the gears, as some of the 'mountain' bikes have one speed only.

AROUND IRINGA
Isimila Stone Age Site
About 15km outside of Iringa off the Mbeya road is Isimila, where in the late 1950s archaeologists unearthed one of the most significant Stone Age finds ever identified. The tools found at the site are estimated to be between 60,000 and 100,000 years old. Although the display itself is not particularly exciting, the area behind is attractive and many people come here on weekends for picnics. While it may look inviting, camping isn't considered safe. There is a Tsh500 entry fee.

Isimila is an easy ride on bicycle from Iringa. Otherwise, take a dalla-dalla heading towards Tosamaganga (Tsh300) and ask them to drop you at the Isimila turn-off, from where it's about a 20 minute walk to the site. Taxis usually charge about Tsh5000 round trip.

A good detour on bicycle is nearby **Tosamaganga**, a pretty town set on a hill with a hospital and mission station.

Kalenga
About 15km from Iringa on the road heading to Ruaha National Park is the former Hehe capital of Kalenga. It was here that Chief Mkwawa had his administration until Kalenga fell to the Germans in the 1890s, and it was here that he committed suicide rather than succumb to the German forces. There is a small museum containing Mkwawa's skull and a few other relics from the era. (See the boxed text 'Chief Mkwawa' earlier in this chapter.)

RUAHA NATIONAL PARK
Ruaha National Park is a vast wilderness area which hosts one of the largest elephant populations in Africa. In addition to the elephants, which are estimated to number at least 12,000, the park has large herds of buffalo, as well as greater and lesser kudo, Grant's gazelle, ostrich, cheetah, sable antelope, and more than 400 different bird species. The Great Ruaha River flows through the eastern side of the park and is home to hippo, crocodile and many water birds.

With an area of almost 13,000 sq km, Ruaha National Park is Tanzania's second largest, and is part of an extended ecosystem that also encompasses the adjoining Rungwa and Kisigo game reserves. Much of the park is undulating plateau averaging about 900m in height with occasional rocky outcrops, and mountains in the south and west reaching to about 1600m and 1900m, respectively.

Large areas of Ruaha are unexplored and undeveloped; one of park management's goals is to preserve as much of the territory as possible in a pristine and undisturbed state. Due to Ruaha's vastness and character, you should set aside as much time as you can spare to visit; it's not a place to be discovered on a quick in and out trip.

Information

Park fees are US$15 (US$5 for children between five and 16 years old, and free for infants) plus a US$30 per day vehicle fee. Camping costs US$20 (US$5 for children).

Endangered Elephants?

In the mid-1980s, the situation for Ruaha's elephants – as well as for those in many other parks in Tanzania and East Africa – looked bleak. Numbers were plummeting due to poaching, and no relief was in sight. Now the picture is much brighter. Since 1986, Ruaha's once dwindling population has more than doubled in number. An additional sign that the population is in recovery is the fact that about 25% of the park's estimated 12,000 elephants are two years old or less. Similar gains have been registered in other protected areas in Tanzania. Much of this progress has been attributed to the effects of a world-wide ban on ivory implemented in 1990 by the Convention on International Trade in Endangered Species (CITES) following a vigorous campaign by conservation groups. An additional factor in Ruaha and elsewhere in Tanzania was Operation Uhai, an anti-poaching initiative of the Tanzanian government in collaboration with the military.

Maintaining these gains, however, will be difficult. In 1997 a decision was made to downgrade the CITES ban for several African countries, permitting limited trade in ivory. Although Tanzania is not among these countries, many worry that the downgrade will simply set off poaching again throughout the continent; some claim detrimental effects are already noticeable in anticipation of it coming into effect in 1999.

Another problem is lack of resources. In large parks such as Ruaha or the Selous Game Reserve in the south-east, vast areas are often inaccessible to rangers, particularly during the rainy season, and poaching is difficult to control no matter how much money is available. Inadequate staff and facilities make things even more difficult. While hunting groups can be an important aid to anti-poaching efforts by monitoring the animals within their concessions, they generally only operate about six months of the year. During the rainy season when they are not around, the way is open for poachers. Entrenched interests complicate the picture. Between the elephants on Ruaha's plains and illegal ivory markets in Asia and elsewhere stand a variety of players including the poachers (often local villagers struggling to earn some money), ivory dealers, embassies, and government officials at the highest levels. The potential gains for all involved lead to ruthlessness, and complicate anti-poaching efforts even more: 1kg of ivory is worth about US$300 wholesale and rhino horn is valued at US$2000 per kilogram (or up to US$30,000 for a single horn).

Some argue that one way of promoting elephant conservation in the face of such constraints would be to loosen restrictions on ivory trade even further. They contend that if trade is legalised but controlled, monies raised from ivory sales could be used to support conservation efforts benefiting both animals and local communities. The traded ivory itself would be gathered from culled elephants or from commercial hunting operations. Others counter such proposals, asserting that controls could never be made tight enough to prevent an increase in poaching.

If you are interested in further information, or in contributing financially to anti-poaching and wildlife conservation efforts in Ruaha and in neighbouring Rungwa Game Reserve, contact the Friends of Ruaha Society (PO Box 2118 Ruaha) or Elefriends (PO Box 238 Iringa).

THE SOUTHERN HIGHLANDS

Park headquarters are at Msembe (Senior Park Warden, Ruaha National Park, PO Box 369 Iringa).

The best time to visit Ruaha is between June and November. During the rainy season many of its roads become impassable.

Petrol is occasionally available at the lodges, but it's best to bring your own especially during the rainy season.

Places to Stay

Ruaha River Lodge, about 15km inside the park gate, has a beautiful setting overlooking the river and accommodation in very comfortable stone bandas. The all-inclusive rate including two game drives per day and airport transfers is US$200 per person sharing. The nonfly-in rate is US$100 per person sharing, full-board (US$85 per person for residents). Game drives cost about an extra US$30 per person for half a day. Bookings can be made through Foxtreks (☎ 0811-327760, email fox@tt.sasa.unep.no, PO Box 84 Mufindi) or through Dar es Salaam travel agents.

Mwagusi Safari Camp is a 16-bed luxury tented camp set attractively on the Mwagusi Sand River inside the park about 20km from the gate. Rates are US$250 per person sharing, all-inclusive. A nonfly-in rate of about US$75 per person sharing, full board and not including game drives may also be available. Booking is through Tropic Africa in the UK (☎/fax 020-8846 9363, email tropicafrica.uk@virgin.net, 14 Castelnau, London SW13 9RU).

There is a camp site near park headquarters with bandas or you can pitch your own tent. You'll need to bring all your own food, and either have your own vehicle or arrange in advance for rental at park headquarters (often not feasible during high season).

Getting There & Away

Air Coastal Travels has scheduled flights three times weekly connecting Ruaha with Dar es Salaam and Unguja (US$300 one way). It also runs flights three times weekly between Ruaha and Selous Game Reserve (US$270 one way).

Road Ruaha is about 115km from Iringa. The road is gravel, and generally in decent condition. For budget transport, there are a few supply trucks which go several times a week from Iringa to park headquarters. Ask around at the market for the schedule of the vehicles, or at Hasty Tasty Too for information. You'll have to make arrangements with the lodges or park headquarters in advance to be picked up at the gate, as well as for vehicle rental once in the park. Hitching a lift within Ruaha is usually not feasible.

MBEYA

Mbeya lies in a gap between the verdant Mbeya mountain range to the north and the Poroto mountains to the south-east. It was founded in 1927 as a supply centre for the gold rush at Lupa, to the north. Today, Mbeya is a regional capital, the major town in south-western Tanzania, and centre of one of the country's most important agricultural regions. Coffee, tea, banana and cocoa are among its major crops.

Mbeya is an important transit point on the main road and rail routes connecting Tanzania with Zambia. It's also a convenient stop for travellers heading to or from Malawi via the Songwe river bridge. For those wishing to stay longer, there are many things do in the surrounding region, especially if you are interested in hiking. Most of the hikes suggested in the Tukuyu section (see later) can also be undertaken from Mbeya.

Information

There is one foreign exchange bureau in town, but it doesn't change travellers cheques; cash rates are about equivalent to those at the bank. NBC and the National Microfinance Bank both accept travellers cheques.

Mbeya lies at about 1800m and the climate is pleasantly cool year-round. The best time for hiking is during the dry season, between July and October.

Kodak film is available at the Professional Photo Shop next to the NBC branch on Karume Ave. Konica is also available at a few shops in town.

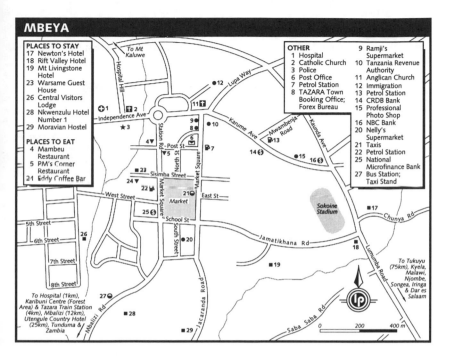

MBEYA

PLACES TO STAY
17 Newton's Hotel
18 Rift Valley Hotel
19 Mt Livingstone Hotel
23 Warsame Guest House
26 Central Visitors Lodge
28 Nkwenzulu Hotel Number 1
29 Moravian Hostel

PLACES TO EAT
4 Mambeu Restaurant
5 PM's Corner Restaurant
24 Eddy Coffee Bar

OTHER
1 Hospital
2 Catholic Church
3 Police
6 Post Office
7 Petrol Station
8 TAZARA Town Booking Office; Forex Bureau
9 Ramji's Supermarket
10 Tanzania Revenue Authority
11 Anglican Church
12 Immigration
13 Petrol Station
14 CRDB Bank
15 Professional Photo Shop
16 NBC Bank
20 Nelly's Supermarket
21 Taxis
22 Petrol Station
25 National Microfinance Bank
27 Bus Station; Taxi Stand

Dangers & Annoyances

As a major transport junction, Mbeya attracts a lot of transients, particularly in the area around the bus station. Watch out for your luggage here and avoid walking alone through the small valley behind the station.

Places to Stay – Budget

If you don't mind being a bit out of town, the best budget lodging is at **Karibuni Centre** (☎ 3035, 4178), about 4km from the centre in Forest Area. It's run by Swiss missionaries, and has nice, clean rooms (doubles only) for Tsh4000 (Tsh6000 with bathroom); meals are available. Dalla-dallas to the centre pass nearby (Tsh100).

In town, the most popular budget lodging is the **Moravian Hostel** (☎ 3263) which has simple, clean doubles for Tsh3600 with shared facilities; there are no meals available. It's on Jacaranda Rd, about 600m from

the market. Several muggings have been reported along this road and locals advise not walking along it after dark. Even during the day, try to walk in a group if possible.

Another cheap choice is **Warsame Guest House** on Sisimba St near the market, although there's nothing to recommend it except its central location. Singles/doubles are Tsh2000/3000.

For those who want to be close to the bus station, try **Nkwenzulu Hotel Number 1** (☎ 2225), which has singles/doubles for Tsh6000/7200 (Tsh9600/10,800 with bathroom), including continental breakfast. It's opposite the bus stand and up the hill, and is not to be confused with the much grubbier Nkwenzulu Hotel Number 3, at the bottom of the hill.

On the other side of the valley behind the bus station is **Central Visitors Lodge** (☎ 2507) with doubles (only) for Tsh4800

(Tsh6000 with bathroom). To get here, it's best to take the longer route through town, rather than the more isolated shortcut behind the bus station.

Places to Stay – Mid-Range & Top End

Newton's Hotel (☎ 4200) on Chunya Rd is a private guesthouse with small double suites for Tsh15,000; they will also arrange a cooking plate for you on request. It's not a bad place, though a bit isolated.

Central Mbeya's most 'luxurious' accommodation is the faded *Mt Livingstone Hotel* (☎ 3331) just off Jamatikhana Rd with singles/doubles for US$40/60 including continental breakfast.

Rift Valley Hotel (☎ 4351, 4429), on the same road at the junction with Lumumba Ave has similar rooms from Tsh11,520/14,400.

About 25km from Mbeya off the Zambia road is *Utengule Country Hotel* (☎/fax 065-4007, email utengule@twiga.com, PO Box 139 Mbeya), a comfortable lodge set among the hills and coffee plantations. Rooms cost from Tsh30,000 per person sharing; special children's rates are available. The hotel has a pool, tennis and squash courts, and other facilities. Payment can be made in US dollars, South African rand, pounds sterling or Tanzanian shillings. To get here, you will need your own vehicle. From Mbeya, take the Zambia road about 12km to Mbalizi. Continue into the centre of Mbalizi and take your first right; follow this road over a small bridge, go left at the fork, and then continue for 9km. The hotel is signposted to your right.

Places to Eat

Mbeya is not distinguished by its dining options. The best local food is at *Karibuni Centre* (see Places to Stay) which serves good, reasonably priced meals daily.

The restaurant at *Mt Livingstone Hotel* has a fairly large selection of more expensive meals.

In town by the market are several local food places. One of the nicer ones is *Eddy Coffee Bar* on Sisimba St. Others nearby include *Mambeu Restaurant* and *PM's Corner Restaurant*.

For self-caterers, the best supermarket is *Nelly's* on South St.

Getting There & Away

Bus Several buses, minibuses and dalla-dallas go to/from Mbeya.

To Iringa, Morogoro, Mikumi & Dar es Salaam Buses go daily to Iringa (Tsh4000, four hours), Morogoro (Tsh8500, four hours) and Dar es Salaam (Tsh10,000, 11 hours), all departing between 6.30 and 7 am. The best line is Scandinavian with buses departing at 7 am sharp. Book at least one day in advance. If you take Scandinavian and disembark at Iringa, you'll need to pay for a ticket as far as Morogoro.

The Hood line runs a bus service most days via Morogoro and Chalinze to Arusha for Tsh15,000. For intermediate stops along the way they charge Tsh6200 to Mikumi, Tsh7600 to Morogoro, and Tsh8600 to Chalinze.

To Njombe & Songea Minibuses go most days to Njombe (Tsh3500, four hours) and Songea (Tsh5500, seven hours); departures are about 5.30 am.

To Tukuyu & Malawi Dalla-dallas go several times a day from Mbeya to Tukuyu (Tsh700) and Kyela (Tsh1500). For Itungi, you'll need to change vehicles in Kyela. There is also daily transport between Mbeya and the Malawi border, where you can pick up Malawian transport heading to Karonga and beyond.

The Twiga and Matema Beach lines each run buses direct from Mbeya to Malawi. Twiga goes on Sunday and Matema Beach on Tuesday and (usually) Friday. It's about Tsh10,000 to Mzuzu and Tsh17,000 to Lilongwe. Departures from Mbeya are in the afternoon, arriving the next day in Lilongwe. For additional information on connections between Mbeya and Malawi see the Malawi section in the main Getting There & Away chapter.

To Zambia & Sumbawanga Minibuses go daily to Tunduma, on the Zambian border (Tsh1500, two hours), where you can change to Zambian transport. There's also a direct bus a few times a week between Mbeya and Lusaka (Tsh17,500). See the Zambia section in the main Getting There & Away chapter for more details.

Several times a week there is a direct bus to Sumbawanga (Tsh8000, at least 10 hours); otherwise, you'll need to change at the junction before Tunduma. The road to Tunduma is deteriorated tarmac. From Tunduma to Sumbawanga, it is unpaved and in poor condition.

Train Tickets for all classes can be booked at the TAZARA town booking office next to the post office (open from 7.30 am to 3 pm on weekdays, though it often closes early). Otherwise, you can book at the station; the window is officially open from 7.30 am to 12.30 pm and from 2 to 4 pm on weekdays, from 8 am to 12.30 pm on Saturday and from 7.30 to 11 am on Sunday and holidays.

See the Train section in the main Getting Around chapter for schedules and fares from Mbeya to Dar es Salaam. See the Zambia section in the main Getting There & Away chapter for information about train connections with Zambia.

Getting Around
Bus & Taxi Some taxis park by the market, though for the better cars you'll have to go to the bus station.

The TAZARA station is about 4km out of town on the Zambia road. Dalla-dallas run there (Tsh150), but are often too full if you have luggage. Taxis charge between Tsh1000 and Tsh1500.

Bicycle Bikes can be rented by the market.

AROUND MBEYA
Mt Kaluwe & Mbeya Peak
Mt Kaluwe (2656m, also known as Loleza Peak), lies just north of Mbeya, and can be climbed as an easy day hike. It's not permitted to go up to the summit, where there is a large antenna, but you'll still be able to enjoy good views over Mbeya and the surrounding area. The walk begins on the road running north from town past the hospital.

Mbeya Peak (2834m), which lies west of Mt Kaluwe, is the highest peak in the Mbeya range. It's possible to climb in a (long) day hike from Mbeya. The easiest way to reach the peak from town is by heading towards Mt Kaluwe and then following the ridge westwards for 7km. If you want to break the trip into two days you'll need to bring camping supplies and all your own food and water.

The Mbozi Meteorite

The Mbozi meteorite is one of Tanzania's more arcane attractions, and is seldom visited by travellers. Yet, the site is significant geologically, and makes an interesting stop if you are in the area. The meteorite, with an estimated size of about 25 metric tons, is the fourth-largest in the world. Scientists are unsure of when it hit the earth, but it is assumed to have been many thousands of years ago. Although the site was only discovered by outsiders in 1930, it had been known to local populations for centuries but not reported because of various associated taboos.

Like most meteorites, the one at Mbozi is composed primarily of iron, with about 8% nickel and traces of phosphorous and some other elements. It was declared a protected monument by the Tanzanian government in 1967, and is now surrounded by a small walkway. The meteorite's black colour is due to its high iron content, while its burnished look comes from the melting and other heating that occurred due to the forces of friction as the meteorite hurtled through the atmosphere towards Earth.

Mbozi is about 65km south-west of Mbeya. To reach the site you will need your own vehicle. From Mbeya, follow the main road towards Tunduma, and then branch off at Vwawa. The meteorite is located on the western slope of Marengi hill.

Lake Rukwa & Uwanda Game Reserve

The remote Lake Rukwa is a large salt lake notable for its diversity of water birds and its large crocodile population. Much of the lake and parts of the lake shore are protected within the boundaries of the Uwanda Game Reserve. As the lake has no outlet, its water level varies significantly between the rainy and dry seasons. Visits are only practical with a 4WD, and even then access to the banks is difficult. The best approach is from Mbeya via Chunya and Saza to Ngomba on the lake shore (about 150km from Mbeya). There are no facilities at the lake, and very little en route.

TUKUYU

Tukuyu is a small town set in the heart of a beautiful area of hills and orchards near Lake Nyasa. While tourist facilities are minimal, the area is one of the best in Tanzania for hiking and Tukuyu makes a good base.

Information

The National Bank of Commerce in Tukuyu will usually change travellers cheques.

Hiking

Hiking is the main activity in and around Tukuyu. The best months are from July to October; during the rainy season the area becomes very muddy.

Between Tukuyu and Mbeya, and to the east of the main road is the 2960m **Mt Rungwe**. You can hike up and down in a day; allow about 10 hours. The climb starts from Rungwe Secondary School, signposted off the Mbeya road about 15km north of Tukuyu. A guide can be arranged at Rungwe or through Langboss Lodge in Tukuyu (see Places to Stay & Eat). Mt Rungwe can also be reached as a day hike from Isongole village between Tukuyu and Mbeya.

Somewhat further north and about 5km west of the main road is the volcanic **Ngozi Peak** (2620m) with an impressive lake lying 200m below the crater rim. To reach here via public transport, take any dalla-dalla heading to Mbeya and ask them to drop you;

there's a small sign for Ngozi at the turn-off. Alternatively, you can reach Ngozi as a day walk from Isongole.

South of Ngozi, and also to the west of the main road, is **Kijungu** (cooking pot), where the Kiriwa river tumbles through a rocky gorge. Nearby is **Daraja la Mungu** (bridge of God), a natural bridge estimated to have been formed around 1800 million years ago by water flowing through cooling lava that spewed out from the nearby Rungwe volcano. The bridge spans a small waterfall.

Other possible hiking destinations in the area include **Masoko Crater Lake** and **Kaporogwe Falls**, both south of Tukuyu. Langboss Lodge (see Places to Stay & Eat following) can assist in arranging guides for any of these hikes.

Places to Stay & Eat

The best place to stay is *Langboss Lodge* (☎ 2080), about 1km east of the town centre. Basic but clean singles/doubles are Tsh2000/3000 (Tsh4000 for a double with bathroom), and meals are available on request. The owner is knowledgeable about the surrounding area and very helpful in arranging hikes and excursions.

Bombay Tea Room, opposite the bank, is good for inexpensive local food.

Getting There & Away

Transport runs several times a day from Tukuyu to Mbeya (Tsh700, one to 1½ hours) and Kyela (Tsh600, one hour) along a scenic, tarmac road.

Two roads connect Tukuyu with the northern end of Lake Nyasa. The main, tarmac road heads south-west and splits at Ibanda, with the west fork going to Songwe river bridge and into Malawi, and the east fork to Kyela and Itungi port. If you are going to Malawi you will have to change cars at Ibanda. For more details, see the Malawi section in the main Getting There & Away chapter.

A secondary dirt road heads south-east from Tukuyu to Ipinda and then branches further eastwards towards Matema.

LAKE NYASA

Lake Nyasa (which is known to many non-Tanzanians as Lake Malawi) is Africa's third largest lake after Lake Victoria and Lake Tanganyika. It is more than 550km long, up to 75km wide, and as deep as 700m in parts. It is also very biodiverse, with close to one-third of the earth's known cichlid species. The lake is bordered by Tanzania, Malawi and Mozambique. The Tanzanian side is rimmed to the east by the Livingstone mountains which form a beautiful backdrop. Few roads reach the towns strung out between the mountains and the shore along the lake's eastern side. The northern end of the lake is one of the most densely populated areas in the country.

Places around the Tanzanian side of the lake where travellers may need or want to pass through include the following (listed from north-west to south-east).

Kyela

There's no reason to come to Kyela unless you arrive late at Itungi and need somewhere to spend the night. It's best not to use a camera here due to official sensitivities about Tanzania's ongoing border dispute with Malawi.

There are several basic, cheap guesthouses near the bus stand. The best one is *Pattaya Hotel*, with clean singles/doubles for Tsh4000/5000.

Minibuses run daily from Kyela to Tukuyu (Tsh600) and Mbeya (Tsh1500), and pick-ups run between Kyela and Itungi (Tsh200).

Itungi

Itungi, about 11km south of Kyela, is the main port for the Tanzanian Lake Nyasa ferry service. There is no accommodation; photography is forbidden. Pick-ups run sporadically to and from Kyela (Tsh200). The road from Itungi as far as Ibanda (at the junction with the paved main road) is in poor condition.

There are usually two ferries from Itungi servicing the villages along the Tanzanian side of Lake Nyasa. The MV *Songea* is the

bigger and better of the two, but it is currently out of service. The smaller, invariably overcrowded, and much more uncomfortable MV *Iringa* departs Itungi once a week on Thursday at about 7.30 am, reaching Mbamba Bay by about noon on Friday. It stops en route at Lumbila, Lupingo, Liuli and several other villages. From Mbamba Bay, the boat crosses over to Nkhata Bay (see Malawi in the main Getting There & Away chapter), then returns to Mbamba Bay, from where it depart Saturday to head back to Itungi. Tickets between Itungi and Mbamba Bay cost Tsh3240 (deck seating only). There's no restaurant on board so you'll need to bring enough food and water for the trip.

Previously, the MV *Songea* departed Itungi port on Monday and Friday mornings, arriving in Mbamba Bay about 24 hours later (Tsh9000/3300, 1st/3rd class); the *Iringa* was just used for shorter runs along the coast from Itungi.

If you are trying to coordinate road and boat travel, bus drivers in Mbeya (or those in Dar es Salaam who drive the Dar es Salaam-Mbeya route) sometimes have information on whether and when the Lake Nyasa ferries are running.

Matema

The beach at Matema is one of the nicest spots on northern Lake Nyasa. The water is considered to be bilharzia free, and it's a popular place for swimming. You can arrange rides in local canoes, or take excursions down the coast. There are some interesting waterfalls and caves in the area.

The place to stay is *Lutheran Guest House*, which has a generator and rooms for Tsh4800 to Tsh6000 per person, including breakfast. Other meals are also available. Before heading down, it's best to check with the Lutheran Mission in Tukuyu (just up from the market on the road to the NBC bank) to be sure space is available.

To get to Matema from Tukuyu via public transport, take a pick-up from the roundabout by the NBC bank to Ipinda. Note that while many drivers say they are going all the way to Matema, they usually only go as far as Ipinda. From Ipinda, pick-ups run only very sporadically to Matema (35km). If you go on a weekend, chances are better that you'll be able to find a lift with a private vehicle. If you are heading to Matema in your own vehicle, the route is via Ipinda (not via Kyela).

Ikombe

The tiny village of Ikombe is notable for its clay pots, which are sold at markets in Mbeya and elsewhere in the region. The mountains around Ikombe are enticing for hiking, although there are no facilities.

Mbamba Bay

Mbamba Bay is the southernmost Tanzanian port on Lake Nyasa. If you get stuck here waiting for onward transport, try *Mabugu Guest House* which has basic rooms for about Tsh1000. See Itungi earlier for details of ferry services between Mbamba Bay and Itungi port. See the Malawi section in the main Getting There & Away chapter for details of ferry connections with Nkhata Bay.

From Mbamba Bay, there are pick-ups to Mbinga (Tsh2000, four hours), from where you can find minibuses on to Songea. The 60km stretch between Mbamba Bay and Mbinga is very bad; you will have to get out

of the vehicle and walk at many spots. During the rainy season the Landrovers that sporadically run this route barely make it.

From Mbamba Bay north along the lake to Liuli the road is in poor condition and there is no regular public transport; your best bet is to try to hitch a ride with a mission vehicle or take the ferry.

If you are entering or leaving Tanzania via Mbamba Bay, you will have to stop at the police station to take care of immigration formalities.

Other Villages

Most of the other villages along the coast including Liuli and Mango have basic guesthouses and food stalls. There is no regular road transport along the lake shore.

SONGEA

Songea, just more than 1000m in altitude, is a bustling, pleasant place and the capital of the surrounding Ruvuma region. The main ethnic group here are the Ngoni, who migrated into the area from South Africa during the 19th century, subduing many smaller tribes along the way. Songea takes its name from one of their greatest chiefs who was killed following the Maji Maji rebellion (see the boxed text).

The Maji Maji Rebellion

The Maji Maji rebellion, which was the strongest local revolt against the colonial government in German East Africa, is considered to contain some of the earliest seeds of Tanzanian nationalism. It began about the turn of the century when colonial administrators set about establishing enormous cotton plantations near the south-eastern coast and along the train line running from Dar es Salaam towards Morogoro. These plantations required large numbers of workers, most of whom were recruited as forced labour and required to work under miserable salary and living conditions. Anger at this harsh treatment and long-simmering resentment of the colonial government combined to ignite a powerful rebellion. The first outbreak was in 1905 in the area around Kilwa, on the coast. Soon all of southern Tanzania was involved, from Kilwa and Lindi in the south-east to Songea in the south-west. In addition to deaths on the battlefield, thousands died due to hunger brought about by the Germans' 'scorched earth' tactics in which fields and grain silos in many villages were set on fire. Fatalities were undoubtedly exacerbated by a widespread belief among the Africans that enemy bullets would turn to water before killing

Things to See & Do

Songea's colourful **market** is worth a visit. About 1km from town on the Mahengere road there's a small **museum** and a monument dedicated to the Africans who fell in the Maji Maji rebellion.

Places to Stay & Eat

One of the better places is *OK Hotel*, opposite the Open University of Tanzania building, with clean doubles from Tsh5000 and a good restaurant.

De Luxe Guest House on the main road near the market is grubbier. Basic rooms cost about Tsh2000.

Getting There & Away

There is daily transport between Songea and Mbeya (Tsh5500, seven hours); the first bus departs in either direction about 6 am. The road is in good condition.

There is also a bus most days direct to Dar es Salaam (Tsh15,000, 14 hours), departing between 6 am and 7 am in each direction.

To Mbamba Bay, buses go most days to Mbinga (Tsh2000, four hours) from where you can find sporadic transport to Mbamba Bay. There is occasional direct transport between Songea and Mbamba Bay during the dry season.

NJOMBE

About 240km north of Songea is Njombe, a district capital and centre of a productive agricultural region. The town lies at the eastern edge of the Kipengere mountain range at almost 2000m altitude and can get very chilly in the evenings. For accommodation, try *Mbalache Guest House* with basic but clean rooms for about Tsh2000, or *Lutheran Hostel*, also inexpensive.

Buses go daily from Njombe to Songea (Tsh3000, three to four hours) and to Makumbako, where you can get transport to Mbeya. There is also a direct bus most days to Mbeya (Tsh3500, four hours).

If you get stuck needing to overnight in **Makumbako**, the best budget accommodation is at *Lutheran Centre Guest House* at the main junction. Otherwise, try the sprawling *Uplands Hotel*, about 500m from the junction on the Mbeya road.

TUNDURU

Tunduru is a dusty, bustling town about halfway between Songea and Masasi. It's in the centre of one of Tanzania's important gemstone mining regions and has a bit of a 'wild west' feel to it. Several gemstone dealers line the main road. The town is also a major truck and transit stop; you will need

The Maji Maji Rebellion

them, and that their warriors would therefore not be harmed – hence the name Maji Maji (*maji* means water in Swahili).

By 1907, when the rebellion was finally suppressed, close to 100,000 people had lost their lives. In addition, large areas of the south were left devastated and barren, and malnutrition was widespread. The Ngoni, a tribe of warriors much feared by their neighbours, put up the strongest resistance to the Germans. Following the end of the rebellion, they continued to wage guerrilla-style war until 1908, when the last shreds of their military-based society were destroyed. In order to quell Ngoni resistance once and for all, German troops hung about 100 of their leaders and beheaded their most famous chief, Songea.

Among the effects of the Maji Maji uprising were a temporary liberalisation of colonial rule and replacement of the military administration with a civilian government. More significantly, the uprising promoted development of a national identity among many ethnic groups and intensified anti-colonial sentiments, kindling the movement towards independence.

to spend at least one night here if travelling between Songea and Masasi

The better guesthouses are at the westernmost end of town. There are plenty to chose from; all are around the same standard.

Landrovers to Songea also congregate at the western end of town. It's best to reserve a seat for onward travel as soon as you arrive in Tunduru, as the vehicles fill up quickly.

Getting There & Away

The road from Tunduru in either direction is in very poor condition, particularly between Tunduru and Songea; it is often impassable during the rainy season. During the dry season, buses run several times a week between Tunduru and Masasi; allow 12 hours for the trip. Between Tunduru and Songea, your only option for most of the year is by Landrover (Tsh10,000, 12 hours). The vehicles run a few times a week, usually departing Tunduru very early, between 3 and 4 am. If you are staying at a guesthouse near the Landrover 'station' you can usually arrange with a driver to come wake you up before departure. There is very little along the route; bring whatever food and water you will need with you.

South-Eastern Tanzania

Tanzania's often forgotten south-eastern corner is a beautiful region of open savanna and spectacular beaches. The continent's largest game reserve, the Selous, is here, as is Tanzania's first marine park at Mafia island. Inland, the Makonde plateau is the home of Tanzania's famous wood-carvers, while on the coast at Kilwa Kisiwani island are the ruins of one of East Africa's most important cities.

Despite its many attractions and rich history, the south-east receives few visitors. One factor has been accessibility; the region has been long neglected by the government, and infrastructure – in particular the road network – is underdeveloped. Although the situation is gradually improving, most roads are in poor condition and many are impassable during the rainy season. The only good, paved road in the entire area is the 200km stretch between Mtwara and Masasi.

Another reason for the lack of visitors is that the south-east was considered to be a sensitive border zone during the Mozambique War and most areas were off-limits to tourists. Although travel restrictions have since been lifted, the region remains in many senses more traditional and reserved than other areas of the country.

For those wishing to visit, the south-east is not a place to be rushed through. While facilities in most towns are more than adequate, journeys can be long and hard, and travellers seeking creature comforts may not enjoy themselves. But for those with an adventurous spirit, sufficient time and a willingness to be open to and respectful of local customs, this unspoiled region can be one of Tanzania's most rewarding.

MTWARA

Mtwara, south-eastern Tanzania's major town, is a sprawling, friendly place in an attractive setting on Mtwara Bay. It was first developed after WWII by the British as part of their East African Groundnut Scheme; a

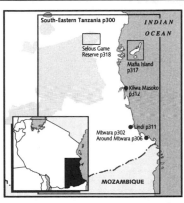

Highlights

South-Eastern Tanzania p300

INDIAN OCEAN

Selous Game Reserve p318

Mafia Island p317

Kilwa Masoko p312

Lindi p311

Mtwara p302
Around Mtwara p306

MOZAMBIQUE

- **Mafia Island** – quiet, palm-fringed and its surrounding marine park
- **Kindani & Lindi** – exploring traces of bygone days in these and other coastal towns
- **Selous** – vast and magnificent, Africa's largest game reserve
- **Ruins** – dating back to the 13th century; Kilwa Kisiwani island

project aimed at alleviating the post-war shortage of plant oils through the implementation of large-scale groundnut production at various sites in the region. Plans were made to expand Mtwara – then a small fishing village – into an urban centre of some 200,000 inhabitants, with Tanzania's first deep water harbour and an international airport.

No sooner had the regional colonial administration been relocated from nearby Lindi to Mtwara and the harbour been completed, when everything came to an abrupt halt with the failure of the groundnut scheme. Although Mtwara's port continued to play a

SOUTH-EASTERN TANZANIA

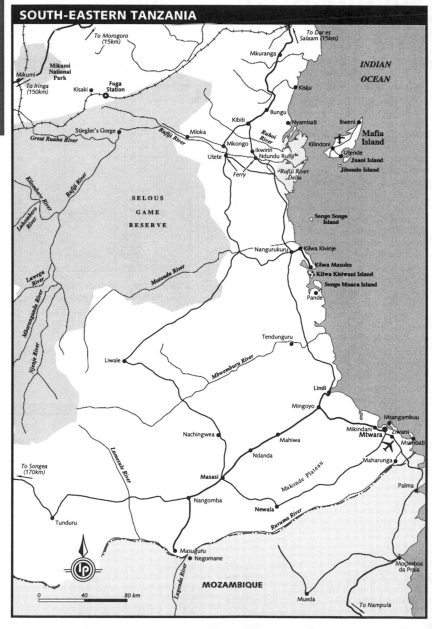

To Morogoro
(15km)

To Dar es
Salaam (15km)

Mkuranga

INDIAN
OCEAN

Mikumi
National
Park

Mikumi

To Iringa
(150km)

Kisaki

Fuga
Station

Kisiju

Bungu

Kibiti

Nyamisati

Bweni

Stiegler's Gorge

Rufiji River

Mloka

Ruhoi
River

Mafia
Island

Great Ruaha River

Mkongo

Kilindoni

Ikwiriri

Kilombero River

Utete

Ndundu Rufiji

Utende

Juani Island

Ferry

Rufiji River

Rufiji River
Delta

Jibondo Island

Lahombero River

SELOUS

GAME

RESERVE

Songo Songo
Island

Luwegu River

Matandu River

Nangurukuru

Kilwa Kivinje

Mbarangandu River

Kilwa Masoko
Kilwa Kisiwani Island
Songo Mnara Island

Njinje River

Pande

Tendunguru

Liwale

Mbwemburu River

Lindi

Mingoyo

Msangamkuu

Nachingwea

Mahiwa

Mikindani
Mtwara

Ziwani

To Songea
(170km)

Lumesule River

Ndanda

Msimbati

Masasi

Maharunga

Makonde Plateau

Nangomba

Newala

Palma

Tunduru

Ruvuma River

Masuguru
Negomane

Moçimboa
da Praia

Lugenda River

MOZAMBIQUE

Mueda

To Nampula

0   40   80 km

Unity Bridge

Since independence, the idea of a 'unity bridge' joining Tanzania with Mozambique, its neighbour to the south, has been under discussion. Yet today, almost four decades later, there is still not a single link – other than by dugout canoe – along the countries' 700km-long common border, defined for most of its length by the Ruvuma River. This situation poses a major barrier to development on both sides of the river. Southern Tanzania and northern Mozambique are markedly underdeveloped, and their agricultural, fishery and tourism potentials untapped. While Mtwara, the major town on the Tanzanian side, is easily reached by air or, with a bit more effort, by boat, many other places in the region are cut off completely during the rainy season and accessed only with difficulty during the rest of the year.

Both sides agree that construction of a bridge, coupled with improvement of road links northwards to Dar es Salaam and south into Mozambique, would be a tremendous boon to the area. It would open new markets, give a boost to the economy and – from a tourism perspective – facilitate development of the entire southern Tanzania-northern Mozambique corridor – a region which has some of the most beautiful coastline, best diving and richest marine ecosystems in East Africa. The problem has been finding resources and keeping political attention focused.

In a positive turn of events, the issue of bridging the Ruvuma moved again to the forefront in late 1998 as high-level Tanzanian and Mozambican delegations visited the border area and put the bridge back on the agenda. The most likely site for the bridge is about 100km south-west of Masasi between Masuguru in Tanzania and Negomane in Mozambique, with connections to Mtwara and Dar es Salaam to the north and the Mozambican towns of Mueda and Nampula to the south. In the meantime, there is urgent need for a ferry further east, to facilitate local movement and commerce in the area south of Mtwara.

significant regional role over the next decades as an export channel for cashew, sisal and other products, development of the town itself came to a standstill. Even today, Mtwara's population numbers only about 80,000, with its oversized layout serving as a reminder of the failed colonial plans.

In recent years, with the reopening of the south-east to travellers, there has been a revival of interest in the tourism potential of Mtwara and the south-east. A few projects for hotel development and rehabilitation of historical buildings are already underway, and others are under discussion.

Orientation

Mtwara is a spread-out place, loosely centred around a business and banking area to the north and the market and bus stand to the south.

In the far north-west of town on the water is the Shangani Quarter, where many of Mtwara's foreign residents live. East of Shangani is the port and a few industry buildings. To the south is Tanu Rd, Mtwara's main north-south street, with district and regional government buildings, the police station, and the Air Tanzania office. Intersecting Tanu Rd is Uhuru St, which together with Aga Khan Rd comprises the main business district. South of Uhuru St are the market and the bus stand, while in the far south-eastern corner of town are the lively areas of Majengo and Chiko Ngola.

Information

There are no foreign exchange bureaus in Mtwara. The National Bank of Commerce on Uhuru Rd changes travellers cheques and cash while the CRDB changes cash only.

The post in Mtwara is fairly efficient; letters to Europe and the USA take about two weeks.

Domestic and international calls can be made at the Telecom Building from 7.45 am to 12.45 pm and 1.30 to 4.30 pm on weekdays, and from 9 am to 12.30 pm on Saturday.

Things to See & Do

In town there is a good **market** with an interesting traditional medicine section next to the main building. Much of Mtwara's fish comes from Msangamkuu on the other side of Mtwara Bay, and the **ferry dock** and adjoining market are particularly colourful in the early morning and late afternoon. The **beach** in Shangani is popular with locals and foreigners on weekends. Mtwara makes a good base for **excursions** to Mikindani, Msimbati, and the surrounding area (see the Around Mtwara section following).

Places to Stay

Nandope Hotel, just off Tanu Rd near the centre of town, is the most popular budget accommodation, thanks to its reliable electricity and water supplies. Simple but clean singles/doubles with nets, fan and shared bath are Tsh2000/3000; food is available on request.

Lutheran Centre Hostel (☎ 333294), at the entrance to town near the main roundabout, also has fairly reliable water and electricity supplies. Decent rooms are Tsh3300/5800 (Tsh5800/8000 with bathroom).

Kwa Limo, down the dirt road opposite the post office, has rooms of a similar standard for Tsh5000 with bathroom; there is also a pleasant restaurant here.

Tinga Tinga Inn at the eastern end of Shangani is a cosy place with nice artwork in the lobby and a small restaurant. Clean singles/doubles with fan, net and shared bath are Tsh5000/7000. As at many places in Shangani, water and electricity supplies can be erratic here.

Finn Club (☎ 333020) in Shangani has spotless air-con rooms from Tsh8000/10,000 including breakfast. Priority is given to aid

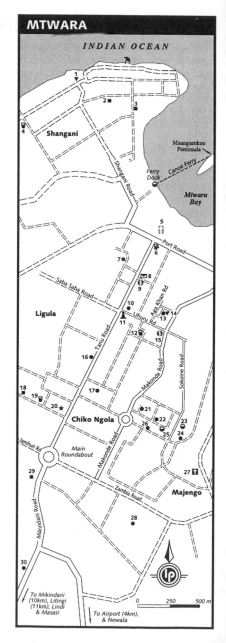

MTWARA

PLACES TO STAY		6	BP Petrol Station	19	Bondeni Pub	
2	Finn Club	8	Post Office;	20	Police	
3	Tinga Tinga Inn		Telecom	21	Canadian Spirit	
7	Kwa Limo	9	CRDB Bank		Booking Office	
18	Nandope Hotel	10	CCM Building	22	MV Maendeleo	
29	Lutheran	11	TAMOFA Monument		Booking Office	
	Centre Hostel	12	Tila Bar	23	Pick-ups	
		13	Maduka Makubwa (Big		to Msimbati	
PLACES TO EAT			Square)	24	Market	
1	Safina Shop	15	NBC Bank	25	Bus & Taxi Stand	
14	Masumeen	16	Air Tanzania;	26	Gem Dealer Shops	
			Tanzania Revenue	27	St Paul's Church	
OTHER			Authority Building	28	Saba Saba Grounds;	
4	CATA Club	17	Regional Block		TAMOFA Office	
5	Cathedral		Administration Buildings	30	Makonde Carvings	

workers. For a temporary membership fee of Tsh500 per day you can avail yourself of the TV room, pool, and tennis and squash courts in the compound.

Litingi (☎ *333635*), about 11km from town off the Mikindani Rd, is Mtwara's up-market accommodation option, complete with its own generator. Doubles (no singles) with bathroom are Tsh15,000 including continental breakfast. There's also an air-con suite for Tsh24,000. To get here, follow the road to Mikindani for about 9km. Just before the Mikindani police station is an unmarked dirt track to the right. Follow this about 2km; Litingi appears out of nowhere. It's near the water but on a mangrove swamp so you can't swim. Taxis from Mtwara charge about Tsh4000. Otherwise, a Mikindani dalla-dalla can drop you by the turn-off (Tsh200).

There are plans to renovate the old Mtwara Beach Hotel as a dive centre and possible regional safari base; inquire in town to see if this has happened.

Places to Eat

One of the best places for street food is the *market* by the Msangamkuu ferry. You can also usually find good grilled *pwezu* (octopus) near the bus stand. *Masumeen*, opposite NBC Bank, has cheap snacks and curries.

Most of the listings under Places to Stay have restaurants. Among the better ones are *Kwa Limo*, which has pleasant bandas and

serves *nyama choma* and other local dishes for about Tsh1000, and *Finn Club*, which serves good meals for between Tsh2000 and Tsh3000.

Mtwara's best dining is at *Litingi*, the only place with any sort of menu selection. Meals average Tsh3000 to Tsh5000.

For self-caterers staying in Shangani, *Safina* has a good selection of basics. In town, there are several fairly well-stocked shops along Uhuru Rd. Throughout Mtwara, prices of packaged foods tend to increase during the rainy season when the Dar es Salaam road is closed.

Entertainment

Popular places for a drink include *Bondeni Pub* near the police station and *Safina* and *Finn Club* in Shangani. The old *CATA Club* in Shangani has seen better days, but still attracts the occasional customer for a drink. *Litingi* has a popular disco on Saturday nights (Tsh1000 admission charge for men).

Shopping

There is a good selection of Makonde carvings at a small market held every Wednesday from 9 to 10.30 am on the grounds of St Paul's church in Majengo.

The family of Makonde carvers on the Mikindani road under the second tree after the airport turn-off also sell good pieces at very reasonable prices.

St Paul's Church

If you happen to be in the lively Majengo area of Mtwara, it's worth stopping in at St Paul's church to view its remarkable artwork. The entire front and side walls are covered with richly coloured biblical scenes painted by a German Benedictine priest, Polycarp Uehlein. These paintings, which took about two years to complete, are part of a series by the same artist decorating churches throughout southern Tanzania and in a few other areas of the country, including the cathedral in Songea and churches in Nyangao, Lindi, Malolo, Ngapa and Dar es Salaam. In addition to their style and distinctive use of colour, the paintings are notable for their universalised portrayal of common biblical themes. The themes were chosen to assist church-goers to understand the sermons and to relate the biblical lessons to their everyday lives.

During the years he worked in Tanzania, Father Polycarp taught several African students. The best known of these is Henry Likonde from Mtwara, who has taken biblical scenes and 'Africanised' them. You can see a good example of his work in the small church at the top of the hill in Maharunga, south of Mtwara near the Mozambique border.

St Paul's is also notable as an example of the positive effects that mission work and development projects can have, given sufficient continuity and commitment. During the 30-plus years that Father Ildefons Weigand, another German Benedictine priest, has been pastor, the surrounding Majengo Quarter has grown from a sleepy community to an area which now boasts a dynamic parish of about 5000, several schools, vocational training programs, and active women's and community groups. During the worst years of the Mozambique War, the parish served as a haven for Makonde carvers who had come over the border seeking refuge; today it continues to provide them warehouse and vending space. The church is now a centre of the community and Father Ildefons' name is known by almost everyone in Mtwara. This growth is even more remarkable when Majengo's vitality is contrasted with the languor that permeates so many towns along the Swahili coast.

Much of this development took place against the backdrop of south-eastern Tanzania's near total isolation during the three decades from Tanzanian independence until the end of the Mozambique War – a time when scarce government resources were directed elsewhere and the region was closed to travellers. The major, and in some cases the only, development assistance reaching many areas came from overseas missions, notably the Benedictine order. Their stations soon became not only focal points of missionary activity, but also important economic centres and catalysts for development. In many cases – the Ndanda mission west of Mtwara is a good example – the missions were the only place where salaried employment was available, or where trade skills could be learned. Education was an equally important dimension of missionary activity, with practically all schools in the region mission-run prior to the 1967 Arusha Declaration.

The vendors at either of these places can help you arrange a visit to outlying villages to watch some of the carvers at work.

Getting There & Away

Air Air Tanzania flies three times weekly between Mtwara and Dar es Salaam (Tsh49,500 one way). Plans for a flight linking Mtwara with both Dar es Salaam and Pemba (Mozambique) are underway, though final approvals are still pending. There is a weekly charter flight (usually on Thursday) between Mtwara and Pemba for US$150 one way. Inquire at the airport for details.

The Air Tanzania office (☎ 333147) is on Tanu Rd.

Bus Buses depart daily from the main bus stand near the market to Masasi (Tsh2400, five to six hours), Newala (Tsh2000, six to

Top Left: Old slave market in Mikindani; plans are underway for its restoration.
Top Right: Iringa market, well stocked with fruit and vegetables.
Bottom: Local boats connect Mtwara with the nearby Msangamkuu peninsula.

Woodcarvings for the craft market in Dar es Salaam.

Women's weaver co-op, Mafia island

10 hours) and Lindi (Tsh1500, three to four hours). During the dry season, buses run several times weekly between Mtwara and Dar es Salaam (Tsh10,000); departures from Dar es Salaam are at 8 am and from Mtwara at about 2 pm. Book a seat in advance as these buses are usually very full. The trip can take anywhere between 24 hours and several days, depending on road conditions and breakdowns. During much of the rainy season, the road to Dar es Salaam is closed.

If you are heading south to Mozambique, there is usually at least one pick-up daily heading towards Maharunga and the Tanzanian immigration post at Kilambo. From Kilambo, you'll have to walk about 5km to the Ruvuma, which can only be crossed by dugout canoe. When the river is high, the crossing can take more than 30 minutes, whereas during certain times of the dry season you can practically walk across. Although locals do this frequently, it's not recommended due to the danger of crocodile and hippo. See the Mozambique section in the Getting There & Away chapter for more details. There are several very basic guesthouses in Maharunga.

Car & Motorcycle The road between Dar es Salaam and Mtwara is in decent condition as far as Kibiti, good tarmac between Kibiti and Ikwiriri, and under construction from Ikwiriri to the Ndundu ferry. From the Ndundu ferry south to Somanga the road is in appalling condition – just a sand track in many places; it can take three hours to cover the 60km stretch, and the road is almost always closed during the rainy season. From Somanga to Nangurukuru, the road is good. From Nangurukuru south to Lindi, the road is in poor condition and is often closed during the rainy season. It improves somewhat from Lindi to Mingoyo; from Mingoyo to Mtwara is good tarmac.

Between Kibiti and the Utete ferry the road is unpaved, but usually in decent condition during the dry season.

There are petrol stations in Kibiti, Ikwiriri, Nangurukuru, Kilwa Masoko, Lindi and Mtwara.

Rufiji River Ferries If you are en route to/from Dar es Salaam, you will need to cross the Rufiji River. There are two ferries. The larger one, used by most buses and trucks, is at Ndundu and operates from 6.30 am to 6.30 pm (Tsh100 per person, Tsh500 for small cars, Tsh2000 for larger 4WDs). Lines can be long, and it is not unusual for buses to get stuck overnight at the river. The second ferry, at Utete, is smaller. Hours of operation are the same, though this service is not as reliable. Neither boat operates during the rainy season as the Rufiji overflows its banks and makes boarding impossible. Construction of a bridge over the Rufiji River has begun midway between Ndundu and Utete, but is not scheduled to be completed for several years.

If you get stuck at Ndundu, the only tolerable accommodation is the *Pentecostal Church Hostel* in Ikwiriri, 7km north of the river. Basic rooms cost Tsh2000/2500 a single/double. It's about 1km to the west of the main road; look for the sign for the 'Ikwiriri Mission Dispensary & Clinic'. If you get stuck on the south side of the river, your best option is to sleep on the bus or in your vehicle.

Boat The MV *Canadian Spirit* runs weekly between Mtwara and Dar es Salaam. Depending on cargo, it usually also stops en route at Mafia island. The boat departs Dar es Salaam on Wednesday around noon, reaching Mtwara around 25 hours later. Departures from Mtwara are on Friday about 3 pm. Fares are Tsh21,300/15,300/12,800 for 1st/2nd/3rd class. If you are coming from Mtwara and want to disembark at Mafia, you will still have to pay the full fare to Dar es Salaam. It's worth paying for 1st class if you want any measure of comfort on this trip. Bookings can be made in Mtwara at the Canadian Spirit office diagonally opposite the main bus stand.

The MV *Maendeleo* sails between Mtwara, Dar es Salaam and Unguja roughly twice a month, but schedules vary. The Mtwara booking office (☎ 333307) is opposite the bus station. Fares between Mtwara and Dar es Salaam are Tsh18,800/12,800/10,800 for

1st/2nd (tourist)/3rd class. The 1st class price is per bed in a four-bed cabin. Fares from Mtwara to Unguja are Tsh22,800/16,800/14,800 1st/2nd (tourist)/3rd class.

There are plans for a boat service connecting Mtwara with Pemba (Mozambique) and Dar es Salaam. For information as to whether it has started inquire at the Tanzania-Mozambique Friendship Association (TAMOFA) office on the Saba Saba grounds off Zambia Rd. There is also a small motorboat which travels sporadically between Mtwara and Moçimboa da Praia; inquire at the port for details. Otherwise, you can find occasional local boats sailing from Mtwara to various destinations up and down the coast. These journeys can be long and risky, and are not advisable.

Getting Around
Taxis to/from Mtwara's airport (6km from the main roundabout) charge Tsh5000.

Minibuses depart from the bus stand, but are useful primarily for getting to outlying villages, rather than around town. Taxis also park at the bus stand; the cost for a town trip is Tsh1000 (Tsh2000 from the centre to Shangani).

Mtwara covers a big area and bicycle is the main means of local transport. If you don't have your own vehicle, the best thing to do on arrival is to rent a bicycle at the main market building or at one of the numerous nearby bicycle shops.

AROUND MTWARA
Mikindani
Mikindani is a tiny but attractive town with an interesting history, lots of coconut groves and a picturesque bay. It makes a good half-day outing from Mtwara.

The town gained prominence early on as a major dhow port and a terminus for trade caravans from Lake Nyasa. By the late 15th century, trade from Mikindani extended across southern Tanzania as far as Zambia and present-day Congo (Zaïre). Following a brief downturn in fortunes, trade – primarily in slaves, ivory and copper – again increased in the mid-16th century as Mikindani came

under the domain of the Sultan of Zanzibar. In the 19th century following the ban on the slave trade, Mikindani fell into decline until the late 1880s when the German colonial government made it their regional headquarters. Large-scale sisal, coconut, rubber and oilseed production began in the area, and the slave trade recommenced. Several buildings from this era remain, notably the boma and the slave market.

With the arrival of the British and the advent of larger ocean-going vessels, Mikindani was abandoned in favour of Mtwara's superior harbour. Today, the town is mainly of historical significance, although it is also still an important port for the local dhows plying up and down the coast.

For Livingstone fans, the famous explorer spent a few weeks here in 1866 before setting out on his last journey.

Things to See & Do The German **boma**, built in 1895 as a fort and administrative centre, is being renovated to house a museum, accommodation and shops. It's scheduled to open sometime in 1999. Down

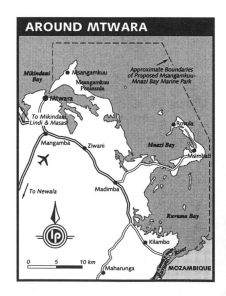

the hill from the boma is the old **slave market**, which is also slated for rehabilitation. The **prison ruins** are opposite the jetty. Not far from the prison ruins is a large, hollow baobab tree that was once used to keep unruly prisoners in solitary confinement. It's a bit difficult to find, so you may need a guide. Throughout town you can still find some carved **Zanzibar-style doors**. See the Conservation of Stone Town section in The Zanzibar Archipelago chapter for more information.

Places to Stay & Eat At present, there is no accommodation in Mikindani. However, once the boma is renovated, it will offer rooms, probably priced mid-range (☎/fax 059-333875 for information).

A cafe is also planned for the boma. In the meantime, the only dining options are several very basic local food stalls in town.

Ten Degrees South Lodge (☎/fax 051-75419, email tendegreessouth@twiga.com, PO Box 4523 Dar es Salaam) is also scheduled to be operating by the time this book is published. The lodge, which is located near the boma, will have comfortable rooms for Tsh3500 to Tsh10,000 and camping for about Tsh2000 per person. A restaurant specialising in seafood and vegetarian dishes is also planned, with meals from about Tsh2000. The owners are knowledgeable about the region and can assist with arrangements for scuba diving, kayak safaris along the nearby coastline and excursions to the Makonde Plateau. They are also willing to facilitate transfers southwards to the Mozambique border and beyond, or westwards across southern Tanzania to Mbamba Bay on Lake Nyasa and on to Nkhata Bay in Malawi. For further information, or for details about getting to the lodge, check out the Ten Degrees South internet site, reached by a link through the website www.africanet.com/njaya/welcome.htm.

Getting There & Away Mikindani is about 10km from Mtwara along a tarmac road, and an easy bike ride. Minibuses run between the two towns throughout the day (Tsh200).

Msangamkuu Peninsula

Msangamkuu peninsula lies north and east of Mtwara town and, together with Msimbati and Mnazi Bay to the south, is slated to become Tanzania's second marine park. Although the park has not yet been gazetted, the proposal (put forth by the Tanzanian government with World Bank support) has received preliminary approval. The area to be covered by the park stretches from the north-west side of Msangamkuu peninsula all the way to the Mozambique border and is considered to have a high level of biodiversity, with more than 400 marine species identified to date. For further information contact Frontier Tanzania Marine Research, the UK-based conservation organisation which has played a major role in identifying the site (☎ 051-153053, fax 112752, email frontier@twiga.com, PO Box 9472, Dar es Salaam) or in the UK (☎ 020-7613 2422, fax 2922, 77 Leonard St London, EC 2A 4QS).

There are some nice beaches, and good diving and snorkelling off the north-west of the peninsula, adjacent to Msangamkuu village.

Camping on the peninsula isn't advised. Your best accommodation option is to arrange lodging with one of the villagers. Fish and basic supplies are available in Msangamkuu village.

Dhows and canoes ply between the Shangani ferry dock and Msangamkuu peninsula throughout the day (Tsh50); the trip takes about 15 minutes with favourable winds.

Msimbati

Msimbati, about 42km from Mtwara on Mnazi Bay, has one of the most beautiful beaches along the Tanzanian coast. Offshore are several still largely unexplored reefs offering superb diving and snorkelling possibilities, although there are no diving facilities yet. The entire area is slated to become part of the new Msangamkuu-Mnazi Bay marine park (see the previous Msangamkuu Peninsula section for details).

Thanks to the work of several organisations, dynamite fishing on the reefs around Mnazi Bay has been significantly curbed in recent years.

About 7km beyond Msimbati town along a sandy track (or along the beach at low tide), is the tiny village of **Rovula**. It was here that the British eccentric Latham Leslie-Moore built his house and lived until 1967 when he was deported for agitating for independence of the Msimbati peninsula (rather than be subjected to the government of newly independent Tanzania). For more information on this era, history buffs can read John Heminway's *No Man's Land* or seek out *Africa Passion*, a documentary film on Moore. Today, Moore's house stands in ruins; the property is privately owned.

Places to Stay & Eat A dive centre with bandas is planned, although at the time of research there were no facilities and camping was the only accommodation option. You will need to bring all your own food and supplies, although you can get basic meals and provisions in Msimbati town. For updated information on the status of the dive centre, inquire at the Finn Club in Mtwara, where there are certain to be some foreign residents familiar with the plans.

Getting There & Away There is infrequent transport between Msimbati and Mtwara. Pick-ups and trucks from Mtwara depart from behind the market and charge about Tsh1000. There is no regular public transport between Msimbati and Rovula. On arrival in Msimbati, it can be helpful to stop in at the police station on the beach and pay a friendly visit to the officers there.

On weekends, many of Mtwara's foreign residents head towards Msimbati, and it's usually not too difficult to find a lift; the journey takes about one hour. From Mtwara, take the main road from the roundabout south for 4km to the village of Mangamba. At Mangamba (not signposted), branch left onto the Mahurunga road; follow this road about 18km to Madimba. At Madimba, turn left again and continue for 20km to Msim-

bati; the road is unpaved, but no problem with a 4WD in the dry season. If you are cycling, the major village en route is Ziwani, which has a decent market.

THE MAKONDE PLATEAU

The plateau, much of which lies between 700m and 900m above sea level, is home to the Makonde people, famed throughout East Africa for their exotic ebony carvings. Individual towns on or near the plateau are described here.

Newala

Newala, the district capital and the main town, is a dusty but surprisingly bustling place with pleasantly cool temperatures and nice views over the Ruvuma Valley.

For comfortable accommodation, inquire about *Sollo's Guest House*, approximately 1km from town on the Masasi road; it's due to open in 1999. Otherwise, there are several local guesthouses in town along the main road. The best one is the nameless *guesthouse* just behind the NBC bank.

There are daily buses from Newala to Mtwara (Tsh2000, six to 10 hours) and to Masasi (Tsh1500, three hours). Both roads are unpaved; the ride from Newala down to Masasi offers good views.

Masasi

Masasi, a long town stretched out along the main road, lies off the edge of the Makonde plateau. It's an important district centre and transport hub for onward travel west towards Tunduru and north to Nachingwea and Liwale. In the late 19th century, the Anglican Universities' Mission to Central Africa (UMCA) came from Unguja to Masasi, where they established a settlement of former slaves.

About 70km east of Masasi on the road to Mtwara is **Mahiwa**, site of one of WWI's bloodiest battles in Africa in which more than 2000 lost their lives.

Places to Stay & Eat Most of the guesthouses are at the western end of town, between the petrol station and the bus stand.

The Makonde

The Makonde, known throughout East Africa for their ebony woodcarvings, are one of Tanzania's largest ethnic groups. They originated in northern Mozambique, where many still live. Beginning in the 18th century, large numbers of Makonde began to migrate northwards across the Ruvuma River and up the coast, as well as onto the Makonde plateau around Newala. Some of these migrations were likely undertaken to escape flooding in the Ruvuma Valley. More Makonde followed later in the 19th century, seeking relief from famine in Mozambique and refuge from the raids of slave traders. The Mozambican War, which was especially brutal in the north of the country, sparked another large influx, with up to 15,000 Makonde coming over the border during the 1970s and 1980s in search of safe haven and better employment. While some returned following the 1992 peace accords, many stayed and have now become integrated into Tanzanian life. In Tanzania, apart from a significant carving community in Dar es Salaam, the

Makonde have settled primarily in the Mtwara, Newala and Lindi districts in the south-east, with the largest concentrations on the Makonde plateau. Although the Makonde on both sides of the Ruvuma are considered to be a single ethnic entity, there are now numerous cultural and linguistic differences between the two groups. It is the Tanzanian Makonde who have been primarily responsible for the development of modern Makonde sculpture.

The Makonde, like many tribes in the south-east, are matrilineal. Although customs are gradually changing, children and inheritances normally belong to the woman, and it is common for husbands to move to the village of their wives after marriage. Settlements are widely scattered – possibly a remnant of the days when the Makonde sought to evade slave raids – and there is no tradition of a unified political system. Each village is governed by a hereditary chief and a council of elders.

Due to their isolated location, the Makonde have remained largely insulated from colonial and post-colonial influences, and are considered to be one of Tanzania's most traditional groups. There is speculation as to why the Makonde chose to establish themselves on a waterless plateau. The relative safety which the area offered from outside intervention (especially during slave trading days), and the absence of the tsetse fly are probable factors. Today, subsistence farming is the basic means of making a living, and the Makonde have developed agricultural techniques to deal with the lack of water. Many Makonde also work as migrant labourers. During the 18th and 19th centuries, the Makonde resisted the encroachments of Arab culture, and today most still adhere to traditional religions, though there are sizable pockets of Muslims and Christians.

Makonde carvings originate in Tanzania, but are copied by artists all over East Africa.

Top Ten Guest House, about 1km east of the bus stand on the main road, has basic but acceptable rooms for Tsh2000/3000. Nearby, opposite the petrol station is *Masasi Hotel* with rooms from Tsh4000. *Siraya*, also near the petrol station, is slightly more upmarket, with rooms from Tsh7500.

Both the Masasi Hotel and Siraya have simple *restaurants*. Otherwise, there are numerous *food stalls* near the market. If you're coming from Mtwara and staying at any of these places, have the bus drop you by the petrol station to avoid having to walk back into town from the bus stand.

Getting There & Away The bus stand is at the far western end of town on the Tunduru road. The road between Masasi and Mtwara is paved for the most part and in generally good condition. Minibuses go between the two towns throughout the day (Tsh2400, five to six hours); the first one leaves from either town at 5 am, and the last about 2 pm. The road from Masasi to Tunduru is in very bad condition. It can take up to 12 hours to cover the 180km stretch; during the rainy season it is often impassable.

Ndanda

About 40km north-east of Masasi along the main road and off the edge of the Makonde plateau, is the town of Ndanda. It is notable for its large Benedictine monastery and the adjoining hospital which serves as the major health clinic for the entire region. The monastery was founded by German missionaries in the late 19th century. About 2km outside of Ndanda towards Masasi is a small Makonde carving workshop where you can get good quality carvings at very reasonable prices.

The only lodging in Ndanda is *Nuru Ndanda Hotel*, at the bus stand and diagonally opposite the hospital. It has basic singles/doubles for Tsh2000/3000 (Tsh5000 for a double with bathroom) and a restaurant.

LINDI

In its early days, Lindi was part of the Sultan of Zanzibar's domain, a terminus of the slave caravan route from Lake Nyasa, a regional colonial capital, and the main town in south-eastern Tanzania. Early in the twentieth century it moved briefly into the lime light when dinosaur bones were discovered nearby (see the boxed text *'Brachiosaurus brancai'* below).

Today, it's a crumbling, quiet, almost listless place, permeated by an air of wistful decay. A few carved doorways, ruins of an Arab tower, and the old German boma are the only reminders of its more glorious past. The town's main redeeming feature is its attractive setting on palm-fringed Lindi Bay, which is still a busy dhow port for boats up and down the coast. With its Hindu temple and Indian merchants, Lindi has a distinctly Asian flavour.

Salt production is the main industry in the area, and you'll see several salt flats along the road into town. There's also a sisal plantation in Kikwetu, near the airfield. About 6km from town off the airfield road is Mtema beach, which makes a pleasant excursion, though watch out for your valuables.

Brachiosaurus brancai

Tendunguru Hill, about 100km north-west of Lindi, is the site of one of the most significant paleontological finds in history. From 1909 to 1912, a team of German paleontologists unearthed the remains of more than a dozen different dinosaur species, including the skeleton of *Brachiosaurus brancai*, the largest known dinosaur in the world. The *brachiosaurus* skeleton is now on display at the Museum of Natural History in Berlin. Scientists are not sure why so many dinosaur fossils were discovered here, although it is thought that flooding or some other natural catastrophe was the cause of their death.

Today, Tendunguru is of interest mainly to hard-core paleontologists. There is little to see and access to the site is difficult, even with your own vehicle. If you do want to visit, you will need to get permission from the District Commissioner in Lindi.

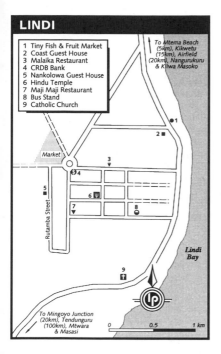

LINDI

1 Tiny Fish & Fruit Market
2 Coast Guest House
3 Malaika Restaurant
4 CRDB Bank
5 Nankolowa Guest House
6 Hindu Temple
7 Maji Maji Restaurant
8 Bus Stand
9 Catholic Church

To Mtema Beach
(5km), Kikwetu
(15km), Airfield
(20km), Nangurukuru
& Kilwa Masoko

Market

Rutamba Street

Lindi
Bay

To Mingoyo Junction
(20km), Tendunguru
(100km), Mtwara
& Masasi

0   0.5   1 km

There is a coral reef running south of Lindi down to Sudi Bay. The area has diverse marine life and has been proposed as a possible protected marine area.

Places to Stay & Eat

The best place to stay is *Nankolowa Guest House* in the centre of town on Rutamba St, about 400m south-west of the market. Clean singles/doubles with nets and fans are Tsh3000/3500, including breakfast served in a cheery dining room. Other meals can be arranged with advance notice.

Coast Guest House has a pretty setting on the beach, but is run-down and unsavoury. Rooms are Tsh1200/1500. No food is available, though there's a small fish and fruit market nearby on the beach.

Maji Maji Restaurant about 500m down from CRDB bank has good local food for about Tsh500 per plate. Another place to try

is *Malaika Restaurant*, about 500m east of the market.

Getting There & Away

Commercial air services to Lindi are suspended. There's an airstrip for charter flights.

There is at least one bus daily to Mtwara (Tsh1500), and minivans throughout the day to Mingoyo junction where you can get transport to Masasi, though you will likely have to wait a while. There are some very grubby guesthouses in Mingoyo, but it's best to plan your travels so you don't have to stay overnight there.

There are also buses most mornings to Nangurukuru (Tsh4000, six to seven hours), from where you can get transport to Kilwa Kivinje and Kilwa Masoko.

The only boats stopping at Lindi are local dhows.

KILWA MASOKO

Kilwa Masoko (Kilwa of the Market) is a tiny coastal town about halfway between Dar es Salaam and Mtwara. It is of interest primarily as a base for visiting the ruins of the 15th century Arab settlement at nearby Kilwa Kisiwani.

The National Microfinance Bank changes cash, but not travellers cheques; you will have to go to Lindi (although you cannot always change cheques in Lindi, either), Mtwara or Dar es Salaam.

Petrol in Kilwa costs Tsh650 per litre.

Things to See & Do

The main thing to do in Kilwa Masoko is visit the ruins either at **Kilwa Kisiwani** or on some of the other offshore islands (see Around Kilwa Masoko later in this chapter). Otherwise, there are a few pretty **beaches** on the outskirts of town. The closest is Jimbizi, to the east behind the health clinic. Check with locals before swimming here, as currents can be strong.

Places to Stay

The two best guesthouses in town are *Hilton Guest House* near the market and *Mjaka Enterprises Guest House & Hotel*, on the main

SOUTH-EASTERN TANZANIA

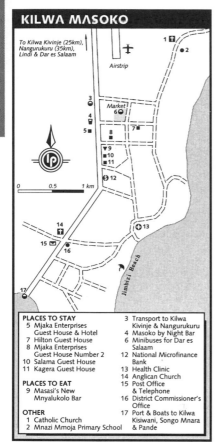

KILWA MASOKO

To Kilwa Kivinje (25km),
Nangurukuru (35km),
Lindi & Dar es Salaam

Airstrip

Market

0   0.5   1 km

Jimbizi Beach

PLACES TO STAY
5 Mjaka Enterprises
   Guest House & Hotel
7 Hilton Guest House
8 Mjaka Enterprises
   Guest House Number 2
10 Salama Guest House
11 Kagera Guest House

PLACES TO EAT
9 Masasi's New
   Mnyalukolo Bar

OTHER
1 Catholic Church
2 Mnazi Mmoja Primary School

3 Transport to Kilwa
   Kivinje & Nangurukuru
4 Masoko by Night Bar
6 Minibuses for Dar es
   Salaam
12 National Microfinance
   Bank
13 Health Clinic
14 Anglican Church
15 Post Office
   & Telephone
16 District Commissioner's
   Office
17 Port & Boats to Kilwa
   Kisiwani, Songo Mnara
   & Pande

road. They're both quite similar, although the water supply and toilet situation (western sit-down style, compared with the Hilton's squat models) are better at Mjaka, while the Hilton generally has a better selection of food. At both, clean rooms with fan and net are Tsh2000 (Tsh3000 with bathroom).

Otherwise, there are several local guesthouses, all charging about Tsh1000 for a basic single. Two of the better ones are *Salama Guest House* and *Kagera Guest House*, both on the main road. A small step

up from these is *Mjaka Enterprises Guest House Number 2*, about one block off the main road, with rooms for Tsh1500 (Tsh2000 with bathroom).

Places to Eat

The food selection in Kilwa is limited. You will be lucky if you find a vegetable during your stay. There are also no bakeries in town; chapatis are standard breakfast fare.

The best place to eat is *Masasi's New Mnyalukolo Bar* on the main road, which does good chicken and chips and has pleasant outdoor tables.

Both the *Hilton* and *Mjaka Enterprises Guest House & Hotel* have restaurants which do fish/chicken/meat with rice, although it is a rare day when you will have a selection of all three.

Entertainment

The best bar is *Masasi's New Mnyalukolo Bar*. Otherwise, you're left with the more tawdry *Masoko by Night*, on the main road up from the market.

Getting There & Away

Air All commercial flights to Kilwa have been suspended. There is an airfield for charter flights. Charter flights from Dar es Salaam cost about US$770 one way.

Bus Road access to Kilwa is completely cut off during the rainy season. During the dry season, minibuses run several times a week between Kilwa Masoko (stopping also at Kilwa Kivinje) and Dar es Salaam's Temeke bus stand (Tsh4500, 10 to 12 hours). Departures in either direction are at 6 am. Before boarding, be aware that it's a long, rough journey! Buses from Kilwa to Dar es Salaam should be booked in advance; the ticket vendors are near the market.

Alternatively, from Dar es Salaam you can take a bus heading to Lindi or Mtwara and get out at Nangurukuru junction, from where you can get local transport to Kilwa Kivinje (Tsh300, 11km) or Kilwa Masoko (Tsh500, 35km). The road between Nangurukuru and Kilwa Masoko is good tarmac.

To go from Kilwa south, you'll have to go first to Nangurukuru, from where minibuses go most mornings to Lindi (Tsh4000, six to seven hours). From Lindi you can find onward transport towards Mtwara. Direct buses between Mtwara and Dar es Salaam stop at Nangurukuru, but it's usually difficult to get a seat.

If you get stuck in Nangurukuru, your only option is the very basic and sleazy *Kilwa Comfort Guest House* on the main roundabout with rooms for about Tsh1000.

Boat Dhows from Kilwa ply up and down the coast, as far as Dar es Salaam. However, safety is questionable – every year several dhows capsize en route to Dar es Salaam – and many boat captains are unwilling to take foreigners.

Getting Around

Kilwa Masoko is easily covered on foot. Pick-ups go several times a day from the main road just up from the market to Nangurukuru (Tsh500) and Kilwa Kivinje (Tsh300).

AROUND KILWA MASOKO
Kilwa Kisiwani

Kilwa Kisiwani (Kilwa on the island) was once East Africa's most important trading centre. Today, the ruins of the settlement are considered to be one of the most significant groups of Swahili buildings on the East African coast. Despite their historical significance, the ruins are not well maintained and there are no tourist facilities. Given the difficulty of getting to Kilwa, the ruins will likely be attractive only to those with a particular interest in archaeology or East African history.

History The coast near Kilwa has been inhabited by humans for several thousand years; artefacts from the Late and Middle Stone Age have been found on Kilwa Kisiwani. However, there were no significant settlements in the area until the end of the 10th century and Kilwa remained a relatively undistinguished place until the early 13th

century when trade links developed with Sofala, 1500km to the south in present-day Mozambique. Kilwa came to control Sofala and to dominate its lucrative gold trade, and before long it had become the most powerful trade centre along the Swahili coast. Its influence extended from Kilwa to Mafia and up to the Zanzibar archipelago. The famous traveller and chronicler Ibn Battuta visited in the early 14th century and described Kilwa as being an exceptionally beautiful and well-constructed town.

In the late 15th century, Kilwa's fortunes began to decline. Sofala freed itself from the island's dominance, and in the early 16th century Kilwa came under the control of the Portuguese. It wasn't until more than 200 years later that Kilwa regained its independence and became a significant trading centre again, this time as a trade entrepôt for slaves being shipped from the mainland to the islands of Mauritius, Réunion and Comoros. In the 1780s, Kilwa came under the control of the Sultan of Oman. By the mid-19th century, the town had completely declined and the local administration was relocated to Kilwa Kivinje.

Information Before visiting the ruins, you will need to get a permit from the District Commissioner's office at Kilwa Masoko. There's no charge, and the permit is issued while you wait; it's best to go in the morning. Once at Kilwa Kisiwani, there is a local guide, although he speaks only minimal English. For his services, he expects a fairly hefty Tsh1000 tip.

For detailed information about the ruins in English, ask at the District Commissioner's office to see a copy of HN Chittick's very informative manuscript. The National Museum in Dar es Salaam has a small display on the ruins at Kilwa Kisiwani.

There are a few small villages on the island, but no accommodation.

The Ruins The ruins are in two groups. When approaching Kilwa Kisiwani the first building you'll find is the Arabic **fort**. It was built in the early 19th century by the

Omani Arabs, on the site of a Portuguese fort dating from the early 16th century. To the south-west of the fort are the ruins of the **Great Mosque**. Some sections date to the late 13th century, although most are from building additions made in the 15th century. In its day, this was the largest mosque on the East African coast. Further south-west and behind the Great Mosque is a smaller **mosque** dating from the early 15th century. This is considered to be the best preserved of the buildings at Kilwa. To the west of the small mosque are the crumbling remains of the **Makutani**, a large walled enclosure in the centre of which lived some of the sultans of Kilwa. It is estimated to date from the mid-18th century.

Almost 1.5km from the fort along the coast is **Husuni Kubwa**, once a massive complex of buildings covering about two acres and, together with the nearby **Husuni Ndogo**, the oldest of Kilwa's ruins. The complex, which is estimated to date from the 12th century or earlier, is set on a hill and must have once commanded great views over the bay. Now much of the original layout is indistinct and overgrown, although the octagonal bathing pool is still in good condition. Husuni Ndogo is smaller and is thought to date from the same time as Husuni Kubwa, although archaeologists are not yet sure of its original function. To reach these ruins, you can walk along the beach at low tide. Otherwise, you'll have to take a slightly longer inland route, for which you will probably need the services of the guide.

Getting There & Away Local boats go from the port at Kilwa Masoko to Kilwa Kisiwani whenever there are passengers. The trip costs Tsh100; for your own boat, it is Tsh1000 each way. Tourists also have to pay a Tsh300 port fee. With a good wind, the trip takes about 20 minutes.

Kilwa Kivinje

Kilwa Kivinje (Kilwa of the Casuarina Trees) is a tiny village with a small but attractive dhow port about 25km north of Kilwa Masoko. Kilwa Kivinje became the regional capital for a brief period in the mid-19th century following the decline of Kilwa Kisiwani. Most buildings from the era are in an advanced state of decay, although you can still see some carved doors and interesting architectural remnants.

Kilwa Kivinje can be easily visited as a day trip from Kilwa Masoko. If you want to stay overnight here, your options are *New Sudi Guest House* on the main road, *Savoye Guest House* by the dhow port, or *Four Ways Guest House* near the market. All have single rooms (only) for Tsh1000, and all are equally basic. For meals, there are several food stalls in town.

Kilwa Kivinje is about 5km off the main road between Nangurukuru and Kilwa Masoko. Pick-ups go several times a day from here to both Kilwa Masoko (Tsh500) and Nangurukuru (Tsh300). The minibus between Dar es Salaam and Kilwa Masoko also stops at Kilwa Kivinje (Tsh4000 from Kivinje to Dar es Salaam).

Dhows go from Kilwa Kivinje to Mafia (Tsh3000) and Dar es Salaam (Tsh5000), but are unsafe and not recommended.

Offshore Islands

Songo Mnara Songo Mnara lies about 8km south of Kilwa Kisiwani. It contains ruins at its northern end that are believed to date from the 14th and 15th centuries, and are considered in many respects to be more significant than those at Kilwa. In addition to the remains of a palace, several mosques and a wall, there are also ruins of numerous houses. On the western side of Songo Mnara, at **Sanje Majoma**, are additional ruins dating from the same period. The small island of **Sanje ya Kati**, between Songo Mnara and Kilwa Masoko, has some lesser ruins of a third settlement, also believed to date from the same era.

There is nowhere to sleep on Songo Mnara. As with Kilwa Kisiwani, you must first get permission from the District Commissioner's office in Kilwa Masoko before visiting.

The best way to get to Songo Mnara is via motorboat from Kilwa Masoko, which can be arranged through the District Commissioner's office. It will cost around Tsh30,000 including fuel for a round-trip excursion. Alternatively, there is a far cheaper motorised local dhow which departs most mornings about 6 am from Kilwa Masoko to Pande, and will stop on request at Songo Mnara. The boat returns to Kilwa Masoko the same day, departing Pande about 1 pm. Although non-motorised dhows go from Kilwa Masoko to Songo Mnara, they can take several hours in low winds and are not recommended. After landing at Songo Mnara, be prepared to wade through mangrove swamps before reaching the island proper.

Songo Songo Songo Songo lies about 25km north-east of Kilwa Kivinje. The island, which measures about four sq km and has a population of about 3500, is covered by low shrub and coconut palms. Together with several tiny surrounding islets, it is an ecologically important area for nesting sea turtles and marine birds. The island is also the site of a significant natural gas field discovered in the mid-1970s; exploration in search of additional fields is ongoing. Despite concerns about possible detrimental effects on Songo Songo's marine habitat, there are plans for a project to convert the gas reserves into electricity for Dar es Salaam; due to funding difficulties, the project is currently stalled.

To get here by sea, you will have to go to Kilwa Kivinje and arrange a local boat there. As with all longer trips by dhow, be aware of safety considerations. The gas companies working on Songo Songo often have charter flights to the island from Dar es Salaam. Check with Dar es Salaam-based air charter operators to find out if there are any extra seats available.

MAFIA ISLAND

Mafia island lies off the Rufiji River delta about 120km south of Dar es Salaam. Owing to its central position along the coast, the island was an important trading post from the 11th to 13th centuries, in the days when the Shirazis ruled much of the East African coastal area. One of the first settlements at Mafia was built during this era at Ras Kisimani, followed later by one at Kua on the nearby island of Juani.

By the time the Portuguese arrived at the start of the 16th century, Mafia had lost much of its significance and had become part of the territory ruled by the Sultan of Kilwa. In the early 18th century, the main settlement moved to Chole island, and Mafia again began to flourish as a trade centre linking Kilwa to the south with Unguja to the north.

During the colonial era, the island was first under the control of the Germans, who had their headquarters on Chole, and then under the British, who made use of Mafia as a naval and air base.

Today, Mafia is better known as a resort island for deep-sea fishing (best between September and March) and scuba diving. It's a superb place to do this as the 200m-deep trough running along the sea bed about 1km off the western shoreline of the island is home to a vast number of aquatic species. The coral formations are best off the small islands scattered around Mafia, particularly the Kitutia and other reefs around Juani and Jibondo islands close to Chole Bay.

Mafia is also notable as a breeding ground for giant turtles, which come up onto the white coral sands to lay their eggs. They do this principally on the uninhabited islands of Shungumbili, Barakuni and Nyororo.

The island's human population is estimated at about 40,000. Most residents are smallholder farmers; crops include cassava, rice, pawpaw and coconut.

Information

For those interested in more details on the history of Mafia, there is an interesting set of articles in the Tanzania Notes and Records reprints edition, *Maritime Tanzania*, available at the National Museum in Dar es Salaam and the Arusha Declaration Museum in Arusha (Tsh6000).

Things to See & Do

The coconut palms and cashew trees that cover much of Mafia were established by

Mafia Island Marine Park

Mafia Island Marine Park encompasses an area of approximately 400 sq km around the southern end of Mafia Island and Chole Bay. Within its boundaries is a unique complex of estuarine, mangrove, coral reef and marine channel ecosystems, including the only natural forest on the island. It is a beautiful area and highly biodiverse, with close to 400 species of fish identified on the surrounding coral reefs.

Although management of the new park has been hampered by lack of experience and funds, several significant achievements have been registered to date, including a notable reduction in dynamite fishing on nearby reefs and increased community awareness of and support for conservation goals. However, many challenges remain. New restrictions on live coral mining and on small mesh nets are proving particularly unpopular with local residents. Many view coral as the only readily available building material that they have, and fishing as their only way to earn a living. Staff are now working with residents of the 10 villages within the park's boundaries (with an estimated total population of between 15,000 and 17,000) to assist them in developing alternative livelihoods.

The park is obviously significant for its role in protecting Mafia's ecosystems. Yet just as important in the eyes of many conservationists is the way the park provides an example for the development of other marine parks and protected areas along the Tanzanian coast. Mafia itself was a long time coming; although Chole Bay, Tutia Reef and some other areas within or near its boundaries were proposed as marine reserves as early as 1975, the park was not officially established until July 1995. This delay was due in part to the fact that there was no legislative framework and no model to be followed as a guide. Now, these basic procedures are in place, with the avent of the Marine Parks and Reserves Act of 1994. Although still lacking in regulatory and enforcement powers, it is hoped that this act will serve as a catalyst for the establishment of future parks.

Mafia Island Marine Park is under the jurisdiction of the Ministry of Natural Resources and Tourism's Fisheries Division (☎ 051-116162 or 0811-340111, PO Box 2462, Dar es Salaam), on the 8th floor of Ardhi House at the eastern end of Kivukoni Front. There are park offices on Mafia in Kilindoni and in Utende; headquarters are planned for Utende.

the Omanis during their Zanzibari heyday, although the soil is poor and the island has never been able to support a large human population.

Mafia's main attraction is its diverse and spectacular natural environment, now protected as part of Mafia Island Marine Park – Tanzania's first, and the largest marine park in the western Indian Ocean. See the boxed text 'Mafia Island Marine Park' for details.

There are ruins on the island of **Juani**, principally those of five mosques dating from the 18th and 19th centuries. Little remains above ground from the early Shirazi settlement.

On tiny **Chole island**, measuring just 1km in length, are picturesque but overgrown ruins, dating from the 19th century, and two short but interesting history/nature trails.

Places to Stay & Eat

The best budget accommodation is at *Lizu's* (☎ *051-116233 ext 96, or Mafia 96*), about a five minute walk from the airfield in Kilindoni, with rooms for about Tsh5000.

There are several options for those with more money. *Kinasi Lodge* (☎ *051-843501, fax 843495,* email *kinasi@intafrica.com, PO Box 3052, Dar es Salaam or PO Box 26, Mafia Island*), is a privately owned

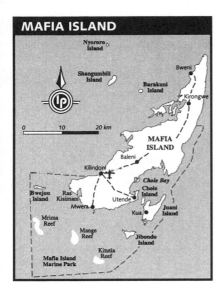

MAFIA ISLAND

32153, fax 33135, email emerson@zanzibar .org). A large portion of the profits from Emerson's On Chole are channelled back into the community, particularly its hospital.

All of the above places can arrange fishing or diving and snorkelling trips. Most also include airfield transfers in their prices; verify when booking.

Getting There & Away

Air The only noncharter service is Dar Aviation (☎ 051-844158/68), which goes three times weekly between Dar es Salaam and Mafia for US$90 one way (Tsh46,000 for residents). Kinasi Ltd (☎ 051-843501) provides an air charter service between Dar es Salaam and Mafia for guests of Kinasi Hotel. The only other option is to charter your own plane (US$500 one way including tax for a three-seater plane from Dar es Salaam or US$740 from Unguja).

Boat The MV *Canadian Spirit* usually stops briefly at Mafia on its weekly run between Mtwara and Dar es Salaam. You will generally be charged the full Mtwara-Dar es Salaam fare. See under Boat in the Mtwara Getting There & Away section for further details. Sailing time between Mtwara and Mafia is roughly eight hours.

Dhows go to Mafia from numerous points along the coast. Two of the closer ports are Kisiju, about 45km south-east of Mkuranga on the Dar es Salaam to Kilwa road, and Nyamisati, about 45km south-east of Bungu, also on the Dar es Salaam to Kilwa Rd. Remember, however, that it is illegal for foreigners to travel in dhows and many captains will not take you.

Getting Around

There is no regular public transport on Mafia. All the more expensive hotels arrange airfield pick-ups for their guests. Budget travellers can contact Mama Shirazi at Lizu's hotel for assistance.

SELOUS GAME RESERVE

With an area of approximately 50,000 sq km, the Selous is Africa's largest game reserve

luxury lodge for 20 guests overlooking Chole Bay. Rooms are US$130 per person including full board. Diving, snorkelling and fishing excursions can be arranged, as can diving certification courses.

Mafia Island Lodge has a good setting on Chole Bay, though its standards are a step down from those at the Kinasi. It's owned partly by the government and partly by the Accor/Tahi chain. Rooms are US$147/210 a single/double with full board. Book through Accor/Tahi (☎ 057-4292, fax 8071, email tahi@yako.habari.co.tz).

Dolphin Island Pole Pole Bungalow Resort (☎ 0811-372532 or 051-843717, fax 051-116239, email archipelago@tanzania .org, PO Box 198, Mafia) is Italian owned and has two-bed luxury bungalows for US$120 per person (US$180 with private bathroom), including full board.

Emerson's On Chole, Chole island, is a comfortable, laid-back place with good tented accommodation for US$40 per person including full board; closed April and May. Bookings should be made through Emerson's House on Unguja (☎ 054-30609, covering 5% of Tanzania's total land area. The reserve provides shelter for more than half of the country's elephant, as well as significant populations of buffalo, wild dog, crocodile and hippo, a rich variety of birdlife, and some of Tanzania's last remaining black rhino.

Parts of the reserve were set aside as early as 1905, although it was not until 1922 that the area was expanded and given its present name (after Frederick Courteney Selous, the British explorer who was killed in the reserve during WWI). The area continued to be extended over the next several decades until assuming its present boundaries in 1975.

One of the main features of the Selous is the huge **Rufiji River**, which has one of the largest water catchment areas in East Africa. In the northern end of the reserve, where the Great Ruaha River flows into the Rufiji, is **Stiegler's Gorge**. The gorge, which averages 100m deep, is named after a German explorer who was killed here by an elephant in 1907. Most of the safari camps and lodges are in this area.

Information

The best time to visit is from June to October, during the cool, dry season, and in January and February when the rains usually break. Much of the reserve is inaccessible from late February to May during the heavy rains. The tourist camps close for at least part of this time, usually during April and May.

The booklet *Selous Game Reserve: A Guide to the Northern Sector* put out by the Selous Conservation Program, is an excellent source of background information. It's available at bookshops in Arusha and Dar es Salaam, or from the Wildlife Division in Dar es Salaam.

The *Selous Conservation Program Discussion Paper Series*, put out by the German Agency for Technical Cooperation (GTZ) and the Selous Conservation Program, is a good resource for those with a scientific or research interest in the Selous. The papers are available from the Selous Conservation Program, PO Box 1519, Dar es Salaam.

In addition to game drives, boat trips up the Rufiji River are offered by most of the camps; guided walking tours can also be arranged.

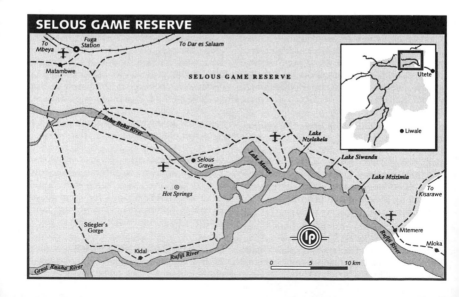

Administration & Fees The Selous falls under the jurisdiction of the Wildlife Division of the Ministry of Natural Resources and Tourism (☎ 866376, 866064, PO Box 25295, Dar es Salaam, Ivory Room, corner of Pugu Rd and Changombe Rd). There are staff bases in the northern Selous at Matambwe (reserve headquarters) and Mtemere.

The entry fee for the Selous is US$20 (US$5 for children between five and 15, free for children under five), plus a US$30 per day vehicle fee. Camping fees are US$20 per person (US$15 for children between five and 15, free for children under five).

Places to Stay

All the reserve's facilities are concentrated in the extreme northern end. In order to prevent the type of high-volume package tourism threatening Tanzania's northern parks, the emphasis is on low-volume/high price tourism. There are no budget facilities in or near the reserve other than two *camp sites*, one at Mtemere and another close to Matambwe at the Beho Beho bridge. Check with the Wildlife Division or reserve headquarters before going to make sure these are open. If you plan on camping you must bring everything with you including camping equipment, food and water.

At Stiegler's Gorge itself is the *Stiegler's Gorge Safari Camp*, which was built in 1977 for Norwegian scientists and engineers working in the area; it is currently closed.

North-east of here on the Beho Beho River is the *Beho Beho Safari Camp* which can be booked through Oyster Bay Hotel (☎ 051-668062, fax 668631, email oysterbayhotel@twiga.com, PO Box 2261, Dar es Salaam). Accommodation is in stone bandas; rates are US$300 per person, all-inclusive.

The exclusive *Mbuyuni Luxury Tented Camp* on the Rufiji River charges US$275 per person including full board. It's run by Selous Safari Company (☎ 051-34802, fax 112794, email selous@twiga.com, PO Box 1192, Dar es Salaam).

Sand Rivers Selous (☎ 254-288 2521, fax 288 2728, email sand-rivers@twiga.com, PO Box 24133, Nairobi) also on the Rufiji River

and even more exclusive, has accommodation in luxury cottages for US$365 per person sharing, full board. Bookings can be made directly or through any Dar es Salaam travel agent specialising in the southern circuit.

Rufiji River Camp, also on the Rufiji, has accommodation in luxury tents for US$230 per person including full board. Book through Hippo Tours & Safaris (☎ 051-36860, fax 75165, PO Box 1658, Dar es Salaam) or through any southern circuit tour operator.

Mbuyu Safari Camp, on a tributary of the Rufiji with excellent views over the river, has luxury tented accommodation for US$235 per person including full board. Bookings can be made through Southern Tanganyika Game Safaris & Tours (☎ 0812-781971, fax 051-116413, email stgs@twiga.com, PO Box 2341, Dar es Salaam).

All of the above prices include game drives, boat trips or walking safaris. Less expensive accommodation-only prices are also available on request.

Getting There & Away

Air Coastal Travels has daily flights to the Selous from Dar es Salaam (US$120) and Unguja (US$120), and three times weekly between the Selous and Ruaha National Park (US$270). All of the lodges arrange airfield transfers.

Bus A minibus leaves daily at about 6 am from Dar es Salaam's Temeke bus stand to Mloka, about 10km from Mtemere (Tsh3500, eight to nine hours). From Mloka, you can usually find a ride with a vehicle from the reserve for the remainder of the trip. Heading back to Dar es Salaam, buses depart Mloka very early, between 5 and 6 am. There's no accommodation in Mloka, so you'll have to arrange something with the villagers. Before arriving this way, contact the reserve in advance to be sure there will be a rental vehicle available when you reach the gate. Trying to hitch a ride within the Selous is not feasible.

Train To reach the Selous by train from Dar es Salaam, take the TAZARA line to Fuga station (approximately five hours). Be sure you board an 'ordinary' train (departures on Monday, Thursday and Saturday from Dar es Salaam), as the express trains do not stop at Fuga. From Fuga, the lodges will collect you in one of their vehicles, but you must make arrangements for this before you leave Dar es Salaam. Being collected won't be cheap unless you're sharing the cost with others.

Car & Motorcycle Those coming by road in their own vehicle have two options. The first is to take the Dar es Salaam to Mkongo road via Kibiti and then on to Mtemere (250km). The road is in poor condition between Mkongo and Mtemere and is sometimes impassable during the rainy season. The last petrol station is in Kibiti. Allow about eight hours from Dar es Salaam.

Alternatively, you can go from Dar es Salaam to Kisaki via Morogoro and then on to Matambwe but this is longer (350km) and will take at least nine hours. The road is good tarmac as far as Morogoro. From Morogoro, drive in the direction of the teachers' training college and then turn right towards Kisaki via a steep, rough road through the Uluguru Mountains. Allow around seven hours for the stretch from Morogoro to Matambwe.

Language

'Standard' Swahili is the language spoken in Zanzibar Town although several other variants, or dialects exist. Written Swahili, the language of newspapers, textbooks and literature, usually conforms to that spoken on the East African coast.

Although Swahili may seem a bit daunting at first, its structure is fairly regular, and pronunciation uncomplicated. You'll soon discover that just a handful of basic words will go a long way, and will rapidly break down barriers between you and the many people you meet on your travels in Tanzania.

If your time is limited, concentrate first on the greetings (of critical importance in Tanzanian society), and then on numbers (very useful when negotiating with market vendors, taxi drivers, etc). The words and phrases included in this chapter will help you get started; for a more comprehensive guide to the language get hold of Lonely Planet's excellent 2nd edition *Swahili phrasebook*. Good luck, and *Safari njema!* (happy travels).

Pronunciation

Perhaps the easiest part of learning Swahili is the pronunciation. Every letter gets pronounced, unless it's part of the consonant combinations discussed in the 'Consonants' section below. If a letter is written twice, it is pronounced twice – or rather, gets extended into two syllables. For example, *mzee* (respected elder) has three syllables: *m-ZE-e* – note that the 'm' is a separate syllable, and that the double 'e' indicates a lengthened vowel sound.

Word stress in Swahili almost always falls on the second-to-last syllable.

Vowels

Correct pronunciation of vowels is the key to making yourself understood in Swahili. If the following guidelines don't work for you, listen closely to how Swahili speakers pronounce their words and spend some time practising. There's also a useful audio pronunciation guide available on the World Wide Web at: http://www.yale.edu/swahili/sound/pronunce.htm.

Remember that if two vowels appear next to each other, each must be pronounced in turn. For example, *kawaida* (usual) is pronounced *ka-wa-EE-da*.

a	as in 'calm' (*dada*, 'sister')
e	as the 'a' in 'may' (*wewe*, 'you')
i	as the 'e' in 'me' (*sisi*, 'we')
o	as in 'go' (*moja*, 'one')
u	as the 'o' in 'to' (*duka*, 'store')

Consonants

r	Swahili speakers make only a slight distinction between **r** and **l**; try using a light 'd' where you read 'r' and you'll be pretty close.
dh	as 'th' in 'this' (*dhambi*, 'sin')
th	as 'th' in 'thing' (*thelathini*, 'thirty')
ny	as the 'ni' in 'onion' (*nyasi*, 'grass')
ng'	as in 'singer' (*ng'ombe*, 'cow'); practise by trying to use the 'ng' sound at the beginning of a word
gh	a guttural sound, similar to the *ch* in Scottish *loch* (*ghali*, 'expensive')
g	as in 'get' (*gari*, 'car')
ch	as in 'church' (*chakula*, 'food')

Essential Greetings & Civilities

Greetings are probably the most important part of the Swahili vocabulary for a traveller to Tanzania. It's worth taking the time to familiarise yourself with the few we include here.

Jambo is pidgin Swahili, used to greet tourists who are presumed not to understand the language. There are two possible responses, each with different connotations: *Jambo* (Hello, now please speak to me in English), and *Sijambo* (Things aren't bad with me, and I'm willing to try a little Swahili).

If people assume you can speak a little Swahili, greetings may involve one or a number of the following exchanges:

How are you? (to one person)	*Hujambo?*
I'm fine.	*Sijambo.*
How are all of you?	*Hamjambo?*
We're fine.	*Hatujambo.*

The word *habari* (meaning 'news') can also be used for general greetings. Among other 'habari' greetings, you may hear *salama* substituted for *habari*, or the habari may be dropped altogether.

How are you?	*Habari?*
What's the news?	*Habari gani?*
Good morning.	*Habari za asubuhi?*
Good day.	*Habari za leo?*
Good afternoon.	*Habari za mchana?*
Good evening. (including night)	*Habari za jioni?*
What's happening with you?	*Habari yako?*
How are you all?	*Habari zenu?*

By memorising these three simple words, you can reply to almost anything:

Good.	*Nzuri.*
Fine.	*Salama.*
Clean.	*Safi.*

There is also a respectful greeting used for elders:

Greetings.	*Shikamoo.*
(response)	*Marahaba.*

Farewells are (by comparison) generally short and sweet:

Goodbye.	*Kwa heri.*
(Until) tomorrow.	*Kesho.*
Later on.	*Baadaye.*
Good night.	*Usiku mwema.*

Small Talk

Please. (if asking a big favour)	*Tafadhali.*
Excuse me.	*Samahani.*
Can you help me, please?	*Tafadhali, naomba msaada.*
Thank you (very much).	*Asante (sana).*
Yes.	*Ndiyo.*
No.	*Hapana.*
OK.	*Sawa.*
Maybe.	*Labda/Pengine.*
What's your name?	*Jina lako nani?/ Unaitwa nani?*
My name is ...	*Jina langu ni .../ Naitwa ...*
Where are you from?	*Unatoka wapi?/ Kwenu ni wapi?*
I'm from ...	*Natokea .../Kwetu ni ...*
May I take a picture?	*Naomba kupiga picha.*

Language Difficulties

Do you speak English/Swahili?	*Unasema Kiingereza/ Kiswahili?*
I don't speak English/Swahili.	*Sisemi Kiingereza/ Kiswahili.*
Do you understand?	*Unaelewa?*
I understand.	*Naelewa.*
I don't understand.	*Sielewi.*
Please speak slowly.	*Tafadhali sema pole pole.*
Please repeat that.	*Tafadhali sema tena.*
How do you say ... in Swahili?	*Unasemaje ... kwa Kiswahili?*

Getting Around

(Remember to always exchange greetings before asking for help or information.)

What time is the ... leaving?	*... inaondoka saa ngapi?*
bus	*basi*
minibus	*daladala*
plane	*ndege*
train	*treni*
Is there a bus going to ...?	*Kuna basi ya ...?*

What time will we arrive?	*Tutafika saa ngapi?*
I'd like to buy a ticket.	*Nataka kununua tikiti.*
How much per person?	*Ni bei gani kwa kila mtu?*
I'd like to make a reservation to ...	*Nataka kufanya buking kwenda ...*
Please tell me when the bus arrives in ...	*Basi ikifika ..., tafadhali unijulishe.*
I want to get off here.	*Nitashuka hapa.*
Drop me off!	*Shusha!*
Stop!	*Simama!*

Where is the ...?	*... ni wapi?*
airport	*uwanja wa ndege*
bus station	*stesheni ya basi*
bus stop	*bas stendi*
taxi stand	*stendi ya teksi*
train station	*stesheni ya treni*

1st class	*daraja la kwanza*
2nd class	*daraja la pili*
3rd class	*daraja la tatu*

ship	*meli*
dhow (traditional sailing boat)	*dhau*
small wooden boat with motor	*mashua*
Where do we get on the boat?	*Tupande meli wapi?*
What time does the boat leave/arrive?	*Meli inaondoka/ inafika saa ngapi?*

I'd like to hire a ...	*Nataka kukodi ...*
bicycle	*baisikeli*
car	*gari*
motorcycle	*pikipiki*
row boat	*mtumbwi*

Directions

Excuse me, I'm looking for ...	*Tafadhali, natafuta ...*
I want to go to ...	*Nataka kwenda ...*

Is it near?	*Ni karibu?*
Is it far?	*Ni mbali?*
How many kilometres from here?	*Ni kilomita ngapi kutoka hapa?*
Turn around.	*Kata/Geuka.*
Turn back.	*Rudi nyuma.*

Go ...	*Kata/Pita/Chukua ...*
left	*kushoto*
right	*kulia*
straight ahead	*moja kwa moja*

information	*maelezo*
there	*huko*
over there	*pale*
next to	*jirani/karibu na*
map	*ramani*
north	*kaskazini*
south	*kusini*
east	*mashariki*
west	*magharibi*

Around Town

Where is the ...?	*... ni wapi?*
beach	*baharini/ufukwe*
bank	*benki*
church	*kanisa*
... embassy	*ubalozi wa ...*
market	*soko*
mosque	*msikiti*
museum	*makumbusho*
park (gardens)	*bustani*
police station	*kituo cha polisi*
post office	*posta*
river	*mto*
tourist office	*ofisi ya watalii*

Is (the post office) open?	*(Posta) imefunguliwa?*
I want to change some money.	*Nataka kubadilisha pesa.*

cheque	*hundi ya benki*
currency	*hela/pesa*

telephone centre	*mahali pa kupiga simu*
I'd like to make a phone call.	*Nataka kupiga simu.*
Is there a phone near here?	*Je, kuna simu karibu na hapa?*

Accommodation

guesthouse	*gesti*
hotel	*hoteli* (note: *hoteli* also means restaurant)

Excuse me, is there a hotel nearby?	*Samahani, kuna hoteli hapa karibuni?*
Do you have a room?	*Je, kuna nafasi ya chumba hapa?*

I want a ... room.	*Ninataka chumba ...*
ordinary	*cha kawaida*
cheaper	*cha bei rahisi*
larger	*kikubwa zaidi*
smaller	*kidogo zaidi*
quieter	*ambacho hakuna kelele*

Is there (a) ...?	*Je, kuna ...?*
air conditioning	*A.C.* (pron. 'ay-see')
bath	*bafu*
electricity	*umeme*
fan	*feni*
key	*ufunguo*
hot water	*maji ya moto*
toilet	*choo*
telephone	*simu*

How much is it per ...?	*Ni bei gani kwa ...?*
person	*kila mtu*
night	*usiku*
week	*wiki*

I'll stay for two/three nights.	*Nitakaa kwa usiku mbili/tatu.*
Can I look at the room?	*Naomba nikiweza kutazama chumba?*
Do you have another room?	*Kuna chumba kingine?*

I need (a) ...	*Ninahitaji ...*
blanket	*blanketi*
mosquito coils	*dawa ya mbu*
mosquito net	*chandalua*
pillow	*mto*
sheet/sheets	*shuka/mashuka*
soap	*sabuni*
toilet paper	*karatasi ya choo*
towel	*tauli*

bed	*kitanda*
bedroom	*chumba cha kulala*
breakfast	*chai cha asubuhi*
lights	*taa*
room/rooms	*chumba/vyumba*

Shopping

Is there a store near here?	*Je, kuna duka hapa jirani?*
Where can I buy ...?	*Naweza kununua ... wapi?*

Where is a ...?	*... ni wapi?*
bakery	*duka la mkate*
barber	*kinyozi*
bookshop	*duka la vitabu*
butcher	*duka la nyama*
chemist/drugstore	*duka la dawa*
clothes shop	*duka la nguo*
fruitshop	*duka la matunda*
vegetable shop	*duka la mboga*
general store/shop	*duka/kioski*
market	*soko*

How much is it?	*Ni bei gani?*
That's very expensive.	*Ghali sana.*
Is there a cheaper one?	*Kuna nyingine ambayo siyo ghali?*
Can you lower the price?	*Tafadhali, upunguze bei.*
It's a fair price.	*Ni bei nzuri/nafuu.*
OK, I'll take it.	*Haya, nakubali.*
I'm just looking.	*Naangalia/Natazama tu.*
I want one/two.	*Nataka moja/mbili.*
I want a larger ...	*Nataka ... kubwa zaidi.*
I want a smaller ...	*Nataka ... ndogo zaidi.*

battery	*betri*
insect repellent	*dawa ya kuzuia mbuu*
razor	*wembe*
sanitary napkins	*Kotex*
soap	*sabuni*
suntan lotion	*dawa ya kukinga jua*
tampons	*OB/Tampax*
toothbrush	*mswaki*
toothpaste	*dawa ya meno/Kolgeti*
water purifier	*chombo cha kusafishia maji*

a little bit	*kiasi kidogo*
a lot	*nyingi*
enough	*bas/inatosha*
too much/many	*mno*
cheap	*rahisi*
(too) expensive	*ghali (mno)*

Health

Where can I find a (good) ...?	*Naweza kupata ... (mzuri) wapi?*
dentist	*daktari wa meno*
doctor	*daktari/mganga*
hospital	*hospitali*
medical centre	*matibabu*

I'm sick.	*Niko mgonjwa.*
My friend is sick.	*Rafiki yangu ni mgonjwa.*
I need a doctor.	*Nataka kuona daktari.*
It hurts here.	*Naumwa hapa.*
I've been vaccinated.	*Nimechanjwa.*
I feel dizzy.	*Nasikia/Nasihi kizun guzungu.*
I feel nauseous.	*Nataka kutapika.*
I've been vomiting.	*Nina tapika.*
I'm pregnant.	*Nina mimba.*

diarrhoea	*harisha/hara/endesha*
fever	*homa*
headache	*umwa kichwa*
malaria	*maleria*
nausea	*tapika*
rabies	*nimeumwa na mbwa wa kichaa*
stomachache	*umwa tumbo*
toothache	*jino linaniuma*
virus	*kirus/virus* (pl)
vomiting	*tapika*

I'm allergic to ...	*Nina aleji ya ...*
antibiotics	*antibayotiki*
penicillin	*penesilini*

I'm on medication for ...	*Nakunywa dawa ya ...*
asthma	*ugonjwa wa pumu*
diabetes	*dayabeti*
epilepsy	*epilepsi*

Emergencies

Help!	*Nisaidie!Jamaani!*
It's an emergency.	*Ni jambo la haraka.*
Call a doctor!	*Muite daktari!*
Call the police!	*Muite polisi!*
Fire!	*Moto!*
I'm ill.	*Naumwa.*
I've been robbed!	*Nimeibiwa!*
Go away!	*Toka!*
Leave me alone!	*Niache!/ Usinisumbue!*
I'm lost.	*Nimepotea.*

aspirin	*aspirini/panadol/ dawa ya kichwa*
condom	*kondom*
contraceptive pill	*kuzuia mimba*
medicine	*dawa*
pill	*kidonge/vidonge* (pl)

Time & Days

What time is it?	*Ni saa ngapi?*
It's ... o'clock.	*Ni saa ...*
half past	*na nusu*
quarter past	*na robo*
quarter to	*kasa robo*
minute	*dakika*

today	*leo*
tomorrow	*kesho*
yesterday	*jana*
now	*sasa*
soon	*sasa hivi*
later	*baadaye*
always	*kila wakati*
every day	*kila siku*
day(s)	*siku*
week(s)	*wiki*

Saturday	*Jumamosi*
Sunday	*Jumapili*
Monday	*Jumatatu*
Tuesday	*Jumanne*
Wednesday	*Jumatano*
Thursday	*Alhamisi*
Friday	*Ijumaa*

Numbers

0	*sifuri*
1	*moja*
2	*mbili*
3	*tatu*
4	*nne*
5	*tano*
6	*sita*
7	*saba*
8	*nane*
9	*tisa*
10	*kumi*
11	*kumi na moja* (lit: ten-and-one)
12	*kumi na mbili*
20	*ishirini*
21	*ishirini na moja* (lit: twenty-and-one)
22	*ishirini na mbili*
30	*thelathini*
40	*arobaini*
50	*hamsini*
60	*sitini*
70	*sabini*
80	*themanini*
90	*tisini*
100	*mia* or *mia moja*
200	*mia mbili* (lit: hundred-two)
300	*mia tatu*
1000	*elfu*
10,000	*elfu kumi*
100,000	*laki*

one million	*milioni*
half	*nusu*

Food
Basics

I'm vegetarian.	*Nakula mboga tu.*
I don't eat meat.	*Mimi sili nyama.*
Is there a restaurant near here?	*Je, kuna hoteli ya chakula hapo jirani?*
Do you serve food here?	*Mnauza chakula hapa?*

I want ... food.	*Nataka chakula cha ...*
European	*kizungu*
Indian	*kihindi*
African	*kiafrika*

Masai Phrases

If you're travelling in the Ngorongoro area, chances are you'll meet some Maasai people. The Maasai speak a Nilotic language which is considered difficult to learn, in part due to the many different forms of address that it contains. The following may help you get started:

Respectful greetings.

(to young woman)	*ndit(h)o ta kwenya*
(to older woman)	*koko ta kwenya*
(to warrior)	*morani ta kwenya*
(to young boy)	*kulalayo ta kwenya*
Response	*iko*
Thank you (very much).	*ah-shuh (nah-ling)*
Peace be with you.	*sih-day*
How is everything?	*su-pai?*
Everything's fine.	*Ibaa*
Where are you going?	*kai oloyto?*
I'm going to ...	*eleto ...*
Where is ...?	*kah-li-ay etee ...?*

I'd like ...	*Nataka ...*
This food has too much hot pepper.	*Chakula hiki kina pilipili kali mno.*
I'd like a milder pepper.	*Nataka pilipili isiyo kali sana.*
Please bring me the bill.	*Nipe risiti tafadhali.*

boiled	*ya kuchemka*
bowl	*bakuli*
bread	*mkate*
butter	*siagi*
cold	*baridi*
cup	*kikombe*
curry	*mchuzi*
egg(s)	*yai (mayai)*
food	*chakula*
fork	*uma*
fried	*kaanga*
glass	*glasi/bilauri*
hot	*ya moto*

hot (spicy)	*hoho*	fish	*samaki*
Indian bread	*chapati*	kebabs	*mushkaki*
knife	*kisu*	lobster	*kamba*
napkin	*kitambaa*	meat	*nyama*
pepper	*pilipili*	meat stew	*karanga*
plate	*sahani*	mutton, goat	*nyama ya mbuzi*
raw	*mbichi*	pork	*nyama ya nguruwe*
ripe	*mbivu*	squid	*ngisi*
roast	*choma*	steak	*steki*
salt	*chumvi*		
sauce	*mchuzi*	**Fruit**	
soup	*supu*	banana	*ndizi*
spoon	*kijiko*	coconut (green)	*dafu*
sugar	*sukari*	coconut (ripe)	*nazi*
sweet	*tamu*	custard apples	*stafeli*
table	*meza*	dates	*tende*
teaspoon	*kijiko*	fruit	*matunda*
waiter	*bwana/ndugu/*	grapefruit	*madanzi*
	mtumishi	guava	*pera*
yoghurt	*maziwalala*	lemon	*limau*
		lime	*ndimu*
Vegetables & Grains		mango	*embe*
aubergine	*biringani*	orange	*chungwa*
cabbage	*kabichi*	papaya	*papai*
capsicum	*pilipili baridi*	passionfruit	*pasheni*
carrots	*karoti*	pineapple	*nanasi*
cassava	*muhogo*	sugar cane	*muwa*
garlic	*vitunguu saumu*	(water) melon	*tikiti (maji)*
kidney beans	*maharagwe*		
lettuce	*salad*	**Drinks**	
maize-meal	*ugali, posho*	(hot) water	*maji (ya moto)*
porridge		drinking water	*maji ya kunywa*
mashed plantains	*matoke*	mineral water	*maji safi*
onions	*vitunguu*	(boiled) milk	*maziwa*
plantains	*ndzi*		*(yaliochemshwa)*
potatoes	*viazi*	(fruit) juice	*jusi/maji (ya matunda)*
rice	*wali*	lime juice	*jusi/maji ya ndimu*
spinach (boiled)	*sukuma wiki*	orange juice	*jusi/maji ya*
tomatoes	*nyana*		*machungwa*
vegetables	*mboga*	pineapple juice	*jusi/maji ya mnanasi*
vegetable stew	*mboga*	soda/soft drink	*soda*
		beer	*bia (baridi)*
Meat & Fish		ice	*barafu*
beef	*nyama ya ng'ombe*	spirits	*pombe kali*
crab	*kaa*	wine	*mvinyo*

LONELY PLANET

Phrasebooks

L onely Planet phrasebooks are packed with essential words and phrases to help travellers communicate with the locals. With colour tabs for quick reference, an extensive vocabulary and use of script, these handy pocket-sized language guides cover day-to-day travel situations.

- handy pocket-sized books
- easy to understand Pronunciation chapter
- clear & comprehensive Grammar chapter
- romanisation alongside script to allow ease of pronunciation
- script throughout so users can point to phrases for every situation
- full of cultural information and tips for the traveller

'...vital for a real DIY spirit and attitude in language learning'
– *Backpacker*

'the phrasebooks have good cultural backgrounders and offer solid advice for challenging situations in remote locations'
– *San Francisco Examiner*

Arabic (Egyptian) • Arabic (Moroccan) • Australian *(Australian English, Aboriginal and Torres Strait languages)* • Baltic States *(Estonian, Latvian, Lithuanian)* • Bengali • Brazilian • Burmese • Cantonese • Central Asia • Central Europe *(Czech, French, German, Hungarian, Italian, Slovak)* • Eastern Europe *(Bulgarian, Czech, Hungarian, Polish, Romanian, Slovak)* • Ethiopian (Amharic) • Fijian • French • German • Greek • Hill Tribes • Hindi/Urdu • Indonesian • Italian • Japanese • Korean • Lao • Latin American Spanish • Malay • Mandarin • Mediterranean Europe *(Albanian, Croatian, Greek, Italian, Macedonian, Maltese, Serbian, Slovene)* • Mongolian • Nepali • Papua New Guinea • Pilipino (Tagalog) • Quechua • Russian • Scandinavian Europe *(Danish, Finnish, Icelandic, Norwegian, Swedish)* • South-East Asia *(Burmese, Indonesian, Khmer, Lao, Malay, Tagalog Pilipino, Thai, Vietnamese)* • Spanish (Castilian) *(also includes Catalan, Galician and Basque)* • Sri Lanka • Swahili • Thai • Tibetan • Turkish • Ukrainian • USA *(US English, Vernacular, Native American languages, Hawaiian)* • Vietnamese • Western Europe *(Basque, Catalan, Dutch, French, German, Greek, Irish)*

Lonely Planet Journeys

JOURNEYS is a unique collection of travel writing – published by the company that understands travel better than anyone else. It is a series for anyone who has ever experienced – or dreamed of – the magical moment when they encountered a strange culture or saw a place for the first time. They are tales to read while you're planning a trip, while you're on the road or while you're in an armchair in front of a fire.

These outstanding titles explore our planet through the eyes of a diverse group of international writers. JOURNEYS books catch the spirit of a place, illuminate a culture, recount a crazy adventure or introduce a fascinating way of life. They always entertain, and always enrich the experience of travel.

MALI BLUES
Traveling to an African Beat
Lieve Joris (translated by Sam Garrett)

Drought, rebel uprisings, ethnic conflict: these are the predominant images of West Africa. But as Lieve Joris travels in Senegal, Mauritania and Mali, she meets survivors, fascinating individuals charting new ways of living between tradition and modernity. With her remarkable gift for drawing out people's stories, Joris brilliantly captures the rhythms of a world that refuses to give in.

THE GATES OF DAMASCUS
Lieve Joris (translated by Sam Garrett)

This best-selling book is a beautifully drawn portrait of day-to-day life in modern Syria. Through her intimate contact with local people, Lieve Joris draws us into the fascinating world that lies behind the gates of Damascus. Hala's husband is a political prisoner, jailed for his opposition to the Assad regime; through the author's friendship with Hala we see how Syrian politics impacts on the lives of ordinary people.

SONGS TO AN AFRICAN SUNSET
A Zimbabwean Story
Sekai Nzenza-Shand

Songs to an African Sunset braids vividly personal stories into an intimate picture of contemporary Zimbabwe. Returning to her family's village after many years in the west, Sekai Nzenza-Shand discovers a world where ancestor worship, polygamy and witchcraft still govern the rhythms of daily life – and where drought, deforestation and AIDS have wrought devastating changes. With insight and affection, she explores a culture torn between respect for the old ways and the irresistible pull of the new.

THE RAINBIRD
A Central African Journey
Jan Brokken (translated by Sam Garrett)

Following in the footsteps of famous Europeans such as Albert Schweitzer and HM Stanley, Jan Brokken journeyed to Gabon in central Africa. *The Rainbird* brilliantly chronicles the encounter between Africa and Europe as it was acted out on a side-street of history in a kaleidoscope of adventures and anecdotes. A compelling, immensely readable account of the author's own travels in one of the most remote and mysterious regions of Africa.

LONELY PLANET

Lonely Planet Travel Atlases

Lonely Planet has long been famous for the number and quality of its guidebook maps. Now we've gone one step further and produced a handy companion series: Lonely Planet travel atlases – maps of a country produced in book form.

Unlike other maps, which look good but lead travellers astray, our travel atlases have been researched on the road by Lonely Planet's experienced team of writers. All details are carefully checked to ensure the atlas corresponds with the equivalent Lonely Planet guidebook.

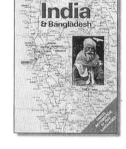

- full-colour throughout
- maps researched and checked by Lonely Planet authors
- place names correspond with Lonely Planet guidebooks
- no confusing spelling differences
- legend and travelling information in English, French, German, Japanese and Spanish
- size: 230 x 160 mm

Available now: Chile & Easter Island ● Egypt ● India & Bangladesh ● Israel & the Palestinian Territories ● Jordan, Syria & Lebanon ● Kenya ● Laos ● Portugal ● South Africa, Lesotho & Swaziland ● Thailand ● Turkey ● Vietnam ● Zimbabwe, Botswana & Namibia

---

Lonely Planet TV Series & Videos

Lonely Planet travel guides have been brought to life on television screens around the world. Like our guides, the programs are based on the joy of independent travel, and look honestly at some of the most exciting, picturesque and frustrating places in the world. Each show is presented by one of three travellers from Australia, England or the USA and combines an innovative mixture of video, Super-8 film, atmospheric soundscapes and original music.

Videos of each episode – containing additional footage not shown on television – are available from good book and video shops, but the availability of individual videos varies with regional screening schedules.

Video destinations include: Alaska ● American Rockies ● Australia – The South-East ● Baja California & the Copper Canyon ● Brazil ● Central Asia ● Chile & Easter Island ● Corsica, Sicily & Sardinia – The Mediterranean Islands ● East Africa (Tanzania & Zanzibar) ● Ecuador & the Galapagos Islands ● Greenland & Iceland ● Indonesia ● Israel & the Sinai Desert ● Jamaica ● Japan ● La Ruta Maya ● Morocco ● New York ● North India ● Pacific Islands (Fiji, Solomon Islands & Vanuatu) ● South India ● South West China ● Turkey ● Vietnam ● West Africa ● Zimbabwe, Botswana & Namibia

The Lonely Planet TV series is produced by: Pilot Productions
The Old Studio
18 Middle Row
London W10 5AT, UK

Lonely Planet On-line
www.lonelyplanet.com *or* **AOL keyword: lp**

Whether you've just begun planning your next trip, or you're chasing down specific info on currency regulations or visa requirements, check out Lonely Planet On-line for up-to-the minute travel information.

As well as mini guides to more than 250 destinations, you'll find maps, photos, travel news, health and visa updates, travel advisories, and discussion of the ecological and political issues you need to be aware of as you travel. You'll also find timely upgrades to popular guidebooks which you can print out and stick in the back of your book.

There's also an on-line travellers' forum where you can share your experience of life on the road, meet travel companions and ask other travellers for their recommendations and advice.

And of course we have a complete and up-to-date list of all Lonely Planet travel products including travel guides, diving and snorkeling guides, phrasebooks, atlases, travel literature and videos, and a simple on-line ordering facility if you can't find the book you want elsewhere.

Lonely Planet Diving & Snorkeling Guides

Known for indispensible guidebooks to destinations all over the world, Lonely Planet's Pisces Books are the most popular series of diving and snorkeling titles available.

There are three series: **Diving & Snorkeling Guides**, **Shipwreck Diving** series and **Dive Into History**. Full colour throughout, the **Diving & Snorkeling Guides** combine quality photographs with detailed descriptions of the best dive sites for each location, giving divers a glimpse of what they can expect both on land and in water. The **Dive Into History** series is perfect for the adventure diver or armchair traveller. The **Shipwreck Diving** series provides all the details for exploring the most interesting wrecks in the Atlantic and Pacific oceans. The list also includes underwater nature and technical guides.

LONELY PLANET

Guides by Region

Lonely Planet is known worldwide for publishing practical, reliable and no-nonsense travel information in our guides and on our Web site. The Lonely Planet list covers just about every accessible part of the world. Currently there are nine series: travel guides, shoestring guides, walking guides, city guides, phrasebooks, audio packs, travel atlases, diving and snorkeling guides and travel literature.

AFRICA Africa – the South • Africa on a shoestring • Arabic (Egyptian) phrasebook • Arabic (Moroccan) phrasebook • Cairo • Cape Town • Central Africa • East Africa • Egypt • Egypt travel atlas • Ethiopian (Amharic) phrasebook • The Gambia & Senegal • Kenya • Kenya travel atlas • Malawi, Mozambique & Zambia • Morocco • North Africa • South Africa, Lesotho & Swaziland • South Africa, Lesotho & Swaziland travel atlas • Swahili phrasebook • Trekking in East Africa • Tunisia • West Africa • Zimbabwe, Botswana & Namibia • Zimbabwe, Botswana & Namibia travel atlas
Travel Literature: The Rainbird: A Central African Journey • Songs to an African Sunset: A Zimbabwean Story • Mali Blues: Traveling to an African Beat

AUSTRALIA & THE PACIFIC Australia • Australian phrasebook • Bushwalking in Australia • Bushwalking in Papua New Guinea • Fiji • Fijian phrasebook • Islands of Australia's Great Barrier Reef • Melbourne • Micronesia • New Caledonia • New South Wales & the ACT • New Zealand • Northern Territory • Outback Australia • Papua New Guinea • Papua New Guinea (Pidgin) phrasebook • Queensland • Rarotonga & the Cook Islands • Samoa • Solomon Islands • South Australia • Sydney • Tahiti & French Polynesia • Tasmania • Tonga • Tramping in New Zealand • Vanuatu • Victoria • Western Australia
Travel Literature: Islands in the Clouds • Sean & David's Long Drive

CENTRAL AMERICA & THE CARIBBEAN Bahamas and Turks & Caicos • Barcelona • Bermuda • Central America on a shoestring • Costa Rica • Cuba • Dominican Republic & Haiti • Eastern Caribbean • Guatemala, Belize & Yucatán: La Ruta Maya • Jamaica • Mexico • Mexico City • Panama
Travel Literature: Green Dreams: Travels in Central America

EUROPE Amsterdam • Andalucía • Austria • Baltic States phrasebook • Berlin • Britain • British phrasebook • Central Europe • Central Europe phrasebook • Croatia • Czech & Slovak Republics • Denmark • Dublin • Eastern Europe • Eastern Europe phrasebook • Edinburgh • Estonia, Latvia & Lithuania • Europe • Finland • France • French phrasebook • Germany • German phrasebook • Greece • Greek phrasebook • Hungary • Iceland, Greenland & the Faroe Islands • Ireland • Italian phrasebook • Italy • Lisbon • London • Mediterranean Europe • Mediterranean Europe phrasebook • Paris • Poland • Portugal • Portugal travel atlas • Prague • Provence & the Côte D'Azur • Romania & Moldova • Russia, Ukraine & Belarus • Russian phrasebook • Scandinavian & Baltic Europe • Scandinavian Europe phrasebook • Scotland • Slovenia • Spain • Spanish phrasebook • St Petersburg • Switzerland • Trekking in Spain • Ukrainian phrasebook • Vienna • Walking in Britain • Walking in Italy • Walking in Ireland • Walking in Switzerland • Western Europe • Western Europe phrasebook
Travel Literature: The Olive Grove: Travels in Greece

INDIAN SUBCONTINENT Bangladesh • Bengali phrasebook • Bhutan • Delhi • Goa • Hindi/Urdu phrasebook • India • India & Bangladesh travel atlas • Indian Himalaya • Karakoram Highway • Nepal • Nepali phrasebook • Pakistan • Rajasthan • South India • Sri Lanka • Sri Lanka phrasebook • Trekking in the Indian Himalaya • Trekking in the Karakoram & Hindukush • Trekking in the Nepal Himalaya
Travel Literature: In Rajasthan • Shopping for Buddhas

LONELY PLANET

Mail Order

Lonely Planet products are distributed worldwide. They are also available by mail order from Lonely Planet, so if you have difficulty finding a title please write to us. North and South American residents should write to 150 Linden St, Oakland, CA 94607, USA; European and African residents should write to 10a Spring Place, London NW5 3BH, UK; and residents of other countries to PO Box 617, Hawthorn, Victoria 3122, Australia.

ISLANDS OF THE INDIAN OCEAN Madagascar & Comoros • Maldives • Mauritius, Réunion & Seychelles

MIDDLE EAST & CENTRAL ASIA Arab Gulf States • Central Asia • Central Asia phrasebook • Iran • Israel & the Palestinian Territories • Israel & the Palestinian Territories travel atlas • Istanbul • Jerusalem • Jordan & Syria • Jordan, Syria & Lebanon travel atlas • Lebanon • Middle East on a shoestring • Turkey • Turkish phrasebook • Turkey travel atlas • Yemen
Travel Literature: The Gates of Damascus • Kingdom of the Film Stars: Journey into Jordan

NORTH AMERICA Alaska • Backpacking in Alaska • Baja California • California & Nevada • Canada • Florida • Hawaii • Honolulu • Los Angeles • Miami • New England USA • New Orleans • New York City • New York, New Jersey & Pennsylvania • Pacific Northwest USA • Rocky Mountain States • San Francisco • Seattle • Southwest USA • USA • USA phrasebook • Vancouver • Washington, DC & the Capital Region
Travel Literature: Drive Thru America

NORTH-EAST ASIA Beijing • Cantonese phrasebook • China • Hong Kong • Hong Kong, Macau & Guangzhou • Japan • Japanese phrasebook • Japanese audio pack • Korea • Korean phrasebook • Kyoto • Mandarin phrasebook • Mongolia • Mongolian phrasebook • North-East Asia on a shoestring • Seoul • South-West China • Taiwan • Tibet • Tibetan phrasebook • Tokyo
Travel Literature: Lost Japan

SOUTH AMERICA Argentina, Uruguay & Paraguay • Bolivia • Brazil • Brazilian phrasebook • Buenos Aires • Chile & Easter Island • Chile & Easter Island travel atlas • Colombia • Ecuador & the Galapagos Islands • Latin American Spanish phrasebook • Peru • Quechua phrasebook • Rio de Janeiro • South America on a shoestring • Trekking in the Patagonian Andes • Venezuela
Travel Literature: Full Circle: A South American Journey

SOUTH-EAST ASIA Bali & Lombok • Bangkok • Burmese phrasebook • Cambodia • Hill Tribes phrasebook • Ho Chi Minh City • Indonesia • Indonesian phrasebook • Indonesian audio pack • Jakarta • Java • Laos • Lao phrasebook • Laos travel atlas • Malay phrasebook • Malaysia, Singapore & Brunei • Myanmar (Burma) • Philippines • Pilipino (Tagalog) phrasebook • Singapore • South-East Asia on a shoestring • South-East Asia phrasebook • Thailand • Thailand's Islands & Beaches • Thailand travel atlas • Thai phrasebook • Thai audio pack • Vietnam • Vietnamese phrasebook • Vietnam travel atlas

ALSO AVAILABLE: Antarctica • Brief Encounters: Stories of Love, Sex & Travel • Chasing Rickshaws • Not the Only Planet: Travel Stories from Science Fiction • Travel with Children • Traveller's Tales

FREE Lonely Planet Newsletters

We love hearing from you and think you'd like to hear from us.

Planet Talk

Our FREE quarterly printed newsletter is full of tips from travellers and anecdotes from Lonely Planet guidebook authors. Every issue is packed with up-to-date travel news and advice, and includes:

- a postcard from Lonely Planet co-founder Tony Wheeler
- a swag of mail from travellers
- a look at life on the road through the eyes of a Lonely Planet author
- topical health advice
- prizes for the best travel yarn
- news about forthcoming Lonely Planet events
- a complete list of Lonely Planet books and other titles

To join our mailing list, residents of the UK, Europe and Africa can email us at go@lonelyplanet.co.uk; residents of North and South America can email us at info@lonelyplanet.com; the rest of the world can email us at talk2us@lonelyplanet.com.au, or contact any Lonely Planet office.

Comet

Our FREE monthly email newsletter brings you all the latest travel news, features, interviews, competitions, destination ideas, travellers' tips & tales, Q&As, raging debates and related links. Find out what's new on the Lonely Planet Web site and which books are about to hit the shelves.

Subscribe from your desktop: www.lonelyplanet.com/comet

Index

Text

A

aardvark 45
aardwolf 49
acclimatisation 239
accommodation 100-1
accordion 162
African civet 48
African elephant 55
African lynx 52
African violet 197
African wild cat 51
Aga Khan Mosque 153
air travel 104-8, 114
   departure tax 104
   glossary 106-7
   to/from Tanzania 104-8
Amboni Caves 195-6
Anglican Cathedral 153
animals, see individual entries
antelopes 59-68
architecture, see Stone Town
arts 32-6
Arusha 212-21, **214**
   immigration 213
   money 213
   travel agencies 214-16
Arusha National Park
   221-3, **222**
Askari Monument 128

B

baboon 43
Bagamoyo 186-9
balloon safaris 229
banana beer 207
baobab 283
Barakuni island 315
baraza 253
barbets 69
bargaining 82
bat-eared fox 53
Bawi island 172-3
beaches 127-8, 139-41, 167-72
bee-eaters 70
Beit al Sahel (The Palace
   Museum) 152
Beit el Ajaib (House of
   Wonders) 151-2
Beit el Amani 156
Beit el Salaam 156

birds 67-72,
   see also individual entries
bicycling, see cycling
birdwatching 201
black rhinoceros 56
blue monkey 43
blue wildebeest 62
boat travel 112-13, 118-19
   ferry 118
Bongoyo island 138-9
books 84-5
   guidebooks 84
   history 84-5
border crossings 108-9
Brachiosaurus brancai 310
Bububu (Fuji beach) 167
Bukoba 258-61, **260**
Burton, Richard Francis 16
bus travel 114-15
bushbabies 42
bushbuck 64
bushpig 57
business hours 99
Butiama 20, 261

C

camel safaris 121, 221
camping 100-1
cape clawless otter 54
car travel 116-17
caracal 52
cash 81
Chagga people 31, 207
Chake Chake 179-80, **180**
Changuu (Prison) island 172
Chapwani (Grave) island 173
cheetah 50
Chief Kimweri 201
Chief Mkwawa 286, 288
chimpanzees 44, 268
chimpanzee sanctuary
   265, 268-9
Chole island 316
Chukwani 166
Chumbe island 173
Chuo cha Sanaa 188
Chwaka 170, 185
Chwaka Bay 174
cinema 35-6
civet, see African civet

climate 23-4
Coco beach 127
coffee 207, 209
colobus monkey, see Eastern
   black and white
common duiker 59
common reedbuck 65
conduct, see cultural
   considerations
conservation, see
   environment
costs 81-2
cranes 70
Crater Highlands 231-2,
   249-50
credit cards 81
cultural considerations 36-7
Culture Musical Club 162
cycling 100, 117, 121

D

dalla-dalla 119
dance 32-3
Dar es Salaam 122-41,
   123, **130**, **139**
   bookshops 126
   entertainment 134-5
   fish market 128
   getting around 137
   getting there & away
      135-6
   history 122
   immigration 124
   money 124-5
   places to eat 132-4
   places to stay 129-32
   safety 127
   shopping 135
   tourist offices 124
   walking tour 128-9
Dar es Salaam Marine
   Reserve System 137
Daraja la Mungu 294
dassies 46
debt 30
dik-dik, see Kirk's dik-dik
disabled travellers 98
diving 77, 100, 128, 139,
   146-8, 307, 315
   responsible diving 77

Dodoma 275-80, **279**
doves 70
drinks 102
duiker, see common duiker
dynamite fishing 27

E

eagles 69
Eastern (Gregory) Rift 22
Eastern Arc mountains 197
Eastern black and white
    colobus monkey 43
economy 30 1
education 31-3
eland 65
elephant 288-9,
    see also African elephant
email services 83-4
embassies 79-80
Empakaai 231, 235
endangered species 25, 289
Engaruka 230, 235
entertainment 102
environment 24-5
        dynamite fishing 27
ethno-linguistic
    composition 39
etiquette,
    see cultural considerations

F

falcons 69
fauna 25-6
    endangered species 25
fax services 83
ferry 188, see also
    boat travel
finches 71
fish market 127
fishing 148, 315
flamingo 68, 235
flora 25
food 101-2
fox, see bat-eared fox
Forodhani Gardens 156
Fuji Beach, see Bububu

G

Galanos Sulphur Springs 196
game reserves 28, **26**
    Kisigo 288
    Mkomazi 196-7

Bold indicates maps.

Rungwa 288
Saa Nane 253
Sadani 189-90
Selous 317-20, **318**
Uwanda 294
Gangilonga Rock 285
gay & lesbian travellers 98
genet 47
geography 22-3
giraffe 59
Gombe Stream National
    Park 268-9
gorilla 44
government 28-9
Grave island, see Chapwani
Great Rift Valley, The 22
Great Ruaha River 288
Gregory Rift, see Eastern
    (Gregory) Rift
guesthouses 101
guides 241

H

habitats 67
Hadimu people 146
Hadzabe people 230, 236
Hamamni Persian Baths 155
hartebeest 62
hawks 69
Haya people 31, 259
health 86-98
Hehe people 285-6
Henry Morton Stanley 268
hiking 281, 284, 294,
    see also trekking
hippopotamus 58
history 15-22
    colonial era 16-17
    independence 17-18
    socialist Tanzania 18-19
hitching 117-18
holidays, see public holidays
honeyguides 70
hoopoe 71
hornbills 69
hostels 101
hotels 101
House of Wonders,
    see Beit el Ajaib
hyaena 48

I

Ijumaa Mosque 153
Ikombe 296
Ilala market 127
impala 61

internet services 84
Iraqw people 31, 235-6
Irente viewpoint 199
Iringa 285-8, **287**
Iringa baskets 285
Isimila Stone Age Site 288
Islam 37-9
    tips for the traveller 38-9
Isongole village 294
Itungi 295
ivory ban 289

J

jackal 53
Jacobsen's beach 265
Jambiani 171-2
Jane Goodall Institute 265
Jibondo island 315
Jimbizi beach 311
Jozani Forest 174-5
Jozani-Chwaka Bay
    Conservation Area 174
Juani island 316
Julius Nyerere 20-1

K

Kalambo Falls 274
Kalenga 288
    museum 286
kanun 162
Kaole Ruins 188
Kaporogwe Falls 294
Karatu 234
Kariakoo market 127
Karimjee Hall 128
Katavi National Park 273-4
kayamba 33
Kendwa 169
Kibo peak 237
Kidero mountains 236
Kigamboni peninsula 128
Kigoma 263-7, **266**
Kigomasha peninsula 183
Kijungu 294
Kikwetu 310
Kilindi people 198
Kilombero Valley 284
Kilwa Kisiwani 311, 313-14
    Arabic fort 313
    Great Mosque 314
    Husuni Kubwa 314
    Husuni Ndogo 314
    Makutani 314
Kilwa Kivinje 314
Kilwa Masoko 311-13, **312**
kingfishers 69

Kiomoni village 196
Kipengere mountains 297
Kirk's dik-dik 60
Kisarawe 137-8
Kisessa 253
Kisigo Game Reserve 288
Kitutia island 315
Kiwengwa 169-70
Kiweni island 183-4
Kizimkazi 174
klipspringer 60
Kojani island 185
Kolo 278
    rock paintings 277
Korogwe 196
Krapf, Johan Ludwig 16, 201
Kuleana Centre for
    Children's Rights 255
Kunduchi Ruins 139
Kyela 295

L

Laetoli 235
Lake Chada 273
Lake Eyasi 230, 236
Lake Katavi 273
Lake Malawi, see Lake Nyasa
Lake Manyara National
    Park 224-5
Lake Natron 235-6
Lake Nyasa 295-6
Lake Rukwa 294
Lake Victoria 251-62, **252**
language 39-40, 321-7
    Afro-Asiatic family 39
    Khoisan family 39
    Maasai phrases 326
    Niger-Congo family 39
    Nilo-Saharan family 39
    Swahili 321-7
language courses 100
laundry 86
Lemagrut 231
leopard 50
Lindi 310-11, **311**
lion 51
Lion Rock 277
literature 34
Little Ruaha River 285
Livingstone, Dr David 16, 268
Livingstone House 156
Livingstone mountains 295
Longido 221
Loolmalasin 231
louries 69
Luguru people 281
Luhombero peak 284

Lupa 290
Lushoto 198-200, **198**
Lutheran Church 129
lynx, see African lynx

M

Maasai land issues 233
Maasai people 31, 232-3, 249
Maasai phrases 326
Machame Route 238
Mafia island 315-17, **317**
Mafia Island Marine Park
    27, 316
Mahale Mountains
    National Park 269-70
Mahiwa 308
Maisome island 252
Maji Maji rebellion 296
Makonde carvings 303, 310
Makonde people 31, 308-9
Makonde Plateau 308-10
Malindi Minaret Mosque, see
    Msikiti wa Balnara
Mangapwani Caves 166
mangroves 176
Marangu 211-12
Marangu Route 242-5, **243**
marimba 33
marine ecosystems 27
marine parks & reserves 27-8
markets 127
Maruhubi Palace 166
Mary Leakey 235
Masasi 277, 308-10
Masek Lake 230
Masoko Crater Lake 294
Masuguru 301
Matema 295-6
Matemwe 169
Mawenzi peak 237
Mazinde Juu 33
Maziwe island 190
Mbaga 203-4
Mbamba Bay 296
Mbeya 290-3, **291**
Mbeya mountains 290
Mbeya peak 293
Mbozi Meteorite 293
Mbudya island 139
Mbugu people 198
Mbweni 139, 166
medical treatment,
    see health
Meserani Snake Park 217
Mikindani 306-7
Mikumi National Park 283-4
Misali island 181

Misali Island Marine
    Conservation Area 181
Mishamo refugees 271
Mkoani 181-2
Mkomazi Game
    Reserve 196-7
Mkuru 221
Mkuu island 185
Mlalo 200
Mnazi Bay 307
Mnemba island 173
Mombo 201
Momela Lakes 222
Momela Route 246-9, **247**
money 80-2
    bargaining 82
    cash 81
    costs 81-2
    credit cards 81
    tipping 82
    travellers cheques 81
mongooses 48
monkey, see blue monkey,
    Eastern black and white
    colobus
Morningside 281
Morogoro 280-3, **280**
Moshi 205-11, **208**
motorcycle 116-17
Mpanda 272-3
Msangamkuu peninsula 307
Msangamkuu village 307
Msasani fishing village 127
Msasani peninsula 127
Msikiti wa Balnara (Malindi
    Minaret Mosque) 153
Msimbati 307-8
Mt Hanang 221
Mt Kaluwe 293
Mt Kilimanjaro 237-45, **238**
    Marangu Route 242-5, **243**
Mt Kilimanjaro National Park
    223-4
Mt Meru 222, 245-9
    Momela Route 246-9, **247**
Mt Rungwe 294
Mtae 200
Mtambwe island 185
Mtema beach 310
Mto Wa Mbu village 225
Mtoni Palace 166
Mtwara 299-306, **302**, **306**
Muheza 196
Murogo 174
music 33-4,
    see also taarab music
    kayamba 33
    marimba 33

ngoma 33
siwa 33
tari 33
Musoma 261
Mwadui 262
Mwanga 204
Mwanza 251-8, **254**
Mweka Route 238

N
national museum 127-8
national parks 26-8, **26**
    Arusha 221-3
    Gombe Stream 268-9
    Katavi 273-4
    Lake Manyara 224-5
    Mahale Mountains 269-70
    Mikumi 283-4
    Mt Kilimanjaro 223-4
    Ruaha 288-90
    Rubondo Island 261-2
    Serengeti 228, **227**
    Tarangire 225-7, **226**
    Udzungwa 284-5
nay 162
Ndanda 310
Ndutu Lake 230
Newala 308
newspapers 85
Ng'iresi village 221
Ngezi forest 184
ngoma 33
Ngomba 294
Ngomeni 192
Ngoni people 296
Ngorongoro Conservation
    Area 230-6, **231**
Ngorongoro Crater 232-4
Ngozi peak 294
Ngurdoto Crater 222
Njombe 297
Nkome island 252
North-Eastern Tanzania
    186-204, **187**
northern circuit 228
Northern Tanzania
    205-36, **206**
Nyamwezi people 31, 153
Nyandira 281
Nyange 174
Nyerere, Julius 17-20
Nyororo island 315

O
Ocean Road Hospital 128
Old Dispensary 156
Old Fort 152-3
Old Slave Market 153
Oldeani 231
Oldoinyo Lengai 231, 249
Olduvai Gorge 234-5
Olmoti 231
oryx 64
ostrich 70
otter, *see* cape clawless otter
oxpeckers 71

P
painting 34
Paje 171
Palace Museum, *see*
    Beit al Sahel
Pangani 190-2
Pangani Falls 191
Pangani River 191, 281
Pange 174
Pare mountains 201-4
Pare people 202
Peace Memorial Museum
    (Beit el Amani or Beit el
    Salaam) 156
Pemba 175-85, **176**
    getting around 178-9
    getting there & away 178
    history 176-7
    money 177
    people 146
    tourist offices 177
Persian baths 166
photography 85-6
pigeons 70
Pingwe 170
pipits 71
population 31
porcupine 46
Poroto mountains 290
porters 241
postal services 83
poverty, *see* debt
pre-dive safety guidelines 147
pre-trek safety guidelines 242
Prison island, *see* Changuu
public holidays 99-100
Pugu hills 137
Pujini Ruins 184

R
radio 85
Ras Mkumbuu 184-5

ratel 55
Rebmann, Johannes 16
reedbuck, *see* common
    reedbuck
refugees 265
religion 37-9
rhinoceros, *see*
    black rhinoceros
Rift Valley 22, *see also* Eastern
    (Gregory) Rift, Western Rift
    Valley
roan antelope 63
rock paintings 278
rollers 70
Rovula 308
Ruaha National Park 288-90
Ruaha River 288
Rubondo Island
    National Park 261-2
Rufiji River 318
Rufiji River Delta 315
Rungwa Game Reserve 288
Ruvu River 281
Ruvuma 296
Ruvuma River 301
Ruvuma valley 308

S
Saa Nane Game Reserve 253
sable 63
Sadani Game Reserve
    189-90
safari guide 42-68,
    see also individual entries
safaris 100, 119-21
    balloon 229
    camel 121, 221
    cycling 100, 121
    responsible tourism 76
    trekking 100
    walking safaris 121
safety 99, 127
Sambaa people 198
Same 203
Sandawe people 277
Sanje Majoma 314
Sanje ya Kati 314
scaly anteaters 45
sculpture 34-5
seabirds 69
Selous Game Reserve
    317-20, **318**
senior travellers 98-9
Serengeti National
    Park 228, **227**
serval 52
Shengena peak 203

Bold indicates maps.

shetani 34
Shinyanga 262
Shira peak 237
shopping 102-3
    paintings 102
    textiles 102
    woodcarving 102
shorebirds 68
Shungumbili island 315
Sigi 195
Singida 277
siwa 33
slave market 307
slave trade 16, 152, 271
snorkelling 100, 139,
    146-8, 307
Songea 296-7
Songo Mnara 314-20
Songo Songo 315
Soni 200-1
South-Eastern Tanzania
    299-320, **300**
Southern Highlands
    275-98, **276**
Speke, John Hanning 16
spice tours 166
springhare 46
St Joseph's
    Cathedral 129, 153
St Mary's secondary
    school 33
St Paul's Church 304
Stanley, Henry Morton 16
starlings 71
State House 128
steenbok 60
Stiegler's Gorge 318
Stone Town 151-6, **154**
street children 255
Sudi Bay 311
Sukuma Museum 252-62
Sukuma people 31, 253
Sumbawanga 274
sunbirds 71
Swahili 16, 39, 321-7
    greetings 321-2
swallows 70
swifts 70

T
taarab music 162-3
    clubs 162
Tabora 271-2, **272**
tama drum 162
Tanga 192-4, **193**
Tanganyika African National
    Union 20

Tanganyika Beach Club 128
Tarangire National
    Park 225-7, **226**
Tarangire River 225
Tarangire Wildlife
    Conservation Area 226
tari 33
taxi 119
telephone services 83
tides 168
Tinga Tinga Art Gallery 217
Tingatinga 34
    painting 35
tinkerbirds 69
tipping 82, 241
Tippu Tib 271
toilets 86
Tongoni Ruins 196
Topi 62
Tosamaganga 288
Toten island 192
tour operators 120, 228
tourism, responsible 76
tourist offices 76
tours, see safaris
train travel 115-16
travellers cheques 81
trekking 100, 121, 203-4,
    237-50, see also hiking
    companies 240
    Crater Highlands 249-50
    Kilimanjaro 237-45
    Mt Meru 245-9
Tukuyu 294
Tumbatu island 173
Tumbatu people 146
Tumbe 185
Tunduru 297-8
turacos 69
TV 85

U
Udzungwa National Park
    284-5
Uhuru peak 237, 239
ujamaa 18, 20
ujamaa motifs 34
Ujiji 267-8
Ukerewe island 252
Uluguru mountains 281
Umbwe Route 238
Unguja (Zanzibar island)
    15, 148-66, **143**
    bookshops 150
    entertainment 160
    getting around 164-6
    getting there & away 160-4

    money 149
    places to eat 159-60
    places to stay 156-9
    safety 150-1
    shopping 160
    tourist offices 148-9
Unity bridge 301
Uroa 170
Usambara mountains
    197-201
Usangi 204
Uvinza 270-1
Uwanda Game
    Reserve 294
Uzi Bay 174

V
Verani beach 183
vervet monkey 42-4
village museum 127
violin 162
visas 77-8, 146
    extensions 78-103
Vuga 201
vultures 69
Vumawimbi beach 183

W
wading birds 68
walking,
    see trekking
Wapare Union 202
warning 104, 120
warthog 58
waterfowl 68
weavers 71
Western Rift Valley 22
Western Tanzania
    263-74, **264**
Wete 182-3, **182**
whydahs 71
wild cat,
    see African wild cat
wild dog 54
wildebeest,
    see blue wildebeest
wildebeest migration
    228
wine 278
women travellers 98
woodcarving 34-5, 309
    shetani 34
    ujamaa motifs 34
woodpeckers 69

Z

Zanzibar Archipelago
142-185
history 142-5
visas 146

Zanzibar island, see Unguja
Zanzibar Serena Inn 163
Zanzibar Town 155, **154**,
see also Stone Town
Zanzibar's slave trade 152-3

Zanzibari doors 254
Zaramo people 138
zebra 57
Zigua people 198

Boxed Text

Air Travel Glossary 106-7
Bagamoyo 188
Brachiosaurus brancai 310
Chagga, The 207
Chief Kimweri 201
Chief Mkwawa 286
Chimpanzees 268
Choosing a Trekking
Company 240
Considerations for
Responsible Diving 77
Dar es Salaam Walking
Tour 128-9
Eastern Arc Mountains,
The 197
Endangered Elephants? 289
Great Rift Valley, The 22
Haya, The 259
Importance of
Acclimatisation, The 239
Jozani-Chwaka Bay
Conservation Area 174

Julius Nyerere 20-1
Kolo Rock Paintings, The 277
Maasai Land Issues 233
Maasai, The 232
Mafia Island Marine Park 316
Maji Maji Rebellion, The 296-7
Makonde, The 309
Mbozi Meteorite, The 293
Misali Island 181
Pare, The 202
Pesky Mangroves? 176
Pre-Dive Safety Guidelines 147
Pre-Trek Safety Guidelines 242
Refugees 265
St Paul's Church 304
Sukuma, The 253
Swahili 16
Tanzania's Coffee Industry 209
Tanzania's Ethno-Linguistic
Composition 39
Tanzania's Fragile Marine
Ecosystems 27

Tanzania's Overloaded
Northern Circuit 228
Tanzania's Street
Children 255
Tanzania's Wine Industry 278
Tanzanian Education 32-3
Tanzanian Shillings versus
US Dollars 81
Tides 168
Tingatinga Painting 35
Tipping Guides & Porters on
Kilimanjaro 241
Tippu Tib 271
Uluguru Mountains, The 281
Unguja vs Zanzibar 15
Unity Bridge 301
Warning 104
Warning 120
Zanzibar Town
(Stone town) 155
Zanzibar's Slave Trade 152-3
Zaramo, The 138

MAP LEGEND

BOUNDARIES

▬ ▬ ▪ ▬ ▪ ▬ ▪ ▬ ▪ ▬ ....International
▬ ▪▪ ▬ ▪▪ ▬ ▪ ....State
▬ ▬ ▬ ▬ ▬ ....Disputed

HYDROGRAPHY

.....................Coastline
.................River, Creek
.................................Lake
.....................Salt Lake
◎ ～✦～.........Spring, Rapids
⫫⫪⫫.....................Waterfalls
.........................Swamp

ROUTES & TRANSPORT

.....................Freeway
.....................Highway
.....................Major Road
.....................Minor Road
═ ═ ═ ═ ═.........Unsealed Road
.....................City Freeway
.....................City Highway

.....................City Road
.....................City Street, Lane
.....................Pedestrian Mall
├─┼─┼─●─┼─...Train Route & Station
─ ─ ─ ─ ─ ─....... Walking Track
─ ─ ─ ─ ─ ─.....................Ferry Route

AREA FEATURES

.....................Building
⚙ ....Park, Gardens
+ + × × ....Cemetery

.....................Market
.............Beach, Desert
.................Urban Area

MAP SYMBOLS

○ **CAPITAL** ....National Capital
◉ **CAPITAL** ....State Capital
● **CITY** ....City
● **Town** ....Town
● **Village** ....Village
○ ....Point of Interest

■ ....Place to Stay
⅄ ....Camping Ground
⛺ ....Shelter
⌂ ....Hut or Chalet

▼ ....Place to Eat
🍺 ....Pub or Bar

✈ ....Airport
⁙.....Ancient or City Wall
∴ ....Archaeological Site
Ө ....Bank
⚓ ....Beach
▥ ....Castle or Fort
■ 🏴 ....Cathedral/Church
⌒...... Cliff or Escarpment
◰ ....Dive Site
○ ....Embassy
⊛ ....Hammam
ⓤ ....Hindu Temple
✛ ....Hospital
⚑ ....Monument

ⓒ ....Mosque
▲ ....Mountain or Hill
🏛 ....Museum
⚘ ....National Park
★ ....Police Station
✉ ....Post Office
❖ ....Shopping Centre
▭ ....Swimming Pool
☎ ....Telephone
▥ ....Temple
❶ ....Tourist Information
⊖ ....Transport
♉ ....Volcano

Note: not all symbols displayed above appear in this book

LONELY PLANET OFFICES

Australia
PO Box 617, Hawthorn, Victoria 3122
☎ (03) 9819 1877 fax (03) 9819 6459
email: talk2us@lonelyplanet.com.au

USA
150 Linden St, Oakland, CA 94607
☎ (510) 893 8555 TOLL FREE: 800 275 8555
fax (510) 893 8572
email: info@lonelyplanet.com

UK
10a Spring Place, London NW5 3BH
☎ (020) 7428 4800 fax (020) 7428 4828
email: go@lonelyplanet.co.uk

France
1 rue du Dahomey, 75011 Paris
☎ 01 55 25 33 00 fax 01 55 25 33 01
email: bip@lonelyplanet.fr
minitel: 3615 lonelyplanet *(1,29 F TTC/min)*

World Wide Web: www.lonelyplanet.com *or* AOL keyword: lp
Lonely Planet Images: lpi@lonelyplanet.com.au